Three Simple Rules

for Following Jesus

Linda Robinson Whited

Abingdon Press
Nashville

Three Simple Rules
for Following Jesus

ISBN 978-1-426–70042-2

Linda Robinson Whited has extensive experience as a writer and editor of curriculum resources, books for clergy and lay leaders, and articles related to Christian education. She is a clergy member of the Mississippi Conference of The United Methodist Church, where she served in local congregations and as associate director of the Conference Council on Ministries staff. She has served on staff with the General Board of Discipleship as an editor for Discipleship Resources and at The United Methodist Publishing House as an editor for children's resources. She also serves as Coordinator of Adult Ministries on the staff of Crievewood United Methodist Church in Nashville, Tennessee. Rev. Whited is the author of *The Promised Land: An Old Testament Activity Book*, *What Every Teacher Needs to Know About The United Methodist Church*, *What Every Leader Needs to Know About United Methodist Connections*, and other resources related to Christian education and formation.

08 09 10 11 12 13 14 15 16 17—10 9 8 7 6 5 4 3 2 1

Printed in the U. S. A.

CONTENTS

Your church can do a church-wide study of the three simple rules by using the youth resource, *Three Simple Rules 24/7*, and the adult resource, *Three Simple Rules for Christian Living*, along with *Three Simple Rules for Following Jesus* for children.

Parents who would like to discuss the three simple rules with their children can download a free list of suggested questions at *cokesbury.com*.

Intergenerational Worship

As you study *Three Simple Rules: A Wesleyan Way of Living* by Reuben P. Job with the children, youth, and adults of your congregation, you may want to plan for group involvement in intergenerational activities. Consider these possibilities:

- Plan a concluding celebration on a Sunday morning that will create a renewed commitment to practicing the three simple rules. Recruit adults, youth, and children to offer testimonies about what they learned and practiced during their study.
- During the study, have the groups learn the song "Stay in Love With God." An intergenerational choir can sing the song during worship.
- Add an intergenerational activity to each session. For example, the combined group might create a group banner for each of the three simple rules. The banners can then be displayed in the sanctuary during worship as a reminder of what the groups have learned.
- Make suggestions of songs or hymns that reflect the three simple rules for those who plan the worship services for the weeks following the study. Have someone name the connections to the three simple rules when the songs are sung.
- Prepare a video or skits that illustrate the three simple rules. Involve actors from all age groups.
- Have children, youth, and adults work together to design a worship altar that reflects the meanings of the three simple rules in the lives of Christians.

Stay in Love With God

Do no harm by an-y word or deed; do

good wher-ev-er there is need. Re -

main at-ten-tive to God's word. Stay in love with

God, stay in love with God.

Words: Raquel Martinez
Music: Raquel Martinex
© 2007 Abingdon Press

DO

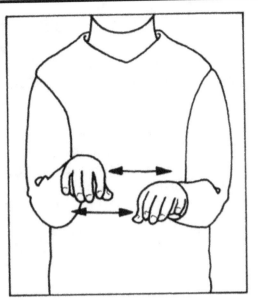

NO

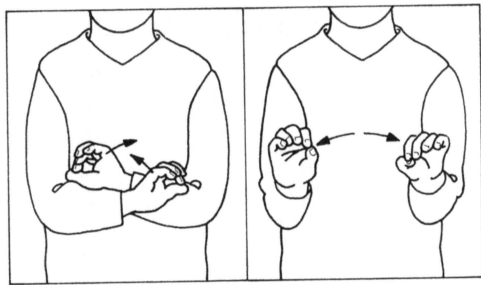

HARM

Art: Brenda Gilliam

DO NO HARM

First Week: **To God's Children**
Second Week: **To God's World**

Objectives

The children will

- recognize rules as tools that can make their lives and the lives of others better;
- learn that following Jesus includes being caretakers of all that God has created;
- experience ways to take care of God's people and God's world.

Bible Story

Genesis 1:1-28, 31a: the story of Creation, including human beings' responsibility for taking care of what God has created.

Bible Verse

Psalm 8:6, CEV: You let us rule everything your hands have made. And you put all of it under our power.

Focus for the Teacher

Wesley's General Rules

John Wesley, the founder of the Methodist Movement that began in the eighteenth century, was ordained as a priest in the Church of England in 1728. As the movement grew, John Wesley organized its members into societies who met weekly to provide mutual accountability for their Christian spiritual growth. Anyone who wanted to "flee from the wrath to come, and to be saved from their sins" was welcome to join. However, a disciplined life was required of those who wished to remain in a society.

In 1743, leaders in the societies asked for guidance. "What should we teach?" they wanted to know. "What guidelines can we follow as we seek to live holy lives in our complex world?" After much thought and discussion, John Wesley answered with what has become known as the General Rules of the United Societies. Even though it has been over 265 years since Wesley's rules were published, these three rules are still basic guidelines for Christians living in the complex world of today. Bishop Reuben P. Job has summarized Wesley's rules as three simple rules: Do No Harm; Do Good; and Stay in Love With God.

Wesley's General Rules are based on the life and teachings of Jesus Christ. The rules are not laws that must be enforced or descriptions of righteous works that must be performed in order for one to be a Christian. Instead, they are guidelines for a way of living that will form Christian character among those who strive to follow them. The goal of Wesley's three simple rules is to help faithful followers of Jesus Christ achieve a goal that Wesley described as a "holiness of heart and life."

For John Wesley, holiness is two-fold. First, there is an inward, personal holiness that seeks a relationship with God that leads to a life of trust, obedience, joy, and worship. Then, there is an outward holiness that shows itself in the ways a Christian shows love for God through acts of love for neighbors. Wesley described this holiness of heart and life in two categories—"works of piety" and "works of mercy."

The second and third of the General Rules—Do Good and Stay in Love With God—are related to Wesley's ideas about holiness. Even before those two important ideas, though, Wesley cautioned those who listened to his teachings to Do No Harm.

Children and Rules

As you begin to explore Wesley's three simple rules with children, be assured that children know about rules! Unfortunately, though, most of the time rules for children come from parents, teachers, or other adults. Children often experience rules as restrictive, pointing out the things that they cannot do. Children often obey rules simply because they know that they have no choice.

Your challenge will be to encourage the children to accept these rules as their own. As you help them to see the picture of what Christian discipleship looks like as they live the way Jesus teaches us to live, children will learn that choosing to follow these three simple rules will make their lives and the lives of others better. When children understand rules in this way, they will experience new ways and new reasons to take care of God's people and God's world.

Perhaps this will be the first time children will hear this rule described as "do no harm." But it will not be a new idea for children. Just as John Wesley learned this idea from the teachings of Jesus, the children will recognize the teachings they have heard in Sunday school and from their parents. In Sunday school they have learned "Do to others as you would have them do to you" (Luke 6:31). "Be kind to one another" (Ephesians 4:32). "God put the man in the Garden of Eden to take care of it" (Genesis 2:15). At home they have heard "If you cannot say something nice, then do not say anything at all." "Do not hit your brother." "Be gentle when you play with the puppies." These are things that children have already learned that have taught them to do no harm. Once they choose these rules for themselves, they will not be easily swayed to abandon the rules that help them live as faithful Christians.

Simple Rule #1: Do No Harm

Although at first glance, this rule seems to point out a simple and obvious way to behave, doing no harm must not be as natural an action as we would like to think. If it were a natural first response to living in God's world and with God's people, imagine what a difference we would find in our daily living.

The Apostle Paul recognized that doing no harm was not always easy. He said, "What I do is not the good I want to do; no, the evil I do not want to do— this I keep on doing" (Romans 7:19, NIV). It seems clear that to do no harm does not come naturally. Instead, it is necessary for us to be intentional about doing no harm as we live each day.

So what is involved as we seek to "do no harm"? In *Three Simple Rules: A Wesleyan Way of Living*, Bishop Job says: "To do no harm is a proactive response to all that is evil—all that is damaging and destructive to humankind and God's good creation, and therefore, ultimately destructive to us. ... To do no harm means that I will be on guard so that all my actions and even my silence will not add injury to another of God's children or to any part of God's creation." (pages 30-31) As you introduce children to this first simple rule, focus on what children can do as they become intentional in their efforts to do no harm to God's creation or to God's children.

God's plan was for an orderly creation and for human lives of peace and joy. The sun would shine; the rains would come; plants would grow; people would take care of the world and treat one another with love, respect, and fairness. When God's plan is distorted, though, the results can be devastating for both the earth and for people. To do no harm is a huge first step toward life as God planned it.

> By doing no harm, by avoiding evil of every kind, especially that which is most generally practiced...
>
> — John Wesley

The Bible in These Lessons

Genesis 1:1-28, 31a
The Book of Genesis tells the story of the world that God created and then gave to human beings to take care of. God declares that everything that has been made—both the earth and people— are "very good." God's people are charged with a responsibility to handle that creation with loving care—a care that begins by doing no harm.

Psalm 8:6, CEV
The Bible verse for these two weeks is from the Psalms: "You let us rule everything your hands have made. And you put all of it under our power." The New Revised Standard Version translates "rule over" as "dominion." Either translation will need to be explained. Neither "rule over" nor "dominion" means being given unlimited control and a freedom to use God's creation in ways that serve selfish needs rather than serving the needs of the created world and the needs of people. These words include a sense of responsibility and care.

First Week: Do No Harm to God's Children

Gather to Explore

Be sure that adult leaders are waiting when the first child arrives. Greet and welcome each child and get him or her involved in an activity that introduces the theme for the day's activities.

Many Kinds of Rules!

- As the children arrive, have them read the rules you have posted. Invite them to post other rules they have seen posted at school or in other places.

- When all of the children have arrived, ask if the rules that are posted were created by people or if they are rules God has given us. If some of the rules the children added are from the Bible, acknowledge that.

- *Ask:* Why do we have rules? (*Rules help us to take care of the world, to respect other people, to warn of danger, and to make our lives easier.*)

- *Ask:* Is it possible that some human rules have been created as a way to help us follow God's rules? (*For example, do we stay off the grass so that we can take care of the beauty of God's world? Do we drive slowly in a school zone to keep God's children safe?*)

- *Say:* During the next six weeks we will talk about three rules from a man named John Wesley. John Wesley's rules will help us follow what Jesus teaches us about the way God wants us to live.

- *Say:* The three rules we will be learning are simple rules. They are: Do No Harm; Do Good; and Stay in Love With God. (*As you name each of John Wesley's rules, add the rule to the other rules posted on the wall. Use photocopies of pages 5, 25, and 45.*)

Who Is John Wesley?

- Call the children together in a circle to learn about John Wesley so that they will understand why we want to listen to what he says about rules.

- *Say:* John Wesley was born in England in 1703. He loved God, and he wanted to live like Jesus taught that we should live. When he grew up, he was ordained as a priest in the Church of England.

  When John Wesley and his brother Charles were in college, Charles organized a group of students who wanted to serve God. John Wesley joined them, and they spent time reading the Bible, praying together, and living the message of God's love through their actions as they took care of others as Jesus had taught.

  Later, John Wesley organized groups that he called societies. These societies were a lot like our Sunday schools today. Wesley wrote three general rules to help them know if they were living as God intended. Those are the three rules we will be learning about.

Prepare

✓ Post familiar rules on the walls. For example:
  - Keep off the grass.
  - No talking.
  - Shoplifters will be prosecuted.
  - Do not touch.
  - Watch for falling objects.
  - Use the other door.
  - Stay to the right.
  - No bicycles allowed.
  - Drive slowly.

✓ Provide paper, markers, and tape.

✓ Make photocopies of the signing pages for the three simple rules (pages 5, 25, and 45).

- Remind the children of John Wesley's three simple rules that are posted with other rules on your wall. Have the children say the three rules aloud with you—Do No Harm; Do Good; and Stay in Love With God.

- **Say:** Although John Wesley was always a priest in the Church of England, the movement he started developed into a new church when it came to America. If you are part of The United Methodist Church—or one of several other churches that grew out of John Wesley's teaching—these three simple rules are a part of your heritage.

Know the Rule

The three simple rules the children are learning will help them to follow Jesus' teachings about how to live. The first step is to know the rule and to recognize why it is important.

Playing Favorites

- **Say:** We all have favorites. Let's find out what some of our favorites are. (*Point out the categories listed on the circles around the room.*)

- Allow a few minutes for the children to go to each circle and write his or her favorite in each of the categories and then return to sit in the circle.

- One by one read the favorites that are listed. Let the children have fun guessing who chose each favorite.

- **Ask:** Is it okay that I like red, but Joey would rather chose blue? Is it okay that Janie loves broccoli, but Ryan would rather eat potatoes?

- **Ask:** Are there any times when it is not okay for us to have favorites? (*As the children answer, remind them of the first of the three simple rules that come from John Wesley—Do No Harm.*)

- **Say:** Today we will talk about how we can do no harm to God's children. It is okay to have favorite colors, foods, songs, or teams. But John Wesley reminds us that God wants us to be careful not to hurt any person. That does not mean that we cannot have best friends, but it does mean that Jesus teaches us that it is important to care about the feelings of everyone, even those we do not know.

Prepare

✓ Cut several circles from construction paper. On each circle name a category: Vegetable, Game, Color, Song, Team.

✓ Tape the circles to various parts of the walls.

✓ Provide pencils.

Declaration of Human Rights

- Open your Bible and read Genesis 1:26-28 aloud.

- **Say:** The Book of Genesis tells us that God created the world. The most wonderful of all God's creation is the creation of human beings. People are created in God's image. Each one is different, and each one is special. God made people who have different likes and dislikes, different talents, different sizes and shapes, different colors. God's people are women, men, boys, and girls.

- Look back at your Bible, and read Genesis 1:31a aloud: "God saw everything that he had made, and indeed, it was very good."

Prepare

✓ Post a sign that says "Declaration of Human Rights" in large letters.

✓ Enlarge the statements on page 22 if possible. Then photocopy them on construction paper.

✓ Cut the statements apart. Cut a few blank strips.

✓ Supply markers and tape.

Simple Rule #1: Do No Harm

- Point out the "Declaration of Human Rights" sign you have posted.

- **Say:** God created people to take care of the world. Taking care of the world includes taking care of one another. Let's talk about the basic rights that all people have because God created and loves them.

- Distribute the statements from page 22 so that each child has at least one strip. (If you have a large class, the children will need to share.)

- **Say:** Let's read these statements one at a time. If we decide that it names a human right that God intends for all people, we will add it to the wall. If it simply names something people would like but is not something everyone has to have, we will put that strip aside.

- Consider each statement one at a time.

- **Ask:** Are there any other basic rights that you think God intends for all people? If so, let's write them and add them to our declaration.

- **Say:** Earlier we talked about playing favorites. We must remember that God does not have favorites among people. God want us to treat every person with respect—even though we each have our special friends. There are some people who do things that God does not like, but we know that God still loves all people. God has given us a responsibility to take care of all people in the best ways we can.

- **Ask:** Do you remember the first of the three simple rules from John Wesley? (*Do No Harm*)

What Is Your IQ?

- **Say:** Let's talk about how to take care of God's people by doing no harm.

- **Say:** One way that we can do harm to other people is by making them feel like we do not like them and that they are not wanted. Let's think about whether we ever do that.

- Give each child a copy of "What Is Your IQ?" (page 23)

- **Say:** Usually when we talk about our IQ, we are talking about a score that we make on a test that measures our "intelligence quotient." Another kind of intelligence, though, is the intelligence we show when we choose to do no harm to others, as Jesus has taught us. Today, our IQ test will measure our "inclusiveness quotient." Our scores will tell us something about how well we are doing at taking care of God's people.

- **Say:** When you write your answers, remember to answer as you really are, not like you think you should be!

- Allow some time for each child to take his or her IQ (Inclusiveness Quotient) test alone. Then talk together about what the children have discovered about themselves.

- **Say:** We do not have to be best friends with everyone, but Jesus taught that all people are God's children. We have a responsibility to respect every person's feelings and show them respect.

Prepare

✓ Photocopy "What Is Your IQ?" (page 23) for each child.

✓ Provide pencils.

Follow the Rule

Discovering ways to follow the rule is the goal of your time with the children. Choose ways for following the rule that match their interests and the time and resources you have available.

Kind Words, Harsh Words

- *Say:* I am hungry. I think I will have a snack!

- Take out a banana, peel it down a few inches, and take a bite. Then act as if you are just noticing that the children do not have anything to eat.

- *Say:* Oops! I am being rude. I should not have started eating this banana in front of you. I am sorry. Let me close it back up.

- Enjoy the children's reactions when you try several methods for closing the banana. Try tape first. When that does not work, pick up a bottle of glue. "Oh no, bad idea—glue is not good on food. How about staples?" Let the children see how messy staples would be and that it would not work anyway. Finally, fold the banana peel down as carefully as you can and put the banana back in the bag.

- *Say:* Once a banana has been opened, there is no way to put it back together. That's a good example to remind us of what happens if we use words that hurt other people. Mean, angry, or insulting words cannot be taken back once they are said. Even if we say "I am sorry," we cannot take back the damage we have caused to the person's feelings.

- *Say:* What situations can you think of when you might be tempted to say words that would make someone else feel bad? (*when you are angry, when you have to do something you do not want to do, when others are making fun of someone, when you are jealous, when you have heard some gossip you want to tell someone else, when you disagree with what someone says*)

- *Say:* Anger, impatience, jealousy, and gossip can ruin our relationships with other people. And when we respond with harsh words, we can hurt the feelings of people God loves. Listen to what the Bible says about kind words and harsh words.

- Invite a child to find Proverbs 15:1 in a CEV Bible and then read the verse aloud.

- *Say:* The Bible tells us that when someone speaks to us with harsh words, we can answer with kind words and stop the anger.

- Let's read another verse from Proverbs. Invite another child to find and read Proverbs 26:20 aloud.

- *Say:* Gossip is another way that we can harm people by using words.

- *Ask:* What is gossip? (*Gossip is talking about people behind their backs, usually saying things that are not true or that we do not know are true.*)

Prepare

✓ Have a banana nearby in a bag.

✓ Provide a CEV Bible.

- **Say:** I am going to describe some situations where we might be tempted to say angry or mean things. I want you to think of words that would be more caring and would do no harm.

- Describe these situations that the children might experience:

1. Your sister is angry and yells at you because you borrowed her iPod without asking. Instead of "You are selfish. You never want to share," what caring words could you say?

2. Your mother is cleaning up and asks you to help pick up your little brother's toys that are in her way. Instead of "I didn't put them there. I shouldn't have to pick them up," what caring words could you say?

3. Your little sister is crying because she cannot go with you to a movie with your friends. Instead of "You are just a cry baby!" what caring words could you say?

4. Someone at school has been telling stories about a kid you do not really like. You do not know if it is true, but you do know that it is gossip. Instead of "Really? What else have you heard," what caring words could you say?

5. Someone at school drops his tray at the end of the serving line. Everyone in the cafeteria starts laughing and saying, "How clumsy can you be?" Instead of joining it, what caring words could you say?

But I Don't Even Know Them!

- Hand out magazines and scissors.

- **Say:** Look through these magazines and cut out 4 or 5 pictures of things you want or need. (*Do not give any more instruction than that!*)

- Have the children cut out the pictures and then put them aside.

- **Say:** Sometimes it is hard to remember to do no harm to the people we are with every day—even our family and friends. It can be even harder to think about how we can avoid doing harm to people that we do not know and have often not even seen. Jesus' teaching as John Wesley expresses it in the simple rule "Do No Harm" is that we have responsibility for doing no harm to those people too.

- **Ask:** How can we harm someone we do not even know? (*Give the children time to think and then give their own answers. You never know, you may learn something new from them.*)

- **Say:** One of the ways our actions can affect the lives of people we do not know is through our decisions about how to use the resources that God has provided. One general statistic reminds us that while the United States includes only about 5% of the world's population, this country uses about 30% of the world's resources. Consider what that means for people in countries that do not have all the food, water, medicine, education, and technology that we have.

- Show the children the poster you have prepared for comparing wants and needs.

Prepare

✓ Prepare a simple poster with a line drawn down the center. Write the heading "Wants" on one side of the line and the heading "Needs" on the other side of the line.

✓ Gather old magazines.

✓ Provide scissors and gluesticks.

- *Ask:* What is the difference between a want (*things that people enjoy but are not necessary for life*) and a need (*things that a person must have in order to live and grow*)?

- Remind the children of the statements they used for their Declaration of Human Rights at the beginning of the session.

- How can we use our understanding of needs and wants to find ways to do no harm to people all over the world?

- Have the children put the pictures they have cut from magazines on the poster under the appropriate headings, considering for each one whether it is a need or a want.

We Are All Special!

- Have the children sit in a circle. If you have a table that all the children can sit around, use it so that the children will have a surface for writing.

```
Singe**R**
    **A**lways Friendly
        **C**
        **H**
Good R**E**ader
        **L**
```

- Give each child a sheet of plain paper and a pencil.

- Have each child write his or her name vertically down the center of the paper, leaving as much space as possible between the letters. If you have a large class, have the children write both first and last names.

- Begin by having the children pass their papers to the left.

- *Say:* Choose one of the letters of the name of the person on the sheet you are holding. Use that letter in a phrase that names something good or special about that person. The letter can begin the first word in the phrase or it can be in the middle or at the end of the phrase.

- When the children have written their phrases, have everyone pass the papers to the left again so that the next person can choose another letter and add some more good words about the person named on the paper. (If the letters run out before the name has gone all the way around the circle, let the children use the same letters again.)

- When the names have gone all the way around the circle, allow time for each person to read the good things that have been written about him or her.

- *Say:* We are all different, and we are all special. It is important for us to recognize the special things in every person God has created. When we remember that God created each person and that God loves each person, we will want to do no harm to any of God's children.

Prepare

✓ Provide sheets of paper and pencils.

Celebrate and Praise God

Following Jesus by learning and following the three simple rules will help the children grow in their relationship to God. Encourage them to worship and praise both as a group and on their own.

Litany of Kind Words

- Call the children together for a time of celebration and praise.

- *Say:* When we follow Jesus, we want to treat others with respect and kindness, just as Jesus would do. Because Jesus has taught us about God's love, we can love others even when we do not agree with what they say or do—and even when we do not know them.

- *Say:* We have learned that the words we use make a difference. When we follow the first simple rule that John Wesley gave to his societies—Do No Harm—we will be careful not to use harsh or unkind words when we talk to or about others. Instead, we will use kind words.

- *Say:* We have also learned that the choices we make about how we use the resources God has provided for the world can affect the lives of people in other places, people we may not even know.

- Teach the children the simple song, "Stay in Love With God" (page 4).

- *Say:* Let's sing this song as our refrain for a closing prayer litany. Let's ask God to help us do no harm to God's children.

Do No Harm

Three simple rules help us remember how Jesus teaches us to live.
(Sing "Stay in Love With God.")

Harsh words create anger and hurt the people God loves. But kind words soothes feelings and show love.
(Sing "Stay in Love With God.")

Gossip stirs up trouble! Where there is no gossip, God's people can live in peace.
(Sing "Stay in Love With God.")

We can respect God's people and treat them kindly, even if they are not our best friends.
(Sing "Stay in Love With God.")

We follow Jesus when we love one another and do no harm to anyone.
(Sing "Stay in Love With God.")

Prepare

✓ Learn the song "Stay in Love With God" (page 4).

Second Week: Do No Harm to God's World

Gather to Explore

Be sure that adult leaders are waiting when the first child arrives. Greet and welcome each child and get him or her involved in an activity that introduces the theme for the day's activities.

Hands on the World

- As the children arrive, show them a globe and encourage them to find the area of the world where they live.

- Then let them find and show one another other places around the world that they have heard about—or maybe even visited.

- As the children continue to arrive, get them involved by having them suggest new places to locate. And suggest some places yourself—perhaps places that the children are hearing about on the news.

- When all of the children have arrived, begin to talk about the globe as a symbol of the earth on which they live.

- *Say:* The globe is a symbol that can remind us of all the wonderful places and things that God has created for us, God's children.

Prepare

- ✓ Display a large globe where the children can gather around it.

- ✓ If you have a large group, you may want to have more than one globe.

Creation Mysteries

- Call the children together into a circle to play a guessing game.

- Hand out sheets of paper and pencils, and have each child number a paper from 1 to the number of bags you have prepared.

- Pass the Creation Mysteries bags around the circle to take turns feeling what is inside the bags without looking inside.

- Caution the children not to say what they feel in a bag, but to write down their guess and pass the bag on to the next child.

- When all the guesses have been made, hear the guesses for the items one by one. After the guesses for each bag, open the bag to reveal the mystery creation that is inside.

- *Ask:* Which thing felt the strangest? Was there an item that you did not guess correctly? What other creation mysteries could we have included?

- *Say:* Everything we have felt and now seen represents a part of God's wonderful creation.

- *Say:* Last week we talked about taking care of God's children. Today, we are going to talk about ways that we can take care of God's world.

Prepare

- ✓ Prepare several numbered paper bags, each with a different item from nature inside. Include as many different types of items as you can. For example:

  - dirt
  - rocks
  - grass
  - tree bark
  - sand
  - sticks
  - seeds
  - sea shells
  - leaves
  - pine cone

  - feather
  - flower
  - sand
  - fake fur
  - star shape
  - an empty bag of air
  - rubber bugs

- ✓ Provide pencils and sheets of paper for guesses.

Know the Rule

The three simple rules the children are learning will help them to follow Jesus' teachings about how to live. The first step is to know the rule and to recognize why it is important.

How Does It Feel?

- Tell the children to close their eyes and imagine themselves in the story you are going to tell.

- *Say:* Imagine that you and your family have planned a wonderful birthday party for your grandmother. Lots of people will be coming to your house, so you spent all day on Saturday cleaning your room and then helping your mother dust and vacuum. It was hard work, but it was worth it because you love your grandmother very much.

  After the house was cleaned, you spent hours blowing up balloons, putting up streamers and a special "Happy Birthday" sign, and helping make the most beautiful birthday cake you have ever seen! Now it is time to go pick up your grandmother and bring her over for the great surprise.

  When you and your family return and pull into the driveway, the guests are just beginning to arrive. Everyone is looking forward to a wonderful party.

  But oh, no! You cannot believe what you see when you open the door. Someone has destroyed all your careful work. The streamers are all over the floor. The balloons are gone, and there are bad words spray painted on the walls. The cake looks like someone tried to eat it with their hands, and now it is lying on the couch in a messy blob.

- Pause for moment of silence as the children picture the scene.

- *Ask:* How does this make you feel? (*Guide the conversation, allowing the children to express their outrage.*)

- ***Then say:*** I wonder how God feels when people trash the world that God created and do not care about the feelings of God's people.

- *Ask:* Do you remember the rule for following Jesus that we talked about last week when we said that Jesus wants us to take care of God's people? (*Do No Harm*)

- Point out the signing poster of the first simple rule (page 5). Help the children sign and say the words.

- *Say:* John Wesley named the three simple rules we are talking about to help people in the societies he formed remember how they could be Christians and live the way Jesus teaches that we should live.

- *Say:* Last week we said that following Jesus means first that we do no harm to God's people. Today we are remembering that following Jesus means that we will be careful that we do no harm to any of the world that God created.

Prepare

✓ Post the signing poster of the first simple rule, Do No Harm (page 5), where the children can see it while they are gathered in a circle.

✓ Practice telling the story.

Caretakers Needed

- **Say:** Let's listen to the Bible story about God creating the world.

- Have the children open their Bibles to the Book of Genesis.

- **Say:** The word *genesis* means beginning. The world was created before there were any people around to take notes and write a report of what was happening. Have you ever wondered how the Book of Genesis, the Bible book about beginnings, came to be? The story was first told by storytellers who passed the story down by telling it over and over to many new generations until the words were finally written down.

- **Say:** We have the story about Creation in many translations of the Bible. Today we are going to hear the story from a modern-day version. As you listen, remember how you felt as you got the house ready for your grandmother's party. Think about God's love for us when the wonders of the world were created to decorate the space where we would live and celebrate all our birthdays!

- Read Genesis 1:1-25 aloud. (If you have a good children's Bible storybook available, consider using that version that is in children's language.)

- Then have the children look up two Bible verses: Genesis 1:26 and Psalm 8:6.

- Ask two children to read the verses.

- **Ask:** What does the verse from Psalm 8 mean when it says that God lets us "rule everything" (or "have dominion" if the children read that translation)?

- Guide the children as they understand that the words of the Bible are describing a responsibility that God has given to us to take loving care of all that God has created. To "rule over" or to "have dominion" is a great responsibility. God has shown great trust in us!

- **Ask:** If you found a want ad in the newspaper that said: "Help Wanted: Caretaker for God's World," what would do you think the person who had that job would be expected to do?

- Make a list of the children's answers on a markerboard or on newsprint. Get them started with a few ideas if necessary, but be aware that the children learn about taking care of the environment, conservation of energy, and recycling in school, so they may already have lots of ideas.

- Group the children into pairs and let each pair work together to create a "Help Wanted" poster that includes a job description for a caretaker of God's world.

- **Ask:** What is John Wesley's first simple rule about following Jesus? (*Do No Harm*) What do the Bible story about God's creation and our job descriptions for caretakers of God's world have to tell us about why he began his three simple rules this way?

Prepare

✓ Be sure that every child can see a Bible, even if it means having two children share a Bible.

✓ Provide a version of the Genesis Creation story in children's language—a modern language Bible translation or a good children's Bible storybook.

✓ Provide a markerboard or newsprint and markers for making a list.

✓ Gather posterboard and markers for the children's posters.

✓ Make decisions about where and how to display the children's posters.

- **Say:** God wants us to appreciate all the wonders that have been created to make our world a beautiful place. If we respect God's creation, we will not do anything to abuse it, to neglect it, or to cause it any kind of harm. We will accept the responsibility God has given us to be caretakers.

- Help the children display their posters in an area where church members can view them.

- If possible, provide a time for the children to be present to explain their posters and to answer questions.

Follow the Rule

Discovering ways to follow the rule is the goal of your time with the children. Choose ways for following the rule that match their interests and the time and resources you have available.

Stop! Caution! Go!

- Call the children together into one group in the center of the room.

- **Say:** Let's consider what we need to do—or stop doing—to follow the first of John Wesley's simple rules and be caretakers of God's world.

- Point out the "Stop!" "Caution!" and "Go!" signs that you have displayed.

- **Say:** I am going to read a series of short scenarios. After each one, I want you to decide whether the person in the story should Stop, Go, or Use Caution. Then go to stand near the sign that names your decision.

- **Say:** It is possible that we will not all agree about some of the actions that should be taken. When that happens, you will have a chance to explain your decision.

- Use these scenarios, or make up some of your own.
  - → "Hey! Don't throw that candy wrapper out of the car window," Danny yelled at his sister Denise. "It is just one candy wrapper; what's it going to hurt?" Denise answered back. *What should Denise do?*
  - → "Hey, Kathy! It is so hot!" Susan complained. "Let's turn on the sprinkler and play in the water." The grass and trees are struggling to survive in a drought. *What should Kathy do?*
  - → You notice that most of the newspapers in the neighborhood end up in garbage cans. *What should you do?*
  - → Your neighbor has offered to pay you to pull the weeds in her garden. Your friend tells you that there is a weed killer that will get rid of the weeds with very little effort. The bottle says, "Do not use around pets, children, or vegetable plants." *What should you do?*
  - → Jimmy's mother has told him to turn the water off while he brushes his teeth, but it is not easy to reach the handles and it will only take a couple of minutes. *What should Jimmy do?*
  - → Courtney's family is leaving the campsite after a picnic. She sees an open tin can with the lid still attached lying in the trees. "Oh, I am tired." Courtney's says. "It's no big deal." *What should Courtney do?*

Prepare

✓ Make 3 signs to display in three separate areas of your class space:
  - a red sign that says "Stop!"
  - a yellow sign that says "Caution!"
  - a green sign that says "Go!"

✓ Choose the scenarios you will use. Choose from the examples or create some of your own.

- After the children have made their decisions, allow time for discussion.

- Even if everyone has chosen the same answer, ask some questions.

- **Ask:** Will God's creation be harmed in any way by my decision? Is this decision one that Jesus would make?

- Help the children consider all the possibilities, including ways people, animals, or plants may be hurt or damaged by some actions.

- **Say:** To do no harm is an important step in following Jesus as we consider ways to fulfill the responsibility that God has given us to take care of the world that God has created for us.

Prevent Harm to God's World

- One effective ways to prevent harm to God's world is through reminding other people about how their actions affect the world. One way the children can help their congregation do a better job of protecting the world from harm is to create an environmental checklist for each family in the congregation.

- Help the children follow these instructions to create the checklist:
  1. Brainstorm a list of things families can do at home and in their community to protect the environment. Have someone write the list on a sheet of letter-size paper.
  2. The list may include such things as
     → Recycle aluminum cans.
     → Compost leaves and grass.
     → Collect and recycle newspapers.
     → Turn off lights when leaving a room.
     → Turn off water while brushing teeth.
     → Use both sides of paper before recycling it.
     → Pick up litter.
     → Put up a bird feeder.

Art: Brenda Gilliam

  3. Have someone quickly make photocopies of the printed list while the children cut pieces of self-adhesive paper to cover their completed charts.
  4. Glue each list to the center of a sheet of construction paper.
  5. Decorate around the edges of the lists.
  6. Cover the chart with clear self-adhesive paper.
  7. Tape a copy of the instructions to the back of each chart.

- Let the children pass out copies of the chart to each family in the congregation.

- Have someone make an announcement to the congregation and/or put an announcement in your church's newsletter to explain the chart the children are providing.

Option for Older Children

Let older children research ways to prevent harm to God's world. If your group has access to computers, they can do research there. Or, perhaps you can plan a field trip to a public library.

Prepare

✓ Provide construction paper, plain paper, a marker, gluesticks, clear self-adhesive paper, scissors, and tape.

✓ Recruit someone to make photocopies when the checklist is ready.

✓ Type the instructions for using the checklist and make a copy to attach to each checklist.

Instructions

Hang this checklist where your family can see it easily. Every day, check off the items your family has done.

At the end of the week, review the items you need to continue to work on.

Then erase the chart with a facial tissue and start over with a new week.

✓ **Caution:** If you use the Internet, recruit additional adults for adequate supervision!

Take Care of God's World at Church

- Help the children choose ways that they can actively be involved in taking care of God's world at their own church. Choose from these options, or plan your own project based on your church's needs.

- *Clean Up the Church Yard.* Take the children outside to pick up trash, sticks, or leaves that litter the flower beds, parking lot, or playground. With knowledgeable adult help, older children can prune bushes or trim lower branches on trees. If the timing is right, the children can plant flowers or weed flower beds.

- *Plan a Recycling Project.* If your church does not already recycle regularly, let the children provide boxes in several areas of the church. There can be a box in the restrooms for toilet paper rolls; one near the sanctuary for used bulletins; several in the kitchen for tin cans and paper packaging; and one near the drink machine for cans. Perhaps the children will want to turn in aluminum cans for money that they can donate to an earth-friendly cause, such as a conservation project or a local animal shelter.

- *Clean Up Inside the Church.* Remind the children that taking care of God's world can also include taking care of the environment inside their church. Let the children clean their classroom. Assign tasks such as dusting the shelves, wiping the table, sweeping the floor, cleaning chairs, or sorting craft supplies. If possible, extend the project to other parts of the building such as the sanctuary or other classrooms.

- *Involve the Congregation in Recycling for Children's Projects.* Let the children wrap a large box with plain paper. Then let them glue on samples (or draw pictures) of items that the congregation can recycle by donating them to your children's supplies closet. Items can include paper towel and wrapping paper rolls, fabric scraps, ribbons, buttons, tissue boxes, pieces of giftwrap, wallpaper sample books, yarn, old pantyhose (washed!), cardboard egg cartons, and so forth. Make an announcement to the congregation and put the box in a location where parents and other church members can make donations easily.

Prepare
✓ Choose the options you will use.

Yard Work
✓ Provide tools needed for the yard work.

Recycling Project
✓ Collect boxes to become recycling bins.

✓ Choose an earth-friendly cause to receive money collected for recycled items.

Cleaning Inside
✓ Provide cleaning supplies: dusting cloths, spray bottles of water, paper towels, brooms, and trash bags.

Recycling for Craft Items
✓ Provide a large box, plain wrapping paper, scissors, tape, glue or gluesticks, samples of craft supplies, crayons and markers.

Celebrate and Praise God

Following Jesus by learning and following the three simple rules will help the children grow in their relationship to God. Encourage them to worship and praise both as a group and on their own.

My Experience With God's World

- Call the children together again for a time of celebration and praise.

- If possible, take the children outside for a silent walk, observing the signs of God's creation around your churchyard. If it is not possible to go outside, encourage the children to spread out as much as possible in your space.

- Whether inside or outside, prepare for a time of private reflection.

Prepare
✓ Make a photocopy of "Experiencing God's World" (page 24) for each child.

✓ Provide pencils and crayons.

- Give each child a copy of "Experiencing God's World" (page 24) and a pencil.

- *Say:* Take some time to consider how you feel about God's world. There are some suggestions on the sheet you have that can help you. Write your answers to those questions first. Then, make notes about anything else that comes to mind as you talk with God about the world.

- *Say:* Think about something that you may need to stop doing because you have learned that it harms God's world. Ask God to help you follow Jesus as you care for God's people and for God's world.

- *Say:* What you write on this paper is for you and God alone. Work in silence. There are no right answers or wrong answers. No one else will read it. Make this time a special time of prayer as you talk to God alone.

- After a few minutes, call the children back together—still in silence—for a closing circle. Be sure to allow the children to put their papers with their private thoughts away before they gather.

Psalm 8 Responsive Reading

Prepare

✓ Provide CEV Bibles, at least one for every two children.

- Divide the children into two groups.

- Give each group enough CEV Bibles for at least every two children to have a Bible.

- Have the children find Psalm 8.

- *Say:* One Bible verse we have used while talking about John Wesley's first simple rule, Do No Harm, is Psalm 8:6. Let's read that verse together.

- Encourage each child to read the verse with the entire group.

- *Say:* Now, let's read all of Psalm 8 to remember all that God has done for us by creating such a wonderful world. As we read, let's think about the responsibility God has given us for taking care of the world.

- *Say:* We will read the psalm together responsively. The group on my left will read the first verse. The group on my right will continue by reading verse 2. Then those on my left will read verse 3. We will continue taking turns through verse 8. Then everyone will read verse 9 together, celebrating and praising God's name.

- When everyone understands the instructions, allow a moment of silence for the children to get ready to read. Then close with the responsive reading of Psalm 8, followed by a brief prayer.

- *Pray:* Loving God, we thank you for the miracle and wonder of all you have created to show us your love. Help us to "rule over" all that you have entrusted to our care. Help us to be responsible caretakers, always being careful to do no harm to your world as we become faithful followers of Jesus. Amen.

Simple Rule #1: Do No Harm

Everyone should be treated with dignity and respect.

Everyone should own his or her own iPod.

Everyone should have enough food to eat to stay healthy and strong.

Everyone should have a safe and comfortable place to sleep at night.

Everyone should be free from abuse and fear of being harmed.

Everyone should be able to stay up to watch TV as late as she or he wants.

Everyone should receive medical care when he or she is sick or hurt.

Everyone should be able to do whatever she or he wants, no matter what the Bible or the law says.

Everyone should receive fair treatment no matter what his or her race, age, gender, religious beliefs, or wealth.

Everyone One should be able to help others who are less fortunate

Everyone should be free to choose her or his own religion.

Everyone should be able to get an education and learn as much as he or she can.

Everyone should have enough money to buy a big house and a fancy car.

Three Simple Rules for Following Jesus

What Is Your IQ?

Do you accept people and include everyone in activities? Or, do you always hang around with the same people and do not accept others who are different? Which of these people would be in your group of friends? Be honest!

5 – Definitely   **3 – Maybe?**   **0 – No Way!**

____ a new kid in the neighborhood
____ a person who is unable to see
____ a student who knows little English
____ a person who is homeless
____ someone from a different church
____ someone who sings out of key
____ someone in a wheelchair
____ a person who has a different color skin
____ a person who lives in a poor part of town
____ a child with only one parent
____ a person who does not go to church
____ a person who did not invite you to his or her last party
____ a migrant worker
____ a person in a lower grade
____ a person who failed last year
____ a person just like you

Add your points to discover your IQ (Inclusiveness Quotient).

66—80   I would like to be your friend—you are inclusive!
56—65   I cannot be sure what you will do. You accept some and not others. It depends!
0—55   You have work to do! What does God want you to do?

Experiencing God's World

The part of God's creation I am most thankful for is

The part of creation I wonder about the most is

The time when I feel closest to God is when

When I think about the world God created,
it makes me sad when I see

One thing I can do to help take care of God's
people and God's world is

Art: Joe Boddy

Three Simple Rules for Following Jesus

DO

GOOD

Art: Brenda Gilliam

DO GOOD

First Week: **For My Family and My Church**
Second Week: **For My Community and the World**

Objectives
The children will
- recognize that following Jesus includes caring for God's world and God's people in active ways;
- discover ways to do good for their family at home and their family at church;
- discover that following Jesus includes doing good even for those we do not know.

Bible Story
Matthew 25:34-40: When we do good for the "least of these who are members of my family," we do good for Jesus.

Bible Verse
Hebrews 13:16a: Do not neglect to do good and to share what you have.

Focus for the Teacher

John Wesley and "Works of Mercy"

"Holiness of heart and life" is the essence of John Wesley's theology. It is a combination of an inward, personal holiness that focuses on a growing relationship with God and an outward holiness that expresses that relationship by engaging in loving acts of care for God's world and God's people. For John Wesley, inward holiness was meaningless if it did not lead to faith in action. In fact, for Wesley, these two were so interrelated that there could be no inward, personal holiness without outward, social holiness. Wesley spoke of the outward holiness as "works of mercy." Galatians 6:10 was an important Scripture for John Wesley. He used this passage at least thirty-three times in his works: "Whenever we have an opportunity, let us work for the good of all, and especially for those of the family of faith."

An examination of Wesley's life tells us that he practiced what he preached to others. One of his greatest concerns was for the poor who lived all around him in eighteenth century England. He saw poverty as a result of poor stewardship of what belonged to God, and he knew that he must do what he could to restore the order that God had intended for the world. There were many ways that he and those who became part of the societies he formed showed God's love by doing good for those who were in need. They provided a school for the poor; regular literacy classes; a medical clinic and drug dispensary; room and board for widows, orphans, and those who were blind; a credit union; and support for cottage industries that provided opportunities for people to help themselves. For example, Wesley enabled a group of women to do meaningful work by initiating a fund that would lend them money so that they could buy looms and material to make cloth. Wesley's concern for God's people was also evident in his support for the abolition of slavery, his care for prisoners, and his opposition to the sale and use of liquor, which he viewed as a wasteful use of grain that could have been used to feed the poor.

"There is scarce any possible way of doing good, for which here is not daily occasion..."
(from Wesley's Journal, 1739)

Children and Doing Good

Compassion for others and a desire to be helpers come naturally to children. Your task is to cultivate those traits by helping children discover ways to express their care in loving ways. In *Three Simple Rules*, Bishop Job speaks of doing good as a way to meet "the needs of my world, my community, my congregation, my family." In these two sessions about the second simple rule—Do Good—you will want to help the children experience what it means to do good in these arenas in which they live.

Children experience caring for others most directly in their families. The practice of doing good things in their families is an important first step as they begin to move into other arenas, such as their church, their community, and their world.

The word *church* will bring many images to the minds of children. They may first think of the building where they gather to worship. When asked again, they will remember the occasions for study and fellowship that are available to them in that building. Help the children think even beyond that, though. Help them recognize that the church is actually God's people. When they do good things for the church, even if it is something for the building, they are doing good for God's people.

Many children live in areas where they never see or interact with the poor, but through their church they can learn to do good for people they do not even know. Children need to know that their church is involved in doing good through community projects to feed the hungry, to minister to those who are homeless, or to care for environmental concerns. Children may have difficulty with the concept of the world beyond their own community, but children learn by watching adults. They will grow in their understanding of their responsibility to care for the entire world as they participate with adults in "works of mercy."

Simple Rule #2: Do Good

This second of the three simple rules is about action—actively seeking for ways to do good. Many posters, books, and websites attribute these words to John Wesley, although he never wrote them in this form:

> Do all the good you can
> by all the means you can
> in all the ways you can
> in all the places you can
> at all the times you can
> to all the people you can
> as long as ever you can.

> By doing good, by being in every kind merciful after their power; as they have opportunity, doing good of every possible sort...
>
> — John Wesley

Although the poetic expression does not belong to John Wesley, the words do sum up the content of his teaching in the second of his General Rules.

Like the first rule—Do No Harm—this second rule appears at first glance to be a simple thing to do. We have already decided that we will do no harm, so how hard can it be to do good? The Bible is filled with stories about Jesus doing good—healing, feeding the hungry, teaching people to pray, and forgiving. However, if we listen closely to Jesus, we discover that it may not be as easy as it sounds.

"Love your enemies," Jesus says, "do good to those who hate you" (Luke 6:27). This is not an easy rule for children, or for adults. Advice from John Wesley may help though. He recognized the challenge of doing good, and he said in *The Character of a Methodist*, "If it be not in [one's] power to 'do good to them that hate him,' yet he ceases not to pray for them."

3 John 11b tells us that "Whoever does good is from God." When we follow God's lead through the example of Jesus Christ and do good, it is not only the lives of those for whom we do good that are transformed, but our own lives are transformed as well.

The Bible in These Lessons

Matthew 25:34-40
While belief, faith, worship, praise, and spiritual growth are important, these words from Jesus name the critical measurement for how we live as faithful disciples as the way we respond to the needs of others. Jesus names those to whom we are expected to do good and then says that by doing good to others, we are doing good to Jesus himself.

Hebrews 13:16a
Hebrews 13:15-16 recalls Jesus' commandment to love God and neighbor. Christians show love for God through continual praise and thanksgiving and confession of faith in Christ Jesus. They show love for neighbor through good deeds of kindness and sharing what they have with God's people.

First Week: Do Good for My Family and My Church

Gather to Explore

Be sure that adult leaders are waiting when the first child arrives. Greet and welcome each child and get him or her involved in an activity that introduces the theme for the day's activities.

A Look at Families

- As the children arrive, give them chenille sticks. Tell each one to use the chenille sticks to create a sculpture to represent each member of his or her family.

- Be careful not to give too much instruction. Let each child decide who he or she wants to include. Some may create only parents and siblings; others may include aunts and uncles or grandparents. Some may also include close family friends. Some will include pets.

- If your time allows, let the children be creative by adding hair, clothes, or objects that identity each person's interests or role in the family.

- When each family sculpture is ready, have the children create a family picture by standing the figures in a lump of clay.

- Have the children display all of their family sculptures on a table where everyone can see the variety.

- Gather the children around the table to talk about what they see.

- **Ask:** Just like all people, families come in different sizes and shapes. What differences do you see in the families we have represented here?

- Let the children talk about the differences they see. If the families among this group of children are fairly similar, help the children think about other family configurations they are familiar with, possibly among their friends or in families they see on television.

Prepare

✓ Provide chenille sticks, scissors, and clay.

✓ If your time will allow it, also provide a variety of other craft supplies that will encourage creativity. Possibilities include:
  - fabric scraps
  - yarn
  - construction paper
  - gluesticks

Our Church Family

- Gather the children in a circle.

- **Say:** I am going to count to three. When I say "three," call out your first name as loudly as you can. Are you ready? Okay, one, two, three. (*Wait for the shouts.*)

- **Say:** I could not understand any of your names! Let's try it again. Shout your name so that I can understand what you are saying. Ready? One, two, three! (*Wait for the shouts again.*)

Prepare

✓ Make sure the signing posters of the three simple rules are displayed (pages 5, 25, and 45).

- *Say:* Okay? Let's try it with your last names. Maybe that will be easier for me to understand. Ready? One, two, three! (*Wait for even louder shouts.*)

- *Say:* All of you have different names. Your families have different names. Let's try something else. This time when I count to three, I want every one to call out the same name. Let's all call out the name "Christian." (*Join in when the whole group shouts "Christian."*)

- *Say:* Wow! I could understand you that time! Even though all of our families have different names, we are all members of Jesus' family. We are all a part of our church families, and our family name is Christian.

- *Say:* Today we are going to talk about how we can follow Jesus by obeying the second simple rule in our two families.

- Show the children the signing posters of the three simple rules. Remind them that the first simple rule is Do No Harm. Let them sign the first rule.

- Then read the second simple rule—Do Good—and teach the children how to sign the second rule.

Know the Rule

The three simple rules the children are learning will help them to follow Jesus' teachings about how to live. The first step is to know the rule and to recognize why it is important.

Putting Love Into Action

- *Say:* What does it mean to do good? Let's play a game of Charades to help us answer that question. In our version of Charades, there will be two groups. One group will act out something, and the other group will guess what they are doing.

- Divide the children into two teams. Decide which team will do the acting first and which team will guess.

- Whisper the name of an animal to the acting team. Explain that the goal is to act out the animal so well that the other team can guess it quickly.

- After a couple of animals have been guessed, let the teams switch places so that the guessers can become actors.

- Switch team positions again. For the next actions, the actors will draw a slip of paper (page 41) that describes a way of doing good.

- *Say:* This time let's do things a little different. Guessers, do not yell out your answers. Instead, when you are sure that you know what the action is, whisper your guess to a teacher. If you are correct, you can join the actors.

- With each action, stop when two or three children have figured it out. (Do not keep going until only one child is left out of the action.)

Prepare

✓ Photocopy page 41, and cut the Charades actions into separate strips that name ways to do good for the family or the church.

✓ Fold the strips and put them in a basket.

Simple Rule #2: Do Good

- Let the children who are still seated become the new actors and draw another action from the basket.

- Let the group act out several ways to do good, depending on how much time you have available.

- *Ask:* What made it possible for you to guess what animal or what way of doing good was being acted out?

- The children will name specific actions. However, lead them to recognize that it was the fact of action itself that made it possible to know what the actors were trying to tell them.

- *Ask:* If there had been no action—if the actors had not done anything—could you have guessed what they were trying to tell you?

- *Say:* It is by our actions of doing good that others can know that we are Christians. It is by showing love in our actions that others know that we love and follow Jesus.

- Open your Bible to Matthew 25:34-40.

- *Say:* Listen to what Jesus says about how we show our love for Jesus through our actions. (*Read Matthew 25:34-40.*)

- *Say:* John Wesley reminds us that even though the first simple rule for following Jesus is Do No Harm, just doing no harm is not enough for us to do to follow Jesus. We must also do good because it is through our actions that we show our love for Jesus and let others know that we love them just as Jesus loves them.

- *Say:* Today we are going to talk about ways we can show God's love by doing good for our two families—our family at home and our family at church.

Follow the Rule

Discovering ways to follow the rule is the goal of your time with the children. Choose ways for following the rule that match their interests and the time and resources you have available.

A Thank-You Surprise

- *Ask:* Has anyone ever said "thank you" to you for something nice that you did? How did it make you feel?

- *Say:* One way that we can do good for our families is to tell them that we appreciate the many good things they do for us. Let's start with our parents. Imagine how good it will make your father or mother feel to get a surprise thank-you card from you!

- *Ask:* What good things do your parents do for you and your family?

- Make a list on a markerboard or newsprint as the children name things like cook great meals, take me to the zoo, help me with my homework, read the Bible with me, or buy me toys.

Prepare

✓ Provide construction paper, crayons or markers, and other craft supplies that may encourage the children's creativity as they make thank-you cards.

✓ Be prepared to make a list with a marker on a markerboard or newsprint.

- The children will probably need help recognizing the many things their parents do, but once you get them started, challenge them to make a really long list.

- *Say:* Now let's do something really fun. First, we are going to make some great thank-you cards. You have probably made lots of thank-you cards in Sunday school. Some of them have probably been for your mother or your father. But here is the fun part: We are going to think of a special place to hide each card so that your father or mother will find it when it is least expected.

- Show the children the supplies you have provided for making the cards.

- *Say:* While you are making a special card, think of a good place where you can hide the card.

- *Say:* Be creative with your card. Think of something that really expresses who you are or something that will be special to your mother or father. There are only two requirements for your card: (1) It must say "thank you," and (2) it must say "I love you." Other than that, be as creative as you want.

- As the children work, talk about where they will hide the cards.

- *Ask:* Do you remember why we are making these cards? (*Be sure that the children make the connection between the cards and the second simple rule: Do Good. Remind the children that Jesus wants us to do good for our families.*)

Coupon Books for Brothers and Sisters

- Remembering to do good for brothers and sisters is often the hardest thing for a child to do. Although siblings are often considered to be "natural enemies," the truth is that there is a loving bond even when children do not recognize it on ordinary days.

- *Say:* The second simple rule is Do Good. Jesus teaches us to love everyone and to do good for all people. Let's think of some simple acts of kindness that we can do for our brothers and sisters. (*Expect some silliness, but also expect some serious expressions of love.*)

- Help the children list some ways they can do good for brothers and sisters.

- Then have each child make a coupon book with at least three coupons (page 42) for each brother or sister. Help them follow these steps:
  1. Write the name of the person who will receive the coupons at the top of each of three coupons.
  2. Below the person's name, fill in a description of a simple act of kindness (read you a book, help you clean your room, let you choose two television shows to watch).
  3. Sign your name and put the date at the bottom.
  4. Stack the coupons, and staple the stack on the left side.
  5. Take the coupon book home to give to your brother or sister.
  6. Remember to cheerfully keep the promises you have made during the next week.

Prepare

- ✓ Be prepared to make a list with a marker on a markerboard or newsprint.

- ✓ Photocopy a page of coupons (page 42) for each coupon book the children will make.

- ✓ Provide markers, stapler, and staples.

- Remind the children that the coupon books will help them remember to follow Jesus and to do good.

Option

Children who want to—or those who do not have siblings—can include moms and dads, grandparents, or aunts and uncles too.

Pew Postcards

- Remind the children of their relationship to one another and to others in your congregation as a church family.

- *Ask:* What is our family name? *(Christian)*

- *Say:* Let's do something good for our church family today. Let's make some pew postcards that will tell the members of our church family that we care about them and that we appreciate what they do for our church.

- Let the children make pew postcards with positive messages for the members of the congregation. Help them follow these instructions:
  1. On a blank index card write a message for the members of your church. Choose messages such as "Welcome to Worship," "God Loves You," "Do Good for One Another," or "It is great to be a part of God's family!"
  2. Decorate the card.
  3. Glue the postcard to a piece of colorful construction paper, cut just a little larger than the card, to make a frame.

- Take the children to the sanctuary and let them place the pew postcards on the pews, in the pew racks, or sticking out from hymnals or Bibles.

Option

- Arrange to have the children straighten the books, pick up bulletins, sharpen pencils, or do some other good deed for their church while they are in the sanctuary.

Plan a Visit

- Many people who are not able to come to the church regularly would welcome a visit from the children. Talk with your pastor about someone in your congregation who would enjoy having the children come to visit.

- *Say:* Do you know that there are members of our church family who cannot come to be with us in Sunday school and worship? Some of them are sick and are not able to attend for a while, but others are not able to come at all. Do you know any of those people?

- What good things do you think we could do for those members of our church family?

Prepare

✓ Provide
  - blank index cards
  - construction paper, cut slightly larger than the index cards
  - scissors
  - gluesticks
  - markers

✓ If the children will help with straightening up the sanctuary, make arrangements with the person who usually does those tasks.

Prepare

✓ Talk with your pastor to identify a church member who would welcome a visit from the children.

✓ Contacts parents for help with planning the visit.

✓ Provide paper cups, clay, short-stemmed artificial flowers, Bible verse strips, and gluesticks or yarn.

- Help the children think about what they would have to do if they want to visit one of those church family members (talk with their parents, find out about who the person is, get someone to drive them to the person's home, decide what simple gift they could make to take to the person).

- *Say:* I will work out the details with your parents and be sure that we have transportation if you will think about what to talk about and make a simple gift.

- Help the children make a simple flower gift. Have them anchor a short-stemmed artificial flower in a small paper cup with clay. Write a Bible verse on a slip of paper and either glue it to the cup or tie it to the flower. Use a simple verse such as "Trust in the Lord and do good" (Psalm 37:3a), "Whoever does good is from God" (3 John 11b), or "Always seek to do good to one another" (1 Thessalonians 5: 15b).

- If you have not already talked with parents about helping with the visit, be sure to contact them immediately and set a date.

Do Good for Your Church

- *Say:* Let's take a trip today to discover ways that we and the rest of our church family can do good for our church.

- Ask an older child to be a recorder for the group so that the children can be reminded later of any ways they discover that they may be able to do good for their church.

- Take the children on a walk around the church—both inside and outside if time and weather permit.

- As the children walk, point out things that members of the church family must do to take care of the building.

- Note some of the things that adults have done, such as buying tables and chairs for the Sunday school rooms; providing a stove and refrigerator for the kitchen; placing altar cloths, flowers, and banners in the sanctuary to make a beautiful place to worship; taking care of the flower beds, trimming the bushes, and mowing the grass.

- Take special note of anything you or the children notice that the children can do to help take care of their church. The children can sharpen the pencils for the pews in the sanctuary, create bulletin covers for special services, keep classrooms neat and clean, greet people who come to worship, give money from their allowances to buy materials for a worship banner, deliver boxes of facial tissues to the restrooms, or take napkins to the trash after a church family dinner.

- *Say:* It takes a lot of people to do all the good that needs to be done to make our church a special place to worship and serve God.

- When the group returns to the class space, encourage the children to talk about ways they will do good to help take care of their church building and their church family in the future.

Prepare

✓ Recruit extra adult help to supervise a children's walking tour of the church building.

✓ Provide paper and pencil for a group recorder.

Celebrate and Praise God

Following Jesus by learning and following the three simple rules will help the children grow in their relationship to God. Encourage them to worship and praise both as a group and on their own.

Do Good For Our Two Families

- Call the children together for a time of celebration and praise.

- **Ask:** Today we have been talking about the second of John Wesley's three simple rules that will help us to follow Jesus. Do you remember the first simple rule? (*Do No Harm*)

- **Ask:** What is the second simple rule—the one we have been talking about today? (*Do Good*)

- **Say:** When we follow Jesus, we want to do good for all God's people. Today we talked about ways to do good for our two families—our family at home and our family at church.

- **Ask:** We all have different family names at home, but we all have the same family name at church. What is our church family name? (*Christian—Expect the answer to be shouted!*)

- Open your Bible.

- **Say:** I am going to read two verses from the Bible. Then I want you to say those two verses with me. The first verse is from the Bible passage we read earlier. Do you remember what Jesus said?

- Help the children remember that Jesus said that when we do good for other people, we are doing good for Jesus.

- **Say:** Jesus said, "Just as you did it to one of the least of these who are members of my family, you did it to me" (Matthew 25:40).

- Help the children say the verse with you.

- **Say:** In the days when the church was first being formed, those Christians remembered what Jesus had said. They reminded one another by saying these words from the Book of Hebrews: "Do not neglect to do good and to share what you have" (Hebrews 13:16a).

- Point out the signing posters of the three simple rules that you have displayed. Have the children read the words and practice the signing for the first two rules.

- Remind the children of the simple song they learned two weeks ago during the first session. It is a part of Bishop Job's *Three Simple Rules* book, and it is printed in this book on page 4.

- **Say:** As we sing this song as our closing prayer, let's sign the first two simple rules when they are mentioned. The rules are: Do No Harm and Do Good.

Prepare

✓ Mark your Bible at Matthew 25:40 and Hebrews 13:16a.

✓ Make sure the signing posters of the three simple rules are displayed (pages 5, 25, and 45).

✓ Review the song "Stay in Love With God" (page 4).

Second Week: Do Good for My Community and the World

Gather to Explore

Be sure that adult leaders are waiting when the first child arrives. Greet and welcome each child and get him or her involved in an activity that introduces the theme for the day's activities.

Where Do We Live?

- Invite your church's mission chairperson to greet the children with you as they arrive and to assist with locating places on the maps.

- First, show the children the map of your town. Point out the push pin that marks the location of your church.

- *Say:* Let's mark the places where each of us lives on the map.

- Assist the children as they identify streets and add their own location pins in the same color as the pins used to mark the location of the church.

- *Say:* Sometimes we call our town and the places nearby "our community." Today we will think about some ways that we can follow the second simple rule by talking about ways we can do good for our community.

- Then have the children focus on the map of the world. Point out the approximate location of your town on that map.

- *Say:* Our town is located in an even larger community. Our church and our town are part of God's world.

- *Say:* Last week we talked about ways to follow the second simple rule by doing good for our families and for our church. Today we will continue to talk about ways we can follow Jesus by doing good for our community (*point to the map of your town*) and for the world (*point to the world map*).

- First, let's review the three simple rules that John Wesley gave to his societies and that help us know that we are following what Jesus teaches us about living as Christians.

- Encourage the children to use the signing posters to tell their visitor about John Wesley's three simple rules that help them to follow Jesus.

- Remind the children to name the rules and to teach the visitor to sign the first two rules: Do No Harm and Do Good.

- Then let the children teach their visitor the song they have been learning about the three simple rules, "Stay in Love With God" (page 4).

Prepare

✓ Invite the chairperson of your church's mission group to meet with the children. (Later in the session, the visitor will talk about ways your church is in mission in your community and in the world.)

✓ Post two maps on the bulletin board—one of your town and one of the world.

✓ Place a push pin at the location of your church on the map of your town. Place a push pin of the same color at the approximate location of your town on the world map.

✓ Provide additional push pins the same color as those for your church and your town for the children to use.

✓ Make sure the signing posters of the three simple rules are displayed (pages 5, 25, and 45).

✓ Review the song "Stay in Love With God" (page 4).

Simple Rule #2: Do Good

Know the Rule

The three simple rules the children are learning will help them to follow Jesus' teachings about how to live. The first step is to know the rule and to recognize why it is important.

Service Project or Mission?

- Introduce your visitor as the chairperson of the group in your church that focuses on ways that the congregation can follow the second simple rule and do good for your community and for the world.

- Invite the visitor to tell whatever he or she wishes about the church's mission group.

- Provide the information below about service projects and mission projects for the speaker to include.

   Ask: When you hear the words "service project," what do you think?

   Say: We often use the term "service project" when we talk about doing good for other people. *Service* is a good word to describe what we do as Christians. One of the important things Jesus taught his disciples was that they—and we—are called by God to serve others.

   Say: There is another word that we use in the church to describe a service project. That word is *mission*. How might you describe the difference between a service project and a mission project?

   Say: Many people participate in service projects. Those projects do good for the people in the community and in the world.

   Say: Some mission projects look exactly like service projects. However, the word *mission* has a special meaning. It means "to be sent," and a mission project has a special purpose. Christians participate in mission projects because they are sent to show God's love to others through loving actions.

   Say: Whether we call what we do "service" or "mission," though, remember that when we follow Jesus by obeying the second simple rule—Do Good—we are responding to Jesus' command to love one another.

Say: Remember what Jesus said. *(Open your Bible.)* "Just as you did it to one of the least of these who are members of my family, you did it to me" (Matthew 25:40).

Say: And in Hebrew 13:16a we read that the early church taught Jesus' followers: "Do not neglect to do good and to share what you have."

Say: Today you will learn about some ways our church is already involved in mission projects in our community and in the world. You will also have an opportunity to participate in some mission projects as you follow the second simple rule: Do Good.

Prepare
✓ Give your missions chairperson information from the lesson plan to use in preparing to talk with the children about mission.

Follow the Rule

Discovering ways to follow the rule is the goal of your time with the children. Choose ways for following the rule that match their interests and the time and resources you have available.

What in the World Are We Doing?

- Have your missions chairperson continue to help you lead the children as they learn more about what their church is doing in missions.

- Point out the poster, the brochures, and the pictures you have gathered to describe the mission projects your church is involved in.

- *Ask:* Are you familiar with any of these projects? *(Hopefully, the children will have heard of some or perhaps helped with some of the projects.)*

- Give the children some time to work together with the missions chairperson to discover what each of the projects does to help God's people in their community or in the world.

- If you have a long list of projects, assign each project to one or two children. Pair younger children with older children who may be better readers.

- Let the children write one or two discoveries about each project beside the name of the project on the poster. (feed people who are hungry, provide housing, collect clothes, provide medical care, send missionaries, teach children)

- After a few minutes, call the group together to talk about what they have discovered.

- *Ask:* What have you learned about how our congregation is already following the second simple rule.

- Have the missions chairperson add interesting details as the children tell what they have learned about the projects.

Sent to Do Good in the World

- Remind the children of the world map with the push pin that marks the approximate location of their town and church,

- *Ask:* What countries do your families come from? Have you ever visited another country?

- Mark any countries the children mention with push pins of a different color from those used for their homes.

- *Ask:* Do you remember the meaning of the word *mission*? *(to be sent)* How, then, might you describe what a missionary does? *(a missionary is sent to show people about God's love)*

- *Ask:* Do you know which countries have missionaries who have been sent there by our church?

- *Say:* Let's find out!

Prepare

✓ With the help of your missions chairperson, make a poster that lists the mission projects your church supports in your community and in the world. Leave space beside each one for the children to write.

✓ Gather brochures and pictures or other information to describe each of the projects. If you do not have brochures, find articles that have been in your church newsletter or information from your church website or the websites of organizations you serve.

Prepare

✓ Write names and locations of missionaries on separate slips of paper. (Some churches have prayer calendars with missionaries' names. Others have names and locations on a website.)

✓ Fold the slips and put them in basket.

✓ Supply yarn and push pins (a different color from those used to mark children's homes and the church's location).

Simple Rule #2: Do Good

- Let each child draw the name of a missionary. Then have the child tape the name on the bulletin board and connect the name to the missionary's location with yarn and a push pin of the new color. If there are missionaries from your local congregation, be sure that the children know about those people. The children will be especially interested if they have met those missionaries or their families.

- *Say:* God calls each of us to be a missionary. Some missionaries, like those we have located on our map, are called to go to other countries to show God's love to people there. We cannot all go to another country, but we can do good by supporting those people who do.

- *Ask:* What do you think missionaries do in other countries?

- Help the children recognize that missionaries are doctors and nurses, teachers, farmers, preachers, and whatever other helpers are needed to do good as followers of Jesus. Missionaries help us follow Jesus by doing good through the work of our church.

- *Say:* Let's write letters to tell missionaries that we appreciate what they do to help all us follow the simple rule to do good.

- Let each child choose a missionary to write.

- When the letters are ready, collect them to mail or send the letters home to be mailed from each family.

Sent to Do Good in Our Community

- Bring out a large cardboard box for the children to decorate with the materials you have provided. Encourage the children to be creative, but tell them that they must use all the pictures.

- Do not offer explanations for the pictures and symbols you have gathered, but encourage the children to think as they work about how they think these things might be related to the simple rule: Do Good.

- When the box is ready, call the children together to discuss what they see on the box they have created.

- *Ask:* Does anything on our box suggest a way that we can do good for our community during the next few weeks

- Encourage the children to identify ways that each picture suggests a way that they can do good for people in their community. For example:
  → *sweater:* give clothing to an group that serves the poor or homeless;
  → *cans of food:* collect food for people who are hungry;
  → *greeting card:* send a note to someone in a nursing home or hospital;
  → *book:* provide children's books for a family shelter;
  → *toy:* clean out closets and give unused toys to a day-care center;
  → *trash bag:* pick up litter in the neighborhood;
  → *dust cloth or rake:* go as a group to help an older person clean up the house or the yard.

- *Say:* We have a box to collect things that can help us do good. Let's get our church members to help us fill the box.

Prepare
- ✓ Provide a large box and a variety of craft supplies.

- ✓ Cut out pictures to represent a variety of ways to do good in the community. (See suggestions in the activity description.)

Three Simple Rules for Following Jesus

- Choose a place to put the box so that members of the church family can bring donations. The task for the children will be to let people know about the box, what kinds of items they can donate, and where the items will be distributed.

- Help the children decide how to advertise their collection. They can design posters, write articles for the church newsletter or bulletin, talk to the pastor about announcements during a worship service, plan visits to adult Sunday school classes to tell what they have been learning about following Jesus by doing good. Wherever possible, let them explain the symbols represented by the pictures on the box.

- Plan for the children to meet again at a later date to sort the items that are collected and, if possible, participate in deliveries.

Do Good for Your Enemies

- Invite two guests to perform the play on page 43 to help the children start a conversation about Jesus' command to love our enemies.

- After the play, invite the performers to join a discussion about how this play is related to the second simple rule: Do Good.

- *Ask:* Why do you think Jesus said "love your enemies, do good to those who hate you" (Luke 6:27)?

- *Say:* This play has taught us about doing good even to those who we do not like, who we disagree with, or even those who have hurt us. Loving our enemies is often a hard thing to do. Loving our enemies does not mean that we allow people to hurt us or bully us. However, Jesus wants us to respond to others by treating them as we want to be treated, even if they do not understand about the rule to do good.

Prepare
✓ Recruit two people to perform a simple play (page 43) for your group.

Do Good Outside the Classroom

- The reality of meeting for an short period of time in a classroom while adults are meeting in a room down the hall limits the opportunities for children to get physically involved in doing good for their community and their world. If you want to help the children develop a habit of doing good for others, as well as a desire to be involved in doing good in the name of Jesus Christ, help them plan a project that will take them outside the church building and into the world.

- Such a project would have to begin with parents—both for permission and for adult involvement. Since we know that parents and children working together in mission is a strong factor in the development of a vital, growing, and lifelong faith for children, you will want consider a project in which parents and children can work together.

- Talk with your missions chairperson. Are there projects already being planned to which children can make a significant contribution? If possible, begin with specific plans so the children can get involved when the talk about the spiritual disciplines of learning, serving, and worshiping with others in a couple of weeks.

Prepare
✓ Contact parents to set a time to talk about a mission project for families.

✓ Talk with your missions chairperson about possibilities for families becoming involved in projects that are already being planned.

Celebrate and Praise God

Following Jesus by learning and following the three simple rules will help the children grow in their relationship to God. Encourage them to worship and praise both as a group and on their own.

Pray for Your Community and the World

- Gather the children around the maps on the bulletin board.

- *Say:* Today we have talked about ways to do good for people in our community and for people who live all over the world.

- Help the children recall some of the projects their own church participates in to do good. Look at the pins on the community map first and name some of the places that are marked. Then focus on the world map.

- *Say:* One of the most important things we can do to care for our community and our world is to pray for the people there.

- *Pray:* Gracious and loving God, we know that you call all of us to be missionaries. You send us out to do good for people all around us. Today, we pray especially for people in our community who are helped through... *(have the children name the places your congregation serves in your community).* And we pray for missionaries all over the world like *(have the children name the missionaries who are named on their map).* Amen.

Prepare

✓ Be sure that the world map and the map of your town are still displayed.

Do All the Good You Can

- *Say:* This second of the three simple rules is about action—actively seeking for ways to do good.

- Give each child a photocopy of page 44.

- *Say:* Many posters, books, and websites attribute these words to John Wesley, although he never wrote them in this form. These words do, however, sum up what John Wesley taught about the second simple rule: Do Good.

- Have the children read the words on the poster in unison.

> Do all the good you can
> by all the means you can
> in all the ways you can
> in all the places you can
> at all the times you can
> to all the people you can
> as long as ever you can.

- *Say:* Let's make a poster to hang at home where your family can see it and remember that one of the ways we follow Jesus is to do good.

- Have each child glue a page to a sheet of construction paper and, as time allows, decorate their posters. If time is not available, encourage the children to complete their posters at home.

Prepare

✓ Photocopy the poster on page 44 for each child.

✓ Provide construction paper, gluesticks, and crayons or markers.

Charades

Set the table for a family meal.
Read a book to a young child.
Pick up litter around the church.
Pray for someone.
Sing in a choir.
Help wash dishes.
Feed your pet.
Fold and put away clothes.
Make a card for your mother's or father's birthday.
Greet people who come to worship.
Help your Sunday school teacher pass out craft supplies.
Invite a friend to come to your Sunday school class.

To _____

This entitles you to _____

_____

From _____ Date _____

To _____

This entitles you to _____

_____

From _____ Date _____

To _____

This entitles you to _____

_____

From _____ Date _____

Art: Brenda Gilliam

Three Simple Rules for Following Jesus

Love Your Enemies—and Do Good

(*A wall made of cardboard bricks is built fairly high. There is a box that contains pizza boxes and gear such as catcher's mask and knee pads. Builder walks in with more cardboard bricks.*)

Greeter: Hello. Can I help you?

Builder: No, thanks. I am just building a wall—to keep people out, you know!

Greeter: But we welcome everyone here.

Builder: (*to self*) Not a good idea, not a good idea.

(*Builder continues to build the wall.*)

Greeter: Who do you want to keep out?

Builder: Enemies. We have to keep enemies out!

Greeter: But this is a church!

Builder: And your point is?

Greeter: Jesus said we should love our enemies and do good to them.

Builder: I think I can love them a lot better if they are not on my side of the wall.

Greeter: Well, maybe it *would* be easier to love your neighbors if you never had to see them or talk to them. But that is pretty unrealistic.

Builder: You obviously never built a wall.

Greeter: But you cannot stay back there forever. Won't you have to come out some time?

Builder: Probably not. I have a cell phone and my computer. I can get anything I need online.

(*Builder disappears behind the wall. Greeter walks off the stage. After a minute, Greeter comes back. Builder stands up, pretending to eat from a pizza box.*)

Greeter: Aren't you getting lonely back there?

Builder: Who, me?

Greeter: I was just thinking that by staying back there by yourself, you have kept out your enemies—but you've also kept out your friends.

Builder: But enemies can hurt you. This brick is for the people who wouldn't let me be on their team. And this brick is for the people who made fun of

the way I look. And this one is for the people who don't believe the same things I do. And ...

Greeter: Yes, there are lots of reasons to consider someone an enemy. God understands that.

(*Builder reaches into the box and puts on protective gear. Then Builder begins to slowly dismantle the wall.*)

Greeter: So, the wall is coming down, huh?

Builder: For now. But I am still not taking any chances. No enemy is going to hurt me!

Greeter: There were people who hurt Jesus. His friend Peter deserted him when he needed him most by saying he did not even know Jesus. And what about Judas? He proved to be an enemy. And Jesus does not like it when your enemies betray you. But Jesus forgave his enemies. Even though they hurt Jesus, he still loved them. And Jesus loves you and your enemies too.

Builder: But that's Jesus! Of course he can forgive!

Greeter: Jesus knows it is not easy for you either—but he understands. He believes you can love them and do good for them!

Builder: I think the wall was easier.

(*Greeter and Builder pick up the pieces of the wall and walk off arm in arm. Greeter returns to the stage and begins to say something to the audience, but Builder comes on stage again with an armload of bricks.*)

Greeter: Oh, no! Not another wall?

Builder: No, no. No walls.

Greeter: Then?

Builder: I thought maybe a bridge.

Greeter: There's an idea!

Builder: I will not always be able to be friends with my enemies, but I can pray for them. And I will try to do good things for them, even if they do not treat me as Jesus teaches. So, let's build a bridge!

Greeter: Awesome!

(*Builder and Greeter start to build together.*)

(Adapted from "Love Your Enemies," *PowerXpress!* Copyright © 2005 Abingdon Press)

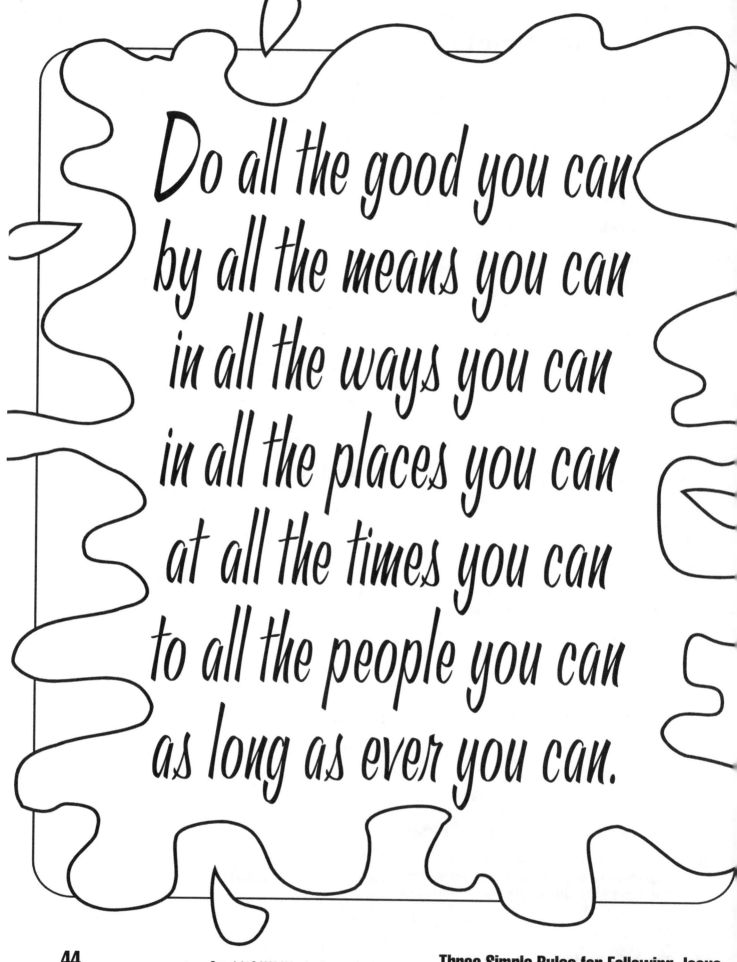

Do all the good you can
by all the means you can
in all the ways you can
in all the places you can
at all the times you can
to all the people you can
as long as ever you can.

Three Simple Rules for Following Jesus

STAY IN LOVE WITH GOD

First Week: **By Spending Time With God**
Second Week: **By Learning, Serving, and Worshiping With Others**

Objectives

The children will
- learn that spiritual disciplines help them develop a growing relationship with God;
- recognize that prayer and Bible study are ways they can get to know God better;
- realize that participating in community with other Christians helps us all live as God's people.

Bible Story

John 21:15-17, 19b: Jesus asks Peter "Do you love me?" When Peter declares his love, Jesus responds, "Feed my sheep."

Bible Verse

1 John 4:21, CEV: The commandment that God has given us is: "Love God and love each other!"

Focus for the Teacher

Wesley and "Works of Piety"

The third of John Wesley's General Rules calls for Christians to respond "by attending upon all the ordinances of God." *Ordinances* is not a common word for most people these days, but Wesley's meaning is clear and his rule is still essential for Christian living. We might define Wesley's ordinances as the spiritual disciplines that keep our relationship with God vital and growing. In *Three Simple Rules* Bishop Job translates Wesley's third rule as "Stay in Love With God." It is this third rule that makes it possible to follow the first two rules—Do No Harm and Do Good.

John Wesley's theology of "holiness of heart and life" includes both "works of mercy" and "works of piety." The works of piety, which Wesley also calls "means of grace," are "outward signs, words, or actions, ordained of God, and appointed for this end, to be the ordinary channels whereby he might convey to men, preventing, justifying, or sanctifying grace" *(Sermon 16, "The Means of Grace")*. Wesley's means of grace include
- public worship of God
- reading and studying the Scriptures
- reading and proclaiming God's Word
- the Lord's Supper
- family and private prayer
- fasting or abstinence
- Christian conferencing.

John Wesley wrote in his journal that holiness is "the life of God in the soul; the image of God fresh stamped on the heart." Consider what it means to be continually recreated in the image of God! That is what Wesley suggests can happen when Christians practice the means of grace. When John Wesley died in 1791, his last words to the friends gathered around him were, "The best of all is, God is with us."

Children and Spiritual Disciplines

Ordinances? works of piety? means of grace? How can children understand the third simple rule with so many terms that describe it? The best course of action is to choose a term that children can relate to and use that one. The term easiest to describe for children, and one they will continue to hear throughout their lives, is *spiritual disciplines*.

When children first hear the word *discipline*, their response is likely to be a negative one. No one wants discipline when it means being punished for doing something wrong. Even the Bible says that "discipline always seems painful rather than pleasant at the time" (Hebrews 12:11). Your challenge then will be to help the children recognize the more positive meanings of the word *discipline* and to help them understand why they should want to have spiritual disciplines in their lives.

Spending Time With God: Children understand prayer as spending time with God. Depending on their ages, though, children may have difficulty with the idea that they can listen to God as well as speak to God. Some may have experienced only memorized prayers or have little experience with prayer at all. The concept of Bible study as a way to listen to God may also be new to some children. They know that the Bible tells stories about Jesus, but some may have never read from the Bible except in Sunday school class. Be patient as children discover that they can spend time with God through the spiritual disciplines of prayer and Bible study.

Learning, Serving, and Worshiping With Others: Children need to experience the church as a community. It is important for them to develop a sense of belonging with others who love God and gather to worship, learn, and serve. As children participate in the church, they can discover that Christian community is a gift from God. Participating in the activities of the church is a spiritual discipline that can help them grow in relationship with one another and with God.

We also know that God will be near, listening and speaking to us when we pray and when we read and study the Scripture. God is with us when we study and pray on own or when we come together in groups where we will be able to hear God's voice through the questions, the insights, and the experiences of others.

When we are in meaningful relationship with God, who created us and loves us, we will find that our passion for seeing God's love and grace revealed to the entire world grows as we see Christ in the faces of those we serve in God's name. Working together as God's family in the community of faith will take on greater importance than ever before.

> By attending upon all the ordinances of God...
>
> — John Wesley

When Christians follow this third rule—Stay in Love With God—their lives are transformed. Then those who are transformed by staying in love with God through the practice of spiritual disciplines are able to respond in ways that transform the lives of others.

Simple Rule #3: Stay in Love With God

"The best of all is, God is with us." Wesley's last words define the heart of the third simple rule—Stay in Love With God. We must be careful not to forget that God's love is the fundamental starting point of all that has value. Remembering God's love and presence reminds us that we must respond with love for God in order for the most important relationship we will ever know to be nurtured and to grow. The ordinances of God are more than a list of things to add to an already crowded to-do list. Without the practice of spiritual disciplines that keep us in a loving relationship with God, little else will have real meaning.

The specific spiritual disciplines that are most meaningful will vary from person to person. The goal of any spiritual discipline, though, is to stay in close relationship with God. One essential practice that keeps us connected to God is worship—especially corporate worship in the community of faith, where we can depend on God to be present.

The Bible in These Lessons

John 21:15-17, 19b

"Do you love me?" Just as Peter had denied Jesus three times, Jesus gave Peter three opportunities to declare his love. It was important for Peter, who had faltered just as we falter today, to stay in love with God through Jesus Christ. Then, as now, it is through relationships between God and God's people that God's goodness, presence, and love flow into the world. Staying in love with God is more than praying, worshiping, and declaring love for God. Staying in love with God comes with a responsibility for caring for God's world, summed up in Jesus' words to Peter, "Feed my sheep."

1 John 4:21, CEV

This verse is a summary of Jesus' answer when he was asked to name the greatest commandment (Luke 10:27). Jesus' answer came from the Hebrew Scriptures as he quoted the Shema (Deuteronomy 6:4-5) and an ancient law from the Book of Leviticus (19:18). Love of God and love of neighbor are the bases for John Wesley's concern for holiness of heart and life.

First Week: Stay in Love With God by Spending Time With God

Gather to Explore

Be sure that adult leaders are waiting when the first child arrives. Greet and welcome each child and get him or her involved in an activity that introduces the theme for the day's activities.

Amen Scramble

- As the children arrive, give a set of letters (in random order) to each group of four children.

- Challenge the children to unscramble the letters to make a word.

- If the children make words like *name, mean,* or *mane,* tell them that yes, that is a word, but you are looking for another word.

- As each group of children discovers the word *amen,* congratulate them. If a group finds the word quickly, let them look for other words while the other groups continue to look.

- When all the children have gathered, talk about the word *amen.*

- *Ask:* When do you hear or say the word *amen? (at the end of prayers)* When do you hear prayers? *(in worship services, at the table at mealtimes, at bedtime, when you pray at other times)*

- *Say:* Today we will begin talking about the third of the three simple rules: Stay in Love With God. Let's sign this rule.

- Show the children how to sign "Stay in Love With God."

- *Say:* Prayer is one of the things we will talk about today as we learn about ways to spend time with God and get to know God better.

Prepare

✓ Make a set of the letters A, M, E, and N, each written on a separate sheet of construction paper, for each four children in the group.

✓ Make sure the signing posters of the three simple rules are displayed (pages 5, 25, and 45).

Prayer and Bible Center

- Let the children work together to create a Prayer and Bible Center in one area of the classroom.

- They can begin with a small table, a tablecloth, a candle and candleholder, and a Bible.

- Provide a variety of other items for the children to work with.

- Encourage the children to come up with their own ideas about how to arrange the space for a worship center.

Prepare

✓ Provide materials for creating a worship table:
- Bible
- tablecloth
- candle and candleholder
- matches
- nature objects (leaves, flowers, an interesting piece of wood)
- quiet worship music and CD player

Know the Rule

The three simple rules the children are learning will help them to follow Jesus' teachings about how to live. The first step is to know the rule and to recognize why it is important.

Discipline—Who Needs It!

- Call the children together to talk about the third simple rule.

- **Ask:** What do you think of when you hear the word *discipline*? (*It is likely that the children's experience with the word* discipline *will be the idea of punishment.*)

- After a short time, hand a good reader a dictionary. Ask him or her to look up the word *discipline*.

- Have the child read the definition that speaks of discipline as punishment or as a method for forcing obedience.

- **Say:** We are all familiar with that kind of discipline. That is not the kind of discipline we are going to talk about today as we consider the third simple rule though.

- Direct the same child to read the definition that speaks of discipline as training that helps us learn so that we can make an improvement.

- **Say:** These two definitions are not really so different. For example, when a parent punishes a young child for running into the street, what is the purpose? (*to improve the child's behavior to keep him or her safe*) The purpose of discipline in this case is to help the child learn something that is good for the child.

- **Say:** Another example of discipline is related to athletes. Do you play a sport? Do you have to exercise and practice to be able to play well? Sometimes athletes call this kind of training "discipline."

- **Say:** The Bible talks about discipline in all these ways. Listen to these words from Hebrews 12:9-11. (*Read the Bible passage aloud.*)

- **Ask:** Can you think of another word that is in the Bible many times that is related to the word *discipline*? Look at the word *discipline*, and you can almost see the word there. (*Coach them if necessary, but the children will likely recognize the word* disciple *quickly.*)

- Now ask another child to look for the definition of the word *disciple* that describes a disciple as a learner.

- **Say:** We are disciples—learners. Today we are going to talk about spiritual disciplines. What do you suppose that means? (*practices that will help us grow in what we know about God and in our relationship with God*)

- **Say:** The spiritual disciplines we will talk about today are some that will help us get to know God better by spending time with God.

Prepare

✓ Provide a Bible and a children's dictionary.

✓ Look up the words *discipline* and *disciple* in a dictionary. Be prepared to direct the one who reads to each definition as it is needed.

✓ If you have younger children, plan to read the dictionary definitions yourself.

Communicating With God

- *Ask:* How do we get to know our friends?

- *Say:* One of the ways is through communication. We talk to them and listen to them.

- *Say:* There are some scrambled words on the walls in our room. All of them are related to ways we communicate. How many can you figure out? Some of them may be hard, so help one another.

- Encourage the children to work together as they create a list of the words that name ways we can communicate.

- Call the group together to talk about what they have discovered.

- *Ask:* Which of these words are ways that we can communicate with God? (Prayer *and possibly* talking *will probably be the children's first responses. Help them to add* music, reading, signing, body language, *and* listening *to the list.*)

- *Say:* Today we will think about ways that we can get to know God better by communicating with God. We talk to God when we pray—sometimes talking through music, signing, or our body language. We can also listen to God when we pray, when we listen to music, and when we read the Bible.

- *Say:* Speaking and listening to God are important spiritual disciplines that will help us learn and grow as we spend time with God and follow the third simple rule.

- *Ask:* What is the third simple rule? (*Stay in Love With God*)

Spending Time With God in Prayer

For Younger Children—Prayer Butterflies

- Help the children follow these instructions:
  1. Place both hands on a sheet of construction paper with thumbs touching and the other fingers slightly separated.
  2. Have someone trace around the hands with a pencil.
  3. Add butterfly antennae at the top of the thumbs.
  4. Write the words "Talking to God" in large letters down the center of the thumbs section.
  5. Write these words on the other fingers, starting from the little finger on the left: "Thanks," "Forgiveness," "My Family," "My Church," "My Friends," "My World," "Myself," "Praise."

- Talk with the children about the various things that their prayer butterflies can remind them of as they pray.

- Have them point to each finger on the butterfly, and help them pray a sentence prayer for each of the ways suggested there.

- Let the children decorate their butterflies with crayons.

Prepare

✓ Write scrambled words that describe ways people communicate on sheets of construction paper. Display them on the walls.

Possibilities:

- alm-ie (e-mail)
- xtte esmgsae (text message)
- kltangi (talking)
- llec hnope (cell phone)
- daori (radio)
- uicms (music)
- drgeian (reading)
- ngsingi (signing)
- dybogulagnae (body language)
- nelitsign (listening)
- rypare (prayer)

Prepare

✓ Provide construction paper, pencils, markers, and crayons.

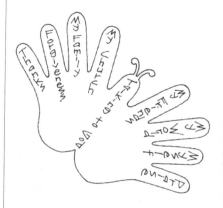

Art: Brenda Gilliam

For Older Children—Rainbow Prayer Fans

- Help the children follow these directions to make Rainbow Prayer Fans:
  1. Copy the names of the ten types of prayers listed at the top of page 61 onto ten different colored construction paper strips.
  2. Cut out the ten descriptions of types of prayers. Place each description beside the name of the prayer that is being described.
  3. Talk with your teacher and classmates about the kinds of prayer. Be sure you all agree on the matching of prayer types and descriptions.
  4. Glue each description on the back of the name of the matching prayer.
  5. Stack the strips with the names of the types of prayer facing up.
  6. Fasten the stack together with a brad on one end.
  7. Flip through your prayer fan each day to remind you of all the many different ways that you can spend time with God in prayer.

Spending Time With God in Bible Study

- **Say:** Prayer is a way that we can talk to God. Spending time with God is more than our talking to God, though. When we spend time with our friends we talk to them, but we also listen to what they say to us. When we spend time with God, we want to listen to God. We do not actually hear God speak to us through our ears, but we can "hear" what God wants us to know if we will listen with our hearts.

- **Ask:** How can we listen to hear what God wants to say to us? (*Give time for some thoughtful answers. Be prepared for some silliness too!*)

- Help the children recognize that we often hear God when we listen to our parents and others who teach us about God. We can hear God when we listen to our conscience and when we learn about what Jesus teaches us.

- **Say:** One of the best ways we can listen for what God wants us to hear is by reading the Bible and listening for what we can learn through God's Word. Reading the Bible is an important spiritual discipline we can develop. Let's experience how that works by hearing and reading a Bible story.

- **Say:** One day after the Resurrection, the disciples were fishing in the Sea of Tiberias when they heard Jesus calling to them from the beach. Peter was so excited that he jumped into the water and swam to the shore. After Jesus had prepared breakfast for the disciples, Jesus and Peter talked. Let's listen to what they said.

- Have the children close their eyes and prepare to listen closely. Then, read John 21:15-17, 19b aloud.

- Have the children open their eyes and find the story in their Bibles.

- **Ask:** What did we hear God say to us as we read the conversation between Jesus and Peter? What did Jesus want Peter to do? What does Peter's story tell you about what God wants you to do?

- **Say:** Hearing what God wants you to do by reading the Bible is an important way to get to know God. Knowing God better helps us to stay in love with God.

Prepare

✓ Photocopy page 61 for each child.

✓ Provide construction paper strips, about 4½-by-2½, in ten different colors for each child.

✓ Provide scissors, gluesticks, and brads.

Prepare

✓ Provide Bibles.

Follow the Rule

Discovering ways to follow the rule is the goal of your time with the children. Choose ways for following the rule that match their interests and the time and resources you have available.

Speak and Listen to God

- Choose one of these activities, depending on the ages and the interests of your children.

Option 1—Prayer Time

- **Say:** When we pray, we need to think not only about what we want God to do but also about what God may want us to do. Listening to God, like listening to our friends, requires that we spend some time being silent. It is not always easy to be quiet, but let's try it.

- Have the children spread out around the room, with each one choosing a personal space for individual prayer.

- Guide the children as they practice speaking and listening as parts of praying. Give these instructions:
  1. Think of something that you want to ask God to help you with.
  2. Take some time to talk to God and tell God what you need or want.
  3. When you hear the music start, choose what you will do while you listen for what God wants you to do in the situation you have prayed about. You can choose to sit quietly with your eyes closed. You can choose to move with the music. Or you can choose to draw to the music, letting the colors and lines express what you hear God saying.

Prepare

✓ Be prepared to play some quiet music that the children can listen to as they listen for what God is saying them.

✓ Provide streamers for those who choose to move to the music as they listen.

✓ Provide paper and crayons for those who choose to draw as they listen.

Option 2—An Ancient Discipline

- **Say:** A spiritual discipline used by people in ancient times and still used today is called a labyrinth. The labyrinth is an ancient sacred design that has been found in many different cultures all over the world.

- Give each child a copy of a labyrinth (page 62).

- **Say:** A labyrinth looks like a maze, but it is different from a maze. A labyrinth has only one path that goes in a circle from the beginning to the end. There are no dead ends. Knowing that you can trust the path makes it possible to relax and concentrate on knowing God.

- Have the children spread out around the room, with each one choosing a personal space for using the labyrinth. Give these instructions:
  1. Find the opening to the labyrinth. It is at the center of the right hand side of the labyrinth.
  2. Trace the path to the center of the labyrinth with your finger, or you can use a crayon in a color that expresses how you are feeling today.
  3. As you follow the path, think about a question you want to ask God. Pray about that question as you follow the path.

Prepare

✓ Photocopy a labyrinth (page 62) for each child.

✓ If your church has a walking labyrinth, be prepared to give the children information about its use, when it is available, and who walks it.

✓ Arrange a time for the children to experience walking the labyrinth if possible.

4. When you reach the center, stay a minute, listening for God.
5. When you are ready, follow the path back to the outside.

- *Ask:* How did it feel to pray while following the path? Did you feel as if God was listening to you and talking to you?

Study the Bible

- *Say:* Let's have some fun while we hear and learn from reading important words from the Bible.

- Divide the group into three teams.

- Give these instructions:
  1. The words of three copies of a Bible verse are hidden in our room. They are hidden, but you will not have to pull things off of shelves or look in boxes to find them.
  2. Your team will be assigned a color. Your task is to find all the words written on that color and to put them together to make a paper chain with the words of the Bible verse in the right order.
  3. When you have figured out where the verse is in the Bible, look it up and check the verse you have created.
  4. When you have finished, have your entire team bring your chain and your Bible to me. Show me where you found the verse, and read the verse aloud from the Bible.

- Assign each team a color matching one of the hidden Bible verses.

- When all the teams have completed their chains, hang the chains on a wall or from the ceiling.

- *Say:* The Bible verse you have found is called the Great Commandment. In the Book of 1 John there is a summary of what Jesus said. Can you find the Book of 1 John?

- Help the children find 1 John 4:21 (CEV) and read it aloud.

- *Say:* When we practice the spiritual discipline of reading the Bible, we can learn what God has to say to us. What do these verses tell us that God wants from us?

Finding Help in the Bible

Say: Reading and studying the Bible is a spiritual discipline that can help us spend time with God and get to know God better. We can turn to the Bible to hear what God has to say to us anytime, but we may especially need to hear from our friend, God, when we have problems.

- Give out copies of "Finding Help in the Bible" (page 63).

- Allow some time for the children to look at the list. Encourage them to look up a few of the verses.

- Tell the children to fold the list in half and keep it handy in their Bibles. It will be available there to assist them when they need to find help from God's Word.

Prepare

✓ Write each word of the Great Commandment on three strips of construction paper in three different colors. Be sure to include the reference for the location of the verse, Luke 10:27.

✓ Hide all three sets of strips around the classroom. Choose hiding places that do not require the children to pull books or toys from the shelves.

✓ Provide gluesticks and three CEV Bibles.

Prepare

✓ Photocopy "Finding Help in the Bible" (page 63) for each child.

Celebrate and Praise God

Following Jesus by learning and following the three simple rules will help the children grow in their relationship to God. Encourage them to worship and praise both as a group and on their own.

Prayer and Bible Study—Two Spiritual Disciplines

- Have the children gather in their Prayer and Bible Center.

- Light the candle on the worship table and explain that the lighted candle is a symbol to remind us that God is with us as we worship together.

- **Say:** Today we have added a third simple rule. Do you remember the third rule? (*Stay in Love With God*) We have learned that one way to stay in love with God is to spend time with God, getting to know God better. One way to get to know God better is by practicing spiritual disciplines. What is a spiritual discipline?

- **Ask:** What two spiritual disciplines did we talk about today? (*prayer and Bible study*)

- Pick up the Bible and open it to the Book of John. Encourage the children to find John 21:15-17, 19b in their own Bibles.

- Help the children recall the story of Jesus' words to Peter: "Feed my sheep."

- Turn to Psalm 119, and help the children find the psalm in their Bibles.

- **Say:** Psalm 119 has only one chapter. It is the longest chapter in the Bible—176 verses! This chapter is also different because, instead of telling stories about what God has done, Psalm 119 praises God's Word. Psalm 119 teaches us that reading and studying the Bible helps us to live as God wants us to live.

- **Say:** Listen and follow along as I read Psalm 119:101-105, which describes God's Word as a light that guides us. (*Read Psalm 119:101-105 aloud from a CEV Bible.*)

- **Say:** Today we have also talked about prayer. What word did we talk about earlier that we often use at the end of a prayer? (*Amen*)

- **Ask:** What does the word *amen* mean?

- **Say:** Saying "amen" means more than that we have come to the end of the prayer. The word *amen* comes from a Hebrew word that means "let it be so." When we end our prayers with "amen," we are expressing faith that God will hear and act on the prayer.

- **Say:** Let's pray together. When we finish our prayer, let's say "Amen." (*Encourage any children who will to pray a short prayer. Then close with your own prayer, emphasizing the "Amen" at the end.*)

- **Pray:** Thank you, God, for ways to communicate with you and to spend time with you. Help us to think of you as a friend we can talk to anytime. Help us learn to listen for what you have to say to us as we practice the spiritual disciplines of prayer and Bible study. Amen.

Prepare

- ✓ Plan to use the Prayer and Bible Center the children created earlier.

- ✓ Provide CEV Bibles, at least one for each two children.

Second Week: Stay in Love With God by Learning, Serving, and Worshiping With Others

Gather to Explore

Be sure that adult leaders are waiting when the first child arrives. Greet and welcome each child and get him or her involved in an activity that introduces the theme for the day's activities.

Describe God's Church

- As the children arrive, show them the large drawing of a church building that you prepared and the craft supplies you have gathered.

- Challenge them to work together to create a montage or collage that illustrates what God's church is like—who is a part of God's church and what kinds of things God's church does.

- The children can cut pictures or words from magazines; draw their own pictures; write words, phrases or poems; or use their creativity to choose other ways to describe God's church.

- As more children arrive, encourage the group that is already working to explain what they are doing and get others involved in the project.

- When everyone has arrived and the project has taken shape, call the group together to talk about the church they have described in their art. Help them talk about the pictures, words, or other items they have chosen.

- As the children talk, notice the many kinds of people who are part of the church. If for some reason a specific group of people has been left out—babies, people with handicapping conditions, poor people, rich people, older adults, people of a variety of cultural backgrounds, and so forth—challenge someone to find a word or picture to add quickly.

- Note the activities that are illustrated. As with the people included, identify activities that need to be included—activities for fellowship, for worship, for learning, for serving—and add those that are missing.

- Continue working until everyone feels that their creation truly represents all of God's church.

- *Say:* Today we will talk about the third of the three simple rules: Stay in Love With God. One of the ways we do that is through our church. When we learn, serve, and worship with other people who love God, our own relationship with God is strengthened.

- *Say:* Let's sign this third simple rule.

- Show the children how to sign "Stay in Love With God."

Prepare

- ✓ Draw a large, simple outline of a church building on mural paper and post it on the wall.

- ✓ Provide magazines, scissors, gluesticks, markers, and an assortment of other craft supplies.

- ✓ Make sure the signing posters of the three simple rules are displayed (pages 5, 25, and 45).

Know the Rule

The three simple rules the children are learning will help them to follow Jesus' teachings about how to live. The first step is to know the rule and to recognize why it is important.

Love the Lord Your God

- Call the children together to talk about the Shema (Deuteronomy 6:4-5).

- **Ask:** Last week we talked about Jesus' Great Commandment. Do you remember what Jesus said when he was asked to name the most important of all the commandments?

- Remind the children that Jesus said, "You shall love the Lord your God with all your heart, and with all your soul, and with all your strength, and with all your mind; and your neighbor as yourself" (Luke 10:27).

- **Say:** Jesus was quoting from the Hebrew Scriptures that he had learned as a child. Those Scriptures are the part of our Bible that we call the Old Testament. Let's read what Jesus learned.

- Have one of the children find and read Deuteronomy 6:4-5.

- **Say:** These words are called the Shema. Jesus added a second verse from the Book of Leviticus in the Hebrew Scriptures. Jesus also said, "Love your neighbor as yourself" (Leviticus 19:18).

- **Say:** The Hebrews bound these words on their hands to remind them of the command to love God. Let's make a wristband to remind us of what both the Old and New Testaments tell us about staying in love with God.

- Help the children make a wristband.
  1. Beginning at the wide end of a paper triangle (1½ inches at the base and 11 inches long), write the words of either the Great Commandment (Luke 10:27) or 1 John 4:21 (CEV), which summaries the Great Commandment.
  2. From the wide end, roll the triangle tightly around a pencil.
  3. Glue the pointed end securely.
  4. Slide the bead off the pencil.
  5. Thread the bead unto a leather shoestring. Tie a knot on each end of the bead to hold it in place in the center of the string.
  6. Tie the leather band so that it fits loosely around your wrist.

- **Say:** Whenever you look at your wristband, remember to stay in love with God!

Prepare

✓ Cut triangle strips (1½ inches at the base and 11 inches long) for younger children. Some older children will be able to cut their own.

✓ Provide a Bible, pencils, gluesticks, and a leather shoestring for each child.

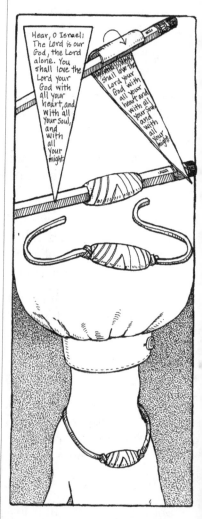

Art: Barbara Upchurch

Follow the Rule

Discovering ways to follow the rule is the goal of your time with the children. Choose ways for following the rule that match their interests and the time and resources you have available.

How Does My Congregation Follow the Rule?

- **Say:** When John Wesley first gave his three simple rules to the societies, he told them to "attend upon all the ordinances of God." *Ordinances* is not a common word for us today, but John Wesley used the word to talk about the customs and practices that make it possible for the relationship between God and people to stay alive and strong.

- **Say:** Last week we talked about prayer and Bible study, two spiritual disciplines that help us grow in our relationship with God. Prayer and Bible study are two of the ordinances that John Wesley said Christians should practice.

- **Ask:** Today, instead of saying "attend upon all the ordinances," we describe this third simple rule as being involved in activities that help us experience God's love together in our church. Through these activities we find ways to follow the third simple rule: Stay in Love With God.

- **Ask:** What activities of our church help us stay in love with God?

- Help the children think about the things they do together as a church, a community of Christians, that help them grow in a loving relationship with God. Guide them to discover that we experience God's love for us and learn to love God when we are part of a community that is learning, worshiping, praying, caring, growing, and serving together.

- **Say:** Let's find out what other members of our congregation do to help them stay in love with God.

- Either show the children your list of interview questions or help the children create their own questions to ask church members about what is important to them about being a member of a Christian community.

- Let the children interview the adults you have invited to be part of the interview experience. Encourage the children to keep notes about what they learn.

- When the interviews are complete, call the children together to talk about what they have heard.

- **Ask:** Did you learn anything new about the church from the members of our congregation? Do you think the people you interviewed know how to stay in love with God?

- **Ask:** What are some ways you are learning, serving, and worshiping in your church?

- **Ask:** How would you explain what John Wesley meant by saying "attend upon all the ordinances" that will help us stay in love with God?

Prepare

✓ Recruit adult members of your congregation to be interviewed by the children. Ask them to prepare by thinking about how the church provides opportunities for Christian growth.

✓ Print a list of interview questions on newsprint or on a markerboard. For example:
  1. How are you actively involved in learning in our church? How and where do you learn other than in Sunday school?
  2. For you, what is the most important part of the worship service?
  3. Has our congregation ever helped you in a time of need?
  4. How do you serve others—either through a church mission project or in the community?

✓ Provide paper and pencils.

Simple Rule #3: Stay in Love With God

Learning With Others

- **Say:** Today is a good day for a picnic! Come and help build a fire.

- Direct the children to gather the scattered wood and the stones to build a campfire. They can form a circle with the stones and then turn the flashlight on and place it in the center of the circle. Help them stack the sticks or logs on top.

- **Say:** Our fire is almost ready. Now, we need some flames.

- Have the children cut long strips of tissue paper to push down into the wood to create flames. Be sure that the flashlight is beaming through the tissue paper to create the illusion of a burning fire.

- **Say:** Ah.... Our fire is ready. Let's sit around the fire and remember a story about a day when Jesus had a picnic on the beach with his disciples.

- If the children remember the story they heard last week, let them tell the story. If you need to read the story, read John 21:15-17, 19b or have a child who is a good reader read the story.

- **Ask:** After Jesus died, the disciples were not sure what they should do next. So, they went back to what had been their ordinary lives before knowing Jesus. What ordinary things did they do in this story? (*fished, hung out with their friends, ate together*)

- **Say:** While they were doing those things, though, Jesus—who had been raised from the dead as he told them would happen—came to them. They were surprised, but they were also happy to see Jesus.

- **Say:** Three times Jesus asked Peter an important question. What did Jesus ask? (*"Do you love me?"*) What did Peter answer? (*"Yes, Lord, I love you."*)

- **Say:** Then Jesus told Peter what he wanted him to do. What did Jesus want Peter to do? (*feed my sheep—take care of my people*)

- **Say:** Everyday there are examples of people doing what Jesus wants. Let's look through newspapers and magazines for headlines, stories, or pictures that tell about people doing what Jesus wants them to do. Cut out those words and pictures and assemble them into a montage on mural paper.

- When the montage is complete, name some things people are doing to show that they love Jesus and want to do what Jesus asks them to do.

- **Ask:** Is there anything that reminds you of a Bible story? Does anything suggest something that you might be able to do to feed Jesus' sheep?

- **Say:** We have been practicing one important way that we can stay in love with God. We have been learning with other Christians. Learning together with others is an important spiritual discipline that helps us remember to follow Jesus' Great Commandment.

- **Ask:** What is Jesus' Great Commandment? (*Let the children look up Luke 10:27. Then have them look up 1 John 4:21, CEV to remember this summary of Jesus' commandment: "Love God and love each other!"*)

Prepare

✓ Scatter small fire logs or sticks and 8 to 10 large smooth stones around the class space.

✓ Provide red, orange, and yellow tissue paper and a flashlight for a campfire.

✓ Provide mural paper, tape, newspapers, magazines, scissors, and gluesticks for a montage.

✓ Have a CEV Bible ready.

Three Simple Rules for Following Jesus

Serving With Others

- Remind the children that another spiritual discipline that will help us stay in love with God is to participate in acts of service with others. We work together through the mission projects of our church.

- Choose a project in which children can participate with hands-on work. If one of the mission projects that your congregation is already involved in includes such things as packing supplies for victims of storms, for children in war-torn countries, or for military personnel, provide the supplies needed for the children to pack some kits.

- If there is not already an ongoing project for your church, check the United Methodist Committee on Relief website (umcor.org) for information about providing kits that help people all over the world. You will find information about creating health kits, school kits, medicine boxes, supplies for babies, sewing kits, and flood buckets.

- *Say:* We cannot actually travel to other parts of the world to show God's love through our loving actions. However, we can do good for people all over the world when we help to provide the supplies they need to survive.

- Tell the children about the needs that the supplies they pack will meet. Help them to understand that although they will probably never know who receives the kits they pack, they can know that by serving with others in Jesus' name, they will grow in their relationship with God and find that they are able to stay in love with God.

- Have the children begin their work by sorting the items for the kits into separate stacks.

- Then they can form assembly lines to pack the kits in an efficient manner.

- Let the children have fun as they work, but also encourage some conversation about the people who will receive the kits. What are their families like? How will their lives be better because of what the children are doing today?

- *Ask:* How does serving with others help us follow the third simple rule and stay in love with God?

Serving Outside the Classroom

- Have you consulted with parents and your missions committee since last week to plan a way for the children to work together with families and other members of the congregation to serve in mission outside the walls of the classroom?

- If so, talk with the children about their opportunity to work with other Christians. Remind the children that learning and serving with others is a spiritual discipline that can help them stay in love with God.

- *Ask:* What makes working together in a mission project a spiritual discipline? (*When we learn to work regularly with other Christians to serve God, we will all grow into closer relationship with God.*)

Prepare

✓ Choose a mission project that will allow the children to have hands-on involvement, such as assembling some kind of missions kit.

✓ Learn as much as possible about the purpose of the project.

✓ Gather the supplies the children will need to complete the project.

Prepare

✓ Have you begun plans for a project that will involve children and families together in serving others?

Celebrate and Praise God

Following Jesus by learning and following the three simple rules will help the children grow in their relationship to God. Encourage them to worship and praise both as a group and on their own.

Worshiping With Others

- Call the group together for a time of closing worship.

- *Say:* For several weeks now we have been talking about how following three simple rules can help us know that we are following Jesus. Let's review these three simple rules.

- Lead the children as they recall the three simple rules, signing each rule as they say it: Do No Harm; Do Good; Stay in Love With God.

- *Say:* Today we have focused on the spiritual disciplines that lead us to learn and serve with others. Let's close our study now by practicing the spiritual discipline of worshiping together. Let's begin by creating a symbol of how we are all connected.

- Give each child a copy of the human chain link (page 64). Encourage each child to choose a figure that is as different as possible from herself or himself.

- Have each child write a word or phrase on the back of the link that names something important the child has learned about following Jesus during these last six weeks.

- Invite the children to complete the figures with multicultural crayons.

- Call the children into a circle.

- Connect your figure to the figure of the child on your left by linking the arms. (*If necessary, use a small piece of tape to hold the figures together.*) As you connect your link, read the word or phrase you have written.

- Let the children continue to the left around the circle, connecting their links and reading what they have written until the chain is complete when the child on your right connects his or her link to yours.

- If the children have trouble holding the linked chain, let them carefully lay the completed chain on the floor in front of them inside the circle and then join hands.

- *Pray:* Loving God, thank you for creating us to live together in Christian community. Remind us that when we are linked together, we can help one another and others to grow in relationship with you. Remind us daily that when we follow John Wesley's three simple rules, we will be following Jesus, who teaches us to do no harm, to do good, and to stay in love with God. Amen.

- Close your time together by singing "Stay in Love With God" (page 4).

Prepare

✓ Make sure the signing posters of the three simple rules are displayed (pages 5, 25, and 45).

✓ Cut out one human chain link for each member of the group (page 64). Older children will be able to cut their own.

✓ Provide multicultural crayons.

✓ Review the song "Stay in Love With God" (page 4).

Confession   **Popcorn Prayer**   **The Lord's Prayer**

Potter's Prayer   **Breath Prayer**   **One-Word Prayer**

Blessing   **Meditation**   **Litany**   **Flash Prayer**

a short phrase said over and over in rhythm with one's breathing	sitting in silence to think about what God may want to say to us
a personal prayer expressed by creating a symbol of a concern or need or thanksgiving from modeling clay	a group prayer in which each person responds to a spoken prayer when moved to participate. For example, a leader says, "God, we thank you for …," and one by one each person names things for which he or she is thankful
the model for prayer that Jesus taught his disciples	a prayer that lasts only one or two seconds—often for someone we do not even know—when we see an accident, hear a siren, read or see a sad story, or see someone who is sad or angry
a group prayer in which each person adds one word to name a thanksgiving, a person in need, or other prayer concern	telling God what we have done wrong and asking for God's forgiveness and for God's help as we try to change our ways
a prayer asking for God's blessing for another person	a responsive prayer in which a leader reads one line at a time and the group responds after each line with a common repeated response

Labyrinth

Art: Paige Easter

Three Simple Rules for Following Jesus

Finding Help in the Bible

When I am lonely > > > > > > Psalm 23

When I am worried > > > > > Matthew 6:25-33

When I am afraid > > > > > > > Psalm 27:1

When I feel that God > > > > > Romans 8:38-39

is far away

When someone dies > > > > > John 3:16

When I am tempted to > > > > 1 Peter 3:13-17
go along with the
crowd rather than
doing what I know
is right

When I have trouble > > > > > Romans 12:14-18
getting along with
other people

When I am discouraged > > > Philippians 3:13-14

When I feel my parents > > > Ephesians 6:1
are unfair

When I have had a > > > > > > 1 Corinthians13:1-7
disagreement with
a brother or sister
or friend

When I feel fear and > > > > > Psalm 31:24
uncertainty

When I am tempted > > > > > 1 John 1:8-9
to blame someone
else for my mistakes

When I do not understand > Romans 8:28
why something has
happened the way it did

When I know that I > > > > > Psalm 37:24
have made a mistake

Three Simple Rules for Following Jesus

CPSIA information can be obtained
at www.ICGtesting.com
Printed in the USA
FSHW011228191119
64252FS

ENTERTAINMENT PROMOTION & COMMUNICATION

The Industry and Integrated Campaigns

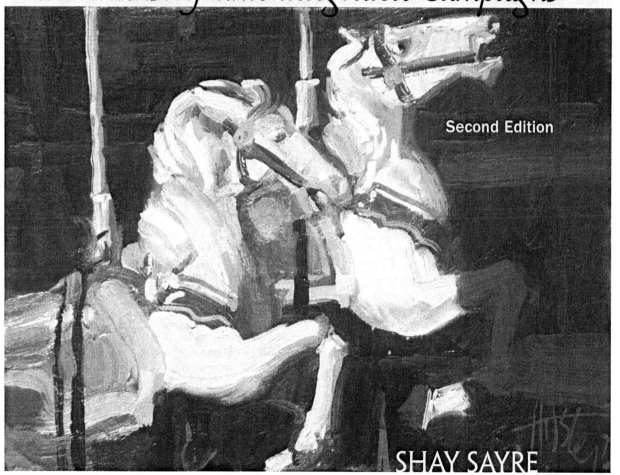

Second Edition

SHAY SAYRE

Kendall Hunt
publishing company

Cover image © Ken Auster, used with permission.

Kendall Hunt
publishing company

www.kendallhunt.com
Send all inquiries to:
4050 Westmark Drive
Dubuque, IA 52004-1840

Copyright © 2010 by Kendall Hunt Publishing Company

ISBN 978-0-7575-7837-3

Printed in the United States of America
10 9 8 7 6 5 4 3 2

Contents

CHAPTER 3
CHARACTERIZING OUR
EXPERIENCE CULTURE   49

CHAPTER 4
VENUE ECONOMICS AND SERVICESCAPES   75

CHAPTER 7
SEGMENTING ENTERTAINMENT AUDIENCES   167

CHAPTER 8
RESEARCHING & MEASURING ENTERTAINMENT AUDIENCES   201

CHAPTER 9
BUILDING ENTERTAINMENT BRANDS   239

POSTSCRIPT
IS THE INTERNET DESTROYING MEDIA
CULTURE AS WE KNOW IT? OR IS IT SIMPLY
RE-SHAPING CULTURE?　　545

AUTHOR PROFILE　　549

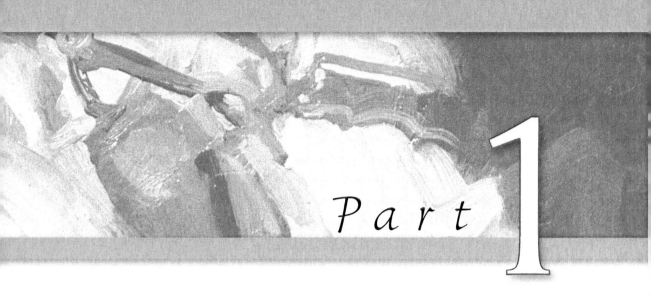

Part 1

THE ENTERTAINMENT INDUSTRY

Chapter 1

AND LEISURE BEGOT ENTERTAINMENT

> *[Leisure] is better than occupation and is its end;*
> *and therefore the question must be asked,*
> *What ought we to do when at leisure?*
> Aristotle

Chapter Objectives

After reading this chapter, you will be able to answer the following questions:

- *What is* entertainment marketing?

- How is entertainment marketing *different* from marketing of products and services?

- How does the concept of *play* figure into entertainment marketing?

- How does today's entertainment *environment* work?

- What *codes of ethics* exist in today's entertainment industry?

LET THE EXCITEMENT BEGIN!

The average American spends more on entertainment than on gasoline, household furnishings, and clothing and nearly the same amount as spent on dining out.[i] Among affluent consumers, more money is spent on entertainment than on health care, utilities, clothing, or food eaten at home. People west of the Mississippi River spend about 20% more on entertainment than the national average. What does the best entertainment buy? On a dollar-to-minutes-of-enjoyment basis, video games are a good value at about 12.5 cents a minute, or fractions of a penny for those who can play "Half Life" their whole life. The worst value in this sense is live opera, which works out to be about 37 cents a minute for a middling seat in the New York Metropolitan Opera house to experience *Aida*. The best value might be a seat at an IMAX Theater to see *Avatar*, which costs a viewer only 7 cents a minute.[ii] People do not make their decisions on costs alone, however. Many variables are at play. The point is this: with such huge amounts being spent on entertainment, marketers must meet the competitive challenge to bring both affordable and enjoyable options to global audiences.

But the way we think about entertainment products—movies, music, TV, video games, or words—must now be regarded as composite bits of information that can be produced and processed and distributed as a series of digits that represent sounds and pictures and texts. Today, technological development provides a common tool for all marketing efforts generated to promote entertainment products.

ENTERTAINMENT EVOLUTION

We begin with a look at the foundations of entertainment experiences before they metamorphosed into today's box office draws. At the heart of entertainment is the concept of *leisure*. The historical concepts of *performance* and *game playing* are also crucial to understanding the meaning of leisure in contemporary life.

Derived from the Latin *licere*, which means to be free, leisure has been described with a variety of state-of-mind characteristics. For Aristotle, the term implied both availability of time and an absence of occupation; in fact, he believed that absence of occupation is what leads to happiness.

In a historical framework, once people could satisfy their basic survival needs, something resembling leisure time was time left over. Leisure activity began as a way to reduce the drudgery of farming and labor. Factory workers in the industrial age escaped the dreariness of assembly lines by playing cards during breaks.

More formal entertainment traces its beginnings to performance and games. Whether games were practiced as religious, mystical or cultural rituals, these activities developed into the theater, games, and sporting events we enjoy today. Street performers advanced to acting on stage; stone-kicking became a game with rules and fans; migration evolved into travel and tourism.

Today, the term **leisure** is broadly used to designate time not spent at work in a profession or in an occupation in pursuit of compensation, or in taking care of children, and the household. Free time is no longer a time reserved for contemplation, nor is it the purview of an elite society. To the contrary, contemporary leisure is time used for going places and doing things. All sorts of consumption activities containing significant elements of amusement and diversion are now considered to be **entertainment**. Simply, **entertainment marketing** consists of the techniques and strategies developed to sell tickets to (or otherwise elicit payment for) activities that amuse and involve us.

Leisure becomes big business

So an attraction to entertainment is based in human needs that have evolved with time. People who pursue leisure activities are our consumers, and entertainment consumers expect what they purchase to produce a pleasurable and satisfying experience. Marketers must address psychological and emotional factors as well as physical and mental ones. With available time as a primary commodity in our attention-based economy, the demand for leisure is affected by the cost of time to produce and consume entertainment products. As such, the cost of time and consumption-time intensity (or "bang for the buck") are significant factors for consumers who select among entertainment alternatives.

Since the Industrial Revolution more than a century ago, leisure time in the United States has been steadily increasing. Although the average work week has not changed dramatically over the last several decades, there has been a natural evolution toward repackaging the time set aside for leisure into more long holiday weekends and extra vacation days rather than toward reducing the hours worked every week. As a result, personal consumption expenditures for entertainment are likely to be intense and compressed instead of evenly spaced throughout the year.

Another factor in the growing demand for entertainment is three broad demographic shifts that have occurred in the past decade. These show 1) the emergence of a technologically savvy teenage audience 2) an increase in the entertainment demands of 18–34 year olds, 3) and a continuation of spending on leisure among baby boomers (35–64). Aggregate spending on entertainment is concentrated in the middle-age groups, whose income is peaking at the same time leisure may be relatively scarce.

1.1 A promoter's job is filling the seats of a venue with audiences.

According to the Fortune 500 largest global industries in 2009,[iii] entertainment ranked 26th, with 5.5% revenue growth. As the 9th most profitable industry, five entertainment corporations dominate the global marketplace. Time Warner, Walt Disney News Corporation, Bertelsmann, and Muruhan were listed as the largest entertainment media in this category. Hotels, resorts and casinos, however, were impacted by the recession and price of fuels, both of which kept tourism revenues down for the same period in 2009. Game revenues, however, continue to grow and are expected to reach $70 billion by 2011 because of increased popularity of online and mobile gaming.

Statistics support the fact that today entertainment and leisure are big business. According to PricewaterhouseCoopers, the global entertainment and media industry will reach $2.2 trillion in 2012, growing at a 2008–2012 compound annual growth rate (CAGR) of 6.6%.

At the wholesale level, entertainment markets are now generating annual revenues exceeding $100 billion. Entertainment has consistently been one of the largest net export categories for the United States.[iv] A notable trend of the 1980s was the association many consumers made between their identities and the brands and products they owned. In the twenty-first century it is consuming experiences—*we are what we do and where we go to do it*—that may underlie consumer identity.

Exhibit 1.1 outlines some historical milestones in the development of both the live and mediated entertainment into the business of entertainment as we know it today.

EXHIBIT 1.1 Historical Milestones

DECADE	EVENT
1930S	• FM radio invented • Federal Communications Commission formed to regulate broadcast content • TV service begins with three networks
1940S	• First computer developed for business use • 33 1/3 rpm* vinyl recordings introduced • First CATV system installed for residential use
1950S	• Disneyland opens in Anaheim, California • First satellite launched by Soviets for communications purposes
1960S	• Sports Broadcasting Act passed by Congress • FM popularized, AM relegated to news, talk

1970S	• Disney World opens in Orlando, Florida • Microprocessors introduced to facilitate smaller computers • HBO begins satellite program distribution • First home video game released for distribution • Atlantic City legalizes casinos and gambling begins • First VCR appears for Betamax formatted films • CNN begins broadcasting 24 hour news
1980S	• Compact discs introduced for personal use • Mirage opens in Las Vegas, strip redevelopment grows
1990S	• News Corporation distributes global TV programming • Internet popularized; search engines develop • Telecom deregulation permits new ownership potential • Digital video discs popularized for film and music
2000S	• Merging of advertising and entertainment functions • Audience-produced content (blogs) invade the Internet • Theming characterizes malls, restaurants, hotels and parks • Technology changes the way people communicate, enjoy entertainment and control content

*revolutions per minute; 78 rpm and 45 rpm single-song records preceded theLong-playing 33 1/3 rpm multiple-song record.

Leisure triad

The way we pass our free time takes various forms, and each category of leisure addresses a particular need or function. We engage in three types of leisure activity: amusement, entertainment, and recreation; all of them are experiential.

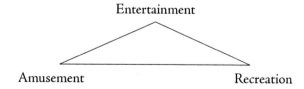

Amusement consists of diversions such as games and the satisfaction derived from playing games. This chapter presents an overview of games and gambling because they play an important role in generating revenues around the world.

Entertainment refers to live and mediated performance experiences such as a concert, dance, or drama, including the pleasure received from comedy or magic.

Recreation consists of activities or experiences carried on within leisure time, either for personal satisfaction or creative enrichment. A recreation industry has developed as recreation activities for adults have expanded, as more and more people seek a break from a cycle of boredom and fatigue. In later chapters we will focus on marketing recreation destinations, such as the luxury resorts and spas consumers visit for health and relaxation, as well as the ways they experience travel and tourism.

Terminology

Although the leisure triad is used in some industry categorization, a better way to view the entertainment industry is content based. Entertainment *content* comes to audiences in three distinct ways: as *live performance* (theater, musical concerts), as *interactive experience* (recreation, amusement parks, travel, gaming) and as *media* (movies, TV). For the purposes of this book, the term *experience* will characterize all forms of entertainment content. To market experiences, then, is to understand all the components of how audiences perceive experiences, and how experiences are promoted and measured.

How we experience entertainment

We experience entertainment in a variety of ways based on our participation and what we derive from the experience. Four realms of entertainment experience are: passive, educational, escapist, and esthetic. *Passive entertainment* occurs when people simply absorb an experience through their senses without much participation; this occurs when viewing a performance, listening to music, or reading. *Educational entertainment* requires the active engagement of the person's mind, the type of involvement that occurs with problem solving. By creating experiences that straddle the realms of education and entertainment, guests absorb the events unfolding before them while actively participating. *Escapist entertainment* experiences involve much greater immersion than other types of entertainment or educational experiences. Escapist entertainment is intended to provide a respite from real life in venues such as theme parks, casinos, and virtual reality games. In *esthetic entertainment*, audiences immerse themselves in a cultural experience but

© *Giancarlo Liguori, 2010. Used under license from Shutterstock, Inc.*

1.2 The aesthetics of a Parisian café.

remain witnesses. These experiences include standing on the rim of the Grand Canyon, visiting an art gallery or museum or sitting in a Parisian café.[v]

As prologue to our treatment of marketing experiences, we need an overview of the theoretical principles that drive the entertainment industry and motivate its audiences. First let's look at how entertainment promotion differs from marketing of products and other services.

WHAT MAKES ENTERTAINMENT PROMOTION UNIQUE

In a world where a plethora of media and distractions compete for our attention, attention becomes a scarce resource. For some, obtaining attention is a way of obtaining positional wealth. Celebrities, for example, gain their status from entourages of fans who form around them, giving them constant attention to their every move. An entertainer must get an audience's full attention to elicit positive responses, such as applause, good reviews, and word of mouth, and, ultimately, the motivation to purchase more tickets.

Social needs and changing demographics require us to refocus on how we market entertainment experiences. To obtain audiences' attention, marketers must deal with the temporal aspects of entertainment brands, mainly *perishability* and *intangibility*.

Experiences are perishable

Changes in trends and tastes by consumers of entertainment are constant. What's in this season is out the next. Because entertainment is a luxury, not a necessity, and because it must be available to audiences when they want it (not a minute sooner or later), entertainment providers are in a constant contest to keep themselves alive. Shelf life is as long as audiences buy tickets. After that, the product disappears and is gone. Think of entertainment content as fruit that ripens, then rots. Once rotten, no one pays to own it!

Combining the best director, top-acting talent, and fantastic set design does not guarantee Broadway success. Even after months of production and in some cases millions of dollars, there are no guarantees that audiences will show up if a play receives bad reviews after its first performance. And if a film isn't a box office buster during its first weekend of release, distribution is reduced and the movie disappears from sight. The crucial time-bound aspect of entertainment is its **perishability**. As in fruit, experiences are time-sensitive and they diminish in importance as time passes.

Experiences are intangible

We buy souvenirs of experience-based entertainment, but we cannot take home the experience itself. It's in our memory, not in our shopping bag. We may purchase a book, but the experience of reading is nonetheless mental. Although the book jacket and graphics may seduce us into buying the book, the experiential pleasure of that book lies in its verbal consumption.

Experiences are not investments like gold or art, and they are not consumables like shampoo. Experiences are **intangible**—of the moment with ever-changing content. Products have utilitarian or intrinsic value and have a presence. Services are performed for a price—dry cleaning services clean your clothes and insurance services protect your car. But neither products nor services are experienced in the same way as entertainment. And that is what we are selling—a piece of time requiring attention from participants.

Promoting entertainment content and experiences that are intangible is a marketer's biggest challenge. The value of the experience is predicated on an audience member's willingness to pay for the opportunity to turn his or her attention toward indulgence in a performance or activity. When was the last time you paid for an experience? If you think about the reasons for your purchase, you'll begin to understand the role of marketing for motivating consumers to purchase an intangible.

Time is attention

Demand for leisure is affected in a complicated way by the cost of time to both produce and consume entertainment products. For instance, reading a book uses more time per dollar of goods (you can spend hours reading for free) than frequenting a nightclub (usually with a cover charge); in other words, it is less expensive for the consumer to read than to party. But partying is more fun! The cost of time and the consumption-time intensity of experience are significant factors when selecting from among entertainment alternatives.

Like money, attention has *instrumental value* because it can get you other things that you might want. It also has *terminal value* because many people want it for its own sake. We value both the attention we give and the attention we receive. Valuable as it is, attention cannot be bought. This is where entertainment comes in because it puts information into a form that can achieve attention. Great ads or musical lyrics take plain, brown paper bag information and put it in a gift box.

Pleasure providers need to capture the attention of audiences and entertainment consumers in order to get them to the venue, destination, or box office. With a constant infusion of mediated messages, most consumers block out promotional white noise by refusing to pay attention to it. A primary function of entertainment marketing is finding ways to attract and hold audience attention in the presence of hyper-real communication, or just too much media stimulation.

One of the most attention-intensive activities is surfing the Web. The number of people communicating through the Web and trying to get attention through it is continuously rising. The growth in the Web's capacity to send out multimedia or virtual reality signals allows marketers to capture user attention through these means. Social networks such as Facebook, YouTube, and Twitter are valuable sources of promotion for producers and promoters of entertainment.

Societal needs matter

With the demands of family and work taking a huge toll on people, many forms of entertainment provide relief from the stress of everyday life. We begin our day with a workout at the gym, catch a glimpse of the morning newspaper, play CDs on the way to work, listen to a radio talk show on the way home, use email to contact friends, play a few online games, eat in a themed restaurant, shop in a mega mall, rent a DVD, see a movie or TV show, and read a mystery novel before falling asleep. Every activity outside of our jobs is a form of entertainment.

Although we cannot avoid or escape encounters with entertainment, we are selective about which forms to use, how often we use them, and how much we are willing to spend on them. Marketing can be used to help direct selectivity, that is, to persuade audiences to watch, listen and buy tickets to the specific experiences that meet their needs.

PLAY THEORY AND ENTERTAINMENT MARKETING

As leisure time proliferates, marketers concentrate on expanding the *notion of play*. According to Huizinga,[vi] in *Homo Ludens*, play existed even before culture itself, accompanying and nourishing culture from the beginning of civilization. He asserts that all the great archetypal activities in human society are permeated with play. To characterize play as a cultural function that separates it from the context of ordinary life, he defined its main characteristics.

Play is different from other types of experiences because it

1. Is a *voluntary* activity—no one forces us to play.

2. Is set *apart from reality*—it is an interlude in the day that provides temporary satisfaction.

3. Is *limited* in terms of its locality and duration—it has a beginning and an end.

4. Is controlled or governed by *rules*.

5. Has a sense of persistent *social community*—sports fans are such a community.

6. Promotes a sense of symbolic *secrecy*—it is different from everyday life.

7. Is a *sacred and profound* activity—it involves rituals, ceremony, and a venue for symbolic representation.

Some aspects of contemporary play may assume different characteristics than those set forth by Huizinga. For instance, as an *extra-mundane activity* (activity outside the parameters of the ordinary), play was thought to provide people with the rewards that they could not find in work or in the consumption of the ordinary world. Yet today, much of our consumption of the ordinary world is filled with all forms of entertainment and play.

Contemporary play is an outgrowth of a devotion to pleasure, known as hedonism. Influenced by the Romantic doctrine, which values individualism, power, and sensitivity, hedonistic consumption designates a conceptual framework of leisure activity, in other words, it's force behind the will to consume a great deal of pleasurable things. Hedonism is expressed in activities that are self-indulgent as well as pleasurable such as game playing and shopping. As a facet of cultural movement, hedonism is a shaping force behind our individual pursuits of pure pleasure and immediate gratification.

Play theory: a strong distinction between leisure and work

Play, viewed as an outgrowth of leisure time activities, gets its definition from the Latin word *ludenic*, which refers to games, recreation, contests, theater, and liturgical presentations. According to William Stephenson,[vii] the spirit of play is essential to the development of culture—stagecraft, military exercises, debate, politics, and marriage conventions are all cultural aspects grounded in play.

Making a strong distinction between leisure and work, **play theory** suggests that work deals with reality and production, while play provides self-satisfaction. This theory goes on to explain how play is pleasure, and pleasure is a concept at various levels:

- physiological pleasure (a massage soothes the body)

- pleasure of associations with objects and the relationship between self and things (riding a favorite bicycle or playing with a special golf club)

- pleasure from objects themselves (film or star-licensed possessions)

- pleasure through communications (discussing a film with friends)

According to the theory, everything not work is pleasure. As a society devoting more time to leisure and play, we are dependent upon marketers to help us sort out the play options for our out-of-work activity.

© cassiede alain, 2010. Used under license from Shutterstock, Inc.

1.3 The pleasure of finding the biggest wave and riding it home.

Playing games

In today's cultural situations, play takes on new meaning. Much of today's entertainment centers around games and gambling. The lure of winning is enough to interest consumers; it's the marketer's job to pull them into a particular gambling venue—a casino. We focus on gaming and gambling for their importance to understanding audience motivations for engaging in this popular form of chance-based entertainment.

Gaming is a term used to reference both games of competition and games of chance. From playing hide-and-seek as children to buying lottery tickets as adults, games have continued to entertain us. Games of competition require skill, such as achieving checkmate, scoring a goal or overtaking an opponent. Gambling activity, on the other hand, is based primarily on chance. Chess is a game, bingo is gambling. No skill involved in rolling dice or playing slot machines. Cards can be either—played without wagers, they are a game; when betting is involved, cards become gambling.

Taking a chance

In gambling, players bet something of value on the outcome of a game or uncertain event whose result may be determined by chance. They risk money in the hopes of winning the game or contest. Gambling activities range in complexity from a coin toss to betting on cards in poker. Outcomes may be determined solely by chance (craps and roulette) or by a combination of strategy and chance (poker). Gamblers may participate while betting on the outcome, or they may be restricted from participation in the cases of lotteries and sports.

To change the negative image of gambling, the industry calls itself *gaming*. A $60 billion industry, gaming has entered the coveted and lucrative mainstream of American entertainment. Online gaming (over 100,000 sites in 2009), has reached $125 billion according to Merrill Lynch. With a year-on-year growth of 17%, the number of unique visitors has surpassed 220 million. Asia, with the world's biggest growth potential, claims over 10 million online players. Houses of gaming have become full-fledged entertainment venues in their own right and have strong client potential for entertainment marketers.

MARKETING PERFORMANCE, INTERACTION & MEDIA EXPERIENCES

The entertainment industry is too broad for an all-inclusive treatment, but there are plenty of experiences to categorize. We will concentrate on those experiences that require planning, communication, and promotion—campaign development—to insure revenue generation. The five entertainment experience genres covered in this text are: 1) live performances, 2) destinations and places, 3) attractions and themed venues, 4) mediated entertainment, and 5) celebrities and stars. Let's take a look at the experiential nature of each entertainment genre.

Enjoying live performances

Dance, opera, musical concerts, theater and the circus are included in this experiential genre where live people perform for live audiences. Often combining media with action, concert promoters are taking their performances to new venues and new dimensions. Sports are

also performed live. In marketing
local, regional, national, or global
performances, reliance on reviews
or star-power is not enough to fill
the house. Audience research and
expectation delivery are key to
developing an effective promotion
strategy for this oldest type of
entertainment, which is most often
performed in a specific venue.
Chapter 13 features marketing live
performances and events.

1.4 Mime with royal flush entertains casino audiences.

Experiencing destinations and places

The places we visit to engage in serious relaxing are part of an exploding tourist industry.
Tourism has long been an important aspect of human geography and is vital to some economies.
Marketing destinations is a primary way that some local economies survive. From the smallest
village promoting arts (Laguna Beach, California) to the most popular city on earth (Paris),
localities recognize the value in developing a recognizable brand that will lure visitors and create
revenue. Laguna Beach markets itself as the home of the "Pageant of the Masters," a performance
presenting the world's masterpieces using human figures.
Local artists display their work in nearby Festival of
Arts, Sawdust Festival, and Art Affair. During the
summer, thousands flock to the city to gaze upon
and purchase art. Combined with the surf and sand
attractions, Laguna's art attracts regional visitors by co-
promotions with hotels, restaurants and galleries, and an
interactive Web site.

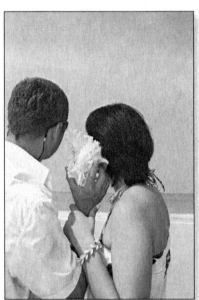

Australia capitalized on the exposure of the film
Australia to promote coming down under with the
2008–2009 promotion slogan, "Come Walkabout."
Their network television and online campaigns
created global awareness and interest for American
tourists who jumped on Quantas Airlines to fly to
Sydney for a glimpse of the famous Opera House,
which is also featured in the country's advertising
campaign. Chapter 14 is dedicated to marketing tourist
destinations and services.

1.5 Much tourism advertising focuses
on beach vacations.

Experiencing attractions and themed venues

For many leisure consumers, it's not just what you do, it's *where* you do it. *Venues* are places—buildings, ships, and centers—where entertainment takes place. Performing arts centers, casinos, spas, resorts, and cruise ships, museums, theaters, cinemas, and theme parks all house entertainment experiences. As private enterprise continues to invest in architectural innovation, performance venues are becoming destinations of their own.

FOCUS ON VENUES

Image 1.6

© *Jupiter Images*

Museums as Movie Stars

Museums are often pieces of art in their own right, such as New York's Guggenheim, a spiral gallery designed by Frank Lloyd Wright (pictured above). This and other museums have provided backdrops for movie scenes, such as *Rocky* (Sylvester Stallone runs up the stairs of the Philadelphia Museum of Art), *Batman* (Jack Nicholson's Joker runs wild in the Metropolitan Museum of Art in New York), and *A League of Their Own* (Tom Hanks' team visits the Baseball Hall of Fame in Cooperstown NY).

What films have you seen that feature museums as props?

As performance competition grows, producers looked to venues to provide a competitive edge over other forms of entertainment. Each event is associated with a physical home or venue specially designed and equipped to maximize audience enjoyment. Rome's Coliseum, Stratford-on-Avon's Globe Theater, and Sydney's Opera House are some of the world's most famous performance venues.

In order to pay for venues, marketers must identify the target market, develop appropriate messages to send them, and implement a successful promotional plan to lure patrons, donors, and guests to these venues in great numbers. Chapter 8 expands upon venue marketing, and Chapter 14 features marketing attractions and themed spaces.

Mediated entertainment

Television and movie marketing requires special skills and strategies to convince potential audience members that the viewing experience is worth their time and money. Unseen mass audiences in dark theaters watching movies—or even more so at home viewing television—are more difficult to identify and reach than other audience types.

Television

Both network and cable stations must promote their programming to attract either advertisers or subscribers. Cable has been able to direct its programming to special audience segments (sports fans, avid enthusiasts) by positioning their brand appeal accordingly. Networks, on the other hand, are struggling to promote news, reality, and, sitcom programming to mass audiences. The changing nature of television technology requires a whole new approach to marketing mediated experiences.

Movies

Major studios rely on trailers, distribution, and product placement to promote blockbuster films. Independents, on the other hand, commonly make do with festival exposure and Internet buzz to gain attention and recognition. In spite of enormous budgets and global distribution, every so often a sleeper film will sneak into theaters for large box office draws. Promotional techniques for new releases require creative merchandising and brand associations in order to reduce the margin between ticket revenues and production and marketing costs.

1.7 Johnny Depp is consistently voted as one of Hollywood's most popular stars.

© Stephane Cardinale/People Avenue/Corbis

Celebrities and stars

We love to love people we consider special or important, those who look good and dress well on the screen and as captured in photographs. Many performances succeed because of the star power they offer audiences. **Celebrities** are people who are exposed by the media or who become well-known through their outstanding accomplishments. Some accidental celebrities capitalize on their temporary status to develop a new business or product (Monica Lewinsky, for example, who started her own fashion design company) that relies on their name brand for success. Celebrity is notoriety; stars are made. Hollywood crafts stars by employing publicists, agents, and image artists. Stars are engineered and become a brand in their own right. Magazines, fan clubs, paparazzi, and celebrity-watch television keep the private lives and loves of stars in front of the public, creating a separate and very lucrative star industry.

THE ENTERTAINMENT INDUSTRY ENVIRONMENT

Entertainment is an industry that depends not only on getting to market before a trend has passed (or creating the trend in the first place), it also depends upon great marketing efforts to create big box office receipts. Major advertising agencies that represent the entertainment industry handle large budgets and intense time frames, and are constantly faced with decisions that can make or break their clients. With mega million-dollar media budgets, large clients keep agencies competitive. Other factors that cause volatility and cannibalization in the industry are its moguls and mergers. Ever unsteady, the shifting sands of ownership and direction create an unsettling environment for creating and distributing entertainment experiences. Their activity further contribute to convergence—blurring the distinction between advertising and entertainment marketing

Global advertising agencies

Advertising agencies represent the largest entertainment companies, vying for huge media budgets that drive marketing programs. As of April 2009, the biggest players and their clients are presented in Exhibit 1.2.

Volatility and cannibalism

A dynamic and changing industry, entertainment entities change ownership regularly, often through unfriendly takeovers. Some of the biggest fish in entertainment shape, control—and often capture through acquisition—the development and delivery of what we experience. Five of the biggest fish in the entertainment tank are Barry Diller, Rupert Murdock, Robert Iger, Judy McGrath, and Leslie Moonvess. The following *Focus on* box profiles the current big entertainment moguls.

EXHIBIT 1.2 Major Entertainment Advertising Agencies

AGENCY	ENTERTAINMENT CLIENT(S)
McCann Erickson	Columbia Pictures
DDB Worldwide	Universal Studios & Theme Parks
Western Media	Disney Studios
Grey Advertising	Warner Bros. Studios, WB Network, *Entertainment Weekly, People Magazine*
TWBA	ABC TV Network
Young & Rubicam	Showtime, Viacom, Blockbuster Video, Sony Electronics Game
Saatchi & Saatchi	News Corp

FOCUS ON THE 'BIG GUYS'

Entertainment moguls

Old Boys

Barry Diller is the Chairman and Chief Executive Officer of IAC, a leading Internet company; the Chairman of Expedia, Inc., one of the world's leading travel service companies; and the Chairman of Live Nation Entertainment, which produces, markets and sells live concerts for artists via a global concert network. Live Nation produces over 22,000 concerts annually for 1500 artists in 57 countries. After merging with Ticketmaster, Live Nation transformed the concert business with the first artist-to-fan platform.

From October 1984 – April 1992, Diller was Chairman and Chief Executive Officer of Fox, Inc., responsible for the creation of Fox Broadcasting Company in addition to Fox's motion picture operations.

Before joining Fox, Diller served for ten years as the Chairman and Chief Executive of Paramount Pictures Corporation. In March 1983, in addition to Paramount, Mr. Diller became President of the conglomerate's newly formed Entertainment and Communications Group, which included Simon & Schuster, Inc., Madison Square Garden Corporation and SEGA Enterprises, Inc. Prior to joining Paramount, Mr. Diller served as Vice President of Prime Time Television for ABC Entertainment.

Rupert Murdock, age 78 in 2010, is capitalizing on the technology that is shifting power away from the established and media elite and giving it to the people. With the $580 million purchase of MySpace, the News Corp.'s. $56 billion constellation includes movie studios (20th Century Fox, Searchlight), TV networks (Fox, FX) publishing (*TV Guide, Weekly Standard*), newspapers (*New York Post, UK Times*), and satellites (SKYE, DirecTV). In 2010, News Corp purchased a 9.09% stake in Rotana Group in the Middle East for $70 million. By generating revenues of $30 billion in 2009, Murdock holds the reins of this entertainment giant and shows no signs of giving it up anytime soon.

Robert Iger became CEO of Disney on December 30, 2005 and immediately agreed to let Apple sell ABC's television shows over the Internet. Iger is bullish on broadband Internet, wireless phone networks and video-on-demand that reach viewers through TV-enabled cellular phones, videogame players, digital video recorders, and the iPod. Under his leadership, Disney projects double-digit earnings growth for its cash cow of ten TV stations and 64 radio stations. Iger acquired Pixar Animation Studios as a companion to Disney's businesses—movies, television, theme parks, and consumer products—to generate revenue for all the divisions around the world. Disney's line of holdings include: ESPN, Toon, SOAPnet, Lifetime TV, A&E, and the History Channel; three record companies; Hyperion book publishing, 15 consumer magazines, 8 parks, resorts, and a cruise line; Muppets and Club Penguins.

New Guy and a Gal

Judy McGrath turned MTV into a cultural phenomenon with 400 million viewers in 164 countries. The former women's magazine writer oversees the MTV Networks empire that includes 100 MTV networks globally, Nickelodeon, VH1, TV Land, Comedy Central, Spike TV, CMT, Nick at Nite, the new LOGO channel serving gay and lesbian consumers, MTV2, The N,MTV, and Nickelodeon Films, and the company's online and digital businesses. On McGrath's watch as chief executive officer, the channels have broken new ground, not just in reality television but also entertainment biopics and animated comedies. Her newest challenge is to revive this MTV channel that has reduced staff and expenses as the economic downturn has cut into advertising revenues and falling ratings.

Leslie Moonves, former president of Warner Bros. Television, joined CBS in 1995 and proceeded to break the Peacock network's hold on Thursday night with shows like Survivor and CSI. CBS, a public company with $13 billion in revenue in 2009, has slightly increased its total primetime viewers over 11 seasons and has the largest number of total television viewership of the big four networks. Moonves is a masterful seller of advertising time, increasing ad revenue more than 6% over its previous season. Earnings at its TV unit were up 4% in 2010 over the previous year with the help of high ratings from shows like NCIS. CBS also owns pay channel Showtime. When not touting his wireless strategy to investors, Moonves will be in charge through 2015.

Others to watch: Sony Picture Chairman **Michael Lynton**, Warner Brothers Chairman **Berry Meyer**, MGM Chairman **Harvey Sloan**, NBC Universal CEO **Jeffrey Zucker,** and Paramount's **Bradley Gray.**

Industry economics

According to a top-ranked entertainment industry analyst,[viii] there are eight frequently observed industry economic characteristics:[ix]

1. In a steady growth phase, profits from a very few highly popular products are generally required to offset losses from many mediocrities. This is especially evident in movies, and network television productions.

2. The unique features of entertainment products must continuously be brought to the attention of potential audiences, causing marketing expenditures per unit to be proportionally large. As lifecycles of entertainment products are brief, marketing typically adds at least 50% to the cost of the average major feature film release.

3. Because almost every dollar of revenue goes first toward recoupment of direct costs, ancillary markets provide disproportionately large returns. For instance, films derive over half their revenues from exposures on cable and home video rather than from initial theatrical release; spinoffs are sources of significant additional income. Price discrimination effects are readily observed in ticket pricing for cultural events and sequencing films through various exhibition windows from screen to DVD to television sequencing of movies through various exhibition windows.

4. Capital costs are relatively high, erecting a formidable barrier to entry by new competitors. Most industry segments thus come to be ruled by large companies with relatively easy access to large pools of capital. These tendencies can be seen in gaming, theme park, cable, film, movies, and broadcasting industries.

5. The cost of production is independent of the number of consumers. And although delivered to consumers in the form of private goods, many entertainment products and services (movies, TV programs) have public good characteristics.

6. Many products and services are not standardized, resulting in considerable freedom for entrepreneurs to originate plays, operas, and ballets. When the production is live performance, it is difficult to enhance productivity, and the costs of creating and marketing entertainment products tends to rise at above-average rates.

7. Technology makes it easier and less expensive to manufacture, distribute, and receive entertainment products and services. The result is more varied and more affordable mass-market entertainment.

8. New delivery methods are constantly evolving, but new entertainment mediums tend *not* to render older ones extinct, as new deliver methods are constantly evolving. The Internet has not kept people away from books, newspapers, and magazines.

9. The economics of each industry segment vary; they are treated separately in Part Three, which includes Chapters 12–16.

Entertainment ethics

For the entertainment industry (as for most industries), ethics provide guidelines or tools for making choices. Not "good" or "right" choices, but choices based on moral criteria, whatever they may be in a particular case.

Ethical Dilemmas

Areas where ethical issues arise and where laws may exist to protect victims include these cases.

- *News*—According to many entertainment journalists, a reporter in Hollywood is only as good as his/her Rolodex is large. To stay well connected and land the big interviews, entertainment journalists have to balance what the actor/agent/publicist/studio wants and the "real" story. There's the quid pro quo—if reporters do a story for the agency/client, they get to interview a sought-after star in return. Compromise may involve unethical practices.

- *Film reviews*—Settlement of a class action lawsuit against Columbia Pictures gave anyone who saw *Hollow Man, Vertical Limit, A Knight's Tale, The Animal,* or *The Patriot* a payment of $5. Why? Reviewer David Manning's quotes filled print and TV ads with praise for those movies while other reviewers trashed them. The problem was that Manning didn't exist; Colombia Pictures made him up.[x]

- *Radio*—The practice of paying off disc jockeys in exchange for favorable airplay of Sony tunes will now cost Sony $10 million. According to former New York State Attorney General Eliot Spitzer, Sony BMG Music engaged in all kinds of flattery in order to secure air time for their music in the form of fixed payola rates for music play. Some stations billed Sony for $1000 after they played a song 75 times. Reportedly, Sony bought 250 "spins" of a Good Charlotte song for $17,000.[xi]

- *Agencies*—The entertainment industry has been concerned about a small but growing problem of unethical talent, modeling, and background agencies. Some of these agencies claim to be part of the legitimate industry but are really in business to defraud thousands of people every year out of millions of dollars. To protect against such frauds, the entertainment industry developed a code of ethics to define roles and set standards.

- *Television*—To deflect parental concerns about questionable program content, the National Association of Radio and Television Broadcasters (NARTB) developed a code of self-regulation for the television industry. The code contributed to the larger process of determining the parameters of "responsible" programming, or what is appropriate for family

EXHIBIT 1.3 Codes of Ethics

One entertainment company's policy on ethics provides a closer look at two most relevant ethical issues of concern in 2010.

A. Conflict of Interest

The primary principle underlying the Company's conflicts of interest policies is that associates and officers in particular must never permit their personal interests to conflict or appear to conflict with the interests of the Company or its customers.

1. *Receipt of bribes, commissions, honorariums, loans, gifts, gratuities, and entertainment are not condoned.* No company employee may accept or give gifts.

2. *Fair competition.* No associate may enter into agreements with competitors affecting pricing or marketing arrangements.

3. *Conduct with competitors.* Employees may not discuss pricing, contract terms, costs, inventories, marketing or product plans, research and capabilities or other proprietary information.

B. Confidentiality

Employees, officers and associates must not divulge any non-public information about the company to any outsider except for a legitimate business purpose with the understanding that that the information is to be used solely for the purpose for which it was given and received. Such information includes salary, personnel information, customer lists, budgets and forecasts, and marketing and sales plans.

viewing in the domestic environment. Ethical issues surface with regard to differences in the definition of "responsible" programming.

Codes of ethics

Entertainment corporations' codes of ethics, while not exactly the same, commonly contain similar areas of concern, especially with regard to conflict of interest and confidentiality. Exhibit 1.3 contains excerpts from one code as an example of the wording and content of such codes.

Although codes of ethics are not legally binding or punishable by law, ethical misdemeanors can results in the loss of one's job or reputation. To avoid punitive reprimands or penalties, take precautions before acting in compromising situations. Ask yourself questions about your duty and intentions: Am I doing the right thing? Am I proceeding with good will? Are my dignity and respect maintained? If you can answer 'yes' to these questions, chances are you have made an appropriate choice.

Finally

The entertainment industry operates with an economic landscape whose foundations are hours at work, productivity trends, expected utility functions, demographics, and other factors that affect the amounts of time and money we spend on leisure-related services. In the United States, spending of disposable income on entertainment has risen to over 10%—very big business indeed. When measured in dollar value terms, entertainment has consistently been one of the largest net export categories for this country.[xii] Are you ready to enter the business? When you finish this book, you will be.

GOT IT?

- Entertainment marketing is the process of promoting amusements, leisure, and recreation to potential and current audiences and travelers.

- Entertainment marketing differs from marketing products because experiences are perishable, intangible and based on time as a scarce resource.

- The seven characteristics of play set it apart from other types of experiences; contemporary play is an outgrowth of hedonistic consumption.

- Five entertainment experience genres include live performance, destinations/places, attraction, and venues, media, and celebrity/stars.

- Five men control most of the entertainment industry and are considered powerful moguls by marketers and corporations alike.

- Ethical issues are important considerations when marketing in the entertainment industry.

NOW TRY THIS

1. Trace a film studio (e.g. Paramount, MGM, 20th Century Fox) from its inception to its place in today's corporate conglomerate structure. How does the studio's evolution reflect the nature of today's entertainment industry structure?

2. Four classifications of Play are: *agon* (competition), *alea* (chance), *mimicry* (simulation), and *Ilinx* (vertigo). Go on line and find out what games and forms of entertainment fit into each classification.

3. Go on line and find out who the other important entertainment moguls are this year. What other women have taken their places among the entertainment moguls?

QUESTIONS FOR DISCUSSION AND REVIEW

1. How have the changes in the way we experience leisure time been reflected in the significant growth of the entertainment industry?

2. Explain the major characteristics marketing all forms of entertainment experiences.

3. What is the role of venues for marketing entertainment performances?

4. What role do ethics and codes of ethics play in entertainment marketing?

5. How have mergers and moguls impacted the entertainment industry in the last year?

MORE STUFF ON ENTERTAINMENT PRINCIPLES

https://www.esrb.org/ratings/principles_guidlines.jsp Guidelines for responsible advertising practices.

www.ugcprinciples.com User-generated content principles.

www.mediastandardstrust.org/ Media Standards Trust present universal principles for media.

[i] Bureau of Labor Statistics, 2005.

[ii] From an article by Damon Darlin in the "Your Money" section of the *New York Times*, Nov. 19, 2005.

[iii] Fortune, April 20, 2009.

[iv] Data from the U.S. Department of Commerce.

[v] From B. J. Pine & J. H. Gilmore (1999), *The Experience Economy: Work is Theater & Every Business is a Stage*. Harvard Business School Press, pp. 30–35.

[vi] Huizinga, J. (1950). *Homo ludens*. Boston: Beacon Press.

[vii] From Stephenson, W. (1988), The play theory of mass communication. New Brunswick NJ: Transaction Books.

[viii] Harold Vogel.

[ix] From Vogel's (2001) book, *Entertainment Industry Economics*. Cambridge University Press, pp. 352–354.

[x] John Horn (2001), "The Reviewer Who Wasn't There; Sony resorts to some questionable marketing practices to promote new movies," *Newsweek* Web Exclusive, June 2.

[xi] arstechnica.com/news.ars/post/20050803-5165.html

[xii] Op Cit Vogel, p. 31.

Chapter 2

PROMOTION IN A MERGING WORLD

> *You've no idea what a difference it makes,*
> *mixing things with other things.*
> Lewis Carroll

Chapter Objectives

After reading this chapter, you will be able to answer the following questions:

- What is the impact of *technology* and the *Internet* on the entertainment industry?

- What role does *globalization* play for the industry's marketing practices?

- How has convergence between entertainment and advertising come about and how does it determine the way the industry functions?

As young people watch films on their wireless phones and download music into their MP3 players, marketers realize that audiences must be reached where they live—and that is where they interact with media and messages. Advertisers develop branded games, branded films and branded contests to entertain potential consumers. At the same time, entertainment accepts brand placements in film, books, and broadcasts to generate revenue. This synergistic relationship is crucial for the success of both advertisers and entertainment. Starting at the corporate level, technology is the driving factor in this joint venture that oversees the fusion of entertainment and promotion. This chapter presents an overview of the current technological and global environment that fuses advertising and entertainment marketing.

ENTERTAINMENT TECHNOLOGY

- Technology, digitalization, and Internet access have had strong impacts on every aspect of the entertainment industry. We can point to four major shifts in the nature of entertainment that have developed since we entered the digital age in the mid-1990s.

- First, we've gone from mass entertainment, which is developed for a common denominator, to *personal entertainment*, where consumers use media tools and content for personal expression. Rather than sitting with a group in a dark theater, audience members preview films online, engage in interactive games, or read chapters on the run with a Kindle or iPad.

- Second, content has changed from being pre-packaged, or simply created for you, to *self-generated*, where you create it yourself. Audiences can now create their own game scenarios, author blogs, publish online fiction, and develop new episodes of old television series.

- Third, experiences have switched from being episodic, with a definite beginning and end, to *persistent*, where entertainment is ongoing and has no clear starting and stopping point. Our phones ring to Beethoven or the Beatles, live billboards enhance our transportation, in-seat movie screens amuse us while we fly, and iPods allow us to conduct our lives with music.

- Finally, entertainment has shifted from a virtual, or separate, experience to an *imbedded* experience, where digital information, images, music, and even experiences are fused with objects in the physical world. Cell phone movies are an example of imbedded information.

The impact of digitalization is most apparent over the Internet, in the nature of games, and how we communicate across borders. This section expands upon those changes.

Connecting online

The Internet provides audiences at home and at work with immediate, continuing access to global information and entertainment. Audiences have taken the Internet on the road; technologies that enable widespread mobile Internet access include long-lasting portable energy sources, low-power flexible displays, Wi-Fi, Bluetooth wireless communications, and global positioning systems (GPS). **Blogs** or Internet commentary and strong search engines such as Google allow audiences to communicate and to connect in ways that both inform and entertain.

Blogs and Vlogs act as promotion and feedback for entertainment providers. For example, in the music industry, these online "conversations" are acting as incubators for new musical talent and can be fertile testing grounds for music labels. A label manager at Vice Records[i] was hesitant to promote a new album by then unknown Norwegian pop star Annie until he saw the positive word of mouth she was receiving on blogs. Blogs also empower audiences; as bloggers, people can really influence content and how products are developed and promoted.

Google, AOL, Yahoo, and Bing search engines provide access to entertainment and simultaneously promote events and venues. Advertising revenues enhance users' ability to access both information and products. Google's brand has become a verb, as in "I googled the applicant for the job," "google this disease," and so forth. And with the addition of Google Scholar, Google Earth, and Google Images, even academics get to have fun searching the Web. The newest search engine, **Bing**, helps find and organize answers so you can make faster, more informed decisions.

Expanding internet usage

Worldwide adoption of Internet technology has connected everyone to everyone else. As of 2009, Asia—with only 9% of the world's population—has the highest percentage of Internet users globally, while Africa and the Middle East have experienced the most increased usage over the past five years.

Game technology fosters creative interaction

Because the cost of producing a video game is $1/20^{th}$ of the cost of producing a film, revenues from game sales outpace the ROI (return on investment) of blockbuster films. Interactivity is the reason why. For example, the fictional, puzzle-solving game known as *The Beast* represents a new genre of alternate reality games sweeping the marketplace.

Games have a grassroots role in entertainment media experimentation. So far, game playing has had enough of an impact to generate a few new social and cultural practices. For example it has changed the way some children and adolescents relate to each other—two boys can sit in the same room playing GameBoy without so much as a word to each other and still be communicating. Games have become part of mainstream culture. We play them on hand-held devices, PCs, mobile phones, TV sets, portable game machines, and in arcades. A $20 billion a year industry, video games have captured 65% of Americans averaging age thirty-five, 40% of whom are female. In 2008, 26% of Americans over the age of 50 played video games, an increase from 9% in 1999. There are Nintendo gaming consoles in over 600,000 hotel rooms and 50,000 airline seats. Game growth overall rose from $2.6 billion in 1996 to $11.7 billion in 2008.

Online Games Played Most Often

PERCENTAGE	GENRE
44%	Puzzle, board, trivia, card, game show
21%	Action, sports, strategy, role play
16%	Persistent multi-player universe
10%	Downloadable-dinu dash
09%	Other

Time Warner's venture GameTap, which offers computer users with broadband connections an opportunity to play hundreds of games on demand, links it with game producers including Activision, Atari, Midway, Namco, Sega, and UbiSoft. Sold by Turner Broadcasting System division of Time Warner, GameTap lets subscribers download and install software from their Web site, which also features free original content like video clips and email cards. The appetite for gaming is further evidenced by the inclusion of products and brands in games from DaimlerChrysler, Kraft Foods, and Orbitz and the decision by filmmaker Steven Spielberg to develop games with Electronic Arts game company.[ii] Although this text does not focus on technology marketing per se, we must acknowledge the competitive role games play when we market entertainment experiences.

Content development and technology

In our global era, necessary focus has been given to the future of digital, satellite, and internet radio as a means to increase the flow of information and culture across geographic boundaries. At the same time, however, radio remains primarily a local experience. Though broadcasting itself can be argued to be a social innovation rather than a technological one, there are two reasons for continuing interest in radio: low-cost and ease of production, access, and broadcast. There is also increasing opportunity for listening, both online and through unlicensed or independent micro radio stations. Important as well is the audience's emotional and cultural relationship with radio. At its best, radio is about the intimacy between the voice and listener.

Marketers are slicing radio audiences into ever narrowing niches of gamers, surfers, and iPod users. Providing additional evidence of convergence, Infinity's Clear Channel and Sirius have pod media on radio, while ABC and NBC produced their own version of a daily headline download, and Scripps-Howard and *Business Week* deliver audio versions of their print products.

Image 2.1 Grand theft auto.

Grand Theft Auto

Parents whose kids spend hours with video games are worried about their influence on behavior. What we consider here is the ethics of exposing violent and sexual content to minors without any censorship capabilities.

Overview

The first installment of the Grand Theft Auto (GTA) video game series released in 1997 gained success from its alleged controversial game play. Throughout the series, players take on the role as a criminal and are free to roam through a large city committing illicit acts including: stealing cars; shooting, and running over pedestrians; taking drugs; and having sex with prostitutes. The game series, considered to encourage violence and degrade women, has received considerable commercial success; it was ranked the top selling game in the United States in 2001, and by 2005 had sold 35 million copies. Two factors are considered to compromise gamers: violence and sexual content.

Violence

According to the Institute for Global Ethics, the key issue surrounding the Grand Theft Auto series is its hyper-violence. Computer and video games have been scrutinized by the mass media for encouraging violent and aggressive behavior, particularly with children and teenagers, and the Grand Theft Auto series contribution to this facet was evident by the moral panic in parents upon its release. Violence against police officers and women are central themes in the series, and it has been considered that the series promotes such actions in real life. After stealing a car, an American teenager shot three people, two of whom were police officers. These actions are thought to have been inspired by playing hundreds of hours of Grand Theft Auto and to resemble a scene from one of the games.

Scholars argue against that notion, claiming that the complexity of a video game such as Grand Theft Auto is actually beneficial for our brains because it challenges our thinking. They further suggest that game violence contextualizes the actions within the game space and the options given in the game are restricted to the game itself, not to reality. Other studies on exposure to violence,[iii] however, suggest that playing violent video games will increase aggressive behavior. A review of the video-game research literature reveals that violent video games can increase aggressive behavior in children and young adults. Research also reveals that exposure to violent video games increases physiological arousal and aggression-related thoughts and feelings among both boys and girls. Playing violent video games also decreases prosocial behavior.

Sexual content

Scenarios relating to sexual activities are prominent in the series, in particular Grand Theft Auto "3" and "San Andreas." In "3," it is possible for a player's character to pick up a female prostitute, have sex with her, and then kill her to take back the paid money. However, actions of this nature are done by the player's choice and the consequences of these activities are punishable by the police within the game.

A "Hot Coffee" modification, when installed with San Andreas, unlocks several mini-games that prompt players to have the game's hero engage in X-rated acts. Rockstar Games, the company behind the series, was reprimanded by the Entertainment Software Rating Board (ESRB) for including this content code in the game without reporting it to the ESRB.

In their defense, game players argue that the material attainable for viewing is not controversial because the sexual content is so overtly ridiculous that it should play as comedy in context.

What do you think?

1. Compare the scholar's argument about violence with the actions of the teenage car thief. Which view do you endorse? Why?

2. What should be the role of a ratings board? Should penalties that include fines rather than mere reprimands be enforced?

Source: Developed by students in New Media Technologies of the Creative Industries Faculty, Queensland University of Technology, Brisbane, Australia.

Podcasting, the practice of downloading and playing live and recorded video through an iPod or other MP3 player, is almost a rebellion against the blandness of commercial radio. It offers audiences more power to raise their voices as a global audience. Inexpensive and with much creative potential, podcasting combines aspects of TiVo and blogging with the added dimension of audio. Podcasting is a logical progression in grassroots media. Podcast downloaders are expected to grow from 9% of Internet users in 2008 to 17% in 2013.

Podcasting is a way to circumvent imposed programming as delivered by corporate-owned stations. Audience members create their own podcasts and become pod stars or Internet radio deejays or talk-show hosts. Radio may not be dead, but it will have to come up with new ways to compete with consumer-controlled media or market itself as more than just syndicated programming. Many stations have joined the movement to become podcast friendly, as did public radio station WNYC, which increased its listeners by 40,000 per week through podcasting. For the top podcasts and a podcast directory, visit podcastalley.com

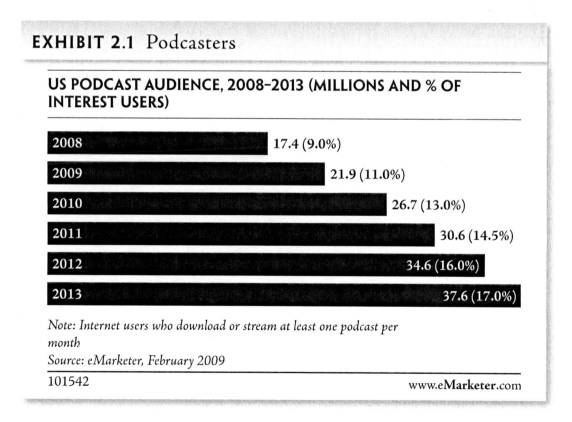

EXHIBIT 2.1 Podcasters

US PODCAST AUDIENCE, 2008–2013 (MILLIONS AND % OF INTEREST USERS)

Year	Value
2008	17.4 (9.0%)
2009	21.9 (11.0%)
2010	26.7 (13.0%)
2011	30.6 (14.5%)
2012	34.6 (16.0%)
2013	37.6 (17.0%)

Note: Internet users who download or stream at least one podcast per month
Source: eMarketer, February 2009

101542   www.eMarketer.com

Watching Their Garden Grow

Client: Wiggly Wigglers, a small mail-order company based in rural Herefordshire England. An English natural gardening supply company Wiggly sells flowers, birdhouses, bird seed, worms—stuff to delight the green thumb set.

Challenge: How to communicate directly and effectively with the 60,000 or so current customers and new customers. In the UK, 12.5 percent of households have gardens. Wiggly's goal is to make those gardens more wildlife friendly.

Implementation: What better way to spark a new conversation than a podcast show where people can respond and comment via email and chat? Unlike radio, podcasts impose no licensing regulations. Long before Wiggly Wiggler's podcasts, the company had an award-winning web site: www.wigglywigglers.co.uk. These days the podcast works together with the new Wiggler blog: http://wigglywigglers.blogspot.com/.

Heather, the host, leads giggly chats with a half dozen employees, the local vet, friends and customers about gardening and related subjects. These conversations are intercut with short reports from Heather's husband Farmer Phil, little Monty (a young friend) and others, about life on the farm. They fashioned their style on NPR's Car Talk-a gregarious back and forth banter about a subject the correspondents obviously love and know well. Part of why Wiggly Wiggler's podcasts worked so well is their focus on subjects of interest to the hosts, not on shilling products they sell. For example, a show discussing birdhouse also included an on-air autopsy by a resident veterinarian to determine why the farm's twin calves died.

Outcome: 1500 regular listeners and thousands of single listeners provide direct feedback on ideas and thoughts, which is valuable market research. Listeners in Luxemburg, Belgium, Canada, and U.S. order bouquets delivered to friends in the UK. Average rating on iTunes and Yahoo Podcast: 5 stars.

Wiggly Wiggler Tips for Building a Successful Business Podcast

AVOID trying to sell. People are fed up with being "sold to" all the time.

Make sure you have a co-host. Co-hosts help keep the conversation going. All the most popular podcasts and radio shows have more than one presenter.

Don't shy away from a little controversy. People like to hear a bit of a row.

Involve your audience. Encourage them to email you, or to make an audio file that you can play on air.

Source: /Excerpted from Ch. 3 of the "Business Podcasting Handbook" by Joe Delvin

GLOBAL EFFECTS

A multi-disciplinary technology revolution is changing the world. The fast pace of technological development and breakthroughs makes foresight difficult, but the technology revolution seems globally significant and is quite likely taking place across all dimensions of life: social, economic, political, and personal. The revolution of information availability and utility will continue to profoundly affect the world in all these dimensions. Competition for technology development leadership will depend on future regional economic arrangement (e.g., the European Union), international intellectual property rights and protections, the character of future multinational corporations, and the role and amount of public and private sector research and development investments.

Currently, there are moves toward competition among regional economic alliances and increased support for a global intellectual property protection regime and a division of responsibilities for R&D funding. Such legal and economic factors have a direct impact on how we develop, market, and use entertainment products and experiences.

Global strategies must mix the right proportion of standardized and customized content and branding. The choices involve sending a single content or brand to a global market, localizing content and keeping the brand global, or localizing both brand and content. Disney has chosen to keep a global brand, image, and content structure while localizing messages and customizing secondary considerations such as food and park layout. Cirque du Soleil, on the other hand, presents standardized global performances marketed locally. By strategically balancing configurations of a global/local message with standardized/customized content, entertainment marketers can maximize box office revenues. Chapter 3 discusses the cultural impact of globalization on entertainment content.

Television is the best medium disseminating global messages without changing content; U.S. soap operas and dramas reach global audiences (often with subtitle additions). Theme park format can remain similar across borders but local food is often incorporated into its content. Films and cruise ships, using standard content, localize their advertising messages. Theater, on the other hand, often customizes its programming and advertising messages with local appeal. Exhibit 2.3 diagrams the global-local relationship between standardized content (same for everyone) and content customized for a local region.

Transnationals: media corporations and entertainment flows

Nationally based media and entertainment companies with overseas operations in two or more countries are called **transnational media corporations (TNMC)**. Exhibit 2.4 presents the major TNMC players. Highly global in its approach to business, a TNMC operates in preferred

EXHIBIT 2.2 Approaching Global Entertainment

Standardized Content

```
                                    ^
                                    ^
Global          TV                  ^              Film, Cruise Ships
message ——————————————————————————^——————————————————— message
Local        Theme parks           ^              Theater
                                    ^
                                    ^
```

Customized Content

markets with an obvious preference and familiarity toward its home market. News Corp., for example, generates 76% of its total revenues inside the United States and Canada, followed by its markets in Europe (16%) and Australasia (8%). Similarly, Viacom generates an estimated 84% of its revenues inside the United States and Canada. The remaining 16% of Viacom's global revenues are generated largely from Paramount Pictures and the company's Music TV international subsidiaries and joint partnerships.[iv]

Global markets are a natural result of transnational business taking place between economies that will mutually benefit. Driven by trends in deregulation and privatization, high-speed technology has helped create new market integration, such as the booming telecommunications business that is currently taking place in India.

Privatization has affected the international TV and film markets with the increasing volume of programs purchased from commercial sources, and increased competition for software products among potential program buyers. The TNMC and the concept of global brands are becoming realities in terms of news, sports, and music entertainment. The importance of the TNMC and co-production ventures are going to foster a programming philosophy based on the assumption that the world can be broken down according to cultural continents, i.e. areas where cultural factors are similar. The next generation of global TV viewers are likely to be people who can simultaneously appreciate world MTV and still have a decided preference for locally originated drama or sporting event.

EXHIBIT 2.3 Internet Usage

WORLD INTERNET USAGE AND POPULATION STATISTICS 2009

WORLD REGIONS	POPULATION	POPULATION % OF WORLD	INT. USAGE	USAGE GROWTH % 2000–2009	% POPULATION PENETRATION	WORLD % USERS
Africa	991,002,342	14.0	67,371,700	1,392%	6.8%	2.5
Asia	3,808,070,503	55.4	738,257,230	546%	19.4%	34.2
Europe	803,850,858	11.4	418,029,796	298%	53%	28.5
Middle East	202,687,005	04.1	57,425,046	1,648%	28.3%	2.2
North America	340,831,831	05.1	52,908,000	134%	74.2%	23.4
Latin America	179,031,479	08.5	179,031,479	891%	30.5%	7.4
Oceana/ Australia	34,700,201	.5	20,970,490	175%	60%	1.8
WORLD TOTAL	6,767,805,208	100	1,733,993,741	380.3 %	25.6%	100

Data provided by www.internetworldstats.com

CONVERGENCE: A SYMBIOTIC RELATIONSHIP

According to Scott Donaton, the editor of *Advertising Age*, the world's largest media publication, what we are encountering is a **Madison and Vine** dynamic that is transforming the way in which media, music, and advertising industries merge to reach their markets. (Madison Avenue in New York is synonymous with advertising, while Hollywood and Vine in California is the symbolic corner of the entertainment industry.)

Mix, match and mold

Convergence comes in a variety of shapes and forms, but six common themes prevail. Stated as rules, they may serve as guidelines for developing a Madison-Vine approach to entertainment marketing.

1. Reject the status quo—change is an economic necessity.

2. Collaborate—deals happen when movie studios, TV networks, ad agencies, marketing firms, and PR agencies work together.

3. Demand accountability—the bottom line gives credibility to return on investment.

4. Stay flexible—adapt branded entertainment models or evolve them into new forms.

5. Let go—market control must yield to audience collaboration with content producers.

6. Respect the audience—marketing is changing from intrusion to invitation, from dumbing down content to respecting the consumer.

One example of convergence was the 2003 Victoria's Secret Holiday Fashion Show in New York City, which featured lingerie-clad runway models wearing angels' wings; performances by Sting, Mary J. Blige and Eve; and an after-show party at which Donald Trump rubbed elbows with P. Diddy.[v] The live show was filmed for broadcast on network TV. Developed to target the sought-after young male demographic, the first annual show drew millions of dollars in free publicity, including the front page of the *Wall Street Journal*. Cloaked as entertainment, was this runway extravaganza simply an hour-long commercial for the Victoria's Secret retail chain? The answer is your call.

Reality television is a second example of convergence where entertainment-advertiser alliances are created, as sponsors take part in program content. Without product sponsors, shows such as *Survivor* could never afford to produce single-run programming (reruns are not an option for reality TV). Wal-Mart, seeking to improve its image, has sponsored an educational reality show called *The Scholar*, which featured intellectual rather than physical challenges for participants.

A third convergence example is BMW's production of a 10-minute commercial designed to show off the capabilities of the X5 sport utility vehicle, part of their series of eight celebrity-studded product films. Assembling acting and directing stars from Hollywood, the Fallon Ad Agency broke the rules by giving commercial directors total control of creative content. The BMW Films became an Internet phenomenon, and the company had

© Louise Gubb/Corbis

2.2 Cast members of the Survivor: Africa reality television show.

to add servers to meet the demand for downloads. The year of the film's releases and two years following, BMW sold a record number of vehicles, beating its own record for three consecutive years. Finally, the series was introduced into the permanent collection of the Museum of Modern Art. So are the films art? Entertainment? Advertising? We contend they are all three—a cool convergence of branding and entertainment.

A fourth example of convergence taps into the music culture, where poor CD sales and strong competition were killing production companies in the early 2000s. The solution? Put brands and logos into the CDs design or lyrics, or use music as background for product advertising. While music tie-ins are more valuable to new artists than established ones, Mitsubishi's commercial music became a popular Internet download. Sting's single "Desert Rose" was both a commercial for Jaguar and for his music. Chapter 3 presents important strategies and tactics that capitalize on the convergence of advertising and entertainment.

Experiential marketing

A further expansion of the convergence notion exists when manufacturers become creators of experiences to connect consumers with their brands. **Experiential marketing** consists of messages designed to increase a purchase intention for a product or service through the fusion of activity with brands. Instead of selling skis from a rack, sport retailers construct sawdust ski slopes where consumers may experience the brand before they buy it. Cuisinart invites shoppers to cook with its kitchen products during classes or special events as part of their experiential marketing program.

During national research conducted in 2005 by the Jack Morton Company, 2,574 consumers in the top 25 U.S. markets completed surveys about their consumption experiences.[vi] Here are the key findings:

+ Experiential marketing drives purchase and consideration across age, gender, and ethnicity.

+ 70% of consumers say participating in experiential marketing would increase purchase consideration.

+ 66% say experiential marketing is extremely influential on brand opinion.

+ 7 in 10 consumers said participating in a live experience would make them more receptive to the brand's marketing.

Implications for entertainment marketers are extensive: fusing entertainment content with products and brands creates excitement about both entities.

Role of the big agency

The *Red Book* contains over 2,500 advertising agencies, yet only a few big agencies control most of the entertainment providers, corporations, and franchises. Total measured advertising

EXHIBIT 2.4 Advertising Revenues Decline

MEDIA SECTOR MEDIA TYPE (SHOWN IN RANK ORDER OF 2009 SPENDING)	% CHANGE
TELEVISION MEDIA	**-9.7%**
✦ Network TV	-4.2%
✦ Cable TV	-2.7%
✦ Spot TV[2]	-27.5%
✦ Syndication–National	0.2%
✦ Spanish Language TV	-15.4%
MAGAZINE MEDIA[iii]	**-20.5%**
✦ Consumer Magazines	-19.2%
✦ B-to-B Magazines	-25.5%
✦ Sunday Magazines	-23.7%
✦ Local Magazines	-25.3%
✦ Spanish Language Magazines	-20.5%
NEWSPAPER MEDIA[iv]	**-25.5%**
✦ Newspapers (Local)	-25.1%
✦ National Newspapers	-28.5%
✦ Spanish Language Newspapers	-21.6%
INTERNET (display ads only)	**8.2%**
RADIO MEDIA	**-26.2%**
✦ Local Radio[v]	-26.8%
✦ National Spot Radio	-31.7%
✦ Network Radio	-11.2%
OUTDOOR	**-14.6%**
FSIs[vi]	**-0.2%**
TOTAL	**-14.2%**

Source: www.tns-mi.com/news/06102009.htm

expenditures in the opening quarter of 2009 plunged 14.2% versus a year before, to $30.18 billion, according to data released by TNS Media Intelligence, the leading provider of strategic advertising and marketing information.

Necessary to support blockbuster films and new TV network and cable program launches, entertainment advertising budgets continue to increase despite economic downturns, making both types of properties attractive and profitable clients. Most of the major agencies use outside firms to supply research, data, direct marketing, trailers, media planning and buying, public relations, Internet and lobbying activities and functions, yet they maintain control over concepts. In addition to the global giants, small and mid-sized agencies provide creative projects for entertainment companies.

Although not all entertainment companies are turning to a single agency for worldwide promotions, an increasing number are lining up their brands with just a few international agencies—a strategy called **alignment fever**. This trend has spelled success for global agency networks; the top ten agencies' combined share of global advertising spending has doubled in the past decade.

As advertising agencies opened up units specializing in entertainment, Hollywood talent agencies have created units specializing in marketing, as have industry lawyers. Product placement firms have reinvented themselves as strategic integration specialists. Former studio, agency, network, talent and marketing executives became backers of specialty companies servicing the entertainment industry. Such consortiums are joining to identify appropriate measurement tools to determine their return on investment.

With lucrative sponsorship, licensing and product placement deals (see Chapters 9 and 16), many clients are forming marketing partnerships with advertising and promotion agencies to develop special applications for branding. And agency billing practices are changing methods of compensation from a percentage of media buys to a share of the profits. Such a practice makes accountability more important, and agencies become partners rather than service providers. The convergence of marketing with entertainment entities is creating unique partnerships, and in some cases building new bridges to connect these very different business for a win-win situation. Agencies and their clients are presented in Exhibit 2.5.

Stealth marketing

Stealth marketing, sometimes called undercover marketing, is an aspect of marketing where an audience is not aware they are being marketed to. Akin to guerrilla marketing that uses a battle strategy, stealth marketing creates scenarios for interacting with consumers without disclosing their promotional intentions. For example, a marketing company pays an actor to talk favorably about the product to people they meet in a social location without those consumers realizing they've been pitched. By working on a person's subconscious, stealth marketers create need for their product that often results in a purchase then or at a later time.

EXHIBIT 2.5 Major Advertising Agencies Representing the Entertainment Industry

AGENCY	CLIENT COMPANY
McCann Erickson	Columbia Pictures
Western Media, Division of Interpublic	Disney Studios
Grey Advertising	Warner Bros. Studios, WB Network *Entertainment Weekly, People Magazine*
TWBA, Division of Omnicom	ABC TV Network
Young & Rubicam, Div of WPP	Showtime, Viacom, Blockbuster Video, Sony Electronics Game
Saatchi & Saatchi	News Corp

When targeting consumers known to be consistent Internet users, undercover marketers have taken a significant interest in using Internet chat rooms and forums. In these settings, people tend to perceive everyone as peers, the semi-anonymity reduces the risk of being found out, and one marketer can personally influence a large number of people.

Whatever the risks, undercover marketing only requires a small investment for a large potential pay-off. It remains a cheap and effective way of generating buzz, especially in markets such as tobacco and alcohol where media-savvy target consumers have become increasingly resistant or inaccessible to other forms of advertising.

Agencies use entertainment to market themselves

Competition among agencies for clients is tough, and some agencies call attention to themselves by breaking traditional client-generating strategies. For instance, to help win some beer accounts, WPP Group's JWT staged an elaborate stunt at the National Beer Wholesalers Convention in Las Vegas. The agency hired a group of actors to perform three days of street theater at the convention to promote a fictitious beverage called Beerka. A wedding was held to marry beer and vodka to produce Beerka. Dressed in wedding gear, the actors spent five hours at the Las Vegas airport on the convention's first day holding signs welcoming the Beerka wedding party. Later they circulated around Bally's Casino where the convention was held handing out wedding invitations to beer executives. When the action slowed down, the actors staged a fight on the convention floor. Conventioneers who wanted to find out more were directed to a Web site. After the convention, JWT sent wedding DVDs to 40 beer executives who had attended the convention. Why? To create a buzz about their agency.

Rather than settle for a buzz, the president of Deutsch Inc. used the entertainment industry to position himself as the voice of the ad business to "give his agency a brand presence in the industry".[vii] Donny Deutsch is a media guy: his show on CNBC, "The Big Idea with Donny Deutsch," and his book, *Often Wrong, Never in Doubt*, have brought attention to himself and the agency. Purchased by Interpublic Group in 2000, Deutsch Inc. has not fared as well from Donny's publicity as Donny himself; the agency lost nine accounts including Bank of America, Mitsubishi, and Revlon with total billings of $849 million. Donny continues to entertain, but neither his clients nor his boss are amused.

FOCUS ON CAREERS

Profile of a PR Intern

As a **public relations intern**, Pauline Perenack worked in the television industry for Boyd Coddington's Hot Rods and Collectibles, one of the features of a reality show called "American Hot Rod." On the show, a car was built from scratch as the cameras rolled. Because of the position's versatility, Pauline worked on location with crews from the Discovery Channel as they film each week's segment, filing a variety of assignments.

Part of her job was writing press releases about upcoming car unveilings and attending to members of the media who cover the show. Pauline also acted as the contact person for media who want interviews or develop feature stories on the show or its stars. With access to one of the most well-know hot rod shops in the country, Pauline watched cars being built from the ground up in preparation for their re-building as part of the reality show that is taped at a later date. "Meeting people from around the world was the most stimulating part of the position," says Pauline. (The show was cancelled after the star's death in 2008).

After graduating from the University of Calgary in 2004 with a major in communication, Pauline began interning to gain experience in television. "Internships allow you to angle your career towards a particular position, or simply walk away if you find it's not the industry for you. Making contacts to use later on to find a job is another advantage of being an intern. Or you can take a job with the sponsor of your internship. After eight months here, my boss offered me a permanent position."

In her words..............

Industry consolidation

Along with the convergence of technology, advertising, and entertainment, acquisitions proliferate. In the 1990s, Sony expanded its technology business by acquiring companies that produce film and TV, and it developed its own movie media entity, Sony Productions. Apple entered the music distribution business after developing the iPod in 2001. Disney branched out beyond parks and resorts by purchasing a sports network and a film production company, Pixar Animation Studios, a television network, forming an Internet group and developing games based on its *Pirates of the Caribbean* franchise. Beverage giant Seagram is now in the theme park and movie business. The gaming software market, while still somewhat fragmented, is consolidating as well. Electronic Arts holds the biggest share (20.8%), which is more than double the share of its closest competitors Activision (8.3%) and Nintendo (7.7%).[viii] In 2009, iPhone games became a huge force for players; on a typical day, six to eight of the 10 best-selling apps are games. One-third of all iPhone owners who use apps had downloaded Tap Tap Revenge by February, 2009, according to research firm ComScore.[ix] That made the music game, which is free in some versions and $4.99 in others, the most-owned app. Twelve of the top 25—and five of the top 10—listed by ComScore are games. Video games that cost less than $10 are a big change. A typical title for a console or PC typically sells for $30 to $60 while handheld games on Nintendo's DS cost $20 to $35.

As large companies continue to gobble up media and entertainment properties, power shifts and empires rise and fall. A few conglomerations run not only the Hollywood studios but also the giant media companies that own the studios. They did create a new version of Hollywood, but they also failed to master the corporate intrigues that would let them rule not just the studio lot, but also the business world beyond. This generation of creative moguls, instead of making Hollywood the center of the universe, gave us a world that is now governed by the wants and needs of 17-year-old boys on any given Saturday night.[x]

Media conglomerates continue to amass, consolidate, and cross-pollinate their interests in publishing, broadcasting, cable programming, movie and TV production, distribution, theme parks, lodging, and real estate. Mergers such as the deal between Disney and Apple to provide ABC TV shows on its iTunes store for playing on the iPod, and the agreement between Apple and Pixar Animation Studios to distribute short animated features are two examples of cross-industry efforts at content development and distribution.

Ties that bind advertising and entertainment

Tie-ins are a way to connect an event or product with another event and/or product, so that both brands benefit from the association. For marketers aiming at the lucrative children's audience, few opportunities are more valuable than the Macy's Thanksgiving Day Parade. More than 50 million viewers watch the three-hour parade on network television, while 2.5 million people line the parade route to watch the event in person.[xi] The parade is a launching pad for promotional campaigns, including product tie-ins involving movies, TV shows, and merchandise.

In 2009, giant balloons were used to promote films and DVDs, including Buzz Lightyear (Disney), Horton the Elephant (20th Century Fox) Sailor Mickey (Disney Cruise Line), Shrek (Dreamworks), Smurf (Sony Pictures), Snoopy (United Media), and Spider Man (Marvel Comics). In 2005, A Scooby-Doo balloon matched plush toys available at Macy's stores nationwide, and a float featuring characters from "Hi Hi Puffy Ami

© Brendan McDermid/Reuters/Corbis

2.3 Macy's Thanksgiving Day Parade float with Spiderman.

Yumi" coincided with the Cartoon Network's promotional campaign for the show. In the 2004 parade, a balloon appearance of SpongeBob SquarePants was timed to the release of the feature-length movie that year; Sponge Bob fans went wild.

Unapologetic commercialism determined most of the event's cast of characters, although a few oldies like M&Ms on Broadway and Sesame Street were featured in the 2009 float parade.

Finally

The advent of a global audience population, digital technology, and the desire of multinational conglomerates for revenue streams, provides a pervasive synergy allows entertainment to be everywhere. Combine technology's reach with businesses' global push and you have messages woven into every aspect of the audiences' lives. The danger, of course, is that the more pervasive the messages, the less consumers are likely to react and respond. A need for authenticity will push audiences towards stimuli that deliver a more creative answer to their needs. Your job as marketer is to entice audiences into venues where they may delight in the sights and sounds of an entertainment experience.

GOT IT?

- Technology has made entertainment in the digital age a personal, self-generated, persistent and embedded element of our society.

- Global intellectual property protection impacts the use and development of entertainment experiences worldwide.

- The convergence of advertising and entertainment, known as the Madison and Vine syndrome, necessitates the marriage of both entities.

- Multinational media corporations are segmenting the globe into cultural continents for program content delivery.

NOW TRY THIS

1. Using the Internet, check out the newest forms of reality games. Develop a franchising idea to carry these games into the workplace.

2. Check out the apps available for iPhones and discuss their entertainment value.

3. Investigate Disney's marketing for their Hong Kong theme park. How did it differ from the way they market Disney parks in the U.S., France, and Japan?

QUESTIONS FOR DISCUSSION AND REVIEW

1. What other examples of the Madison and Vine syndrome (the merging of advertising and entertainment) can you identify as useful for marketing experiences?

2. How does 'experiential marketing' differ from marketing experiences?

3. How has digitalization changed the focus of entertainment for providers of children's television and gaming?

4. What is the role of the big agency for entertainment marketing?

OTHER STUFF ABOUT GLOBAL MERGING AND CONVERGING

www.mindshareworld.com *Ad Age* interviews with small agency leaders on changed media.

www.mediaweek.com Consumer insights and innovative campaigns.

www.carat.com Independent media agency network.

www.mediaconvergence.org/blog Conversations of convergence.

[i] From an article by Brian Montopoli, "Little Known Brands Get Lift Through Word-of-Blog", *New York Times*, June 6, 2005.

[ii] Reported in the *New York Times* by advertising columnist Stuart Elliott on Oct. 17, 2005.

[iii] C. A. Anderson & B. J. Bushman (2001), "Effects of violent video games on aggressive behavior, aggressive cognition, aggressive affect, physiological arousal, and prosocial behavior: a meta-analytic review of the scientific literature," Iowa State University, Department of Psychology.

[iv] From Richard Gershon, "The Transnationals: Media Corporations, International TV Trade and Entertainment Flows" in Ann Cooper-Chen (ed) (2005), *Global Entertainment Media*. Lawrence Erlbaum.

[v] From "Madison Avenue is Getting the Beat" by Brian Steinberg for the *Wall Street Journal*'s Advertising column, June 23, 2005.

[vi] From a Jack Morton Worldwide (division of Interpublic) corporate promotion piece written by Liz Bigham who describes the survey and its findings.

[vii] From Devin Leonard's Media Bubble column in *Fortune*, Oct. 31, 2005, p. 46.

[viii] Reported by Geoff Keighley's article, "Could This Be The Next Disney?" in *Business 2.0*, January, 2003.

[ix] Alex Pham for the *LA Times*, April 13, 2009

[x] "In Hollywood, All Players but No Power, *New York Times*, August 8, 2005.

[xi] From Julie Bosman's Advertising column in the *New York Times*, Nov. 23, 2005.

3

CHARACTERIZING OUR EXPERIENCE CULTURE

> *Culture has always been driven by the marketplace.*
> *It's just that today the marketplace, having invaded every*
> *nook and cranny of our lives, is completely supplanting culture;*
> *the marketplace has become our culture.*
>
> Tom Robbins[i]

Chapter Objectives

After reading this chapter, you will be able to answer the following questions:

+ What makes entertainment an *experience industry?*

+ How does *service marketing* differ from entertainment marketing?

+ How does entertainment marketing address *timing* and *attention?*

+ What *convergence strategies* work for marketing both experiences and brands?

+ How does *audience fragmentation* underlie the marketing challenge?

+ What *global paradigm* can be used for understanding cultural differences?

Chapter Two showed us how merging technologies and corporations affect the way audiences receive entertainment. This chapter grounds our understanding of how entertainment marketing differs from product and service marketing. As a way to delineate the unique characteristics of entertainment marketing, we will look at aspects of services marketing and entertainment marketing as they converge in the hospitality industry. We also will discuss the cultural dimensions of entertainment marketing and the volatile characteristics of today's fragmented entertainment audiences.

ENTERTAINMENT IS AN EXPERIENCE INDUSTRY

Entertainment is an experience industry. So, is it a service industry as well? Entertainment as a commodity involves service *only* when its core product is *customer service* satisfaction, which is an essential component of operating resorts, lodging, spas, and performance venues. Such experiential venues must have a service culture that differentiates them from the competition; they must become the *provider of choice* for visitors.

According to a Marriott executive, "if a company takes care of its employees, they will take care of its guests." The hospitality industry's philosophy focuses on attracting and retaining quality employees. In this industry, customer expectations are higher because of the service comparisons they can make within industry segments such as restaurants and lodging. Venues such as concerts, theme parks, and museums also adhere to this customer service philosophy.

In *The Experience Economy*, authors[ii] Joseph Pine and James Gilmore present a view of staged experiences as *experience realms* of engagement, organized by type and level of involvement. Exhibit 3.1 diagrams this experiential view. Four levels of audience participation—passive and active (horizontal axis) and absorption and emersion (vertical axis)—describe connections that unite customers within an event or performance. Coupled with these dimensions are four realms of a single experience—entertainment, education, escape, and estheticism. These realms are mutually compatible domains that often commingle to form uniquely personal encounters. The *entertainment* realm contains the type of passive absorption experience that is provided by mediated and staged performances. Absorbing activity that gradually unfolds, such as what visitors experience in museums, falls into the *educational* realm. Audiences may participate in the *escapist* realm by actively participating in immersive environments such as theme parks, casinos, and Internet chat rooms. Although passive, immersion in art or visual delights carries audiences into an *esthetic* realm. Marketers can use this realms model to understand the relationship between an experience and its target audience.

Marketers may enhance the "realness" of a particular experience by blurring the boundaries between realms to promote an immersive venue of entertainment experiences. Ontario Mills

EXHIBIT 3.1 The Experience Realms

Absorption

Entertainment   *Educational*

Passive   *   **Active**
Participation   **Participation**

Esthetics   *Escapist*

Immersion

Source: The Experience Economy, 1999, p. 30

shopping center in Southern California was designed to merge aspects of all four realms. First, it provided businesses that offer both staged entertainment and escapist experiences—a 37-screen movie house, an arcade/restaurant, and Spielberg's Gameworks. Then it laid out these businesses on distinctive streetscapes with neighborhoods to provide some esthetic and educational experience. The result is a cumulative adventure that really transcends shopping by itself. By marketing all levels of an attraction—educational, escapist, esthetic, and entertainment—a generic space becomes a mnemonic place that creates memories and fosters play. As we will see in later chapters, successfully staged marketing events involve more than just offering an experience; success is contingent upon the qualities inherent in successful service businesses that accompany entertainment experiences. So in many instances, service and entertainment marketing intersect. They are, however, different entities as the next section illustrates.

DISTINGUISHING BETWEEN PRODUCT, SERVICE AND ENTERTAINMENT MARKETING

All forms of entertainment rely to some degree on service elements. And although some entertainment content is considered product, experiences are not products, services, or commodities. By comparing the dimensions of products with those of entertainment, we can identify the challenges presented to experience marketers. Exhibit 3.2 outlines the differences and the implications of marketing products and experiences.

Because entertainment is delivered as an *action*—a performance, experience, or event—it cannot be felt, seen, tasted or touched in the same way as tangible products. Entertainment is *intangible*. As such, it presents marketing challenges due to fluctuations in demand. Seasonality, tour schedules, film releases, and performance dates often drive experience promotions. Also, because it is not a tangible product, the actual cost of a "unit of experience" is hard to determine and to price.

EXHIBIT 3.2 Products vs. Entertainment

PRODUCTS	EXPERIENCES	IMPLICATIONS
Tangible	Intangible	Entertainment cannot be inventoried Pricing is difficult
Standardized	Context-dependent	Audience satisfaction depends on unique delivery and many uncontrollable factors
Production and consumption separate	Simultaneous production and consumption	Audiences participate in transaction Audience members affect each other Employees affect audience satisfaction Mass production difficult Experience cannot be returned or resold
Nonperishable	Perishable	Hard to synchronize supply & demand with experience Entertainment cannot be returned or resold

McDonald's standardizes it hamburgers and its fries, but entertainers rarely present the same performance twice (every version is different), and no vacation, theme park visit, or shopping spree is ever experienced the same way. Satisfaction is context-dependent and predicated on how the experience is delivered as much as the content of the performance. A rude usher can ruin a ballet for an audience member. No two participants have the same expectations or standards for experiences; and often the experience is dependent upon the actions or behavior of other audience members. Therefore, ensuring consistent experience delivery quality is very challenging for marketers.

Products are produced or manufactured, then sold and consumed; experiences are sold first, then produced and consumed simultaneously. A theme park can provide an experience only after the ticket has been purchased; the production satisfaction comes from audience interaction with the production and consumption experience. Danish developers of LegoLand theme park began with a product—children's building blocks—and morphed that product into an experience where participants travel around the park to view cities and environments made entirely of Legos.

Workstations provide kids with an opportunity to construct Lego creations of their own or with friends and parents. And of course, everyone is encouraged to purchase Legos to take home.

Experience providers and audience members interact with one another as entertainment is literally consumed, and a better quality entertainment experience is the result. The real-time nature of entertainment means that marketers can customize offerings for individual audience segments by changing venues and content to fit audience needs.

The major distinctions between products, services and experiences are summarized in Exhibit 3.3. Unlike products or experiences, **services** are intangible activities customized to the individual request of known clients. Services accomplish specific tasks, and products supply the means. Most advanced countries have shifted to a service economy where consumers prefer to purchase services rather than commodities. However, whenever a company uses services as the stage and products as props to engage a consumer, it sells experiences.

Some distinctions between products, services, and entertainment are less obvious than others. What's the distinction between intangible and memorable, for instance? Intangible means that service is bestowed, not built, and can be delivered well or poorly. Memorable means that an experience stands out among others for its unique qualities. Services are customized to the needs

EXHIBIT 3.3 Economic Distinctions Between Products, Services and Experiences

OFFERING	PRODUCTS	SERVICES	EXPERIENCES
Economic function	Make	Deliver	Stage
Nature of offering	Tangible	Intangible	Memorable
Key attribute	Standardized	Customized	Personal
Method of supply	Inventoried after production	Delivered on demand	Revealed over a duration
Seller	Manufacturer	Provider	Stager
Buyer	User	Client	Guest
Factors of demand	Features	Benefits	Sensations

Source: Pine & Gilmore, *The Experience Economy*, 1999, p. 6

of a consumer group, while experiences are ours alone. While subtle, these service distinctions are what render experiences as the most pleasurable form of leisure-time entertainment for participants—the better the service, the more enjoyable the experience.

Entertainment experiences cannot be saved, stored, resold or returned. If you miss the play, it moves on to another location or performance venue. Marketers cannot inventory *perishable* experiences—events that exist in real time. They can only use past research to predict box office receipts. Thus, forecasting and planning for capacity venue utilization are challenging decision areas for entertainment marketers.

The GAPS model of service quality[iii]

In many instances, services contribute to experience satisfaction. Tourist services such as resorts, spas, and certain other venues package experiences around products and services that, while perishable, have a sustainable foundation. Success is measured in terms of audience satisfaction. One key model developed to help experience providers assess their satisfaction strategy is based upon closing the gaps that exist between *audience expectations* and *audience perceptions*. **Expectations** are standards or reference points the audience member brings to the experience, and **perceptions** are subjective assessments of the actual experience. Sources of expectations come from marketing factors such as pricing, advertising, and promotion, and from personal experience such as needs, competitive offerings, and word-of-mouth communication.

The GAPS model of service quality suggests that four *gaps* that negatively affect service may occur within a providing organization. The four provider gaps are based on the organization's lack of effectiveness with these factors: 1) not knowing what customers expect, 2) not selecting the right experience designs and standards, 3) not delivering experience designs and standards, and 4) not matching performance to promises. A GAPS audit is used to evaluate the difference between expectations and perceptions.

Provider gaps occur most often in hotels that are now considered places to experience entertainment and live performance. Las Vegas hotels, themed and infused with museum exhibits, live shows, gambling, and shopping, must measure their own performance to distinguish themselves from the plethora of competition.

Measuring service quality at the venetian hotel

In order to dramatize how the GAPS model is applied to a resort experience, we'll look at one client's particular experience at the Las Vegas Venetian Hotel. Built by Steve Wynn, the Venetian has enjoyed high occupancy and positive publicity in the recent past.

When selecting a hotel for a family reunion with her mother, sister, and daughter, our client had high expectations that were predicated on several sources: a Travel Channel show on Las

Vegas, an article in the Sunday *New York Times* Travel section, the hotel's Web site, and positive word-of-mouth from a friend who said the Venetian was "her favorite place in all of Las Vegas." Complete with gondola rides on its indoor/outdoor canal and canal-side restaurants, the Venetian received reviewers' praise for its enjoyable Madame Taussault's Wax Museum and its distinguished Guggenheim art exhibits.

When booking, our client asked for a handicapped suite to accommodate her mother who is in a wheelchair, and beds for three adults. She was assured there would be adequate handicap accessories in the suite, two king-sized beds, and a pull-out sofa. She reserved five days and nights in the hotel at $425 per night.

The group's experience-based perceptions of the services they should have received did not meet their expectations. Here's how the GAPS model can be applied to characterize the hotel's deficiencies as our client and her family experienced them.

Gap 1: Not knowing consumer expectations.

Our client had four expectations of service that the hotel did not meet: 1) Handicapped accommodations to code, 2) safe harbor for a garaged car, 3) careful loading and unloading of luggage, and 4) remuneration for any damage caused by hotel employees. The Venetian did not meet our expectations according to these GAPS factors of analysis:

1. *Inadequate marketing research orientation to understand how to respond to consumer needs.*

   • The Council on Aging has specific guidelines for providing handicapped lodging, and these were obviously ignored. Our client had to order a special toilet seat and make arrangements for a wheelchair that would fit around large beds.

   • Hotel valet parkers took our client's SUV in the hotel parking garage; when retrieved, it had a dented front fender and soiled seats for which no one took responsibility.

   • The bellman allowed packages to fall off the luggage cart and smash to the cement; he laughed as he picked up the parcel and put it into the trunk.

2. *Lack of interaction between management and patrons.*

   • Requests to management for remuneration were either ignored or passed along to another department.

   • Letters to the operations manager of the hotel went unanswered.

3. *Lack of market segmentation.*

   • Because a large percentage of Las Vegas visitors are handicapped or have disabilities, a hotel serving this demographic should focus on the segment's needs.

4. *Inadequate service recovery.*

  + Management did not acknowledge the problems that occurred or the client's dissatisfaction and failed to provide a remedy.

  + After days of endless dialog following the unhappy visit, our client received a letter informing her that damage reports must be filed before leaving the hotel premises.

  + Our client never received compensation for the damage to her car or reimbursement for a glass platter that was dropped and broken by the bellman/valet as he loaded the car for departure.

Gap 2: Not having the right service quality designs and standards

Our client's expectations for high-quality service design may be due the following standard deficiencies as characterized by these factors of the GAPS model:

  1. *Absence of customer-driven standards.*

  + Over half the vacationing population is over 60 years of age, yet the Venetian has not made adequate changes in their hotel design configurations.

  + Slot machines have fixed chairs, prohibiting use by wheelchair-bound patrons.

  2. *Servicescape design doesn't meet customer needs.*

  + Unsecured parking structure.

Gap 3: Not delivering on service designs and standards

Our client's expectations for careful employees and responsive management may be a result of this GAPS factor:

  1. *Deficiencies in human resource policies.*

  + Hiring of incompetent staff.

  + Inadequate training of personnel.

Lack of published service standards.

Gap 4: Not matching performance and promises

Our expectations for quality performance could have resulted from these GAPS factors:

  1. *Absence of strong internal marketing program.*

  + Employees had a different agenda from that of the hotel management.

2. *Lack of adequate education for customers.*

   - No signage or literature stating a policy that damages incurred on the premises must be reported before leaving that premises.

3. *Overpromising.*

   - Advertising and personal selling overstated the hotel's ability to provide necessary equipment for handicapped, safety for garaged vehicles, and care for guest belongings.

The GAPS model brings an understanding of the nature and extent of the gap between customer expectations and perceptions of experience. The model stresses the importance of the providing organization's need to focus on the audience and to use knowledge about the audience to drive business strategy. Another measurement tool developed to assess quality is profiled in Exhibit 3.4.

TIME AND ATTENTION

Once we acknowledge the importance of advertising for entertainment, we need to look to what makes promoting entertainment so different from promoting products. The cultural industries—recording, arts, television, radio—commodify, package, and market experiences as opposed to physical products or services. Their stock and trade is selling short-term access to simulated worlds and altered states of consciousness. Unlike products with tangible qualities, entertainment brands rely heavily on intangible assets, not bricks and mortar, to generate future net cash flows.

Intangible assets of experience-based brands are: franchises, licenses, royalties, goodwill, copyrights, trademarks, and the brand or logo itself. Customer relationships, employee skills, and management strategies drive profits in this business. The value of entertainment enterprises depends first and foremost on the marketing and communication used to create excitement and generate revenue.

Using a network-based approach to organization, the Hollywood culture is the prototype for capitalist systems. In other words, it depends upon forming relationships for raising capital. The entertainment industry, which deals with the risks accompanying perishable and intangible products, must find a quick audience for each unique experience in order to recoup its investment. In this climate, transnational companies stay on top by controlling finance and distribution channels, while pushing off the burdens of ownership and management of physical assets into smaller entities.

Marketing's role is that of impresario of cultural productions. Marketers help entertainment producers create elaborate fantasies from the bits and pieces of contemporary culture and sell them as live experiences. Our job is to find new themes for eliciting human response. The unique

EXHIBIT 3.4 SERVQUAL Instrument for Measuring Quality

KEY ELEMENTS OF ENTERTAINMENT SERVICES MARKETING

Access: approachability and ease of contact with venue or destination.

    Example: *Locating a stadium near a freeway off ramp.*

Communication: two-way conversations; listening to audience feedback.

    Example: *Conducting exit interviews and implementing changes suggested.*

Competence: skills and knowledge to provide advertised experience.

    Example: *Superior visuals and acoustics for staging an opera.*

Courtesy: respect for audiences by experience providers.

    Example: *Helpful ushers, pleasant tour guides.*

Credibility: provide honesty and reputation.

    Example: *Make refunds available for dissatisfaction or missed performance.*

Reliability: ability to perform promised experience on a consistent basis.

    Example: *Last visit provides the same pleasure as the first.*

Responsiveness: immediate adaptation to audience preference changes.

    Example: *Expand the number of box seats to meet demand.*

Security: freedom from danger and risk in a venue or at a destination.

    Example: *Regular maintenance of park rides.*

Tangibles: appearance of physical facilities, personnel, visual materials.

    Example: *Interior ambiance creates a sensual experience.*

Understanding consumers: know their lifestyle considerations.

    Example: *Aging population requires more elevators, wheelchair access.*

Source: SERVQUAL, *Delivering Quality Service,* 1990

aspects of entertainment marketing are overviewed here with the caveat that each plays a major role in how promotions are executed in the entertainment industry. *Immediacy* and *attention* are key business elements in entertainment marketing.

Timing is crucial for branded entertainment promotion

Purchasing products is primarily a need-based activity; when you're out of toothpaste, you go buy more. With entertainment, however, need is not the driving factor. No one needs to hear a concert or see a play. So marketers promoting entertainment must create desire in order to stimulate purchase activity.

And because entertainment is available 24/7, marketers must know when and to whom a promotional message will be directed. Many entertainment experiences are time-sensitive, such as a concert that only plays for one night, or a play for several weeks. Therefore, planting the seed and creating desire are time-sensitive as well. Once the concert or play has gone, no amount of awareness or desire can impact past sales.

Immediacy is key

For movies, the opening weekend makes or breaks the film, so promotional messages must begin as teasers even before the film is complete. Trailers, licensed products, and product tie-ins must be conceived and implemented well in advance of release. True, the film has an afterlife on DVD and rental, but the brand changes from hype to holdover.

Audiences are used to having a plethora of entertainment options whenever they want them. When they decide to act on a desire to see a concert, they consult reviews, schedules, and past brand associations. Each of those influences must be positive to close a sale. In order to make a sale, marketers must manage messages and monitor impressions for maximum exposure. Audiences who cannot find what they need to make an entertainment choice will select another option. And once the selection opportunity passes, it's gone.

To entice audiences, try the *Sayre 3T technique*: tickle, transfer, trap. *Tickle* audiences with excitement or suspense well in advance of the event. *Transfer* that tickle into the desire to attend with product tie-ins, celebrity endorsements, and clever promotions. Then *trap* the audience by offering an easy and immediate way for them to purchase tickets. With several successful completions, your branded experience has a good chance of becoming a hit.

The attention principle

With numerous technological options available today, information is no longer a scarce resource—attention is. In the workplace, computer screens juggle messages, text documents, PowerPoint presentations, spreadsheets, and Web browsers all at once, forcing people to multi-task and become masters of constant interruption. This condition of *continuous partial attention*[iv] allows workers to connect with each other and the world. Like workers, consumers are subject to thought interruptions, and messages that will get attention are selectively chosen.

Before marketing can be effective, it must grab a consumer's attention. Attention is a valuable and scarce commodity—an attention economy is based upon getting the "ear" of an audience first, before a message can be transmitted. Whether you are promoting a play or a casino, you must gain the interest of your audience so they will pay attention to your marketing message. Messages directed at entertainment promotion must either educate or motivate, and they must convince consumers that your activity or venue is worth their attention. This is not easy in a world where every other brand promoter is trying equally as hard to capture your consumer's attention with a competitive message.

Once we get consumers' attention, marketers must create awareness about an event, celebrity, destination or venue. Without knowledge about the when and where of entertainment activities, audiences cannot attend. A primary function of entertainment marketing is getting news of the event into the consumer's *evoked set* of experiential brands. An **evoked set** is all the experiential brands and activities known to an individual audience member that are used when making purchase decisions. Unless information reaches the target segment, audience choice is severely limited. Reaching audiences effectively requires riding the *trend wave*. What interested audiences yesterday may not interest them today.

Holding audience's attention is another marketing challenge. While audiences will pay for entertainment, and even pay well, entertainment providers who produce the plays, build the venues, and play the music will often find it difficult to make a profit from the sales of that content alone. Similarly, concert venues and theaters often do not make a profit from ticket sales alone. Instead, they may make their money through concession sales—the food, beverages, and souvenirs you buy while you are there. Thus, while corporations may not be able to buy audience attention directly, they do so indirectly, by covering the costs of the entertainment "bait" that will capture consumer attention for them.

A CLOSER LOOK AT ETHICS

Alternative Reality Branding

To introduce Audi's 2006 A3 model, the McKinney & Silver advertising agency used a variety of untried methods to suck the public into its campaign based on a fictional drama. It began with a staged car theft at a New York City dealership and resumed with handbills seeking information about the theft that were posted at the International Auto Show. Augmenting the stunt were ads placed in major magazines, blogs and streaming videos featuring fictional people purporting to capture moments of the theft.

Actors from this cyberspace play showed up at major music festivals in character to stage fights, thefts or escapes in Los Angeles at the E3 Expo show for the interactive media industry. Because of the campaigns risky elements, Audi employed a full-time lawyer as part of the ad team. The unorthodox campaign combined aspects of real events, fiction, online video, blogs, journalism, and even some conventional print and TV ads. A unique form of branded entertainment, the campaign skated across multiple media platforms and live events to attract young consumers who had all but turned their backs on 30-second spots and static Internet banners or print ads.

Like alternative reality gaming, the campaign blended factual events with the imaginings of game creators. The actor hired to play the role of a computer hacker and partner in a company that recovers lost and stolen art, sees that a notorious art thief has stolen an A3 from a Manhattan dealership, and the stolen car contains his computer files. He tracked the car to a New Jersey chop shop, and stole the car back from the thieves. In the meantime, the dealership turned into a 'real life' crime scene complete with police tape, a smashed glass door, and security officers standing guard.

Fake ads that looked like those for real companies specializing in art recovery were placed in wired, *Esquire, Robb Report* and *USA Today*. Actors advanced the plot and the story was followed by fans who tapped into emails, security films viewable on the net, and blogs that the characters used to communicate within the story. Over 125,000 followers on various Web sites created by Audi. Fans launched Web sites, such as Smirkbox.com and Argn.com, that enabled devotees to follow the action.

The online play eventually made it to Coachella, the Indio California music festival where the actors, who showed up in character, were barraged by gamers who forced the online video producer to change the script to incorporate some of the fans into the story. When Audi's A3 ads began to run on TV, they were directly tied into the game, asking viewers to report any information of the stolen car's location to report it on Audiusa.com/a3 Web site; print ads were tagged with the same plea.

The target—men 25 to 34, college-educated earning over $125,000 a year—thought the "Heist" campaign was cool, proving that buzz marketing, designed to create word of mouth, can surpass traditional media campaigns by maintaining consumer brand interest.

What do you think?

1. Some consumers thought this was a "bad marketing idea" because it made light of an illegal robbery. Is Audi treading on ethical 'thin ice' here?

2. What dangers can develop from creating fictional action within a real setting?

Source: David Kelly, *Business Week* May 16, 2005

Weaving products and services into experience is one form of convergence. However, when we think about marketing experience, another form of convergence occurs: the marriage of advertising and entertainment. This union is not likely to be dissolved in the near future. In fact, the symbiotic relationship between product and entertainment promotion has economic cement bonding the entities for all time. Once acknowledged, convergence must be approached strategically and viewed as a powerful marketing tool.

CONVERGENCE MARKETING STRATEGIES

Chapter 2 introduced the notion of convergence between different business genres that provides the backdrop for entertainment marketing while this chapter expands the discussion with convergence strategies that are essential for entertainment marketing. One of the dangers of convergence is the development of experiential content first with a specific advertiser in mind, then seeking an audience as an afterthought. Success resides in creative quality that serves both the advertiser and the audience. In order to capitalize on convergence, marketers must develop appropriate strategies that can lead to providing audiences with quality content. Collaboration with advertising agencies is the first step for entertainment producers and distributors.

Advertising's role

The role of advertising for entertainment cannot be underestimated since it's not only essential, it's crucial for success. Entertainment companies marry themselves to advertisers because each company is owned by the same conglomerate. Advertising and entertainment convergence takes place in a variety of configurations, including theater advertising and product placement. We bring this point up again to expand on the specific ways marketers use entertainment to promote brands, and how brands in turn rely on entertainment to sell themselves. Media and entertainment's use to promote products is discussed first, then we focus on the reverse scenario: how products are used to promote entertainment.

Media, entertainment and stars are paired to promote branded products in these ways:

1. 'Advergames' that combine games and marketing content served up on the Internet. (Mitsubishi's driving game)

2. 'Advertainment' pairing stars with branded products. (Rolling Stone featured on a calendar with GM's Chevy; Peter Max's art on designer handbags)

3. Integration of product messages into scripted sitcoms & soaps and unscripted talk and reality show television programming. ("So I grabbed a bottle of Bud Lite and climbed into my Beemer")

4. Product placement in film and TV shows, video games and novels. (Hummer driven by *CSI Miami* star)

5. Product advertising on TV, DVDs, and the Internet, and in theaters and magazines. (Aflack's talking duck, animated pop-up ads, Coke spots in "First Look" movie theater ads)

6. Service advertising in printed inserts. (AIG Insurance company put a small book of poems into *New Yorker Magazine*)

7. Blogs created to promote products. (Volvo blogs hype the safety of their cars)

8. Music tie-ins. (Sinatra and Elvis music used to promote Las Vegas hotels)

One example of the fusion between advertising and entertainment was produced by New York City-based Screenvision in the form of a "pre-show" presented on over 1,000 digital screens via satellite at Loews, Pacific, and Crown theaters. An October, 2005 pre-show program, which featured a branded entertainment deal with sponsor Samsung, promoted a "Scream Your Way To Hollywood" sweepstakes that sent the winner of a contest for the best recorded scream and a guest to a Hollywood movie premiere. The game was part of an in-cinema advertising campaign. These campaigns are part of a number of tactics that have become increasingly attractive to marketers over the last few years, especially for the 18–34 demographic. According to the Cinema Advertising Council, in 2008, U.S. box office was $9.79 billion, an increase of 1.7% in total domestic box office figures over 2007. The studios helped to drive attendance by releasing a whopping 610 new films, up 1.8% over 2007.

Leo Burnett USA has integrated rock stars and artists into its advertising agency. Known as the birthplace of Tony the Tiger, Burnett began an "artists in residence" program in 2005 to bring guest musicians, songwriters, and producers into the Chicago agency's headquarters to meet with staffers on a quarterly basis. The hope is that ground-level collaboration can help ad agencies cut through some of the red tape and financial obstacles surrounding use of pop music for weaving songs into advertising messages. (Led Zeppelin's "Rock and Roll" was used to sell Cadillac, and Apple's iPod Shuffle advertised to the beat of Caesars' "Jerk it Out.") Based on the fact that songs can sell ads and ads can sell songs, the agency-artist alliance is further evidence of the inevitable convergence of advertising and entertainment.[v]

The Dora the Explorer brand has extended, licensed, merchandized, and partnered with a plethora of other brands and franchises. In 2010, however, the Dora brand is getting a rock 'n' roll makeover in a bizarre co-branding scheme. Former Guns-n-Roses guitar player Slash has agreed to team up with the cartoon brand's parent company, the Nickelodeon Network, to design a limited-edition Dora the Explorer backpack. The rock star and his iconic black top hat will be part of the design for a bag featuring Dora the Explorer that will be auctioned this year to raise money for the Children's Defense Fund.

Products are used to promote mediated and live entertainment in these ways

+ Licensed merchandise (Warner Brothers' characters and New York Yankee's clothing)

+ Advertiser funded programs (GE sponsors public broadcasting shows)

Brands and Songs

So many composers incorporate brands into their songs that an entire Web site named amiright.com has been dedicated to making fun of music and branding's love affair with one another.

A few of the postings include:

- Kenny Loggins' *Alive 'n Kickin's* lyrics refer to the cover of the *Rolling Stone* magazine.

- Weird Al Yankovic's *Ringtone* lyrics talked about his wife smashing his iPhone with a brick.

- Sheryl Crow's *All I Wanna Do* lyrics mention Bud bottles twirling on the floor.

Cadillac is probably the best example of how a traditional brand can keep aware of youth culture without trying to exploit it. Their recent success has been partly due to a healthy respect for hip-hop culture, which they understand without seeking to exploit.

Image 3.1

© *Laurent Renault, 2010. Used under license from Shutterstock, Inc.*

The lyrics that reflect those sentiments include:

- Young Buck's *Shorty Wanna Ride* that says Cadillac trucks can take you places you've never been.

- Ludacris' *Get Back* says it's the knick-knack-patty-whack who are still riding Cadillacs.

Pink Cadillac by Bruce Springsteen is a famous tune that equates car brands with love. He says his love is bigger than a Honda and a Subaru and is best demonstrated with a party in the back seat of a pink Cadillac.

Source: AmericanBrandstand.com, 2005

- Bottle cap and can tops with premiums (Dr. Pepper tops redeemed for prizes)

- Supermarket discount coupons (half off of LegoLand admission fee)

Many of the online games that were once embedded in advertisements now have Web sites of their own. Research shows that computer users spend an average of 3.5 minutes playing each game and e-mail game recommendations to a total of 1.8 million friends a year. Game Websites include elements of mainstream advertising campaigns plus interactive capabilities that include game show hosts and player messaging. Capitalizing on the growing interest among computer users in so-called casual gaming, **advergaming** encourages consumers to engage in a branded experience—to spend time voluntarily with an ad.

Because advergames break through the clutter into all demographics and create a memorable brand experience, marketers find bit returns from game profits. More than half the U.S. population plays online games and the entire gaming market is expected to be worth $68 billion by 2012. Consumers have moved beyond traditional media and want to engage with their brands.

FOCUS ON ADVERGAMING

Marketing entertainment with play

Get The Glass: Got Milk

Helping the **Adachi family** steal milk from "**Milkatraz Island**" is the task in this advergame created by Goodby, Silverstein & Partners and North Kingdom. This Flash 3D advergame has a dark 3D model appearance with wonderful animations, but the game is deceptively challenging. It's your roll of the dice...

Stride Gum Game Trio

Here are three "**point and click**" games designed to let players improve their gum extraction skills for June 20, the longest day of the year. Using flash technology, StrideGum.com features a Chew Challenge, a Gum Fly, and Moving Chewers. Let the dentists beware!

The Day The Office Melted

Set in a comic book style world, TAMBA's new game players use a mouse to help Mr. Heatbuster stop arch enemy Ms. Dee Hydration from melting his office. My clicking on a heated object, a pulsing target will appear; another click will allow players to cool office items and prevent meltdown. The object is to foil Ms. Dee Hydration's dastardly plot, and survive the day the office melted? Try it at: http://www.thedaytheofficemelted.co.uk/

Volkswagen Snake

Achtung! launched its new game on a Nokia phone. The main idea is to discover VW prices and collect bonuses that lower the price. Play the game at http://www.volkswagensnake.nl

Source: www.advergamez.com

Advergames turn play into profit for entertainment marketers such as History Channel's *Warriors* and National Geographic Channel's *Hooked*.

Orbitz travel company offers Sink the Putt and Swing for the Fences on its site (orbitzgames.com), and is integrating travel-related games like Run for Your Flight and Pick Your Path with action-oriented and puzzle games. Like other companies, Orbitz wants to convince people that their brand is the way to win at the travel game. One risk in advergaming is that sponsors may become better known for games than for their products or services.

Not only do advertising and entertainment have a symbiotic relationship, their convergence is accompanied by a fusion of TV and the Internet, and advertisers hope the Web will reinvigorate the endangered commercials. With the fusion, viewers don't skip ads because they're digitally integrated into the shows themselves. Internet Protocol TV (IPTV) is transforming advertising as we know it, or once knew it.[vi]

This technology transforms video content into digital files and makes TV a two-way experience where viewers chat on their screens or use their phones to program the DVRs remotely. In addition to using video game product placements and text messages on wireless phones, advertisers are looking to the Internet to provide the same targeting and measurement capabilities from IPTV that they get from the Web. Because IPTV is a point-to-point service, not a broadcast, every TV can potentially receive a different advertisement based on the shows the viewer has watched and other demographic information. And if you want to travel to a place featured on your TV, just click to make reservations.

On-demand entertainment gives providers an opportunity to reduce costs for viewers, but they must have a high tolerance for watching ads. For instance, the *New York Times* is free online, but readers must also endure a plethora of advertising on the site. If you can tolerate the ads, you get free stuff, which could actually make TV free again. *Forbes Magazine*'s Sam Whitmore predicted that by 2010, advertising conglomerates WPP, Omnicom, and IPG would produce 80% of what America watches.[vii] Chapters 9 and 12 present more extensive examples of promotional convergence tools as they are used in an entertainment integrated marketing campaign.

CHANGING LANDSCAPE OF THE AUDIENCE

Similar to marketing products and services, experiential marketing has to contend with ongoing changes in the way consumers are categorized, reached, and measured. Some especially crucial changes involve audience products, audience fragmentation, and new audience group configurations. These are discussed briefly here.

Audience as product[viii]

Consumers, media organizations, and audience measurement firms together produce the **audience product** that is central to the audience marketplace. The process of producing and selling the audience product begins with audience consumption of media products, as shown in Exhibit 3.5.

Consumer interaction with media firms takes place as media consumption choice; consumers' interaction with audience measurement firms takes place as their consumption habits are monitored. Measurement is made with a small sample of consumers, and their behaviors are generalized to the population as a whole. Both media and measurement firms are essential to the process. Without media firms, no audience exists to be measured and without measurement firms, no audience data exists to sell to advertisers.

Because they purchase audiences before they are actually produced, advertising's demand for audiences has a tremendous influence on the structure and behavior of media organizations *by shaping the content media provide to consumers*. Advertisers' demand for certain types of audiences dictates that media produce product that caters to the types valued most highly by advertisers. Audience measurement firms are also influenced by advertisers' demand for specific types of data about media audiences—techniques are altered to best serve the clients who purchase the data. A reciprocal influence relationship bonds media organizations with measurement firms. Media organizations are major clients of measurement firms. When the industry demands better approaches to measuring media, they too influence the nature of measurement. Conversely, when measurement firms introduce a new method, such as People Meters, the resulting changes in how audiences are measured produce a different profile of the television audience and change the competitive dynamics of participating media organizations in the marketplace.

Audience transactions begin with **predicted audiences**, which are particularly difficult to characterize because they are constantly changing. A marketer predicts the audience segment most likely to view or attend. The shelf life of a predicted audience is exceptionally short, lasting for the

EXHIBIT 3.5 The Audience Marketplace

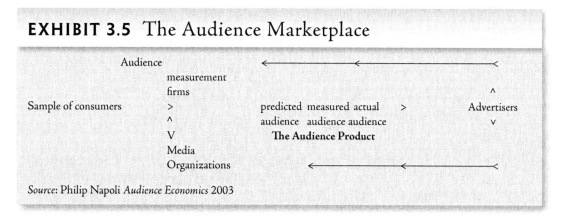

Source: Philip Napoli *Audience Economics* 2003

period in which a media product is consumed. The marketing challenge inherent in the audience product is that, while media audiences must be sold before the product has been distributed and consumed, the size and composition of a media product's audience cannot be determined until after the product has been consumed, when buying or selling that audience is no longer possible. Buyers and sellers in the audience marketplace devote much time and effort to forecasting audiences and maximizing the degree to which these forecasts correspond to the subsequent measurement data.

Predicted audience data represent **measured audiences**, the starting point for audience transactions among buyers and sellers. The data that defines a measured audience are used to determine the estimated size and composition of the audience reached to determine how much an advertiser spent to reach a particular size and type of audience. The mix of content and basis of dollar allocation of advertising result from measured audience data. Measured audiences are the central economic currency in the audience marketplace.

Because measurements are uncertain, the **actual audience** represents the invisible deal in the marketplace—the unknowable. Its ambiguity renders the actual audience a highly contestable component of the audience product. In spite of that fact, buyers and sellers generally treat measured audiences as accurate representations of actual audiences. The nature of an audience product, however, is increasingly difficult to commodify because of its global fragmentation.

Audience fragmentation

No longer can advertising reach a mass of people at a single time. Audiences have split off into thousands of separate zones, requiring a whole new approach to message delivery. The proliferation of media choices has fragmented audiences, making it harder and harder to reach them through traditional means. The fragmentation of the old mass markets into mass-market *groups* both creates a budgetary advantage and allows for a more target-specific marketing plan. And the global marketplace offers more opportunities to market to more audiences in different ways.

With a merging of popular and high culture entertainment genres, audiences no longer fit into traditional demographic classifications. Attend a Grateful Dead concert and witness an audience made up of many generations of fans, including dedicated "Deadheads" with their children. We see kids attending operas and grandparents loving the circus. Not only do audiences attend a wide range of entertainment experiences, they are constantly changing their performance priorities.

The largest disposable incomes belong to Boomers, a generation that, in entering their sixties, has free time and patronizes a very diverse set of entertainment venues and experiences. As marketers, our only option to approaching such a fragmented group of potential audiences is to segment. Segments, or niches, allow us to focus a specific message to a small group of folks. Because people attend entertainment for different reasons, marketers must be able to present the benefits of a single experience to the segment that fits the benefit.

A cross section of audience members from a recent orchestral performance at the new Disney Center in Los Angeles illustrates the diverse range of motivations for attending: a woman in her fifties liked the musical program; a man in his sixties favored the conductor; a thirty-something woman came to experience the architectural venue; twenty-something parents brought their kids as a way to introduce music into their lives; and a teenage girl enjoyed the opportunity to dress up for a special occasion.

Audiences no longer act as a single entity, they form according to individual preferences. An understanding of each audience segment's motives provides marketers with valuable insight about what the performance means to people and so how to appeal to them. The choices are varied: appeal to parents with messages directed toward integrating music into the family experience and the child's cultural development; appeal to adults with a combination of venue-artist-program messages; appeal to music lovers by providing attendance incentives. It's our job to discover individual preferences and craft messages that appeal directly to a particular segment or niche.

Think of the process as promoting a 24-slice pizza, each slice with a different topping. Sure, it's a pizza, but one piece doesn't please all. In order to sell every slice, we must market that pizza 24 different ways. We can begin by grouping consumers according to eaters and non-eaters, extolling the category benefits of convenience and family adaptability to non-eaters. Next, focus on product benefits such as fat content and crust thickness for eaters, then direct attention toward grouping consumers by preferred features such as meat, vegetable options, cheese type and combinations. Finally, we can target party packagers for the economy of slice-based distribution. The promotional combinations are endless—hooray for mass specialization.

CULTURAL DIMENSIONS AND GLOBAL PARADIGMS

Although entertainment is considered to be universal, cultural considerations play a major role in experiential content that will cross ethnic and language borders. Differences also require that marketing media, messages, and promotional tools are appropriate for use in the targeted country or audience group. Geert Hofstede[ix] identified five dimensions that may be used for looking at how well or how poorly content and marketing messages will translate to other cultures: long-term orientation, power distance, individualism/collectivism, masculine/feminine and uncertainty avoidance. Here is a brief overview of those dimensions and their application to marketing entertainment.

Long-term orientation

This dimension focuses on the degree the society embraces long-term devotion to traditional, forward-thinking values. A low orientation indicates the country does not reinforce the concept of tradition (parts of the US, for instance); a high orientation indicates the country prescribes to the values of long-term commitments and respect for tradition (e.g., Japan).

3.2 Marketing to Muslim couples requires cultural sensitivity.

Entertainment example: A film about Samurai, a tradition that may be unclear to many Western audiences, should be marketed by incorporating messages about the significance of honor and ritual.

Power distance

The degree of equality between people in the country's society is this dimension's focus. A low distance means the society de-emphasizes the difference between citizen's power and wealth (e.g., China); a high distance means that inequalities of power and wealth have been allowed to grow within the society (e.g., India).

Entertainment example: Branded marketing and product tie-ins will be much more effective in countries where wealth and status are represented by exclusive brands (Western nations and Japan) and avoided where social status is not measured by possessions (Africa and the Middle East).

Individualism/Collectivism

This dimension illuminates the degree to which a particular society reinforces individual or collective achievement and interpersonal relationships. A high rank suggests that individuality and individual rights are paramount within the society (e.g., U.S.); a high rank typifies societies of more collective nature with close ties between individuals (e.g., Japan).

Entertainment example: Western films are easily marketed to German audiences who appreciate the notion of individualism, but more difficult to market in parts of Asia where family and groups are revered.

Masculinity/Femininity

This dimension indicates how much a society reinforces the traditional masculine role model of achievement, control and power. A high level of masculinity indicates the country residents experiences significant gender differences (e.g., Mexico, Iran); high femininity in a country's population reflects dominant values of caring for others and quality of life; feminist cultures treat both sexes equally. (e.g., Sweden, Russia).

Entertainment example: Macho marketing will succeed in places where men make entertainment decisions (Latino-based cultures), but will be rebuked by countries where females have an equal or primary role in selecting entertainment (U.S. and European cultures).

Uncertainty avoidance

This dimension focuses a society's level of tolerance for uncertainty and ambiguity in unstructured situations. A low rank means the country's population has less concern about ambiguity and uncertainty and has more tolerance for a variety of opinions (e.g., France); a high rank means the country has a low tolerance for uncertainty and ambiguity in their everyday encounters (e.g., Germany).

Entertainment example: Marketing entertainment to Germans requires stating explicit times, dates, and profiles, where French audiences are more captivated by ambiguous visual communications.

In short, entertainment marketers must familiarize themselves with cultural nuances when promoting media and live performances on a global level. Advertising agencies always maintain local agencies with native speakers to service clients in specific countries in the most informed manner possible. Because we are no longer nationally focused, marketing messages and promotions must reflect a thorough understanding of cultural differences if they are to achieve profitable box office receipts.

Finally

Experiential marketers must develop expertise in bundling—promoting winning combinations of products and services into memorable experiences. Obstacles to overcome when promoting experiences include tangibility and perishability. Marketers must gain the attention of audiences for immediate buying responses if box office receipts are to be profitable. And marketers must be good shots, target practice is essential for reaching audience segments with a message that incites buying behavior across borders and across cultures.

GOT IT?

+ The experience industry must deal with issues and aspects of tangibility, context, production/consumption and perishability.

+ Immediacy and awareness are key elements in marketing entertainment experiences.

- Services, measured with the GAPS model, are different from experiences in the nature of their functions, offering, attributes, method of supply, and factors of demand.

- Product placement, games, media-integrated messages and blogs are among the most popular convergence strategies for blending brands with entertainment.

- Attention principle says that everyone is vying for your time, and our attention economy is based upon getting the 'ear' of an audience to tell them something.

- Hofstede's five cultural dimensions are valuable for developing marketing communications that cross ethnic and national borders.

NOW TRY THIS

1. Go one line and identify at least two marriages or convergences between advertisers and entertainment. Now check to see if both the product and entertainment genre are owned by the same conglomerate. What can you conclude from your investigation?

2. Using the SERVQUAL instrument, rate a branded hotel you have visited on the key elements of entertainment marketing. What improvements can you suggest?

3. Analyze two experiences you have had as each relates to the Customer Gap; what were your expectations and perceptions of each experience and how did the difference between the two influence your satisfaction with each experience?

4. Using Hofstede's cultural dimensions, profile a country you've never been to and determine how that country's dimensions differs from those in the U.S. What marketing accommodations would be necessary to promote a concert in that country?

QUESTIONS FOR DISCUSSION AND REVIEW

1. Discuss the ways in which marketers incorporate products and services into both mediated and live experiences (TV and travel, for instance).

2. How might you use the GAPS model to improve consumer perceptions of an older theme park like Six Flags that has failed to keep up with the competition's promotional efforts?

3. How would you convert interruptions into opportunities for capturing a consumer's attention?

4. What aspects of a feminine culture would help you to promote a rock concert?

5. How would buying a 30-second spot during the Super Bowl to announce a new Nintendo game be ambushed by audience fragmentation?

OTHER STUFF ABOUT THE NUANCES OF ENTERTAINMENT MARKETING

www.gmnhome.com A global marketing forum.

www.informaworld.com Articles from *Journal of Global Marketing*.

www.businessweek.com Up-to-date information on global marketing and brands.

[i] From *Fierce Invalids Home from Hot Climates*, Bantam Books, p. 194.

[ii] B. Jospeh Pine II and James H. Gilmore (1999), *The Experience Economy: Work is Theatre & Every Business a Stage.* HBS Press, chapter 2.

[iii] From V. A. Zeithaml, A. Parasuraman & L. L. Berry, *Delivering Quality Service: Balancing Custsomer Perceptions and Expectations*, Free Press, 1990.

[iv] A phrase coined by software executive Linda Stone, as reported by the *New York Times*, Oct. 16, 2005 by Clive Thompson.

[v] Ibid p. 61.

[vi] From an article by Stephanie Mehta (2005), "How the Web Will Save the Commercial," *Fortune Magazine*, Aug. 8.

[vii] From S. Whitmore (2005), "The Era of the Mixmaster," *Forbes.com*, August 3.

[viii] A concept developed by Philip Napoli (2003), in *Audience Economics*, Columbia University Press.

[ix] G. H. Hofstede, *Cultures and Organizations: Software of the Mind.* McGraw-Hill, 1991.

Chapter 4

VENUE ECONOMICS AND SERVICESCAPES

> *If it wasn't a business,*
> *they would have called it show-show.*
> Woody Allen

Chapter Objectives

After reading this chapter, you will be able to answer these questions:

+ What distinguishes the various types of entertainment *venues?*

+ When does a venue become a *servicescape?*

+ What are the main *economic considerations* in marketing experience venues?

+ What *financial elements* underlie calculation of a venue's bottom line?

ENTERTAINMENT CONTENT

The expansion of entertainment business follows the growth of leisure time and disposable income. It is consistently one of the largest net export categories in the U.S. economy. Real expansion has resulted from technological development, which in turn has changed the way we think of entertainment products. Performances and experiences are processed in the human brain as feelings and emotions. Media content including movies, music, TV shows, video games, and words now function as composite bits of information that can be produced, processed, and distributed as a series of digits. Entertainment has three distinct types of content: performance, experiential, and media-dependent.

Performance content, is developed around music, dance, and theater (or combinations such as opera) for presentation by bands, quartets and orchestras, or theatrical and production companies. Performances are presented in specific venues in single locations or by touring. Once completed, the specific live rendition cannot be repeated in exactly the same way ever again, as costumes, performers, conductors, and set designs may be altered or changed. Even venue acoustics may render similar performances differently.

Experiential content occurs in or at attractions, resorts, spas, casinos, theme parks, and travel destinations. As with performance content, it cannot be packaged for duplication. Each visit to a branded theme park creates a new adventure; museums change their exhibitions regularly; and destinations capitalize on seasonal elements for their unique urban, rural, or seaside offerings. Many arts organizations are nonprofit, requiring subsidization from government and private foundation grants and patron contributions.

Experiential content, which includes gaming and wagering activity, attractions that charge admission fees (such as exhibits and parks), and destinations are dependent upon tourism boards for promotion and local and global businesses for visitor accommodations.

Media-dependent content is considered **property**, a tangible item that is created, sold to a studio, and produced for distribution. The output is the basis for branded products sold in a variety of formats (DVD, Internet, cable, on-demand purchase, and so on). Although audiences experience media-dependent content in real time (at the time of viewing), tangible duplications of copyrighted property can also be purchased for repeat viewing, gifting, or archiving.

Media-based content involves "deals" for financing, producing, distributing, marketing, and advertising. Each function requires raising and investing money, assessing and insuring production costs and risks, and planning and executing marketing and advertising campaigns. Media content, except for cinemas, is provided in a variety of distribution centers rather than a single venue, and as such is featured in a later chapter.

This chapter focuses on the various types of venues and dimensions used for offering performance and experience-based content, including commercial service venues. It also examines criteria for venue aesthetics, explores price setting and pricing strategies, and gives an overview of distribution strategies. We also give you a heads up on the types of piracy invading the content marketplace.

ENTERTAINMENT VENUES

Much of what is offered to audiences is performed in a specific place or space. Performance and experience places are profiled here for their importance to entertainment marketing.

Performance venues

These are places where stage activities or media are housed and offered to audiences.

Theaters, performing arts centers and cinemas

Before the invasion of movie multiplexes, theaters functioned to house live performances. Plays, musicals, dance, and orchestral concerts still perform in elaborate centers catering to the entire live performance experience. Many venues are specially designed to be used for specific entertainment, such as the Magic Castle in Los Angeles, where magic is performed. Outdoor amphitheaters, such as Tanglewood in Massachusetts, and parks, such as Ravinia in the Chicago area, are warm-weather venues. Communities take pride in their arts centers, and as such they pay careful attention to design and brand image.

Some may think of theater as Broadway—essentially the theater district in New York City. Off-Broadway and other commercial theaters, however, provide entertainment for millions of audiences annually. In addition, non-profit or regional/repertory theaters funded by subscriptions, grants, and contributions also vie for audiences.

Symphony halls are grand in stature and saturated with ritual. Today, some 1,600 orchestras play in the United States, the most famous in Boston, Chicago, Cleveland, Los Angeles, New York, and Philadelphia. Popular music and jazz concerts are often performed in venues usually operated as stadiums or sports arenas.

Only four major opera companies perform in the United States: Metropolitan, San Francisco, Chicago Lyric, and New York City Operas; smaller companies in Los Angeles and Houston are becoming prominent opera providers. Dance companies include New York City Ballet, San Francisco Ballet and the American Ballet Theater, as well as a dozen important modern dance groups.

Out of favor in North America, the circus is still considered a major form of entertainment in Europe and Asia. Venues range from tents to arenas rented for traveling performances by established troupes. A hybrid of performance genres, Cirque du Soleil came out of Canada from regional tent performances and grew into several different extravaganzas performed in Las Vegas venues; tented versions are written for global appearances.

Cinemas—media-dependent experiences—are franchised conglomerates that control film distribution and duration. Only a handful of independent cinemas operate today, and many require fundraising and donation solicitation to keep the venue healthy for audiences who prefer viewing off-Hollywood productions. Chapter 16 features marketing for media-based content.

Experience venues

These are places where audience members become actively engaged with the activity that is offered or provided.

Casinos

Casinos are legalized establishments where commercial gambling operators make their profits by regularly occupying advantage positions against players. Concentrated in pockets around the world, casinos locate in areas with relaxed legal restrictions enacted by governments to derive tax revenues from gambling and control cheating.

Casinos typically offer card games such as poker, baccarat, and blackjack. Many also have slot machines and roulette as well as wagering on sports events. Casino operators are not in the business of providing on-line gambling, although they maintain websites for marketing and reservation systems.

Locations worldwide are fast incorporating gambling into their national economies. In developing countries such as Slovenia, casinos are positioned adjacent to Italian border towns and cater to Italian gamblers by accepting lire and using Italian-language dealers. International destinations such as Macao near Hong Kong, Isla De Margarita off the Venezuelan coast, and Bermuda tempt tourists from around the world to gambling tables. Casinos have the potential to lure travelers and bring tourism to areas devoid of natural wonders, historical monuments, or recreational resorts. Chapter 14 has more on marketing casinos.

Spas, luxury resorts, and cruise ships

The Golden Door Spa, the Montage Resort, and Princess Cruise Lines are examples of venues where people go for vacations. Spas focus on health and well-being, while resorts combine recreation, food, and lodging, and cruise lines pack all forms of entertainment aboard ship. Each venue type has grown exponentially over the past five years, and there is no end in sight. Canyon Ranch, a stand-alone spa in Arizona, has packaged its products for use in hotel-based spas such as the Venetian in Las Vegas. Other resorts are building their own spas to provide guests with treatments and products that complement their brand image and contribute to profit revenues. Chapter 14 expands upon tourist destinations and services.

Cruises are packaging trips for a variety of markets: seniors, couples, gays, families with children, singles, and every other demographic configuration possible. While on board, travelers may gamble, dine, swim, and engage in a variety of physical and intellectual pursuits. Conventions and business meetings are held on board ships chartered specially for large corporations and trade organizations.

Spa, resort, and cruise experiences all require branding, packaging and promoting, making venue marketing a necessary element for selling vacation concepts.

Museums

From places that used to be considered storage rooms for the stuffy and dead, museums are reinventing themselves into competitive entertainment venues. Within the past ten years, rapid expansion of the Guggenheim Museum franchises in Venice, Las Vegas, Berlin, Bilbao, Paris, Berlin, and Geelong (Australia), has spirited other museums into the content development business. An alliance between the Hermitage Museum in Russia and The Museum of Modern Art in New York created an independent for-profit e-business to curate international exhibitions drawn from both collections.

The integration of ancient artifacts and modern aesthetics renders museums attractive to post-modern audiences who combine past with present. Museums generate revenue by hosting parties, charity events, and fashion shows among their antiquities. Recognizing the necessity to compete with all other entertainment product offerings, museums are turning to marketers for creative packaging and innovative promotions.

Theme parks

Theme parks are places where families go to be entertained. They are considered safe places to experience fun. As such, park management and marketing teams work together to maintain the trust and patronage of visitors. Employee training, crisis management, and environmental design are key elements for successful park maintenance. Disney has an entire marketing staff to oversee quality control and insure consistency among all park services. Chapter 14 expands upon marketing themed spaces.

Zoos

In San Diego, the Zoological Society sells memberships for its animal habitats: the zoo and wild animal park. Packages for tours, seniors, and kids help lure visitors to experience the zoo's gorillas and the park's wild lions in natural habitats. A recent marketing strategy that gave the zoo national recognition included late-night television appearances of some of the zoo's personnel showing unusual pets.

Arenas and stadiums

Special activity venues are built to house hockey teams (arenas) and football teams (stadiums), but often are sites for performances such as concerts and touring family shows. Often built for a large price tag, these venues must market themselves to lure performances that create gate revenues.

The verdict is still out as to whether we consider events such as rodeos and drag races live performances or sporting events. Either way, they are performed in arena and stadium venues across the country and need to be branded, positioned, and promoted to compete with other competitive forms of entertainment.

VENUE AS SERVICESCAPE

A hybrid of performance and experience venues, marketplaces and consumption sites are built environments called **servicescapes**, a term proposed by consumer researcher John Sherry.[i] Window shoppers and serious buyers wander around these spaces looking for myriad delights. Shopping is no longer a mere transaction, it is a transformation. The themed *purchase performance* transforms audiences into visitors to other centuries and other countries. Producing the enjoyment of a tactile and visual shopping experience is a retailer's mission. Whether housed within a mall offering different experiences or uniquely placed for individual discovery, retail has entered the entertainment age.

Shopping centers and retail superstores

Mall of America, the largest shopping center in the U.S., combines retail with kids' camps, live entertainment, hotels, restaurants, gardens, and rides and games for a complete consumption experience. Smaller centers rely on a consortium of shops to provide an advertising budget, sponsor events, and provide community activities during off hours.

Designed for display and branding more than consumption, *super retailing* has become a specialty of designers such as Armani, who bought an entire block in Hong Kong to offer shops with Armani everything, including fresh flowers. Here, the store is the marketing and the marketing happens in the store. Attraction marketing is discussed later in this chapter and in Chapter 14.

Malls and shopping experiences

Urban arcades of the nineteenth century stimulated both the growing consumer culture and development of a consumer self by providing a fantasy-driven landscape of shopping. These arcades were the early version of our shopping malls and galleries.

Being in the mall is a distinct experience that is shaped significantly by its architectural and aesthetic elements. Malls have become, by default, the dominant public space of advanced capitalism. Various approaches to strategic retailing illustrate the ways brands are staking out their own identity in the marketplace. One approach is creating *flagship* stores, which provide prime city spaces to promote the brand's image. The flagship's antithesis is a series of neighborhood outlets that address local experiential needs. *Stand-alone retail* presence is accomplished in a self-contained space and maintains an independent image. *Identity venues* choose from among formats such as factory outlet, theme store, or various hybrids to communicate their brand strategies.

Flagship stores as retailing business cards

As walk-in 3-D advertising, flagship stores must be co-financed by advertising budgets; as landmarks for the city, they are often featured in travel guides, lifestyle magazines, and TV shows. Flagship store formats are: *sacred*, such as Nike's awe-inspiring museum-like edifice; *lifestyle-oriented*, such as Crate & Barrel where you can find everything for your yuppie home; and a *mega* such as Costco, where you can pick up everything from peanuts to pots and pans. All types of flagship venues are likely to provide visitors with experiential retailing that is both entertaining and image-generating.

The six-story Barbie Shanghai, Barbie's first worldwide flagship store, is an exclusive shopping destination with products and activities designed especially for girls. The flagship store has a fashion runway, full-service day spa, doll design center and more than 1,600 Barbie products, including apparel, jewelry, skin-care, toys, electronic products, cosmetics, games, and other goodies for girls of all ages.

Located in the restored 1901 Denver Tramway building, the REI Denver Flagship is a complete outdoor resource, a historic landmark and an award-winning architectural accomplishment. Interactive features include mountain bike trails, a 45-foot climbing wall.

Concept store

Concept stores are in the business of making merchandising fun. By turning lifestyle gadgets into a recurring theme, concept stores display goods as games that are to be experienced.

Nokia introduced special venues to enable consumers to experience the full potential of its mobile technology. Completely interactive, each store features a high-energy space dedicated to educating customers and pairing them with the perfect mobile device. Nokia boasts 18 different

© Daniel Nyvlt, 2010. Used under license from Shutterstock, Inc.

4.1 REI provides climbing experiences for patrons at larger retail outlets.

experiential stores around the globe. Apple Stores operating on a similar assumption—if consumers can interact with the product in an entertaining fashion, purchases are imminent—Apple Stores have made shopping for electronics more than simply shopping.

Using an *affect phenomenon* where shoppers know exactly what they are looking at, concept retailers use shop-in-shop areas as walk-on stages that turn shopping areas into entertainment districts. Flexible display units and stylized carrier bags are a few elements that render an aesthetic avant-garde to concept shops.

Destination malls

In the spirit of the Mall of America in Minnesota, regional shopping centers are increasing their impact as tourist destinations. South Coast Plaza in Orange County California, for instance recently became trademarked as the "ultimate shopping resort." The designation gives Plaza a marketing edge to draw both retailers and consumers to its location. Among the largest revenue generating malls in the U.S., South Coast Plaza is surrounded by a performing arts center, parks, hotels, and commercial and residential complexes. A desired destination for Asian shoppers, the mall caters to chartered groups by providing transportation from four adjacent airports, including Los Angeles International Airport.

FOCUS ON SERVICESCAPES

Retailers Partner with Movies and Music

Movie with your Burger: Coupling itself with an impending blockbuster, McDonalds offered an interactive *Avatar*-based game that let players explore the movie's computer-generated planet Pandora and offered a set of on-package cards that could put consumers in virtual space.

Before *Avatar* was released, diners who bought Big Macs received one of 8 different *Avatar* 'Thrill' Cards. Using a Web cam, viewers see a McD Vision augmented reality software that interacts with the lush jungle landscapes generated for the movie. PandoraQuest. The cards let global players find hidden objects in three Pandoran landscapes; the objective – to win a membership in the "RDA Research Team" featured in the film. American players could unlock bonus features as scenes from the movie. German and UK players on line had the chance to morph photos of themselves into the blue-skinned creatures. Australians received cup and tray lines with hidden codes that acted as entry into the *Avatar* sweepstakes.

Prior to the movie's debut, McDonald's ran a Twitter-based buzz campaign where entrants decoded word scrambles and entered solutions online. The prize? A Big Mac lunch with the producer, Landau (even though he is said to prefer the Quarter Pounder).

Source: promomagazine.com/contests/news/mcdonalds-avatar-campaign-1215/?imw=Y

Music with your Coffee: Starbucks formed a partnership with the William Morris Agency to identify music, film, and book projects that it could promote and distribute from its retail outlets. The effort was a bid to enhance the overall entertainment experience for its millions of dedicated coffee drinkers.

As drivers for consumer interest in music, Starbucks touted its national footprint of stores, strong passion from its huge customer base, and its track record with word-of-mouth marketing, to partner with music labels and studios. But in July of 2008, Starbucks music came to a screeching halt when the company announced the termination of their Hear Music label along with six hundred retail locations. Carly Simon sued Starbucks after the demise of the record label, on which she appeared, for breach of contract; the suit is pending as of this writing.

In 2009, Starbucks coffee shops began offering songs for free at the iTunes Store each week, no strings attached. iTunes' Facebook began offering free music from Starbucks "Pick of the Week" Sampler that included Moby, Metric, Ben Sollee, and Sting.

Image 4.2 Starbucks as music venue.

© Dziekan/Retna Ltd./Corbis

SPACE AND PLACE: VENUE DESIGN AND MANAGEMENT

Research on the effects of environment and atmosphere concludes that careful and creative management of service venues contributes to achieving marketing goals. By observing audiences as they move about entertainment venues, researchers can determine the benefits and delights of consumption at every level.

Location-based entertainment

In order to leverage brand equity, create product outlets, and increase brand awareness, investors from retail, restaurant, real-estate development, and entertainment industries are combining entertainment experience with location-based products. For instance, Sega partnered with MCA Universal and SKG DreamWorks to create GameWorks, a concept that combines food and entertainment with a high-end range of games and simulation, packaged in a venue with a highly-themed environment designed to look like the inside of an old factory. Often anchored by cineplexes, urban entertainment centers like Irvine Spectrum Center, a huge (at 1.1 million square feet) retail and

4.3 Experience Music Project in Seattle, a Frank Gehry design.

© oksana perkins, 2010. Used under license from Shutterstock, Inc.

entertainment complex in California, optimize the chances for repeat visits by offering clustered experiential venues in a single location. **Co-opetition** is a term coined for these joint ventures, where companies working together can optimize opportunities in local and global locations.

Experience venue guidelines

According to the author of *Brand Lands*, experiences are designed using strict guidelines. They must: 1) be high exposure landmarks, 2) provide places for visitors to explore and move about freely, 3) develop experiences along a specific conceptual line, and 4) contain a core attraction.[ii] Those guidelines are explained here.

+ *Landmarks* are physical symbols that help guide audiences to a particular location. They may be on storefronts (yacht model above nautical gear store), in building interiors (REI climbing wall), or they may be decorative items or replicas (Outback Steak House Australian artifacts).

+ *Malls* are places that encourage strolling so visitors may discover merchandise and items of interest on their own time. To stimulate strolling, retailers create and emphasize hubs, such as lavish bouquets in hotel lobbies or dramatic staircases. Every venue should have a clean, dramatic entrance.

+ *Conceptual (or concept) lines* provide direction and suspense. Creative design of venue atmosphere puts audiences almost inside a brand's image. Image contrast has become a successful concept, such as the now-familiar café in the midst of your local bookstore. Authentic theming tells a story that can be used to transport visitors into an imaginary world. Designed theming casts one element in a starring role, such as a sushi bar aquarium.

+ *Core attractions* are a means of walk-in advertising that encourages browsing in retail spaces A wine tower in a bar, for example, produces a "wow" effect. Neon signage creates a "show" effect that renders Times Square unique.

Design and aesthetics

We are visual, tactile creatures, and the look and feel of things tap deep human instincts. **Aesthetics** is your sense of beauty as we experience it through your senses. It's behind why you buy one thing and not another, and why you choose to patronize one venue over another. Entertainment relies on the immediate perceptual and emotional effects of aesthetics to entice and maintain audiences. According to industrial designer Hartmut Esslinger, *form follows emotion*.[iii] Everywhere is now designed, and whoever determines look and feel controls a great deal of economic value. Also, because our entire physical landscape has improved, people generally have become more critical as an audience.

The aesthetic approach was born when manufacturers began to realize the importance of extending advertising into products and experiences themselves. Because functional ideas are so quickly copied, global competition has mandated prioritizing aesthetic over functional design. When used with consumers in mind, aesthetic design can help to differentiate otherwise similar venues and cut through clutter to communicate quality differences. One of the most important dimensions of entertainment satisfaction is reliability; the failure to deliver a promised experience dependably is a direct function of failure in service delivery system and design.

Architectural theming

Architectural elements and design contribute to the ultimate shopping, eating, and gambling experiences. In pseudo-authentic backdrops, visitors understand the signs and symbols used to communicate a specific location, era, or ethnicity.

Lifestyle stores provide a new environment where shoppers experience style and ambience. In a retail outlet called Anthropologie, cast-iron columns and other relics of loft architecture form a theme and signal a lifestyle. Anthropologie features Asian items, bric-a-brac, fashion, candlesticks, home fashion items, informal women's clothing, all set against used brick walls and beneath high ceilings with iron beams.

Replica construction, as it might be called, enables retailers, restaurateurs and hoteliers to create fantasy ambiance for their visitors. Rainforest Café delivers exotic drinks to patrons who sit in bamboo chairs among jungle greenery listening to bird calls. Gamblers in Las Vegas may choose from among a variety of global cityscapes for their gaming pleasure. An extensive discussion of the role of theming for experiential marketing is covered in Chapter 15.

Room-in-room principle

Originally conceived for trade shows, room-in-room retail configurations allow different spaces to grow out of the floor of restaurants and shopping areas. Inside, the mini-venues are presented in different true-to-life *taste worlds*. Room-in-room spaces give expression to lifestyle by incorporating warm woods and other luxurious materials into the areas. A modular framework unifies the overall appearance by tying together the open room-in-room architecture with seemingly floating ceiling structures.

Furniture for watching

In order to create the pleasure of watching what goes on around you, furniture designers have put wheels and swivels on seating in experiential environments. Casinos, restaurants, and performance centers are realizing the value of "seated freedom," a design that creates a sense of community among audience members. People watching in malls, airports, and parks may prolong the time they spend in a single location, enabling marketers to deliver promotional messages in specific, high-traffic locations.

Convenience and safety

Even though form should follow fun, form must also adhere to function (Louis Sullivan and Frank Lloyd Wright are early proponents of this notion). Venues must provide accessible parking, clean restrooms, and safe environments for audiences, visitors, and consumers. Attached parking garages bring people to venues even in hostile weather.

FOCUS ON CAREERS

Profile of a Venue Marketer

As a **marketing coordinator** for the Dodge Theater and U.S. Airways Center, Kent Walls is responsible for promoting and managing concerts, shows, and sporting events. Kent reports to the Vice President of Marketing and Advertising for the venue that is home to the Phoenix professional sports teams.

A large part of Kent's time is spent developing cross promotions with downtown businesses in Phoenix. He creates PR campaigns that include writing and distributing press releases to state media for both venues, and he edits the venue's Website. Kent must develop and maintain favorable relationships with local television networks, radio stations, newspapers, artist's management, and promoters.

Although he loves his job, Kent thinks the hours he must keep and intensity levels he must maintain can be tough at times. "Long hours are part of the industry, and you learn to adapt," he says.

Following graduation with a degree in marketing from Arizona State University, Kent interned for the Arizona Diamondbacks in game operations and marketing. After doing some part-time work with CBS Arizona Entertainment Weekly as production coordinator, Kent signed on to his current position. One of his most exciting experiences was acting as a script assistant for ABC Good Morning America's 2006 Oscar coverage, an opportunity he "couldn't resist."

In his words..............

Accomplishment of note

The lack of a professional PR staff provided an opportunity for me to make an impact within the organization. In the last year, I have focused on building relationships with the local media and establishing a solid base for this very important aspect of marketing within the entertainment industry. The more you can offer clients in terms of marketing and PR services, the more likely they are to return to your venue, which results in increased revenue. I have received compliments from several national promoters commenting on how impressed they are with our venue's emphasis on public relations.

ENTERTAINMENT VENUE ECONOMICS

As Publilius Syrus said in the first century BC, *Everything is worth what its purchaser will pay for it.* The problems marketers must solve are: what is a performance worth and what do we charge for it? Then, what do we spend to promote it so audiences will pay what we ask?

Entertainment products and services have universal appeal, cutting across cultural and national boundaries, and incremental revenues derived from international sources have an important effect on profitability. Profitability begins by setting the right price.

Steps in price setting

For entertainment performances, pricing decisions are made as information becomes available about costs, competitors, and consumer demand. Seven steps are suggested to determine appropriate pricing.[iv]

1. As with every other marketing aspect of entertainment, pricing decisions begin by *setting pricing objectives*. Profit, sales, and status-quo goals are among the most frequently used objectives. *Profit maximization* is a difficult objective because it requires knowledge of demand and is difficult to predict. Some venues prefer to seek a satisfactory profit or fair rate of return; profit goals are expressed as *target rate of return*. Increasing market share and increasing profit are also pricing objectives. In times of flux, venues may choose to maintain status quo pricing but exercise aggressive marketing efforts in one area of the 4 Ps.

2. The next step in pricing is *estimating demand*. Elasticity of demand reflects the speed at which demand changes in response to price changes. Movie houses that have discounted matinee fares have experienced an increase daytime traffic among seniors. Since elasticity is influenced by the number of alternatives available, theaters must compete with one another to achieve attractive pricing incentives.

3. *Calculating costs* involves considering demand, but costs to provide the entertainment experience are equally important. Monetary costs include fixed, variable and incremental costs. *Fixed costs*—overhead like rent, interest, and taxes do not vary with output; they are incurred even if no performances are held. *Variable costs* are the expenses associated with each production; they increase or decrease with the amount of output as labor and technological upgrades. Managers often employ a breakeven analysis to determine what prices might be charged to cover the cost of production. *Incremental costs* are those involved with selling one more seat. The cost of selling an empty seat just before a performance starts is close to zero, so the incremental revenue of each empty seat sold is, in effect, the price of the seat. This is the economic justification for offering day-of-performance discounts, student rush tickets, and other promotions that sell otherwise unsold seats at a deep discount.

4. *Analyzing competitors' prices* is another important step in calculating price. The fact that oligopolies (a market controlled by a few corporations) and monopolies (such as Time Warner) exist can make direct price competition a moot point. One way to avoid price competition is to differentiate the venue. Because markets are becoming increasingly subject to global competition, entertainment franchises cannot expect consumers to pay higher prices in the long run.

5. *Selecting a pricing policy* involves determining whether to offer a single price or different prices, and whether to price at, below, or above market. One-price policies treat all audience members equally, which is not an industry practice. Variable pricing allows for differences based upon single or group purchases, audience member age, time and day of performance or activity, and seat location. Pricing options are elaborated upon in the pricing strategy section.

6. *Determining price-setting methods* is not a large factor for entertainment venues, but some methods allow airlines to offer lower prices at off-peak hours, for example, or theaters to offer last-minute discounts on remaining seats. Marketers may conduct breakeven analyses to determine what will happen to profits at various price levels.

7. *Deciding on a final price* is the final step. The list price is quoted to buyers, but typically a variety of discounts are made for wholesaler or retailer cooperation. *Trade discounts* are offered in return for services performed. *Quantity discounts* are made to stimulate larger purchases to consolidators for buying in volume. Airlines, hotels and theme parks with lower demand during off-seasons offer *seasonal discounts*.

Actual and perceived costs to audience members

The price of the ticket is only one of the costs an audience member has to pay in order to attend a performance or to subscribe to a series. The actual and perceived costs of a proposed exchange can be defined as the sum of all opportunity costs (what the person alternatively could be spending the money on) as well as any expected negative outcomes, such as difficulties in parking, child care, uncomfortable seats, inadequate restroom facilities, or lengthy transportation.

Perceived value represents the margin of difference between the producer value and what an audience member feels the offering is worth regardless of its production cost, and it varies by audience segment. Some people are willing to pay high prices for self-actualizing experiences delivered with the certainty of planning ahead; others see value in waiting for last-minute pricing for the discount.

Choosing a ticket pricing strategy

A broad variety of strategies are available for planning. Here, let's examine two major strategies: competition and discriminatory pricing options.[v]

1. **Competitive pricing strategy** occurs when the presenting organization is likely to account for the cost of engaging artists or performing groups. This is called *going-rate* or *imitative pricing*. Many managers feel that conforming to a going price is the least disruptive of industry harmony that pays the house first.

2. **Discriminatory pricing** occurs when an organization sells a performance at two or more prices that do not reflect a proportional difference in cost. This practice of price discrimination can go a long way toward maximizing audience size and revenue. Several options exist for discriminatory strategy.

   + *Consumer segment pricing* charges audience groups different prices to acknowledge differences in their willingness or ability to pay. Senior and student discounts are examples of segment pricing. Group sales are another form of segment pricing, because discounts are given to groups purchasing a block of tickets for a single performance. Gift certificates and subscriptions are offered at a special price to encourage current patrons to draw in friends and family.

   + *Performance pricing* is applied to performances featuring stars or celebrities. Operas staring Pavarotti, for instance, cost more to produce than the same program performed by an unknown singer.

   + *Image pricing* is based on the fact that some audiences will pay a higher price to see a performance in an outstanding venue, pay premiums to attend an opening night gala for its excitement, or incur higher prices for hit or long-run performances.

   + *Location and time pricing* places orchestra and box seats at higher prices than those on the main floor, or sets evening or weekend prices higher than tickets for matinees or weeknights. Timing also includes the time of purchase; subscribers and early birds pay less for their tickets, while last-minute buyers incur even better discounts during "public rush" offerings.

Other factors to consider in developing strategies are the role of scalpers and discount ticket booths, as well as other opportunities for surplus maximization and conditions for price discrimination.

When the experience is highly valued, *ticket scalpers* buy in advance and sell outside venues to audience members who are willing to pay a premium; no additional revenues are generated for the organization with these transactions. *Half-price ticket booths* discriminate in favor of people who are willing to wait in line for hours to save money.

Certain conditions create *opportunities for surplus maximization.* Tickets can be priced at higher levels for opening night performances, special events, and celebrations and holiday performances. Outdoor venues that present concerts in an open area may offer higher prices for audiences who prefer pavilion seating to lawn viewing or listening.

4.4 Disney concert center in Los Angeles uses image pricing to offer visitors more perceived value.

© Jennifer Cheung/Corbis

If price discrimination, selling a performance at two or more prices that do not reflect a proportional difference in cost as described above, is to work, certain conditions must exist. First, the market must be segmentable, and the segments must show different intensities of demand. Second, members of lower price segments must not be able to resell to a higher price segment. Third, the cost of segmenting and policing the market must not exceed the extra revenue derived from price discrimination. Finally, the practice must not cause consumer resentment nor be illegal.

Choosing a ticket distribution strategy

For most audience members, the nature and ease of access to tickets is central to their purchase decisions. Options such as sales through the organization's own box office, centralized ticket agencies, Internet booking, and alternative community outlets all offer distinct sets of benefits.

The venue box office provides a key link to consumers, but is time-consuming at performance time and may be inconvenient. Centralized ticket agencies (Ticketmaster and other intermediary agencies) save having to staff a ticketing office. The downside is that agencies do not share audience names, addresses or purchasing behavior with performance providers; venues sacrifice valuable marketing information for efficient distribution.

Internet booking brings convenient purchase and seat selection to audience members. Most systems also provide the option to print tickets, allowing audiences to avoid will-call pick-ups prior to the performance. *Automated ticket machines*, similar to those in airports, are available in many urban locations to streamline purchasing activity.

Most performance venues and event marketers consign with wholesalers and *consolidators* for a percentage of ticket prices. Tickets to events, destinations, and performances are sold online through Web sites such as TicketsPlus, CheapFlights, and Expedia. Another option is the resale ticket market.

StubHub, an open marketplace dedicated to tickets, allows fans to buy and sell tickets to sporting, concert, theater, and other live entertainment events. Connecting sellers and buyers through a secure ticket fulfillment service, StubHub's partners include sports teams in the NFL, NBA, and NHL; media companies like AOL and Knight Ridder; and leading artists such as Britney Spears, Coldplay, and Alanis Morissette. Audience members use credit cards to purchase and print e-tickets at home.

Again, performance content and experiences are delivered to audiences, but the goods sold to audiences are in the form of tickets and subscriptions. Two other forms of goods that are available in venues and help extend the bottom line are franchising and licensing.

Franchising

To extend brand profits and exposure, entertainment enterprises engage in a variety of partnerships, the most profitable of which are licensing and franchising. **Licensing** gives manufacturers the right to put your brand on their products; **franchising** means paying for the brand's name and concept and running the business independently.

Franchising entertainment brands involves the integration of media with licensing and merchandising. Business format franchising resulted from parent companies realizing that their intangible assets—the concepts and brand names—are of far greater value than the franchisees' tangible assets—plant, facilities, and so on. The idea is to mass produce concepts rather than merely products, making franchising the most important form of business organization in the twenty-first century. In every geographic region of the world, the franchising phenomenon is replacing traditional independently-owned single businesses. This relationship's operating premise pulls the commercial agenda away from broadly distributed ownership of independent business and toward a regime made up of wholly-dependent lessees sharing access to networks of powerful suppliers. Such organization shifts the scheme of sellers and buyers into a *system of suppliers and users* where intangible assets count for more than physical ones. According to Jeremy Rifkin of the Foundation of Economic Trends, this metamorphosis from ownership to access is now a reality.[vi]

4.5 Former star Wayne Gretsky franchises his hockey rinks.

Through franchising, the culture of media entertainment is being infused with new modes of authorship, production, marketing, and consumption that are characterized by Internet fan clubs, online producer-consumer affiliations, and real-world legal controversies over the proprietary ownership of digital bits of information. Entertainment franchises are more prolific these days than hamburgers. Withf burgeoning franchises, entertainment companies have begun to delve deeper into marketing strategies that enable them to connect with their customers across their whole range of properties and communications divisions. Chapter 9 has more on franchising as an entertainment marketing tactic and brand extender.

FINANCIALS AND THE BOTTOM LINE

Entertainment marketers have valuable decision-making tools at their disposal for calculating the bottom line. The **balance sheet** shows the company's assets, liabilities and net worth at a single point in time. Profit and loss or operating statements present a summary of sales and expenses over a specific period of time and serve as a major tool for analyzing a company's financial performance.

Operating statements for entertainment-related companies have six main calculations:

- *Gross sales*—total revenue received during a specific time period
- *Net sales*—revenues retained after subtracting the amount paid to customers for tickets returned
- *Cost of tickets sold*—expenses for retailers or wholesalers, labor, venue operation, and maintenance
- *Gross margin*—obtained by subtracting the cost of tickets sold from the net sales
- *Operating expenses*—costs incurred during the statement period, including marketing expenses and performers' fees
- *Net income before taxes*—calculated by subtracting total operating expenses from gross margin; the bottom line

Performance ratios

Operating statements also provide data for figuring important **analytical ratios**, which are points of information that enable marketers to evaluate a company's performance by comparing it with their performance in previous operating periods or against performances of competing companies. Gross margin ratio, operating expense ratio, and net profit ratio are a marketer's most valuable calculations.

- *Operation ratio* is the percentage of net sales. It is obtained by dividing each item on the operating statement by the amount of net sales.

- *Gross margin ratio* is the percentage of net sales dollars available to cover operating expenses and to provide a profit after paying for the cost of tickets sold. The higher the gross margin, the more dollars left for expenses and profit.

$$\frac{\text{Gross margin}}{\text{Net sales}} = \text{Gross margin \%}$$

- *Operating expense ratio* is the percentage of each net sales dollar needed to cover operating expenses. If high, the salary, commission or advertising expenditures may be excessive.

$$\frac{\text{Total operating expenses}}{\text{Net sales}} = \text{Expense \%}$$

- *Net profit ratio* is the percentage of each net sales dollar that is left after all expenses have been paid, but before payment of federal and state income taxes.

$$\frac{\text{Net income before taxes}}{\text{Net sales}} = \text{Net profit \%}$$

Return on investment (ROI)

ROI an analytical ratio that compares profits with the amount of investment needed to sell tickets. Investment is a company's total assets (venue, land, equipment), minus the liabilities. ROI shows how well a company or venue has used its assets to generate ticket sales and make a profit. Marketers use both the balance sheet and operating statement to calculate the ROI. The formula for calculating the ROI is:

$$\text{ROI} = \frac{\text{Net profit}}{\text{Net sales}} \times \frac{\text{Net sales}}{\text{Investment}}$$

In order to be effective, marketing efforts should include an analysis of operating statements and balance sheets to determine performance in relation to industry averages.

Determining promotion budgets

Although setting budgets and allocating funds is always a challenge, marketers can rely on a few practical methods. These strategies are invoked for campaign planning and often are determined by the client rather than the promoting agency.

Percent of future sales

By evaluating past sales and future goals, budgets can be determined as a percentage of anticipated revenues. If a five percent increase is expected in performance box office sales, then the same increase should be given to last season's budget. For destinations, increases in inbound traffic form the basis of calculation. Shopping malls typically have a promotion consortium through which each retailer contributes a percentage of its expected sales for combined advertising and public relations efforts.

Competitive comparison

Using trade association studies of industry averages, venues and performance companies may opt to meet their competition's promotion budget. This method is not as useful for services as for products, because no venue or performance has specific competitors. Genre competitive spending—say in regional theater—may provide indications of what audiences are willing to pay, but figures vary by demographic, performance type, and season.

Objective task method

This is the most practical method of budgeting for entertainment, because it is tied to future objectives rather than predicted or competitor sales. Once promotion objectives are set, the tasks necessary to reach those objectives and their costs are calculated for each aspect of the promotion mix. Creating brand awareness is the most expensive objective, because the most frequent objective task, achieving desired media reach and frequency, is expensive. Measuring attitude changes tied to experiential branding, while not inexpensive, is a more direct and measurable objective than media messages. The task of connecting audiences to brands through positive experiences involves a variety of options, including sponsorship and event marketing, each of which can be a more economically efficient objective task than media buying.

Piracy

Every year, the motion picture industry loses in excess of $4 billion in potential worldwide revenue from piracy. Because piracy undermines the revenues needed to launch marketing programs and produce content, it has a related impact on marketing efforts. Piracy takes many forms, depending on the medium. The most prevalent examples are:[vii]

+ *Optical disc piracy* involves laser discs, video compact discs and DVDs, which are inexpensive to reproduce and have a fast turnaround time.

+ *Internet piracy* is the use of copyrighted movies for sale, trade, lease, distribution, uploading for transmission, transmission, or public performance of a movie online without consent.

+ *Downloadable media*, digital files that allow movies to be compressed and uploaded for direct download onto computers over the Internet, can be pirated.

+ *Hard goods*, copies of movies in any non-downloadable media format, may be stolen for illegal sale, distribution and/or trading.

+ *Streaming media* may be illegally delivered to online users in real time.

+ *Circumvention devices* allow someone to secure copyrighted content by going around protection devices such as encrypted software.

- *Camcording*, the use of video cameras to record movies from theater screens, is a form of pirating.

- *Screeners* are illegal copies made from advance copies used for screening and marketing purposes.

- *Back-to-back Copying* is the connection of two VCRs to copy an original video onto a blank cassette.

- *Theatrical print theft* entails stealing film to make illegal copies.

- *Signal theft* is illegal tapping into cable TV systems or satellite signals.

- *Broadcast piracy* involves over-the-air broadcasts of bootleg videos of a film.

- *Public performance theft* is showing a tape or film to customers without permission.

- *Parallel importation* is importing goods authorized for distribution but imported without authority of copyright owners.

Finally

Bringing audiences to an attractive venue and pricing experiences correctly are important keys to successful entertainment marketing. Pricing strategies must respect objectives to maximize bottom line profits. Promotion budgets are determined by behavioral and communication objectives set for the performance, experience, or media venues. And although piracy is responsible for undermining ROI, clever marketing strategies act as an insurance policy for entertainment businesses and franchises.

GOT IT?

- *Performance content* is developed around music, dance, and theater for presentation by bands, orchestras, and other musical groups, or theatrical and production companies; *experiential content* occurs in or at attractions (resorts, spas, casinos, theme parks) and through travel destinations; *media content* is property that is created, sold to a studio, and produced for distribution;.

- Servicescapes provide *purchase performance* that can imaginatively transform audiences into visitors to other centuries or countries; flagship stores, concept stores, and destination malls drive shopping experiences in unique ways.

- Setting pricing objectives, estimating demand, calculating costs, analyzing competitors' prices, selecting a pricing policy, determining price-setting methods and deciding on a final price are the essential components of a pricing strategy.

- Promotion budgets may be determined by percent of future sales, competitive comparison, or the objective task method.

NOW TRY THIS

1. Check out frontrowtickets.com and ticketmaster.com online and compare each Internet booking service's pricing and ease of purchase for the Broadway show or local concert of your choice. Now go directly to the box office where the event takes place. How does their ticketing procedures compare to the ones you found with ticket brokers? Which do you prefer?

2. Find the Web site for a mall in your area. What attributes of an ideal servicescape does the mall offer? What can you suggest to improve the shopping experience for this venue?

3. To sample a venue experience, visit the Web site of any museum designed by Frank Gehry (Guggenheim in Bilbao, Spain; Seattle's Experience Music Project). Alternatively, research a hotel designed by Philippe Starck (Clift Hotel in San Francisco, Mandarin Hotel restaurant in Hong Kong). How does the architecture add distinction to these spaces?

QUESTIONS FOR DISCUSSION AND REVIEW

1. Compare performance and experience content for their dependence on venues. Which type of content is more difficult to market? Why?

2. Discuss the various aspects of venue aesthetics and give examples of each from your home city or state. Explain which is most attractive and why.

3. Which of the three methods for figuring bottom line profits is most effective for theme parks? For concert venues? For destination cities?

4. What are the pros and cons of determining promotional budgets using the comparison method?

5. Which types of piracy are most difficult to control? What policing mechanisms can you suggest for international piracy?

6. Is showing a copyrighted video in class considered to be piracy?

OTHER STUFF ON CONTENT, VENUES, AND PRICING

www.buzzmedia.com Tips on venue advertising and related topics.

www.aarkid.com 3D architecture and venue marketing case study for Glasgow Science Center's corporate facility.

www.exhibitoronline.com Corporate event magazine and case studies.

[i] John Sherry (ed.) (1998), *ServiceScapes*. New York: NTC Books.
[ii] Christian Mikunda (2004), *Brand Lands, Hot Spots & Cool Spaces*. London: Kogan Page, Introduction.
[iii] Virginia Postrel (2003), *The Substance of Style*. Perennial, p. 10.
[iv] See David Rachman (1994), *Marketing Today*, 3rd ed. Dryden, chapter 12.
[v] For more details, see Philip Kotler & Joanne Scheff (1989), *Standing Room Only: Strategies for Marketing the Performing Arts*. Cambridge MA: Harvard Business School Press, Chapter 9.
[vi] Jeremy Rifkin (2000), *The Age of Access*. New York: Tarcher/Putnam, p. 72.
[vii] Al Lieberman (2002), *The Entertainment Marketing Revolution*. New York: FT-Prentice Hall, pp. 304–307.

Part 2

ENTERTAINMENT CAMPAIGN PLANNING AND EXECUTION

Chapter 5

PRODUCING AN INTEGRATED/CONVERGENT COMMUNICATIONS CAMPAIGN

*When society requires to be rebuilt
there is no use in attempting to
rebuild it on the old plan.*
John Stuart Mill

Chapter Objectives

After reading this chapter, you will be able to answer these questions:

+ What choices and changes drive *integrated* campaigns?

+ What role does *research* play in planning a campaign?

+ What are the *ten steps* for planning a campaign?

+ Why is *evaluation* of the integrated mix and campaign important for accessing campaign effectiveness?

+ When does a campaign warrant a *globalized execution*?

COMMUNICATING ENTERTAINMENT BRAND MESSAGES

The objective of all marketing communications efforts is to present a coordinated, cohesive, unified branded message to a specific target audience. **Integrated promotional communications**, (called **IMC** by marketers) is the management of all brand contact points through an integrated, audience-driven strategy. The difference between expectations and delivery—the gap discussed in Chapter 3—is what distinguishes a well-executed experience from a poorly executed one. Audience expectations are shaped by both uncontrolled and management-controlled factors, yet audience needs are the main factor for influencing expectations. Messages delivered through advertising, promotions, sponsorships, PR, and Internet communications are vital to the success of an experience. All of these communication devices must be crafted to represent the entertainment genre as accurately and specifically as possible.

From integration to convergence

Hollywood has always been creative in reaching its audiences. What it hasn't always been good at is crafting a unified message across all of its communication vehicles. Message delivery is not simply sending out a piece of advertising, a press release, and a direct mail solicitation that have similar graphics. Integration ideally results in a metamorphosis of advertising, promotion, and merchandising that presents the same message and the same brand image throughout all audience contacts. Convergent communication adds the branding message to the mix.

Exhibit 5.1 shows the natural progression from a traditional IMC strategy to an integrated or convergent communications strategy. Both approaches are based on similar principles and goals, but by planning for convergence, brand benefits are maximized through specifically directed communication. Ultimately, all marketing will make the transition to convergence.

EXHIBIT 5.1 Integrated vs. Convergent Communications

TRADITIONAL IMC		CONVERGENT COMMUNICATIONS
Marketer's need to synchronize programs	< reason for being >	Create programs that address consumers' needs w/impact
Common strategy, look, theme	< approach >	Common elements, but modified according to medium's capacity to communicate benefit(s)

Consistent advertising, PR, direct response, etc	< Communications created >	Consistent advertising, PR direct response, etc.
Well-coordinated marketing communications program	< End result >	Well-coordinated program with maximum benefit communication

Source: Lynn Upshaw, Building Brand Identity, Wiley (2005), p. 212.

CAMPAIGN PLANNING, STRATEGIES AND TACTICS

Campaigns are developed to solve problems. Because marketing problems for the entertainment industry usually center around revenue generation, most campaigns are designed to promote new content, venues, and destinations. Some campaigns focus on bringing back pre-released content and properties, or changing attitudes about an attraction or destination. The nature of the promotion problem determines the campaign's objectives. This section presents a step-by-step approach to planning and developing an integrated or convergent communications campaign for performance, experiential, and mediated entertainment and their venues.

Promotional tools are constantly changing in response to technology's rapid advances. Marketers constantly monitor audience preferences in message delivery. Which media channels should be purchased to develop a relevant promotional campaign? Research is necessary to negotiate the plethora of delivery options. How are audiences learning about entertainment options and where are they buying their tickets? The Internet continues to play a major role in information distribution and purchase facilitation. What's the best way to pay attention to Web sites and online advertising?

Research options

This section is addressed in Chapter 6 and is one of the first steps in developing a campaign. Both primary and secondary research are conducted as part of Step Two in campaign planning.

Primary research uncovers problems that campaigns are designed to circumvent. Using qualitative techniques (focus groups and in-depth interviews), marketers determine the nature and extent of problems as well as the audiences consumption habits, preferences, and attitudes. Dollars spent on marketing research have increased, largely because of the need to understand audience involvement against the backdrop of ever-expanding delivery and purchase channel options.

Secondary research comes from outside sources that provide market, company, and audience statistics from research and business reporting services and tourist bureaus. Some of the most useful *free resources* are:

- ESOMAR world research organization for global markets, consumers, and societies

- Greenbook (greenbook.org), a directory of worldwide marketing research and focus group companies

- Hoovers Research

- Internet World Statistics

- Market Research Association (mra-net.org)

- Market Research Library (export.gov)

- Market Research Portal (marketresearchworld.net)

- U.S. Government Bureau of Labor Statistics (bls.gov)

Syndicated services

Secondary research that is subscription based is called syndicated research service. Audience usage data are available only through subscription affiliations. Most advertising agencies subscribe to

FOCUS ON CONVERGENCE

Orchestrated Efforts, Harmonious Results

As marketers and academics dispute the merits of integrated services, we provide reasons why the convergence of planning and implementing a campaign will drive twenty-first century entertainment marketing efforts.

Entertainment promotion has gone from marketing oriented to market driven

The mass market and its traditional techniques of mass marketing have been rendered obsolete. In its place, the incredible explosion of technology of the last two decades has become the driving force of consumer control of what, where, and how they want to purchase tickets. Technology has changed both the way consumers make their purchasing decisions and how companies market their entertainment products to consumers. The audience's role has become so dominant that companies have shifted their focus to a market-driven strategy. Marketers must establish and maintain a strong and consistent voice across all media in order to appeal to consumer sophistication, media proliferation and mass-market fragmentation.

Marketers switch to an audience-oriented approach

For any promotional communication campaign to produce effective results, it must be solidly based on a deep understanding of the consumer audience. Entertainment brand communications programs now incorporate segmentation/aggregation, customer valuation, and database management for directing effective messages that affect audience behavior.

Planning is a crucial element for implementing audience-based promotion

The added value of a comprehensive plan is established through a conceptual promotional communications plan. Such a plan evaluates the strategic roles of a variety of communication disciplines—for example, general advertising, direct response, sales promotion, and public relations—and combines these disciplines to provide clarity, consistency, and maximum impact through seamless integration of targeted messages.

Convergence requires a collaborative strategy

Coordination of strategy and tactics yields an effective convergent plan. To be effective, collaboration must embrace an understanding of the different roles that all forms of communication techniques play in the promotion process (e.g., promotion might prompt trial but only once public relations has raised awareness).

Each component of the promotion mix should work together to leverage the strengths of other components and present a consistent set of benefits and images to the audience member. Selecting an appropriate combination of promotional communication tools that will achieve the brand's communication objectives is the key to a successful integrated approach.

Convergence is not a management fad

An integrated approach is a fundamental and marked shift in thinking and practice of promotional communications by clients and advertising agencies. A critical issue regarding convergence is the evaluation and measurement of integrated programs. Because traditionally advertising, sales promotion, direct marketing, and the public relations disciplines have developed separate and distinct measurement approaches, this task is a difficult one. The measurement of integrated programs, which is designed to estimate the synergy between elements, is a totally new field that remains relatively undeveloped.

Integrated planning, still an emerging discipline, exists today as a transition between the historical product-driven outbound marketing systems and the new information-driven, interactive, consumer-focused marketplace of the twenty-first century.

Source: Manoj Khatri for *strategicmarketing.com*

syndicated services to determine media buying expenditures. The best-known services are A.C. Nielson, Harris Interactive, and Simmons.

Designed to understand the market as a whole, syndicated research is often conducted on a national scale and involves hundreds, if not thousands, of participants. The idea behind syndicated research is sharing the cost among a broad base of users. Prices for syndicated research can range from roughly $300 for a subscription to a newsletter-style report to more than $11,000 for the rights to get a peek at the data on, say, the online buying habits of Quake-playing retirees. Syndicated research is a good way to shape long-term strategies, and it can be an excellent jumping off point. Two of the biggest providers in the online arena are Forrester Research and Jupiter Communications.

TEN STEPS TO DEVELOPING YOUR CAMPAIGN

There are many approaches to developing a comprehensive campaign to promote an entertainment brand, performance, or mediated property. This text recommends a 10-step approach to developing an integrated communications plan for entertainment companies. In addition to describing these steps, you'll see an example of how they are applied to a campaign developed for the national Public Broadcasting Service (PBS).[i] This example, featured after the plan outline, will show you how to craft an appropriate campaign plan for an entertainment client.

Step 1: State the problem and campaign objective

Why is the client conducting a campaign? State the reason as a problem clearly and succinctly.

Supporting facts

Look at relevant data regarding the problem situation. Such evidence comes from consumer research and client or brand statistics.

Campaign objective and duration

The reason the campaign is being conducted and length of implementation needs to be formulated. Answer the question "What outcome does the client want from this campaign? (e.g., higher box office gross, brand awareness from a niche audience)

Step 2: Conduct a situation analysis (see Chapter 6)

An analysis of the current marketplace is the means for identifying the most important factors in campaign development. Situation analysis begins with an industry overview that includes a determination of its size, sales volume, growth trends, and attendance statistics. Company background, target market, and current marketing mix are included in this section. Once these data are determined, you must review significant and mitigating factors that impact the industry.

Industry overview

Begin with a broad stroke of your client's entire industry segment and where it is today. Focus on developments and trends within the industry by enumerating the most important aspects, such as a saturated marketplace.

Corporate history

Include your client's most recent company or corporate data here. Rather than repeat what the client already knows about itself, elaborate on important events in the company's past and its current status in the marketplace. What events have altered or enhanced the client's brand image (such as Toyota recalls in 2010)?

Economic, technological, political, social, and legal environments

Because technology, circumstances, and unforeseen events change today's entertainment marketplace, you use secondary research to determine what uncontrollable factors may impact the campaign (for example, the 2009 global economic downturn).

Competitive analysis

Analyze the major competitors to your client and their market shares. Look at the strengths and weaknesses of the competition, plus threats they may pose. Prioritize the number of competitors to the ones most closely associated with your client's business or genre. Sometimes competitors exist outside the usual suspects; for instance, train ridership competes with branded airlines and busses but also with personal cars as modes of transportation.

Step 3: Conduct a SWOT analysis of the property or brand

Using primary research on your client's audience, determine the brand's strengths and weaknesses and identify the opportunities and threats to the client, both internal and external. Internal threats are controllable, while external threats are not. Exhibit 5.2 illustrates how these variables are plotted for analysis. Use Chapter 6 to guide you.

Step 4: Characterize the target audience

Using both client information and psychographic profiles, describe the overall target market and profile the specific audience targeted by this campaign. Present as much information about them and their perceptions about the brand as possible. Use primary research to determine how audience members or consumers feel about your client's brand. *Perceptual maps* can dramatize audience perceptions of the client's brand in relationship to competitive brands. Exhibit 5.3 is an example of the configurations used for perceptual mapping for designer clothing based on status and conspicuousness. Chapter 6 will help you prepare questionnaires and/or surveys necessary to develop a perceptual map to visualize audience perception of your client and its competitors.

EXHIBIT 5.2 Components of a SWOT Analysis

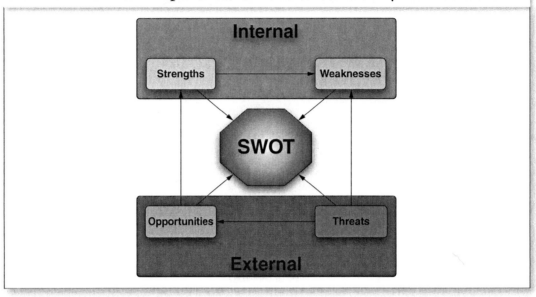

Source: hrmadvice.com/assets/images/swotanalysis

EXHIBIT 5.3 Perceptual Mapping

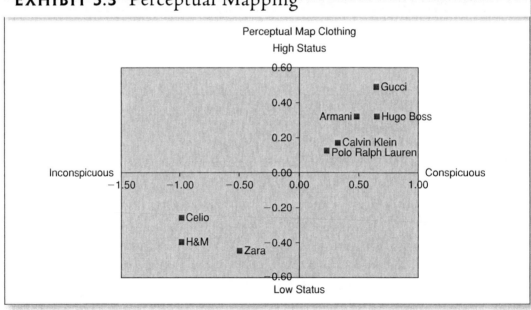

Source: www.palgrave-journals.com/bm/journal/v16/n5/images/bm20091f2.jpg

Step 5: Determine the brand positioning strategy

Use your competitive analysis and audience research to determine how to position your client's brand in the marketplace. The alternatives suggested in Chapter 8 for constructing a positioning strategy are:

+ Position on a *specific feature*, such as a Frank Gehry architectural venue, Cedar Point's highest roller coaster, or state-of-the-art staging technology

+ Position on *benefits*, such as Six Flags' excitement, thrills, adventure and so forth

+ Position for specific *usage occasion*, such as Saturday afternoon concerts, Christmas showing of the Nutcracker's Suite, or Tanglewood's summer outdoor theater

+ Position for *user category*, such as gay and lesbian weekends on a Carnival Cruise

+ Position *against other brands* in the category, such as Golden Door touting itself as the "most expensive spa experience in the U.S."

+ Position *as number one*, such as Paris' claim to be the most visited city in the world

+ Position as *exclusive*, such as PBS unique status as the only nonprofit broadcasting entity

FOCUS ON VIRTUAL PROMOTION

Digital Utopia for Corporate Research

User engagement in virtual worlds has contributed to the economic success of sites that invite social interaction. Second Life, a virtual world designed primarily for user-generated content, has also become a hot spot for real world businesses that have entered the virtual marketplace. The usage rates for virtual worlds have increased rapidly, suggesting that by 2011, 80% of Internet users will have created avatars for both work and play. By 2012, over half of all U.S. companies are anticipated to have digital offices or "networked virtual environments." An important place for meetings, hiring, communication, and collaboration, a virtual "work" world will replace face-to-face interaction. Brick and mortar businesses have entered the virtual marketplace through Second Life's virtual world of user-generated content.

As of 2008, Second Life has 11.8 million residents, 50,000 of which operate a virtual business. Second Life, home to an economy based on the Linden dollar (260L per USD), has sold over 75 million square meters of virtual land. Corporate players such as IBM, Reuters, Playboy, Dell, Comcast, Telstra/Bigpond (an Australian Internet service provider), and many other companies have created virtual presences in Second Life.

Linden Labs, site owner, leases "land" to tenants for around $20 a month per acre or $195 a month plus a one-time fee of $1,250, for a private "island." The most important activities on Second Life are aimed at social groups rather than individuals. Shopping, dancing, and clubbing are popular, and corporations with the highest traffic ratings host such social events to drive and maintain site traffic. Corporate sites host concerts, radio shows, lectures, and other activities that provide social reasons for people to visit the corporate site.

Corporations also conduct consumer research on Second Life. Aloft (a division of the W Hotels brand) obtained feedback from prospective guests prior to building the actual hotel, which opened in 2008. Sony BMG's building offers fans the opportunity of listening to tunes or watching videos before purchasing them online; the specific rooms devoted to popular musicians facilitate the interaction. Online press conferences and corporate events further enable pre-release testing for entertainment companies.

Retaining and training IT developers, architects, and infrastructure, security, and, integration professionals on complex concepts using the Second Life virtual world, Michelin's enterprise architecture group is a leader in the field. Trainees participated in both traditional presentation-style learning and interactive hands-on exercises. According to program participants, it doesn't take long to learn how to use the virtual environment to simplify complex concepts through an immersive experience that helped increase their engagement in the learning process. Even educators, such as Dr. Paul Lester at California State University, Fullerton, conduct classes in an auditorium on Second Life purchased by the university for distance learning.

Source: pc.joystick.com; wiki.secondlife.com/wiki/Other_Second_Life_Studies; www.onetooneinteractive.com/wp-content/uploads/2009/07/otoinsights_serious_games_report.pdf

Step 6: Structure campaign objectives

Remember that objectives drive strategies and tactics at all stages of promotion planning. This step helps you determine specific objectives and the amount of funds needed to achieve those objectives. Develop specific marketing, advertising, media, promotion, and action objectives in this section. You can pick and choose which objectives are relevant to your campaign. Chapter 10 will direct you in this task.

Marketing objectives

Marketing objectives are relevant when your client specifies sales, revenue, profits, or market share as a campaign objective. Remember, these must be measurable. Clients determine their marketing objective based on slow sales, declining profits, and competitive growth. These objectives help to determine which promotion strategy to use.

Advertising/communication objectives

Specify communication objectives as category need, awareness, attitude, or purchase intention. As explained in Chapter 10, objectives must include a measurable component that is attainable by the campaign's conclusion. If you can't measure it, it's not a valid objective.

Media objectives

When and if you use traditional media, specify media objectives based on reach (percentage of demographic), frequency (number of impressions), continuity (continuous, flights, or pulsed).

Promotion/Action objectives

For each consumer aggregate your campaign targets, specify what action(s) you want from each audience aggregate. Action objectives are what you want consumers to do after being exposed to the campaign, such as buy a ticket or take a trip.

Step 7: Allocate a budget

Chapter 9 explains how using the objective-task method will assist you in determining the resources needed to produce and deliver a promotional campaign for your client. Most appropriate for limited budget campaigns, the objective-task method determines the resources needed to accomplish media and promotional objectives. If the objective is to raise awareness by 5%, the budget reflects media costs and expenditures for promotional activities needed to accomplish that task.

Step 8: Select promotion mix you need to reach campaign objectives for delivery strategies and tactics

Selecting from the options described in Chapters 6, 9, and 12, decide on a promotion mix for your communications.

Media advertising

After comparing all mass media alternatives, select the appropriate vehicles for reaching your campaign audience. Determine media selections through localized focus groups with target audience members. Nationally syndicated resources on demographic media usage (such as Simmons) inform your media choices.

Product placement

Determine places where the logo or property can be imbedded into a form of entertainment or activity.

Licensing

Use garments and products produced by other manufactures to feature brand logo. Licensing is both a profit-generating activity and method of spreading brand awareness.

Sponsorship/PR

Sponsoring an event generates media coverage and creates a favorable association with the audience's preferred activity or cause. Resulting exposure improves brand image and increases awareness. See Chapter 11 for details.

Internet

Creating a Web site to induce audience interaction and build positive audience relationships is mandatory in today's global marketplace. Website design and maintenance costs, although typically separate from the marketing budget, are necessary elements for the campaign's overall effectiveness.

Publicity

Editorial commentary in print and broadcast media must appear concurrently with advertising and promotion. To insure adequate coverage, you must deliver publicity materials to editors and producers in advance of campaign activities.

Promotions/Incentives

Develop promotional incentives using both push and pull strategies. Dollars spent on incentives is insurance against non-participation and increases opportunities to reach revenue goals.

Direct response

Design personal contact with audience members to induce responses that result in a positive relationship with the brand.

Step 9: Develop message strategies

As explained in Chapter 10, create appropriate messages for each consumer aggregate that will be targeted in the campaign. Messages are designed to attract audience members and speak directly to their needs.

Step 10: Set evaluation criteria

Campaign effectiveness can be determined only through research conducted by the client, the advertising agency, or an outside research firm. Evaluation methods include but are not limited to:

- Pre and post tests to measure attitude changes
- post-campaign sales data and market share statistics

- contest and sweepstake entries
- exit polling from venues
- attendance measures
- Web site traffic counts
- revenue indicators from box office sales, merchandise purchases, and subscriptions

Once the plan is completed, the creative team develops concepts for all promotional vehicle executions (commercials, Websites), and the plan is implemented. At the campaign's conclusion, outcomes are measured to determine levels of success or failure. The plan can also serve as the basis of a new campaign or modifications to the previous effort.

Example of a campaign plan for PBS

The following campaign follows the above outline, and provides an example of what the bones of a campaign plan should look like. All plans should be supported with visual illustrations of proposed creative when possible.

INTEGRATED CAMPAIGN FOR PUBLIC BROADCASTING SYSTEM

Problem and campaign objective

Research determined that many PBS services go unnoticed and unused because of a lack of information about programs and performances. Many audience members think PBS is purely educational with no entertainment value for them. The campaign objective is to raise awareness of PBS entertainment options.

Supporting facts

There is a high awareness among children regarding kids' programming and among seniors who watch BBC sitcoms. On the other hand, many parents, teachers, teens, and young adult audiences remain unaware of PBS entertainment offerings.

Campaign objective and duration

Develop awareness among teens and young adult audiences of PBS entertainment offerings and expand viewership among that age demographic by the end of the six-month campaign.

Situation analysis

Industry overview

Most broadcast companies are privately owned and provide programming on network TV stations funded by advertising or paid subscription services sold through cable and satellite companies. PBS operates as a nonprofit enterprise, funded solely by donations from members, individual donors, corporate sponsors, and foundation grants.

Corporate history

Founded in 1969, the Public Broadcasting Service is a private, nonprofit corporation. PBS, headquartered in Alexandria, Virginia, whose members are America's public TV station affiliates. PBS oversees program acquisition, distribution, and promotion; educational services; new media ventures; fundraising support; engineering and technology development; and video marketing. There are 170 non-commercial educational licensees operating 349 PBS member stations. Licensees include 87 community organizations, 57 colleges or universities, 20 state authorities, and six local educational or municipal authorities. A trusted community resource, PBS uses

Sponsorship Sectors and Percentage of Whole, 2008

Financial	15%
Auto	15%
Insurance & Real Estate	13%
Gas % fuel	08%
Retail	08%
Building construction	06%
Packaged goods	07%
Computer software	06%
Beverages	03%
Chemical	03%
Other	16%

the power of non-commercial television, the Internet, and other media to enrich the lives of all Americans through quality programs and education services that inform, inspire, and delight. Available to 99% of American homes with televisions and to an increasing number of digital multimedia households, PBS serves nearly 110 million people each week.

PBS' operating revenue was cut back by $3.4 million in 2009, resulting in staff reductions and pay cuts. Leading sources of revenue included: station assessments (47%); CPB and federal grants (24%); royalties, license fees, satellite services, and investment income (14%), and educational product sales (12%). Leading expenditures for PBS in fiscal year 2009 included: programming and promotion (72%); member and educational services (15%); satellite interconnection and technical services (9%); general and administrative (4%).

Economic, technological, political, social, and legal environments

Because of the economic recession, contribution to arts and nonprofit organizations has declined. Technology has enabled television viewers to receive programming over hand-held devices as well as computers, DVDs, and large-screen plasma TVs. Governmental support is also declining, although regulations have not significantly affected programming selection. Mature adults actively participate in philanthropic campaigns and exhibit social responsibility for people who are less fortunate. Social trends vary by demographic group.

Competitive analysis

Competition includes:

+ Nature, news, history, and lifestyle channels
+ Network television and broadcast programming delivered by cable and satellite

Competitive advantages:

+ Paid advertisers to subsidize broadcast costs
+ Ability to develop content and properties

Disadvantages:

+ Advertiser control
+ Viewing disruption by commercials

Share of television viewership:

+ 30% Network TV
+ 60% Subscription or pay channels
+ 11% Public television

SWOT analysis of the brand

Strengths

1. Educational services

   + "Ready To Learn" helps to increase school readiness for all of America's children with programming and short educational video spots. These programs are enhanced through outreach services including workshops, free children's books, a magazine, and other learning resources to help parents, teachers and child-care providers prepare young children to enter school ready to learn.

   + "TeacherSource" helps preK-12 educators learn effective ways to incorporate online tools in the classroom through nearly 5,000 free lesson plans, teachers' guides, home-schooling guidance, and other resourceful activities correlated to national and state curriculum standards.

   + "TeacherLine" provides professional teacher development through more than 90 online facilitated courses in reading, mathematics, science, curriculum development, instruction techniques, and technology integration.

   + "Adult Learning Service" provides college credit TV courses to nearly 500,000 students each academic year.

2. Programming Activities

   + The National Programming Service is the major package of programs that PBS distributes to its member stations. It features television's best children's, cultural, educational, history, nature, news, public affairs, science, and skills programming.

   + Programs are obtained from PBS stations, independent producers, and sources around the world. PBS offers news, science and history, as well as nature, life, and culture programming to its viewers.

3. Digital Leadership

   + PBS.org is not only one of the most visited dot-org Websites in the world, it is also the home of comprehensive companion Websites for more than 1,000 PBS television programs and specials, as well as original Web content and real-time learning adventures.

   + Member stations are digital television leaders, from groundbreaking work in interactive TV and a monthly schedule of original high-definition programming (on the PBS HD Channel) to the PBS YOU multicast services.

4. Brand Equity

   + Award-winning news, documentary and children's programming; Website; educational activities; logo and member loyalty.

Weaknesses

+ Dependence upon outside sources for funding and programming

+ Stodgy image among teens and young adults

+ Limited programming directed at teens and young adults

Opportunities

+ Add affiliates and college licensees

+ Solicit more corporate sponsorships

+ Attract a more solid teen and young adult audience base

+ Increase sales through the online store and other outlets

Threats

+ Ever-increasing programming competition

+ Decreasing government subsidies

+ Economic downturn

Target market

The current public TV audience reflects the social and economic makeup of the nation. PBS and its member stations reach nearly 90 million people each week through on-air and online content.

Target audience

The campaign will target teens and young adults of all demographics in major urban metropolitan areas. Secondary targets are parents and teachers of the primary demographic.

Audience perceptions

Primary research determined that the campaign audience's perceptions of the entertainment brand are not ideal. While the brand's image evoked adjectives such as educational and informational, they did not convey a sense of excitement or relevance for this demographic. Audience members characterized the brand's personality as being introverted, serious, and playful for kids.

EXHIBIT 5.4 Perceptual Grid for Mapping PBS Teen Audiences

```
                        Entertaining
                             |
              MTV            |            ESPN
                             |
Fun _____|_____ Factual
                             |
                             |
            Discovery        |            PBS
                             |
                        Educational
```

Brand position—exclusive strategy

The nation's only nonprofit broadcasting alternative that provides uncensored, original entertainment programming for all audience segments.

Positioning for campaign audience—benefit strategy

Information television that entertains.

Marketing objectives

+ Increase online sales by 5%

+ Increase revenue generated by corporate sponsors by 7%

+ Increase television viewing market share by 1%

Advertising objectives

+ Increase awareness of PBS programs directed at teens and young adults by 20%

+ Improve positive attitude toward PBS among teens and young adults by 25%

+ Increase intention to purchase merchandise from PBS Website by 11%

Media objectives

+ Reach 40% of teens and young adults five times using a pulsing strategy

Promotion/Action objectives

+ Current PBS viewers: maintain current financial loyalty and introduce teens to PBS programming

+ Emerging PBS viewers: play games on the PBS Website; become a member and compete in online games

+ Competitive viewers: Incorporate PBS into viewing selections

Budget allocation

National budget for promotional spending is generated from 5% of revenues from governmental subsidies and global corporate sponsors, and 3% of profits from sales of DVDs, tapes, and related formats featured and sold via online store. Once that number is determined, the campaign budget is to be used for media and promotions directed at teens and young adults.

Media advertising

National media buys for general PBS game contest and sweepstake promotion; does not include affiliate promotions.

+ 30 second TV spots on "Nick at Night", ESPN and MTV

+ Full-page magazine ads in Seventeen, Teen, and Skateboarder magazines

+ 2 column inch newspaper ad in New York Times, Wall Street Journal, Los Angeles Times, Chicago Tribune and Boston Globe calendar or entertainment sections

Product placement

Logo images are displayed on television screens turned on during sitcoms and reality shows on ABC, NBC, CBS; PBS logo can be seen on Tony Hawk skateboard used in competitions.

Licensing

Some toys and clothing feature Sesame Street characters.

Sponsorship/PR

+ Co-sponsor a contest with Tony Hawk skateboard manufacturer for teens to design an online game for the PBS Website. The winner receives a skateboard.

+ Participate in a skateboarding event where PBS logo decals are given away to competitors.

Internet

+ Feature skateboard and teen reality games on the Website.

+ Promote the Website using sponsored links on skateboard manufacturer websites.

+ Put a campaign together using social media like Twitter, Facebook, and YouTube.

Publicity

+ *Develop press kits for dist*ribution to teen and young adult magazine editors to create a buzz about the skateboard game contest.

+ Send out news releases to both print and broadcast media announcing skateboard-related programming.

Promotions/Incentives

+ Provide funding incentives for affiliates who join sponsorship activities.

+ Offer skateboard prizes as incentives for teens and young adults to enter contests and sweepstakes and play games on the PBS Website.

Direct response

Using databases from skateboard and teen magazines, mail out PBS contest entry forms that direct entrants to the Web site.

Audience message strategies

+ Current PBS viewers: Turn your friends on to PBS Web site.

+ Emerging PBS viewers: Find excitement on PBS; enter a game contest; visit the Web site.

+ Competitive viewers: Enter PBS sweepstakes on line.

Campaign evaluation criteria

Objectives will be evaluated using:

+ number of Web hits as tabulated by eMarketer

+ contest and sweepstake entry totals

+ Internet-generated teen surveys to measure post-campaign attitude changes toward PBS.

5.1 Tony Hawk skateboards as event co-sponsor.

Warner Bros./Photofest, © Warner Bros.

Image 5.2 Loonatics

Developing a Campaign to Raise Ratings

PROBLEM: *WB television network's children's (6-11) program lineup has slumping ratings; the company turns to research to see how they can improve the product.*

OBJECTIVE: *How can WB breathe new life into the animated Looney Tunes franchise?*

Agency Research Proposal

Methodology—use focus groups and in-depth interviews to probe audience thoughts and feelings about the following:

- Plot: Loonatics series set in the year 2772.

- Characters who retain personality quirks of the original. Featured character is Buzz Bunny who is the natural leader of the Loonatics' spaceship; the new Daffy remains confident that he is the one who should be in charge.

Report format—agency meeting, written results

Budget—includes research and re-drafting cartoon images

Primary research results provided WB's advertising staff the direction for creating a new campaign, which is outlined below.

Campaign Plan
Campaign problem

Traditional images and animation, story lines, and characters are not appealing to audiences in the age range; need to promote the new versions that testing selected

Current market analysis

Japanese animation techniques, video games, cartoon networks, Disney Channel, and technological innovation has rendered WB cartoons obsolete and uninteresting to its audience; kids market is weak globally; Saturday morning viewership down 26% among children between the ages of 5 and 9 since last year

Trends

Slicker characters, craftier plots, and continuing innovation will drive entertainment; Loonatics and Buzz Bunny will improve cartoon viewing on Saturday morning

SWOT analysis

- Strengths: Cartoon history, recognizable characters

- Weaknesses: Outdated images and plots

- Opportunities: Find a fresh way to tap the funny bone of an audience raised on Bart Simpson and SpongeBob; expand WB line of characters

- Threats: Competition; past bombs, in particular "Looney Tunes: Back in Action", the WB movie that failed last year

Behavioral objectives—stimulate children's audiences, who are finicky and get itchy for something new, to bond with WB characters

- Current viewers—Keep tuned to WB programming and make it a preferential viewing selection

- New viewers—Develop a relationship with the newly image characters and request WB channel

- Competitive viewers—Tune in and experience the new characters

Budget—objective based

Determine preferences in character style and plot structure through a series of focus groups and in-depth interviews with children who watch television cartoons. Budget reflects cost of focus groups and analysis as determined by an outside research company.

Mix needed to promote new characters

- PR: editorial about new configurations in WSJ and NYT
- Licensing: new images on clothing for sale at WB stores
- Home video: Loonatics DVDs
- Advertising: cartoon trailers on WB channel and other kid-based channels
- Print: coloring books distributed through restaurants and schools that feature new characters
- Product placement: New Bugs will appear in branded product ads
- Sponsorship: Run for cancer and other marathon races to feature sprinting bunny
- Internet: Interactive games featuring New Bugs

Evaluation techniques

- Neilson ratings
- Recognition surveys
- Attitude surveys

What do you think?

1. How would you create a buzz about the new Bugs?
2. In addition to licensing, how would you merchandise the updated character?
3. What other promotional methods are appropriate for the new Bugs?

TAKING CAMPAIGNS GLOBAL

Entertainment properties, franchises, performances, destinations, and attractions have global appeal and can demand global campaigns. The global mindset is a fundamentally different perspective from international, multinational, and pan-regional, because it encompasses all cultures or nationalities. Global and cross-regional considerations include delivery systems, market regulations, agency options, logistics, and campaign scope.

Global delivery systems

Of all the challenges facing promoters of global entertainment, media advertising may be the greatest. Availability and usage complicates the problem of deciding which combination of media will achieve the desired coverage of a market.

Newspapers, the most localized worldwide medium, provide the best programming information; however, they require the greatest amount of local market knowledge. Global magazine coverage is expensive, and the cost of full coverage in publications in a variety of languages is often prohibitive for all but the most profitable entertainment genres.

Global television networks using cable and satellite technology provide the best media availability and coverage. One of the largest networks, Viacom's MTV, reaches over 400 million households worldwide. MTV Network offers an efficient means of reaching Generations X, Y, and Z around the globe, facilitating international campaigns for many global brands. Direct broadcast by satellite is available through systems like SkyPort, which sends transmissions through low-cost receiving dishes. Satellite Television Asian Region (STAR) sends BBC, U.S., Bollywood, and local programming to 53 countries across Asia; it's on its way to becoming one of the world's most influential broadcasting systems.

Global market regulations

Depending on the market, advertising regulations can impose limitations on the kinds of data that can be collected from consumers, the types of message appeals used, languages and talent, and national symbols and taxes. Some promotional tactics like couponing and loyalty rewards programs may also be restricted or regulated, which directly affects the hospitality and tourism industries.

Global advertising agencies

Entertainment promotions can be directed by a global agency, an international affiliate, or a local agency. The big four global agency groups, Omnicom, Interpublic, WPP, and Publicis, have each assembled a network of diverse service providers to deliver global brand promotions. International affiliates in foreign markets provide local market expertise. Managed by foreign nationals, affiliates provide knowledge about local markets and help avoid resistance to foreign ownership. Local agencies have well-established contacts for market information, production, and media buying. They are knowledgeable about competitive brands, culture, and conditions in a particular market.

Advertising agency affiliations

The top two global corporations, Omnicom and Interpublic, have acquired the largest advertising agencies.

OMNICOM GROUP	INTERPUBLIC GROUP
BBDO Worldwide	Foote, Cone & Belding Worldwide
DDB Worldwide Communications	Deutsch International
TBWA Worldwide	McCann-Erickson Worldwide

A CLOSER LOOK AT TRAVEL CAMPAIGNS

Grey's Asian Office Delivers
Client: Incredible India

The Challenge: Craft an India experience for premium tourists. Most travelers to India are backpackers and know India as a land of elephants and the home of the Taj Mahal. The objective was to give India a brand—as a place for physical and mental rejuvenation, cultural enrichment, and spiritual evaluation within a modern infrastructure.

India has incredible diversity; 27 different languages and people who look different in every region. That's why the experience could be promoted as 'incredible.' Color is unique to India—it is always brighter and more vibrant than the rest of the world that has predominantly grey hues. Color is primary in the campaign's delivery.

The Campaign Objective: Increase the India share in the tourism market from 3% to 4% and increase tourism spending.

The Strategy: Promote India as a cure for twenty-first century stress.

Promotion Mix:

- *Website:* Featured colorful traditional Indian costumes, festivals, and attractions with 18 microsites. See versions of their video spots on www.youtube.com/user/india.

- *Global TV commercials:* are directed at different traveler segments.

- *Outdoor advertising:* Bus wrap in Beijing, China; Mega skyscraper ad in Dubai.

- *Trade Shows:* Booths in Germany, Thailand, and other nations where shows were held.

- *Festivals:* Indian food festivals in Ankara, Turkey; Road Shows in Muscat and Bahrain, Dubai.

Results: Go to http://incredibleindiacampaign.com/ to view the campaign images

Best campaign award from National Tourism Council; individual traveler expenditures next largest to U.S. Arab travelers voted India as their favorite destination. Recognizable brand Incredible India using an exclamation mark in place of the I in the campaign slogan. Increased web destinations from 400 in 2002 to 1,600 destinations by 2008.

Sources: Naresh Gupta, Grey Advertising SE Asia region; www.incredibleindia.org/emailers/
Newsletter%20April%20May%2009.pdf

What do you think?

1. For a new campaign, on which of India's attributes should Grey focus to differentiate its brand from other country travel brands?

Global logics

The entertainment industry faces global logics in the form of competition, industry, size, and regulations that must guide marketing decisions. Here are some details.[ii]

- *Competitor logic*—The entertainment industry consistently encounters many of the same competitors, resulting in a chess-game activity with the world as its game board. A country-by-country position is called for when marketing live performances, parks, and destination locations.

- *Industry logic*—Transferring an experience from one country to another means taking key entertainment industry success factors and applying them across the globe.

- *Size logic*—*Critical mass* can be achieved in global markets to drive profitability. In the motion picture industry, for instance, foreign sales are the only way to achieve profitability.

- *Regulatory logic*—Government can significantly affect global marketing strategies. In several entertainment industries, recent trends toward deregulation have opened up markets to foreign competitors and encouraged globalization. The telecommunications industry has been most affected by recent deregulatory activity that has given them access to many new markets.

Global logic patterns are rarely symmetrical, and it is important to understand the global logic that dominates your particular entertainment problem. For each global logic force, a situational marketing strategy can be adopted.

Campaign scope and branding

Universal expectations for entertainment and travel enable experience marketers to globalize their messages and their promotions across borders and cultures more easily than marketers of products. Entertainment brand campaigns can be globalized to take advantage of cost savings and creative strategies. Conditions that support globalized campaigns include:

+ Global communications—worldwide cable and satellite networks and the Internet

+ Global youth market with commonalities of travel norms and entertainment values

+ Universal demographic and lifestyle trends

+ Americanization of entertainment content

Branding plays a subordinate role in promoting specific performance genres, film titles, or television programs because global audiences seek experiences that are not brand-dependent. Conversely, destination, venue, theme park, and resort promotions must focus on branding to entice global travelers and local visitors, and to develop brand loyalty.

Finally

Campaign development is essential for marketers of entertainment experiences. But unlike flashy, original brand and product campaigns, entertainment advertising most often relies on editing produced content rather than original material. Nonetheless, research into audience needs, wants, and attitudes drives campaign messages and delivery systems. Whether global or locally focused, entertainment campaign planning requires an in-depth understanding of media, advertising, and consumer behavior.

GOT IT?

+ Data gathered from quantitative and qualitative research ground campaign planning activities; syndicated services provide national research data by subscription.

+ The marketing problem helps determine the campaign's overall objective; marketing, advertising, media and promotional objectives drive the campaign budget.

+ A situation analysis involves gathering corporate and industry data as well as determining the social, economic, technical, political, and legal environments in which the campaign is situated.

+ A SWOT analysis acts as an accounting of the brand's marketplace equity.

+ Campaign evaluation is the key to understanding how well objectives are achieved.

+ Universal demographics and lifestyles, as well as the Americanization of entertainment content, facilitate the use of globalized campaigns.

NOW TRY THIS

1. Log on to the Web site of Japanese agency Dentsu (www.dentsu.com) and note the specific services the firm offers its clients. Would you characterize Dentsu as a local, national, or global agency? Why?

2. Find examples of successful entertainment brand campaigns (films, theme parks) and see if you can identify the overall campaign objective. What media were used to deliver the campaign's main message?

3. Go online to www.studio2B.org. How does the activity on this site reflect the teen demographic? What can marketers learn about message delivery to teens from this site?

4. Peruse www.pc.joystiq.com and read about how the Internet fuses marketing with entertainment opportunities. What ideas can you suggest for testing a theme park ride in Second Life's virtual universe?

QUESTIONS FOR DISCUSSION AND REVIEW

1. What are the major differences between marketing and communication objectives? Which are more important for promotional message delivery?

2. Name the elements of the situation analysis and give an example of how each element influences the final form of an entertainment campaign.

3. What forms of evaluation are important for determining the success or failure of a campaign for a destination such as Australia?

4. If you were creating a global campaign for Six Flags Parks, what emphasis would you put on newspapers in executing your strategy? What factors complicate their value for achieving broad market coverage?

5. What factors make consumers around the world similar to one another? What factors create diversity among consumers in different countries?

MORE STUFF ON DEVELOPING INTEGRATED ENTERTAINMENT CAMPAIGNS

www.pbs.org/mediashift/2009/10/8-tips-to-make-sponsored-tweets-work289.html How to promote a brand using Twitter.

Shay Sayre (2005), *Campaign Planner for Integrated Brand Communications*, 3rd ed. Thompson/South-Western.

[i] All PBS information retrieved from pbs.org in November, 2005.
[ii] From Jeannet Hennessey (2001), *Global Marketing Strategies*, 5th ed. Houghton Mifflin, Chapter 7.

Chapter 6

UNDERSTANDING ENTERTAINMENT AUDIENCES

> *He always hurries to the main event and whisks*
> *his audience into the middle of things*
> *as though they already knew.*
>
> Horace

Chapter Objectives

After reading this chapter, you will be able to answer the following questions:

+ Who is the *entertainment audience* and how are they motivated?

+ What *attitudes* do audiences hold toward entertainment?

+ How do *involvement levels* impact entertainment purchases and how are they measured?

+ Why are audience *perceptions and satisfactions* important for planning a campaign?

+ What are *fan subcultures* and why are they profitable niche markets?

+ What factors distinguish fan subcultures from *cults*?

Before planning a campaign, promoters must research, analyze, and understand members of entertainment audiences. Campaigns are directed at specific target audiences, members of groups, who are potential entertainment consumers. By understanding the motives that drive their purchase decisions, promoters can direct messages to that audience that create behavior changes.

Without audiences, there would be no entertainment industry. Every performance, game, destination, and venue is dependent upon the people who patronize these activities and places. To successfully promote entertainment, we must understand the needs and motivations of our audiences, spectators, and fans. This chapter is devoted to describing audiences, presenting their motivations, and determining their level of involvement. Only through an understanding of what brings people to an activity or place and why they come back can we effectively market to them.

WHO'S IN THE AUDIENCE

We think of entertainment audiences as *people who come together in one place to give attention to live performance, gaming, or viewing a spectacle.* Audiences have been characterized from a variety of perspectives according to where they watch, what they watch, and with whom they watch. Venues, programming or content format, and membership all determine how groups form.

For instance, concert goers may attend every event at the new Disney Performance Center simply because they enjoy the enthralling environment of the building. Or, the most recent Cirque du Soleil performance may attract those who appreciate acrobatic innovation. Some people attend an event for social reasons connected with business, others because in some way it is the "place to be seen," while still others enjoy going with a group of fellow season ticket holders.

Audience formation is most often characterized in terms of mass media—people who watch a particular form of mediated entertainment. Audiences of mass media are important primarily because media institutions are in the business of delivering audiences to advertisers through the vehicle of *ratings*. Entertainment marketers, however, are also interested in delivering and promoting experiences to groups of live entertainment consumers, and this involves *generating box office revenues* rather than delivering high ratings. (For our purposes, we exclude sport audiences from our discussion because they are covered extensively in other books.[i])

Unlike a media audience, whose members are masses of viewers dispersed across a multitude of settings, participants in a live entertainment audience are commonly associated with a particular venue or location where the entertainment takes place. The audience is a consumption community, and marketers are focused on the revenue that can be generated from members' attendance. Increasingly, the dominant meaning of the term *audience* has practical significance and clear market value.

Audience members form groups because of a merging of common interests. Rather than being defined traditionally according to their socio-economic background, new audiences function as *taste cultures*. **Taste cultures** are dependent upon entertainment products—outcomes of form, style, presentation, or genre that match the lifestyle of an audience segment. Rap music can be called a taste culture, gaining its identity from the music, fashion, and lifestyle of the genre. Within every taste culture, three types of audiences predominate. They are labeled as spectators, participants, and fans.

Passive audience members as *spectators* are caught up on the awe of performance, a temporary but not deeply involving activity. Spectators at an orchestral concert applaud and perhaps involve themselves in the performance ritual of attendance, but their interaction with the performance's content and the performers remains minimal.

Active audience members as *participants* represent a group likely to be playful or personally committed in one way or another to the entertainment activity. Members actively engage in the activity (blackjack players in a casino), performance (as actors in an interactive play such as *Tony and Tina Get Married*), or spectacle (dancers in the rituals of the Burning Man Festival). These active audience members are also characterized by what they do during an experience. Participant labels include: *attendee* (of a concert), *visitor* (to a museum, national park), *shopper* (buying at a themed mall), and *guest* (staying at a themed hotel), which are synonyms for audience members that marketers encounter.

Members of the most active audiences in various taste cultures are categorized as *fans*; fans enthusiastically support particular music or genre sub-cultures, as described in detail later in the chapter. Because of their brand loyalty, fans are a highly sought-after target market.

Audience and identity

A person's self-concept is his or her perception of identity. Crucial for gaining a sense of self are role models, material objects (i.e., collections) and one's own ideas, beliefs and values. Psychologists recognize both the *I-self*, who is the information processor, and the *me-self*, who is the person we see in the mirror. For the I-self, one's own decisions are preeminent; for the me-self, the opinions of others are most important. Collections, objects, and physical things to which we are attached are considered to be part of the self that Russell Belk calls the *extended self*.[ii] For instance, in the U.S., women see their bodies as more important for their identities than bodies are to men's sense of identity. Audiences may construct their identity from all these forms of self, and marketers' understanding of each part is essential for effective communications.

Identity construction is about projecting a sense of one's self through an engagement that draws the attention of others.[iii] In other words, it is the process of making oneself known. Using a model known as the *spectacle/performance paradigm*, Abercrombie and Longhurst advocate a notion of identity in which being a member of an audience is intimately bound up with a construction of the person.[iv] If this sounds difficult, the simplest way to phrase this idea is,

"You are what you attend." Critical to the meaning of audience membership is the concept of *performance*, which is an interactive relationship developed between performer and audience. According to these authors, performance occurs at four levels of audience types: *simple, mass, diffused,* and *postmodern.* All levels have significance for marketers because they provide insight into purchase motivations.

Simple audiences

Marketing to simple audiences is usually accomplished locally through a particular venue or location. **Simple audience** members attend concerts, plays, festivals, carnivals, sports, and religious events; all of these events are live and most have a substantial ceremonial quality about them. *Ceremony* implies a certain physical and social distance between performers and audiences. *Convention* demands high attention and a condensed experience from simple audiences who congregate in specialized venues. Identity levels vary for this group, whose members are our primary entertainment consumers.

Mass audiences

Marketing to mass audiences involves a mediated advertising strategy. Unlike simple audiences, **mass audiences** are invisible because they are entertained at home or in movie houses. Events aimed at mass audiences do not involve special venues and deal with indirect communication with less ceremony and little performance interaction. Attention for mass audiences is low, as they move in and out of attention. Because we are a media-saturated society, we cannot help being part of the constant presence of mass communication.

Diffused audiences

Marketers to this group must embrace the notion that everyone is an audience all the time. **Diffused audiences** are a factor of our "performative society where human transactions are complexly structured through the growing use of performative modes and frames".[v] This means that people involved in everyday events come to see themselves as performers—as tourists, for instance, as we view spectacles, others view us as spectacles. (Don't you notice other people photographing the same monuments and streetscapes at which you are clicking away?) So in this sense, we constantly play a role and all social life is considered performance. Shakespeare said it first in *As You Like It*: "All

© Kim Ludbrook/epa/Corbis

6.1 Postmodern Burning Man festival in Arizona combines ancient ritual with modern rave.

the world is a stage and all the men and women merely players". The diffused audience becomes an imagined community, bounded only by the common role of performers in an imaginary life play.

Postmodern audiences

Many of today's audience members identify with a *postmodern self*, a concept of identity that is continuously in flux.[vi] Postmodernism is the confluence of past and present, new and old in the context of mass media and advanced technology. Take a look at the buildings of Frank Gehry, an architect whose post-modern style mixes materials and combines structures from the Renaissance and from outer space, to get a better understanding of the postmodern condition. With regard to marketing, a postmodern self allows each consumer to construct his or her own identity from a catalog of cultural options. Marketers must match today's technologically savvy, post-modern audience with a variety of technologically savvy, post-modern marketing strategies!

Characteristic of postmodern entertainment are role-playing games and activities, such as participating in computer-generated games, Renaissance Fairs, or an annual rendezvous of Mountain Men. An entertainment culture provides many opportunities to experiment with personal identity; tours of national monuments, participation in community festivals, or attending ethnic or national holidays can all serve this end. Postmodern audience members know they can select from a variety of (at least temporarily) identity-constructing options. As such, they allow marketers the flexibility of promotional diversity.

Marketers prefer simple and postmodern audiences because they provide significant sources of revenue. We should not, however, factor out the competitive role of media for getting the attention of audiences as global consumers of entertainment. And in spite of the prevalence of an entertainment economy, the plethora of competing entertainment options requires marketers to motivate consumer purchases of their experiences over those of the competition.

WHAT MOTIVATES AUDIENCES?

The foundation of any entertainment marketing effort is an understanding why audiences attend entertainment events. Motives are reasons for carrying out a particular behavior; consumers are motivated by a desire to satisfy their needs. While there are many definitions of need, marketers define need as a *perceived lack*. Merely lacking something does not create a need, but a consumer's realization that he or she lacks something means that the need is acknowledged. Once people feel the unease produced by an unfilled need, a series of events take place in the consumer's mind; the theory has it that these events lead to purchases that fulfill the needs. Needs are classified as either *utilitarian*, which are functional needs such as relaxation, and *hedonic needs*, which involve the pleasing and aesthetic aspects of experience. A common utilitarian entertainment need might be stress relief; the hedonic entertainment need is most often enjoyment.

A *want* is a specific satisfier for a need. We might need to relax but we want to attend a concert so we can relax. Motivation is the force that makes a person respond to a need. Audience purchase motivations, while similar to other types of consumer purchase motivations, have special applications to entertainment consumption. Here we discuss both emotional and physical motivators that are performance purchase determinants.

The psychology of motivation

Everybody has needs. Recognizing this fact, psychologist Abraham Maslow developed a model that illustrates how people progress from physiological necessities to objects of desire to satisfy their self-esteem. Promoters use this pyramid-shaped model, called Maslow's Hierarchy of Needs, to understand purchase motivation that is driven by a particular need at a particular time.

Maslow identified consumer-driven needs as physiological, safety, social, esteem, and self-actualization. The first four needs are "deficit-driven," meaning they must be fulfilled before going on to the next level. Entertainment experiences fulfill social needs through group activity,

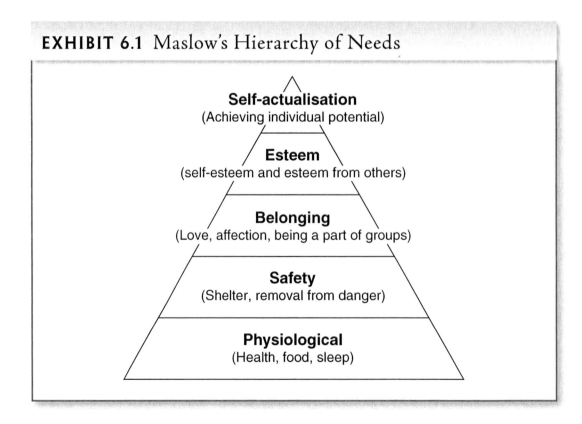

EXHIBIT 6.1 Maslow's Hierarchy of Needs

Self-actualisation
(Achieving individual potential)

Esteem
(self-esteem and esteem from others)

Belonging
(Love, affection, being a part of groups)

Safety
(Shelter, removal from danger)

Physiological
(Health, food, sleep)

and fulfill esteem needs by providing special experiences to reward loyal patrons. The final need, self-actualization, is a level of maturity at which a person is beyond striving for basic needs and can "be all they can be." Self-actualized audience members represent an important market for performing arts attendance because of their philanthropic utility—they donate money.

Two motives specifically are associated with purchasing entertainment experiences: diversion and stress relief.

+ *Diversion* is accomplished by getting away from work or the drudgery of everyday life. Diversion happens when people attend special events, visit parks and amusements, or travel.

+ *Stress relief* comes from letting go of pressures through relaxation and use of leisure time for sensory pleasures.

Adapting Maslow's hierarchy to suit promotional purposes, entertainment marketers have identified significant emotion-based audience motivations: achievement, power, novelty, affiliation, and self-esteem.

+ *Achievement* is one of the most studied motivations. Defined as the drive to experience emotion in connection with evaluated performance,[vii] achievement can be individually oriented or socially oriented, where the goal is to meet the expectations of significant others. Winning at Blackjack may gain praise from family members for the player. Individuals may strive to attend all the concerts of a certain performer to achieve their personal achievement goals.

+ *Power* is defined as the drive to have control or influence over another person, group, or the world at large.[viii] An aspect of this motive—to create excitement—is situation dependent. One method for achieving power is to collect prestigious possessions or symbols of power. A purse from Cher's closet is worn for social status; an autographed photo of Prince is displayed to indicate star proximity.

+ *Novelty* is a motive common to people living in cultures that stress independence and uniqueness. The need to perceive oneself as different from others is strong in Western cultures, and differentiation can be accomplished by experiential participation. Having climbed Mt. Everest or attending an Elton John concert at the Acropolis in Greece are novel experiences that position the participant as unique.

+ *Affiliation* is the drive for association with other people. In order to overcome feelings of detachment that a mediated society often foster, audience members connect with each other through fan communities and groups of people who enjoy similar entertainment activities.

+ *Self-esteem* in this context is the need to maintain a positive image of oneself. High self-esteem occurs through association with popular entertainment genres, attendance at gala events, winning at craps, or navigating a foreign city. Some audience members want to be associated with what's happening, what's hip and what's hot to improve their self-image.

Audience risk and uncertainty

Entertainment consumers must negotiate a balance between risk and uncertainty. Audiences naturally want to minimize risk, which involves not only the possible loss of the ticket price, but also some consequential losses such as physical injury from active participation. Audience members are faced with a greater degree of uncertainty when purchasing entertainment because it is intangible and variable, and there are no guaranteed performance outcomes. A possible response to consumer dissatisfaction with a performance is to refund the price of the ticket. With consequential loss from injury, venues must avoid lawsuits by ensuring that risks are explained beforehand, placing disclaimers in contracts, and carrying liability insurance.

Another risk is audience misunderstanding about the nature of the entertainment content. This risk is understood as *cognitive dissonance*, a theory that involves post-decision regret—having made the wrong choice. After spending $250 on opera tickets, an audience member may question her judgment and feel discomfort about her purchase decision, especially since her partner is not an opera lover and only agreed to accompany her out of kindness. She has two options—vowing never to repeat the choice or seeking out information to confirm the high value of her action (such as "opera offers a new experience to my partner; the critics raved about this performance"). Appropriate advertising and publicity may serve to dissipate such dissonance for audience members, especially as television commercials and reviewer comments.

With regard to developing future audiences for the performing arts, the debate focuses on core audiences, potential audiences, and non-audiences. *Core audiences* are more likely to take risks on attending unproven shows, where as *potential* and *non-audiences* wait for proven stage successes before they make a commitment to attend. Unlike the retail business, the performing arts "product" is not conceived in response to a consumer demand, and therefore enjoys a different relationship with its audience. A full house is not just about the economics—artists need audiences to see their work, and there is a "feel-good" factor for everyone in the venue when shows do well. Audiences loyal to a specific performance or venue may take the risk of attending even if an incoming troupe has received poor reviews.

Venues as physical motivators

Physical motivators are often stimulated by the performance venue itself. Fabulous performing arts centers and museums are being built around the country by corporations interested in revenue enhancements and by cities vying for tourists. Venue attractiveness factors range from location to architecture and aesthetics. Variables such as newness, access, comfort, cleanliness, food, and souvenir offerings determine the venue's popularity. According to research, the more favorable the audience's attitude toward the venue, the higher goes the attendance rate.

Location determinants include the general atmosphere—*entertainmentscape*—of the venue. Audiences want easy access to public transportation, or on-site parking with access situated near freeway ramps. They expect to find adjacent restaurants where they might dine before or after events; and they want safe, friendly environments. Facility aesthetics, both interior and exterior, contribute to a venue's desirability. Architectural distinction enhances attractiveness; interior comfort (seating, layout, lounge areas, access options, décor, lighting, and so on) is vital for satisfaction and enjoyment. Such amenities, while no guarantee of return visits, certainly enhance the prospect of sell-out performances.

Internet audience motivators

Internet users are highly involved with a heavily interactive medium that is not tied to a venue. According to a study of usage motivations for commercial Websites,[ix] five factors motivate audiences to go online: search factor, cognitive factor, uniqueness factor, sociability factor, and entertainment factor. Each is briefly described here.

+ *Search factor*—enjoyment from locating the latest informational updates, shopping sites, and travel/hospitality resources; Google.com and craigslist.org are the most frequently used search sites.

+ *Cognitive factor*—motivation lies in Web-based learning and information seeking; check out adrants.com, for example, to keep up on Madison Avenue's ups and downs.

+ *Uniqueness factor*—a "what's new and exciting" appeal, including new programs and software; paidcontent.org tracks the latest developments for delivering entertainment; endgaget.com is for gadget lovers; Slashdot.org is a favorite blog covering tech issues.

+ *Social factor*—satisfaction through blogging, chat room participation, and even dating; social networks like match.com, Facebook, and Twitter keep users linked together.

+ *Entertainment factor*—fun through games, poker, and movies found online; e-Bay.com bidding is also a source of entertainment for many Web surfers.

Virtual communities are constructed as places for audiences to be "alternative people," or just to feel like they could be someone else for a few hours. Myspace.com, founded in 2003, listed 36 million users after only two years. By 2005, when Rupert Murdock acquired the parent company for $580 million, it was the 4th ranked Web domain in page views worldwide. MySpace, like other social networks, contains all five motivation factors for hours of audience engagement. In 2009, MySpace was second in members only to Facebook. The table below shows the social network rankings by monthly visits as of February 2009.

EXHIBIT 6.2 Social Networks

TOP 25 SOCIAL NETWORKS RE-RANK

(Ranked by Monthly Visits, Jan '09)

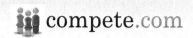

RANK	SITE	UV	MONTHLY VISITS	PREVIOUS RANK
1	facebook.com	68,557,537	1,191,373,339	2
2	myspace.com	58,555,800	810,153,536	1
3	twitter.com	5,979,052	54,218,731	22
4	flixster.com	7,645,423	53,389,974	16
5	linkedin.com	11,274,160	42,744,438	9
6	tagged.com	4,448,915	39,630,927	10
7	classmates.com	17,296,524	35,219,210	3
8	myyearbook.com	3,312,898	33,121,821	4
9	livejournal.com	4,720,720	25,221,354	6
10	imeem.com	9,047,491	22,993,608	13
11	reunion.com	13,704,990	20,278,100	11
12	ning.com	5,673,549	19,511,682	23
13	blackplanet.com	1,530,329	10,173,342	7
14	bebo.com	2,997,929	9,849,137	5
15	hi5.com	2,398,323	9,416,265	8
16	yuku.com	1,317,551	9,358,966	21
17	cafemom.com	1,647,336	8,586,261	19
18	friendster.com	1,568,439	7,279,050	14

19	xanga.com	1,831,376	7,009,577	20
20	360.yahoo.com	1,499,057	5,199,702	12
21	orkut.com	494,464	5,081,235	15
22	urbanchat.com	329,041	2,961,250	24
23	fubar.com	452,090	2,170,135	17
24	asiantown.net	81,245	1,118,245	25
25	tickle.com	96,155	109,492	18

WHAT'S INSIDE THE AUDIENCE?

Once we understand audience needs and purchase motivations, we must address another important strategic level of audience behavior—members' attitudes toward the entertainment experience. Audience attitudes are functions of the purchase process: they can be formed, changed, and measured.

Forming and changing audience attitudes

Attitudes are evaluations of a performance, venue or activity that express some degree of favor or disfavor; attitudes are context dependent. Motivations to attend performances are often the result of a positive attitude toward an entertainment genre. For instance, asked whether or not you enjoyed your trip to Disneyland, you might include a variety of aspects in your answer. Your enjoyment might be season-based, or it may depend upon the people who joined you. Enjoyment-based feelings are nested within both cultural and social contexts.

According to the functional theory of attitudes,[x] five factors contribute to forming opinions about entertainment: knowledge about the activity, usefulness of attending, personal values, ego, and social adjustment. Attitudes help us organize and simplify experiences, help us act in our own self interest, provide a way to express personal values, provide defense against threats to self-concept, and facilitate social relationships.

Of the many theories about attitudes, the *theory of planned behavior* is most applicable to understanding entertainment audiences. This theory recognizes that an audience member's perception of how easy or difficult it is to attend a performance, visit a venue, or engage in an activity underlies his or her motivation to attend. Because many entertainment decisions are made impulsively, it is important for marketers to develop a positive attitude among consumers about the ease of attending an experience or performance.

Audience members use simple strategies for making decisions about attending: strategies of brand preference (for the place, performer, or program), genre familiarity (the more one knows about opera the more likely one will attend), country of origin (cultural and geographic derivation of the performance), and price-related considerations (cost of attending). Before deciding about the value of an event, audience members anchor their judgments on an initial impression then adjust their attitudes with additional information. Entertainment consumers collect information and weigh the alternatives before making an attendance decision. The ultimate decision is based on the largest net benefit in terms of the exchange resources at issue—what they get for their money. The more expensive the ticket price, the stronger the attempt to select an option they are least likely to regret. Will they be sorry they paid $125 for a seat in the balcony to attend a symphony? Or will the overall experience be well worth it?

Marketing message content is important for forming or changing audience attitudes. Information is key to audience understanding, and providing a strong knowledge base allows consumers to form positive attitudes about attending performances. Only after creating favorable attitudes or changing negatives to positives among consumers can entertainment marketers expect to deliver effective motivational messages. The more we educate audiences, the more they will understand; understanding yields positive attitudes; the more positive the attitude, the more likely they are to buy tickets.

Audiences as consumers

Audiences consume entertainment experiences. In the entertainment buying process, three basic functions occur: buying, paying, and consuming. The *buyer* makes the ticket purchase, the *payer* finances it, and the *consumer* is the one who has the experience; sometimes one person fulfills multiple roles. By understanding the allocation of these roles, marketers can create different buying/paying/consuming scenarios. Exhibit 5.2 presents examples of the possible relationships between participants in the buying process.

Audience buying roles

The implication of these roles suggests that the buyer's decisions appear to be related to when he or she is reimbursed, both to the degree to which the buyer takes into consideration the payer's preferences versus his or her own preferences, and to situational variables such as the system of reimbursement.

Here is a sample scenario: suppose a teenager wants to take his grandmother to a *Lion King* performance for her birthday. If the parents are paying for the tickets but not buying them or attending, the teenager will probably select seats in the orchestra section without regard to price. If the parents are both buyers and payers, they may select the mezzanine for grandma because she might have a better view from above. On the other hand, if the teenager were buying, paying, and attending the performance, he or she may opt for the cheapest balcony seats. You can see marketers care who buys, who pays, and who goes. Each function requires a different marketing message to motivate a decision.

EXHIBIT 6.3 Audience Buying Roles

DIFFERENTIATION OF FUNCTION	BUYER'S ROLE	PAYER'S ROLE	CONSUMER'S ROLE
All three held by same person	←————————————individual buyer————————————→		
Each of the 3 held by specific person	teenager	parent	grandparent
One person is payer and buyer. Another is consumer	• family buyer • gift purchaser ←————— • intermediate purchaser ————→ • host		• family consumers • gift receiver • invited guest
One person is buyer & consumer; other is payer	• buyer-consummer of free or paid services • invited person	• supplier of free services • reimburser • host	• buyer-consumer • invited person
One person buyer; other is payer and consumer	mandated	←————————mandatory————————→	

Source: Bon & Press, in Lambkin, Foxall, Van Raaif & Hielbrunn (eds), *European Perspectives on Consumer Behavior,* 1998, p.120

This approach is useful for a segmented marketing approach and has applications for various venues, activities, and travel destinations where buying, paying, and consuming roles are not always carried out by the same person.

Tying in audience research

Although research is covered in depth in Chapter 6, here we address it as it relates to understanding audience identification, needs, wants, and satisfactions. Three challenges drive efforts to develop reliable audience research:

1. *Closing the gap between what people say they do and what they do in practice* To eliminate the do/say gap, researchers have developed ethnographic techniques to understand behavior using audience stories. Ethnographers use observations and in-depth interviews to gather data for comparison between members and across segments. Marketers have used the

shopping stories of head-of-household women to focus communication messages on the concerns and problems articulated in the stories.

2. *Interpreting the relationship between the experience and an audience member—i.e., examining the process as it relates to various forms of media and genre* Variations in audience experiences have led to segmenting audiences for purposes of addressing specific needs through marketing communication. In addition, audience research has grappled with questions of demography—the distribution of meanings and practices across a diverse population. For instance, we try to answer the question, "How do various audience segments react to performance conversions?" One example would be adapting "Phantom of the Opera" stage play to a film. Different groups will have different reactions to the same question. Hence, how people feel before, during, and after a performance reveals their symbolic, emotional, and cognitive engagement with the experience.

3. *Determining the effects of entertainment/media upon audiences* Although effects research (media's impact) has never proven a connection between content and behavior, researchers continue to probe the relationship between entertainment content and audience actions. The impact of advertising on young children is a hot topic in effects research and will ultimately determine what promotional messages can be delivered to children within the context of programming to that segment.

Laddering technique

An effective method for developing motivational communication messages is through a research technique called **laddering**. Entertainment audiences buy experiences for various reasons; laddering provides a means of digging beneath the surface to uncover layers of consumer meanings that reveal audience motivations for purchasing those experiences.

A researcher begins by posing a question to an entertainment consumer, such as: "Assume you wanted to surprise a friend with tickets to a musical performance. What factors do you consider when you are deciding what concert to attend?" During this part of the interview, the respondent narrows

Image courtesy of WestGroup Research, Phoenix, AZ. Used with permission

6.2 Focus group facility houses clients and participants in entertainment research.

down the list of important factors to the two that are considered most important. This is where the laddering process begins as the interviewer keeps asking *Why?* (Why is that important; what does the factor give you? Why? Why? Why?) until the informant exhausts his or her ability to respond further. Hopefully, this process will yield a particular value (e.g., affiliation, status, excitement, or convenience) that is important to audience members for making the decision about which concert tickets to purchase. By using a small sample of respondents, researchers can draw out important values that can direct marketing strategy development. If a senior segment values convenience when attending concerts, for instance, messages must emphasize adjacent restaurants and on-site parking. A successful laddering interview will identify major points for developing effective communication vehicle content.

Research always forms the basis for making marketing decisions. Theme park managers, for instance, commission research on a continuing basis in order to understand engagement levels and to sustain close relationships with visitors. Each year, Disney park management conducts over 200 different external surveys and dozens of focus groups to track satisfaction and demographic profiles of its visitors. When its research revealed high levels of frustration with long lines, Disney initiated and marketed the FastPass, which permits visitors to bypass lines at rides and attractions.

KEYS TO AUDIENCE INVOLVEMENT AND PARTICIPATION

Motivation for consumers of entertainment is designed to foster an involved and participatory experience. When personal needs, values, or self-concept are stimulated in a positive way, consumer involvement is activated. Products, brands, ads, media, and activities are all objects of consumer involvement. Participation levels are useful for developing appropriate marketing messages.

Characterizing by involvement levels

Audience involvement in selecting entertainment choices can be cognitive (thinking), affective (feeling), enduring (long-term), or situational (time-specific). All three aspects of involvement help consuming audiences make decisions about entertainment brand, product, and activity consumption. Marketers distinguish entertainment purchases by their level of involvement.

Low involvement audience members

Low involvement purchases involve a small financial commitment and have an insignificant consequential outcome for making the wrong choice. If a listener pays a $15 cover charge to hear a jazz group that turns out to be unsatisfactory, the listener has not compromised a great deal of money or time for the bad decision. Decisions at the movie or a cover charge level are low-involvement, easily made decisions.

High involvement audience members

High involvement purchases require higher levels of decision-making and financial commitment. A $200 opera ticket or a $10,000 trip to Africa are considered high involvement expenditures that involve informational sources for comparing options before making a decision. Here, consumers spend considerable time researching options prior to making their final purchasing commitment. With entertainment, consumers purchase experience through admission costs or ticket prices, and depend upon reviews, buzz, and ratings to help evaluate the alternatives. Purchasing entertainment experiences involves substantial financial and emotional involvement for audience members, which can be characterized around loyalty toward a brand or genre. Four highly involved audience groups are: loyalists, information seekers, routine buyers, and brand switchers.

- *Loyalists* are music fans who try to always attend concerts by specific artists, or travelers who regularly patronize a particular airline or hotel brand, or theme park attendees who subscribe to season passes. They are a prime marketing segment in every experiential brand and genre category.

- *Information seekers* love a particular genre, say jazz, but are not loyal to a specific jazz artist or jazz band. This niche segment is ideal for targeting genre-specific marketing messages.

- *Routine buyers* don't necessarily attend every genre-specific performance, say popular music, but are very likely to attend concerts by a favorite artist, such as Elton John. Performer-based brand marketing works well with this segment.

- *Brand switchers* attend whatever their mood dictates—genre and brand are insignificant for determining their choices. This group is the hardest to identify and target—price promotions are useful motivational tactics here.

As a marketer, you must consider involvement levels when developing marketing objectives, in order to craft an appropriate message for each group. By targeting audiences based more on involvement levels than on usage, entertainment marketers are better able to understand consumer motivations.

Audience involvement scale

High Visibility, a book dedicated to celebrity marketing, identifies eight levels of audience involvement.[xi] We will discuss these briefly for their relevance to understanding how audiences identify and bond with famous people in every experiential genre.

- *Invisible* consumers confine their interest in celebrities to locally prominent folks, such as a popular minister or city council member.

- *Watchers* have a passive celebrity consumption pattern—they observe but don't chase famous people.

- *Seekers* are more likely to want more intentional contact with celebrities by attending performances. The largest group, seekers spend the most money, so they are the most desirable audience for the celebrity industry.

- *Collectors* attend events and purchase souvenirs and memorabilia.

- *Fans* are distinguished by their need for interaction with celebrity.

- *Insiders* are groupies who seek to achieve the ultimate form of identification by becoming their friends.

- *Entourage* members are those who move inside celebrity circles; they have authorized positions in their support systems. Team doctors and star lawyers are among the entourage group; some have a special connection by virtue of their social or professional status.

- *Ensnared* members have the most intense relationship with celebrities and have the potential to become obsessed and lack discretion.

Participation levels and marketing messages

Three involvement levels help marketers understand entertainment consumption and in turn determine appropriate message strategies. Audiences are labeled as passive spectators, focused experiencers or absorbed experiencers. For each level, we determine which message strategy is the most appropriate for use in marketing communication. Message strategies determine whether communication is developed to educate, to promote, or to inform. By understanding audience participation segments, marketers get clues to audience dispositions or reasons for being part of an audience so they may craft effective messages. Message development and strategies are expanded upon in Chapter 10.

Passive spectators

Watching and listening are visual and auditory activities that routinely accompany audience participation. Because they have become routine, however, these senses often dull the level of active involvement in an entertainment activity. Passive audience members are merely receptors, having minimal focus on and identification with the activity they are experiencing. This barely there syndrome characterizes *passive spectators*. These folks occupy seats at a play but forget the plot a week later. They ride a ferris wheel but upon reflection, cannot distinguish one amusement park from another. They are present at concerts but their thoughts are elsewhere. Passive spectators attend because someone takes them along, or because they have free tickets, or perhaps because they are duty-bound to show up. They are light users of entertainment products.

For these folks, the *message strategy must educate*. Information about a play's creator, the nuances of a particular park, and the uniqueness of a musical genre contribute to enjoyment. By providing knowledge, marketers produce a more informed audience. Opera performances have become more user friendly by presenting crawling translations (subtitles); pre-concert lectures by a conductor enable first-time concert-goers to get acquainted with composers and their music. Informational messages must occupy advertising copy and promotional materials directed at passive audiences.

6.3 Passive spectators or active audience?

The objective is to convert passive spectators to active audiences through a continuing message strategy of education. Studies have shown that children growing up with parents who patronize the arts, or who were introduced to the arts as part of their elementary education, are much more likely to attend performances as adults than people who had no previous contact with the arts. For people who have not been introduced to the arts as children, marketers must provide information and promotional opportunities for developing appreciation for a particular entertainment genre.

Focused experiencers

The more audiences understand what is being performed, the more likely they are to engage in cheering, applauding, and standing ovations during and after a performance. We call members of this educated audience *focused experiencers* for their active attention to the performance. This group is composed of knowledgeable, appreciative entertainment consumers who attend because they enjoy performance. They engage themselves in the moment, they purchase souvenirs, and they help create a buzz around the activity or experience. Consumption levels range from moderate to heavy usage of entertainment activities.

Members of this segment can be loyal to the genre, to the brand, or to the venue—maybe even all three. But they are discriminating, and they consider their choices carefully; brand switching is common. They operate within a specific budget, plan ahead, and actively seek out activities they want to attend. In a study undertaken to determine how men and women select their entertainment options within a specific budget, researchers learned that women select for their families or partners, while men choose activities for themselves, stretching their entertainment budget to include a variety of options.[xii] Gender-based marketing is used to connect specific entertainment genres with their most likely purchasers.

The *message strategy for this group is promotional.* Communications must contain critical reviews, audience testimonials, and bold assertions that attract the attention of potential audiences. Although they are actively engaged once they arrived, getting focused experiencers to reserve tickets requires a competitive approach to marketing. Incentives can be used for this segment as well, adding an additional reason to select your entertainment over someone else's offering.

Absorbed identifiers

When entertainment consumers pose a high level of identification with a particular group, genre, place, or activity, they are members of the group labeled *absorbed identifiers*. Their motivation for attending is self-evident—identity by association. They not only love what they do, they actively engage in the activity and often join in the production of that activity.

Brand loyalty is common among this segment. They follow a specific band or type of music, get season passes to parks, have memberships at museums, hold subscription to performance seasons, fly the same airline, or stay in the same casino repeatedly. They respond to loyalty programs designed to reward patronage, and can be counted on to devote a significant amount of time and financial resources to their entertainment passion. We consider them heavy users of entertainment.

Absorbed identifiers are experts when it comes to knowing about their passion. They subscribe to related publications, may join an online community, and often provide word-of-mouth promotion for their favorite events and performers. They enjoy being part of performances at a greater level than simple applause—they immerse themselves in the event to the greatest extent possible for an audience member.

Message strategy for this group is informational; communication should be frequent and special. They should receive advance notices of performances, get special subscription rates, enjoy restricted lounge areas, and benefit from complementary services. This segment of revenue-generating consumers is the bread and butter of the entertainment industry, and they must be treated accordingly. Our marketing objective is to keep these consumers attending, playing, or participating. Members of this segment often become avid fans, and as such slip into another dimension of active consumption. By way of summary, refer to Exhibit 6.4 for a comparison of involvement group characteristics.

EXHIBIT 6.4 Audience Participation Groups

AUDIENCE INVOLVEMENT CHARACTERISTICS					
GROUP	LOYALTY	INVOLVEMENT	USAGE	ACTION	MESSAGE
Passive Spectators	none	low	light	convert to active	educational
Focused Experiencers	med. to high	moderate to heavy	med.	reserve tickets	promotional
Absorbed Identifiers	loyal	high	heavy	keep attending	informational

In the exhibit above, actions are what promotions are designed to achieve with specific message strategies.

+ An *educational strategy* is designed to convert passive audiences to active ones by providing new and relevant information they care about.

+ A *promotional strategy* is created to convince audience members to reserve or purchase tickets and often includes incentives.

+ An *informational strategy* is intended to persuade loyal patrons to keep attending performances by providing a schedule.

Consumer experience model

To help marketers further understand how audiences experience entertainment, models are often used as a guide for strategy development. [xiii] The consumer experience model uses audience experiences to develop a consumer-oriented marketing strategy. The strategy is built upon two main aspects—perception and satisfaction—and their specific components.

1. A set of perception, judgment, and choice processes used in making a consumption decision has four components:

   + Psychological component of information processing and choice (motivation)

   + Economic component of consumption experience and its evaluation (cost/value)

   + Consumer knowledge component (information)

   + Market information component (promotional message)

2. The consumer's satisfaction with consumption experience itself is its own value.

An audience member's internal knowledge base and external information provided by marketers are combined with consumer perceptions and consumer satisfactions to develop preferences and are important elements of the repurchase cycle. This model is predicated on interaction—what consumers take from the marketplace they also give back in future ticket revenues and favorable recommendations. One's internal knowledge base is important, as the consumption cycle is repeated and audience experience grows.

Consumer perceptions are both analytic and synthetic; information is selected out, then synthesized into a world-picture using elements from memory. Audience perceptions are based on three factors: selectivity, expectations, and past experience.

+ *Selectivity* depends on how much is going on in the environment, and on the person's interest and motivation regarding the entertainment genre. The more entertainment activities available the more selective the consumer becomes.

+ *Expectations* of quality play a huge part of perception; with expectations of high quality or high ticket prices, audience members may select evidence that supports their view and ignore evidence that does not. The more costly the ticket, the higher the audience's expectations.

+ *Past experience* with a venue, destination, or content genre also helps consumers make quality judgments. A favorable experience usually results in repeat behavior, while a negative experience will likely terminate the user's desire to attend again.

An example of one customer experience model is Walt Disney World's *customer orbit*. Disney uses this progression scenario to improve visitor experiences and to identify opportunities for repurchase:[xiv] The consumer orbit is circular and describes a holistic plan for recruiting and retaining park visitors. These steps involve: using marketing to attract visitors and act upon their questions through internet responses to facilitate purchase; making the booking process pleasant and efficient; insuring visitor enjoyment by controlling and monitoring visitor/employee interactions, and encouraging visitor referrals with promotions and discounts for repeat visitors.

The heart of the consumption experience is the visitor's enjoyment of all components of the Disney Parks. Satisfaction measurement systems are used to monitor and improve the customer's experience. The customer orbit relies on market information provided by satisfied visitors to increase opportunities for continuing the repurchase cycle.

Measuring involvement and attitudes

Audience motivational research is accomplished with qualitative methods as just described. Involvement levels of consumption experiences are measured using quantitative techniques. Researchers use semantic differential scales to measure involvement on a continuum; the most common instrument is called the Revised Personal Involvement Inventory (RPII), shown in Exhibit 6.5. Both cognitive (thinking and processing) and emotional items can be measured using a 5-point scale.

Measuring attitudes

Audience enjoyment is a result not only of their involvement but of their attitudes as well. The *theory of reasoned action* says that consumers consciously evaluate the consequences of alternative

DISNEY'S CONSUMER ORBIT

Attract visitor > respond to visitor inquiries > book tickets > track visitors' experiential enjoyment > use promotion to book more tickets > attract visitors

EXHIBIT 6.5 Personal Involvement Inventory

RPII FOR OBTAINING MUSEUM AUDIENCE OPINIONS

Think about the Museum of Modern Art's gift shop and rate your opinions using the following scale:

Cognitive items

Important	____	____	____	____	____	Unimportant
Relevant	____	____	____	____	____	Irrelevant
Means a lot	____	____	____	____	____	Means nothing to me
Valuable	____	____	____	____	____	Worthless
Needed	1	2	3	4	5	Not needed

Emotional items

Interesting	____	____	____	____	____	Uninteresting
Exciting	____	____	____	____	____	Unexciting
Appealing	____	____	____	____	____	Unappealing
Fascinating	____	____	____	____	____	Mundane
Involving	____	____	____	____	____	Not involving
	1	2	3	4	5	

Source: J. Zaichkowsky (1994),"The Personal Involvement Inventory: Reduction, Revision and Application to Advertising," *Journal of Advertising* 23 (4), 59–70

behaviors then choose the one that will lead to the most favorable consequences. The theory assumes that consumers perform a logical evaluation procedure for making decisions about purchasing tickets or attending performances. Measuring attitudes is of interest to marketers, since attitudes play such a major role in consumer purchasing behavior.

Marketers use the Fishbein and Rosenberg models of attitude measurement to develop survey instruments. Rosenberg's model[xv] has two main components: perceived instrumentality and value importance. *Perceived instrumentality* is the capacity of the performance to attain the value in question, i.e., the usefulness of the experience. *Value importance* is the amount of satisfaction derived from attaining a particular value or achieving the expected result from the experience. Taken together, these components are good predictors of behavior that is illustrative of attitude.

The Fishbein model[xvi] focuses on the consumer rather than on the experience. For Fishbein, attitudes can be predicted from beliefs and evaluations; this is not compatible with Rosenberg's model. In Fishbein's view, the consumer's belief in the experience replaces the perceived instrumentality aspect. If we combine the two models, we are able to determine three distinct aspects of attitude:

+ Perceived instrumentality ("I think the Beatles are the most harmonious band ever recorded")

+ Evaluative aspect or affect ("I like harmony")

+ Value importance ("Harmony is very important to me")

Note that the second two are not the same; you can like something without it being very important to you. Marketers prize audiences with high involvement levels and positive attitudes toward entertainment experiences; we know them as fans.

FOCUS ON MEDIA ETHICS

Radio News: When to Use a Person's Name

Roger Levine had just started his senior year at a California University to pursue a career in journalism. In fact, he already had a job lined up after graduation at a major newspaper that he had interned with over the summer. On campus, Roger was involved with KXYZ, the campus radio station, and had become the head of the organization when he was a senior. In spite of the huge responsibility, Roger loved working in radio news. After a month into the school year, Roger perceived that the newspaper was running smoothly. He had developed great rapport with his new staff and, as of yet, he hadn't encountered any major issues.

One Monday morning, as Roger was reviewing the weekend's campus safety report, he got a phone call from his friend John who worked at the university's student newspaper. John told him that on Saturday, a female student reported that a local worker had attempted to rape her. In order to verify the information, Roger called the Police Department and was transferred to the officer covering the case. He told Roger that the report filed by the woman had been called into question.

An hour later, the police officer called Roger and said that officers had determined the report was false – the young woman had made up the story in an attempt to implicate the local worker. Roger wasn't sure what to do with this latest piece of information. He knew that KXYZ had to cover the story, but he didn't know if the female student's name should be used.

Recognizing that the woman obviously made her report as a result of some perceived wrongdoing, Roger also knew that she allegedly committed a crime by making a false report.

Roger faced a lose-lose situation: Running her name would label the female student and embarrass her, but not running the name could be construed as a cover-up.

After discussing the issue with his staff and his faculty advisor, Roger decided that KXYZ would not withhold her name because it would set a poor precedent, so he advised his staff to reveal her identity.

As a dedicated journalist, he felt he couldn't confront these issues on a casual basis where exceptions were easily made against the principle that favored disclosure.

When Roger picked up school paper that week, he saw that it had the same story of the false report, but had chosen not to run the girl's name. Although this caused some questioning in Roger's mind, he still felt he had done the right thing by full disclosure.

Discussion questions:

1. What are the benefits and harms of disclosing the name of the female student?

2. Is there any significant difference between disclosure in a newspaper or on the radio?

3. Do you agree with Roger's decision to disclose the name? Why or why not?

4. Ethically, who took the right course of action—KXYZ or the campus newspaper?

Source: Jessica Silliman, Hackworth Fellow at the Markkula Center; http://www.scu.edu/ethics/dialogue/candc/cases/radionews.html

THE FAN SUBCULTURE

Fans are a marketer's delight because they are the most involved segment of audience members. If, as suggested above, audience membership is closely tied to the construction of personal identity, then fan activity helps us define ourselves. A form of skilled audience, the fan audience is composed of highly prized members of the consuming public. Usually followers of a specific taste culture, fans are avid followers of musical groups, sports teams, celebrities, and mediated genres.

On the extreme end, fans can be pathological in their actions through an intense fantasy relationship with a celebrity figure, or as a frenzied member of a crowd shouting at a rock star or sports team. But more common fans are organized around stars or media images who are heavy users of the genre, and who engage in a variety of socially acceptable communal activities. Enthusiasm, which involves reciprocity and forms of exchange, is almost always linked with fan activity. Fan identity and activity, and cults, are the focus of this section.

© Pedro Nogueira, 2010. Used under license from Shutterstock, Inc.

6.4 Musician signing autographs for a fan.

Fan identity

Recall our discussion of performance and identity at the beginning of the chapter. Unlike many audience members whose identity emanates from the I-self, much of what unites fans is their collective identity—basically a grouping of me-selves. Fans make meanings of social identity and social experience from the resources of the fan cultural commodity—their extended selves.

Madonna fans have dressed like the star, for example, to construct an empowered identity for themselves in their social circles. Such temporary attachments can be ultimately transformed into the star's identity. Fans' identification with "their" star evolves from devotion to adoration to worship, and it focuses on the construction of the star's image. **Images** are mediated constructions resulting from publicity and exposure. This means that the connection between escapism and identification is built with aspiration and inspiration. When the boundary between self and star is less than fully separate, the fan fantasizes about becoming the star and sharing the star's emotions. Here the fan transforms reality into star identification. Pretending in this way can even involve taking on the identity of the star in blatant imitation. At the point of physical transformation that involves copying and imitating, fans become part of a cult community.

Fans who dress in tie-dyed shirts and attend Dead Head concerts are bound together by their symbolic allegiance to the music and culture of this 1960s rock band. Fans such as these have become interpretive communities that are sought after by marketers for their patronage and support. Describing the concept of the musical *scene*, Barry Shank said:

> Spectators become fans, fans become musicians, musicians are always already fans, all constructing the non-objects of identification through their performances as subjects of enunciation—becoming and disseminating the subject-in-process of the signifying practice of rock'n'roll music.[xvii]

Because identity formation and reformation is an important aspect of contemporary life, fan activities may be increasingly important in the consumption of entertainment preferences as a form of identity construction. Where a fan is seen and with whom may determine the nature of entertainment preferences. According to Sartre, identity formation consists of doing, having, and being. Using this model, entertainment-marketing messages directed to fans must emphasize the unique experience of attending entertainment activities (doing), the necessity of buying branded memorabilia (having), and the exaltation of associating with the scene or event (being). By addressing every aspect of fan identity construction, marketers meet the association-based needs of fans and cultists.

Fan activity

Fans are most often the objects of marketing attention; they are ideal consumers because their habits can be highly predicted by the culture industry. Although fans do not know each other or have similar backgrounds or shared demographics, they do share their interest in the object of their "fanship."

Fan activity is an inter-textual affair featuring consumption of both textual materials and media technologies. In other words, fans derive their sense of reality from a variety of printed and electronic media. Fan activity is characterized by:

1. emotional proximity and critical distance in which they act

2. critical and interpretive practices they use

3. consumer activism

4. production of alternative texts (other ways of communicating or producing stories and star encounters or original material based on a person, program, or film)

5. creation of an alternative social community[xviii]

Fans of television science fiction, especially shows such as *Star Trek*, exhibit these traits: Trekkies go to conventions, dress up as Dr. Spock and Captain Kirk, write and perform celestial songs, produce music videos, and gather in virtual fan clubs over the Internet. After the television show was cancelled, *Star Trek* fans demanded and thus stimulated four more television series, ten big screen movies, countless television specials and hundreds of conventions—and all without the Internet! Today, entertainment virtual communities are the water cooler of the new millennium, as evident with the release of *Avatar* in 2010.

Countless forums, Websites, and wikis devoted to all things *Avatar* were created immediately after the *Avatar* movie was released. Enthusiastic fans could visit the "Learn Na'vi" Web site to study the language spoken on the mythical world of Pandora. On sites like "Naviblue," fans discussed their relationship with the film and turned to fan sites like "Avatar Forums" for advice on how to control their *Avatar* nostalgia.

Fueling similar fandoms, the Internet, blogs and social media have allowed sites to spring up more rapidly and effortlessly than ever before. In addition to finding each other faster, media fans are linking up on a global scale. The highest grossing film ever, *Avatar* is an example of fandom as a global phenomenon.

Fan hysteria surrounding *New Moon*, the second installment of *Twilight*, was also a global activity. Twi-hard global fans used Facebook and Twitter to connect with each other prior to the film's release. Fan fiction, archived on FanFiction.net, has produced more than 128,000 stories connected to the vampire legend.

Once situated on the fringe, fan groups are now more public and diverse, enabling just about anyone to become a member of a fan community. Like "Trekkies," the ardent *Star Trek* fans that emerged in the 1960s, fans are looking for a way to deepen their engagement with the fantasy world that became an integral part of their lives.

Virtual communities are symbolic communities that seek out other fans with whom they interact. A social hierarchy of fans exists in every fan community. Moderators of message boards or creators of Websites devoted to the show or celebrity are at the top of the hierarchy. The next level includes the community members who have been around the longest, and then comes the newer members. Such a hierarchy has allowed virtual communities to be analyzed according to the social structures formed by and through their interactions.

Fan sites not only help to establish communities, they also provide sources for fan-based entertainment. Echo Station, a *Star Wars* fan site, sells costumes, art, miniatures and collectibles, games, and books. Fans can watch new episodes and read editorials, interviews, reviews, and convention news; they can work crossword puzzles, send postcards, and enter trivia contests on this fan site.

One element of a fan community is fan appropriation of content and text. Fans are not just consumers but producers as well. They are proactive and they participate in cultural production of Webzines, stories, and other artifacts—they are producers of the very texts they love to consume. Fan communities are ready-made sources for ticket revenues.

According to Stephen Brown, "[Fan commodities] are imbued with evocative patina of the past …. many products, whose life cycles have long since run their course, have been successfully raised from the dead … such are the tie-in products from re-runs of old television series."[xix] Also called "symbolic capital," fan memorabilia has a cognitive foundation that rests upon knowledge and recognition (fame, prestige).[xx]

Collecting is the acquisition of objects and experiences that derive meaning from the act of collecting and the collection itself. One items become part of a collection, they no longer serve their intended function; they become objects of personal significance. For instance, the 152 cookie jars collected by Andy Warhol were not used to store cookies, they were objects of fascination for him; the collection eventually sold for $247,830. There exists a market for media tie-in memorabilia or collectibles—an excellent example of the 'dialectic of value' or fluctuation of worth as things move in and out of the commodity state. eBay offers commodities that should be defined as 'exchange-value' merchandise—stuff with monetary value. But because of the fans' desire to own merchandise that is often no longer being manufactured, they become use-valuations, or stuff that converts to personal worth.[xxi] Elvis memorabilia, for example have become speculative investments as hedges against inflation because they cannot be duplicated. In order to understand the motivations and collecting behavior of fan communities, researchers study these groups as sub-cultures. Sub-cultures exist among musical genre enthusiasts (Strait Edgers), bands (Dead Heads), brand users (Harley Davidson riders), and star worshippers (George Clooney fans). Ethnographic research techniques similar to those used by anthropologists help marketers understand fan sub-cultures so they might tailor appropriate promotional messages to these unique audience segments.

Fan intensity ladder

A tool called a **fan intensity ladder** illustrates the hierarchy of flow from one level of celebrity involvement to another; from there it can be used to develop marketing strategy.[xxii] For instance, TV and radio stations pull their audiences up the ladder with promotions, contests, and reality programming to generate revenue by developing watchers into seekers, collectors, and fans.

Promoters and publicists in the celebrity industry seek to get their celebrities featured in magazines, interviewed on television, chosen as a spokesperson for a cause, or selected to endorse a product in a commercial. They also create celebrity Websites (celebrityalmanac.com, celebrityweb.com, celebritysighting.com) that provide fans with access to the latest information about celebrities' activities, love life, and upcoming appearances.

The cult audience

Cults are advanced subcultures whose highly organized members exhibit explicit attachment to celebrities and stars. According to a talk radio host in San Diego, Michael Jackson fans are cultists "who worship the star—turning fandom into something comparable to idol worship of ancient Egypt. It's almost like he became the new, worldwide god-like pharaoh."[xxiii]

Elvis cult fans attend annual birthday celebrations at Graceland and organize look-alike contests in Las Vegas. Elvis's death shifted his status from being a capitalist-controlled commodity to being a fan-controlled icon; in death he became a truly popular medium—a vehicle through which people tell stories about their past and present day lives.[xxiv]

Cult geographies[xxv] are places of sacredness and "para-spatial" interactions where special meaning is ascribed to a location. When fans valorize cultural places such as Graceland and Neverland Ranch, these spaces transform cult fans into interpretive communities where private sentiments and attachments are shared. Although cult members are desirable as active consumers, cults are the final phase of fan communities where excess may tarnish the image, place, or the object of their adoration.

Fans and cultists are skilled entertainment consumers who typically possess technical, analytical, and interpretive expertise. Cult members are knowledgeable about the technology of performances they favor or games they follow; they have genre-specific analytical skills; and they can interpret performance, games, and

© *Yuri Arcurs, 2010. Used under license from Shutterstock, Inc.*

6.5 Fans.

spectacle by comparing them with others of like kind. Fan interactions enable fuller and more reasoned judgments of entertainment activities, venues, and performers. Yet make no mistake, fans communities would not exist without the entrepreneurial complicity of sections of the entertainment industry; fan clubs are dependent on their own commercial significance. Unlike entertainment consumers who are increasingly followers in their tastes, fans and cultists tend to take leadership roles in promoting and supporting particular stars and musical groups. They buy tickets and branded merchandise in bulk and they produce new artifacts for consumption by other fan members.

Sometimes fans' aggressive enthusiasm poses problems for entertainers, venue managers, and promoters. Mob mentalities may form and converge upon performers. Even extreme behaviors such as star stalking may result from intense fan-based enthusiasm. One fan subculture known for its occasional aggressive enthusiasm, Straight Edgers are popular with younger audiences as shown in the Closer Look section below.

FOCUS ON FAN COMMUNITIES

The Straight Edge Subculture

Music has become a powerful social influence today, and many subcultures have developed as a response to societal events that confuse or dismay them. One such group, the Straight Edge movement, began as a sub-creation of the punk rock music scene and has become a global phenomenon.

Straight Edge is a group, scene, and subculture very much like any other; they provide identity for members through self-expression, lyrics, tattoos, signs, symbols and ideology. One symbol is the letter X, which resulted from attending punk rock concerts where alcohol was served. Establishments drew a large black X on the tops of the hands of adolescents to signify their under-age status to servers. Over time, X emerged as a symbol of solidarity among these rockers who chose not to drink. Today the X is displayed in numerous forms on clothing, hands and in band logos. The symbol identifies the community and gives concert-goers a sense of belonging and identity. Members also form their identity through tattoos and piercing, which serve as symbols of their devotion to the edge. By transforming their lives into artwork, Edgers become living symbols of their own identity. According to on 22-year old Edger from Southern California, piercings help remind him that he is in control of his own life at all times, and they "help keep things in proper order."

Straight Edgers describe their culture as a way of life; a longing for uniqueness and a strong desire to be heard. Straight Edge is about enthusiasm of beliefs, integrity and individual involvement rather than natural talents or inherent traits. Members live a clean lifestyle without drugs, smoking, and sex; many are vegans or vegetarians. A website* explains that Straight Edge is not an Internet phenomenon; it is hardcore, and it is about music. It's about fellowship and about being drug free. Members agree: the prevailing sentiment for this lifestyle is that death, dying, and destruction of integrity in this world has forced a need for positivism. Adolescents enter the scene to escape realities and harshness of the world and reject forms of addiction as an avenue of escape. Their philosophy is depicted in H2O's 2002 song, "All We Want," that proclaims their desire to be wanted. They're screaming for attention and claim that is all they want.

As the song ("As the Line Between Machinery and Humanity Blurs", written by a Straight Edge band Atreyu) states, this youth culture doesn't want to be controlled, babysat, or mediated by television; they have grown tired of the cold mechanical nature and idealistic images of today's media.

Marketing to these teens begins with research conducted to understand what drives and motivates these kids to participate. Next, it entails providing awareness about upcoming concerts, such as the Ozzfest tour where Straight Edge metal bands prevailed, in media they choose. Small, grass roots or garage labels organize the work of promoting, selling, and publicizing their own releases. Straight Edgers themselves typically run independent hardcore music labels; they call these labels DYI, "do it yourself." These vehicles provide the only acceptable way to produce CDs and make them available to the hardcore scene. Victory Records, Indecision Records, and Equal Vision Records are the three largest and most influential independent labels of the past decade.

All DIY record labels use fan zines to advertise and get the word out; they consist of band interviews, CD reviews, and record label advertisements. Content includes music, philosophy, attitudes, vegetarian recipes, and animal rights topics. Distributed to local record stores and concert venues, these zines are advertising supported and free to readers. *Maximum Rock & Roll*, a printed extension of a punk radio show, focuses on scene reports and advertisements for record companies. Such fan zines are important for transmitting the Straight Edge culture to its audience.

Internet based webzines are also popular, allowing bands to directly communicate with their audience with publicity and venue concert listings. The site www.revhq.com provides an extensive catalog of Straight Edge CDs and merchandise through mail order.

What do you think?

1. How does the notion of personal identity apply to this subculture?

2. Would you describe the Straight Edgers as a cult or a fan community? Why?

Reprinted with permission of Michelle Weber.

WHO KNOWS WHAT'S NEXT?

Will audiences of the future be much more participatory than voyeuristic? Are they likely to commit themselves to the active experience and abandon viewing one-way mass media? Madison Avenue certainly wants answers to these and other questions about audience behavior. Hoping to get a better handle on fast-changing audience habits, Interpublic Group's PR unit formed an alliance with trend-spotting guru Faith Popcorn; WPP Group hired a trend forecaster as well. These newly formed unions reflect the increasing interest in the advertising and marketing industries in identifying trends as rapid changes in technology make audience behavior hard to predict. Called futurists, Popcorn and others keep tabs on emerging trends, relying on experts from a variety of industries and extensive consumer interviews. According to marketing consultant Al Ries, "If you want to predict the future, you have to study the past."[xxvi] One problem with looking to the past, however, is that it never had technological advances quite like the kind we are experiencing in the second half of the century's first decade.

No entertainment genre is immune to advances, which may render the updates in this book a bit archaic. Nevertheless, we present the most recent trends in each aspect of entertainment promotion. As you read each of the succeeding chapters, try to determine what changes are likely, then check to see if the experts think as you think, or if their ideas are already obsolete!

Finally

This chapter explains why audience interests, motivations, and levels of involvement are important to entertainment marketers. Audiences are developed, nurtured, and rewarded; they can be both fickle in their loyalty and zealous in their support. In order to prepare adequately, marketers must begin every planning and strategy session with current audience-based research—for as goes the audience, so goes the industry.

GOT IT?

+ Audiences are classified simple, mass and diffused; all levels of audience involvement impact each member's personal identity.

+ Stress release and diversion are two of the strongest emotional motivators for entertainment audiences; physical motivators reside in venue aesthetics.

+ According to the functional theory of attitudes, five functions contribute to forming opinions: knowledge, utility, value-expression, ego-defense and social adjustment.

- Three challenges have driven the search for methodological rigor in audience research: 1) the gap between what people say they do and what they do in practice; 2) the relation between experience and audience member; and 3) the question of entertainment/media consequences or effects.

- Audiences may be classified, segmented and measured by their levels of involvement.

- Fans and fan subcultures are audiences who have a strong emotional identification with particular media, stars and performance genres.

NOW TRY THIS

1. Think about an event you attended recently. How would you characterize your participation level? What involvement segment best describes you? Before attending the event, what was your attitude about the performance genre? Did attending change your attitude? How would you rate the venue using the variables discussed in this chapter?

2. Go to your Internet browser home page and click on 'entertainment'. What kind of messages do you find there? At which loyalty segment are they directed? What improvement can you suggest to make the messages more focused toward knowledgeable audience members?

3. Go to an Internet fan sight for a particular celebrity or musical group you enjoy. What types of memorabilia are available for sale? How is the fan community developed (chat rooms, discussion boards, conventions, etc.)? Describe the texts (songs, videos) produced by fan members. Would you characterize this fan group as a cult? Why or why not?

4. Using the RPII, survey ten people about their rational and emotional reactions to a particular band or popular music style. What did you learn about their involvement with the band or style? What message strategy would you use to motivate those with low involvement to attend a performance?

QUESTIONS FOR DISCUSSION AND REVIEW

1. Discuss the main motivators for audiences to attend a performance, engage in an activity or visit a venue.

2. What message strategies would you suggest to develop a positive attitude among light users of an entertainment venue such as a local museum or performing arts center?

3. If attendance has dwindled at your theater in the past year, what measures would you take to analyze the reasons for this decline? Once identified, what actions might you take to correct the problems? What messages would you send to your data-base of past patrons?

4. Under what circumstances would you use the laddering technique to determine consumer motivations for selecting a particular casino? Who would you interview? How would you use the results of the research?

5. How would you characterize audiences of the next generation?

MORE STUFF ABOUT AUDIENCES AND FANS

www.onlinefandom.com News and perspectives on fan communication and online social life.

www.citizenreviewonline.org News and commentary on entertainment and current events.

www.newsblaze.com Real-time news on the entertainment industry and business.

S. Sayre and C. King (2010), *Entertainment and Society: Influences, Impacts and Innovations*, *2ⁿᵈ Edition* Routledge.

[i]See M. Shank (1999), *Sports Marketing*, Prentice-Hall; D. McQuail (1997), *Audience Analysis*, Sage.

[ii]From E. Arnould, L. Price & G. Zinkhan (2004), *Consumers*. McGraw-Hill/Irwin.

[iii]Andy Ruddock (2001), *Understanding Audiences*, Sage, p. 169.

[iv]From N. Abercrombie & B. Longhurst (1998), *Audiences*. Sage, p. 37.

[v]In B. Kershaw (1994), 'Framing the Audience for Theater'. In R. Keat, N. Whitely & N. Abercrombie (eds), *The Authority of the Consumer*. Routledge, p. 167.

[vi]C. Thompson & E. Hirschman (1995), "Understanding the Socialized Body", *Journal of Consumer Research* 22, 139–53.

[vii]D. McClelland (1953), *The Achievement Motive*. Appleton-Century-Crofts Inc, p. 79.

[viii]D. Winter (1973), *The Power Motive*. Free Press.

[ix]From T. A. Stafford & M. Stafford (2001), "Identifying Motivations for the Use of Commercial Web Sites. *Information Resource Management Journal* 14, 22–31.

[x]See G. Maio & J. Olson (1995), "Relationships between Values, Attitudes and Behavioral Intentions: The Moderating Role of Attitude Function," *Journal of Experimental Social Psychology* 31, 266–85.

[xi]I. Rein, P. Kotler & M. Stoller (1997), *High Visibility: The Making and Marketing of Processionals into Celebrities*. NTC Business Books, p. 108.

[xii]Study conducted as part of a graduate research project at California State University, Fullerton, Spring semester, 2004.

[xiii]Taken from M. D. Johnson (1998), *Customer Orientation and Market Action*. Prentice Hall, p. 46.

[xiv]V. Oberle (1995), "Operationalizing the Voice of the Customer in Disney's Educational Strategies. Paper delivered to the American Marketing Association's 5ᵗʰ Congress.

[xv]M. J. Rosenberg (1960), *Attitude, Organization and Change*. Yale University Press.

[xvi]M. Fishbein (1980), "An overview of the Attitude Construct," in G. B. Hafer (ed.), *A Look Back, A Look Ahead*. American Marketing Association.

[xvii]B. Shank (1994), *Dissonant Identities: The Rock'n'Roll Scene in Austin, Texas*. Wesleyan University Press, p. 131.

[xviii]In H. Jenkins (1992), *Textual Poachers: Television Fans and Participatory Culture*. Routledge, p. 278.

[xix]S. Brown (1995), *Postmodern Marketing*, Routledge, pp. 116–118.

[xx]Based on a theory presented in P. Bordieu (1991), *Language and Symbolic Power*. Polity Press.

[xxi]See the discussion on Appadurai's theory in M. Hill (Ibid), (2002), p. 35.

[xxii]Ibid p. 118.

[xxiii]http://www.760kfmb.com/Global/story.asp?S=10662499

[xxiv]From G. Rodman (1996), *Elvis After Elvis: The Posthumous Career of a Living Legend*. Routledge, p. 13.

[xxv]See D. Horton & R. R. Wohl (1956) "Mass Communication and Para-Social Interaction," *Psychiatry* 19, pp. 215–29.

[xxvi]From an article by advertising writer Suzanne Vranica for the *Wall Street Journal*, Nov. 11, 2005.

Chapter 7

SEGMENTING ENTERTAINMENT AUDIENCES

Do unto others as you would have them do unto you.
Their tastes may not be the same.
George Bernard Shaw

Chapter Objectives

After reading this chapter, you will be able to answer these questions:

+ What are the *criteria* for developing audience segments?

+ How do *demographic, geodeomographic and psychographic* segments apply to maketing U.S. based entertainment?

+ How do *global lifestyle segments* affect target audience marketing across borders?

+ How are *global demogaphics* used to promote entertainment performances, attractions, and destinations?

+ What *audience segments* are applicable for promoting marketing entertainment to all types of audiences?

+ How important are *aesthetics* to audiences of enertainment activities?

+ Why is audience *segmentation* important to a campaign plan?

As we saw in the last chapter, audiences vary in motivation, attitude and involvement levels. This chapter describes the way we segment audiences for regional, national, and global targeting. We characterize typical lifestyle segments and the branded product constellations with which they identify. Global demographic segments are explained, and we define several segments that are applicable to all audience types.

AUDIENCE SEGMENTATION

Audience segmentation enables marketing managers to divide total markets into component parts in order to target and deal with them more effctively and more profitably. From among the many **segmentation** possibilities, marketers must determine which approach works best for their client's needs. Although there are many ways to segment entertainment audiences, all segmentation schemes should possess these characteristics.[i]

+ *Mutual exclusivity*. Each segment should be conceptually separate from all other segments.

+ *Exhaustiveness*. Every potential target member must be placed in a viable segment with other members of like kind until everyone has an appropriate group.

+ *Measurability*. In order to make appropriate targeting decisions and track strategy effectiveness, the segment's size, purchasing power, and profile should be readily measurable.

+ *Substaintiality*. Each segment should have a large enough potential membership to be worth pursuing.

+ *Actionability*. The degree to which the segments an be effectively reached and served through some form of communication.

The importance of audience segmentation for planning promotional campaigns

As more and more audiences express their individuality rather than fit into mass markets, segmentaton takes on growing significance. The more people preceive themselves as different, the greater is the competition between entertainment producers to increase their own share of the same market, and the greater is the need for segmentation.

With visitor attractions, the basic product is essentially the same for all audiences. There are always different ways, however, to promote to subgroups around a segment's identified needs. The use of museums for functions and events outside normal hours is one form of segmentation that illustrates this point. Segment identification is also crucial for message development and delivery. Each group of audience members attends events for different reasons, as detailed in Chapter 6. Precise segmentation enables copy writers to select and create effective group-specific informational and/or motivational messages.

Some specific benefits can be defined. Market segmentation:[ii]

+ provides valuable insight into the design of products and services to more accurately reflect market demand

+ gives direction in pinpointing advertising messages

+ yields substantial cost savings from more accurate service design and promotional message placement

+ enables focusing on various competition's strengths and weaknesses by reducing marketplace variables

+ fosters the production of more informed strategic marketing plans and assists in the investigation of changing and developing markets.

The first step in strategy development for promoting entertainment and venues is determining the most appropriate group or groups to target. There are three options.

1. *Undifferentiated marketing* uses the shotgun approach, ignoring differences between segments and offering a single marketing mix to the entire market. Rarely used by entertainment marketers, this strategy is best applied to products with global similarities in usage.

2. Experential promoters prefer *differentiated marketing*, which targets multiple segments, each with a different incentive and message.

3. *Niche marketing*, which targets small groups of like audience members, works with companies such as Bang & Olufsson that sell high-end stereo products to audiophiles, or the Lincoln Center that promotes Wagner to opera buffs. This strategy concentrates all promotional media on a single segment to maximize impressions and impact. The Grateful Dead also used this approach. According to the late Jerry Garcia, "You don't merely want to be considered just the best of the best, you want to be considered the only ones who do what you do."[iii]

Entertainment marketers most often use a differentiated approach, targeting groups of audience members most likely to attend performances or buy tickets to attractions. Occasionally, niche marketing is used when a definitive, finite audience group's potential yield justifies the marketing expenditure to reach them. Movie promoters use niche marketing to target Screen Actors Guild members prior to the Oscars, asking them to vote for a specific film, actor(s), or director.

Selling Small-Budget Films to Millenials

As the independent film industry is forced to compete with Hollywood studio cinema, it faces the challenge of reaching its intended audience. Filmmaker and director Benjamin Morgan successfully targeted a teen audience by using new media to market his film on kids and graffiti, *Quality of Life*.

Although U.S. the box office gross for corporate studios was approximately $758 billion in 2005, independent studios grossed a mere $1.05 billion to market a small-budget film about graffiti artists in San Francisco, Morgan targeted younger crowd for which the movie's theme would resonate—the Millenial generation, specifically those born between 1985–1994, with an age range of 12–21. Millenials, who do not have college degrees and make under $30,000 per year are a-typical audiences but are nonetheless very willing to spend their entertainment dollars on independent films.

Using non-traditional methods such as Instant Messaging technology and notices on CraigsList and MySpace to attract actors, investors, and viewers, Morgan was able to tap into a technologically savvy, urban, and hip audience that are the newcomers to independent films. For the *Quality of Life* filmmakers, authenticity was key in attracting a Millenial audience that would understand the film and, at the same time, tell the narrative of two graffiti writers to a larger audience.

He continued: "The whole idea of *Quality of Life* crimes is so offensive. It's like the suburbanization of the urban space. Literally a whitewash over real problems." (Morgan, p. 28)

Referring to their movie as an "ultra-indie" film because of its extremely low budget, filmmakers also used unorthodox fundraising methods such as selling screen credits for $100, writing a book about the process to give other ersatz filmmakers a how-to guide to filmmaking, and holding graffiti art shows in which they split the proceeds with the artists. Audience members were alerted to the film by everything from websites, to newspapers to postcards.. The audience was also reached through a Web site that celebrates street art and graffiti (www.woostercollective.com) to promote their film.

Director Benjamin Morgan's book *Putting the pieces together; A behind-the-scenes look at the making of Quality of Life*, provided valuable insight into independent filmmaking, and served as a primary promotion vehicle.

According to Brant Smith, producer and writer, festivals are key to promoting independent films:

> *"Well, I mean, for those of you who don't know, the Berlin film festival is literally one of the top four festivals in the world. Up there with Sundance and Toronto and Cannes, so, getting into Berlin, I compare it with ending up with the silver medal at the Olympics. Cause not only did our film go to Berlin, we actually ended up winning an award there, which is huge. So, one the one*

hand, it was really good because we were able to get a little more money, and get more people interested making it happen, cause otherwise, nobody's going to care about our movie. It gave us validation. That's what the festivals do, is they give you validation."

Industry data suggest we are seeing a younger audience for independent films, but *Quality of Life* filmmakers said they still had to contend with the older filmmaking gatekeepers at the international film festivals. Smith theorized that they didn't get into most film festivals because producers don't understand the youth market.

According to industry experts, increasingly, more independent movies are adopting models of grass-roots marketing. Unable to compete with the multimillion-dollar advertising budgets of studio blockbusters, small movies are instead targeting localized niche audiences as a way to gain traction. That platform allows a film to open small and then potentially build momentum through word-of-mouth. Marketers attempting to reach potential independent film audience members can utilize Internet sites already available to independent film fans, including Netflix and Fandango websites in celebration of street art and graffiti.

What do you think?

1. Urban Millenials were thought to be an ideal niche market for these San Francisco filmmakers. Given the prominence of graffiti in cities, how would this film translate to rural youth audiences?

2. How else might Smith and Morgan reach their audiences with a small budget?

3. Was publishing a 'how-to" book a good promotional strategy? Why?

Reprinted with permission of Steven Chen.

REGIONAL & NATIONAL SEGMENTING APPLICATIONS

Traditional U.S. market segmenting practices adhere to five general categories: psycghographic, geodemographic, demographic and cohort, behavioral, and benefit segments. The most popular and frequently utilized segment by marketers and advertisers is psychographics, or lifestyle segmenting. This discussion centers around regional and national segments, then focuses on global audience segments according to their importance for entertainment marketing. Because cultures differ, some segment structures are only applicable to a single national or local geographic region. We will discuss demographic, geodemographic, and psychographic segmentation for their importance to entertainment marketing.

Demographic segmentation

Every piece of information on your driver's license reveals a demographic segment of interest to marketers. Some demographic segments, such as some based on age and gender, have special needs and are marketed to because their lifestyles have unique requirements. As a group, *mature adults*, for instance, may have more enjoyable (or even possible) visits when attention is paid to dietary needs ambulatory assistance, or visual and auditory adjustments in service. Because many in this segment have unlimited resources of time and money to devote to entertainment and tourism activities, many are sought after and catered to by marketers of events, performances, and tours.

7.1 Global teens is a demographic segment.

Three American consumer demographic groups—American baby boomers, Generation Y and global teens—are changing the way U.S. entertainment is marketed.

Baby boomers

The American *baby boomer* segment, people born between 1946 and 1954, ages 50–58, total around 78 million consumers with 25 million of them now over the age of fifty. Representing 27.5% of the entire U.S. population, the boomer demographic has an estimated annual spending power of $1 trillion.

Our largest group and biggest spenders, *baby boomers* are doling out huge amounts of cash to amuse themselves. As boomers are freed from work, they become ever more engaged in all forms of activities, morphing free time into "all the time." With considerable financial resources at their disposal, 75 million boomers are eager for advice on what to do with their money. As entertainment marketers, we must be willing to and eager to help with their spending decisions by providing unique entertainment experiences.

Heavy purchasers of vacations and vacation homes, boomers are also big travelers.[iv] Taking advantage of this traveling demographic, the Hong Kong Tourist Authority runs an annual large-scale contest with 50Plus.com to increase awareness of Hong Kong as a travel destination and build a database of mature travelers interested in receiving ongoing information. A promotional campaign centered around a Hong Kong trip giveaway for two and featured hundreds of thousands of banner and button impressions, travel email newsletter mailings and Featured Destination sponsorship in newspaper travel sections. The contest generated thousands of entries, indicating that members of the 50-plus segment—the most powerful consumer travel demographic—are very interested in researching travel and interacting online. The promotion confirms findings of research studies that concluded that the 50-plus age group loves contests, free offers, and incentives.[v]

The heads of virtually every major film studio, record company, and TV network—all boomers—have contributed to shaping the culture in ways that were different from those of their predecessors. As boomers came of age in the 1960s and 1970s, good economic conditions provided a blank canvas for pursuing what seemed like unlimited opportunities. To understand how to market to baby boomers, marketers must understand the large role the concept of *self* plays in the lives of this generation. The sheer numbers of people who experienced childhood at the same time has created a collective memory that encourages nostalgia.

Boomers were the first generation to be raised with television in the background. They are characterized as independent learners who grasped the goal of self-improvement. Often described as the "me generation," boomers still relate to the music that underscored their "growing up" years, such as the Doors and Beatles. Whether self-made, inherited from trust funds, or enriched by generous retirement plans, boomers' spending power continues to render them a highly desirable and responsive market segment. And as they move into middle and older age, boomers are taking their entertainment habits with them.

They key word to promoting entertainment to this segment is *benefit*—like other segments, boomers want a sense of value from their experiences. One of the best attention-getting devices for boomers is packaging nostalgia. Convertibles, war protests, open relationships, and recreational drug use are often parodied in all forms of entertainment, while music is designed to give boomers a soundtrack for their everyday lives. Films, books, and vintage clothing allow boomers to touch base with the past. Targeting the baby boomer segment should bridge images of a rich past, positive images of today, and visions of what can be.

Aging baby boomers or *empty nesters* are early retirees who have both the financial resources and leisure time to take advantage of entertainment activities. Using geographic databases, marketers are able to pinpoint these affluent consumers and target them with communications that provide performance schedule information and incentives for purchase.

© De Visu, 2010. Used under license from Shutterstock, Inc.

7.2 Baby boomers grew up touting peace and love.

Generation Y

Another important segment for entertainment marketers—Generation Y—are young adults with big numbers and big bucks. These "echo boomers" represent an exciting new opportunity for marketers of entertainment. Diversity in race and family profile makes marketing to this segment a challenge. Dependent upon the income or estimated net worth of a parent or head of household, Ys are more difficult than boomers to qualify as prospects. They are the most computer-literate, media-savvy younger generation in history.[vi] Their medium of choice is the Internet, and they enjoy logo-imprinted clothing and accessories from favorite films, shows, and brands—ripe for entertainment promotion. Entertainment marketing strategy, in part, can be developed based on the group's branding needs and its propensity toward rebellion.

FOCUS ON DEMOGRAPHIC SEGMENTATION

Using Social Marketing to Target Young Adults

Promoting entertainment fiction for young adults has spanned multiple platforms, especially the Internet's social media networks. These networks of online youth sociability exist in a mutually beneficial relationship with global media industries. The young adult demographic has been identified as the major target to be reached through social media campaigns.

Approached as a trend conscious consumer force, book packagers and concept marketing efforts are directed at the young adult audience. Their goal is to mobilize interest in entertainment fiction artifacts to young consumers who are unlikely to be "heavy" readers with specific genre preferences. Readers with specific preferences, however, rely on the viral communication of peer trends through social media. Such marketing of entertainment fiction relies on the "hook" of a blockbuster trend, in addition to more traditional preferences. Characterized by promoters as romantic individualists, new media audiences are not part of the old notion of taste culture.

An analysis of online discussions of *Twilight*, Stephenie Meyer's vampire and teen-romance series, concluded that traditional blockbuster promotional strategies need to be enhanced by viral marketing through selected online channels and applications. Such digital retailing is strengthened by superstar artists and blockbuster titles. *Twilight* fan groups on Facebook, Twitter, and MySpace overwhelmingly looked to other readers' thoughts about which supernatural boyfriend the heroine should end up with, or relay information about upcoming *Twilight* related events. The phenomenal market success of the *Twilight* series was due in part to the unconventional coverage appearing in viral and non-commercial sources. And although online marketing only represents a part of the promotional budget, there is an increasing trend toward using strategies aimed at the teen market through Internet channels.

Promotion tactics

Some of the promotion vehicles include title-specific sites, sending books to bloggers, producing podcasts or video trailers and author interviews for official fan sites. PR efforts organize chat sessions with authors on their *MySpace* pages based on questions from readers. An author's self-promotion should parallel the publisher's campaign to build lines of communication and rapport with the fan base. User feedback enables publishing and media industry stakeholders to make projections about the potential of merchandising or cross-platform products associated with their literary properties.

A redesigned Website for the *Twilight Saga* in 2007 included discussion boards, a reviews blog, an application to find author media appearances, and additional images. In order to sustain readers' involvement and suspense around the series' closure, fans were invited to speculate on which suitor, vampire Edward Cullen or werewolf Jacob Black, the heroine would choose. A poll, used to build reader engagement, was supplemented with fan-contests and competitions involving user-generated video auditions for roles in a made-for-DVD version.

Fan communities and merchandising

Fan clubs have become a place for a fan's emotional investment and goals of financial rewards for the industry. Since the publishing industry has historically spent less money promoting young adult books, their authors must rely on personal relationship building with audiences through correspondence with readers. The *Twilight* readership expanded rapidly from its outset because it was connected to other, non-literary, cultural forms. An increasingly popular hybrid blends audiences for paranormal fantasy, teen subculture, and romance/melodrama that had movie predecessors such as *The Lost Boys, Buffy the Vampire Slayer, Angel*, and *Charmed*.

The phenomenal growth in popularity of the *Twilight* series is attributed to the use of online applications that showcased the author's star potential, and merchandising. Character merchandise (t–shirts, posters, online assets) was made available on author Websites and fan-organized sites, such as *Twilight Lexicon*. And the books themselves became fetishized objects. As book sales escalated along with celebrity-oriented Internet fandom, the blockbuster teen vampire movie took over the prime theater release date previously slotted for the sixth Harry Potter adaptation. Once it became a celebrity commodity, the series fueled Internet communities of intersecting, cross-media stardom.

The Internet has facilitated a coming together of formerly separate youth taste cultures, such that literary, screen and graphic fandoms that have now overlapped. Young adults who might previously have been thought of as "light" readers of entertainment fiction have been recruited to reading through their engagement with celebrity culture. An initial investment in the image of a celebrity performer has become a recruiting tool to entice young readers to a fictional series. Marketing popular teen fiction through the Internet and social media is most effective when it disguises a promotional intent that simulates a non-commercial conversation of sociability in online channels.

Source: From an article by Leonie Rutherford, "Industries, artists, friends and fans: Marketing young adult fictions online" featured in First Monday, V14, (6), April 2009.

Teenagers

The teen market's prevailing use of technology, "word of mouse," and their tendency to share things online make them an elusive and challenging group to reach with traditional marketing strategies, Their intense interest in music keeps electronic innovations alive, and the fact that the movies are one of the few activities they can do outside the home make them a prime audience for selling films. Their real strength is in their global power, which is discussed later in this chapter.

Geodemographic segmentation

By combining geographic location with other demographic information, researchers have developed geodemographic analysis that spans a wide range of marketing and site location applications, including: neighborhood description, customer and prospect analysis, facility planning, advertising, direct mail, and multi-channel marketing. The chief advantages of neighborhood segmentation are 1) the inherent simplicity of the technique and 2) its ability to synthesize vast amounts of data into manageable pieces.

One system, PRIZM lifestyle segmentation, enables marketers to target audiences on a regional level. Every U.S. neighborhood is described with 62 clusters based on census data, consumer surveys, and other research methods. Clusters highlight audiences in terms of buying habits and media patterns. Venue and region-based entertainment marketers can access data for particular zip codes by lifestyle segment. Developed by the Claritas Company of San Diego, California, PRIZM software (zip codes) may be useful for developing prospect lists for direct mail campaigns, or it could be used to suggest appropriate media for targeting advertising messages. For instance, zip codes of affluent neighborhoods can be targeted with promotions for lifestyle-based entertainment and travel. Wilderness Safari Company uses this method to distribute adventure-based vacation catalogues to boomer-occupied zip codes in metropolitan areas.

The UK's ACCORN (A Concise Classification of Residential Neighborhoods), which provides an analysis of census data to supplement survey research, is a British PRIZM equivalent. Classifications—ranging from least prosperous areas to most prosperous—include striver, aspirer, settler, riser, expander, and thriver categories. A newer system, U.S. MOSAIC, is the latest in a series of neighborhood classifications built by Experian and Applied Geographic Solutions (AGS). Their international lifestyle segmentation research spans over twenty years and nearly twenty-five countries; over 40 consumer segmentation systems have been identified.

The geographic aspect has been enhanced in recent years by computerized mapping techniques based on satellite technology that are linked with customer databases provided by census and market research survey data. These tools are capable of targeting individual buyers and households with great precision. They have value for direct marketing and local media selection for entertainment promotional messages.

Psychographic segments

Psychographics are based on lifestyles, and lifestyles imply a pattern of behavior that is reflected in the consumption of product clusters or combinations. These clusters are groups of specific brands, products, or consumption activities that relate to one another.

We measure lifestyle through psychographics that link individual psychological factors to characteristic patterns of consumer behavior, enabling us to identify and profile a market segment. Preferred over simple demographic information, psychographic segments provide information about the *why* of audience preferences. Behavioral characteristics of lifestyles that can be quantified are consumer *activities*, *interests*, and *opinions*.

Psychographic segmentation is quantified through extensive item batteries that cover activities, interests and opinions (AIO-studies), and lifestyle surveys. VALS, owned and operated by Strategic Business Insights, an SRI International spinout, is the most common U.S. psychographic classification system. VALS classifies people into segments based on their level of resources such as income, education, self-confidence and primary motivation: ideals, achievement and self-expression as shown in Exhibit 7.1. Visit the VALS website in the source line to see descriptions of each segment and to find out your own VALS type.

One model of lifestyle grouping, developed by Stanley Plog[vii] for the tourism market, classifies the U.S. population according to psychographic types along a continuum from psychocentric to allocentric traits. *Psychocentric*, or self-centered travelers, tend to be self-inhibited and non-adventuresome. They like familiar places, avoid risk-taking, prefer guided tours, don't speak other languages, prefer standard hotel accommodations, and buy souvenirs to record their visits. *Allocentrics*, on the other hand, have interest patterns that focus on varied activities. These travelers try new places, enjoy a sense of discovery, have high activity levels, enjoy meeting people from all cultures, seek little-known hotels and restaurants, and want a variety of destinations. By understanding the wants and needs of such travelers, marketers can direct specific promotions at particular segments. For instance, senior segments respond to cruise ship marketing that contain messages assuring cruisers of low-risk, inclusive, English-speaking vacations that address the psychocentric needs of that market. Promotions

EXHIBIT 7.1 VALS™

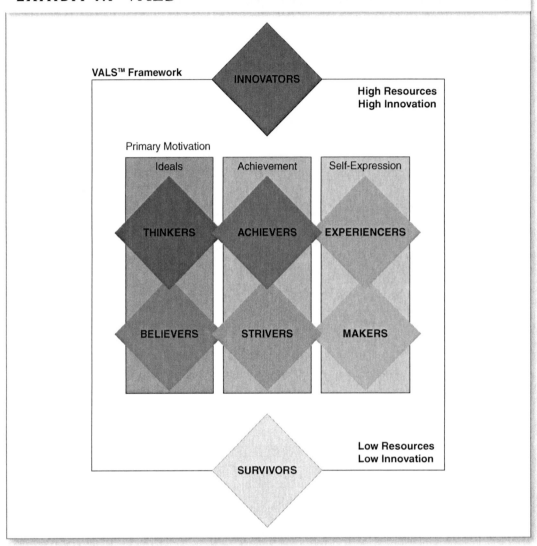

VALS™ Framework

INNOVATORS

High Resources
High Innovation

Primary Motivation

| Ideals | Achievement | Self-Expression |

THINKERS

ACHIEVERS

EXPERIENCERS

BELIEVERS

STRIVERS

MAKERS

Low Resources
Low Innovation

SURVIVORS

Source: Strategic Business Insights (SBI); www.strategicbusinessinsights.com/VALS. Reprinted by permission.

that include rock climbing, shore activities and multi-cultural cuisine are designed to attract a more active group of allocentric cruisers, who tend to be younger and more physically fit.

Four additional classifications have application for experience-based entertainment:

+ *Psychocentric consumer* motivations involve ego enhancement and a quest for status; most likely to visit amusement parks

- *Midcentric consumer* motivations include health and shopping; enjoy national and state parks, health spas, and malls
- *Near-allocentric consumer* motivations include trying new lifestyles; prefer; sports, theater tours, and special entertainment

Allocentric consumer motivations include learning and a sense of power and freedom; frequent gambling casinos and resort hotels.

Lifestyle segmenting for entertainment centers on experiential activities; marketers must figure out what goes with what (creating service assortments) for a particular lifestyle to maximize opportunities for promotional contact. *Product combos* have implications for media preferences and merchandise that might be marketed in conjunction with particular activities or at specific venues. Combining Budweiser duffle bags with baseball audiences is one example. By pairing educational learning with adventure travel, Eddie Bauer sponsorship has provided product assortments that complement both lifestyle segments. As indicators of consumer preferences, combos are somewhat insensitive to geographic location, education and occupation. Exhibit 7.2 presents product combinations grouped around specific entertainment experiences.

Cohort segmentation

Age cohorts are groups of people who grew up in the same time period, who age together, and who are influenced by events occurring during their formative years. Cohort analysis looks

EXHIBIT 7.2 Product Combos Oriented Around Performance Preferences

OPERA	GAMBLING	LOTTO PLAYING	ADVENTURE TRAVEL	ROCK MUSIC
Armani suit	Dockers	Levis jeans	LL Bean	Kid Rock
Jaguar	Corvette	Ford pickup	Subaru	VW van
French wine	Jack Daniels	Bud	Evian	Miller
Rolex	Seiko	Timex	Swiss Army	Swatch
New Yorker	*Casino Player*	*People*	*Outdoor*	*Entertainment Weekly*
AmEx card	Bijon	Marlboro	Cabella	iPod

Segments of Travel Consumers

Travel market researchers have identified types of travelers and given them appropriate names to designate their lifestyle preferences. Among them are:

Galloping Groupies: This group consists of couples and singles who make reservations to travel with tour groups. They account for 52% of all reservations, preferring to leave everything to the experts. Groupies carry cameras, like to shop, and never wander into unfamiliar territory without their guide. Sturdy walking shoes, telephoto lenses, and currency changers accompany them everywhere. Tour expenditure segments, which last from one to three weeks, record the highest amount of spending per capita.

Rough Riders: These consumers are singles or pairs of adventuresome travelers seeking excitement and thrills. They plan their own trips to climb mountains, white-water raft, trek in the wilderness, or scuba dive. These folks camp out or stay in remote lodgings. They prefer cutting edge activities in exotic locations, and inspiration fuels their enjoyment. Their adventures last from ten days to six weeks, but spending is limited to advance purchases of supplies and gear.

Eco-Lovers: Eco-lovers are older adults who want to experience nature without harming it. Whale watching is one type of eco-tourism in this emerging sector of tourism. Eco-tours promote photographic safaris to the Galapagos Islands, Alaska, and Africa. Often buying packages or travel in pre-arranged small groups, eco-travelers have abundant leisure time and a desire to spend their money on animal gazing.

Histrionics: This group consists of mature couples or adult family groups who want to trace their ethnic origins or wish to experience a different culture. They visit museums and historical monuments, learn the language, and they eat local cuisine. Education is complemented with mementos purchased to record discovery. Their travels range from day trips to multi-week migrations where they contribute to the coffers of cultural venues.

Cruisers: These consumers are couples on honeymoon, families, singles on the loose, or retired adults in search of luxury without the hassle of moving locations. Cruise ships provide an all-inclusive opportunity for gourmet dining, live entertainment, and outdoor activities. This growth segment spends top dollar on their trips that last from three days to six months.

Ties that Binders: Families and family members who travel to visit their relatives make up this segment. Sixty-six percent of all travel is made by members of this category. They prefer to travel by car, stay with relatives, and drive straight through when possible. Some take planes or trains, but rely on friends and relatives to provide the lodging. They spend less on travel than any other segment.

at how specific groups, such as baby boomers, will influence the entertainment marketplace. Because of this aging cohort's free time, disposable income, and desire for adventure, travel and tourism revenues continue to grow. And because boomers listened to the Beatles and Bob Dylan as teenagers, their appetites for listening to rock and popular music is not expected to decline. Venues such as Cleveland's Rock 'n Roll Hall of Fame and the Experience Music Project outside Seattle serve this audience's quest for music from their past.

To anticipate trends, **cohort analysis** is a useful tool. Cohorts are people who grew up together, or who had parallel experiences during the same time period. One of the most valuable segments for entertainment marketers is the older audience. Boomers have 77 million members of their generation cohort, presenting a formidable challenge for marketers. Rather than looking at cognitive age (how we see ourselves; usually ten years younger than our actual age!), mature markets are best segmented by lifestyles. Older audiences often require special access, more intermissions, and brighter lighting. Advertising for cruise lines and learning tours features older models to reflect the lifestyle of this aging target segment.

Generational influences—life stage, cohort experiences, and current condition—are indicators of the values, preferences, and marketplace behaviors of consuming audiences. *Life stage* is where one is in life physically or psychologically; *current conditions* are events that affect what people buy; and *formative experiences* are shared traits that define and differentiate generations. The phrase, "you are who you are because of where you were when" may describe the power of generational influences.

7.3 Life stage audience members.

The *Yankelovich Report on Generational Marketing*[viii] looks at the power of the most significant generations, Matures, Boomers, and GenX; these broad groupings reflect the MONITOR data that provide the most accurate view of developing trends and best explain ongoing events in the marketplace. Developed in 1971 and repeated annually, MONITOR remains the longest running and most complete continuous tracking study of American values, lifestyles, and buying motivations. The study tracks changing social climate and translates that data for marketers. The report illustrates how generational factors provide a framework for understanding the entertainment marketplace.

GLOBAL LIFESTYLE SEGMENTS

Global Market Segmentation is the process of dividing the world market into distinct subsets of customers who have similar needs. Criteria for global market segmentation is based on the same criteria as national segments; demographic and psychographic are the most relevant marketing segments for global consideration.

Global demographic segments

Although not a significant determinant of global marketing, demographics may illuminate specific trends among a specific age group that span nationalities and international boundaries. One such segment is the teen market. Youth marketing has been a focus of Asian marketing for quite a while, because in the West, clearly, youth is such a high-value market.

Teens

Thirty-two million strong, the teen market (12–17 year-olds) is a force to be reckoned with. Teens are active consumers in terms of the money they spend, as well as in the influence they wield in their families and on societal trends. Despite being raised in a period of rapid change, they display a remarkable self-confidence in their judgment. Teens do their research prior to making large purchases because they want to make informed decisions; in addition, they are particular about what they spend their money on. Teens trust advertising in magazines more than through television, the radio, or the Internet. Teens tend to multitask less when they read magazines than they do with other media. Teens are a diverse, vibrant, growing, and crucial market in the world today. Their beliefs, attitudes, and behaviors will affect the future entertainment marketplace. Teens understand the need to be able to turn on a dime and be spontaneous because they live with short-term change and volatility on a day-to-day basis. Unlike previous eras, today's teens also live with paradox, realizing that their choices are filled with a mix of good and bad.[ix]

A C Nielsen's work on Thai teen consumer behavior provides some illumination, as does McCann Erickson's study on Malaysian teens in general and their Internet behavior in particular. Research reports from Ogilvy and Mather are confirming that Japan is seen as the fashion center for many Asian teenagers (Thailand, Hong Kong, and Singapore specifically) and trends often start there. (Several worldwide trends have also originated in this part of the world, for example, the *Pokémon* and *Hello Kitty* rages.) In short, Asian teens are influenced by a complex mix of East Asian, Western, and their own cultures.

Four other important global demographic segments are profiled for the importance to entertainment marketing—gender, religion, economics, and ethnicity.

FOCUS ON GLOBAL TEENS

MTV Reaches Out

Teens are growing up in a digitized and exciting ad world where U2 promotes their iPods, McDonald's gets them to see *Avatar*, and an EverQuest II video game delivers them Pizza Hut. But with all these branded entertainment campaigns, what's working and what is doomed to turn off the savvy teen today? Entertainment marketers worldwide should know how to craft youth-focused, buzz-worthy branded entertainment programs. Here are ways to tap into this market.

1. Know what's hot.

Teens are passionate about electronics and entertainment; products such as iPod accessories and Wii are in; Target, is the place to be seen; NetFlix is how to watch movies; and vampire dramas are must-see TV shows for teens.

2. Pick music over film any day.

Music is something that does not have a shelf life of more than three weeks. In comparing music with films, films are great, but there is a buzz about a film last for three weeks and then it disappears. The buzz about an album can last for a year or more.

3. Turn off the TV.

TV is something that is in the background for teens as they are instant messaging with friends or doing other things. TV is "there" and present, and it's something they pay attention to, but it does not define who they are.

4. Get into their social networks.

In a recent survey, 89% of the teens polled in a recent survey said they were fine with friends sending them info about products through My Space, but on the flip side, 92% of them were not fine when advertised to directly on My Space.

5. Integrate causes that matter.

Cause marketing is very important to teens. They care about changing and improving the world for the better.

6. Let them explore and discover.

Teens are the "Google Generation" because Google is more than a search to them. It's a window to things that they may not have accessed so easily before.

7. Give them the tools to customize and document.

Young people are really big on owning their own universe, and being able to document it and share it with friends, which is why uploading photos or writing music are big trends.

8. Keep them communicating and connecting.

Teens are creating their own communities, or "pods." Instead of just having a big group of trendy friends, young people exist in their own pods, mixing and mingling. Facebook and YouTube are their global links to one another.

9. Find them on their cell phones.

Since teens are on their cell phones more than ever, traditional research practices should be cellphone based.

10. Be funny, cool, and on the Internet.

The company called "Jib-Jab" is a great example. Teens forward its sites around to their friends right away, because it was the funniest thing they had seen.

Source: Tina Wells, Buzz Marketing Group, 2005

Gender segmentation

The cultural definition of *gender* is behavior appropriate to the sexes in a given society and cultural capital (i.e., possessions associated with a set of gender roles.[x] Gender differences in information processing offer marketers an opportunity to reach audience members by appealing to gender-specific leisure, sports, and shopping needs. Gender roles affect purchase and consumption. In travel marketing, a focus on the male gender role would emphasize functional benefits of travel (self-orientation), while a focus on female gender role would emphasize social aspects of travel (other-orientation).

In a study of male and female entertainment consumers, researchers found that women select entertainment that can be enjoyed by the entire family, while men most often chose activities for themselves.[xi] And although gender roles differ from culture to culture and often country to country, gender-based meanings and symbols are often used to tailor entertainment genre messages. In India, for instance, the $90 million traditional music cassette/CD industry remains gender-specific in terms of performers and audiences.

The recognition of gay men and lesbian women as ideal targets for leisure and entertainment marketing is a result of their economic clout and distinctive value orientation. IKEA was one of the first retailers to feature a gay couple in their furniture commercials. Cruise ships offer gay and lesbian cruises, and music venues provide entertainers who reflect the preferences of their gay clientele. The leisure industry has recognized the potential revenue generation to be gained from addressing distinct sex or gender-based groups with messages tailored to their needs and values.

Religious segments

Useful in markets where religion is an important component of identity, segmentation by religion addresses consumers' value systems. Jewish people are noted for their philanthropy, Catholics for their consumption of holiday icons, and Buddhists for their abstinence from meat. Marketers use knowledge about the preferences of religious groups to craft media messages that will not offend the segment. Conversely, religious sects use the media to deliver spiritual entertainment; Trinity Television Network provides 24 hour programming including game shows, talk shows, concerts, and soap operas to viewers nationwide. Targeting Christians worldwide, TTN has capitalized on this huge segment to generate revenue and proselytize their theologically based messages through broadcast entertainment.

Symbolic capital

Income levels are often determinants of the kind of promotion and message content used to market entertainment. It would be foolish to advertise an exotic African vacation to working students, and no millionaire is interested in bargain rates at the Holiday Inn. Marketers note that it's not only what, but how people of varied income levels consume entertainment (tux or T-shirt for the opera?).

To segment consumption across segments on the basis of how potential audience members compete for status, we look at an audience's **symbolic capital**.[xii] Financial resources (economic capital), memberships and social connections (social capital), and aesthetics, status, and education (cultural capital) combine to form a person's symbolic capital.

People with symbolic capital can use it to cross social segments in which a particular cultural knowledge is valued. Film stars such as Chow Yun Fat from Hong Kong or Hrthik Roshan from India can trade their national appearances as symbolic capital for Hollywood credibility. Arnold Schwarzenegger was able to translate his film star credibility into access to political networks and was elected governor of California. To some extent, the nature of entertainment activities is status-oriented consumption for the participant, laden with status symbols that indicate a person's position, class, or group. Opera goers who sit through three nights of Wagner's "Rings" consume the activity as a badge of elite consumption. Marketers must position status symbols for different economic and social segments in different ways to accommodate differences in how people consume symbolic capital.

Ethnic segmentation

Multicultural marketing programs differentiate the interests of one group from another. *Ethnicity* implies common origin, a self-perpetuating population, shared cultural values, a field of communication and interaction with a common language, and members who define themselves as a distinguishable category.[xiii] Successful ethnic marketing depends on appealing to the basic motivational drive through benefit and values-based segmentation. In the U.S., entertainment marketers target Asian and Hispanic consumers differently because of their different attendance motivations. Asian families value education-based entertainment, whereas Hispanic families are more interested in shared emotional experiences. Venues that advertise in Spanish are more apt to attract Hispanic audiences than those that do not; 53% of Hispanic consumers say they pay more attention to brands that are advertised in Spanish.[xiv]

7.4 Ethnic segmentation.

© *Konstantin Sutyagin, 2010. Used under license from Shutterstock, Inc.*

Global migration has resulted in groups of ethnic cultures living in every country. By addressing these groups individually and using distinct promotional messages, entertainment marketers can establish valuable relationships and build brand loyalty.

Global psychographics

Worldwide, marketers are using lifestyle segmentation to develop promotional communications. The Japanese VALS system identifies four important dimensions: exploration, self-expression, achievement, and tradition. Other highly developed schemes include France's COFREMCA Sociostyles and Denmark's Minerva scheme, which uses color to identify segments. A study by D'Arcy Massius Benton & Bowles identified four lifestyle groups of European consumers: successful idealists, affluent materialists, comfortable belongers, and disaffected survivors. Cultural differences are important to understand because they impact the way promotional messages are developed.

Japanese VALS are also used to clarify the processes of social change and innovation diffusion in Japanese society. It also identifies the consumer segments at the core of most consumer markets:

+ **Integrators** (4% of population) are highest on the Japan VALS measure of Innovation. These consumers are active, inquisitive, trend-leading, informed, and affluent. They travel frequently and consume a wide range of media print and broadcast, niche, and foreign.

- **Self Innovators** and Self Adapters (7% and 11% of population) score high on Self-Expression. These consumers desire personal experience, fashionable display, social activities, daring ideas, and exciting, graphic entertainment.

- **Ryoshiki Innovators** and Ryoshiki Adapters (6% and 10% of population) score highest on Occupations. Education, career achievement, and professional knowledge are their personal focus, but home, family, and social status are their guiding concerns.

- **Tradition Innovators** and Tradition Adapters (6% and 10% of population) score highest on the measure of Traditional Ways. These consumers adhere to traditional religions and customs, prefer long-familiar home furnishings and dress, and hold conservative social opinions.

- **High Pragmatics** and Low Pragmatics (14% and 17% of population) do not score high on any life-orientation dimension. They are not very active and not well informed; they have few interests and seem flexible or even uncommitted in their lifestyle choices.

- **Sustainers** (15% of population) score lowest on the Innovation and Self-Expression dimensions. Lacking money, youth, and high education, these consumers dislike innovation and are typically oriented to sustaining the past.

Global Scan, a more universal and comprehensive lifestyle scheme, was created by Backer Spielvogel and Bates Worldwide. Global Scan measures a wide variety of attitude and consumer values, media use, and buying patterns by conducting annual surveys in over 18 countries. From their research, BSB concluded that five global segments describe the combined population: adapters, traditionals, pressureds, achievers, and strivers. As their names imply, these groups are categorized by their primary motivation: adapting, maintaining tradition, trying to keep up, getting to the top, and making a difference.

Another scheme, Global MOSAIC, classifies over 800 million of the world's consumers and is composed of thirteen lifestyle types that can be found in every modernized country. It is based on the simple proposition that the world's cities share common patterns of residential segregation. Each has its low-income inner city area, upscale suburbs, and rural communities. Using highly localized statistics across eighteen countries, Experian has identified thirteen types of residential neighborhoods, each with a distinctive set of values, motivations, and consumer preferences. The *global* MOSAIC serves as the common analytical currency among and between *country* MOSAIC typologies. MOSAIC types in every country can be cross-referenced to one of the Global types on the basis of four primary attributes: age structure, family structure, extent of urbanization, and income structure.

Using one or more of the local or global typologies enables marketers to craft and deliver motivation-specific messages to their desired audiences. Audience research that ground these groups continutes to be developed in countries new to capitalism.

Lifestyle segmentation in emerging capitalist nations

Within the past seven years, two countries developed their first consumer segments in response to global marketing demands. Turkey's scheme included both males and females, but males still dominate purchase decisions. In China, women are a strong force in the consumer marketplace, as indicated by the female-oriented segmentation scheme presented here.

Turkish research identified three lifestyles:[xv]

+ Liberals/trend setters—college educated and high-income earners

+ Moderates/survivors—predominantly male wage earners

+ Traditionalists/conservatives—those concerned with price over prestige and style

In China, females' lifestyles were reported as four segments:[xvi]

+ Conventional women—family is a priority

+ Contemporary females—combine work and family as main priority

+ Searching singles—career and image-oriented, postpone marriage

+ Followers—low involvement in social, cultural, and physical activities

Problems with global lifestyle profiling

There are many problems inherent with research across borders and cultures. Lifestyles change, environments are vulnerable to natural disasters, and economic fluctuation creates instability that underlies dramatic swings in circumstances for consumer groups. Another problem is that central concepts in this type of research are not universally defined, and it is not always clear why particular segments express particular consumer preferences. Additionally, current lifestyle measures are not very good at capturing the fluidity of lifestyle segment membership, especially in emerging free markets such as Turkey and China. Finally, there is a low level of correlation between lifestyle segments and particular behaviors such as brand or product preference, which vary widely across global geodemographics.

Some improvements can be made to address the problems, including: strengthening the link between micro-motives and macro-behavior, that is, between lifestyle segmentation and macroeconomic data; extending data coverage on ongoing lifestyle changes, both voluntary and unintended; analyzing the emergence of a global consumer culture using case and comparative studies.[xvii] Only with continuing efforts can research remain current and address cultural nuances; marketing is held hostage to available data and must rely on academics and scientists to improve the accuracy and currency of that information. Without lifestyle information, the effectiveness of marketing would diminish dramatically.

GENERIC SEGMENTATION FACTORS

Regardless of where audiences are located geographically, demographically, or psychographically, they can also be segmented according to usage behavior, price, benefits, and aesthetics. Niche marketing is also utilized to reach global audiences on a narrow-cast, or pinpointed basis. This discussion helps marketers identify which segmentation strategy is best for their clients and for developing appropriate audience messages.

Usage segmentation

Audience members are divided into groups on the basis of differences in their knowledge, attitude, and use of or response to an experience. This type of segmentation focuses on how often people buy tickets or use entertainment genres, when they use them, and their usage patterns. Although usage behavior varies among global audiences, we can generalize based upon usage in most world locations by rate, occasion, and loyalty.

+ *Usage rate segments.* Usage rate segmentation sorts audiences by the amount of entertainment they consume. Very often, the best predictor of future behavior is past behavior. Using the 80-20 rule (80% of ticket purchases are made by 20% of a potential audience base), we call the 20% group *frequent* or *heavy users*; the remaining 80% are *light* or *nonusers*. Marketers know that it's much easier to stimulate increased attendance by current patrons than to attract those who never attend. A study by the Cleveland Foundation and Pew Charitable Trust[xviii] found that *frequent users* placed a high value on leisure-time activities that spark the imagination or are new and different. To the other extreme, *light users* were defined as those who attended at least one activity of a particular genre during the year. Central to users' decision-making processes were cost, comfort, and convenience, as was social interaction. *Nonusers* reported that their activities must be fun and entertaining, informal, involve friends, convenient, and inexpensive. According to Sidney Levy, *nonparticipants* "harbor many inhibiting images of the arts as relatively austere, effeminate, esoteric, inaccessible, and too demanding of study and concentration."[xix] These folks are targeted at a *point of entry* that is familiar and accessible to potential audience members. Educational messages are an important consideration when attempting to recruit nonusers.

+ *Occasion-based segments.* Occasion segmentation divides audiences according to when they attend a performance, travel to a destination, or visit a venue. Buyers can be distinguished according to the occasions when they develop a need, purchase a ticket, or encounter the experience. Performing arts centers increase demand by promoting season tickets as birthday and holiday gifts, and movie theaters provide coupons for gifting as well. Holiday performances, evening concerts, and society fund raisers are among the occasions marketers use to segment audiences. New occasions may be created, such as hour-long rush hour performances to attract commuters. Marketers should consider the many possible occasions when audiences might attend performances, parks, and attractions and create messages and incentives to promote attendance at those times.

- • *Loyalty status segments.* A market can be segmented by consumer loyalty status. Strategy to promote a special concert to loyal season subscribers differs significantly from the strategy to promote the same concert to those who have only attended once before. This segmentation method functions with the aid of computerized databases, which allow marketers to direct their promotions to the appropriately loyal users.

Segmentation by price

In general, buyer behavior in entertainment activities in all countries appears to be highly price sensitive, and many venue marketers (such as spas, casinos, and resort hotels) still act on the assumption that price is the key segmentation variable. In the resort industry, high-price band venues (i.e., concert halls and stadiums) require feasibility studies to identify the ability and willingness of sufficient customers to pay the prices necessary to generate the level of revenue required to pay back investment, cover fixed costs, and create targeted profits. Segment-targeted tactical pricing is important, although limits are set by the strategic marketing mix decisions, costs of operation, and consumer satisfaction. Although pricing is not as important as the other variables discussed in this chapter, it continues to motivate large numbers of entertainment consumers.

FOCUS ON PERFORMING ARTS VENUES

Segmenting Performance Audiences

Segmentation is the engine that drives audience building for the performing arts. Recognizing that the audience is not a homogeneous mass, we treat them as a collection of distinct and discrete segments each with different needs, attitudes, and expectations. One approach[ix] advocates engaging with and addressing the needs of all attendees, not just the reliable core audience, by segmenting the current audience into groups of attendees with similar needs. As with traditional segmentation, as described above, such approaches are most useful when prospecting for new customers or when little is known about current purchasers.

Most arts venues, however, know a great deal about their audiences: how long members have been a attending performances, what type of shows they like and which they avoid, how often they come, how many people they normally attend with, whether any of them are children or senior citizens, where they like to sit, how much they're prepared to pay, and how far in advance they will book. From this information, a venue marketer can track an audience's past behavior, predict its future behavior, and tailor its communications to meet audience members' very different needs.

Venue analysis identifies the two primary defining variables as *frequency* (number of bookings over time) and *degree of difficulty attempted* (based on a classification of the accessibility of each show). Both of these are based on behavioral data routinely collected by the box office system. This means that the development of each booker (i.e., the increase in frequency and/or degree of difficulty attempted) can be easily measured and tracked. The degree of difficulty is closely correlated to psychographic or attitudinal data, which is widely used in other marketing sectors. By combining behavioral data with psychographic profiling, a comprehensive picture begins to emerge of each audience, making it easier to target it with an effective marketing campaign.

Here are typical definitions of existing live performance genre types broken into five categories according to *difficulty to market*. They are in order from most to least difficult.

1. *new writing*: work by unknown or obscure playwrights; work that is outside the mainstream

2. *serious drama*: Ibsen, Chekhov, Shakespeare's tragedies and histories, for example

3. *mainstream work*: plays that many people know (such as Tennessee Williams's *A Streetcar Named Desire*); or productions featuring well-known actors

4. *accessible work*: musicals such as *Chicago* that have catchy tunes and appealing story lines

5. *family shows*: major, immensely popular productions such as *Lion King* and *Cats*

CHICAGO: *Easy to market on broadway and in the movies*

Frequency of attendance is broken into four categories of audience members by number of performances they attended:

1. once in the past 12 months

2. two or three times in the past 12 months

3. four or five times in the past 12 months

4. six times or more in the past 12 months

The Audience Climbing Frame[xi] makes the frequency/degree of difficulty strategy practical and possible to implement using the two primary defining variables set against each other on the axes of a matrix. The combination of the two variables produces a number of discrete segments, each includes members who hold different attitudes from those in other segments. This framework helps to effectively target prospective audiences according to their past behavior. Those who have attended in the past are more likely to attend in the future than those who have not. Databases are built on behavioral measures for most performance audiences marketing functions. More details on this audience-building typology are discussed in later chapters.

Benefit segmentation

This segmenting method addresses the additional value consumers seek from purchase decisions. What one attendee seeks from an experience may differ substantially from the benefits sought by another. Benefits take a variety of forms, from social and functional to health and safety, and have global application. For instance, attending a free performance of Rigoletto in Central Park provides benefits that might look like this those listed in Exhibit 7.4.

Each benefit can be marketed to entice an audience segment to attend the concert. Benefits are derived through audience research to determine the nature of why people attend a variety of entertainment activities and performances.

Segmenting by aesthetics

Aesthetics play an important role in all of our lives, and audiences often choose their form of entertainment based on their aesthetic interests. Northwestern University professor Sid Levy's audience research identified six factor adjectives used by audience members to describe what the important objects in their lives should be like.[xxii]

+ *Factor 1* suggests that people in general want stimulation, movement, and excitement. Men chose *thrilling* and *awesome* more than women to describe their favorite experiences; stimulation adjectives were most pronounced among younger adults and middle class indviduals

+ *Factor 2* is a realism factor; most strongly preferred by working class and disadvantaged people; they use words like *special* and *expensive* when describing pereformance experiences

+ *Factor 3* suggests a conventional sex identity dimension with traditional masculine (military metaphors such as *wipe out*) as opposed to feminine (relationship metaphors like *loving*) terminology; predominant among high-income groups

+ *Factor 4* yielded references to shapes such as *round, flowing,* and *curved* indicating preference for visual stimulation; occurred among all demographics

EXHIBIT 7.4 Targeting Messages by Benefit Segment

MESSAGE-BASED COMMUNICATION BASED ON AUDIENCE BENEFITS	
AUDIENCE SEGMENT	**BENEFIT**
Non-opera goers	Introduction to the opera genre
Opera lovers	An opportunity to experience the opera again
Students	A cost-free form of entertainment
Office workers	A chance to be outdoors
Teenagers	Socialization without parents
Tourists	A unique way to be part of New York City
Families	Occasion for a family activity
Tourists	Unique cultural exposure

- *Factor 5* is oriented toward social status; high-income respondents preferred *comfortable* and *luxurious*, while disadvantaged and working class respondents were more focused on *sentimental* and *customary*

- *Factor 6* deals with seriousness and frivolity; women and young adults tended to prefer *funny* and *pretty*, *crowded*, *soft*, and *musical*; men, older adults and high-income earners were inclined in the opposite direction

Adjectives yielded by such research were used to develop promotional messages that would relate directly back to actual audience descriptors.

Experience location, design, and appeal are reasons why aesthetics play an important role in marketing entertainment. Open to creative interpretation by performance marketers, these factors are strong indicators of the relevance of aesthetics for venue interior design, collateral material design, and message strategy.

Segmenting by action

One group, believed by some people in the industry to be the most powerful consumer segment of all, is called the **prosumers**. Several definitions of *prosumer* exist:[xxiii] **1.** A consumer who is an amateur in a particular field, but who is knowledgeable enough to require equipment that has some professional features ("professional" + "consumer"). **2.** A person who helps to design or customize the products they purchase ("producer" + "consumer"). **3.** A person who creates goods for their own use and also possibly to sell ("producing" + "consumer"). **4.** A person who takes steps to correct difficulties with consumer companies or markets and to anticipate future problems ("proactive" + "consumer"). The text usage is occasion-specific, but always implies a step beyond the notion of a traditional consumer.

Regardless of how they're defined, prosumers as a group are turning the heads of marketers worldwide. Euro RSCG, a big international agency, completed a nine-country study of prosumers that said prosumers can represent 20% or so of any particular group or marketing segment. They can be found everywhere, are at the vanguard of consumerism, and what they say to their friends and colleagues about brands and experiences tends to become mainstream six to 18 months later. They also vary by category: a wine prosumer, for instance, will not necessarily be a prosumer of cars.

Prosumers often reject traditional ads and invariably use the Internet to research what they are going to buy and how much they are going to pay for it. Half of prosumers distrust companies and products they cannot find on the Internet. If they want to influence prosumers, companies have to be extremely open about providing information. Further, promoting to the prosumer has taken on conflicting spins: the business sector sees the prosumer as a means of offering a wider range of products and services, whereas activists see the prosumer as having greater independence from the mainstream economy. Either way, prosumers present a challenge for marketers of entertainment and experiences.

The *cluetrain manifesto* (a futurist publication) noted that "markets are conversations" with the new economy "moving from passive consumers ... to active prosumers." For instance, Amazon.com emerged as an e-commerce leader, partially due to its ability to construct customer relations as conversations rather than simple, one-time sales. The emergence of producer consumers (prosumers) and the rise of the Consumer-to-Consumer (C2C) economy has been enabled by easier access to the internet (open source software, blogs, message boards, and so on) and the availability of selling forums (eBay, for example).[xxiv] To accommodate prosumers, entertainment marketers must establish and maintain a dialog with audiences that provides more than a simple schedule of coming attractions.

Segmenting by personas[xxv]

Consumer models called **personas** are a set of fictional archetypes based on the behaviors, attitudes, and goals. A good persona (or user archetype) is based on research, is memorable, and includes actionable information. Personas have names, personalities, pictures, personal backgrounds, families, and, most importantly, goals; they are not "average" users but specific characters. A persona is a stand-in for a unique group of people who share common goals; at the same time, persona characteristics encompass those of people in widely different demographic groups who may have similar goals.

For example, people across all demographics have similar goals when traveling by air—getting from one place to another easily. These goals can guide an airline advertising campaign to refine the scope of the target audience, and even uncover new market niches for a specific travel route. Personas bridge the gap between market segments and experience definition.

How do promoters select the right personas? Researchers interview stakeholders, customers, and users to gain insight into the experience domain and user population. This information feeds directly into the types and characteristics of the personas.

Personas and market segments provide different kinds of information. Market segmentation is a breakdown of the user attitudes and potential buying habits, while personas provide an analysis of user behavior including motivations for buying and usage patterns.

By informing each other, both market segmentation and personas provide useful information that provides a rich, complementary set of user and consumer models. Together, these tools can create a useful and more successful product definition than either could by itself.

Niche markets

People worldwide with special interests are considered niche markets. Originally utilized by magazine publishing, today's niche markets are also useful targets for Internet promotion. Directed Internet messages can reach larger worldwide audiences with lower initial cost than satellite TV channels. And although specialized offerings may appeal to a small number of people, cumulatively they represent a large market that can be easily aggregated on the Internet. Shows with dedicated small audiences that could never make it into prime time use what is called *silvercasting*.[xxvi]

For example, Sail.tv (a boating site) attracted 70,000 viewers in its first month of Web casts. OutZone.com has gay and lesbian programming created in conjunction with PlanetOut, an entertainment company that focuses on that audience. HGTVPro offers programming aimed at contractors and builders, and Discovery Communications offers video clips from its library of documentaries and other educational programs to help students with their homework. Instructional videos are also available on the Internet by TotalVid, including videos that teach everything from how to play a guitar to the best yoga poses.

Immigrants and expatriates are two niche audiences that are both large and attractive to Internet broadcasters

7.5 Yacht racers are a profitable niche market for advertisers.

who provide news and entertainment from the audiences' home countries. Toronto's JumpTV, for instance, offers live Internet transmission of television station broadcasts from more than 60 countries to expatriates around the world.

As the global population increases, so does the trend toward niche marketing. No longer a world of mass-mediated viewers, niche audiences dominate the landscape with special needs, wants, and motivations. Successful marketing identifies niche segments to receive promotional communications focused on their specific interests.

Finally

Although there is no single right way to segment a market, the implications for segmentating audience characteristics, before, during, and after attending entertainment events are great. Segmentation is a dynamic process; new segments emerge as older ones disappear or are no longer viable because of market changes. For this reason, segmentation justifies a considerable and continuous commitment to audience research, as explained in the next chapter.

GOT IT?

- There are many ways to segment entertainment audiences, but all segmentation schemes should possess the same criteria: mutual exclusivity, exhaustiveness, measurability, sustainability, and actionability.

- Performance differentiation allows marketers to concentrate promotional strategies on a single segment or niche market to maximize impact and stimulate ticket purchase.

- VALS 2 is an important marketing tool that segments the U.S. population into finaicial resource-based lifestyle segments that focus on principle, status, and action orientations.

- PRIZM software clusters U.S. audiences by zip code according to buying habits and media patterns; MOSIAC's U.S. neighborhood classifications enable marketers to target buyers and households with greater precision. GlobalScan and global MOSIAC are based on lifestyle types appropriate for most world metropolitan areas.

- Gender, religion, economic, and ethnic demographic segments are important for developing global entertainment marketing strategies.

- Segmenting by price, behavior, and benefits help entertainment promoters craft communication messages to the needs of these audience groups.

NOW TRY THIS

1. Go to the Claritas web site at www.yawyl.claritas.com and look up your own zip code. Do the PRIZM clusters for your code make sense? Why or why not?

2. Go to www.thematuremarket.com/.../metlife_mature_market and revisit the American baby boomer market. What geographic locations are best suited to marketing leisure and entertainment activities? What does the group's racial and ethnic composition contribute to marketing strategy?

3. Select and compare an advertisement that portrays gender stereotypes with one that does not. Would the target audiences for these ads be similar or different? Why?

QUESTIONS FOR DISCUSSION

1. As the manager of the Bolshoi Ballet, your job is to develop a marketing strategy for their upcoming world tour. What global segments would you target for promotional messages? Provide a rationale for your decision.

2. Discuss the value of cohort segmentation for targeting mature consumers for a vacation destination.

3. Which system, PRIZM, MOSIAC, and MONITOR, would be best for promoting season subscriptions to an outdoor music venue for summer concerts in Massachusetts? Why?

4. What new market segments may emerge for global audiences in the future?

MORE STUFF TO READ ABOUT
MARKET SEGMENTS

www.seniormag.com provides insights for marketing to seniors.

www.hispanicmarket.net has information on Hispanic marketing.

www.sri.com is an independent international nonprofit research firm.

www.demographicsnow.com is a source for US demographic data.

American Demographics Magazine prints the latest research on segmented marketing.

[i]P. Kotler and J. Scheff (1998), *Standing Room Only: Strategies for Marketing the Performing Arts.* Harvard Business School Press, pp. 108–9.

[ii]Michael Walker (2005), *Marketing to Seniors*, 2nd ed. 1st Books Library, p. 52.

[iii]J. F. Engel, R. D. Blackwell & P. W. Miniard (1995), *Consumer Behavior* 8th ed., Dryden Press, chapter 3.

[iv]Statistics provided by MetLife's Mature Market Institute, Westport CT, 2003.

[v]From 50Plus.com online case studies.

[vi]Joe Marconi (2000), Future Marketing. NTC Business Books, p. 107.

[vii]S. Plog (1991), *Leisure Travel: Making It a Growth Market … Again!* Wiley.

[viii]Presented in J. W. Smith & A. Clurman (1997), *Rocking the Ages.* Harper Business Books.

[ix]From Mediamark Research Inc.'s teen market profile, 2004.

[x]From K. M. Palan (2001), "Gender Identity in Consumer Behavior Research," *Academy of Marketing Science Review*, p. 10.

[xi]Study conducted by graduate students at California State University, Fullerton using the *Sunday Los Angeles Times Calendar* as selection criteria and $500 as an entertainment budget for 25 women and 25 men who were asked to plan a month's entertainment.

[xii]This discussion is taken from Arnould, Price, Zinkhan, Op. Cit. p. 578.

[xiii]Arnould, Price, Zinkhan Op Cit p. 595.

[xiv]From J. Fetto (2002), "Targeted Media," *American Demographics*, July/August.

[xv]O. Kucukemiorgllu (1999), "Market Segmentation by Using Consumer Lifestyle Dimensions and Ethnocentrism: An Empirical Study," *European Journal of Marketing* 35 (5–6):1–9.

[xvi]J. Tam & S. Tai (1998), "Research Note: The Psychographic Segmentation of the Female Market in Greater China," *International Marketing Review* 15 (1): 25–51.

[xvii]Fritz Reusswig Hermann Lotze-Campen Katrin Gerlinger (2005), "Changing Global Lifestyle and Consumption Patterns", Potsdam Institute for Climate Impact Research (PIK) Global Change & Social Systems Department.

[xviii]Philadelphia Arts Market Study, Pew Charitable Trusts, 1989 and Marketing the Arts in Cleveland, commissioned by the Cleveland Foundation, 1985.

[xix]Sidney Levy (1980) "Arts Consumers and Aesthetic Attributes" in M. Mokwa, W. Dawson, E. Prieve, (ed.) Marketing the Arts. Praeger.

[xx]From Morris Hargreaves McIntyre's *Audience Builder* schema.

[xxi]From the key note address made by Gerri Morris, & Morris Hargreaves McIntyre at the 2005 Arts Marketing Association conference in Belfast on 22 July, 2005.

[xxii]Sid Levy, OpCit.

[xxiii]As defined by www.wordspy.com.

[xxiv]From www.futurematters.org.uk

[xxv]Elaine Buchen report located at cooper.com/newsletter, Feb–Mar. 2002.

[xxvi]Saul Hansell (2006), "Much for the Few," *The New York Times*, March 12.

Chapter 8

RESEARCHING & MEASURING ENTERTAINMENT AUDIENCES

> *If you can't measure it*
> *you can't manage it.*
> Anonymous

Chapter Objectives

After reading this chapter, you will be able to answer these questions:

+ What is *applied research* and what types of studies fall into this category?

+ How do *projective techniques* enable audience disclosure?

+ How do *new audiences* differ from past audience members?

+ What are the various methods of *audience measurement*?

+ How is *advertising research* different from other forms of evaluation?

+ Why is *methodological convergence* necessary in today's marketplace?

+ How is audience research *analyzed?*

Every promotional plan requires primary research to determine what consumers want and how they perceive a client's brand. Understanding audiences can only be accomplished through field studies, focus groups, and questionnaires. And although the people who promote entertainment are not always the same people who conduct the research, marketers in the entertainment industry must understand the research process in order to effectively utilize the results. Applied research is conducted with all types of consumers and audiences of entertainment for planning and predicting functions. This chapter details the most relevant qualitative and quantitative research techniques and their value for use in entertainment research. We also review audience satisfaction measurements and the use of syndicated services.

WHY, WHAT, AND WHO OF RESEARCH

The purpose of applied entertainment research is *discovery*. Discovery consists of three aspects: it is a process of finding out and *describing* what it is, it is a way of *explaining* why things are the way they are, and it is a method of *evaluating* performance satisfaction. The chapter is organized around these three approaches to discovery, which are carried out using two distinct research techniques. Quantitative audience research, the first technique measures how many people attend, watch, listen, and visit performances and venues, and most of it is conducted to determine what to charge advertisers. In such a competitive industry, entertainment producers must understand not only how many, but *why* audiences attend concerts, visit resorts and casinos, and enter performance venues. To answer the why questions, qualitative research methods, the second technique, are employed.

Why we conduct research

Discovery is conducted for a variety of reasons, mostly to learn more about audience preferences and wishes. Both qualitative and quantitative methods of data collection are appropriate. Three aspects of discovery and their purposes for audience research are explained here.

Finding out and describing

Research conducted to find answers to audience-related questions is called **descriptive research**. Common in the leisure, entertainment and tourism areas, descriptive research helps marketers keep up with a constantly changing landscape. Field research is used to track basic patterns of behavior as needed for market profiles or needs assessment. Statistics gathered by syndicated services are also used to describe market conditions.

Explaining

Explanatory research seeks to answer the how and why questions and use the answers for predicting future trends. Going beyond description, this form seeks to explain the patterns and trends observed: Why is a particular destination losing popularity? How do casino developments gain approval against the wishes of a local community? Why do some social groups and not others patronize the arts? What venue modifications will make the consumption experience more enjoyable? The focus is causality, and knowledge gained is used to predict behavior. Prediction is a key aim of much of the research that takes place in entertainment.

Evaluating

Evaluative research arises from the need to make judgments on the success or effectiveness of programs developed or in place—for example, whether a particular advertising campaign for a performance has been cost-effective. Evaluative research measures success and failure. Because audiences have monetary value, promoters measure them using ticket receipts, exit polls, advanced reservations, and past performance. To measure audience satisfaction, venue managers solicit feedback through exit surveys or postcards for service evaluation. Resulting numbers determine advertising rates and predict revenues. Research giants such as Neilson compile and syndicate purchase and attendance statistics for a monthly charge to manufacturers and advertising agencies.

Purpose of research

Research plays a key role for all organizations in the entertainment industry that engage in policy making, planning, and managing resources to achieve their goals. Outcomes and examples of research efforts include: *policies* for an arts center to encourage contemporary composers; *plans* for a casino to increase visits by a particular audience demographic; *management systems* to implement user-pay programs for a national park.

Who conducts research

Three groups that conduct research for entertainment organizations are important: government agencies and commercial organizations, consultants, and venue managers.

Using their own in-house researchers, government agencies conduct censuses, which tourism bureaus use to tally departures and visitations. Because of the magnitude of these studies, few independent organizations can undertake them, yet they are invaluable resources for entertainment researchers. Advertising agency in-house research teams and private research companies collect data for entertainment providers.

Consultants establish specialized areas of research and are occasionally linked with academic institutions. They work on a project-by-project basis with industry clients and advertising agencies.

Managers of entertainment venues and attractions see research as a vital part of their responsibilities. Managers supervise research on customers, staff, performance, competitors, and products that is used to make strategic decisions. For example, resort managers routinely receive information on usage levels from sales figures or bookings, while an urban park district manager conducts specific data-gathering exercises to determine attendance levels.

Foundations and government agencies provide free resources for analyzing consumer data, such as:

+ *Pew Internet & American Life* provides unbiased research that explores the impact of the Internet.

+ *U.S. Census Bureau* contains an endless supply of information on people and businesses, including the Economic Census with industry information from many countries including quarterly financial reports. The bureau's American FactFinder focuses on demographics and features a population counter; Statistical Abstracts Fact Sheet provides a summary of demographic data compiled by city, state, county or zip code.

+ *U.S. Department of Labor's Bureau of Labor Statistics* has a demographic section that slices data by age and gender. Consumer Expenditures report categorizes how much was spent on what.

APPROACHES TO ENTERTAINMENT-FOCUSED RESEARCH

Similar to standard market research, entertainment researchers rely on empirical research for decision-making tasks. Empirical research can be theoretical or applied.

Theoretical research is conducted to draw general conclusions about a phenomenon under study. Most theoretical research is deductive, starting with the explanation or hypothesis, then gathering descriptive data to test a theory or explanation, and finally analyzing the data to test the hypothesis against it. Academics conduct theoretical research, which may ground future study for a variety of marketing and consumer research applications.

Applied research, commonly recommended for entertainment, makes use of existing knowledge to find solutions to particular problems. Applied research is inductive, beginning with observation and description and utilizing data analysis to explain what happens. The ability to induce explanations from observational data is most appropriate for entertainment research.

Empirical studies, both theoretical and applied, are the building blocks of research and knowledge, because their conclusions are based on specifically collected information. Studies following a *positivist tradition* are most often used in the natural sciences to prove a hypothesis from observed data. For social science, an *interpretive model* is adopted for its reliance on the people who are studied to provide their own explanation of their situation or behavior.

This flexible approach to data collection involves qualitative methods and uses an inductive approach to entertainment research. Our discussions of research methods are devoted to applied techniques appropriate for learning about *new audience* members. Applied research is invoked to prepare the situation analysis section of the promotional plan.

Two Branches of Empirical Research

THEORETICAL (SCIENTIFIC)	APPLIED (PRACTICAL)
Deductive	Inductive
Hypothesis testing	Descriptive studies, projective techniques, Explanatory studies, evaluative studies

A CLOSER LOOK AT MUSEUM RESEARCH

Sydney's Powerhouse Museum

PROBLEM: When attendance levels dropped by 20% in two years, the Powerhouse Museum in Sydney (Australia's largest museum) conducted an inductive study to determine what people wanted from a museum experience. During in-depth interviews, visitors and members described what they wanted in experiential concepts, learning opportunities, and exhibits. The information is summarized here.

Experiential concepts:

· Hands-on (active) experiences

· The ability to use all the senses

· Something to take away from the visit

Learning opportunities:

· To start from familiar concepts and things and move to unfamiliar

· To control their own experiences and amount and depth of information they access

· To cater to all levels of learning, for different age groups, and for adults and children

· Exhibitions that help them to learn something

Exhibits:

- To touch objects and displays

- Not too much reading

- Computer interactives that enhance knowledge; beyond button-pushing

- To get up close to objects and displays

- Exhibits that are well maintained and working at all times

- Staff on the floor to answer questions and bring the exhibition alive

- Exhibits that are realistic

- Places in exhibitions where they can sit down and "'take it in"

- Exhibitions that encourage sharing among a group

RESULTS: In-depth-interviews yielded information that was used to reinvigorate the museum. Innovations and improvements raised attendance levels by 23%, showing a net 3% gain in the number of visitors the following year. Membership increased by 9% overall, a healthy sign of growth for the museum.

What do you think?

1. What other research might be conducted to supplement the museum's original study?

2. How often should organizations conduct preference research with its audiences?

What's a new audience?

We conduct audience research because we can no longer depend upon our previous levels of continuing and devoted attention to a specific entertainment brand. Today's audiences are challenging. Not only do the audience members have hundreds of entertainment forms and brands to choose from, they have access to endless performance and brand information through the Internet.

Current audiences are pressed for time, have short attention spans, and don't trust mass media to provide the most reliable information. New audiences value genuine experience, not simply a mere performance commodity. Compare this idea to the difference between a Broadway play and the film version of the same play; many people prefer the original delivery system. In their quest for experience, today's audiences are *individualistic* in their needs and wants, as well as *involved* in their purchases, *independent* in choice selections, and *informed* about experiential performance options.

To understand new audiences, entertainment marketers commission or conduct applied research. The next three sections characterize the techniques used for collecting data from audience members: descriptive, explanatory, and evaluative. Descriptive studies are useful for portraying situations and experiences, while explanatory studies reveal the whys and hows of those situations or experiences. Evaluative studies analyze effectiveness and allow marketers to reconfigure entertainment experiences based upon consumer input.

DESCRIPTIVE STUDIES

Description involves direct observation, what can be seen on site and while the action is happening. Researchers must get out into the field, which means meeting and talking with audience members as they experience all forms of entertainment. Anthropologists have shown us methods applicable for conducting entertainment research where it happens, rather than in a controlled or laboratory situation.

One of the most effective ways to describe and understand what's going on in entertainment environments is to employ **ethnographic** research to describe consumer cultures. The ethnographic approach to entertainment research draws on a variety of qualitative techniques to understand the world through the eyes of your research subjects. In leisure studies the approach has become particularly associated with cultural studies. Researchers use observation and conversation to study people's behavior in everyday contexts—what we call field research. Being in the field means integration into a particular consumer entertainment culture. We use *unstructured* data collection to focus on a specific group or culture—say a group of seniors experiencing a museum, or music fans. Analysis involves interpreting the meanings and functions of human action.

Like anthropologists who go into the field to research cultures, ethnographic researchers go into entertainment environments to understand how audiences behave at plays, in venues, and while shopping. For instance, Hilton Hotels gave business travelers cameras to capture their feelings about hotel rooms. They learned from the photographs that business guests want wireless Internet connections and a well-stocked bar. At LegoLand, researchers posed as park attendees to observe families as they experienced rides and activities. Children were observed straining to see animals over rails and barriers. This information caused park officials to replace barriers with floor-to-ceiling glass, providing young children with

© Tomasz Trojanowski, 2010. Used under license from Shutterstock, Inc.

8.1 Consumer ethnographer documents household brands.

unobstructed views of wildlife. By putting themselves in the consumers' shoes, researchers learn important information that is useful for entertainment brand enhancement.

Ethnographic research focuses on an *emic* perspective. This type of research seeks to present an insiders view by using a non-judgmental orientation to cultural practices. The researcher "hangs out" in a particular location, relying on visual symbols and consumption rituals for insight. He or she works with an informant or "native speaker"—a member of the culture under study—to answer questions and validate assumptions. To better understand the hip-hop musical culture, a researcher merges into the group. Identifying a particular group of hip-hoppers and spending time watching them is a first step. Next, it's important to meet and talk with group members about their music. An informant helps the researcher understand the group's dress code, language, and musical rituals.

The Museum of Modern Art (MoMA) used the ethnographic technique of observation to learn about the special needs of older visitors (Over 60 market segment), as presented in our focus on the senior audience segment.

FOCUS ON RESEARCH ETHICS

Senior Spies

The Museum of Modern Art saw a decline in senior volunteers and visitors during the recent exhibition season. To ascertain reasons for the decline, they placed a research team posing as museum docents to observe senior visitors for three months. The information would be used to develop new programs and recruit volunteers to maximize the museum's relationship with this audience group.

The spies gained an understanding of the particular wants and needs of this audience segment while working at the museum with a veteran docent who acted as their informant. Presented below is a list of discoveries the docent-spies make, as well as their recommendations for addressing the needs of this special group. Using research results, museum officials implemented the recommendations that caused a 17% increase in visitor satisfaction over the next six months.

Discovery	Recommendation
· Unfamiliarity with museum environments	Offer guided tours for new visitors
· Disrupted by noisy children	Schedule visits for early mornings
· Difficulty standing in ticket lines	Modify ticketing system
· Frequent fatigue	Provide seating and catalogs to read

• Inability to go with the flow	Limit numbers in gallery at one time
• Interest in stories and material from the era 1910–1960	Focus exhibitions on early decades
• Limited information access	Promote activities through age-specific channels
• Hours of uncommitted time	Recruit and train docent volunteers; reward their efforts with service symbols

What do you think?

1. How ethical is spying on mature audiences without their knowledge or permission?

2. How should the privacy issue be handled by museum officials?

Descriptive research has enabled entertainment providers to pinpoint the needs and wants of its audiences. This first step in understanding consumer motivations should be expanded with another type of research that probes more deeply into the culture of entertainment consumption. To do that, we turn to explanatory research.

Critical incident technique and trailer calls

Two of the most popular methods of evaluation important for determining the success or failure of an experience are the critical incident technique and trailer calls as characterized in Exhibit 8.1.

In **critical incident techniques** (CIT), end users are asked to identify specific incidents which they experienced personally and which had an important effect on the final outcome of an interactive experience. The emphasis is on incidents rather than opinions, which can be vague. The context of the incident may also be elicited. Data from many users is collected and analyzed qualitatively.

Study participants are requested to follow the three stages described below in the same order:

1. Focus on an incident, which had a strong positive influence on the result of the interaction and describe the incident.

2. Describe what led up to the incident.

3. Describe how the incident helped the successful completion of the interaction.

There will be some variation in the number of positive and negative incidents to which users respond. Begin with a positive incident in order to set a constructive tone with the user. Hotels,

EXHIBIT 8.1 Service Marketing Research Elements

ELEMENTS OF AN EFFECTIVE MARKETING RESEARCH PROGRAM ON EXPERIENCES[1]			
TYPE OF RESEARCH	**RESEARCH OBJECTIVE**	**METHOD**	**FREQUENCY**
Complaint solicitation	Identify dissatisfactions Locate service failure points	qualitative	continuous
Critical incident studies	Identify 'best practices' Identify audience requirements	qualitative	periodic
Requirements research	Inputs for qualitative research regarding audience requirements	qualitative	periodic
Relationship survey, SERVQUAL survey	Monitor & track service performance Access expectation/perception gaps	quantitative	annual
Trailer calls	Obtain immediate feedback on performance of transaction	quantitative	continuous
Service expectation meetings	To create dialog with audiences Identify audience segment needs	qualitative	annual
Process checkpoint evaluations	Determine audience perceptions Identify and solve service problems	quantitative	periodic
Market-oriented ethnography	Research audiences in natural settings Study global audience cultures	qualitative	periodic
Mystery shopping	Measure employee performance	quantitative	quarterly
Audience panels	Monitor changing audience expectations Provide forum for audience input	qualitative	continuous

| Future expectation research | Forecast audience expectations Develop & test new ideas | qualitative | periodic |
| Database marketing research | Identify audience requirements | quantitative | continuous |

amusement parks, and public television stations use CIT to gather perspectives in the customer's own words.

Trailer calls capture information about key service encounters with a customer. In this method, customers are asked a short list of questions immediately after a particular transaction about their satisfaction with the transaction and contact personnel with whom they interacted. Hotels use this method because visitors presume the call is followed up on to ensure that they are satisfied, so it serves both as a research tool and a form of customer service.

EXPLANATORY STUDIES

The concept of sharing information is an optimistic one if audiences are not as forthcoming as we'd like them to be. With privacy concerns, audiences are often reluctant to disclose details that may later come back to haunt them. People worry that information may be used in ways other than those intended by the research.

When conducting consumer research, challenge begets innovation. If we are to understand the whys and hows of entertainment brand or product perceptions, we must develop clever methods for probing the minds of our audience. So we do the prudent thing—we borrow from past success. Psychologists developed inkblots to probe the innermost thoughts of their patients. By showing them a series of patterns, therapists listen while patients interpret what they see based on past experiences or familiar associations. They disclose information about a topic rather than responding to directed questions. In one sense, they *project* their feelings on to an unrelated task, thus avoiding uncomfortable associations to them.

Projective techniques

Audience researchers use the same type of projective techniques as those developed by psychologists. We give respondents a task to perform that provides us with insights without directly asking them to disclose their personal or private experiences. And we can make it fun. If ballet is the subject, bring out your respondents "inner child" by asking them to draw and color their renditions of a ballerina, or to name the celebrity who might dance in that role. From their drawings we gather information to use in promotional media that capture the humor and satire of the playful drawings.

Projective techniques uncover a person's innermost thoughts and feelings by allowing him to project his beliefs onto other people or objects. The notion is that unconscious desires and feelings can be explored by presenting participants with an unthreatening situation where they are free to interpret and respond to various stimuli.

This technique is especially useful for uncovering subtle differences in how consumers feel about brands in categories where no obvious differences exist. For instance, opera is a genre of performances with similar audience expectations, but opera as an experience may invoke a variety of associations that are based on specific consumer experiences or media promotions. Audience experiences, gathered through a series of projective techniques, may reveal that audiences choose to attend a specific opera based on the venue in which it is performed rather than on the quality of the performance. Armed with this information, promoters might present the *venue* as the star instead of the specific opera for their next performance. The new Disney Concert Hall in Los Angeles is such a venue, selling out seats a year in advance to audiences who are more curious about Frank Gehry's architectural creation than they are music aficionados.

© Jupiter Images

8.2 Bubbles provide researchers with ways for consumers to interpret perceptions.

© Kheng Guan Toh, 2010. Used under license from Shutterstock, Inc.

8.3 Rorschach ink blot test.

Projective techniques differ from traditional methods because they allow information to emerge from the research rather than from questions posed directly to audience members. Like all research techniques, however, projective methods require a problem that research can solve and a concise research question for focus. The only difference between traditional and projective research techniques is the way we go about getting answers to solve the problem.

As early as the nineteenth century, inkblots, known as Rorschach tests, were used to probe the minds of crime suspects for signs of guilt. Projective techniques were therapeutic in nature and consisted of five types: constitutive (modeling with clay), constructive (building blocks), interpretive (word association), cathartic (play), and refractive (expressive behavior). It wasn't until after World

EXHIBIT 8.2 Components of Haire Study that Create Projection

GOOD WIFE SHOPPING LIST	LAZY WIFE SHOPPING LIST
Pound and a half of hamburger	Pound and a half of hamburger
2 loaves Wonder bread	2 loaves Wonder bread
Bunch of carrots	Bunch of carrots
1 can Rumford's Baking Power	1 can Rumford's Baking Powder
Maxwell House coffee (drip ground)	Nescafe instant coffee
2 cans Del Monte peaches	2 cans Del Monte peaches
6 lbs. potatoes	6 lbs. potatoes

Source: Zeithaml, Bitner & Gremler, *Services Marketing*, McGraw-Hill 2006, p. 144

War II that psychotherapy was applied to market research. A famous study by Mason Haire used projective techniques to gather consumer attitudes toward Nescafe instant coffee by developing two shopping lists with a single ingredient difference. One list featured Nescafe instant coffee and the other included Maxwell House drip coffee. All the other items were the same on both lists.

Fifty women were asked to describe the woman who developed each list. The woman who listed Maxwell House coffee was characterized as a "good housewife" for buying fresh roast for her husband, but the woman who listed Nescafe was labeled as "lazy" for purchasing instant coffee for her family. Results of that study were used to develop an advertising campaign where instant coffee was portrayed as rewarding to a family and socially acceptable to serve guests.

Entertainment researchers might compile two lists of entertainment preferences with a paired variable, such as the opera and musical theater, and ask two groups to describe the list's developer. Results will produce the images that opera and musical theater project for a specific demographic, enabling managers to develop promotions to either change or strengthen those images.

One advantage of using projective techniques today is their cost efficiency and compatibility with in-depth interviews and focus groups. With increased audience choices in the entertainment marketplace, researchers must find selling hooks to differentiate one brand from another. It's a researcher's job to uncover subtle differences that can be used for effective promotional communication.

EXHIBIT 8.3 Research Games

The Great Dinner Party

In order to better understand the fan-worship response of audiences, celebrity industry researchers give interviewees these instructions:

"You have been invited to five dinner parties, all scheduled for the same night. For logistical reasons, you can attend only one. From the hosts listed below, choose the one whose party you would attend and give the reasons for your decision."

1. *Elton John: musician, performer*

2. *Madonna: entertainer*

3. *Mickey Mouse: Disney star*

4. *David Letterman: talk show host*

5. *Sean Penn: film star*

Source: Rein, Kotler, Hamlin & Stoller, *High Visibility*, 1998

Here's still another situation. The choices given in Exhibit 8.3 may seem runners in a mere popularity contest, but the respondent's reasons for attending should reveal the motivations behind his or her choice and provide insight into the celebrity's image.

By comparing the celebrity's perceived image with the real image as reported by the Dinner Party respondents, marketers can develop appropriate strategies to close the gap between perception and reality.

Projective techniques used to research audience motivation

By asking consumers to talk about other people or solve other people's problems, researchers have obtained insightful information that was not obtained through other methods. Other-directed research can successfully elicit self-disclosure rather than mere description. Four of the most common techniques used in projective research are word association, symbolic association, thematic apperception, and object sorting. Here are some situational examples of how these psychological tools can work for understanding audience motivations.

- Let's say New York's Kennedy Center wants to develop a creative concept for advertising the upcoming opera season. Using *word associations*, researchers ask for types of performances that come to mind when they hear words such as foreign language and *old fashioned*. Or they ask what words best describe genres such as ballet and musical. The results may help position opera away from negative connotations consumers have for such performances.

- *Symbolic associations* are made between an object and its meaning to a consumer. A casino may symbolize crime to one consumer and fun to another. Venue researchers may show respondents a party scene around a craps table to determine their perceptions about gambling. This information is valuable for developing brand messages about their casino and its activities to a specific audience segment.

- Story scenarios are gathered from consumers as part of **thematic apperception testing (TAT)**. Using a picture of people sitting in their cars in freeway traffic, we ask consumers to tell us a story about a time when they were in such a situation, or develop a story about what the other drivers are thinking as they crawl along the freeway at five miles per hour. Responses can be used in print advertising to show how commuting on Amtrak allows riders to relax rather than riot.

- Researchers may ask consumers to group items of like kind together to tell how drivers perceive types of entertainment. In one study, participants in **object-sorting** activities could not place Cirque de Soleil in either the circus or the dance categories, opting for a new category instead. From this research, Cirque decided to classify itself as a hybrid form of entertainment to avoid unfavorable associations with either of the other two alternatives.

Four standard approaches to uncovering layers of consumer thoughts have been improved to expand our understanding of the motivations and brand preferences of today's audience. Visualize peeling an onion.

Using projective techniques to peel the audience onion

Sophistication and discrimination are adjectives used to describe the audiences that marketers must confront when peeling the information onion. To penetrate the layers of consumer thought, researchers must provide a stimulus to generate an understanding of the meanings consumers associate with that stimulus. Constructing an effective stimulus requires a great deal of creativity on the researcher's part.

Using open-ended formats, projective techniques are classified according to the type of information they yield—either diagnostic or descriptive. Whereas the use of projective techniques for psychotherapy is most often therapeutic, the intentions for marketing and audience research are *rich description* and *self-disclosure*. Five types of projective techniques are available: free association, choice ordering (ranking), completion, construction, and expressive (role playing).

Free association

Researchers use **free associations** to understand consumer relationships with a brand or product by asking for words, images, and thoughts in response to a specific stimulus. Word association has served as an effective elicitation technique for decades. *Neutral words* that have nothing to do with the brand—theme park, performance, casino– are used to mask the actual identity of the brand. *Key words* that directly relate to a venue brand—comfortable, spacious, easy to access—are useful for expanding neutral responses.

Brand-specific associations are best accomplished with *personification* techniques. Planners ask, "If Sea World were a celebrity, who would it be?" Visual personification, called *photo sorting*, requires participants to match pictures of people with a brand that reflects the brand's personality. This technique pairs facial expressions in photographs with brands in a single category to draw out a brand's personality. Brands that elicit smiling faces can be further grouped and sorted for distinctive characteristics.

Laguna Museum's photo sorting research results showed that visitors matched the museum's brand with pictures of older audiences, enabling the museum to develop a trend-setting campaign that appealed to younger audiences, changing consumer perceptions about attending museum functions. Tattoo art, motorcycle artifacts, and surf culture exhibits replaced traditional offerings; percussion bands replaced string quartets at function openings, and the gift shop added jewelry and ceramics to its retail inventory. These audience-appropriate entertainment innovations enabled the museum to increase its membership and exhibit attendance.

A *photo-and-tale* technique used for Denny's Restaurants struck gold when consumer collages showed an association between their restaurant and overweight, old-fashioned men and women. Researchers used photo sorts to obtain self-image portrayals of mid-priced restaurant consumers. Subjects were given a group of 40 photographs featuring people of varying sizes and shapes, modes of dress, levels of occupation, and economic status. They were instructed to place the photos of people who were most likely to appreciate food preparation and appearance in one pile and photos of people who were unlikely to care about those features in another pile. By analyzing the similar responses of the folks in their likely-to-care piles, researchers found that their target audience cast themselves as intelligent, physically fit, and well-dressed. Research yielded the concept for a new campaign featuring stylish folks with discriminating taste in their ads with the tag line, "The meal that dictates the fashion."

Word associations generate adjectives usually associated with a brand, and personifications help researchers identify the images audiences and consumers hold of a brand and its competitors. Association techniques are also useful for determining the effects of brand slogans, logo designs and sponsorships Exhibit 8.4 shows word associations shoppers made for the Mall of America, located near Minneapolis.

Ranking

For this technique, consumers rank, or choice order, brand preferences and explain why certain aspects are more important than others in their entertainment brand selections. When respondents rank brand benefits from most to least important, researchers can probe their reasons for choosing those benefits. Knott's Berry Farm theme park research revealed that female consumers ranked LegoLand ahead of their brand because of the tactical factor involved in building blocks. Marketers used the findings to focus a tactile-based advertising message ("Knotts will keep your feet moving and your hands busy") to women in gender appropriate magazines.

EXHIBIT 8.4 Associations Made for Mall of America

ATTRIBUTES *(what the brand/experience has)*		
PRODUCT-RELATED ATTRIBUTES	**USER IMAGERY**	**BRAND PERSONALITY**
Multiple shopping options	Fashionable, trendy,	Fun, adventuresome, outgoing,
Ample parking	stylish, unisex	athletic, artsy
BENEFITS *(what the brand/experience does for consumers)*		
FUNCTIONAL BENEFITS	**EXPERIENTIAL BENEFITS**	**SYMBOLIC BENEFITS**
Big names, wide range of prices, product variety	Greenery, escalators, kid activities, cafe smells	Feeling of self-expression and self-assurance

Ranking is a simple yet effective technique for understanding relationships between brands, benefit preferences, and other measurable characteristics.

Completion devices

Audience needs and values surface by using **completions**, techniques that ask respondents to finish sentences, stories, conversations, or arguments.

Using a *first-person scenario*, planners ask participants to complete the phrase, "When I think of ballet ————." Responses were stereotypical. When they used *third-person scenarios*, ("When an average person thinks of ballet ————."), respondents were more likely to reveal their innermost feelings. People are much more willing to talk about an average person or a friend than themselves for fear of negative connotations associated with an admission about one's self.

Hotel and hospitality researchers often employ sentence completions to understand "whether or not" and "why" issues associated with visiting their venues. Look at the difference in responses the New York Hilton received by changing from first- to third-person scenarios. Asked in the first person, a respondent filled in the blanks like this:

+ When in New York, I would stay at the Hilton *because* I like the restaurant.

+ I'd stay at the New York Hilton *if* it were across town.

Brand personality profiles

Ratings are ideal for assessing brand personality traits. Jennifer Aaker developed five factors of brand personality: sincerity (wholesome, cheerful), excitement (daring, up-to-date), competence (reliable, successful), sophistication (upper class, charming), and ruggedness (outdoorsy and tough). She asked consumers to rate the descriptiveness of each personality trait for brands using a seven-point scale (1 = not at all descriptive; 7 = extremely descriptive). Five of the 37 brand profiles are presented below.

	APPLE	CNN	LEGO	LEXUS	MTV	SONY	VISA
Sincerity	.92	.99	1.11	.87	.70	.87	.90
Excitement	.95	1.02	1.10	1.12	1.27	.94	.87
Competence	1.07	1.18	1.01	1.07	.82	1.02	1.02
Sophistication	.86	.93	.87	1.27	1.02	.89	.87
Ruggedness	.92	1.01	1.10	1.03	.93	.90	.87

Some brands were strong on one factor (MTV with excitement, CNN with competence), and other brands were high on several factors. For global destination brands Japan and Spain, a "peacefulness" dimension emerged for Spain in place of the "competency" dimension for Japan.

Source: Jennifer Aaker, "Dimensions of Brand Personality." *Journal of Marketing Research* 34 (8) (1997), 347–366, and Jennifer Aaker, Veronica Benet-Martinez & Jordi Garolera, "Consumption Symbols as Carriers of Culture:, *Journal of Personality and Social Psychology* 81 (3) (2001), 492–608)

From this set of responses, researchers understand that the restaurant is better than the hotel, or that it is in the wrong location. If they made changes based on this information, they could incur unnecessary expenses.

By asking questions in the third person, however, Hilton got these responses:

+ When my neighbor is in New York, she stays at the Hilton because she likes to show off.

+ My neighbor would stay at the New York Hilton if she had the money.

The second set of responses indicates that this consumer perceives the Hilton to be prestigious and expensive, answers not probable when using the first-person orientation. This consumer is much more willing to be truthful when projecting her feelings onto the neighbor than admitting her own feelings.

Completions work well in individual interviews and for group interaction. Focus group leaders use completion techniques to begin discussions by asking participants to talk about what they were thinking as they finished the exercise. Because they don't require extensive facilitation, completions are easily developed and administered by researchers at all skill levels.

Construction techniques

Requiring a more complex and controlled intellectual activity, **construction** techniques ask consumers to develop a story from a specific stimulus. One of the most effective techniques builds on consumer metaphors. The Zaltman Metaphor Elicitation Technique (ZMET) requires consumers to assemble a *collage* of magazine pictures to represent their feelings about a brand or a venue. Upon completion, the collage provides a launching pad for consumers to discuss their feelings in detail with the researcher about the brand as portrayed by the metaphorical pictures they chose.

Cartoons also provide a creative mechanism for learning about consumer perceptions. Nicknamed *bubbles*, drawings of people in relevant branding situations are used to generate a response to a comment made in the cartoon. In the wake of a population explosion in Mexico, such cartoons were used to elicit information from Hispanic men about their attitudes toward practicing birth control. The fill-in-the-bubble cartoonish nature of the pictured questions looked like a fictional story rather than an incriminating personal admission for the respondents. Researchers learned from the cartoons that men, in order to retain their *machismo*, refused contraception, which resulted in producing large families that many of the men were unable to support financially. This revelation provided the input for a public education campaign using a macho cartoon penis character to extol the virtues of contraception.

Role playing

Stories, myths and legends are the stuff of consumer research. To generate consumer narratives, role-playing works well in situations where consumers cannot describe their actions or behaviors, but maybe they can act them out. Assuming the role of flyer and flight attendant, Virgin Atlantic Airways passengers acted out a typical scenario between a rude attendant and frequent flyer. Researchers learned that flyers prefer discretion to "being scolded for using the wrong toilet," yet they want attendants to keep passengers sober by refusing to serve them additional alcoholic beverages on long trips. Virgin repositioned its attendants as "flight consultants" and trained their employees to respond to consumer requests rather than to initiate interaction.

Consumer *stories* are useful for gathering information based on specific situations. Virgin Atlantic also used a thematic apperception test (TAT), which as we discussed earlier presents an ambiguous situation where the consumer assumes the role of a person in a photo or cartoon and constructs a story about what the person is thinking, saying, or doing. First class flyers were asked to elaborate on what led up to and what followed a scene depicting the inside of a cabin during a flight from London to Miami. As a result of customer stories about aching backs and stiff necks from sleeping upright, VAA now features seats that become flat beds, a bar and bartender, and a chance for a massage. When passengers land, the airline provides them with a shower and a shave in a special revival lounge before taking advantage of a free limousine service. Themes were developed from participant interpretations and used for naming individual upper class flights; the Miami to London flight is known as The Trance Atlantic. "The transportation business has become the experience business," claims the VP of marketing for Virgin, "and we strive to provide our premium passengers with an experience they won't forget."

Brand obituaries

By asking consumers to develop **brand obituaries**, researchers are presented with a holistic conceptualization of brand's impact. Writing on Disneyland, consumers used phrases like "cartoon stars," "animated ears," "American icon," and "mouse mania" to eulogize the park. One writer said, "Disneyland is survived by a mouse and a park full of kids standing in long lines!" Such obituaries are useful for generating messages to communicate an entertainment brand's equity and perceived value for collateral materials and advertisements.

Consumer brand tales help companies understand how the brand is perceived in the minds of consumers. Here a brand obituary of the Pontiac as the automobile company serves as an example of how such research might be insightful for entertainment brand managers.

Although normally developed after the brand is dead (as in the above), obituaries can also be conducted before a brand's demise to determine how consumers perceive its current image and its future potential.

Cool searching techniques

The Look-Look Network, a Los Angeles marketing firm that focuses on youth culture, forges relationships with its target audience by monitoring dialog and interpreting trends and brand attitudes. Using their database of 35,000 14–35 year olds, the company surveys can develop peer friendships through lifestyle images produced by amateur photographers.[i] In other words, people relate to other people who look like them.

The company also helped Latino Telemundo research the youth network mun2 with ethnographic studies of 24 youths across the United States. It enlisted 24 others to create blogs, and both groups were then studied for marketing opportunities. Look-Look provided in-depth investigations on Latino youth culture that resulted in successful promotional campaigns.[ii]

Image 8.4 RIP Pontiac

Eulogizing Pontiac

Pontiac—the car taking its heritage from Chevy and Buick, attempted to build consumer excitement for decades. But in 2010, it is gone from General Motors forever.

The brand's survival resulted by combining Chevrolet components to achieve cheap production costs. When GM was consolidated into three divisions, Pontiac was packaged with Buick and Oldsmobile, forcing dealers to sell all three or none at all.

The Pontiac brand kept its sporty design that included its classic "speed streaks" along the fenders. Still, until the 1960s Pontiac remained an also-ran company. Consumers were turned on to the brand when the GTO was introduced. In 1968, the Pontiac Firebird gave the brand a Camaro-based pony car and in 1971 began providing drivers with the Firebird Trans Am performance cars.

Then a rapid increase in gas prices hurt the brand that had no small car alternative to its performance guzzlers. There wasn't much to be excited about Pontiac until the 1990s when the brand regained some consumer interest, from American muscle car fans, with the funky Firebird. Athletic flair was added to a mundane GM platform to produce a redesigned Grand Am, and Bonneville got a new front end with cat's-eye headlights. By the mid-2000s consumers were unimpressed by the ugly and underpowered GT, although the GTO's performance held its own. The brand's best seller became its G8ST sport truck until it was replaced with a rebadged Aveo called the G3. Unfortunately for Pontiac, its death spiral occurred soon after its first step toward consumer satisfaction.

EVALUATIVE RESEARCH AND AUDIENCE MEASUREMENT

Providers of entertainment rely on measurement data to determine the relative success or failure of a performance or activity. Box office receipts, or paid attendance, provide a baseline for calculating profits after promotional expenditures are deducted. Other common forms of entertainment measurement are rating services, the Q Factor, and incidental measures. This section looks at how and why marketers need to keep their fingers on syndicated and outsourced data for calculating the success of an entertainment venue, destination, or experience.

Media and the ratings game

Promotion success or failure is measured quantitatively at regular intervals in the entertainment industry. One of the most common measurement techniques is **audience analysis.** Managers who need to know if their advertising campaign budget effectively promoted an event or performance rely heavily on audience analysis provided by a variety of measurement companies such as Nielson and Arbitron. Information they collect is conceptually straightforward: they record people's exposure to media.

Ratings measure audience exposure to media for use in assessing audience viewing behaviors. Television and radio industries define *exposure* as program choice rather than attention or involvement with programming. These exposure databases reveal nothing about the effects of the exposure or viewer motivations. If researchers know what determines exposure and can predict patterns of use likely to emerge under given circumstances, then they can interpret the data provided.

Exposure is measured in two distinct forms: with gross measures, which do not depend on tracking over time and cumulative measures, which have a temporal quality in the data.

Gross measures

Gross measures, or estimates of audience size and composition at a single point in time, include: audience ratings, market shares, circulations, Web site traffic and sales (attendance, rentals). These measures provide a snapshot of a population without any definitive sense of repeat consumers. Gross measures of exposure are expressed in *Gross rating points* (GRPs), which summarize ratings over a schedule, and simple cost calculations such as *cost per point* (CPP) and *cost per thousand* (CPM). The most common audience summaries reported by syndicated research companies, gross measures are best known and most widely used audience measurements. Their main drawback is a failure to capture information about how individual audience members behave over time. For such information, we turn to cumulative measures.

Cumulative measures

Cumulative measures deal with *cume ratings* (a station's total audience), *reach* (how many viewers are targeted), *frequency* (how often the message is delivered), and *audience duplication* (channel loyalty, repeat viewing). Media planners work with these tracking measures to maximize audience exposure to a sponsor's message.

Producers who craft media content use these measures when monitoring popular culture trends to determine what viewers prefer in entertainment programming. Program preference research reveals a linkage between content and audience age and gender demographics; women prefer romance, teenage boys like action-adventure. Trend monitoring helped programmers anticipate the popularity of reality TV, for example, and allowed them to develop a variety of demographic-based program for the reality genre.

Advertising research

People's use of electronic media has been the focus of audience researchers by advertising agencies, economists, and social psychologists. Both individual and structural factors are key determinants of audience behavior. As a collection of individuals, audience choice is of interest to communication studies and marketing; mass audience behavior is most used by sociologists, but has applications for marketing and advertising.

One model used to organize thinking about media audience behavior, shown in Exhibit 8.6, was designed to guide the analyst in considering all relevant factors. Entertainment organizations can use the resulting analysis to make decisions on where to place advertisements.

Techniques used for advertising research allow researchers to perform these functions.

+ They can measure who sees ads through *audits of circulation or audiences* and *Web cookies*, which yield quantitative data on a representative sample and users' choices.

+ They can determine how audiences respond to broadcast commercials and/or print advertising through *consumer surveys, in-depth interviews* and *focus groups*. Response narratives provide an understanding of how audiences react to print and broadcast advertising.

+ They can evaluate if the ad sold the product using *mail orders, coupons* and *responses, retail surveys*, and *bar code scanner* data to measure success; such data link consumer responses directly to advertising promotions.

EXHIBIT 8.5 Audience Behavior Model

AUDIENCE FACTORS	EXPOSURE	MEDIA FACTORS
Long-Term Development of Technologies, Programming Services, Strategies		
Structural	*Group Measures*	*Structural*
Potential audiences	Audience ratings	Coverage
Available audiences	Market shares	Content options
	Circulation	
	Web site traffic	
	Total sales	
Individual	*Cumulative*	*Individual*
Preferences	Cume ratings	Technologies owned
Group vs solitary	Reach	Subscriptions
Awareness of options	Frequency	Repertoires
	Audience duplication	
Long-Term Cultivation of Tastes, Expectations and Habits		
Source: Webster, Phalen and Lichty (2003), *Media and Audiences*, Open University Press p. 191		

Two of the most common data collection methods are focus groups and surveys. Protocols are lists of questions or instruments for gathering information using these methods, which are briefly described in this section. For more information, refer to the suggested reading section at the end of this chapter.

Focus group protocols

Conducting a focus group requires a skilled moderator and a question protocol that addresses a client's needs. Comprised of five to 12 participants, focus groups are usually chosen from a panel of people who make themselves available to researchers because of their interest in a particular experience or use of a brand. The usual procedure is to visually record the discussion and for the researcher to produce a summary from the recording. The moderator's role is to guide the discussion, ensure that everyone has her say, and make sure that the discussions are not dominated by one or two members of the group. Advertisers use groups to develop concepts or to evaluate commercials; behaviorists use groups to collect reactions to content. Focus group protocols include all the information needed to address the client's research questions. Points are not necessarily covered in a specific order, but are used to stimulate discussion and draw out participants opinions and attitudes.

Survey development

Questionnaire surveys developed for advertising, tourism, and entertainment research can be completed by interviewers or respondents, although there are some advantages to having an interviewer conduct the survey. Interviewer completed surveys are more accurate, get a higher response rate, and obtain more complete answers; drawbacks are higher cost and less anonymity. The most common types of surveys are: household, street, telephone, mail, site/user, and captive group surveys. Exhibit 8.6 provides a summary of types and characteristics.

EXHIBIT 8.6 Types of Questionnaire/Survey Characteristics

TYPE	COMPLETION	COST	SAMPLE	LENGTH	RESPONSE RATE
Household	self/interviewer	expensive	whole pop.	long	high
Street	interviewer	medium	most of pop.	short	medium
Telephone	interviewer	medium	most of pop.	short	high
Mail	respondent	cheap	general/specific	varies	low
On-site	either	medium	users only	medium	high
Captive gp.	respondent	cheap	group only	medium	high
Internet	respondent	cheap	most of pop.	varies	high

Source: A. J. Veal, *Research Methods for Leisure & Tourism*, 2nd. Ed. Prentice Hall, 1998 p. 149

An effective survey consists of four parts: introduction, instructions, questions, and respondent demographics. The brand is NEVER mentioned at the beginning of the survey, only the brand category. By keeping the survey short (ten questions), researchers can obtain higher numbers of responses. Incentives are usually a part of the completion process if response rates are important. These are the essential survey protocol components:

+ *Introduction* includes the purpose of the survey and identifies the interviewer or organization conducting the research.

+ *Completion instructions* must be included for every question or set of questions using the same format to avoid confusion or marking answers incorrectly.

+ *Questions* best address information necessary for attitude surveys by using scaling methods that allow respondents to quickly mark the degree to which they agree or disagree with statements made. Open-ended questions are more difficult to analyze but are most useful for eliciting in-depth responses.

+ *Demographic information* is requested at the end of the survey, and only variables necessary for the topic under study should be asked; respondents are usually reluctant to answer income-related questions.

The survey protocol presented in Exhibit 8.7 is typical of those used for entertainment research. Note that demographic information is collected at the end of the survey.

EXHIBIT 8.7 Survey Protocol

This is an example of a survey developed to determine the Internet's role in making travel plans and to identify the most popular sites.

Introduction

This survey, sponsored by the city's travel council, is designed to find out how you plan your travel vacations. When you return your completed survey, you will receive a $10 coupon good for redemption for ticket purchases on any domestic airline traveling to this city.

Questions

For each of the questions below, write in the number that best represents your level of agreement with the statement using this raking system:

1. agree completely
2. agree somewhat
3. no opinion
4. disagree somewhat
5. completely disagree

1. _____ I usually make travel plans months in advance.

2. _____ I consult Internet sources to plan my travel.

3. _____ Price is my first criteria for selecting an airline or hotel.

4. _____ Customer comments play an important role in my destination considerations.

Fill in the blank

5. When I think of an Internet travel websites, the brand that comes to mind is _____.

Check all the words that apply

6. Adjectives that best describe my experiences with Internet travel services are:

____convenient   ____time-saving   ____confusing   ____invasive to my privacy

____lengthy   ____time-consuming   ____simple   ____better than a travel agent

Rank your preferences from 1 to 5, 1 being your most favorite

7. Which agencies are your favorites?

____Travelocity   ____ORBITZ   ____Hotwire

____Expedia   ____Cheap tickets

Check the appropriate answer

8. How likely are you to log on to one of the above travel websites in the next 3 months?

____very likely   ____likely   ____unsure   ____unlikely   ____very unlikely

Demographics

Tell me about yourself by checking the appropriate answer:

9. I am   ____female   ____male

10. I am age   ____ 20–35   ____ 36–50   ____ 51–65   ____ over 65

Thanks for taking the time to complete this survey.

Measuring convergence

Measurement standards are still being developed to determine the return on branded entertainment investments where advertising and entertainment converge. While there is not as yet an agreed-upon currency (dollar valuation) system for branded entertainment, there have been several attempts to attach value to such convergence deals, at least in the television space. Nielsen Media Research, for instance, introduced a program in 2004 to track product placement ratings for broadcast networks and in 2005 put that service into movies as well. IAG's In-Program Performance service uses a panel of consumers who respond to online surveys designed to measure their recall of and reaction to product placements and sponsored program. Brandchannel.com and *The Wall Street Journal* also keep tabs on top brand placements in entertainment media. Such measurement systems help both advertisers and entertainment producers calculate their return on investment (ROI).

A recent measurement tool introduced by research company Audible Inc. tallies Podcast audiences.[iii] As we learned, podcasts are Internet-based audio shows that are downloaded to listeners' computers. This technology puts measurement capability in iPods and other MP3 players. Using a tracking service available to outside podcasters, Audible charges three cents per downloaded podcast to report whether a downloader listened, and for how long. These tools provide a bona fide rate card for advertising on podcasts, enabling advertisers to get a handle on how many people are actually listening to shows, not just how many times a show is downloaded. These data give podcasters some audience information based on the same technology used for distributing newspapers, books, and other printed material into audio format.

The Q factor[iv]

In order to measure how much a performer or celebrity is liked or disliked by the public, and how familiar the public is with a celebrity, the **Q rating system** allows audiences to grade celebrities with a 6-point scale. In Exhibit 8.8, a Q Factor question elicits a specific opinion on a performer's "Q"uality.

Using the Q Factor method, researchers provide audience members with a questionnaire listing a sample of personalities. The scale yields dimensions of *familiarity* and *appeal*. Every year since 1964, over 1,600 personalities have been evaluated by a national sample and categorized into 17 groups such as comedians, fashion designers, sportscasters, film stars, and so on, which are syndicated to marketers. The report tells what kind of impression the celebrity makes on an audience.

Polling and incidental measures

Polling research provides popularity measures regarding audience perceptions about celebrities and their image. Athletes, musicians, destinations, and venues are measured using pre-testing

EXHIBIT 8.8 Q Factor Question

In your opinion, the performer is ....
1. one of my favorites
2. very good
3. good
4. fair
5. poor
6. someone you've never seen or heard

and post-testing designs to scan public attitudes about believability, compatibility with products, and potential to change public attitudes. Polls help match celebrities with products, events, and organizations for sponsorships, endorsements, and advertising. Audience sector polls conducted by Audience Studies Inc. can report an audience pull for a specific celebrity in a specific role, but they cannot predict the vehicle or role where that celebrity would be successful.

Incidental measures are vast numbers of subjective data in the form of a celebrity's popularity indicators that include: size of fan base, speaking invitations, videos or DVDs sold, mentions in gossip columns, number of magazine covers, and number of log-ins to celebrity home Web pages. Marketers use these data for image management and visibility indicators.

Best bang for the research buck

Qualitative methods provide the most efficient method for discovering and explaining audience behavior. Regardless of the techniques selected, qualitative research enhances our ability to understand entertainment consumers and the consumption process. The success of qualitative techniques, however, depends upon the information-gathering process. Unlike questionnaires, structured interviews, and directed focus groups, ethnographic techniques are appropriate only for situations where elaboration is possible. Projective techniques can be incorporated into individual and group situations, paired with technology, or as a stand-alone methodology. Developing focused yet entertaining techniques is a challenge every researcher faces. By incorporating popular culture with innovation, researchers are in a unique position to produce projection devices that result in *Ah-ha* discoveries.

Because of the complexity of the task, entertainment promoters often outsource research to private companies. Although the expense may be substantial, research efforts are validated by the profits generated when the entertainment venue, brand, or experience becomes more desirable.

Although researchers have learned a great deal about media audiences, there is much more to discover about the behavior of Internet audiences. Typically characterized as individuals seeking information and amusement, Internet audiences are active and have unlimited potential for purchasing entertainment programming. By studying long-term relationships between the Internet and its users, we may be able to develop a useful framework for collecting and evaluating ratings data.

Analyzing audience research

Researchers usually analyze consumer stories collected during interviews, but in the case of projective techniques, consumers play a significant part of the analysis process. With the researcher's guidance, participants interpret their own responses. Researchers then make connections that will uncover marketplace opportunities.

Methods

Both quantitative and qualitative analysis methods are appropriate for analyzing projective data. Consumer interpretations are *categorized* qualitatively to identify emerging themes. Alternatively, content may be classified into categories that are given a numeric value. Categories are counted for frequency of responses. Here is an example.

Results of research conducted on luxury cruises will yield dining (food quality and variety) and activity (types and difficulty level) aspects of cruise brand preferences. All references to activity aspects are grouped into one category, while another group is created for dining features. By counting consumer references to each aspect of the cruise, researchers can identify important features consumers' use for making their selections. If comfort is mentioned many times in conjunction with stateroom aspects of ship life, we know our target segment values cabins with amenities. Few mentions about swimming pools indicate that this feature is unimportant for selecting cruise options for our segment. This method is useful for uncovering response frequency, looking at "top of mind" preferences, or plotting conceptual maps. This technique does not, however, help you understand *why* consumers have certain preferences. This is where the participant comes in to help you learn the answers to the why questions. Probing consumers' reasons for making the choices they did helps expand their answers.

Projective technique results can also be analyzed through interpretation of *patterns* that reveal meanings behind the projections. Again, researchers achieve the most insightful results by asking participants what their answers mean. Similarities and differences that emerge show inherent patterns indicating how a particular market segment really feels about the brand or service.

Triangulation

To validate or reinforce findings, researchers often use an additional technique to see if similar patterns emerge from a second or third round of projective research. The use of different methods to check results is called **triangulation**. One way to accomplish triangulation is by using three groups from a single target segment and a different method for each group. Results for all three groups should generate similar patterns, which then verify your conclusions and give you confidence that your research yielded consumer truths.

Using three different researchers to gather the data can also triangulate research. Hopefully, similar patterns will emerge regardless of the person administering the projective technique. Triangulation is like insurance in that it offers a protection device against response aberration. If wide differences are detected, research can be repeated until dominant themes prevail. The only research constant must be the consumer segment. Creative treatments are developed specifically for a particular consumer group and are rarely applied to the public at large.

Hawaii as a Vacation Destination

Problem:	The Hawaiian tourism board statistics reveal that tourists are choosing destinations other than Hawaii for their vacations.
Research Objective:	To learn about visitor perceptions of Hawaii to see if the islands' image is part of the reason for reduced traffic
Research Question:	What comes to mind when travelers think about taking a Hawaiian vacation?
Technique:	Photo sorts to generate visual consumer perceptions about Hawaii
Method:	Ten groups of 10 people who were planning a vacation within the next year were asked to participate in selecting photographs taken of the Hawaiian Islands to produce brochures advertising the destination. None of the participants had ever been to Hawaii.
Findings:	As participants selected photos for their brochures, they explained to researchers the reasons for their choices.

Brochures from each group contained photographs of

- 146 beach scenes
- 99 palm trees
- 34 luaus
- 18 sailboats
- 13 pineapples
- 6 sunsets

Conversations validated what the brochures revealed:

People think the only thing to do on in Hawaii is go to the beach.

Use:	An advertising campaign called "*1001 things to do in Hawaii when you're not at the beach*" was developed to change consumer perceptions about the destination.
Result:	Tourism increased by 22% during the first year of the campaign.

What do you think?

1. If research also showed that people want the beach to be a good part of their vacation agenda, would you include beach activities in the next advertising campaign? Why?

2. How would you test the campaign to see how it might be updated?

USING THE INTERNET TO CONDUCT AUDIENCE RESEARCH

In order to minimize costs and travel, entertainment researchers are beginning to utilize technology to collect interviews. There are two main ways of doing qualitative research on the Internet: synchronous and asynchronous. *Synchronous* is "all at the same time," or the online equivalent of a focus group. *Asynchronous* software (email, instant messaging) lets people respond whenever it is convenient for them. The main use of synchronous Internet research is through chat groups, listservs, threaded discussions, groupware, and forms with open text entry boxes. Here's what you can expect from the various modes of online inquiry.

Chat groups

People use chat groups to meet online at a specific Internet location. A moderator asks chat room participants to discuss a particular issue and later studies the transcript for common themes. Websites available for free chat groups are:

- www.parachat.com
- www.talkcity.com
- www.chat.zoho.com
- www.paltak.com

Some researchers find that chat room conversation is more stilted and does not flow as well as in-person focus groups. Others swear by the efficiency of obtaining results using the Internet.

Listservs

Researchers can send email to a group of people with listserv software. Anybody can reply, either to everybody else or to the organizer. Some providers of free listservs are:

- http://www.topica.com Database of over 84,000 listservs plus tutorials for beginners. Create your own free listserv discussion group.
- http://netpals.lsoft.com
- http://netpals.lsoft.com
- www.mhhe.com/socscience/comm/group/.../new_com.htm
- www.coolist.com
- www.eGroups.com

Listservs without advertising that charge usage fees are: www.listhost.com, www.sparklist .com and www.lyris.net. Many ISPs also have such software available for their clients; Majordomo is widely used, but it's not very user friendly. Listservs are best used for participatory interactive research where it's an advantage for people to see each other's responses. Listserv discussions can run for up to a week, giving motivated respondents time to provide thoughtful their answers.

Groupware

Groupware is software that a group of people can use to communicate between themselves. Research can be conducted through, bulletin boards, guestbooks, forums (newsgroups), threaded discussions, ICQ (instant messaging), and conferencing software.

Threaded discussions

First developed in Internet Newsgroups as a form of hypertext, these forums are discussions on a particular theme or thread. Each thread is made up of a number of contributions. Some of the best packages for threaded-discussion software are:

- www.discusware.com

- drupal.org

- www.wimba.com—Based on spoken messages and requiring speakers and microphones on computers.

Threaded discussion systems work well for answering specific questions, but the sheer number of threads makes reading a whole set of contributions very difficult. This discussion vehicle is best suited to a large number of participants—100 or more—mostly making occasional contributions.

Guestbooks

A guestbook is the computer equivalent of a hotel or bed-and-breakfast book that invites guests to sign in and write their comments. Researchers use this format to get visitors' reaction to a venue using questions such as, "Of the venues in your city, which do you like to attend most for musical concerts and why?" Here everyone can see everybody else's responses, resembling a group discussion in that respondents will influence one another. Many ISPs provide guestbook software for their clients, but numerous websites offer free or low-cost software. Some popular providers are:

- Bravenet (www.bravenet.com)

- Site Gadgets (www.sitegadgets.com)

Social networks

Two sites that provide users with blogs collected hourly from the Internet also allow users to rate the blogs and bookmark their favorites. Two social bookmark sites are:

- www.del.icio.us

- www.digg.com

Researching online compared with face-to-face discussions

A big advantage of online discussions is that it's always possible to comment on what somebody else has said. Normal focus groups can be fairly expensive and require people to meet at a specific location. By using the Internet, researchers access a broad population, and often participants do not need to be paid. Online participants have more time to consider their responses than live groups forced into 90-minute sessions. A major disadvantage of online groups is that researchers are not privy to emotional and non-verbal content of discussions. Also, meanings are not as clear as they are when tone of voice and expressions are part of the dialog. Emoticons or *smileys*, keyboard-created pictures, can be used to some extent, but only if respondents agree on their usage beforehand.

Online measurement

Two methods exist for measuring online audience measurement, panel and census. A panel-based method gives more detailed demographic and behavioral data, but critics believe panels'

FOCUS ON RESEARCH TOOLS

One of the easiest ways of doing qualitative research on the Internet is to adapt a normal Web survey for obtaining open-ended responses. Most participants who use the HTML form respond coherently and in detail to open-ended questions if the population is right, the questions are well worded, and the subject is of interest to the sample. Try the free www.surveymonkey.com for your next open-ended format survey.

© vinston, 2010. Used under license from Shutterstock, Inc.

Image 8.5 Free survey web site.

narrow a sub-section of visitors is a drawback. The census analytics-based approach relies on Web cookies to provide information across a broader section of a Web site's audience. The Web cookie approach could lead to overestimating visitor counts and underestimating visitor frequency metrics when users delete or block cookies.[v]

In an attempt to reconcile discrepancies that exist between the two forms of online audience measurement forms, Nielsen/NetRatings created a combined system. Called Data Integration, the system pairs results from a NetView panel and its SiteCensus Web analytics approach. This method results in an Integrated Audience number that delivers reach and frequency and audience demographic profiles for pre-and post-campaign analysis tools. Different types of measurement systems are currently under development by other companies as of this writing.

Finally

So, from this chapter about applied audience research, you now see how discovery, explanatory, and evaluative research methods are used to understand entertainment audiences and consumers and help prepare your campaign plan. Qualitative methods are ideal for collecting stories about branded entertainment experiences. Innovative projective techniques stimulate discussion and generate large amounts of rich information. To evaluate media audiences, managers use syndicated measures to gauge exposure and predict attendance trends. Once collected in person or on the Internet, data are analyzed for themes and patterns that help us to understand the relationship between the consumer and the entertainment brand.

GOT IT?

Entertainment research can be descriptive, explanatory or evaluative; it is designed to measure satisfaction with the entertainment experience and to understand audience motivations for attending.

- Empirical research using inductive methods is most appropriate for conducting entertainment studies.

- Projective techniques are developed to gather consumer stories about their entertainment experiences; limits are set only by the creativity of the researcher.

- Results from projective techniques can be analyzed quantitatively and qualitatively and used for developing creative marketing concepts.

+ Gate receipts, media audience ratings, Q Factor and incidental measures are used to determine profits, attendance numbers, viewing patterns, celebrity popularity, and performer image.

+ Audience analysis provides useful measures for developing entertainment programming and predicting audience behavior.

+ Triangulation of methods or researchers will insure result reliability.

+ The Internet is a valuable data collection resource for entertainment research.

NOW TRY THIS

1. Develop a bubble cartoon for a client who owns a chain of hotels to help him understand how consumers feel about national brand lodging as opposed to boutique accommodations.

2. Create an online projective method for generating self-disclosure from female consumers with children about how they use theme parks.

3. Design an audience satisfaction survey for an entertainment event of your choice. Compare it with those designed by classmates. What did you miss? What did they miss? How would you administer the survey, in person, or over the Internet? Why?

4. Have a group of five theme park visitors select pictures of people from those you provide who would most likely patronize each of three specific park brands. Then group the pictures by park brand and identify patterns of similarities and differences across the pictures. From the patterns, come up with a description of the type of person who prefers each brand theme park.

QUESTIONS FOR DISCUSSION AND REVIEW

1. What is the best method for researching declining attendance at a local performance venue? How would you design the data collection and analysis?

2. How would you use the Internet to gather information on satisfaction with service at a specific spa resort?

3. What ethical issues are involved in gathering personal information from attendees or participants of events? How can they be overcome?

4. How can technology contribute to developing new research techniques? What advances in research methodology can you predict for the future?

OTHER STUFF TO READ ABOUT AUDIENCE RESEARCH TECHNIQUES

S. Sayre, S. (2001), *Using Qualitative Methods for Marketplace Research*. Sage.

http://sociology.camden.rutgers.edu/jfm/tutorial/main.htm tutorial on some basics of online research methods.

www.socialresearchmethods.net has instruction on qualitative methods.

www.socialpsychology.org/methods has links to experimental design, data analysis and research ethics.

[i]Stephanie Kang for the *Wall Street Journal*, Oct. 13, 2005.
[ii]Gina Piccalo for the *New York Times*, Oct. 9, 2005.
[iii]From an article by Sarah McBride for the *Wall Street Journal*, Nov. 16, 2005.
[iv]From a brochure advertising the "Syndicated Performer Q Study," 1996, Marketing Evaluations, Inc.
[v]By Kevin Newcomb (2006), www.clickz.com, September 9.

Chapter 9

BUILDING ENTERTAINMENT BRANDS

> *The term* science *should not be given*
> *to anything but the aggregate of recipes*
> *that are always successful.*
> *All the rest is literature.*
> Paul Valery

Chapter Objectives

After reading this chapter, you will be able to answer the following questions:

+ What modifications must be made to convert marketing's *4Ps* for use in the entertainment marketing mix?

+ What are the significant elements of *audience based brand equity*?

+ How are brands positioned?

The marketing mix has long been the standard approach to delivering products and services. The brand, a crucial element of the product component, gives the parent company or entertainment franchise its identity and power. This chapter focuses on these two important entertainment marketing considerations: the mix and the brand. We will investigate some revised mix typologies as they apply to experiences, and look into the key role of branding in audience relationship building.

Taken together, the marketing mix and brand concepts provide a recipe for successful entertainment promotion. To review briefly, the **marketing mix** is the optimal combination of marketing variables an enterprise can use to generate the most revenue from its target market. To determine the weight or emphasis placed on each variable in the mix, the marketing manager takes into account the actions of competitors, reworking the balance of variables according to prevailing marketing conditions. Since the first days of radio and television, brand concepts and theories have been incorporated into marketing strategy. **Branding** is a way to identify, guarantee, structure, and stabilize an entertainment property, entity, or company. Because the primary capital of many entertainment businesses is its brand, marketers realize the importance of developing a branded "landmark" for their audience members.

MIXING AND MATCHING: UPDATING OLD STANDARDS

Most university business schools embrace the teachings of two early marketing pioneers, Edward McCarthy and Philip Kotler. Let's quickly look at how we got from there to here.

McCarthy to Kotler

In 1970, McCarthy[i] developed the classic four-variable system on which marketing management decisions should be based: *product, price, place, and promotion.* This system was standard practice for almost three decades. As the economy changed, however, it became more and more clear that McCarthy's model virtually ignored the consumer. So, in 1999, Kotler[ii] restated the mix's variables, adding a component for the consumer that reflected the consumer orientation necessary for marketing in a service economy.

Today's experience-based promotion mix

Principles of the entertainment marketing mix are similar to McCarthy's model. Entertainment terminology and applications are different from those of traditional marketing, however. Exhibit 9.1 defines the entertainment marketing mix, showing how consumer buying and paying take on new meanings when they are applied to entertainment audiences. In the next section, we'll characterize the transition from a product-based orientation to consumer-based orientation.

EXHIBIT 9.1 The Experience Promotion Mix

4PS RECONFIGURED FOR ENTERTAINMENT SERVICES		
MARKETING ELEMENT	WHAT IT MEANS	HOW IT APPLIES TO ENTERTAINMENT
Target Market	who buys	audience usage segment
Product	what they buy	audience experience
Price	what they pay	audience investment
Place	where they buy	venue, destination, Internet
Promotion	why they buy	information, persuasion and incentives

Target market as audience usage segment

Traditional marketing theory segments consumers by demographics, psychographics, and loyalty dimensions. Most times, however, an entertainment experience crosses gender, age, and lifestyle segments. Entertainment simply is available to anyone who wants it. Entertainment marketing, therefore, must address the needs of audiences. To reach an audience, marketers focus on users of the activity, performance, or destination.

Product as value of audience brand experience

A consumer product's value lies in its consistency and brand association. An entertainment product's value, on the other hand, is the form the experience takes; it's what audience members get when they attend or play. **Audience value** is the audience's assessment of their experience as weighed against the ticket price or investment and compared to other entertainment options. For entertainment, experiential components include component design, venue style or ambience, service element, and identity through branding.

+ *Component design* is how the experience is assembled for consumers, such as a four-day spa package that includes meals, treatments, and lodging.

+ *Venue style and ambience* is the character of the place where the entertainment or activity is performed, which aligns with brand image and price. The ambiance of the Golden Door Spa in Escondido, California, for example, is minimalist, food is vegetarian gourmet, and treatments are professional. Price is the highest in the spa resort category. In this and every case, guests must determine if the venue is worth the price charged.

+ *Service element* of the staff includes the work and attitudes of all persons engaged in delivering the experience to audiences. Front desk receptionists, servers, ushers, hot dog vendors, massage therapists, reservation takers, and so forth are all part of the service element of an entertainment experience.

+ *Brand identity*, the primary focus of communications, identifies an experience by making known a particular set of values, a logo, an image and an expectation of the entertainment to be delivered.

Price as cost to the audience for entertainment brand purchase

Price in a formal sense is the negotiated value (translated into money) that an audience member is willing to pay for experiential content provided by the producer, who in turn takes into considerations sales volume and revenue objectives. Price simply is what we pay to experience something. In marketing some experiences, travel for one, price is sometimes considered a personal investment rather than an expenditure. **Promotional pricing** of entertainment is common. This approach responds to the requirements of a particular audience segment or the need to stimulate demands that fluctuate by season or competition resulting from overcapacity. Disneyland, for instance, offers discount coupons to residents during the winter season to offset tourism decline during that time. During peak season, however, many venues typically raise prices in anticipation of high demand.

Place as convenience and comfort of venue or distribution access

A location or attraction venue includes all points of sale that provide prospective audiences with access to entertainment experiences. This expanded idea of place, a **servicescape** (see Chapter 4), is a physical space where audiences come together to enjoy and experience a consumption activity. **Convenience of access** is how easily audience members may access the venue, what hotels are available to make their stay more pleasant, and how simply can they make reservations. The Internet is a convenient way for audiences to acquire tickets and make reservations for performances, parks, and travel destinations.

Promotion as information, persuasion, and incentives

For communicators, promotion is the number one variable—it includes everything the entertainment marketer needs in her bag of tricks: advertising, direct mail, sales promotion, merchandising, sales force activities, brochure production, Internet communication, and PR activity. Promotional communications can make consumers aware of products, stimulate demand, and provide incentives for purchase. (These actions or results will be explained more completely in Chapter 9). Reinforcing awareness and building a positive attitude helps potential customers make purchasing decisions and stimulates repeat purchases.

Every element in the marketing mix is an organizational expenditure that has direct implications for pricing and sales revenues. Exhibit 9.2 illustrates how the marketing mix works for specific entertainment venues.

In the exhibit, you can see that the mix is adaptable to a variety of entertainment experiences. For instance, the *spa experience* is dependent upon each component: content is judged on the

EXHIBIT 9.2 The Marketing Mix for Entertainment Venues

	SPA	MUSEUM	CONCERT	CASINO	PARK
EXPERIENCE AS PRODUCT					
Content	Treatment/food	exhibit	group/style	game variety	rides
Packaging and design	location/buildings/facilities/décor/food/ambiance/light	building/design/lighting/space/café/shop/display	venue/lighting/sound/seats/lobby/lounges/refreshments	building/glitz/rooms/ambience/theme	location/rides/food/rest areas/theme
Service	staff/masseuse/attendants	docents/director/staff	ushers/servers/ticket window	dealers/waiters/staff	characters/security
Branding	Golden Door	MOMA	Lincoln Center	Monte Carlo	Six Flags
Image/position	luxury/budget	global/local	state-of-the-art	high/low	roller friendly
INVESTMENT OR EXPENDITURE AS PRICE					
Normal	rack/corporate	adult/senior	orchestra/loge/balcony	minimum bet*	adult/kid
Promotional	online discount/package price	group/children/member rate	group/subscriber	regular client	group/partner

VENUE OR DESTINATION SALES AS PLACE					
Reservation systems CRS, 3rd party retailers, Web sites	CRS/ Internet	Internet/ hotels/ tourist offices	CRS/ box office/ retailers	Internet/ phone	CRS
PROMOTION					
Ad media, Merchandising, PR, brochures	brochure/ print ads/ feature stories/ soaps, towels	print ads/ PR/event calendar/ tote bags, books	brochure/ print, radio ads	outdoor, print, web ads/ t-shirts	radio/ tv ads clothing

quality of treatments and food; packaging manifests itself in the way food is presented and the design of the treatment rooms; service is measured through personal attention to individual needs; branding is the spa's logo or mark; the positioning places it in the consumer's mind as luxury, affordable, rural, urban and so forth. A visitor's expenditure is dependent upon both normal and promotional offerings, such as day packages or weekend specials. Spa sales are accomplished through the Internet and reservation systems. Promotion takes the form of glossy brochures and products sold at the spa as well as feature stories and spa reviewers. The trick is making the most effective selection for your client. And as the next section details, the mix is *always* audience dependent and must be viewed within the context of specific audience needs and characteristics.

MIX IN CONTEXT

At the core of all marketing mix decisions is the audience member, the ultimate consumer. Think of the consumer as the core of an onion. The first layer that is formed around the consumer contains the *mix decisions* (which elements to use); the next layer consists of the *organizational resources* (financial, personnel, operations, branding, location, and all physical assets); and the outer layer consists of the *external factors* that make up the entertainment environment and influence all the other components. The external factors are technology, distribution channels, competition, political, social and environmental attitudes, legal and regulatory framework, and any trends that motivate consumer actions. Each element of the mix circles around a core, or audience, called a locus of control. Marketers must anticipate possible uncontrollable external factors that affect decisions, and they must use the organizational resources that they can control to develop an appropriate mix. Using the layers of the marketing mix onion helps you plan the entertainment experience. The process begins with a situation analysis of *external factors*—those conditions over which managers have no control—against *internal resources*, factors that can influence management decisions and fall under the organization's direct control. Both external and internal factors are needed in planning marketing strategies.

The missing P

It's *people*. As identified by Kotler, the most important component of the marketing mix are the people directly involved in the production and presentation of the entertainment event. Three groups of participants are most important to marketing functions:

+ *Audiences* are groups of individual consumers of entertainment content; audience interactions are an inseparable part of the satisfaction the experience provides. You *market directly to audiences*, who then use the power of word-of-mouth to determine an experience's fate. Happy audiences keep the lights on and the curtain rising; unhappy audiences shut the place down.

+ *Employees and staff* include both front-line workers who deal directly with audience members and non-contact workers who provide support. Third-party suppliers are also represented in this group.

+ *Community* consists of the residents of neighborhoods where large venues such as amusement parks, outdoor concert theaters, or casinos are located; they often interact with audiences informally.

Mix extenders

Marketing management can extend the mix in three important areas. First, because *front-line employees* so closely interact with audiences during their entertainment experience, their attitudes are vital to audience satisfaction and ultimately the success of the event. In fact, it's been said that managers must operate with the belief that employees are "walking billboards from a promotional standpoint."[iii] Second, *internal marketing* is an important way to effectively address employee concerns and promote value. Finally, *physical settings* are crucial to both audience enjoyment and employee satisfaction. Let's review and examine these areas in more detail and provide a few examples.

+ *Front line or contact employees* must reconcile the internal operational requirements of an organization with the expectations and demands of audiences. This is a difficult task. Not only must contact employees show empathy with visitors, they must do so within the organization's rules and regulations. A museum docent may be torn between adults' interests and those of noisy parties of children. Dealing with conflicts between visitors is often stressful, so training for employees in developing strong interpersonal skills is essential.

Profile of a People Finder

As a **people finder** for Young and Rubicam Brands, James Rosetto handles recruiting responsibilities for the agency's Irvine, California office. Screening and interviewing for temporary and permanent hires, Rosetto negotiates contracts with temporary employee agencies, headhunters, talent agents, and production companies.

Much of James' time is spent identifying key candidates for positions in account and project management, IT, and creative (writers and artists). Identifying "talent" for television commercials and appropriate experts to produce them is a large part of this activity. "Finding the right candidate for the job makes a hiring manager happy," says Rosetto.

After graduating with a B.A. degree in advertising from the University of Central Florida, James worked in broadcast production, graphic design, and advertising sales before joining Y&R in 2004.

In his words...............

Recruiting is a great way to get a full 360-degree view of the advertising industry. Seeing people across different disciplines grow into their jobs is very rewarding—you get to know all the winners and scammers. I act as a matchmaker, trying to fit the perfect person into the perfect position. When it works it's fantastic—when it doesn't it's a disaster!

Pitfall to forget

One of our large automotive clients was under a deadline to deliver dealership promotions, which coincided with the untimely departure of our account manager. I scrambled around to locate someone with similar expertise who could fill the bill. A colleague at another agency recommended a promotion guy who had interviewed with them a month before, so I called him in for an interview the next day. Because we were in a rush, I hired him on the spot, assuming my colleague's agency had checked out his references. Unfortunately, it wasn't the case. Instead of taking over, he took off after two weeks, leaving us in the lurch. And I was to blame. After the fact, I learned that the guy had a terrible reputation among his former employers– and there were many—for being a flake. People tend to move around quite a bit in this business, but his resume read like a phone book. Wish I'd let my fingers do the walking!

Advice

To learn about job openings in the advertising field, consult *AdWeek* and *Advertising Age* trade publications' job opportunity postings in print and online.

Reprinted with permission of James Rosetto.

- *Internal marketing* (promoting to those within the company or organization) is an often-neglected extension of the marketing mix, yet has value for harnessing employee potential. As organizational stakeholders, employee needs must be addressed, and this process starts with assessing levels of job satisfaction, identifying problem areas, and recognizing their ideas for product improvement.

- For entertainment, the *physical setting* or venue can be the *raison d'etre* for audience attendance. As we saw in Chapter 4, a venue acts as the experience's packaging; it communicates messages about quality, positioning, and differentiation that help determine and reach audience expectations.

C words proliferated: Lieberman's view

A veteran of entertainment marketing, Al Lieberman characterizes the entertainment industry with an entirely different set of words from the P-word version, the C-words.[iv] He describes the industry structure as content, conduit, consumption and convergence.

Content is the entertainment product delivered to the consumer. Part of the creative process involves copyright protection, a legal transaction that gives content creators and their assignees exclusive rights to reproduce, distribute, and make the most of their original works.

Conduit

Conduit refers to the where and how the performance is delivered—the venue.

Consumption

Consumption is the result of advertising and promotional activities that result in the purchase of tickets and performance attendance.

Convergence

Convergence is the experience created when live performance is converted to a digital format. Convergence is very much a part of the present as well as the wave of the future, especially where advertising and entertainment are fused to deliver both an enjoyable experience and brand awareness as a simultaneous activity.

BRANDING EXPERIENCES AND PLACES

What is a brand? To many audience members, brands aren't just IN the culture, they ARE the culture.[v] Brands have become the tools with which people construct their personal and social identities. Our post-modern culture is thrusting people and brands together at warp speed. A new ethos of brand participation is emerging; people see brands as shared cultural property, where familiarity breeds ownership.

Bikers who choose to be buried in Harley-Davidson-branded caskets are just one example of the results of the collision between brands and fans. When people think they own brands, they do funny things—like wear brand tattoos, form Internet brand tribes, and use brands to characterize themselves in personal ads. Brands as a type of cultural infusion are here to stay, and, as a result, entertainment franchises *must* adopt a special view of what their brands are and what they mean.

9.1 Harley Davidson is an international **cultural brand**.

Branded everything

Branding involves creating mental structures and helping audiences organize their knowledge about entertainment experiences in a way that clarifies their decision making and provides value to the producer. With products, brand distinctions are related to specific attributes or features and product benefits. With entertainment, although venues have specific features, the benefit of all experiences should be an enjoyable emotional association. Brand symbols help make intangible or abstract experiences more concrete. Here are some of the ways entertainment is branded.

+ *Venue brands* such as Hilton Hotels, Disneyland, and Museum of Modern Art.

+ *People and organizations* such as Madonna and MGM. Some celebrities even become product brands in their own right (Newman's Own salad dressing, Glow by J Lo).

+ *Sports teams* where marketing is a highly sophisticated combination of creative advertising, promotions, sponsorship, direct mail, and other forms of communication.

+ *Bands and films* such as the Rolling Stones and *Avatar*.

+ *Geographic locations*, such as Paris, whose strong image has drawing power.

By tying brands to an entertainment-driven experience, marketers can connect brands with consumers as personalities, not just products. Experiential branding takes core values of the brand and introduces them into an actual environment; good branding is the conversion of entertainment and marketing.

Audience-based brand equity

Brands gain their equity from audiences. The **customer-based brand equity model (CBBE)**[vi] approaches brand equity from the perspective of the consumer or audience member. Its basic premise is that the power of the brand lies in what audiences have learned, felt, seen and heard about the brand as a result of their experiences over time. Best applied to products, this model is nonetheless a valuable approach to building knowledge about entertainment genres with potential audiences. To illustrate how audience-based brand equity works in practice, you can compare and contrast customer expectations with the actual entertainment experience.

Brand awareness

Repeated exposure through personal association with a performance experience creates familiarity with a brand. *Brand recognition*—the ability to identify a particular mark as belonging to a performance category—is the most basic form of awareness. If you see *Bolshoi* and know it as a ballet brand, you have just experienced brand recognition.

Brand recall, on the other hand, is more difficult to attain because it requires an audience member to come up with the brand without prompting. If you ask a person what ballet company is her favorite and she replies "Bolshoi," you are witnessing brand recall. Visual and verbal reinforcement through communication avenues such as advertising and promotion, sponsorship and event marketing, publicity and public relations, and outdoor advertising contribute to improving brand recall.

Brand image

Marketing programs create a brand's image with a strong creative message that links favorable associations of the brand with a person's memory. Brand associations are created directly through experience, commercial and non-partisan sources (e.g., reviews), and word of mouth, and indirectly through identification with a company, country, or event. Image development grows primarily from *brand benefits*, which are the characteristics of value and meaning that audience members attach to the entertainment form. Venue image results from descriptive features or *brand attributes* that characterize a location of entertainment performances.

Integrated marketing communication programs contribute to brand equity by encouraging favorable brand associations. To make an association favorable and create desire for a target audience, marketers depend on a brand association's *relevancy*, *distinctiveness*, and *believability*. A brand's image must be unique and distinguished from competitive brands with meaningful *points of difference* that cause audiences to choose it over other brands. Brand associations can also be equal in favorability with competing brands and function as *points of parity*, which are jumping-off places for negotiating points of difference. Points of parity are easier to achieve than points of difference, which are needed when the brand must demonstrate clear superiority. Not all brand associations are considered important or viewed favorably by audience members, and not all brand associations will be relevant for a consumption decision. Points of parity and difference for a variety of entertainment locations are presented in Exhibit 9.3.

Entertainment genres often are communicated as brands. Continuing the ballet analogy, you may consider ballet a brand of dance; the parity is that all dance involves people performing to

EXHIBIT 9.3 Brand Associations

LOCATION	POINTS OF PARITY	POINTS OF DIFFERENCE
Theme park	Rides, food	Largest roller coaster in the world
Hotel	Rooms, pool	5-star luxury with spa
City	Buildings, shopping	Winding canals and gondolas
Concert venue	Seats, crowds	Outdoor amphitheater
Theater	Rows face front	Seating in the round
Casino	Wheels, tables	500 quarter slot machines

music on a stage; the difference is that ballerinas dance on their toes. The individual dance troupe may also be a brand. Bolshoi is, like other troupes, a touring dance company—a point of parity. But it differs because it features traditional dance with a Russian heritage—a point of difference.

A distinct *brand identity* distinguishes the Bolshoi and attaches *meaning*: The troupe's Russian dancers (identity) with a history of intrigue where dancers fled the Iron Curtain for sanctuary in America (meaning). How an audience member feels about that brand is the *emotional response* generated by the association. Finally, a connection between that brand and the audience creates a *relationship* between them.

Creating relationships between audience members and various forms of dance may begin with the familiar and accessible: local presentations of Tchaikovsky's *Nutcracker* ballet during the holiday season. If the experience, a ballet that's easy to share with children and other family members, is favorable, marketers can extend that feeling to another ballet story and educate audiences to understand and appreciate more ballet performances.

Brand imagery can also be developed through associations with the type of person who uses the brand. If audiences think ballet-goers are stuffy and boring, ballet's brand image is unfavorable. Marketers must demonstrate that ballet has universal appeal and is exciting and beautiful. To create a favorable association, ads may feature ballet lovers as young and vibrant families.

Brand loyalty

Branded products work toward developing a habit of repeat purchasing. With branded entertainment, loyalty may not be an important factor because of the temporal nature of the product—here today, gone tomorrow! How many times can we expect one person to purchase tickets for the same play?

The exception is building a fan base to create loyalty to a sports team or music brand. Like sports stars and teams, musicians work to develop loyal fans who attend their concerts and purchase their music. In the book *Brands that Rock*, authors Roger Blackwell and Tina Stephan focus on how bands create loyalty and devotion in their fans. Converting consumers into fans requires an understanding of human behavior. The devotion of long-time fans to their favorite performers, from Frank Sinatra to 50 Cent, illustrates that it takes a deep-level connection to develop brands that audiences incorporate into their lives. To make an emotional connection with audiences, marketers must figure out what makes them tick. Successful bands break through the clutter to become long-term industry leaders, by creating awareness and targeting a single market segment to generate high profits.

The Internet plays a crucial role in cementing fan status through interactivity. Fans come together to support bands, create new songs for them, and build relationships with other fans through their common love of a particular group, vocalist, or musical type. Fans act as "spotters," keeping other fans abreast of news about group appearances and star gossip.

Music marketing

Blackwell and Stephan present prime examples of how performers blend music and marketing. Elton John turns brand equity into sales, whether he is promoting his latest CD, concert, Broadway show, or commercial endorsement. KISS broke the record industry's traditional mindset with pyrotechnics and fireworks. The Rolling Stones created a unique experience built on the personality of Mick Jagger that people paid big bucks to see. Aerosmith involved fans in rejuvenating their band and transforming it into a stronger brand than its predecessor. Lessons for branding bands include:

- Stay fresh
- Focus on the entire experience
- Package talent well
- Create realistic expectations
- Match the message with the mission and the audience
- Exude energy and passion
- Define the band with functional and emotional attributes
- Monitor brand adoption
- Play for cultural adoption
- Resist the temptation of overexposure
- Empower your fans

Exhibit 9.4 shows the distinctions that music marketers make between various audience members.

EXHIBIT 9.4 Who Watches Rock?

ROCK BAND AUDIENCES		
CUSTOMERS	**FRIENDS (REPEATERS)**	**FANS**
Price driven	Value driven	Experience driven
Shop opportunistically	Shop purposefully	Shop for pleasure
Need a reason to buy tickets for band	Prefer to buy from band	Devoted to band
Surprised by good experience	Had some good experiences	Expect good experiences
Drop band if disappointed	Give band a second chance	Express disappointment, will forgive and forget
Indifferent to band	Feel rational/emotional connection	Actively invest in relationship—and $$
Don't talk about band	Casually recommend band	Praise band

Source: Blackwell & Stephan, *Brands that Rock* (2002), p. 5.

BRAND POSITIONING AND EQUITY

As an entertainment marketing manager, once you have segmented and selected your audience, you must promote the experience's most appealing aspects. Developing a focused positioning strategy means *designing an image to occupy a distinct place* in the audience member's mind. Imagine that all the entertainment options in a particular genre or category were set upon a step ladder, each occupying its own position. Audiences could easily distinguish one rung from another and make choices. That's the role of positioning, which involves creating a real differentiation and making it known.

First, you establish the *category membership* of the performance, or simply the genre or the type of entertainment—dance, opera, music, and so on. Category membership is communicated through benefits, by comparing exemplars (the best of what is available) and by relying on experience descriptors. Positioning is established and maintained over time using a means-end chain.[vii] In this chain, attributes lead to benefits, which in turn lead to values. Audience members select a performance that delivers an attribute that provides benefits that satisfy values. Using a laddering progression, we see how the progression flows in the means-end chain:

Brand >>> Attribute >>> Benefit >>> End Benefit (Value)

Let's say an audience member selects to attend a performance at a venue because of its marvelous acoustics (attribute) that provides fantastic sound (benefit), she values because it designates her as an aficionado of music, making her feel great—enhanced self-esteem is the result. Marketers use this chain to appeal to the desired value, in this case self-esteem, when promoting the venue's orchestral performances. Another example is Disneyland, which provides life-size cartoon characters (attribute) that delight children (benefit) and satisfies the parent's family values of sharing experiences. Disney promotes family fun in its advertising. Exhibit 9.5 illustrates the means-end chain concept.

Brand positioning strategies

Every entertainment brand needs a focused positioning strategy so that its intended place in the total market—and the audience member's mind—is clearly reflected in its communications. The strategy requires coordinating all the attributes of the promotion mix to support the brand's position. Seven alternatives for selecting a positioning strategy are:

1. *Specific feature*—the Venetian Hotel's canal or a theater's reclining seats

2. *Benefit*—the excitement of visiting a foreign destination or the self-esteem received from attending an opening night performance

EXHIBIT 9.5 Means-End Chain for Theme Parks

BRAND	ATTRIBUTE	BENEFIT	END BENEFIT (VALUE)
Disneyland	Mickey Mouse	Delight	Sharing
Six Flags	Roller coasters	Thrill	Adventure
LegoLand	Legos	Activity	Education
Universal Studios	Movie sets	Fantasy	Esteem
Wild Animal Park San Diego	Wild animals	Wonder	Nature

3. *Usage occasion*—summer concerts in the park or special matinee performances

4. *User category*—senior and single vacation cruises or family nights at the circus

5. *Against another brand, performance, venue or destination*—a television network claiming it has better news coverage than another network

6. *As number one*—an assertion by an orchestra that it is the best in the country

7. *Exclusivity*—a spa that claims to restrict membership to the most upscale guests

Brand equity strategies

Promoting entertainment events requires developing a strategy to either *push* tickets to the consumer through a retailer or middleman or *pull* bookings directly from audience members. The Internet has made both strategies popular; you can go to a ticket broker (Ticketmaster) or directly to the venue to purchase tickets.

With a push strategy, venues rely on the retailer to deliver a full house. With a push strategy, venues promote their own distribution center. Using both strategies, however, yields the highest return. Push strategy commonly requires indirect channel use of retail segmentation and cooperative advertising; pull strategy uses direct channels, such as venue ticket sales. Both strategies take advantage of the Web to integrate and maximize selling power.

Brand contacts

Messages about the brand must reach the audience at each point of contact—thinking about buying, locating a place to buy, actually buying tickets, and attending the performance. At each stage of promotion, a positive brand image must be communicated to the target audience in promotional materials, staff, reviewers, media, and personal contact. By managing the consumer's total impression of the brand, you control the contacts you can, influence the ones you can't, and allocate dollars to the most important contacts available. Chapter 5's ten steps for developing an integrated promotion communications plan show you how to build brand equity through contact management.

Brand and line extensions

The most powerful tool for maintaining brand equity is through **brand extensions** and **line extensions**. To extend the brand, entertainment producers enter another category. For instance, a film studio goes into the recording business, or Donald Trump adds condominiums to his hotel brand; these are brand extensions. When extending the line, producers offer the same brand in a different way within the category; when Hilton adds a new location to its hotel chain, it makes a line extension. MTV has extended its line of television music programming globally, while Disney has extended its brand to include films, recordings, and hotels.

Brand extension is part of entertainment product synergy—morphing one product into others. The Harry Potter brand was extended from books into the film genre, while the *Lion King* film was made into a stage play. Both extensions were merchandised by translating the brand into thousands of spin-off retail items.

Licensing

Another form of brand extension, **licensing**, allows a brand to use its image and logo to change genres. *National Lampoon* magazine had a million subscribers in its heyday during the 1970s.[viii] Lampoon Inc.'s first film, *Animal House* was the highest grossing comedy of its time. Taking its writers, performers, and attitude from the Lampoon company's example, late-night TV spoof "Saturday Night Live" was touted for changing the world of comedy. Few people knew that *National Lampoon* deserved much of the credit. The magazine's organization was effectively responsible for launching the careers of actors John Belushi, Bill Murray, and Chevy Chase.

FOCUS ON LICENSING

Creating Characters for Sale

California artist Debby Carman, president of Faux Paw Productions, creates characters and product concepts for licensing in niche markets to a variety of goods manufacturers. U.S. gift company Russ Berrie and Company licensed over 50 different products from her *Bowzers & Meowzers™* character series. These same characters are supported by published children's books and their stories have been animated into short digital films for presentation in Cannes, France for introduction into the vast entertainment and digital markets.

A license works as follows: Characters or a unique product or property collection is developed and depending on it's variety of applications in varying markets (i.e., gift, tabletop, home décor, textile, paper goods, stationary, accessories) a license is

Image 9.2

negotiated with a manufacturer. A manufacturer will secure a license to produce, market and distribute that property collection in the form of finished goods, and pay the licensor a royalty based on sales. Royalty fees differ depending on the type of product and the market. Plush animals and ceramic products generally may command a 5–10% royalty on wholesale sales. Fabric and textile licenses may range from 3–15%. Typically, an advance against royalties is negotiated in good faith and in advance of the goods being sold.

Books may translate into licensing opportunities as the characters achieve brand recognition with readers and as they transcend into entertainment and toy product licensing. Other entertainment media opportunities exist for characters building brand recognition in their potential for digital content, interactive games, DVD, cartoon series, animated film shorts or TV network programs. Consider the Sponge Bob Square Pants property licensed for TV and appearing on hundreds of varying manufactured products. Sponge Bob Square Pants is expected to generate in excess of $3.5 billion licensing revenues in 2006.

After working in magazine and movie genres, *Lampoon* moved on to a radio show and recorded a musical parody of *Moby Dick* in the style of a Maine community theater.

Brand characters

Characters have been successfully developed to bring heightened awareness and brand association to products and services. One of the most famous characters of all time, Mickey Mouse, has symbolized family fun for decades. Ronald McDonald and the MGM roaring lion are also associated with fun and entertainment.

In keeping in the same tradition, GEICO and Aflac insurance company brand characters have become advertising icons. GEICO's gecko is a wise-cracking amphibian who uses humor to help audiences remember the company's difficult brand (the character corrects mispronunciations people make between "gecko" and "GEICO"). Video and print messages motivate potential customers to call or go to the Web for more information. A vocal duck that screams "Aflac!" in commercials to consumers who are having difficulty solving their insurance problems, began as a mnemonic

© Gene Blevins/LA Daily News/Corbis

9.3 Michelin Man is a brand character.

device so viewers could simply connect the duck's honk with the company name. As the campaign progressed, the duck took to synchronized swimming and more antics. Once the campaign was successfully established, synergy infused all aspects of the brand.

Brand synergy

The payoff of brand synergy evolves from licensing, merchandise retailing, and sponsorship. Effective marketing strategy results in revenue streams that enhance the bottom line. Licensing is a $100 billion industry[ix] in the U.S. alone. Revenues from licensed-based merchandise retailing generate funds for future performances and maintain shareholder value in this competitive segment of the world economy. Fashion is well integrated into the growth of sponsorship sales for the entertainment industry—Armani-sponsored events, including a retrospective of his design at the Museum of Modern Art in New York, is just one example of fashion as entertainment. Runway shows are themselves entertainment performed for producers of the fashion industry and consumers of branded designs. Product placements and product tie-ins link fashion and food with entertainment products and brands. Branding as a long-term strategy is a huge commercial support system that creates synergy. We will continue to discuss branding strategies and synergies in more detail in later chapters.

Brand slogans

In its heyday, advertising jingles and slogans ruled the airwaves. Today, slogans still help position a product or service. Take MasterCard's "Priceless" campaign. Thanks to the popularity of retro ad campaigns, many old slogans are still recognizable. See if you can identify these experience-based slogans from the past:

1. When you care enough to send the very best
2. Reach out and touch someone
3. You're in good hands
4. Think outside the bun
5. Mmm Mmm good
6. Diamonds are forever
7. The ultimate driving machine

Check the end of the chapter to see how many you guessed correctly!

Interactive branding

Brands adapt to new selling environments in different ways. By assessing the potential of interactive platforms to assist in ticket sales, branded entertainment can improve its volume and increase its usefulness to audience members.

Creating interactive messages takes a different set of writing skills than developing a script for television commercial or copy for a brochure. Interactive scripts for CDs, DVDs, and Web sites require the marriage of the identity crafting talents of traditional agency creative directors, direct marketing skills, and knowledge of appropriate content development disciplines.

When producing convergent communications, brand messages must be coordinated among the various interactive platforms to develop a consistent stream of strategically compelling content. Concentrating on how a brand's overall identity is presented to individual consumers within the framework of their needs is the best strategy for integrating approaches. The next section will continue to explore and develop the topic of convergent communications.

Finally

Marketing mix elements and branding principles from product and service marketing are a departure point for those who will promote experiential content, venues, and destinations. These principles provide a grounding for strategy development and campaign planning that are necessary for structuring effective entertainment promotions. When the creative product succeeds, models and theories can't be far behind.

For years, marketers have coordinated graphic and message elements for campaigns; only recently has convergence made more sense than simple integration. By focusing on audience benefits, entertainment promotion efforts can utilize all elements of the promotion mix for effective message delivery before, during, and after campaign implementation.

GOT IT?

- McCarthy's 4Ps are reconfigured for entertainment as 5Ps: audience usage segment, audience experience, audience investment, performance venue or destination, and communication and incentives.

- A marketing mix locus of control is the consumer or audience member; management controls mix decisions and influences organizational resources, but it has no control over external factors that can affect ticket sales.

- Audience-based brand equity insures that expectations of performance and venue are met; brand awareness, image, and loyalty are important factors for developing brand equity.

NOW TRY THIS

1. Go to the Web site of your favorite musical group. How does the group distinguish itself through logo, type style, and graphics? How does the site contribute to or detract from the band's brand image?

2. Check out the brand blogs on http://web.mit.edu/cms/bcc/2005_04_01_brandculture_archive.html, especially the archives such as "Baby's recognize brands," or other branding reports. What does the site contribute to your understanding of entertainment and branding?

3. Now try using http://brandnoise.typepad.com/ to see what's new in branding strategy. What role does advertising play?

4. Using two museums of your choice, enumerate their points of parity and points of difference. What do these points suggest for positioning strategies for each of the museums?

QUESTIONS FOR DISCUSSION AND REVIEW

1. Which typology would you choose, McCarthy's re-crafted 4Ps or Liebermann's 4Cs to characterize the entertainment industry? Why?

2. How would you explain the difference between integrated and convergent communication strategies to a client who asks?

3. Which positioning strategy is best for a new product that is emerging into a large category of entertainment brands?

Answers to brand slogan quiz: Hallmark, AT & T, Allstate, Taco Bell, Campbell's Soup, DeBeers, BMW.

MORE STUFF TO READ ABOUT BRANDING

Roger Blackwell & Tina Stephan (2004), *Brands that Rock*. Wiley.

www.brandweek.com has the latest branding news.

www.brandchannel.com reviews branding promotions.

[i]E. McCarthy (1981), *Basic Marketing: A Managerial Approach*. 7th edition. Irwin Publishing.

[ii]P. Kotler and g. Armstrong (1999), *Principles of Marketing*. 8th edition. Prentice-Hall.

[iii]V. Zeithaml and M. Bitner (1997). *Services Marketing*. McGraw-Hill, p.304.

[iv]A. Liebman (2002), the *Entertainment Marketing Revolution*. Prentice Hall.

[v]Quoted from Andrew Zoli (2004), "Brands, Consumer Behavior, Trends." *American Demographics* 27 (9), p. 44.

[vi]Based on K. L. Keller, (2003) *Strategic Brand Management* (2nd ed). Prentice Hall, Chapter 2.

[vii]From M. Vriens & F. T. Hofstede (2000), "Linking Attributes, Benefits and Consumer Values," Marketing Research, Fall, pp. 3–8.

[viii]From Jake Tapper (2005), "National Lampoon Grows Up by Dumbing Down," *New York Times*, July 3.

[ix]Licensing Institute of America report for June, 2004.

Chapter 10

DEVELOPING COMMUNICATION OBJECTIVES AND MESSAGE STRATEGIES

> *If you would hit the mark,*
> *You must aim a little above it.*
> HW Longfellow

Chapter Objectives

After reading this chapter, you will be able to answer the following questions:

+ How do communication *objectives* frame the marketing message?

+ What three *messages types* are used to serve delivery functions?

+ Which integrated *strategies* help you reach audiences, develop creative, position the brand, and buy media?

+ How can you best *compete and communicate* in a global marketplace?

Message development is about communicating the brand to audiences, and promoting entertainment is about developing informational, persuasive, and reminder messages for current and emerging audiences. This chapter is designed to help you prepare message strategies that fit the needs of a particular group of audience members by the way they use the brand, and to construct messages that create excitement about that brand.

Every promotional effort begins with objectives. Communication objectives, unlike marketing objectives, cannot be measured by sales, market share, or profit. Instead, pretests given prior to and post-tests given after an advertising or public relations campaign serve to measure objectives for awareness and attitude. To achieve the communication objectives that have value for the advertiser, you must execute your creative concepts. This section outlines the principles that drive message development, looks at message strategies that apply to experiences, and defines management strategies for developing a well-executed message delivery system. Also, because we live in a global marketplace, we'll look at competitive communication strategies that are appropriate for international audiences.

Audience aggregates

+ To determine what to say to whom, we speak to one particular group at a time. The most effective groups are called **audience aggregates**. Audience aggregates are groups of consumers expressed in terms of usage or visitations by a group of like kind. Aggregate-directed messages are essential for effective promotional communication. *Current audience members* can be divided into heavy, medium, and light users of entertainment venues, performances, and destinations. In all usage levels, current users receive *reminder messages* to keep them coming to the venue.

+ *New* or *non-audience members* are potential users who have not yet experienced a performance genre or others who can be developed into users through *educational or incentive messages*.

+ *Users of competitive entertainment* genres are also potential users who must receive specialized *promotional messages*. Promotional messages are tailored to each aggregate according to designated communication and action objectives, and then user aggregates are subdivided for more focused targeting.

Notice how, in Exhibit 10.1, that while the behavioral outcome remains the same (ticket purchase), the message for each audience aggregate is adapted for their stage in the usage matrix.

Communication objectives

Communications is directed toward a particular audience need, which becomes our objective—something we need to do to reach a particular audience aggregate. Necessary components of

EXHIBIT 10.1 Tailoring Messages About Legoland To Each Audience Aggregate

AUDIENCE AGGREGATE	MESSAGE THEMES ABOUT LEGOLAND
Current users	We appreciate your patronage; Try our new off-season bargains. (Reminder message)
New/non users	Why not try an alternative to standard theme park experiences with our interactive play? Mom gets in free on your first visit. (Educational/Informational message)
Competitive users	You owe it to yourself to experience a new kind of park. LegoLand offers father-son workshops on weekdays for half off. (Promotional message)

objectives require that they are measurable, time sensitive, target audience directed, and behavior specific. Measurable determinants of communication objectives are: category need, awareness, attitude, and purchase intention.

Category need

Before audiences can be convinced to buy tickets, they must have some understanding or desire for the specific experience genre. For instance, non-users of ballet performance will likely not respond to ticket promotions since ballet is not in their evoked set of entertainment criteria. To put ballet into this evoked set, communications must deliver generic information about ballet and the benefits of watching. Like the "Got Milk?" milk campaign designed to put milk onto a shopper's list of things to buy, a generic campaign about ballet (got tu-tu?) introduces the notion of attending to people unfamiliar with this kind of dance. Only after audience members agree to consider attending do you switch from a generic message to messages with brand-specific objectives.

Awareness

After an audience member is familiar with a performance type, communication must make him aware of specific entertainment brands, which can be movies, musical groups, dance performers, and so on. Awareness has two levels: recognition and recall.

Recognition is the easiest awareness behavior to achieve. By placing impressions of the brand in front of the public, marketers establish visual or aural recognition. If you're shopping movies on the Internet and you recognize a director's name (brand) or film title (brand), you might find out where the movie is showing and even purchase tickets. Recognition occurs at the time of purchase and is usually delivered through mass media.

Recall is more difficult to achieve because it requires that a person bring up the brand in advance of purchase. For instance, when shopping a movie, you would hunt for one directed by Oliver Stone because you remembered his name. Recall occurs before purchase and requires more directly targeted repetition of the marketing message.

Attitude

The aim of the attitude objective is to develop, maintain, or change attitudes about an entertainment experience, venue, person, or destination. Introducing a new entertainment brand requires marketers to create a specific and positive attitude toward that brand. If research determines that brand attitudes are already positive, messages must maintain that momentum. Messages can also change a negative attitude to a positive one, or dispel attitudes that are based on misinformation. Important for public relations as well as advertising campaign, this objective is key to achieving purchase behavior.

Purchase intention

Although communication objectives cannot be measured by actual purchases, they can help marketers determine whether the campaign has stimulated the intention to buy tickets or make reservations. Promotional messages help activate purchase behavior, and special pricing acts to stimulate immediate response.

10.1 Converting movie browsers to ticket purchasers is a communication objective.

© Diego Cervo, 2010. Used under license from Shutterstock.com.

Writing objectives

Measurable, time sensitive, usage-based, target audience-directed, and behavior-specific components of a *written objective* enable marketers to focus on exactly what must be achieved and by when. Here is a handy formula for writing an awareness objective:

Communication will _____ among _____ % of _____

objective   *measure*   *target audience/usage based*

within _____ that _____ will do something.

time limit   *brand*

Example: Communication will <u>create awareness</u> among <u>60%</u> of <u>regular theater-goers</u> within <u>two weeks</u> that *Avatar* will be appearing at their local 3D movie theater.

An objective created to change attitudes may be phrased like this:

Communication will <u>improve negative attitudes</u> about <u>Six Flags Park</u> among <u>40%</u> of

objective   *brand*   *measure*

<u>theme park visitors</u> within <u>two months</u>.

target audience   *timelimit*

Unless objectives are specific, they cannot be measured; all four components are necessary for formulating written objectives prior to campaign development. Communication objectives drive integrated campaigns for entertainment content and destinations before creative concepts are developed or media and delivery vehicles are selected.

Action objectives

Communication objectives determine the success or failure of message delivery; action (or behavioral) objectives determine the success or failure of promotion efforts. Actions are behaviors that result in buying tickets or redeeming promotion incentives that result in usage. As with communication objectives, action objectives are developed for each audience aggregate and are measured by box office receipts.

Entertainment industries are interested in getting consumers and audiences to take these actions:

+ Buy a ticket

+ Subscribe to a season

+ Travel to a destination

+ Book reservations to a resort

+ Visit a park or attraction

+ Play in a casino

Action objectives propel the bottom line. Most actions require behavior modification, which involves persuasive messages with purchase incentives. Message development is crucial for achieving action objectives.

MESSAGE DEVELOPMENT

Audience-based messages serve three functions: *to inform, to persuade,* and *to remind.* The messages delivered through media, buzz, the Internet, and in person must be directed by action objectives. Informational messages are designed to stimulate curiosity and increase understanding about the experience among non-users or light users; similar informative messages are developed to drive ticket sales among medium and heavy users. Persuasive messages use sales promotions to provide incentives that drive buying behavior for all audience collectives. Reminder messages trigger buying behaviors in audience members who are regular experience visitors.

Informational messages

If you want young adults to understand the nuances of opera so they may consider ticket purchases, you provide informational messages that create excitement about the genre and encourage self-enlightenment. To communicate schedules and information about artists to heavy users of opera so they will purchase tickets, you also use informational messages, but for renewal or reuse motivations. Information also acts as an educational tool for new or non-audience members who may not know that crawling subtitles and librettos simplify their ability to understand operas presented in other languages.

To view JetBlue's 'BigWig' advertising campaign, log into http://www.jetblue.com/deals/welcomebigwigs/

Persuasive messages

When incentives are needed to stimulate timely ticket sales, persuasive messages can provide light and medium users with a reason to purchase immediately. Promotion-driven messages can be combined with informational messages for cases where both action components—selecting venues and buying tickets—are necessary, such as in subscription drives and group sales. Incentives are important components of persuasive messages and are designed to entice new or non-audience members to try a performance genre, visit a venue, or travel to a particular destination.

In 2009, JetBlue launched an ad campaign with Christmas ideas for non-JetBlue flyers. The ad campaign relied on simplicity and the notion that fewer seats are better because they provide more leg room for passengers. See the ad on http://lessisbetter.net/, or the complete collection of ads on JetBlue's Facebook page.

Reminder messages

Reminder messages are used to communicate subscription renewals, season opening performances, and loyalty program information (awards or point totals) to user aggregates. Best delivered on the Internet or by mail, reminders are used to provoke action.

There are two questions to ask when developing all forms of communication messages.

1. *Is the message actionable?* Unless you ask people to do something, they'll file your message and possibly never refer to it again. Audiences must be able to take action—buy tickets, make reservations, subscribe—or your message is of no use for marketing purposes.

2. *Is the message easy to understand?* People are only able to grasp one idea at a time. The more simple the message, the more apt the audience is to respond to it. Use visuals when every possible and adhere to the old KISS principle: keep it simple stupid.

In Exhibit 10.2, we differentiate between objectives and strategies recommended for current, new/non and competitive audience groups.

Message strategy

Consisting of objectives and visual techniques, message strategy defines advertising goals and how they will be achieved. Methods involve the mode of delivery and form the message takes. Unlike product ads, entertainment promotion relies less on brand recall, scare tactics, and brand image for audience persuasion than on product promotion. Awareness, attitude and purchase intention objectives can be achieved by using advertising that creates *emotional resonance* with audiences.

EXHIBIT 10.2 Objective/Strategy Grid for Live Performance Audience Aggregates

	AUDIENCE AGGREGATE:		
	CURRENT	**NEW/NON**	**COMPETITIVE**
COMMUNICATION OBJECTIVE	Maintain positive attitude	Create recall awareness Develop positive attitude	Change attitude
ACTION OBJECTIVE	Buy more tickets	Try one performance	Compare options
MESSAGE STRATEGY	Inform, remind; Loyalty rewards	Education, inform; Incentives	Inform, persuade: Incentives

The most effective strategy for venues and performance companies, as well as tourist bureaus and some media, **affective advertising** incorporates celebrities, music, costumes, and visual delights to make emotional connections with audiences. Sharp editing in movie trailers and video performance previews, regional music for travel ads, and close-ups of sensational costuming presented in plays and opera performances are techniques used to tease audiences into purchasing tickets.

MANAGING COMMUNICATION STRATEGIES AND TACTICS

To be successful, marketers absolutely must develop appropriate management strategies to insure their messages are properly created and directed. Managing the audience, the creative, the brand's image and extensions, and the media are important aspects of developing and executing a successful entertainment marketing campaign.

Manage the audience

Audience relationship management involves conducting ongoing research and using the results to communicate and update. To track audience activity, venue and performance marketers use data-based mechanisms that pinpoint where a consumer is in the buying cycle. Customer interactions are managed with regular contacts that attempt to educate, inform, remind, and persuade. Providing regular contact without inundating aggregate members is effective audience management.

Performing arts centers and concert venues mail out regular subscription and special performance notices to audience members who have attended previous performances or who are present or past subscribers, as well as to potential audiences who have visited the center's Web site. Tourist bureaus use the Internet to send notices of special attractions to consumers who have requested information online, or who have downloaded travel brochures. Museum and theme park and attraction visitors also receive direct mail and Internet messages; past and current ticket buyers are informed about new exhibits, new rides, and seasonal promotions. Unless a relationship can be maintained, audience members will drift to other sources of entertainment that value their patronage. Because it is more efficient to maintain current patrons than to recruit new ones, managing these vital audience relationships is a first priority of every marketing program.

Manage the creative

Creative strategy drives advertising by delivering a memorable concept to audiences. Creative development centers around three factors, information, emotion, and motivation. *Informational*

EXHIBIT 10.3 Tailoring Messages about LegoLand to Each Aggregate

AUDIENCE AGGREGATE	MESSAGE THEMES
Current users	We appreciate your patronage; Try our new off-season bargains. (Reminder message)
New/non users	Why not try an alternative to standard theme park experiences? Mom gets in free on your first visit. (Informational message)
Competitive users	You owe it to yourself to experience a new kind of park.LegoLand offers father-son workshops on weekends. (Persuasive message)

strategies are appropriate for all audience aggregates; *emotional* strategies are designed to excite and involve potential audience aggregates; *motivational* strategies provide promotional incentives to drive ticket purchases by infrequent or new audience aggregates.

Regardless of the nature of the creative strategy, all communication must be linked by a single concept through unique and exciting executions. "Creative for creative sake" may win awards for ad agencies, but it does nothing for the entertainment's bottom line. Creative concepts and executions must achieve the campaign's communication goals in order to be effective.

To market its 45 regional theme parks, Six Flags developed a creative strategy that unified the brand's image and strengthened brand awareness. Six Flags' ad campaign featured a dancing senior who became the park's brand, helping to position the regional parks against national competitors. Moving to the beat of "We Love to Party," the brand character helped deliver the brand's emotional message—Six Flags is the "ultimate release" from schedules and pressures of work and home. This emotional creative strategy that used humor and music drove park attendance way up, surpassing both the communication and action objectives developed for the advertising campaign.

Manage the brand

Brand management is usually associated with product brands, but entertainment brands also require attention to aspects of branding. Let's look at positioning, image, and extensions.

Brand positioning

As we saw in Chapter 9, effective entertainment brand management requires creative and relevant positioning. An effective position will:

+ leverage existing brand strengths

+ focus on perceived consumer benefits

+ go where the competitors are not

+ establish a credible fit between expectations and receipts

+ update the position to fit growth strategy[i]

Brand positioning is audience driven. All the theme parks featured offer thrills, chills, and food; we call these *points of parity* (POP). To stand out in consumers' minds, each park must distinguish itself from the others with a position determined by audience feedback and message management; we call these *points of difference* (POD). Exhibit 10.4 shows the ways in which amusement park brands differentiate themselves.

To develop advertising that reflects positioning strategy, advertising themes must convey points of difference. Advertisers may select from benefit, user and competitive positioning themes for their promotional messages.

"Excitement you can count on" is an example of a *benefit* positioning theme; what the audience gets is the ad's single focus. Benefits are functional, emotional, and self-esteem oriented. Spas and resorts may declare relaxing and restoration as a functional benefit of their location. Audiences

EXHIBIT 10.4 Positioning a Theme Park

THEME PARK	POSITION/POINT OF DIFFERENCE
Cedar Point	Roller coaster capital
Disneyland	Fantasy and family fun
LegoLand	Hands on learning
Six Flags	Regional excitement
Sea World	Animal habitats
Universal Studios	Hollywood backstage

derive both emotional and self-esteem benefits from performance and destination-based entertainment.

User positioning themes revolve around the target audience. Disneyland always features families in its advertising because the parks are positioned as family entertainment. Carnival Cruise Lines often cast mature travelers in their vacation promotions to attract affluent seniors.

Competitive positioning can benefit casinos, resorts, and destinations, but is rarely selected by performance venues, parks, or attractions because gaining audience loyalty is not really a factor for these types of entertainment brands. Since tourism promotes all theme parks, it would be counterproductive for parks to position themselves against competitors. Visitors to California may combine their trips to Disneyland with stops at Knott's Berry Farm or LegoLand. Messages presenting subtle advantages of casinos, resorts, and destination imply superiority rather than directly referencing the competition. Mandalay Bay competes with Wynn casinos in theory, but it rarely uses that strategy in its advertising.

Manage the media

Media selection and buying (see Chapter 11) are important for creating awareness through advertising, but there are other important ways for entertainment marketers to manage the media. Public relations is a key factor in managing brand image. Audiences respond to editorial information, and they may be likely to buy tickets as a result of buzz of word of mouth rather than pure advertising. Networking with arts and entertainment writers, reviewers, and editors is important to generating publicity and exposure. Good managers understand how to use the tools outlined below to their advantage.

ZAGAT

Entertainment promoters must not underestimate the role Zagat Ratings are for entertainment success. Since 1910, Zagat Survey has been the restaurant, hotel, resort, spa, entertainment, shopping movie, music, theater, golf, and travel bible for many consumers. A best-selling publisher of guides, Zagat's approach separately rates the distinct qualities of a restaurant (food, decor, service, and cost), hotel (rooms, service, dining, and public facilities), and other leisure categories based on a 30-point scale. This format allows people to search for and find the best places to meet their individual needs based on a variety of criteria.

Zagat has also developed business relationships with over 3,000 companies, including entertainment entities such as AOL, MGM, Microsoft, News Corp, and Verizon. Since Zagat relies on online voting, it offers a subscription-based site with all Zagat Survey's ratings and reviews, as well as maps, driving instructions, monthly e-newsletter, and the ability to vote and shop online. Now the world's leading provider of consumer survey-based date, Zagat has more than 250,000 voters participating worldwide.[ii] Not all is written in stone, however. Like all quantifiable data, results may be manipulated to serve specific interests.[iii]

Media reviews

Media critics comment on every form of media in an attempt to influence audience selection. Critics are routinely in opposition to one another, so no one review should act as criteria for buying tickets to a performance. Several sources combine reviews to present a well-rounded approach to criticism.

In spite of the fact that journalistic reviewers see any given film only once and have a day or two to formulate opinions, they have an important impact on the success of film. The exceptions are mass-marketed action, horror, and comedy films that are not greatly affected by a critic's overall judgment. For prestige films such as most dramas, the influence of reviews is extremely important. Poor reviews will often consign a film to obscurity and financial loss.

With so much riding on reviews, studios often work to woo film critics with press kits or small gifts. Studios offer to fly a group of critics from cities across the U.S. to New York or Los Angeles for a weekend that includes a screening of the studio's news film. Following the screening, critics are asked to write short reviews. It is from these reviews that advertising blurbs are drawn. Some of the most renowned critics are Roger Ebert of the *Chicago Sun-Times*, *New York Times'* A.O. Scott (who also co-hosts *At the Movies* on ABC with Michael Phillips), and Peter Travers of *Rolling Stone*.

Web sites that seek to improve the usefulness of reviews by compiling them to ascertain general opinions are Rotten Tomatoes and Metacritic. Log on to www.rottentomatoes.com/ for reviews of entertainment products categorized by source, critic, date, or rating. Reviewers are from the *New York Times, Los Angeles Daily News, Boston Herald, Cinema Em Cena, Filmfocus, Christian Science Monitor,* and *Rolling Stone* among many other publications and Web sites. Approved Tomatometer critics, who review each film, meet the standards of accredited media outlets and online film societies for consistent and unbiased reviewing. However, a recent academic study[iv] claimed that buzz, regardless of good or bad reviews, is more important for box office determination than any other factor. According to researcher Dr. Liu, word of mouth influences people by affecting their awareness, not their attitude.

Smaller film releases, however, are more closely tied into a circle of reviewers that influence the success or failure of independent offerings. One such group is Rogue Reviewers, a select group of B-movie review Web sites dedicated to bringing reviews to and by members on their "movies under the bed" roundtable. Schlock Audio Theater is dedicates a Web site to producing "madcap audio productions of the world's cheesiest B-Movies."[v] Schlock takes its format from the traditional cablevision show that features an eccentric host who provides colorful commentary as the program progresses. One of the recent episodes is "Attack of the Giant Leeches," a Web article in a zine covering the world of independent and cult cinema.

Performing arts, books, video games, and destinations are all reviewed by a particular set of critics, guidebooks, and Web sites that give power to audience members for selecting entertainment.

COMMUNICATING ACROSS BORDERS

Most entertainment content is designed for global distribution. Only a few Middle Eastern countries ban imported content, and, volume for volume, this is more than compensated for by China's and India's thirst for Western entertainment vehicles. In order to market content to a variety of destinations, you must understand the challenges and restrictions involved in distributing content across borders. This section addresses some of those concerns.

Strategies for competing in global markets

The U.S. exports more entertainment product than any other nation. Organizations and franchise corporations must decide how to market across national, international, and cultural boundaries to maximize ticket sales and profits. Four general strategies prevail.

10.2 All Disney's theatrical productions of the *Lion King* contained the same costuming, music, and promotional communications aimed at a global audience.

© *Ralf-Finn Hestroft/Corbis*

Same product/same communication

When Broadway shows, such as the *Lion King*, and musical groups, such as Jimmy Buffet, go on tour, their products are essentially the same each time they are presented. *Lion King* features the same actors, costuming, set design, and language. Promotional materials follow the same format away as at home, using English as the primary language. Controlled promotional tactics may vary slightly by city for Buffet, but generally audiences receive the same advance hype, syndicated ticket sales, and media advertising. Margaritaville, Buffet's official Web site, provides radio, online chatting, café locations, and recipes for his tequila concoctions. Both play and performer have extended their brand with licensed products.

Same product/different communication

Destinations like the Grand Canyon and Paris, France are permanent experiences, but promotional messages are directed to specific audience demographics. When promoted to Europeans, Grand

Canyon brochures feature spectacular vistas and Western-style lodging; promotions to Australians focus on hiking, camping, and visits to American Indian sites. Paris is touted as a romantic destination to Americans, while marketing to Europeans takes into account the city's proximity and Euro-based economy. Promotional materials are produced in the language of the audience and produced with cultural considerations in mind.

10.3 The name's the same, but Blue Man Group performances and actors vary by concert location and audience.

Different product/same communication

Each Hilton Hotel is a different experience, but all are promoted under the same brand. Graphics for the chain depict a variety of locations featured on Web sites and newspaper ads. Communications direct audiences to Web sites and travel packagers. The Blue Man Group, which began in New York and Chicago with three guys and some drums, changes its show to suit the location and the audience. They use vaudeville techniques—like catching thrown gumballs in their mouths—with tribal rhythms hammered out on contorted PVC pipe for matinees and families. Evening performances from their Las Vegas location include more sophisticated musical interpretations.

Different product/different communication

If you like soul, blues, rock and roll, or jazz, you've probably purchased a CD from Ace Records. Boasting the largest and most active back catalogues of any record concern, Ace produces high-quality reissues. Its promotions are targeted toward aficionados of each musical genre. In most cases, album cover designs act as the primary promotional graphic. Boasting 25 labels, Ace's Web site provides an introduction to the music the company releases, as well as background on the artists and a list of top ten recordings. Their music is played on BBC2 and MTV, reviewed in 26 magazines, and played on radio stations in Great Britain, Ireland, Scotland, and the United States. The NFL also uses this strategy: one league and 16 different teams means promotion to fans with different tastes and reasons for attending football games. Team advertising, public relations, and merchandising are tailored to home and visiting cities according to fan preferences.

Global communication strategies

Strategies for both the delivery system and the message content must be set prior to developing creative concepts. Audience reception is predicated upon an understanding of the audience's needs, wants, perceptions, and expectations—in each location where the entertainment experience takes place.

Promotional communication can be produced in a central location, in several locations, or in a combination depending on audience diversity and corporate policies. We'll look at three options.

Standard/central

The Australian Tourist Board has produced a standard message ("A Different Light") from their headquarters in Sydney. Their Web site features 10 language selections and offers 410 locations from which to choose your viewing point. Yet the logo, graphics, jumping kangaroo, and message presentation are standardized. This is a typical of case of standardized messages emanating from a single location to a global audience.

Decentralized/autocratic

Music and programming developed for MTV is produced autocratically at each of its 24 locations around the world. Only the logo and graphics unite the stations, which connect youth to music in a variety of sounds and content. The music is promoted to its targeted audience and controlled by each affiliate independently of the home office.

Central/locally produced

In the case of Disneyland, all communications are developed at corporate headquarters but are produced with local actors and targeted to local audiences. Hong Kong, Tokyo, and Paris locations, however, must have approval from Disney for all of their message development and delivery. Central control enables Disney to maximize the quality of the experience for all of its visitors worldwide.

Cultural considerations

Communicating across cultures and borders is a necessity for global entertainment companies. Structuring messages that persuade audiences to buy tickets, attend performances, and travel to destinations is predicated on acknowledging specific differences among cultures. Here are some of the considerations marketing communications must address in global promotion.

Language

Americans like to believe that the world is learning to speak English, but the truth is global audiences prefer to be communicated to in their own language. Literal translations have caused embarrassments for advertisers in the past, so native speakers craft messages for local offices of global agencies. Web sites with global entertainment products provide visitors with language options to enhance their usability.

Collective or individual perspective

Japanese prefer to travel in groups; Australians like lone adventures. The way you promote depends on your audience's mindset and preference for engaging in experiential entertainment. You market to collective societies by extolling the benefits of engaging with family and friends. To societies where individual preferences rule, you highlight activities for singles or the virtues of going it alone. Individualistic cultures such as the U.S. generally use a direct mode of communication in which intentions and meanings are displayed clearly and expressed explicitly. Audiences in collective cultures prefer a less direct communication based on a trust-generating orientation and nonverbal acts that are not threatening or unsettling to their sense of self.

Expression

Communication is inextricably bound up with meaning. Cultures where people have extensive information networks among family and friends are considered high context. In high-context cultures, people collect information from their networks. They are recognized by the use of indirect communication using less copy and more symbols. In low-context cultures, people without information networks require a great deal of detailed information from other sources. Low-context culture audiences tend to need more copy, augmentation, facts, and data than their high-context counterparts. To communicate effectively across cultures, you must ascertain the correct level of context for each audience you address.

Social norms and cultural values

Social norms are standards that define what is considered an appropriate or normal way for a society's citizens to be and act. A **value** is a single belief that guides and determines actions, attitudes, and judgments. Norms are related to a culture's *instrumental values*, which are the basic values that motivate members of the society to reach desired ways of being, called end-states of existence. **End states** are also known as *terminal* or *core values*, simply values that bring the state of existence that everyone in the society wants to achieve—be it enlightened, financially secure, successful, or incredibly smart. The notion of a value system implies a rank ordering of terminal or instrumental values along a single continuum and can be used to compare people along different measurement systems.

Values are learned and are enduring. For instance, Americans share values of freedom, equality, fairness, achievement, patriotism, democracy, and luck. Japanese share values of group unity, education, and loyalty. Cross-cultural communication requires an understanding of the audience values for each segment targeted. Rather than featuring symbols of independence as American advertisers do, Japanese communications feature symbols that express their preference for group collectiveness.

Gender roles

In addition to individual roles determined by sex, gender differentiations can be country-specific. A strong role differentiation exists in so-called masculine cultures, while a subtler role differentiation is present in cultures where women have a dominant social presence. Gender stereotypes are more pronounced in countries that score high on the masculinity index (Japan) and less pronounced in countries labeled as feminine (Thailand). Cultures can be matriarchal (some African-American cultures) or patriarchal (some Hispanic cultures). Men and women in feminine cultures are seen as more responsible and caring than in masculine cultures were decisiveness and ambition are present. Communications must be gender-sensitive to be effective.

Finally

Each element of the marketing integration process—objectives, message strategy, management support, and global considerations—is necessary to insure an effective marketing communication message. The challenge is determining which element to emphasize and which to minimize; when determined correctly, the results yield a solid bottom line and client satisfaction.

GOT IT?

- Communication objectives—category need, awareness, attitude, and purchase intention—are used to measure advertising effectiveness. Objectives must be measurable and include a behavior, specific audience segment, and time limit. They are measured with pre- and post-campaign testing.

- Promotion-oriented messages inform, persuade with incentives, or remind; they must be actionable and easy to understand. Action objectives are developed to stimulate ticket sales and are measured with box office receipts.

- To develop advertising that reflects a positioning strategy, advertising communication themes must convey points of difference. Advertisers may select from benefit, user, and competitive aggregate positioning themes for their promotional messages.

- Global marketing requires an understanding of cultural differences and gender roles across borders and ethnicities.

NOW TRY THIS

1. Compare the promotional messages used to promote two travel destinations from either their Web sites or travel brochures. What structures do the messages take—informative or incentive? What action objectives are communicated by these messages?

2. Using the Internet, compare the points of parity and points of difference for two performance venues in your area. Which strategy would you suggest for each one?

3. Read or listen two three reviews on the same film or live performance. Which one seems the most credible? Why? How much importance would you place on these reviews for actually purchasing tickets to the movie or event?

QUESTIONS FOR DISCUSSION AND REVIEW

1. Awareness is generated through recognition and recall. What are the key components of each type of awareness generation?

2. How would you state a communication objective for promoting travel to Mumbai, India to active seniors who like to travel?

3. Why are communication objectives rather than marketing objectives used to measure advertising effectiveness?

4. Why are cultural considerations important for message construction?

5. When are different product/different communication strategies most effective?

MORE STUFF ON PROMOTIONAL COMMUNICATIONS

J.R. Rossiter & S. Bellman (2005), *Marketing Communications*. Prentice-Hall.

www.adage.com has articles on communication campaigns.

www.ijoc.org is the *International Journal of Communication*, which has articles on all aspects of studying global communication.

www.globalissues.org provides information on global media.

[i] Scott Davis (2000) *Brand Asset Management.* Jossey Bass, p. 117.
[ii] Information from zagat.com/about/about.aspx
[iii] From fairness.com/resources/
[iv] Alex Mindlin, "What Counts at the Box Office is the Buzz," *New York Times*, July 24, 2006.
[v] From rouguereviewers.com, August 6, 2005.

Chapter 11

USING ADVERTISING AND PR TO PROMOTE ENTERTAINMENT

> *Promise, large promise, is the soul of an advertisement.*
> Samuel Johnson

Chapter Objectives

After reading this chapter, you will be able to answer the following questions:

- How are *advertising media* used in integrated and converged communications?

- How has the *Internet* changed the way entertainment is promoted?

- Why has *product placement* become such big business for the entertainment industry?

- How do *promotion, merchandising and licensing, and personal selling* factor into the entertainment marketing mix?

- What role do *public and media relations* play in promoting experiences?

- How are *events and sponsorships* integrated into an entertainment brand or corporation's overall marketing strategy?

As you know, the original promotion mix had four components: advertising, public relations, sales promotion, and direct sales. Today, the list of promotional mechanisms for delivering persuasive messages is endless. The formula for mixing the perfect communications creation is dynamic—it changes with social trends, audience preferences, and budgetary concerns. Because your entertainment product is experiential, you must deliver the message to audiences in unique formats that can achieve specific action-oriented behaviors. For every entertainment organization or franchise, perhaps the most important yet challenging part of managing brand image involves coordinating all the communication vehicles that send information to audiences and consumers. This chapter presents an overview of all the promotional tools available to entertainment marketers for sending those messages.

ADVERTISING

Advertising is any paid form of nonpersonal promotion by an identified sponsor. In today's mediated world, however, the *identification* part may be illusive, as many advertisements are disguised as print editorial and electronic content. As you know, television, radio, newspapers, magazines, outdoor signage, movie theaters, and the Internet are dominant advertising vehicles. Product placement is catching up in a major way. It's the most current innovation now capturing the imagination and dollars of advertisers.

In years past, a company spent a major portion of its promotional budget buying media. Today, advertising has extended beyond traditional media locations to become *place based*. **Place advertising**—ads that appear where the buying takes place—allows consumers to purchase insurance at airports, see demonstrations of tools in hardware sections, and even order made-to-measure jeans in retail outlets. This chapter reviews and updates the basics of advertising as it coordinates with and converges with entertainment. The downside of convergence is the movement toward increasingly fragmented advertising venues, so marketers must make innovative use of all avenues to make sure their messages reach target audiences.

The traditional tools of print and broadcast advertising are purchased to reach a specific target audience over a specific period of time with measurable results. Entertainment companies and advertising agencies choose media to create a buzz and to deliver scheduled messages in a timely fashion. Media are invaluable sources of mass communication and achieve broad reach and frequency objectives for advertisers.

Media are never purchased in a vacuum—reach (number of audience members targeted) and frequency (number of times message is delivered to a target audience) measures extend to global audiences. Regulation and accessibility are two factors advertisers consider when purchasing both national and international media time and space. Media target both mass audiences and niche markets, where audience members have a distinct commonality. Let's quickly review print and broadcast media with an eye specifically toward how they can direct promotional communications to current and potential entertainment audiences. Refer back to Chapter 10 for specifics on message development.

Developing persuasive messages

The AIDA approach to creating advertising messages in every media—attention, interest, desire, and action—still holds true for configuring ads today. However, the process of getting attention, creating interest, fostering desire, and stimulating action (buying tickets, going to a Web site) must be tailored to the sophistication level of the target audience.

Advertising messages delivered by any mass or personal medium are broadly classified into three types:

+ *Informative*—conveys information to raise awareness; educates with news and performance updates

+ *Persuasive*—creates desire and stimulates purchase; often used in conjunction with ticket promotions, special offers, and discounts

+ *Reminder*—reinforces existing knowledge and benefits; appropriate for long-running performances and annual or subscription-based events; includes entertaining ads that reinforce brand image

As you saw in Chapter 10, each of these classifications is used to develop messages for each audience aggregate in your target market.

Print advertising

Print media include newspapers, magazines, mail brochures, packaging, and all forms of printed message delivery systems that carry theme park and resort brand names, for example, or museum exhibition and movie logos. Print advertising is especially useful for entertainment because of its timeliness and wide availability.

Newspapers

Regardless of readership decline, newspapers can play a vital role in announcing performances to local audiences and posting schedules and locations. Short lead time and low production cost maximize the potential of newspaper advertising for most entertainment experiences. Coverage can appear as part of a special calendar or entertainment section of metropolitan newspapers.

Newspapers with full-sized pages like the *New York Times* are called **broadsheets. Tabloids** are half the size with a more sensational focus. Entertainment reviews, features, and biographies are treated more favorably in tabloids, but editors of the entertainment sections both types of papers rely on news releases provided by public relations firms representing entertainment-oriented companies.

Of the basic types of advertising—classified, display, and supplements—only two are appropriate for experience marketers; **display ads** are used most frequently. Sold by column inch (2″ × number of columns), the standard advertising unit (SAU) for display ads is 40 column inches. Occasionally, theater or blockbuster movie advertising will take advantage of free-standing inserts to promote an upcoming spectacular event.

Newspaper advertising is bought on a market-by-market basis, anticipating a metro penetration of around 35% and community penetration as high as 85% of households. Standard Rate and Data Services (SRDS) provides media buyers with profiles, production requirements, and advertising rates. With daily circulations, most metro newspapers are a source of timely information for loyal subscribers and pass-along readers. Even within a life span of one day, newspapers play an invaluable role in of publicity and promotion. Newspapers are the most personal and localized media.

Consumer publications/magazines

Classified by publication frequency (weekly, monthly, bimonthly, and quarterly) and by audience type (consumer, business, trade, and professional), magazines are distributed by paid circulation or by controlled circulation (distributed free to readers of a given profession or organization). Magazines focus their coverage on a specific subject area, and advertising can be tailored to reach interested readers in niche markets.

Several entertainment trade publications (*Entertainment Weekly* and *Variety*) bring news and features about films, stars, and revenues to members of the industry. *Fade In, Interview,*

FOCUS ON TIE-IN ADVERTISING

Cover Ad Mimics Newspaper Front Page

On the day *Alice in Wonderland* was released in theaters, the entire first page of the *Los Angeles Times* was an ad that looked like the front page of the newspaper, blurring the boundary with news. A wrap-around ad featured a garish image of Johnny Depp as the Mad Hatter that was surrounded by actual news articles. Borrowing a practice from Web sites that have ads covering the entire home page, the *Times* lent its name and content to the advertiser. Although blending advertising and editorial content isn't new, some reporters worry that readers will misinterpret the paper's intentions.

To view the ad featured in the *LA Times*, go to the *Huffington Post* article at: http://www.huffingtonpost.com/2010/03/06/los-angeles-times-front-p_n_488593.html

Rolling Stone, *Talk*, and *Wired* are among a variety of consumer-oriented magazines. Advertising is purchased by page (or page part) and location—covers cost more. Branded entertainment messages can appear in gatefolds, tip-ins, and pop-op advertising designed to grab readers' attention. Major metro areas also have city magazines that include calendars of events.

Standard Rate and Data Systems (SRDS) publishes two magazine directories (consumer and business) for media buying. Space is sold in portions of a page—quarter, half, and full page, as well as double-page spreads—by salespeople working directly for the publication.

Trade publications

The entertainment and advertising industries have a variety of trade publications where service providers place **business-to-business** advertising. Some of the best known of these trade publications are:

- *Advertising Age*
- *AdWeek*
- *Amusement Business*
- *Billboard*
- *BrandWeek*
- *Broadcasting & Cable*
- *Emedia*
- *Hollywood Reporter*
- *Variety*

Broadcast advertising

Broadcast commercials are more intrusive than print ads, and they can be quickly passed by changing channels or TIVO. Creative approaches to broadcast advertising are key. Broadcast time is sold in units (30-second and 60-second spots) based on the **daypart** (prime, drive, and so on) and the audience size. Ad rates are more negotiable than rates for print, because commercial time is both fixed and perishable—there are only 24 hours in the day, and once the spot airs, it's gone forever. (You may want to review Chapter 6 on broadcast audience measurement.)

Television

Nothing has the visual impact of television, especially for capturing the excitement of a performance or the glamour of a resort. With the broadest exposure of any medium, television reaches a large audience and can deliver messages with highly dramatic effects. Networks offer fragmented audiences, while cable or satellite offer more selective viewers with specific interests. For instance, blockbuster movie trailers are featured on networks, while independent films find their audiences on cable channels. Not surprisingly, the biggest users of television advertising are the networks themselves; they heavily promote their own season lineups and returning series.

With traditional 30- and 60-second spots under assault by TIVO and other recording services that allow zapping (editing out ads by the viewer), television networks are scrambling for new ways to lure marketing dollars. Potential customers are reached through interaction. Advertisers take advantage of program DVDs, the Internet, and mobile phones to promote their shows. E-mail lists, Web chat rooms, and contests are sold on all these technological venues.

Many shows offer a cable or network-organized Web stream or message board, conversations carried out on the Web through updates by fans. For example, ad deals by Disney's ABC allow *Alias* fans to watch video clips on various Internet sites and purchase show memorabilia online. Lifetime TV offers viewers of the *Beach Girls* summer drama a chance to download ring tones heard on the show from their Web site. Such alliances put advertisers in touch with consumers in ways that may not be as disruptive as a traditional commercial.

The next step might be giving a computer and video camera to a participant in a network reality show so the person could operate a blog. This would provide product placement opportunities for both the computer manufacturer and the camera maker on the Web and TV. The more contacts are used in concert with products, the stronger the impact on viewers.

Television time is sold to advertisers by **dayparts**, which include: early morning, daytime, early fringe, early news, prime access, prime time, late news, and late fringe. Prime time and late news are the most expensive commercial dayparts. The high cost of production is not a detriment for entertainment advertisers who often use performance segments or edited trailers as opposed to specially scripted and produced commercials. Cable station time is purchased locally, and network media buys can be local, regional, or national in scope. Subscription channels have a range of purchasing location options.

Radio

Radio provides a soundtrack for your daily activities. It is the most reasonably priced cost-per-thousand broadcast medium in advertising. The good news is that it's always on; the bad news is that often no one is paying attention. One advantage is that each radio station has a specific kind of programming or format, such as country, Top 40, jazz, or talk, which improve targeting capabilities. Also, on-air personalities can be brands in their own right; some are quite attractive, live promotional tools for entertainment events.

Another advantage is radio's ability to broadcast from remote locations where sponsored events provide live audiences. Disc jockeys broadcast live from community fairs, festivals, and street exhibits, urging listeners to "come on down" to the event. Contests and giveaways can promote movies, concerts, and live performances in conjunction with radio stations. Entertainment providers offer free tickets to stations in exchange for on-air promotion, which simultaneously benefits the station, its listeners, and the entertainment provider.

Many entertainment marketers prefer radio when they need to deliver a localized and cost-effective ad, as programming, with either a music or talk show program format, can easily target specific audiences. With short lead times and minimal production, radio is ideal for announcing events and promoting performances. Announcements to audiences whose entertainment preferences are synonymous with station content can be made on time and with accuracy.

Humor can contribute to successful message delivery. Musical and humorous commercials fare best; soundtracks from movies and musical events are ideal sources commercials for radio advertising. Morning drive time, which boasts the largest listening audience, is the most expensive daypart on which to purchase radio advertising.

FIGURE 11.1 Comparing Media Advertising for Entertainment Brands

MEDIA SELECTION CRITERIA					
MEDIUM	REACH	FREQUENCY	CPM	PRODUCTION TIME	COVERAGE
Newspaper	limited	limited	high	short	local/ national
Cons. mags.	niche	unlimited	high	long	regional/ national
Trade pubs	specific	good	medium	long	regional/ national
Network TV	broad	unlimited	medium	long	national
CableTV	niche	unlimited	low	medium	local/reg/ nat/global
Radio	broad	unlimited	low	short	local/ national

Subscription radio permits listeners to select musical genres without commercial breaks, as well as commercial stations in a variety of geographic markets. Without censorship, program content can stretch the boundaries of control by the Federal Communication Commission (FCC) in the same way cable and satellite television does. The growing popularity of subscription radio indicates that listeners are willing to pay for greater selection and programming choice. In 2008, Sirius and XM merged to provide subscription services for listeners. Car dealers often provide it for their new customers as part of a purchase package.

Direct response advertising

Communicating directly with audience members brings a personal dimension to promoting entertainment products. Direct response marketing is unfortunately synonymous with the pejorative term *junk mail*, It functions as a connection between the marketer and the audience,

---

FOCUS ON ADVERTISING ETHICS

Choosing Between Client and Content

As a member of a popular radio station management committee, you are caught between the conflicting demands of your most popular consumer program and your sales representative. Your station's *Consumer Watch* program has been following a series of critical reports on defects of one automaker's brand and on court cases against a particular car model. Your sales rep is concerned because a dealership who sells this car is a major sponsor of the station.

The client told the rep to stop the continuous exposure or lose its advertising. If the station keeps running the programs, it risks losing substantial sums of badly needed income to sustain the broad range of other station activities.

During a meeting on the dilemma, the program team said that the car's problem is important consumer information, that the station should not be promoting a dangerous car, and that no commercial operator should be able to dictate station policy.

The sales team insisted that if the station is to reach revenue target goals, this advertiser must be mollified and *Consumer Watch* must drop this particular item. It does not have to shut down altogether, rather just switch to other issues.

What do you recommend?

1. Should you ask the sales team to find alternative advertisers? Why?

2. Should you ask the program team to switch to other equally important topics? Why?

---

bypassing sales reps and retail outlets. In direct response, audiences respond to infomercials and interactive marketing vehicles via phone or Internet. Responses are most often fulfilled using toll-free numbers or through Web addresses.

The most crucial component of direct marketing is reaching the right audience. Success for direct mail pieces is based on the effectiveness of the **mailing list**, the group of names and contact information that defines the target audience. Member names, addresses, and relevant information must be captured and organized in a company's database to deliver appropriate messages.

Direct marketing's primary objective is to elicit a response to an offer. Blogs, cell phones, and e-mail alerts are useful for increasing ticket solicitation and performance reminders. Performing arts venues, amusement parks, and travel companies advertise ways for consumers to purchase tickets and book reservations by direct response. Internet ticketing programs require attention making an offer to targeted prospects, order fulfillment, and customer service.

On-screen advertising

Advertising on the big screen has been standard procedure in European theaters for year, but it's relatively new to American movie houses. According to the Cinema Advertising Council, on-screen advertising revenues grew 19% in 2007 for $540 million, and off-screen promotions—including revenue from in-lobby promotions and concession area marketing—was up 43% from the previous year. Providing an attractive alternative to television advertising, theaters are an ideal canvas for quantifiable ad messages. Theaters can demonstrate reach, frequency, and recall, all of which lead to a very good return on investment.

According to the Cinema Advertising Council,[i] many advertisers are taking advantage of the extensive off-screen options cinema has to offer. These can be used in tandem through integrated campaigns—on-screen advertising combined with off-screen marketing in the theater—that can double or triple the impact a brand can make on the moviegoer. More than 28,000 of the total 38,000 movie screens in the U.S.-run cinema advertising. The audience educational levels and spending power are attractive to marketers. Vonage, a broadband phone company, ran a special 30-second animated spot on a trial basis, and executives were so pleased with the results they signed up for a month's worth of advertising for the brand. A special presentation called "The Twenty" presents 20 minutes of advertising prior to the feature presentation in many California cinemas. Not always welcomed by movie-goers, cinema advertising nonetheless has gained in popularity. As long as box office receipts are up, it's worthwhile for makers of branded products and services. Exhibit 11.1 shows the expenditures of entertainment advertisers.

Place-based (out-of-home) advertising

Reaching people where they eat, shop, and exercise has become the preference of entertainment promoters who haven't succeeded with media—even when the product is mediated! **Out-of-home**

Exhibit 11.1

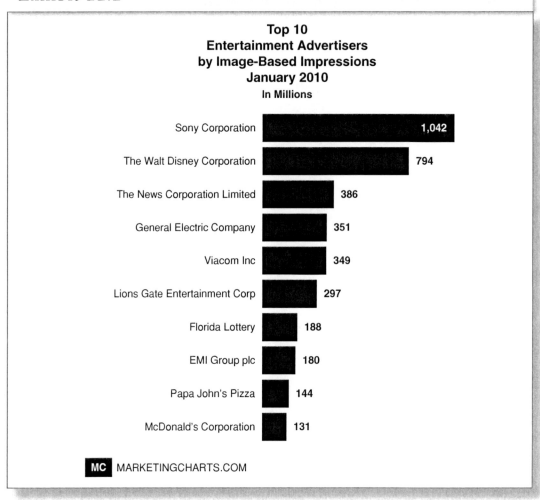

**Top 10
Entertainment Advertisers
by Image-Based Impressions
January 2010**

In Millions

Advertiser	Millions
Sony Corporation	1,042
The Walt Disney Corporation	794
The News Corporation Limited	386
General Electric Company	351
Viacom Inc	349
Lions Gate Entertainment Corp	297
Florida Lottery	188
EMI Group plc	180
Papa John's Pizza	144
McDonald's Corporation	131

MC MARKETINGCHARTS.COM

Source: The Nielsen Company, AdRelevance

media—purchased signage on taxis, busses, trucks, and trains—include outdoor advertising (billboards) and posters that work well for advertising long-run performances, theme parks, and resorts. Digitized running messages capture pedestrian attention in large cities. Designed to reach mass audiences, out-of-home media extends both reach and frequency of an entertainment branded message. There are more than 200 out-of-home formats in use today.[ii] Brands are built on our roadways, where billboards telegraph their messages to America. They act as guides, directing us to hotels, eateries, and amusements. They help us find businesses and services and help businesses find customers. Nike's interactive display on a 23-story digital billboard in Times

Square allows passersby to temporarily control the billboard and design their own shoes on the huge screen by using their cell phones.

Digital signage and Digital Out-of-Home (DOOH) advertising offers advertisers reliable, measured dynamic media presentation with very concise market, location, timing, and demographic targeting at a scale and price that makes DOOH one of the best advertising tools available.

According to the editor of DigitalSignageToday.com, digital out-of-home is a growing medium—a significant statement in a time when traditional media outlets are struggling Network aggregation services are emerging and allowing media buyers one stop to place ads to targeted demographics down to the screen level.

One of the fastest growing mediums in North America, DOOH spending will hit $4.53 billion in 2013, up from $2.6 billion in 2009, accounting for 44.1% of all OOH spending. There are approximately 180 DOOH network in the United States and 30 in Canada that carry third-party advertising. Collectively, there are active media screens in over 70 venue types each with unique audience and media characteristics. The landscape will continue to aggressively grow in capacity and market coverage.

© James Leynse/Corbis

11.1 Bus wrap ad for Pepsi.

Advertising as *street furniture*[iii] offers protection from the rain to transit riders, acting as a consumer magnet. Big, bold, and night-illuminated, the ads are magazine pages come to life. Whether providing broad-based coverage in many markets or targeted to a single neighborhood, street furniture (such as bus shelters) is perfect for entertainment promotion.

Advertisers who go directly to the places where audiences buy related services and products maximize message impact. Here are some are ways in which place-based advertising targets consumers.

+ *Airports* carry advertisements for products related to travel as well as destinations and hotels that serve travelers.

+ *Point of purchase* displays help tourists choose destinations by providing travel brochures and attraction promotions.

+ *Cell phones* have become a new music-buying venue, Samsung's "Anymotion," a musical ad produced to promote its $600 Anycall telephone, sold more than three million copies (at $2 each)[iv] as a cell phone-only download. In other words, people will pay to hear an ad for a cell phone delivered to them via cell phone!

Outdoor signage goes global

Out-of-home advertising, long considered a backwater on Madison Ave., is getting tougher to ignore as it branches out beyond national borders to gain a global presence.

In India, which produces the largest number of films of any country in the world, films and movies are prominently advertised on large silhouetted cutout figures, which rise into the air above their billboard frames.

Even Moscow is becoming a city of billboards as building-size ads transform the Russian capital into its own version of Times Square. In the city's downtown area, advertisers from around the world vie for consumer attention with size and color. Russia's $3.8 billion ad market is the world's fastest growing, and it's expected to keep expanding by 30% per year (compared with 4% in the U.S. and Europe).

Aerial advertising

Airplanes pulling signs, skywriting, and branded blimps direct gazes upward to entertainment messages. Virgin Lightships rents small blimps to advertisers for around $200,000 per month. The Family Channel and NASCAR are frequent blimp users, receiving high brand recall for their advertising dollars.

11.2 *These gigantic posters are simply "Wallpaper without the WOW factor," according to a creative director in the Russia office of Saatchi & Saatchi.*

Specialty advertising

A huge business, specialty advertising uses clothing and all sorts of products for displaying logos, brands, and company names. Useful products targeted at a specific audience create loyalty and stimulate recall for potential purchasers. Golf resorts, for instance, inscribe balls, hats, shirts, and towels with the resort logo. Guests literally take the brand home and wear it as advertising for the place as well as for themselves (as evidence of being in a special place).

Non-traditional advertising

Balloons, restroom art, sidewalk messages, mouse pads, and roving characters are but a few of the attention-getting media designed to carry advertising messages to people in unconventional forms.

Examples of such promotions include Jim Carrey's face on peel-off stickers attached to California apples promoting *Liar Liar*, entertainment brands embossed on the sails of feluccas (traditional sailboats) as they travel up the Nile River in Egypt, and actors dressed as butterflies who skate around New York to promote MSN.com. In Chicago, ads were attached to manhole covers to promote the Museum of Science and Industry's U-505 German submarine exhibit.

INTERNET ADVERTISING

Online advertising is on the rise due to consumers' changing preferences in media. A full 80% of Internet users are there because of the entertainment factor. Unlike clutter from banner

FOCUS ON NON-TRADITIONAL ADVERTISING

Attention-getting Promotions

Here are just a few examples of non-traditional forms of taking a message to audiences that have worked for promoters of entertainment experiences.

- To promote their new series, the **History Channel** gave diners at Greek restaurants brochures along with free salads on premiere day of *Alexander the Great*. Screenings in Atlanta, Boston Greek Festivals, and spot radio helped secure a 2.8 rating for the channel.

- The **Mexican Tourism Board** lured travelers to Mexico by putting a beach (complete with swim-suited models) inside Plexiglas trucks and placing them at street corners in wintry New York, Chicago, Montreal, and Toronto; they reported consumer 410,000 interactions.

- **Verizon** produced wildly colored Chinese take-out cartons and handed them out to consumers at Chinese restaurants in dozens of markets across the U.S. where hundreds of thousands of containers were distributed.

- Toy maker **Hasbro** sponsored a unique series of make-believe newspaper classified ads to promote a new version of Monopoly board game. Hasbro's agency, Arnold Worldwide, created ads featuring photographs of the new game's tokens that mimicked actual houses, boats and cars featured in corresponding classified ad sections of two popular consumer publications, *Deals on Wheels* and *Yacht Trader*. One ad read, "1935 classic. Just upgraded. Low mileage. Mind condition. Chrome finish. Runs like a dream in Monopoly 70th Anniversary Edition, the best board game money can buy. Go to monolpoly70th.com."

Source: Promomagazine.com, Sept. 9, 2005 and Stuart Elliott's advertising column in the *New York Times* Nov. 25, 2005.

ads that were measured in click-through rates, today's Internet advertising is *search-based.* ADWords, a pay-per-click advertising service provided by Google, allows advertisers buy the "search" rights to words and terms related to their business. When consumers type in one of the keywords, the advertiser' URL appears beside the search results. Payment occurs when a user clicks on the ad. For only about 5 cents a click, advertisers are linked with prospective buyers.

Pop-ups, banner ads, interstitials, and browser placements promote global entertainment, venues, and attractions to the masses over the Internet. Because many forms of Web advertising have become irritating to consumers, new formats such as *advergaming* and *addressable media* are more user friendly. *Advergames*, brought to the Web by Orbitz to advertise their Internet travel service, are pop-ups with charm. Their first game, Pluck the Chicken, yielded a golden egg for expert feather pluckers and gave Orbitz three times the response as their pop-ups without the game. Orbitz rationale for advergames: travel today is a game and they want people to know Orbitz is the way to win that game.[v]

Addressable media serve as communication vehicles for offers to consumers by e-mail. With the correct messages, this medium develops a more intimate relationship between entertainment providers and audiences. E-mail campaigns are most successful with permission—consumers who request communication are much more likely to pay attention than to unsolicited or spam messages, which are often filtered out by junk-filtering software. Sent as ads and publicity, e-mail advertising is effective for specific communication objectives such as recognition or recall. Ads with streaming video provide audiences with previews of performances, movies, and special events these are effective for getting audiences to the brand's Web site. E-mailed news releases distributed online to editors encourage immediate publicity. Spending on e-mail marketing hit $13.4 billion in 2010 year, according to the latest Communications Industry Forecast.

Traditional entertainment advertisers had to book slots in advance for web messages. As of 2010, companies like Google, Yahoo, and Microsoft let advertisers buy ads in milliseconds between the time someone enters a site's Web address and the moment the page appears. This 'real-time-bidding' allows advertisers to study site visitors one by one and bid to serve them ads almost immediately. For example, while a woman searches for a bicycle on eBay, eBay can follow that woman's activities in real time and decide where to show her personalized ads for bicycles throughout the Web. If she bought a bike on another site, eBay can update the ad to show her bike accessories or offer her a cycle vacation in France. Ad colors can even be changed for male cycle buyers.[vi]

Another form of Internet advertising, **rich media**, combines flash animations and streaming video and is predicted to grow faster than the search market. Similar to television advertising, rich media is easily coordinated with its video counterpart.[vii] One example of rich media bundles television, film, and the Web. In conjunction with its "Be Cool" movie co-promotion and product integration, Cadillac launched a five-second film contest that ultimately drew an amazing 2,648 entries and boosted Cadillac.com traffic 458% over a six-week period.[viii]

A virtual version of the weekly local circulars usually found in newspapers gives national advertisers a way to reach online readers in local markets with promotions tied to neighborhood stores. PaperBoy, devised by a unit of Gannett called PointRoll,[ix] is accessed through newspaper Web sites by using a mouse to roll over a branded message. The ad expands on the screen to become a miniature, animated version of a newspaper circular. Readers may check prices or products at other locations by entering another zip code.

Book publishers are using Internet and TV to draw buyers under 35. Aimed exclusively at the 18–34 crowd, Viacom Inc.'s Simon Spotlight Entertainment used cross-promotions with TV shows and bookstores as well as ads in college newspapers and radio stations giveaways to promote novels, books on poker, and Japanese *manga* titles.

Entertainment marketers add online advertising and Internet TV to their mixture because they recognize that managing their media strategy as a whole maximizes campaign effectiveness. If revenues are any indication of profits, Internet advertising will continue to be a key factor of integrated communications. For Internet advertising standards, check out the Internet Advertising Bureau, iab.net, the organization that provides industry information for ad agencies, entertainment companies, and media buyers.

Viral advertising

Viral advertising is a way to distribute commercial messages over the Internet by circulating individual emails through a desired audience—like a virus. By producing an entertaining and compelling commercial or spot, advertisers not only get viewers to watch, they get them to send the ad on to friends, who in turn send it to their friends. These pass-along ads are spread by word of mouse: the goal is to make ads so funny, charming, sexy, or controversial that viewers e-mail or post them to Web sites.

New Line Cinema, Anheuser-Busch, and the Gap created commercials that lived only on the Web. By invoking frogs that sing and dance about beer, a strip poker game for Victoria's Secret, and "confessions of a self-admitted pooper" for dog food, these advertisers found that entertainment was the best way to create attention for their products. The more crude and less like traditional ads, the more the audience seems to like them. To promote movies online, film trailers allow people to upload headshots and replace the movie stars' faces with their own.

A Boston-area entrepreneur streams a weekly game show over the Web to choose players from among the audience in the entire Internet. Eric Friedberg got a strong enough response that he was able to garner sponsorship from a sporting goods retailer and the Jolly Time popcorn brand. Viewers log in 20 minutes before the game "State Your Case" goes live, and the first 5,000 people to show up make it into the Web audience.

One of them gets to take part in the 20-minute game, which asks players to guess which state license plate is in one of 40 different suitcases on display, for prizes ranging from $50 to $1,000. The show attracted a total audience of more than 8,000 since its October, 2009 debut and draws 200 new viewers for each show. For the eyes it's bringing to the ads placed on the Easy to Win Web site, apparently that price is right.[x]

Marketers like viral videos because of their low cost—they only pay to produce the videos, not to buy airtime. Although there are no accurate measures in place, Web hits and interactions indicate millions of watchers and participants with Internet advertising. Traits outlawed elsewhere—sexual innuendo, juvenile humor, and crass language may be the reasons viewers send the ads to others. Despite the frowns some traditionalists may make, giving viewers advertising that's interesting is what works.

For instance, transmitters mounted on billboards are beaming out text messages asking people to watch video clips on their Bluetooth-equipped cell phones in UK train stations and shopping malls[xi]. By asking first, advertisers avoid annoying consumers. One promotion introduced a new album from rock band Coldplay with 30-second spots of interviews and clips from their music videos, adding new clips to phone screens daily.

Blog advertising

Using the Internet to generate awareness for a specific audience segment was particularly successful for Budget Rent-a-Car. Impax Marketing Group in Philadelphia created a $20,000 campaign for Budget using ads on 177 Web logs, or **blogs**. The ads directed readers to visit a Web site and enter a treasure hunt held for four weeks in 16 cities; cash prizes of $160,000 were awarded. Appropriate for Budget's young, tech-savvy audiences, these blogs featured cartoon characters urging readers to enter the contest. Ads appeared on popular sites such as Blurbomat, BoingBoing, CityRag, Daily Heights, DCist, Gothamist, IndieWier, and That Is Broken. Blogs were screened to cull inappropriate content and were successful enough for Budget to sign up for another blog campaign and contest. Preliminary counts indicated that blog pages where Budget ads appeared had 19.9 million impressions, which generated about 60,000 click-throughs to the Budget blog.[xii] Read about how one movie studio used blogs to promote an upcoming film in the *Focus on* column below.

Promoting a Film on Twitter

A member of Internet site ehow.com posted these five tips, which are abbreviated here, to help promote movies using social network tactics. By incorporating photo graphics software and T-shirts into the promotion, even an amateur can use Twitter accounts to create buzz for a new film.

Step One: Invoke cast member participation and assign them specific days for using Twitter. Rather than social networks that require multiple account management, select a single Twitter account for the film and schedule each cast and crew member to participate in the participation during weeks leading up to the movie's release. By spending at least one hour per week, cast members can build excitement for the film and bring in new followers.

Step Two: Give away free background graphics. With its increase in popularity, Twitter users may be tired of the same format. Users are encouraged to find new ways to customize profiles and promote films. Build graphic backgrounds and make them available for free on your movie website or blog and place the website URL in a prominent place. Members using your designs on their profile will be helping to promote the movie indirectly as new users see the URL in the background.

Step Three: Make memorable avatars and add them to every contributor's profile. The avatar will create recognition on every link or widget related to the media website. Create avatars that display a Twitter URL for the film that feature scenes or stars. Avatars prominent on blogs, forums and social media websites are effective promotional vehicles.

Step Four: Hand out "Follow me on Twitter" shirts that promote the movie. Partner with popular websites and social media users to give away free movie t-shirts printed with the Twitter URL and a message directing viewers to follow the movie profile on this social website. Pay students, actors or models a small fee to walk around in public wearing these t-shirts to promote the film during public events like concerts and football games.

Step Five: Hold special promotions for Twitter followers so they become loyal fans and promoters by providing discounts on merchandise. If your movie is screening at a film festival, offer free tickets to the first Twitter follower who responds to your tweet. You can also give special discounts on merchandise like limited edition t-Shirts, DVDs and Downloads. Coupons and exclusive discounts can be an effective way to promote a movie on Twitter.

Source: msnicole, *eHow Member*

Social networking

Most everyone in the twenty-first century has been exposed or has joined a social network such as YouTube, Facebook, or Twitter. Heavily trafficked by teenagers, these sites are attractive to advertisers, who spend tens of thousands of dollars to build profile pages that promote brands and entertainment experiences.

In addition to advertising, social networks allow companies to learn from fans about what they like and what they are interested in. Social networks like dig.com and del.icio.us allow visitors to search and rate blogs collected instantly from Internet-generated information. Agencies use these sites for advertising to thousands of visitors who receive and send information from the privacy of their virtual spaces.

Social or word-of-mouth advertising uses research to determine their effectiveness. Research metrics important, explained below, provide important building blocks for measurement and evaluation.

- **Conversation volume and share:** One of the basic building blocks of any research effort, conversation volume measures the overall amount of word of mouth about an entertainment brand. It is the word of mouth equivalent of audience size. Measurement of conversation share looks at the amount of conversation each brand enjoys versus the total for all the brands combined. It is the equivalent of market share analysis.

- **Reach:** Reach measures the number of people who have been exposed to word of mouth content.

- **Sentiment analysis:** An analysis of a speaker's tone when talking (or posting) about a brand or product (e.g., positive or negative), and the intensity of opinion.

- **Content:** Monitoring what is being said about a brand during online or offline conversation. Verbatim comments can be read as qualitative insight into conversations in which we look for things like passion words or the "everyday" language that consumers use when talking about a brand that can be used in promotional messages.

FOCUS ON CAREERS

Profile of an Advertising AE

After receiving a scholarship from the Lifeguard Foundation toward his college education, Matt Smart surfed right into a job as account coordinator for Team One Advertising. Of course he graduated first—from Cal Poly State University in San Luis Obispo, California—as a journalism major, knowing he wanted to write for a living. But instead of writing for a newspaper, Matt ended up writing advertising copy.

Matt first served as Account Coordinator for the Lexus Dealer Association, then as an Assistant Account Executive for Lexus National and Lexus Collateral. As a key player in the development of "MY '05 Brand" television and print advertising for Lexus, Matt created and presented the campaign's advertising analysis, dealership displays, fliers and special edition posters. Matt was also an Account Executive for the Ritz-Carlton, in charge of creative solutions for North East and South East properties.

To learn about the advertising business, Matt attended the Los Angeles Advertising Agencies Association's Advertising University, and a year later, completed a program at the Institute of Advanced Advertising Studies presented by the American Association of Advertising Agencies. Currently, he is working toward his M.A. degree in Communications. "The best part of my job is traveling and being able to see interesting places and meet fascinating people," says Matt.

In his words ...

Planning for disaster

"Last year, in preparation for a big new client presentation in Maryland, our team planned out how we were going to get all the presentation materials to the hotel. We packaged it off and sent it UPS to the hotel our executives were staying at for next day delivery. The executives boarded the plane, landed and checked-in to the hotel. No meeting materials had arrived. And they never arrived. The plane with our materials was grounded for mechanical issues. We asked our account coordinator, who was in her second day on the job, to fly to Washington D.C. on a red-eye and carry the new materials to the director at her hotel near the Capitol. The entire day was used to create new materials. With 45 minutes to spare every material was recreated. Such moments of disaster are really opportunities for major success. Those hours at work from the moment we found out our materials were not going to arrive to the moment they were delivered into the hands of our director were filled with tremendous team work and camaraderie. That was exciting.

Getting ahead

Go the extra mile. Get the job done. Exceed expectations.

Many people in today's workforce are there to cover the expenses of life. Find what you enjoy doing and you will have an easier time succeeding at it.

It is important to approach assignments with a lot of humility. You will be asked to do things that you know your supervisor can do. You are right. But that isn't the point. It is your turn to do it. And do it again. And again. That is why they call it work. That is why you get paid for it."

Reprinted with permission of Matt Smart.

- **Advocacy:** Galvanizing consumers to advocate for a brand is a top priority. Advocacy measurement identifies all of the different ways people verbalize their advocacy, isolating advocacy terms and emotions from general positive sentiment.

- **Actions taken:** This measure (which should reflect campaign goals) determines the extent to which positive word of mouth or brand advocacy links to behavior.[xiii]

Web site marketing

The Internet is a brand-message expander. Ads, publicity releases, and events can direct audiences to an entertainment brand's Web site for more information and possible ticket purchase. Creative, interactive, and fun Web sites enjoy frequent hits and extended stays. Interactivity is key; by using games and feedback vehicles, sites can be entertaining as well as informative and persuasive. By registering the Web site with multiple search engines, industry franchises gain visibility and site visits. As with other media, marketers must create awareness of the site, then give visitors a reason to go there.

A company's Web site is its consumer communication vehicle. It should reflect the look, feel and content of a company and be coordinated in theme and content. The company of course must match service delivery with promises.

Web sites give entertainment providers a cost-effective way to distribute brand information and provide online ticketing to worldwide audiences. Theaters, events, destinations, and theme parks use online ticketing because it's fast, convenient, and easy. Audience members can print out tickets from home, along with information such as schedules, maps, and updates.

Measuring online activity

Web sites traditionally measure their traffic using click-through and unique visitor measures. For an entertainment venue to determine how well its Web site is performing, some of the following measurements, fairly standard in the industry, are used. The factors here relate to a performing arts venue or a movie Web site.

- *Lift:* How many additional ticket purchases were made by season ticket holders who visited the venue's Web site? What is the ratio between trailer hits (number of times site visitors clicked on a movie preview, or trailer) and box office attendance?

- *Conversion rate:* What percentage of non-subscribers signed up for season tickets after visiting the Web site? How many trailer viewers purchased online tickets after viewing?

- *Brand knowledge and perception:* What percentage of site visitors thought more positively about the venue compared to those who did not visit the site?

- *Number of visits:* How many viewers hit, either through a search or a click on a URL, to visit the Web site? This number is useful in determining the level of interest in performance schedules and movie plots. Hits and click-throughs, while creating brand awareness, may generate misleading measures with regard to actual purchase.

+ *Length of time on site*: How long did viewers remain to explore the Web site? The longer viewers stay, the more likely they are to learn about the brand and purchase tickets.

+ *Number and types of inquiries*: How many and what kind of responses were collected? Interaction and dialogue engage visitors and stimulate purchase.

PRODUCT PLACEMENT AS ENTERTAINMENT

The practice of placing products in every medium has become so widespread that it has fostered in industry of its own. Movies themselves have become advertisements; product placement has turned the movie screen into a moving billboard.

Annual retainer fees paid to specialty placement agencies range from tens of thousands of dollars a year for an emerging brand to a few million a year for major automaker.[xiv] The Entertainment Marketing Association acts as a trade association for groups that have a vested interest in the practice of product placement. Advertisers include:

1. corporations looking to get their brands placed into entertainment vehicles

2. studios and production companies seeking to defray costs with products 'comped,' or placed in their projects

3. placement agencies

Brands (product and place) are placed in at least five different ways.

+ silent props or *creative placements* (Kellogg's cornflakes on a kitchen pantry shelf or on a table during a breakfast scene)

+ props that provide dimension to a scene, called *on-set placements* (Marlboro cigarettes to signify American male freedom)

+ props the advance the plot, or *embedded placements* (BMW chase car for James Bond)

+ props that star or *feature placement* (Caesar's Palace from *Rocky III*, or a geographic location that figures in the central plot of a program of film)

+ *virtual placements* (outdoor boards seen in *Law & Order*, an NBC series); permits visual manipulations and allows for intra-brand comparisons

+ *in-game* advertising on X-Box and PlayStation video games (Coke logo in *SWAT 4*, updatable graphics in networked games such as *Anarchy Online*) where racing game players can test-drive a Porsche or outfit their characters in Rocawear's new fall line[xv]

Products for the Pope

Promoters looking for pontifical product placements were delighted when the Pope was spotted wearing Serengeti-branded sunglasses, carrying an Apple iPod, and wearing red loafers rumored to be made by Prada in 2006. What was next for branding a Pope?

They decided to test the lengths of exploitation for hyping products by creating a papal association with over a billion Catholics, a placement worth at least 100 times more than an A-list celebrity. But unlike movie stars who can command huge sums for product endorsements, the papal moral and spiritual leader who endorses holiness and chastity was unlikely to accept the huge sums of cash commanded by movie stars to endorse products.

Image 11.3 Mercedes Popemobile.

© Getty Images

The method used to plant brands is simple—donate the product, then promote on a photograph showing him using or wearing the brand. But pursuing the pope-and-product juxtaposition poses risks. Risking backlash from Pope followers, companies and their brands must be careful not to appear opportunistic.

According to the research director of an international advertising-research firm, product placement on such luminaries as the Pope raises many questions in terms of company ethics. Even ethical issues, however, have not quelled the interest in papal brand placement, as illustrated in the Mercedes Benz association captured in the photo above.

Following Benedict XVI's election in April 2005, Italian shoe company Geox gave the papal spokesman several pairs of Uomo Light loafers as a present for the new Pope, and were delighted when word got out that he was wearing them. Apple's gift of a Nano engraved with "To His Holiness" and packed with Vatican Radio programming was considered a real coup. Natuzzi leather created the internal upholstery for a golf cart that GE gave the pope, and issued a joint news release to let people know about the vehicle that is used inside the Vatican gardens.

Volkswagen and BMW both jockeyed to replace the Mercedes as the next maker of the Popemobile, arguably the world's most visible SUV. Although BMW hoped the pope would use the bulletproof X5 it donated to the Vatican, he is still seen waving from the Mercedes in 2010.

What do you think?

1. What ethical issues does BMW face by donating its SUV to the Pope?

2. Should the public be made aware of branded accessories worn by the Pontiff? Why?

3. Who should be responsible for selecting what the Pope drives and wares?

4. What considerations must the Vatican make before accepting donations?

Source: Stacy Meichtry for *The Wall Street Journal*, April 25, 2006.

Past studies have shown that the more likeable the product's user (film star), the more likely the viewer is to remember that product. According to consumer memory authorities, the less overt the placement the more likely it is to be retained. Placements occur on television, in print, in music, movies, games, and even staged settings.

Someone at Alcatraz, the island museum that used to house a maximum-security prison, placed an empty package of Marlboro cigarettes in a cell that was designed to replicate an actual incarceration cubicle to reflect authenticity. No one will divulge whether the tobacco company paid for the placement, or if park providers dressed the set using their own idea of what was an appropriate prop.

The next step in product placement, **product integration**, occurs when advertisers move from being clients to becoming partners and program development and production costs are subsidized. Integration is closer to **sponsorship**, where financial backers or sponsors get involved in tuning content to the goals of their brands, while making commitments to provide advertising support. Television programming is often a result of product integration.

A talent management agency in Beverly Hills merged with a brand-placement shop to facilitate access among their respective client bases. The talent agency clients include Leonardo DiCaprio, Cameron Diaz, Martin Scorsese, and Snoop Dogg. Citing "organic product-integration efforts as the strategy to place clients" brands into films and TV programs, the firm helps talent firms break through the clutter of advertising with branded content. Other talent firms are merging their clients as well. Endeavor, which represents Adam Sandler, Matt Damon, and Drew Barrymore, works on behalf of American Express and AOL. William Morris agency, which represents Russell Crowe and Halle Berry, handles Anheuser-Busch, GM, and Saks Fifth Avenue. That merger involved getting Saks a key role in the movie *Shopgirl*. A partnership between ABC and MindShare (WPP Group) media was formed to develop content that offers WPP clients a deal to have their ad messages embedded into the programming.[xvi]

It's often difficult to separate the ad from the entertainment. For instance, on *Harlem Heights*, a new reality show on BET, the young stars swish Listerine, treat their allergies with Zyrtec, and sweeten their coffee with Splenda. Welcome to the new generation of product placement where brands are no longer just occasional props on TV shows and movies, as they were until about five years ago. Now, as part of more elaborate marketing deals, advertisers are increasingly working with writers, producers, and the networks to incorporate products into the story lines of both scripted and reality shows. Even news shows are doing it, raising difficult questions about journalistic integrity.

In 2009, the characters on *CSI: New York* gathered around video-conferencing screens to share information about a shooting, but really to promote Cisco Systems' TelePresence video-conferencing system. The same year, characters on the ABC soap *One Life to Live* spent the month talking up the health benefits of Campbell's soups. [xvii]

Digital technology has made it easy and inexpensive to dub product placements into overseas versions of the same movie[xviii]. Product dubbing is largely confined to still shots where the brands are little more than props in the background. This technique was first used in 1993 action movie *Demolition Man*. Pepsico bought a major role for its Taco Bell brand in the film's U.S. release, while its overseas version featured Pizza Hut, another Pepsico brand. Refrigerator magnets were switched in *Spider-Man 2* from one touting Dr Pepper to another for Mirinda when the film moved beyond the U.S. Since foreign markets contribute as much as 60% of the box office take for most Hollywood pictures, so the practice of tailoring product placements for international markets is a mainstay of a studio's global marketing campaign. By taking a can in someone's hand and changing it from one brand to another, studios open up new avenues of revenue generation.

Product Placement Snippets

+ *Can to imprinted logo*—*American Idol*, known for the visible Coke can on the panel's desktop, changed to using Coke branded glasses for drinking liquids of any kind. Coca-Cola also has a digital branded logo on screen for selected segments in the show.

+ *The biggest apple*—In 2009, the Apple brand dominated the product placement industry. Apple's logo or products appeared in 18 of 44 box-office hits. In addition to movie appearances, Apple had TV placements on shows like Jimmy Fallon and Regis and Kelly.

+ *Smartest phone*—Real-time product placements are being generated through Smartphone advertisements. Gaming company Booyah designed a campaign for H&M stores that activates the game when consumers are near the outlets. Games feature H&M branded products that gives discounts to shoppers who show the product on their phone.

Source: www.productplacement.biz/News/Product-Placement/

Most placement agreements are made 18 to 24 months before a film's release. Costing between $10,000 and $100,000 to dub a logo into a short scene, big brand film promotion for Europe is one way to leverage films as promotional tools. To build international sales, a movie-marketing group, LA office, hosted an international meeting of brand marketers designed to help spur overseas product placement and promotion. You'll find more examples of product placement in Chapter 14.

FOCUS ON THE ETHICS

Selling in the Movies

Three films in the past decade illustrate the impact product placement has on movie industry economics. With advertisers complaining about the difficulties of measuring product placement ROI, movie *Sideways* reported outstanding results that demonstrate the powers of placement persuasion. Snubbing Merlot, the protagonist created over-the-top sales of pinot noir in the first month after the film's release: traditionally an ignored varietal of wine, sales of pinot noir increased 22%. Blackstone Pinot Noir, for instance, saw sales increase by almost 150% after the film opened. Merlot, the brunt of disparaging criticism, received a decrease in sales for months after the film's release. However, tourism to California's wine region increased substantially, driving business up 30% at The Hitching Post, a restaurant featured in the film. *Sideways*, a 2004 Oscar nominee, showed very measurable results for its placements.[xix]

Stephen Spielberg's 2002 *Minority Report* is said to have "compromised the merger of commerce and content."[xx] More than 15 real-life sponsors reportedly paid more than $25 million—approximately a quarter of the futuristic film's budget—to become featured brands. *Minority's* star Tom Cruise had a Lexus speak to him, used a Nokia phone, wore Reeboks, got splashed by an Aquafina billboard, visited the Gap, and celebrated his American Express membership since 2037. And footage from FedEx covered approximately 80% of *Cast Away's* budget in exchange for its plot presence in the 2000 film.

So what's wrong with such blatant product placement? Opponents of advertising's "overbearing invasiveness" claim that we cannot escape the deep editorial influence brand sponsors foist upon us. They allege that because our commercial media landscape continually demands higher profit margins, advertisers and studios, networks, publishers, and music labels have too much control over what we watch, hear, and read.

What do you think?

1. Is your viewing experience compromised by the appearance of brands on the big screen? Why?

2. Should legislation be enacted to prohibit paid placement in fictional stories?

3. Can you make an argument for freedom of brand expression in all mediated content?

Source: www.brandchannel.com/brandcameo_brands.asp.

SALES PROMOTION, MERCHANDISING, AND PERSONAL SELLING

Sales promotion is a function that offers a tangible added value designed to motivate and accelerate a purchase response. Sales promotion is best used when sales are low, performances are nearing their completion, or when new destinations are being introduced. Promotions can be directed at middlemen (retailers and distributors) who *push* tickets on to their own customers, or directly to audience members themselves with a *pull* strategy. Performance, experience, and venue providers use both trade and consumer promotions to encourage purchase.

Trade promotion

When targeting members of a distribution channel, marketers use a **push strategy** to motivate retailers—business that act as go-between among content providers and audiences—to promote branded entertainment products to their customers. Entertainment producers provide incentives to ticket distributors, such as Ticketmaster and Expedia, to promote their shows, venues, resorts, theme parks, performances, and concerts on retailers' Web sites.

Trade promotions are designed to encourage retailers to push entertainment products directly to audience members. These promotions include *bulk discounts* on tickets and *spiffs* as sales incentives for retailers. Other sales promotions for the trade include *incentive travel*, which rewards top producers with vacations. Carnival Cruise Lines, for example, conducted online sweeps entries for travel agents for each cruise booked using Visa, their advertising partner. Participating agencies sold 12% ($1.3 million) more than other agents.

Consumer promotion

Marketers promote directly to audience members or ticket buyers with a **pull strategy**. Direct mail brochures announcing season performances is an example of a consumer promotion that pulls audience members into a venue. Multiple-ticket discounts and premier seating premiums function as incentives for audiences to subscribe or purchase tickets.

In an era of economic downturn, coupons—especially those downloaded from Internet sites—have gained popularity as one of the most effective consumer promotion tools. Coupons, two-for-ones, premiums, and contests are the primary vehicles of promotions for experiential brands. Safeway Grocery chain gave out discount tickets to Disney's California Adventure when it first opened to help stimulate traffic among locals. Subscribers and season ticket holders often receive bonuses (free parking or a special lounge area) as audience member promotions.

Sales promotion tools used in the entertainment industry are similar to consumer product promotional tools. Sweepstakes and games are especially popular for promoting experiences and often involve tie-ins with product brands with the same target audience. Here are some examples.

+ *Premiums are* free items given with purchase to reward a buying behavior. Season subscribers to an outdoor concert series may receive a branded stadium seat, or frequent hotel guests are presented with logo-embossed robes as a thank-you for purchasing or booking. Movie figures, included in fast-food lunches reward your family trip through the drive-thru as they encourage you to see the film. Such premiums often become collectables, encouraging multiple purchases. Premiums are successful if they 1) appeal to the target audience, 2) have perceived value, 3) are relevant to the brand image, and 4) create a buying response.

+ *Specialties* are given free to the customer but not intended to stimulate immediate buying behavior. Typically, t-shirts, visors, pencils, and mugs are provided to audience members to keep the brand's name top-of-mind. Usually inexpensive and distributed to a mass audience, specialty items can also be higher priced gifts to valued customers.

+ *Coupons* are certificates that offer a stated price reduction on a specific performance or attraction. Coupons can be paired with most consumer goods. With the purchase of $100 in groceries, supermarkets may give out coupons good for $3 when redeemed at a local theme park. Off-season hotel sales can be stimulated with coupons for breakfast with a room booking, or reduced admission at a nearby museum. Coupons are delivered in stores, newspapers, magazines, and electronically online.

+ *Sweepstakes*, or drawings, are used by vacation packagers in conjunction with radio stations to draw attention to the brand. Hotels, theme parks, and motion picture studios commonly use sweepstakes. For example, film promoters may offer the winner an evening with the film's star or a trip to Hollywood for the premiere showing.

FOCUS ON MOBILE MOVIES

It's a Movie—No, It's a Game!

In an age of participatory media and cross-media promotions, just watching a movie doesn't suffice. People want to experience it, to live it on the go. So for iPod Touch and iPhone owners, an enhanced move experience comes in the form of games from the App Store. Ten film-inspired games were available in 2010:

1. *The Dark Knight: Batmobile* Game; racing/driving game to see how quickly you can get Batman through a maze of obstacles in Gotham City.

2. *The Day the Earth Stood Still: Aphid Attack;* action game to control a swarm of aphids and use them to destroy landmarks worldwide.

3. *Days of Thunder;* racing/driving game lets you compete in six races and vie for the winner's cup.

4. *Hellboy II: The Golden Army*—Tooth Fairy Terror; action game to see how many carnivorous tooth fairy creatures you can squash.

5. *Iron Man: Aerial Assault;* action game in a battle against Iron Man's foes in the unfriendly skies.[xi]

6. *Race to Witch Mountain;* racing/driving game that challenges you to get to the mountain without being forced off the road.

7. *Rounders;* poker/role-playing game that uses poker to move through a version of the movie.

8. *Saturday Night Fever:Dance!;* dance game where player earns points for helping characters dance like stars.

9. School of Rock; music game where you play along with classic rock songs on various instruments.

10. Watchman: Justice is Coming; action/fighting game where players create their own hero and dispense justice on the mean streets.

Source: Sam Costello, "Movie tied-in iPod touch games" About.com/guide

Games are popular for use with entertainment attractions because they are conducted over an extended period of time and keep the branded experience alive after the game ends. Usually played on the Internet, games are often used for promotion. For instance, posters at Office Depot let customers know they were an official sponsor of NASCAR using an instant-win game. Customers get scratch-off cards for a change at an instant prize. A grand prize winner received a VIP race experience with drive Tony Stewart at the Charlotte Motor Speedway in May, 2010. Another received a trip for two to Stewart's 'Smoke Show' fantasy driving experience at Texas Motor Speedway. The promotion was featured on the front page of a Sunday insert distributed to 40 million households, national radio, online media, and Office Depot's Facebook page and Twitter accounts.

Contests require skill and involve a brand. Crate & Barrel brand built their registry business with a wedding contest where couples open an in-store registry account and go online to win votes and the help of a wedding planner. The "$100,000 Ultimate Wedding Contest" offers as a grand prize the services of top-shelf wedding planner Jo Gartin and a $10,000 Crate & Barrel gift card as parts of a deluxe $100,000 marriage ceremony. To enter, couples—including same-sex couples—must create a registry account and profile on the brand's Web site and upload a photo of themselves with a statement about their love story or description of their dream day. At the end of the submission period, 50 entries with the most votes were considered for the grand prize by a panel of judges. The grand prize winners were selected on the basis of the originality and creativity of their entry and the ranking it received in the public voting.[xxii]

Price reductions, rebates, and sampling are product-specific, consumer-oriented promotions that have little value for experiential products. Cross promotions and tie-in promotions are more applicable to entertainment marketing.

Cross promotion

The promotion of two or more brands together, such as a beverage and a movie, allows the brands to share promotional costs while they benefit from each other's image. CBS and Campbell's soup produced a joint print promotion that included the network's fall line-up schedule on the back of the piece and inside pages devoted to various shows and corresponding meal suggestions. Campbell aligned its soups with different shows, such as pairing the *NFL Today* show with its hearty line.

Movie promotion deals offer two-way advantages: consumer-goods companies benefit from brand exposure without paying a licensing fee, and studios get a compelling chance to put the movie's name and image into heavily trafficked retail spaces.

Tie-in promotion

Linking of two products through advertising and in-store merchandising typically occurs between movies and their characters in fast-food restaurants. More unique was the tie-in with *Avatar* and eXpo's 'killer app', a detachable mobile projector as a mobile phone feature. A campaign microsite features some video spots showing the product and Avatar scenes. LG worked with video game manufacturer Ubisoft to sponsor content for the platform-based tie-in movie game. Registered Gamspot users were able to get secret weapon game add-ons for Xbox and PlayStation Platforms. Although the microsite targeted 20 to 30 year-olds, it gave all ages an opportunity to see the eXpo phone and *Avatar* scenes.

Partnerships developed between organizations are designed to promote both brands. Most are carried out during summers and holiday seasons. Universal Pictures *The Grinch Whole Stole Christmas*, for instance, was partnered with Sprite, Nabisco, Hershey, and Wendy's on some $85 million in marketing support. In addition, the partners made an agreement with the U.S. Postal Service to identify the Grinch's fictional town of Whoville with cancellation stamps for over 6 billion pieces of holiday mail.[xxiii]

Social Media and Promotional Tie-Ins

Some promotions use all and every promotional tactic available for a blanket strategy that works with specific audience segments. Dippin' Dots campaign integrated tactics for a movie tie-in that benefited both the retailer and the film box office.

CAMPAIN OBJECTIVE: Invigorate their web presence and to drive visits and gather email addresses and consumer information.

PROMOTION TACTICS: A nationwide promotion between Dippin' Dots and New Line Cinema/Warner Brothers 3D feature film, *Journey to the Center of the Earth* to include in-store activation and online sweepstakes. POP signage featuring star Brendan Fraser was created to attract attention, and 'Creature Cards' were developed from film images of threatening monsters. Traffic was driven with a viral marketing campaign that leveraged multiple social media platforms, networking communities, forums, and blogs. A totally buzz-focused campaign created without paid advertising. Weekly prizes included movie tickets, posters and an adventure trip for four to Iceland where the film was made.

New Line/Photofest

Image 11.4

What do you think?

1. Would similar promotional tactics work with a film for mature adults? What changes would be necessary?

2. Did promoters miss any tactics you can suggest?

Source: Matrixpictures.com.

Loyalty programs

Keeping audience members coming back is best achieved by rewarding them with more of what they purchased—in other words, more of the same experiences. Hotels reward their frequent guests with extra night stays or nights at another facility of the same brand to keep occupancy rates high with a minimum of promotional expense. Designed to build repeat usage, loyalty programs are the preferred promotions of theme parks, attractions, casinos, and resorts. In 2010, program updates were developed to attract new members and add excitement to standard programs. Member points, for instance will be enhanced with an option to use those points to enter contests and win prizes like trips and flat-screen TVs.

Merchandising and licensing

Merchandising involves creating or licensing others to produce merchandise that is based upon a movie, performance, destination, or character. Disney, master of merchandising, produced 186 items associated with *The Lion King* movie. Brands, such as Batman or Rugrats, are lumps of content that can be exploited through film, broadcast and cable television, publishing, theme parks, music, Internet, and merchandising. Movie soundtracks are another form of profitable merchandising. Most entertainment content and experience providers are heavy users of merchandising, which often makes up for box office losses. Merchandising and licensing are covered more extensively in Chapter 14.

FOCUS ON MOVIE MERCHANDISING

To Sequel or Not to Sequel

After *Proposal* with Sandra Bullock grossed $315 million worldwide and only cost $40 million to make, it became the perfect film for a sequel. But since Bullock action figures can't be sold, and a *Proposal* theme park ride can't be built, what was Disney to do for an encore?

As part of Disney's new edict to produce only two kinds of films, they're giving preference to a $150 million-plus blockbuster with lots of merchandising or filling the movie with young, cheap, on-the-cusp movie stars. Extremes rule, and for Disney, everything in the middle is tossed.

After Disney CEO Robert Iger admitted publicly that 2009 had been "awful": *Confessions of a Shopaholic* (domestic gross: $44 million), the flop *G-Force* (domestic gross: $119 million), and the Bruce Willis action flick *Surrogates* (domestic gross: $38 million) all fell short of revenue forecasts, he had to take action to improve the brand.

To help recuperate the $10 billion Disney spent acquiring Pixar and Marvel, Iger decided that its films had to sell heaps of spinoff merchandise as well as producing box office successes. The world's largest licensor of consumer products, Disney 2008 sold some $30 billion worth in 2008, and none came from selling Sandra Bullock hand towels!

New studio president Rich Ross—formerly the Disney Channel's worldwide president responsible for making Hannah Montana and the Jonas Brothers household screams—was brought in to enhance the company's value with a high-quality Pixar or Marvel film under the Disney brand. Two projects in the making that reflect the new mission are blockbusters *Tron* and *The Black Hole*.

A new Muppet movie and *Jungle Cruise*, a project based on little more than its Disneyland ride namesake, were slated as the next money makers, and both films are sure-fire merchandise extenders. *Pirates of the Caribbean*, a franchise that has so far grossed $2.68 billion worldwide with much of the profits generated by merchandising, has its sixth sequel ready for release in 2011.

Source: Claude Brodesser-Akner at nymag.com/daily/entertainment/2010/02/the_middle_is_toast_at_disney.html

Personal selling

Face-to-face presentation by a company's representative builds customer relationships and completes sales. Group sales for performances and incentive travel companies make use of personal selling to optimize volume and guarantee box office or tour success. Employees of hotels and resorts also act as personal sales representatives by referring guests to house services and sponsored events. Performance subscriptions are commonly solicited by phone, a process that's also an aspect of personal sales. Personal interaction with audience members is a vital component of many promotional mix strategies. Discussed as a tourist service, personal selling is presented in Chapter 13.

PUBLIC AND MEDIA RELATIONS

For entertainment companies, public relations are invoked to create good and a positive image between the organization and its stakeholders. Public relations is one of the most important parts of the promotion mix for entertainment marketers. Serving as a source of information about the organization, **public relations**, or PR, is a system that uses a variety of media to bring news and attention to a product, service, or experience. Marketing PR and brand publicity are the functions most relevant to the entertainment industry. "The deliberate, planned and sustained effort to establish and maintain mutual understanding between and organization and its public" is the definition provided by the Institute of Public Relations. An entertainment company's *publics* include the following groups, among others.

- the community
- employees
- government
- financial community

- distributors
- audience members
- opinion leaders
- media

When connected to entertainment promotion, PR employs a variety of tactics to manage audience perceptions about an experience. These aspects of the public relations operate separately and in tandem to maintain positive communication about a specific celebrity, venue, performance, attraction, or destination. Here are the major components of PR activities.

Media relations

One of the most important activities of PR is to use non-paid media messages to deliver persuasive branded communications to potential and current audience members. No entertainment experience can survive on paid advertising alone. A well-placed editorial will catch the attention of potential and current audiences and provide objective reviews. News releases and feature stories delivered to newspaper editors and broadcast station producers can result in more positive exposure than advertising, and for far less cash.

A good publicist—one who has an inside track to media gatekeepers—is worth her weight in gold. Publicity supports brand communication and promotion directed at prospects. All experiences require some amount of *buzz*, a hard-to-define quality that essentially says, "people are hearing about your product," and buzz is developed and dispatched through constant publicity and media coverage. PR objectives seek to build awareness and visibility, create or change attitudes, create buzz, influence opinion leaders, and generate a sense of involvement for audiences and other publics.

The value of public relations is the perception that it provides branded entertainment with third-party endorsements. Audiences believe that communications presented by a media source that has no vested interest in the success or failure of the brand is more credible than paid advertising. The success of many performances comes from positive advance reviews, feature stories, and news segments prior to their debuts.

To receive timely and frequent coverage, entertainment PR professionals must maintain positive relationships with the media. Paid space and time guarantees advertising messages; not so with PR. The only way to insure coverage of an event or news item is to deliver it personally to a reporter who covers the entertainment or travel beat, an editor of the features section of major newspapers or magazines, or a television producer of entertainment news.

Courting reporters, editors, and producers involves providing timely, credible, and interesting news. Media professionals don't want to hear a story they could have gleaned from an ad. Creative and innovative news must be crafted for the audience of each medium, and presented to the gatekeeper (e.g., a reporter) in a way that demonstrates the benefit of delivering the story. Media relations works well when relationships are built upon honest communications.

Publicity

Publicity is editorial written about a brand—it's getting mentioned in print or over the airwaves. Publicity's strength is its ability to reach audiences that are difficult to reach with advertising, such as business professionals and groups with limited exposure to traditional commercial messages. Publicity, especially over the Internet, is very cost effective and is perceived to work better than advertising in many cases. For instance, movie goers are more likely to go to a reviewer's Web site than to respond to a pop-up ad on that film. Motion picture studios provide media with a steady flow of quotes, research data, photographs, trailers, interviews and access to directors in order to generate positive coverage of a film in advance of the film's release. Tourism bureaus dispatch segments to travel channels, distribute feature articles to major newspapers, and offer free trips for editors to experience the city for themselves, which is standard practice in the industry. Publicity tools used by PR practitioners are listed in Exhibit 11.2.

Again, you'll find that public relations are an essential element of all marketing plans for entertainment-based product promotion, *especially when your news has value.*

EXHIBIT 11.2 Basic Publicity Tools

+ *News release*—print, visual, or broadcast news delivered by a franchise or corporation
+ *News kit*—packet of information with photos, histories, biographies, feature stories, and a fact sheet about an attraction, event, or destination.
+ *Press conference*—event where corporate officials meet with media with a major news story
+ *Media tour*—scheduled live appearances to promote a film, performance, or experience
+ *Media event*—special event to generate coverage and involve company publics
+ *Speeches*—ghostwritten statements provided for media use
+ *Pitch*—story idea proposal for an editor or reporter
+ *Fact sheet*—information to provide background data for media use in story preparation

Creating Buzz

Buzz is the natural, authentic version of hype—the CNN of the street! Hype is intended to promote, whereas buzz often is truthful about an entertainment product and therefore higher in credibility. And while hype takes time, effort and expense to circulate, buzz can move like wildfire through a community. PR professionals' role is to generate buzz, not create hype, surrounding a new entertainment innovation.

Corporate PR

PR is used to develop positive relationships between a brand (film, performance, destination, attraction) and its audience. Typical corporate PR functions include:

- *Corporate communications* focus on identity, reputation management, and management counseling. Publicity functions include monitoring public opinion, addressing community concerns, informing public officials and regulatory agencies, and engaging in activities with the industry itself. Hotel chains, media conglomerates, and entertainment franchises consider this an important function for maintaining brand equity.

- *Employee relations* are internal communication programs to build morale, acculturate, and reward positive activities. Theme parks like Disneyland rely heavily on their employee community for delivering favorable experiences to park visitors.

- *Investor relations* provides information programs for investors and members of the industry's financial community. This functions is especially important for the motion picture industry, which secures its funding through venture capitalists and private individuals.

- *Philanthropy* is comprised of corporate giving and non-profit or cause sponsorship has become part of corporate brand identity. Giving back to the community is not only good business, it is an excellent marketing strategy. By becoming advocates for medical research, educational scholarships, public broadcasting, or curing disease, entertainment corporations bring attention to another side of their enterprise—a caring presence in the community at large. Marketers should never lose sight of the "greater good" philosophy when developing a promotional campaign. Campaign planners should always propose a philanthropic partner for their client as a way to increase brand recognition and good will.

Crisis management with PR

One function of PR that often goes unheralded is the important task of managing crises. A crisis plan is vital for theme parks to put into action when a patron is injured or killed on a ride, or for venues to use in anticipation of uncontrollable crowd actions, or on a large scale for destination cities should they be struck by a natural disaster or terrorist attack. When Magic Mountain roller

Sony Supports Local Communities

Sony Pictures Entertainment is a major supporter of arts education and community involvement, and the spirit of philanthropy is imbedded in the culture of Sony in America. Every philanthropic activity provides countless opportunities for feature stories that work to maintain Sony's positive brand image.

Listed below are a few of the company's philanthropic associations with arts education, cultural organizations, film festivals, health and human services, and community outreach.

Arts educational program: New York University's Tisch School of the Arts, among others, has received generous support from Sony. The school is one of the nation's leading centers of undergraduate and graduate study in the performing and media arts.

Museums and other cultural organizations: American Film Institute, American Museum of Natural History, Holocaust Museum, John F. Kennedy Center for the Performing Arts, Metropolitan Museum of Art, Muhammad Ali Center, El Museo del Barrio, and the Smithsonian Institution are a few organizations that have all benefited from Sony's support.

Film Festivals and Awards Shows: Los Angeles Asian Pacific Film & Video Festival, Los Angeles Latino International Film Festival, and OUTFES have received help from Sony.

Health & Human Services: Support from Sony has gone to Recording for the Blind and Dyslexic and the T.J. Martell Foundation, which is dedicated to raising funds for the initial and ongoing research into the treatments and cures of leukemia, cancer, and AIDS.

Civic and Community Outreach: The company has a program that matches the donation employees make to the non-profit organizations of their choice.

Source: sony.com/philanthropy

coaster injured a rider, Disney had a plan in place for interfacing with the media to report the status of the rider's health and measures being taken to insure the ride's safety.

Most recently, Nielson Media Research, the television ratings arbiter, spent hundreds of thousands of dollars fighting groups objecting to their ratings system, which they say has undercounted minority viewers and hindered the development of shows geared to those audiences. News Corporation, whose Fox television stations produce shows for special audiences, mounted a campaign to determine why people meters were failing to register the viewing preferences of many black and Hispanic homes. Nielson has paid lobbying firms to coordinate a campaign to reach out to blacks and Hispanics, including the sponsorship of the annual

GoldenPalace Online Casino

Bodacious brand-building is about performing crazy acts just to generate publicity. GoldenPalace online casino bought a haunted walking cane ($65,000), a collection of Michael Jackson puppets ($15,099), and the privilege for being able to officially name a new monkey species after the site—*caallicebus aureipalatii* ($650,000) The biggest and most recent purchase was a "Pope Mobile," a VW Golf formerly owned by Pope Benedict XVI on eBay for a mere $244,591.

A somewhat crass marketing strategy, bidding for bizarre items is effective in an industry where advertising is controversial. Since online gambling is considered illegal, GoldenPalace's $20 million budget still runs plenty of traditional and online ads, but PR stunts are a cheaper and better way to build name recognition. Press mentions regarding its eBay purchases are equivalent to at least $30 million in ads. Plus, middle-weight boxer Bernard Hopkins was paid to stamp the GoldenPalace brand on his back for a Madison Square Garden bout, resulting in multiple lawsuits—which were covered by media outlets such as *USA Today* and The Howard Stern Show, of course!

Promotion strategy for GoldenPalace, one of the world's top three gambling sites, has also included hiring people to streak naked during some thousand sporting events, from Wimbledon to Pamplona's running of the bulls, all with the Web site's name on their bodies. After a man with the brand's URL streaked through half-time of the 2004 Super Bowl, visits to the site jumped by 380%. With 2.4 million U.S. visitors per month to the site, revenue—upwards of $80 million—was growing at 5% a month.

What do you think?

1. When buying eBay's odd objects loses its luster, what can GoldenPalace do to trump itself?

2. What are the merits and pitfalls of using publicity stunts as the main marketing strategy?

Source: Elizabeth Esfahani, *Business 2.0*, July, 2005, p. 60.

Real Men Cook, a charity devoted to encouraging African-American men to stay involved with their families.[xxiv] This is a type of crisis that highlights the need for entertainment corporations and franchises to anticipate and arm themselves against negative publicity with a effective plan.

EVENT PROMOTION AND SPONSORSHIP

Event management and sponsorship activities, sometimes the purview of public relations efforts, work because they are experiential rather than mediated. Both activities connect a brand with audience members. Because consumers prefer to purchase lifestyles, experience, and emotions rather than products, events, and sponsorship opportunities provide a large component of the promotion mix for entertainment companies.

Event promotion

Event promotion is a fast-growing, high-profile industry and a very successful marketing strategy. Events provide a promotional occasion that attracts and involves the brand's target audience. Billions of dollars pour into sponsorships of entertainment, sports, venues, and attractions annually. Events marketing integrates the corporate sponsorship of an event with a whole range of marketing elements such as advertising, sales promotion, and public relations for these reasons[xxv]:

- Companies can break through the advertising clutter by creating a brand image associated with an event.
- Both the event and the brand profit from the pairing a financial partnership with an advertising budget and added leverage to sell tickets.
- Sponsorship allows for profitable, "ownable" territories that can be leveraged, catering to audience members who purchase experiences.

Event marketing offers companies the flexibility to reach specific geographic and demographic audiences for a depth of exposure. Important considerations are event selection, return on investment, terms of agreement, marketing integration, execution, and results. You must make certain that the expenses incurred in presenting an event will generate enough revenue to turn a profit.

Live event marketing experienced a renaissance in 2009 as more marketers recognized its power to engage audiences and deliver the all important 'experience' that develops and cements brand loyalty. The increasing number of events taking place, the trend for media groups to strengthen print and digital portfolios with live events and the growing involvement of leading brands has seen marketing budgets shift toward the sector.

Companies earmarked an average 25% of their 2009 budgets for event marketing. Media and entertainment promotions lend themselves local to events for creating attention and media coverage. Savvy brand promoters say that the right combination of persistent public relations and event creativity can deliver national—even global—results from a local event. A 2009 promo survey showed that trade shows were used as venues by 50.8% of agencies and their clients. General entertainment events were used by 37.4% of those responding, with sports events at 23% and music events at 18.4%. Retails events ranked just behind entertainment at 36.3%.

Media entertainment marketers also use local events in their mix. To promote their fall series *Three Wishes*, NBC played the role of fairy godmother to boost viewership. During the

Virgin Takes Flight

Client: Virgin Galactic

Event: Maiden voyage of Virgin Spaceship Enterprise and the unveiling of first-ever commercial space plane. Eight hundred VIPs and members of the press were invited to the Mojave, California desert where Sir Richard Branson once again proved that no one sets the bar higher for innovative publicity stunts.

Challenge: Held in the middle of the harsh Mojave Desert environment with no amenities or infrastructure.

Logistics: Two months before the event, party domes from China were imported to give the site a moon-base look and feel, they also provided a warm party zone after the press conference. The conference itself was in a huge clear-sided tent that highlighted the desert's colors and desolate sand-scape as background for the presenters. Because of the unpredictable wind, cold temperatures and rain, a contingency plans was crucial to the planning process.

After VIPs and 800 paying guests ($200,00 for the space ride) arrived at the nearby Mariah Country Inn at noon on event day, they were driven into what appeared to be a no man's land just outside the airport. While guests enjoyed wine, beer, and champagne, they received Virgin Galactic gear, including warm jackets, caps, and gloves, provided by Puma.

At the height of the event, a deluge pounded the plastic tent for about 20 minutes, bringing the temperature down another five degrees. To dazzle the guests, a high-intensity spotlights lit a silhouette of Daedalus in flight accompanied by booming sounds and icons. Enhanced by a music crescendo, *VSS Enterprise* appeared at the end of the runway, suspended underneath the *Virgin Mother Ship (VMS) Eve*. Nature's unplanned finale culminated the event with 110 mph winds that uprooted the press structure and ended the ceremony.

Outcome: Success. The event generated more than 17,000 news articles, about $7 million in media value, according to Susan Newsam, head of marketing production at Virgin Galactic. They even got a thank you note from Governor Schwarzenegger, who said he had a wonderful time and was glad to have been a part of the experience.

Source: Kenneth Briodagh @ www.eventmarketer.com/article/virgin-galactic-takes-flight

week of September 12, the network traveled to 15 markets and granted three wishes—two at various retailers and one at a local charity in each market. NBC surprised shoppers and restaurant patrons by picking up the tab at select retailers, including grocery stores and restaurants. The campaign was part of NBC's newest grassroots effort to reach consumers in an engaging way and create buzz around a new series. As part of the campaign, NBC paid retailers with stickered $1 bills, which cashiers distributed to customers with their change. The sticker was intended to drive recipients to a *Three Wishes* section on the NBC Web site and encourage consumers to use the marked dollars to fulfill another person's wish to coincide with the show's theme. Following the campaign, NBC tracked how consumers used their *Three Wishes* dollars by asking consumers on its Web site how they received the dollars and how they used them to grant someone else's wish. Input could be used for another network promotion.

Across gender, age, and ethnicity, audience members indicate that experiential marketing is more likely to influence both consideration to purchase tickets and actual ticket purchase than other forms of marketing tested. Events engage audiences, and for that reason alone justify their existence.

Sponsorship

Sponsorships are always financially motivated: an organization or individual trades financial support for publicity and mutually beneficial association. Sponsorships add value and differentiate brands by developing unique associations. Events, sports teams, celebrities, entertainment venues, and causes lend themselves to sponsorship activities.

Entertainment brands that serve as event sponsors display their brand and logo, target a self-selected audience, create awareness, improve brand image, encourage purchases, and achieve product mentions in media coverage of the activity.

Obtaining financial support by providing branded placement has become the promotion of choice for both product and experience providers. Sporting events prominently display beverage logos, and special events provide a multitude of exposure opportunities. Auto racing and fan conventions provide the most lucrative venues for brand placement.

NASCAR, the granddaddy of sponsorship opportunity, has soaring TV ratings, flowing corporate money and exploding crowds. Which is why entertainment companies are lining up to get logos placed on cars. With 84 television cameras on a 2.5-mile track, no aspect of the 43-car, 400-mile race escapes viewers. Beginning with a two-day tailgate party, the Indy 500 race draws a quarter of a million fans to the track of commerce. Racetracks have become profitable commercial venues and are the second most-watched sport on TV after pro football.

Unfortunately, the economic downturn caused Speedway Motorsports Inc's (owner of 12 Cup races at seven tracks) overall revenue to decline by 9.9% in 2009 from $611 million to $550 million. Drops also occurred in admissions revenues and event related revenues (sponsorships, merchandising, etc.) fell by 15.5%. Broadcast revenues, however, increased 3.3%.[xxvi]

Image 11.5

© *Kabik/Retna Ltd./Corbis*

NASCAR's Economic Dilemma

What does it take to become a NASCAR sponsor? The best teams in the sport can charge up to $25 million for a full-year sponsorship. That's about $500,000–700,000 per race! The lower-tier teams ask for about $8 million–10 million for a full season, which is still a large sum of money. Even with the economic downturn, sponsors of the 2010 season of new and renewed sponsor deals were:

- GoDaddy spent well into eight figures to sponsor Mark Martin's No. 5 Sprint Cup car for a majority of the 36 races in 2010.

- Michael Waltrip Racing had 100% sponsor renewal from the 2009 season, with TUMS as a new primary and associate sponsor.

- Richard Petty Motorsports moved Best Buy to the No. 43.

- Stanley was the primary sponsor for Elliot Sadler.

Sponsors Allstate, Jack Daniel's, and Jim Beam did not sponsor NASCAR teams after 2010, spending their money elsewhere. The big questions for upcoming seasons are: Can drivers retain their current sponsors or will the signing team have to find new sponsorship deals? With all of the uncertainty for future sponsorship dollars what can be done? Should NASCAR implement more changes to reduce the cost to run a team full time? Is there anything that can be done?

Question: What can you suggest to revive NASCAR sponsorship?

Source: blog.chadsfantasynascar.com/2010/01/01/2010-nascar-sponsorships-how-economy-is-affecting-sponsors/

Primary sponsorship of a NASCAR team costs $350,000 to $500,000 per race, which gives them the opportunity to choose the paint scheme of the car, put the logo all over it, and use the driver's likeness in advertising for the product or service they want to promote. It's possible to be the primary sponsor for just one race, and for the half a million-dollar investment, the car will change its appearance for just that one venue.

Allocating the promotion budget

Promotion planners must prioritize which tactics meet campaign objectives and deliver a reasonable return on investment (ROI). Using a promotion pie chart, allocate percentages of the total budge that will be used in a campaign. Once you have a visual image of priorities, the actual dollar amounts can be assigned for each promotional tactic. Here is a sample budget prepared for promoting the release of a science fiction film (excluding merchandising):

Internet buzz and blogs	35%
Television	20%
Social networks	30%
Staged events	10%
Tie-ins	05%

Finally

Promotional strategies are not simply a recipe for mixing and matching random tactics; they are carefully coordinated efforts to deliver timely and persuasive messages in a variety of strategically placed locations. While budgets many dictate the extent to which mass media and sponsorships are invoked, you can create effective yet economic campaigns with public relations and nontraditional or viral advertising. By understanding an audience's habits and desires, you can deliver behavior-changing messages that result in high box office receipts and profitable attendance.

GOT IT?

Here are the important points from this chapter on integrating promotional elements:

+ Place-based and out-of-home media bring performance messages directly to consumers where they eat, shop, and travel. Nontraditional advertising puts messages where they are not expected to be, reaching audience almost anywhere.

+ Viral, online, and Web site marketing provide invaluable opportunities for marketing performance, venues, media, destinations, and resorts.

- Direct marketing takes advantage of customer lists to solicit subscription renewals and sell tickets to performance audiences.

- Product placement not only puts products into films, it also promotes venues and destinations that appear in movies.

- Sales promotions, including cross-promotions and tie-ins, link brand constellations or brand pairs to consumer needs and stimulate purchase.

- Public relations tactics use mass media to create buzz for entertainment experiences. Sponsorships and event marketing provide entertainment brands with vast opportunities to reach audience niche markets.

NOW TRY THIS

1. Locate a specialty promotions company on the Internet and identify creative ways in which they deliver nontraditional messages. Which ones are relevant for entertainment marketing?

2. Visit the NASCAR Web site as a potential advertiser and explore the variety of opportunities to expose a particular entertainment brand for under $100,000. What do the opportunities suggest with regard to budgeting and company size?

3. Peruse the calendar or entertainment section of your local newspaper. How much of what appears has been placed there by public relations efforts (features, reviews)? Advertising efforts (paid display)? Which element offers readers the most persuasive messages? Why?

4. Check out the *Wall Street Journal's* update on the most-placed products in media. Is Apple still in the top ten? What does this say about placement as a marketing tactic?

QUESTIONS FOR DISCUSSION AND REVIEW

1. Of the many product placement opportunities discussed in this and previous chapters, which method is the fastest growing and receives the least amount of consumer resistance? Why?

2. How do sales promotions differ from loyalty programs? Aside from hotels and airlines, what entertainment experiences might benefit from loyalty programs? How would they be administered?

3. If hotel guests at an upscale resort became infected with an airborne virus that made news headlines and resulted in hotel evacuation, how would you handle the crisis? What PR tactics would make most sense for recouping occupancy rates?

4. How do a sponsorship and an event differ in their approach to branding entertainment? Which provides the best opportunity for television or movie promotion?

OTHER STUFF TO READ ABOUT THE PROMOTION MIX

Mary-Lou Galican, ed. (2004), *Handbook of Product Placement in the Mass Media*. Best Business Books.

www.adweek.com has articles on all aspects of advertising promotion.

www.brandcameo.org features best promotions.

www.oppapers.com/subjects/**promotion-mix**-page1.html provides free essays for students on the promotion mix.

[i] www.marketingcharts.com/interactive/top-10-entertainment-online-advertisers-by-image-based-impressions-january-2010-12122/

[ii] From Mike Esterl (2005), "Going Outside, Beyond the Billboard," *Wall Street Journal* July 24, p. B3.

[iii] "Street Furniture" is a term used by TDI Primetime Media, who also provide examples for this chapter as found on www.tdiworldwide.com.

[iv] From A. O. Scott (2005), "Post-Popism," *New York Times*, August 8.

[v] From Stuart Elliott's Advertising column in the *New York Times*, Sept. 21, 2005.

[vi] Stephanie Clifford, "Instant Ads Set the Pace on the Web," *New York Times* March 12, 2010.

[vii] From a Technology Spotlight, in V. Zeithaml, M. J. Bitner & D. Gremler (2006), *Services Marketing* 4th ed. McGraw-Hill, p. 498.

[viii] From AdAge.com, case study brief, July 2005.

[ix] Reported by Bob Teedeschi for the *New York Times*, Oct. 31, 2005.

[x] Brian Quinton for http://promomagazine.com/contests/0109-weekly-game-show/

[xi] Reported by Aaron O. Patrick for the *Wall Street Journal*, Aug. 22, 2005.

[xii] Reported by Stuart Elliott for the *New York Times*, Nov. 25, 2005.

[xiii] Ed Keller for http://promomagazine.com/viralmarketing/news/0212-social-media-womma/

[xiv] B. Klayman (1998), "Driven to Stardom: Product Placement in TV and Film Extends to Cars and Trucks." *Toronto Star*, May 23.

[xv] John Gaudiosi (2006), "Product placement to Die For: The Rise of In-Game Advertising." *Wired*, April, p. 136.

[xvi] From Ethan Smith and Suzanne Vranica's Advertising column in the *Wall Street Journal*, July 6, 2005.

[xvii] www.thefreelibrary.com/Is+it+a+show+or+a+commercial%3f+Increasingly%2c+it's+both%2c+a s+advertisers...-a0199683357

[xviii] From Charles Goldsmith (2004), "Dubbing in Product Plugs," *Wall Street Journal*, Jan. 6, B1.

[xx] Jennifer Pozner (2004), "Triumph of the Shill," *Bitch Magazine*, Winter, p. 51.

[xxii] http://promomagazine.com/contests/news/0311-crate-barrel-builds-registry/

[xxiii] D. Finnigan (2001), "Marketers of the Next Generation: Beth Goss." *Brandweek* 42 (13), p. 32

[xxiv] Lorne Manly & Raymond Hernandez (2005), "Nielsen, Long a Gauge of Popularity, Fights to Preserve Its Own. *New York Times*, August 8.

[xxv] B. Avrich (2002), *Selling the Sizzle*. Maxworks Publishing, p. 80.

[xxvi] Bob Pockrass for SceneDaily.com, March 10, 2010.

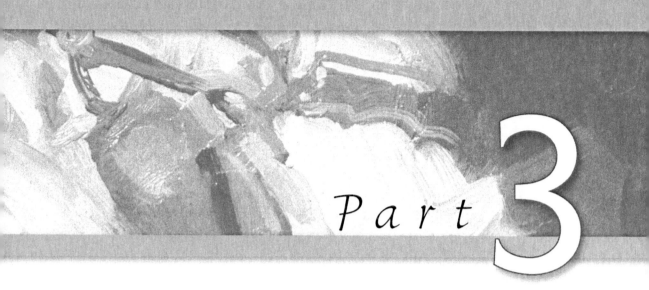

Part 3

ENTERTAINMENT INDUSTRY APPLICATIONS & MINI-CAMPAIGNS

PROMOTING LIVE PERFORMANCES AND EVENTS

> *It's an odd job, making people laugh.*
> Moliere

Chapter Objectives

After reading this chapter, you will be able to answer these questions:

- What is the importance of *drama* to entertainment marketing?

- How do we market *theatrical performances?*

- How do we market *live performances* and *concerts?*

- Which marketing strategies have worked for *bands* and *recording artists?*

- Which practices maximize an organization's brand image through *public relations* and *planned events?*

- What *communication objectives* and *strategies* can best meet goals and reach performance audiences?

The performing arts are constantly challenged by low attendance, shrinking audience patronage, spiraling expenses, and reduced government support. Nonetheless, live performances provide audiences with exciting and vibrant experiences that cannot be duplicated by mediated entertainment. This chapter looks at marketing theater and live concerts, bands and musicians, the economics of audience development, and the role of public relations and planned events for generating a positive organizational brand image.

MARKETING THEATER AND STAGED PERFORMANCES

All the world is a stage, as evidenced by twenty-first-century presentations that circle the globe and become cultural manifestations. Whether on Broadway or on a street corner, theatrical performances have been entertaining audiences since the beginning of history. Venue attendance data indicate that two-thirds of Broadway audiences are university-educated females averaging 42 years of age who attend 5 shows per year. Who else goes to theater and how can we reach them? Let's take look at how performances in residence and on tour are marketed to local audiences.

What's on stage

The business of theater requires one essential ingredient: a great product. Good scripts have become scarce resources, a fact that plagues many theatrical venues. Producers are trying to rebound from the lack of new product and improve their chances at success by mounting revivals of previous hit shows. They are cultivating audiences by appealing to new segments. Theaters' newest targets are kids and their parents. *Lion King*, *Beauty and the Beast*, and *Cats* were overwhelming successes because of their family appeal. Whether on Broadway or in a local venue, live theater is the ultimate shared experience, representing a brilliant composite of promise, escape, survival, and satire.

In spite of the economic downturn, audiences seemed to love live theater more than ever before. According to the League of American Theaters and Producers, 12.15 million tickets were sold in 2009 and 43 new productions were introduced. Compared with 2008, ticket sales were down slightly from 12.27 million, although gross revenues were up by $7 million. Those theatergoers paid an average of $68.86 a ticket, about $2.75 more than the previous year.

That box office successes were due to three elements:

+ targeted productions (i.e., The Lion King to family and female demographics)

+ premium seat pricing (discounting to various demographic groups and last-minute discounts

+ the appearance of Hollywood stars in shows (i.e., Christopher Walken or Helen Mirrin)

Like all marketing efforts, promoting stage performance involves influencing the behavior of a market segment. Creating, building, and maintaining communication and message exchanges are the foundation blocks of effective marketing.

With advertising trying to stand out of television, Internet, and mobile devices, choosing the right Broadway campaign often means finding a look that is flexible enough for different platforms—one that catches on quickly. For a 2010 revival of "La Cage aux Folles," the producer hung poster candidates on her office walls to see if endurance change their appeal. She had to choose between three poster alternatives: something simple and witty, images from 1940s France, and another with disco graphics. To decide on the final option, readers and fans were asked to vote on their favorite version at nytimes.com/theater. Such involvement resulted in non-paid promotion for the revival that stimulate advance ticket sales and excitement.[i]

What's on tour

The touring business gives producers an opportunity to recoup their Broadway investment and make money by exploiting key markets. Touring often makes shows into international phenomena, and the road business has created a market for theater everywhere. Also, with changing Broadway economics, producers need the backup of a road tour to give investors assurance that there is a plan B.

Success means branding the experience of a first-class Broadway show across the United States and internationally. Some new theater centers rival the New York and London stages. Toronto is third ranked as producer and exporter of world-class theater.

In the 2008–09 season, touring shows across North America grossed $883 million, representing more than 14 million tickets. Touring shows of varying sizes were presented in more than 250 cities across the country. Touring Broadway productions contributed a cumulative $3.25 billion to the metropolitan areas that hosted shows.[ii]

When theater productions tour, 69% of the audience is female, the average age is 46, and patrons are affluent, white, and well educated. This group attends six productions a year, lives less than 50 miles from the venue, and generally responds

© Bruno Passigatti, 2010. Used under license from Shutterstock, Inc.

12.1 Phantom of the Opera is one of the most successful shows to take its act on the road.

to advertising and word-of-mouth recommendations. Knowing this, regional venue managers are eager to book touring performances for their loyal audience members of similar demographics.

The first step of taking a show on the road is **selling off**, which is the process of securing the dates with local promoters, who receive a royalty and a profit participation in exchange for mounting the production. Another option is self-presenting, known as **four walling**, which involves renting a theater in each market and assuming all the risks of mounting the show.

In addition to theater, single acts also prefer touring to a stationary venue.

Bob Dylan, for instance, has left the big cities to perform in state fairs, corporate events, urban street fairs and American Indian casinos. Since 1988, Dylan has performed 1,700 shows, reintroducing himself to fans using a keyboard instead of a guitar and turning his act into one of the most unique road shows in rock.[iii] Dylan seems almost anti-promotion; there are no themes, little publicity, and no tractor trailers—he just plays the shows in as many venues as possible, even playing successive nights in different theaters and clubs in larger cities. Unlike most highly choreographed rock concerts that charge hundreds of dollars, the singer's small ensemble plays from among his huge repertoire in an unscripted format, and his tickets are moderately priced at under $50.

Other road shows include regional performances of Broadway flops and discards, shows that have lost money on Broadway and have little name recognition.[iv] Crowds from Providence to Sacramento love revivals of shows like *La Cage aux Folles*, which won a Tony but closed after a six-month run at two-thirds capacity. *Bombay Dreams*, which lost all of its $14 million investment on Broadway, played to a full house during its 20-week tour in regional theaters. Shows can be victims of harsh reviews by powerful critics or fail to connect with audiences in spite of good reviews. Nonetheless, regional markets provide a rousing second act.

Road shows do have their risks, however. They are expensive, with trucking cost alone running to $20,000 per move, or $1 million for a typical 50-city tour. It's still cheaper for regional theaters to import fully realized productions rather than mounting multimillion-dollar ones from scratch. A presenter who brings in a road show typically pays an upfront fee to the original producer, ranging from about $225,000 to 300,000 per week. In return, he gets a 10–40% cut of the gross—which can run as high as $1 million a week. For producers, this is better than busting down sets and going home. Ideal audiences are people tired of amateur revivals and willing to see big shows irrespective of their Broadway fate.

Summer tends to be a slow time for Broadway productions, both in New York and on the road. So regional theaters use celebrities and recognizable titles from other media as draws for their own revivals. Local theatrical productions, performed by less-known actors for smaller crowds, were well attended in 2009–10, partly because of lower ticket prices and proximity to annual subscribers.

Internationally acclaimed sketch-comedy troupe Second City took itself on the road from Chicago to perform in local theatrical venues. A second regional-specific show was performed in Laguna Beach, CA in March 2010. During its 50-year history, the troupe has fostered such legends as John Belushi, Bill Murray, Dan Aykroyd, Gilda Radner, Stephen Colbert, Mike Myers, and Tina Fey.

Promoting stage performances

The best philosophy is to get audiences to move beyond the reviews and into the theater, and advertising, promotions and direct mail are the strategies of choice. Marketers typically work with budgets of about ten percent of the productions' potential weekly gross. Producers can spend up to $1 million for a dramatic performance's pre-opening publicity, and up to $75,000 each week on advertising and promotion. Musicals are the most popular form of entertainment in the world; they require far less of a marketing budget to get audiences to buy tickets than drama or comedy.

In theater, the creative elements always start with commanding artwork and poster design. Logos become the brand identification for the show. Great artwork results from studying scripts, listening to the music and talking with the writer or director long before the show begins rehearsals. One or two line summaries provide direction for creative; themes are developed using fashion styles, advertising, or art from the time period of the performance.

Once developed, themes should take a variety of forms so newspaper advertising can be changed on a weekly basis to keep the show looking fresh. Two types of advertising—*review ads* and *quote ads*—make use of positive narrative from reviewers and audience members to position the show in print as a winner. Review ads feature more extensive favorable commentary that ads with shorter and more positive quotes from media critics. Electronic advertising is essential for effectively launching a musical. Radio and TV spots promote the quality of production values of sets, costumes, and cast. Television and radio commercials are ultimately the show's communication. When good reviews appear, producers will often increase the weekly advertising budget to send out the message in a big way.

Developing a plan for theater promotion

After the demographics and on-sale date are determined, your plan needs to have the following integrated components:

+ Press announcement—releases and press conference

+ Group sales—begin when exact dates are determined

+ Subscription or show sponsor campaign—precede public on-sale period

+ On-sale period—exact date tickets go on sale to general public

Image 12.2 A scene from the off-Broadway production.

© Getty Images

A Long Life for Avenue Q

Jeffrey Seller is a theater producer with an uncanny ability to market unconventional musicals such as *Rent* and *Avenue Q* with tactics that include offering a limited number of $20 front row tickets to attract young adults. For the adult puppet show called *Avenue Q*, he used emails and ads that said: "Warning: Full Puppet Nudity," as well as airline-style pricing of theater seats to ensure there's always a full house. He even incorporates ads into the set, usually seen as heresy for serious theatrical production.

Unlike the standard approach to selling a play with radio spots, newspaper ads and posters, Seller's marketing strategy involves Broadway's No. 1 sales tool—the Tony Awards. The Best Musical campaign was an aggressive push targeted at the 730 people who vote for the Tonys that included parties, advertising and gifts. As part of the campaign, Seller and his partners targeted voters from outside New York, who normally vote as a block, by wooing them with an argument that couldn't ignore—selling the play in regional theaters. He positioned *Avenue Q* as a quirky little musical up against a glitzy Hollywood-backed production. *Avenue Q* won the Tony.

Seller's marketing strategy is drumming up media coverage—especially on TV because, he says, "Nobody young reads newspaper ads." One stunt—a staged political event in Times Square—generated coverage by 14 television stations, including two in Japan. The crowd munched free popcorn and a CNN reporter covering the event chatted with "Rod," a closeted gay Republican puppet. His strategy is to make news that gets them off the arts page and into mainstream exposure.

His other tactics include keeping theater seats filled during slow months by selling seats at lower prices close to show time, advertising on ethnic radio stations and handing out fliers in bars and nightclubs. They even spent thousands of dollars distributing textbook covers featuring artwork of their shows to high-school students.

Produced at a cost of $3.5 million, *Avenue Q* grossed $36 million in its first two years of production. After winning the Tony, Seller signed an exclusive agreement with the Wynn hotel in Las Vegas for a second production (which was replaced after one year with *Spamalot*). A third production opened in London in 2006. After their 6-year run on Broadway, the musical began performing off Broadway in 2009 at New World stages nationwide.

Source: Brooks Barnes for *The Wall Street Journal*, March 10, 2005
Ben Brantley for *The New York Times*, Oct. 22, 2009

+ Promotions—tied to sponsors or media presenters; opening night galas, anniversaries and holiday seasons

+ Advertising—pre-opening, post-opening and sustaining media schedules prepared

The role of advertising and publicity are crucial for introducing a new play. Media sponsorship, audience development, database marketing, and licensing play out as equally important components of marketing theater.

Advertising's role

Advertising is directed to the primary audience, one that is most economically and easily reached. The pre-opening period builds and creates anticipation. Launching the campaign on a weekend drives Monday sales. Once reviews are generated, the post-opening period begins with media to scream victory and declare the show a hit. A sustaining campaign follows opening night to maintain awareness and stimulate sales. Newspaper ads should have a consistent presence and be placed at least once per week in the entertainments sections with the highest circulation. Short flights of radio and TV allow a continuing presence in the market.

Media companies can align themselves chosen theatrical productions in what are called *presents deals*. Three sponsors, each representing a separate medium, sign on to stretch marketing dollars. The most common tactics are:

- Broadcast or Internet contest with tickets as prizes; winner gets an opening night package with limo, dinner, and tickets

- Run of show tickets for daily call-in radio contests

- Media logo identification on playbill

Such promotions get airtime or space valued at two to three times expenditures to drive the contests. Bonus airtime or space at a value equal to the face value of tickets, as well as editorial coverage in the form of opening night and feature stories, are among the benefits of presents deals.

Publicity's role

The publicity machine begins with a call to local entertainment columnist to leak a rumor that the show is coming to town. By persuading journalists to write about the show, promoters gain hype that leads to box-office or ticket sales. As free advertising, publicity plays a crucial part of promoting the production. Publicity arms audiences with information, and provides most of what they want before committing to purchase tickets. Photographs and marquee posters, playbills and production notes, actor and director biographies, and ticket sale information are used to develop press kits. Journalists are in the audience on opening night.

Publicists create fun, media-driven promotions and opportunities for publicity that hopefully result in lots of editorial coverage. T-shirts, soundtrack giveaways, and midnight box-office openings that accompany opening night backs up the publicity hype. Other tricks used to promote shows include:

- Media events with local auditions and local casting (*King and I*)

- Contests and giveaways on cereal boxes (*Phantom*, Canada)

- Trivia contests to generate entries and awareness (*Phantom*)

- Television promotion asking viewers to guess the location in the city of an actor staring in the show, with prizes including tickets (*Fiddler on the Roof*, Tampa)

Audience development

Performance venue marketers use a variety of pricing strategies to change audience perceptions that live performances are out of reach. These discrepancy pricing strategies include:

- Internet pricing discounts

- student subscriptions

- pay-what-you-can pricing

- rush seating one hour prior to performances

- lottery seating in the first two rows for persons who cannot afford full-price tickets

- mini-subscriptions and special packaging

Any booking over 20 tickets is considered a group. Group sales to tour operators, booking agencies, schools, and private organizations are an essential part of selling tickets. Groups usually receive incentives such as discounts, preferred seating, promotional materials, and pre- or post-show events. Brochures present the stars, schedules, and ticket prices and include a bold call to action and clear reservation deadlines.

Advertising to outlying areas is another essential audience builder. Theater education programs, special family performances, and co-branding with airlines and hotels can all can bring audiences to the performance.

Unlike movies and television, there is no after market for theater. However, astute marketing can produce an event that allows audiences to share a live experience, regardless of how large or small the production.

Database marketing

Live performance requires personal contact with audience members based on active contact information. An audience database is an information-intensive, long-term marketing tool that serves as the cornerstone of message delivery and audience management. More than a simple list of patrons, a database contains lifestyle, demographic, and financial information; purchase transaction records; and promotions and media response characteristics

Using databases as the central tool for marketing communications includes several critical elements and functions:

- Loyal patron identification—frequency of attendance and subscription purchases

- New audience development—consumer profiles developed and used to recruit by common characteristics

- Message delivery—communications targeted to groups based on usage patterns and motivations for attending

- Program development—behavior patterns analyzed to identify musical or performance preferences that can be used to develop a new season's program

List creation results from collecting information on audience members who have expressed some level of prior interest. Coupon ads may offer a purchase discount, and respondents are added to the database. Radio broadcasts can make similar offers that result in new names; lead cards can be left at box office or on a table in the lobby, placed in programs, or distributed at corporate sponsors' offices, area restaurants, and local libraries. Arts organizations should go beyond their own lists to maintain a full range of lists and update them on a regular basis.

House lists, external lists, and specifically created lists maximize database marketing. **House lists** are current patrons who can be segmented into categories of: single-ticket buyers, first-year subscribers, two-plus year subscribers, lapsed subscribers, group sales buyers, and special plan or event buyers. **External lists** are obtained from a variety of outside sources, such as exchanges with other organizations whose patrons match demographics, performance preferences, or attendance patterns. **Rental lists** can be purchased from commercial sources such as video rental stores, magazine subscribers, mail-order houses and museums.

Lists must be prioritized according to likely response rate, and lists with lowest response rates should be eliminated on a regular basis. House lists can be rented to other organizations to generate revenue, charging fifty cents per name; a 50,000-name mailing list will gross between $12,000 and $25,000 per year. Professional list managers implement a selective list rental program, advertise its availability, collect revenues, and monitor use. A financial commitment from organization's management and continuous updating of the data and system in response to the dynamic environment are two essential factors.

Licensing theater

Stage productions are taking advantage of licensing agreements that often yield more revenue than the performance itself. *Wicked*, a musical that flopped in 2003, was a money-making machine by 2005, thanks to a strategy that took it to the launch pad for a much broader brand. Backed by Universal Pictures, the musical tapped into a new mother load for the theater business—worldwide touring and licensing. By using the initial production as a platform for building a global franchise, the musical about teen witches scored a hit with audiences from teens to grandparents.

Success evolved from a licensing deal between *Wicked*'s producer and Stila, a cosmetics company that developed a line of clothes to sell at theaters. Karaoke contests at malls offered people a chance to win tickets by "auditioning" for parts in the show.

© Robbie Jack/Corbis

12.3 *Wicked* marketers flipped a flop into a fortune; on the road in Sydney, Australia.

Revenues for the cast album and advance ticket sales for a 30-city national tour in 2007 allowed *Wicked* to license its way to achieving the status of a cultural phenomenon. Other revenue streams include a movie version and tie-ins with Sprint cell phones and green M&Ms; a 192-page coffee table book is also popular among fans.

When it opened in St. Louis, Wicked sold $1.5 million of tickets in the first 48 hours after they went on sale. Sales for future shows, based on the *Wizard of Oz*, stand at about $30 million. Weekly sales of products—everything from $20 'Wicked' golf balls to $35 themed necklaces—exceed $300,000, which is more than most Broadway plays gross in a week.[v]

Audience economics

Performing arts operate under somewhat different economic assumptions than other types of entertainment. In the 1990s, syndicates owned chains of theaters and controlled bookings and fees. Today, producers select a play, raise funds, and hire a director and cast, while theater owners generally handle box-office personnel and stagehands, advertising and sales functions. Gross receipts from commercial theater presentations on the road have overshadowed gross receipts on Broadway. This shift in economic balance has led to the development of publicly owned companies that specialize in the production and staging of off-Broadway performances.

Returns on investment in a major musical production are high and long lasting, even in comparison to potential returns on popular films. Touring reproductions of musical and restorations of past Broadway hits have accounted for more than 80% of total commercial ticket sales. Resident or repertory theaters around the country are supported by a combination of subscription fees, foundation grants, individual contributions and ticket and merchandise sales, and are often the source of new productions. Exhibit 12.1 shows typical financial participations of major players in the production process.

EXHIBIT 12.1 Typical Financial Participations in Theater Productions

GROSS PARTICIPATION	(%)
Playwright	10
Lead performer	05
Director	02
Theater manager	25

PROFIT PARTICIPATION	(%)
Playwright	5–10
Director	05
Lead performer	5–10
Other performers & mgr	10
Producer	15
Investors	50–60
Source: Entertainment Industry Economics	

Financing for new commercial theater productions closely resembles financing for films. The producer acquires the rights to a play or literary property for adaptation to the stage, and prospective investors are sought for financing. Broadway runs are more likely to be funded by large entertainment companies than by individual investors. Financing may be available in the form of sale of stock in a corporation organized for production of a play, or as a development investment granted by film studios in return for movie rights. Broadway theater owners often take profits through limited partnerships or limited liability company arrangements.

A major star in a small play can receive weekly guarantees plus increasing percentages of gross after receipts reach certain levels. Directors may receive upfront fees and smaller percentages of weekly grosses. Playwrights normally earn at least a minimum author's royalty of 10% weekly, and the general manager receives weekly salary and perhaps a small percentage of net profits. High fixed costs of operation mean a large leveraged effect on profits. This creates either a smashing hit or a crashing failure—not much falls between the extremes.

PROMOTING LIVE PERFORMANCES AND CONCERTS

Live performances come in a variety of forms other than theater. You'll need specialized marketing strategies and tactics to promote ballet and dance, opera, classical, and popular music, and the circus.

Promoting ballet and modern dance

New York City, San Francisco, and the American Ballet Theaters dominate domestic ballet performances. At least six important dance groups feature modern dance, a format that's usually dependent on a single choreographer and small groups of financial benefactors.

Traditionally, marketing budgets for promoting dance have consisted of immeasurable educational and outreach programs along with media advertising. Studies have found, however, that this approach works only when the target audience does not require a reward of some kind.[vi] Cooperative marketing efforts are an additional avenue for increasing return on investment of the company's marketing dollar.

Choreographer Michael Smuin learned from gigs in nightclubs and musicals that audiences don't have much patience. His recent effort called *Fly Me to the Moon* was an unembarrassed homage to Frank Sinatra, mixing Sinatra trademarks like trench coats and high-crowned hats with toe shoes. Smuin claimed that his old-fashioned ballet is new nostalgia, like a prom night for adults. And it sold out, even in Italy. What was his positioning strategy? Differentiation.

Promoting opera

One of the problems for opera, the most expensive type of live performance to produce, has been the economic downturn that caused a drop in philanthropic contributions for the arts. People whose wealth was decimated by the Madoff scandals, the collapse of investment banking houses, or the halving of equity and real estate values, were contributors to the arts and other cultural activities in years past.

Two primary reasons for the current and impending decline in funds for opera performances include:[vii]

1. Subscriber pushback: as resources decline or fail to increase, what this group thinks and does is an increasingly important concern to opera managements.

2. Ticket price inflation: American opera managements have reconciled to the reality that, even with some brilliant marketing and popular offerings, their revenue bases will decline The hope for the future is in reining in and substantially decreasing costs.

As the economy improves, there will be a visible increase in philanthropic giving, but what appears to worry producers is that the numbers of philanthropists willing to give opera companies large gifts with or without strings attached, appears to be declining. As potential mega-donors switch their donations to other priorities opera companies focus their attention and energy on generating funds.

Four major opera companies operate in the U.S. today: the Metropolitan, San Francisco, Chicago Lyric, and New York City. Companies in Los Angeles and Houston have emerged as profitable in spite of inherent problems of sustaining payroll for singers, chorus, dancers, orchestra, conductor, and extras. With over 200 professionals on a payroll sustained by 4,000 seats in most venues, it is not surprising that more cities do not have permanent grand opera companies.

Unfortunately, the complexity of opera performances, which require a cast of principals and orchestra, a conductor, usually a chorus, and sets and costumes requiring platoons of backstage personnel, generates expenses so high that the costs of production exceed the revenue generated, even if houses are sold out every performance.

A CLOSER LOOK AT OPERA

The Victoria Opera

Venue research provides valuable insight into who attends, how often and why. Once the audience segments are characterized, appropriate media are bought to deliver relevant messages. This Australian investigation of 104,000 patrons revealed that their opera audiences had these demographics:

- 61% were women

- 45% had a college degree

- 36% were aged 35–49

- 30% belonged to the Socially Aware Value segment*

The Socially Aware segment of the Australian population, based on lifestyle, motivations, and attitudes, provides valuable insight into opera's most relevant segment who are:

- the most educated segment of the community

- up-market professionals, often in areas where they can influence others

- politically and socially active and environmentally aware

- pursuing stimulating and progressive lifestyles

These audience members are 'information vacuum-cleaners', are attracted to the new and different, and seek opportunities for training, education and knowledge. They take a thoughtful and strategic approach to life. Their attraction to innovation and passionate commitment to ideas can also lead to a relative disregard for price.

This is the segment most likely to perceive the arts as an integral part of their daily life, and their arts attendance is both regular and high. They have a strong orientation towards the interpretive and innovative in art, and are attracted to art that is genuinely new and different—not simply remakes and re-presentations. They have a preference for intellectual stimulation over entertainment or relaxation as such, and for form and structure.

Recommended media: Their desire for information makes them heavy consumers of newspapers, particularly national newspapers, and of magazines presenting information not available in the mainstream media.

Information source breakdown:

- Daily metropolitan or national newspaper (72%)

- Friend/relative (36%)

- Television (19%)

- Local/suburban newspaper (15%)

- Notice/brochure/pamphlet in mail (15%)

- Radio (10%)

Advertising: They respond to stylish, tasteful and intelligent appeals, rather than hype and cliché, and prefer Internet reminders and informative web sites to written communications.

Decision-making factors

Who mostly go with

- Spouse/partner (57%)

- Friends (52%)

- Children (13%)

Who mostly decides what to see

- Self (84%)

- Of which 57% are female & 43% are male

- Spouse/partner (37%)

- Friend (22%)

Motivation for attending opera

- To see a particular performer/show/group (28%)

- Entertainment (25%)

- Part of a subscription (14%)

- It's an old favorite (11%)

Reasons for not attending more often

- Cost

- Don't have time to go

- Competing leisure time activities

- Too far to travel

- Don't like what is currently available

What do you think?

1. Based on the information learned from audience research, what messages would you communicate and to whom about a special opera performance?

2. What form should advertising take to reach this segment?

Source: www.arts.vic.gov.au/arts/general/archives/factsheet 12/05/05

San Francisco Opera's promotes opera premieres throughout the city with lectures, panels and exhibits; most events became a "must attend" for opera buffs in the Bay Area and from around the world.

In its first advertising campaign since the 1970s, New York's Metropolitan Opera put promotion pieces in telephone kiosks, lamp posts, subway entrances and the sides of city buses to announce its 2006 season. Why now? The Met is finding it harder to fill 4000 seats with people willing to purchase tickets that range from $15 to $320.[viii] The $500,000 advertising campaign blanketed street-level New York with images from "Madame Butterfly," the season opener. Aimed at younger people who may find opera intimidating, the campaign aimed to demystify opera by reaching commuters and pedestrians on transit. By bringing Lincoln Center performance awareness to the masses, the venue hoped to convince potential audiences that opera is also a vibrant form of entertainment. And Next door at the Lincoln Center, the New York City opera sells every seat in the house for $25 on eight evenings during the season.[ix]

Ticket sales at the Met rose 7.1% in the 2006–07 season, the first ticket sale increase by season in six years. Tickets for the Met's high-definition broadcasts of operas in about 400 movie theaters around the world helped bolster interest in the opera company. The U.S. led all countries with 35,014 tickets on 179 screens, followed by Canada with 16,535 on 60 screens. Tickets to live broadcasts also were sold in Denmark, Sweden, Germany, and Japan.

According to director Peter Gelb, future plans for the Met include increasing the number of live telecasts and offering a broad menu of ways in which to enjoy the Met outside the Met, is stimulating an interest in the Met. Gelb has lured performers outside of opera to join its productions, including Oscar-winning film director Anthony Minghella for "Madam Butterfly" and Isaac Mizrahi for costume design for "Orfeo et Eruidice."

12.4 The Sydney Australia opera house is one of the most famous venues where traditional and modern opera perform to sell-out crowds.

"The days of a Luciano Pavarotti or a Placido Domingo selling out a performance on their own are no more," Gelb said. "The future of opera is going to be secured through presenting combinations of star artists, an attractive repertoire and acclaimed directors."

For a model of how to open a new opera house, promoters might copy the Royal Danish Opera in Copenhagen. The strategy to dedicate their modern $441 million home was to open with an audacious new work. It drew mixed reactions but played to sold-out houses. As evidenced by past successes, promotional draws center on new work, new buildings, and new locations.[x] Taking opera out of the concert hall into other, more accessible venues is a strategy now embraced by the Houston opera, which sings at baseball games, and San Francisco opera's free concerts of popular arias in Golden Gate Park.

New opera means omitting the word *opera* from promotion materials, according to high-art American composers who come from the world of music theater. Opera is trying to speak more clearly to a new generation. Some recent titles are San Francisco Opera's production of "Dead Man Walking," and the Michigan Opera Theater's production of "Margaret Garner." If the momentum generated can be sustained by subscriptions and guest appearances throughout their annual seasons, opera should be able to hold its own against other classical forms of entertainment.

Promoting classical music

The American Symphony Orchestra League categorizes approximately 1,600 orchestras in the U.S. according to the size of their budgets. In addition to large concert hall productions, many local and regional performances are presented each year; their success depends upon timely and effective promotion. Even the nation's oldest and wealthiest, the Boston Symphony Orchestra, uses promotional strategies to recruit audiences. By offering half price tickets for performances of new works and pairing composers from different centuries, the orchestra keeps classical music alive for Boston and for the world.

Audiences' motivations are supported by the desire to see and hear a particular performer, conductor, or orchestra, and to support the organization. Emotional appeals play into those motivations by featuring a star performer—the bigger the star, the larger the box office. Promotional materials may use "all time favorite" messages. Brochures and advertising clue the audience in on something special or interesting about the performance, or, position it exclusive or distinctive from the competition.

Classical music is confronted by long-range challenges that will not solve themselves. Recording contracts for orchestras have dried up. Audiences resist what is loosely called contemporary music. Patrons no long purchase full season subscriptions, and audiences are growing grayer. To cover rising costs, tickets keep becoming more expensive. In short, classical music is jeopardized and marginalized, and there's no easy fix.

One innovator who manages Carnegie Hall in New York has taken serious measures to generate revenue in new ways. Since recording companies are not offering to make CDs, he decided to do the recording himself by sharing the risk of financing them. Starting with the London Symphony Orchestra, he designed the self-produced series as an orchestra-controlled alternative to a studio recording system. The label, nicknamed LSO Clive, now offers 32 discs. As part of a Mahler series, the San Francisco Symphony released its first new recording under its own label. By pricing CDs at slightly under $10 so they were accessible to everyone, LSO orchestras sold 25,000 copies in the first year of release. The recordings have won prestigious prizes. The LSO made its entire catalog available for download online on iTunes in 2005.

Another business-model strategy transforms unusual programs into events. One event packaged a Shostakovich festival, featuring cellist Rostropovich conducting all 15 symphonies; it played to full houses. A discovery series used the orchestra to illuminate the obscurities of modern music. Education is also used to help audiences understand classical music. During a London symphony Orchestra production intermission, the orchestra demonstrated how Stravinsky constructed the work in rhythmic chunks, then returned to perform the piece uninterrupted.

Carnegie Hall developed a Sound Insights series for audience education. The Carnegie administration has ambitious orchestra residency program of eight-day visits from outstanding world philharmonic orchestras; the administration spends $8 million each year on education. Finally, Carnegie Hall created an intermediate-sized basement space, Zankel Hall, which has 600 seats, to present innovative artists who aren't mainstream enough to fill the 2,800 seat main auditorium. Following in their lead, regional performing arts centers are conducting capital campaigns to provide smaller, more intimate venues with lower prices and reduced overhead.

According to studies conducted by the Brooklyn and Fort Wayne philharmonics,[xi] thematic and crossover programming brings in more first-timers. Results were unclear, however, whether such concerts would lead to more regular subscriptions. In this study, education—like more Web material, pre-concert lectures, and expanded program notes—did not increase ticket sales at all.

Trying nonmusical methods to lure concertgoers have included producing shorter and earlier concerts, adding onstage commentary, and offering film-score programs for a broader appeal. More recent innovations include video screens in the concert hall, hand-held electronic devices to provide running commentary, and musical programs built around pop culture themes such as film soundtrack music.

Guaranteeing sales for any classical performance requires splashy telemarketing, flexible subscription packages, a mini-season of popular titles, reasonable prices, catchy print ads, and powerful radio ads. Using unique locations, such as the Denver symphony performing in venues like a basketball arena, is another innovation. Ultimately, orchestral delivery systems must provide an entertainment experience. Marketer of classical music must focus on what the audience wants, loosen the definition of classical music, offer lots of visual stimulation, and pay more attention to social functions for drawing younger adults. In our times of electronic media, *out-of-venue performances* and *lobby attractions* are the best tactics for maintaining interest in classical music concerts.

FOCUS ON CLASSICAL MUSIC

New Overtures at the Symphony

As audiences seem to grow older and the public turns its attention away from concert-going, orchestras around the country are adopting a wide array of marketing strategies to bring more people into the concert hall—mainly audiences who are neophytes, dabblers and the un-gray. Some of their innovations are presented here as indications of what can be done to invigorate lagging attendance.

- *Classical Connections* series where the under-40 set can speed date, take salsa lessons or exchange resumes before a performance, a shortened concert with onstage commentary and occasional videos (Milwaukee).

- *Friday night mixer* puts chamber music in the first half of the program, then provides a choice of chamber music or jazz in the lobby for the second half (St. Paul).

- *Seven 18 Club* series for young professions with pre-concert drinks and post-concert socializing with young orchestra members (St. Louis).

- *Shorts* of four 20 minute concerts in one evening, each one hour, from 7–10:00 PM (Miami Beach).

- *Beyond the Score* series offers a live documentary on a major piece—film clips, an actor reading letters, comments from the conductor and musical examples from the orchestra—followed by a performance of the piece in the second half of the program (Chicago).

- *Fun factor Thursday* series provide free buffet dinners in the hall's ballroom and *College Nite* concerts that feature post-performance parties where students nibble appetizers and listen to a local band (Cincinnati).

- *Symphony with a Twist* series of four concerts preceded by martini bars and jazz in the lobby (Baltimore and Atlanta).

- *Fourth Ring Society* for the MTV crowd with $10 balcony seats for ballet performances (New York City).

- *Popular themes* from movies such as the *Lone Ranger* and *Star Wars* were used for packaging classical programs (San Diego).

Source: David Waken for *The New York Times*, Aug. 21, 2005

The music business

Musical concerts geared to young adults are their own special case. Concert marketers have a direct link to the recording industry. Concerts are organized as seasonal line-ups of regular acts. Promotional players include: a *promoter* who is responsible for booking acts, paying for ads and venues, and setting performance details; the artist's *personal manager* who selects tours, dates, venues and markets; an *agent* who works with the manager to book tours, hire promoters and plot the tour route; and a *road manager* to look after the details. The genre comes with its unique problems—producers and marketers must anticipate and overcome crowd control, unruly fans, venue design, and ticket scalping.

The least expensive form of entertainment to market, concerts are usually limited to short engagements. Managers budget for three modules: on-sale period, sustaining period, and the panic period when goals have not been met. During the *on-sale* phase, print ads, and a short flight of radio ads are used to promote the sales date on week prior to the performance. Radio promotions help to clean out the inventory left over from the on-sale period.

Timing is an important factor in marketing concerts. Ticket sales for smaller acts need a six- to eight-week advance along with a large advertising budget. When multiple concert dates are scheduled, each show should sell out before the next one is promoted. Booking should be matched with album release dates, and the use of 'wild posting' heightens interest.

Publicity is crucial to box office success. Press releases must use a creative hook so media can promote the venue. Newspaper and radio entertainment calendars must be notified, and interviews are arranged with the press by phone or in person just prior to the concert. Merchandising giveaways in the form of T-shirts and stickers accelerate hype; retail exposure for albums, POPs, and joint promotion with record chains work well for promoting popular bands and individual performers.

A CLOSER LOOK AT BAND BRANDS

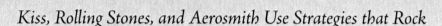

Kiss, Rolling Stones, and Aerosmith Use Strategies that Rock

In their book *Brands that Rock*, Blackwell and Stephan tell business leaders what they can learn from the world of rock and roll. This focus highlights three bands that re-emerged after falling from grace by implementing unique promotional strategies that are relevance for entertainment marketing.

KISS

Elements that allowed the band to re-emerge successfully: band members made personal connection with the audience and packaged themselves in Kabuki makeup for differentiation; sensory overload brought surprise to the stage.

Strategy:

- Induce trial in the right markets

- Rollout concert tours with performances in rural locations

- Court the press

- Merchandise makeup kits and games for fans

- Create an MTV special to remove Kabuki makeup

- Hold a KISS convention starring the original band members

- Change musical content as fans change by using a migration strategy

Image 12.5 KISS.

© Bettmann/Corbis

ROLLING STONES

Elements of success and remaining relevant: adhering to the business side of music revenue-generating areas such as album sales, royalties, and touring; creating a brand image with merchandising, tours, books, and corporate endorsements.

Strategy:

- Change and evolve style and music at a rate that doesn't alienate fans while keeping the band relevant to new fans

- Generate buzz with online ticket sales

- Develop corporate partnerships

- Feature new songs in commercials

- Use CDs as marketing tool rather than as revenue generators

- Invoke discriminatory pricing strategies

- Alternate performance venues with a variety of prices and musical content to include stadiums, arenas and theaters

- Generate revenue from sky boxes, bus tours, TV appearances, merchandising and cross promotions

- Co-brand with E*Trade on the Internet

- Adapt performances to baby-boomer wants and needs

Image 12.6 Mick Jagger of the Rolling Stones.

© Yves Herman/Reuters/Corbis

AEROSMITH

Elements of reinvention and marketplace reentry: getting clean and sober; perform with funky clothing, long hair and painted nails; loyal male audience; combination that featured newness and familiarity.

Strategy:

- Use grassroots marketing

- Implement a unique tour strategy by playing a concert and then returning in three weeks to play again

- Cater to fans of other band brands

- Create *angel fans* who discover bands before they become stars

- Invoke a trickle-up theory of cultural adoption

- Reverse audience intimacy by monitoring fans' behaviors during concerts and focusing on ways for fans to know the band better with *remote staging*, travel packages and 'meet and greet' backstage visits for fans

What do you think?

1. Which band strategy relied on an established fan base to make its comeback? Why was this an advantage?

2. What lessons can concert marketers learn from the brand successes?

Source: Blackwell & Stephan, *Brands that Rock*, 2004

Image 12.7 Aerosmith performs in London.

© Cookie Rosenberg/Retna Ltd./Corbis

Bands and artists

Concert tours are typically the primary marketing vehicle of bands and artists. Tours provide the exposure that can leverage sales. One of the newest forms of promotion for touring musicians is VIP pricing for concert tickets. By offering VIP packages at high prices, artists may maximize grosses and reap some of the markup value of resale sites like StubHub.com. According to an executive of AEG Live, VIP pricing is the biggest negotiation in any tour deal because the collapse of record sales has forced artists to rely on touring for most of their income.

"Jessie's Girl" and Rick Springfield sold 'schmoozing time' before and after his shows for $1000, which also included a seat on stage. For $800, Christina Aguilera posed for a picture; VIP fans paid $1750 for front row seats to see Bon Jovi that included a folding chair with his logo on the cushion. Intended to reward loyal fans, VIP pricing offers two benefits: high prices up front subsidize lower price seats and, because they are not part of general advertisements, artists profits soar without the stigma of being high priced.[xii]

Besides touring, marketing campaigns to promote music sales may involve cooperative advertising with local retailers, in-store merchandising aids (e.g., posters, T-shirts), radio and TV commercials, and promo press kits (free cuts are usually sent to radio stations). Marketing costs can often reach $100,000 for a standard release and in excess of $500,00 for a release by a major artist.

Promotional efforts focus on 200–300 radio stations nationwide. Tip sheets and trade papers such a *Billboard* and *Radio & Records* serve as measuring points. Music companies have their own staffs of trackers, whose job it is to know which songs and CDs are being added to or deleted from play lists of stations and syndicated radio companies around the country. Competition is intense: each year an estimated 7,000 (nonclassical) albums are released.

The Internet and music downloads have changed the industry by providing an ideal distribution channel. Older forms of distribution are rapidly becoming less and less important, so marketing expertise will be needed to distinguish content and break through the clutter.

File sharing

For those music fans who are tired of the entertainment industry treating them like a criminal for wanting to share music, Electronic Frontier Foundation is fighting for a constructive solution that gets artists paid while making file sharing legal.

The irrational war on P2P is not generating a single penny for artists. In fact, despite lawsuits against many P2P providers and over 20,000 music and movie fans, file sharing is more popular than ever in 2010. Yet the lawsuits have forced listeners to pay thousands of dollars to music and movie industry lawyers, while many innocent individuals have been caught in the crossfire. Many recording artists have turned against the lawsuits, and over 60 million people in the U.S. have used file sharing, which is more people than there were voters in the past presidential election.

Terry McBride of Nettwerk Music Group believes that, rather than suing file-sharers and using digital rights management (DRM) to protect the copyright, the industry should "give up control." McBride's new paradigm centers on "mobilizing the fans" by using a band's fans as a marketing team to spread the news about artists through word-of-mouth. In addition, downloads could be made freely available, either subsidized by pop-up ads or paid for by a minimal fee paid by subscribers to mobile phone or Internet services. "Let the market establish what the price is and the revenue litigation has never won. People who pirate music and make a profit should be sued out of existence," says McBride. "But file-sharing is our future."

The music marketing mogul[xiii]

Jimmy Iovine, who runs Interscope/Geffen/A&M, is an executive with musical talent. Although he is a manager with Universal Music Group, the biggest music firm in the world (owned by French conglomerate Vivendi), artists regard him as much more than just another "suit." Iovine has street credibility, which may be the key to his success as a businessman.

Big music labels, known as the majors, used to have talent-spotting music executives at the helm—not any more. A television producer and a journalist head the second biggest music firm, Sony BMG. A group of private-equity firms own a big chunk of Warner Music Group. EMI's chairman used to run a biscuit company. Iovine is a different breed. He created the record label Interscope, which has consistently been on the cusp of some of the most profitable trends in American music.

Iovine got his first break from working with John Lennon during his solo career. He then produced Bruce Springsteen, Tom Petty, and Patti Smith, among others. His techniques were innovative; he lent an air of Hollywood to the music with expensive videos and billboard advertisements. Iovine advanced the careers of artists from U2 to Eminem.

Iovine, recognized early that music marketing needed to be more sophisticated and advocated partnerships with the ad industry to benefit both sides. He saw marketing as a tool to combat piracy and overcome some of the built-in problems of the recording industry's business model.[xiv]

His reputation for giving artists more money than other record labels includes making lots of 50/50 joint-venture agreements with musicians' own labels—so his artists tend to have more of a stake in their success than other labels' artists do. When Steve Jobs was developing iTunes, Iovine helped persuade the other labels to sell him their music alongside that of Universal Music. Iovine's latest idea for Universal Music is to earn money from sources beyond recorded music, such as Dr. Dre endorsed headphones and HP laptops.

In 2009, A&M chairman Iovine built a television studio across the street from Interscope that is a performance-nightclub facility where new content is created on a daily basis. Club Beats's in-store technology hub was created in partnership between Dre, Monster and Best Buy.

His mission for saving the music industry from digital sound—making better speakers and headphones so music can be experienced with the production precision.

Planning points for concert promotion

Using much the same planning process as for any performance, concert plans have four key functions:

1. Identifying what will make the product stand out and be noticed (unique selling proposition)
2. Positioning the event ahead of the competition
3. Staying current by reading trade magazines (*Billboard, Performance*) and consumer magazines (*Rolling Stone, Spin*)
4. Knowing the audience well

Planning is key for developing and implementing successful marketing strategies.

Crafting a MySpace Page for a Band

Many music fans roam MySpace in search of good indie music. But with so many options, how do visitors choose whose music site to visit? MusicDish talent scout Anne Freeman checks two things:

1. Photo/graphic

2. Band Name

The first thing consumers do when confronted with a list of potential bands is look at their photo or graphic. The second thing is to look at their name. The third thing is look at their photo/graphicagain. That's it, period.

What that says to marketers of indie labels and band/artists is: Be very careful about your photo/graphic selections. If you're just starting out, pay attention to the name you choose if you have a band. Promote yourself to catch a potential fan or music industry professional in a few seconds.

Her advice? Use a graphic or photograph that best communicates the band's *primary artistic sensibility*. Here are some examples:

The Pink Spiders used a photo of band members that is eye-catching with bold colors. The art conveys musical fun and creates a 'must hear' from browsers to MySpace. Their site (www.myspace.com/thepinkspiders) is a perfect match for their pop/punkish music. Everything on the site contributes to their look and sound.

Creech Holler's band name confirms the intrigue and stimulates a click to their site. Their ominous graphic recons back to the old snake handlers of the deep South, so buffs know it's a southern blues or folk band from both the name and the image. They've effectively married their music with their look and style. www.myspace.com/creechholler

Probably the bigger challenge on a site like MySpace is for the individual artist who is trying to stand out, and this is especially for artists in acoustic-based music. Individual artists have a much more difficult time of it when trying to establish a presence.

Carie Pegeon is an example of an acoustic-based artist whose photograph created an eye-catching image of a strong female, acoustic-singer/songwriter with a hard, confessional edge. Her photo is well composed and interesting to look at, and should convince others to visit her site.

Networking sites are important for both new and established artists. Most consumers base their decisions whether or not to visit a site on the same two pieces of information: graphic and band name.

What marketers, managers and record labels must think through carefully is how to use those two portals to an artist's site, whether the browser is a fan or a music industry professional.

Band marketers should be very clear about primary artistic sensibility to ensure that every decision made for the site contributes to the band or artist's cause. If each choice is not actively contributing to the site, then it's actively detracting from the artist. There is no neutral ground in this game.

Need a name for a band? Check out the Band Name Generator, a link with 10,000 names generated by MIT students and a computer.

Source: MusicDish Network, August 5, 2006

Message development

Word-of-mouth is a big factor in popular music. Promotional messages directed at concert goers are best delivered through friends, family, or just anyone who might influence targeted buyers. Unlike theater goers who wait for expert channels to review a performance before purchasing tickets, music fans are excited by the buzz created around a concert. Among young adults, opinion leaders—those whose opinion matters to a defined social group—have legitimate power by virtue of their social standing. Live concert performance marketers try to stimulate word-of-mouth exposure by providing opinion leaders with free tickets or special perks so they will spread the word and stimulate ticket purchases.

Promoting the circus

Circuses are considered to be one of the major performing arts in Europe, where they commonly receive government subsidies. In the United States, circuses are operated by private, for-profit organizations. As such they have become permanent traveling forms of commercial theater, operating with a blend of economic features seen in both theater and theme-park operations. Given the size and structure of the spectacle that must be assembled and disassembled every few days, circuses are only marginally profitable. Still, the ten major domestic circuses enjoy attendance from over 40 million people each year.

The once-classic three-ring Ringling Brothers and Barnum & Bailey Circus now presents its new show to audiences without any rings at all. New for 2009, Ringling Bros. and Barnum & Bailey's Red show debuted "Zing, Zang, Zoom," the Circuses 139th edition! The show will have a number of new acts including a disappearing Elephant and other illusions.

Circus executives attributed the overhaul to market research. The circus's family audiences, primarily mothers of kids 2–11 years old, say their lives are already three-ring circuses, so they

Innovation vs. Tradition

Two circus giants, Cirque de Soleil and Ringling Brothers, have suffered and/or benefited from the economic downturn in very different ways. Entering a financially unattractive industry, Cirque du Soleil was able to reinvent the industry by challenging conventional assumptions about how to compete. By changing demographics from kids to adults, Cirque drew from the distinctive strengths of alternative industries, such as the theatre, Broadway shows and the opera, to offer a totally new form of entertainment to more mature and higher spending customers. Cirque du Soleil's business model succeeded in part from its relationship with MGM Mirage that provided capital investment for shows located in their casinos. As a magnet for traffic for an exclusive clientele that spends large amounts of money at the casinos, Cirque invigorated the resort and created a new platform for its performances.

Image 12.8 Ringling's elephants perform.

© Bo Zaunders/Corbis

The more traditional Ringling, however, has fallen behind since the down economy took a toll on its audience—working-class families. Competitors from Cirque and New York's Big Apple Circus, and angry animal-welfare protesters against circus mistreating its elephants has stagnated attendance. As never before, Ringling is under siege in spite of declaring its shows recession-proof. They maintain, however, that families are trading expensive Disney trips for smaller, less costly alternatives such as movies and circus where value is king. Taking advantage of excess railroad capacity for global transportation and collapsed oil prices, Ringling's mile-long circus trains have continued to roll at a cost reduction.

However, the disposition of the company's 54 Asian elephants depends upon the outcome of the 2010 court's interpretation of the 1973 Endangered Species Art. Ringling maintains innocence of mistreatment, saying that their $5 million, 200-acre conservation center in Florida has given birth to 22 elephants since 1992. Maintaining that elephants have been domesticated to work for humans for centuries, the circus claims that the animals are their most valuable assets, and that they receive care exceeding federal regulations.

Although Ringling has a history of contesting animal-rights challengers, the company been disparaged in comparison to Cirque du Soleil's high-end shows in the United States, Europe, and South America. The privately held Montreal-based Soleil, however, has always rejected the notion that it competes with Ringling.

Source: Glenn Collins for *The New York Times*, March 23, 2009

want something less distracting. They also wanted to connect with a story in an emotional way. Ringling expected 11 million people to watch their shows in one of 79 markets a year during a recent two-year tour.

Audiences also respond to smaller circuses with extraordinary formats, such as the Dream Circus Theater in Los Angeles that offers a new kind of creative space for promoting tribal trance parties performed by a band of "Burning Man" types that melds a club scene, rock scene, and arts scene in its venue for emerging talent.

Financing live performances

It is almost impossible to raise substantially the productivity of live performances, which are themselves end products. Productivity lag in the arts becomes more pronounced as productivity in other economic sectors decrease and operating costs escalate. Ticket prices have risen at higher rates than the consumer price index, and indications are that higher prices reduce demand. Revenue sources that go beyond box office revenues, especially for nonprofit organizations, are desperately needed. The most prevalent funding source is donations from individuals and corporations.

Donations and subsidies

Contributions to the arts by individuals and estates are the performing arts largest single source of voluntary funding. Orchestras and operas receive proportionately more regular contributions than theater or dance. Performing arts subsidies from state and local arts councils and through the National Endowment for the Arts are vital, but in the U.S. they are much less significant than in Europe Private corporate support of cultural activities may stimulate local commercial activity as it may provide new business opportunities.

Because of the tremendous costs of establishing and continuing live performances, corporate philanthropy is an important source of revenue. Marketers establish liaisons with corporations by demonstrating to them a perceived benefit from associating with arts performances.

Support for the arts, regardless of the source, is normally dedicated to the development of specific facilities or to the patronage of fixed dance, orchestral, and opera groups. Usually no return on investment is expected. Always on a financial precipice, performing arts organizations are subject to audience size limitations and the expense of coordinating an effective production with venture capital from those willing to invest in risky ventures. With advances in technology, revenues derived from new media are becoming significant considerations in financing the arts.

MAXIMIZING PUBLIC RELATIONS TO PROMOTE PERFORMANCES

Marketing is an integrated effort. One of the most significant components of integrated marketing is public relations, for many reasons. By integrating a program consisting of research, publicity and lobbying, public relations efforts provide a coordinated effort for reaching the organization's publics. PR's merger with marketing functions enables the delivery of persuasive and influential unpaid promotions. By developing sound objectives, creating a positive image, and using event marketing, public relations becomes a star performer.

Synchronizing objectives

Promotion's goal is to influence *behavior*; PR's task is to form, maintain or change public *attitudes* toward the organization or performance genre. Publicity can make a profound impact on public awareness by placing stories in the media that bring attention to performances and performers. Publicity yields high rewards for improving an organization's image and visibility.

The benefits of public relations include high credibility, extending advertising's reach, and reinforcing messages sent by other delivery systems. Media coverage is an important component of image development. PR requires a fraction of the cost of media advertising. In the face of shrinking arts coverage, PR managers can place features in alternative newspaper sections (food, travel, home, news), develop collaborative feature stories, and capitalize on holidays for image enhancement.

Event promotion

A fast-growing, high-profile industry that began as an offshoot to PR, event marketing ties product brands with entertainment events to deliver a lifestyle experience to audiences.

From world platforms like the Olympic games to local marathon races, event marketing integrates the corporate sponsorship of an event with a whole range of marketing elements such as advertising, sales promotion and public relations. Events enjoy a growth rate of 20% each year, which points to their high level of success. Companies break through the advertising clutter with image association that drives awareness and sales. Sponsorship caters to audiences who have switched their allegiance from buying products, to enjoying lifestyles, experiences and emotions. Events can take many forms: international, such as the Olympics, or local and regional events that provide a captive audience both face-to-face and through live media coverage.

Why develop an event?

According to a recent IEG Sponsorship survey of 280 events,[xv] sponsors' key objectives include establishing:

+ Corporate identification through displays of brand names or logos on event signage

+ Target marketing to reach a select audience

+ Promotional tie-ins to gain attention and drive purchase

+ Entertainment for clients

+ Sampling of a product or service through coupons or teasers distributed at the event

+ Brand awareness from frequent impressions

+ Usage stimulated by event promotions

+ PR for brand mentions in media coverage of the event

Planning events

Tactical and detailed plans ensure a positive return on investment. Following these six key elements helps to insure success:

1. Select an event that meet business objectives and enhance the brand's image and try to lock in a long-term relationship to build high recall.

2. Tightly define the target audience to insure the development of a good match between them and the event.

3. Leverage the sponsorship by integrating marketing programs to include product sampling, on-site signage, logo placement, and cross-promotions.

4. Negotiate favorable terms and protect them in a contractual agreement that includes brand exclusivity, brand role in relation to other sponsors, brand protection measures,

right of refusal for future events, and benefits such as complementary tickets and logo inclusion in advertising.

6. Deliver relevance for your audience in order to build the brand's reputation.

7. Use the Internet to promote the event, maintain continuous communication with the target audience and follow up with the audience after the event.

Events are best used to create an emotional tie with participants and spectators, and to increase brand awareness for an entertainment franchise or corporation. When the entertainment brand is the sponsor, selecting appropriate product brand partners is crucial for maximizing the audiences' lifestyle expectations. Brand constellations—brand groups valued by a specific target audience—must package brand images that are compatible with the event, the sponsors, and the audience.

The Sponsors Report, which tracks the number of times a sponsor's name is mentioned or viewed in a broadcast, adds up the exposure time and multiplies it by the cost of the advertising time to arrive at an overall figure. Broadcast time for elements such as logo, on-screen graphics, verbal mentions, uniform or clothing signage, and banners is valued, then totaled, to determine the equivalent value provided by the event.

For non-profit organizations, special events in the form of benefits or galas are a popular fund raising strategy. By selling an event at a premium price, organizations can link their mission and goals with coming events; a theater's dinner benefit may feature vignettes from an upcoming musical or comedy. Events are especially effective for attracting potential donors and new patrons to the organization, and improving an organization's image. Costly to run and highly labor-intensive, events nonetheless generate enthusiasm for a venue or organization that may out-weigh individual fund-raising efforts.

FORMULATING A COMMUNICATIONS STRATEGY FOR PERFORMING ARTS

As previously discussed, the communication process is:

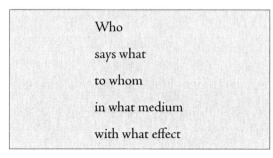

Who

says what

to whom

in what medium

with what effect

To communicate effective promotional messages, the sender must successfully deliver a message using an understandable set of symbols to the audience so that it is understood and acted upon. A process of coding and encoding takes place, concluding with a feedback loop that allows the sender to determine whether or not the message was successfully understood. Sounds simple enough, but marketers are not always able to achieve effective message development or feedback mechanisms. This explains how to set objectives and craft messages for performing arts. Delivering messages over the Internet and to editors and reviewers is also discussed here.

Setting objectives

Our objectives for communicating to performing arts audiences are to achieve *purchase stimulation* and *performance satisfaction*. A long process of decision-making, purchase behavior begins with an understanding of how to move the audience to a higher state of purchase readiness. Buyer readiness has six levels:[xvi]

1. *Awareness*—let the audience know that a new opera will debut, a popular performance is back in town, or a new venue is opening.

2. *Knowledge*—convey the benefits of attending a particular performance to a specific audience segment.

3. *Liking*—the disposition toward a performance by the audience is either a point for emphasis or a problem to overcome.

4. *Preference*—with many stay-at-home viewing options, marketers must convince audiences that seeing live performance is the most preferred choice.

5. *Conviction*—marketers often must convince audiences that attending is fun and exciting; incentives are often necessary to reach this level.

6. *Purchase*—advertising or email reminders help deliver audiences to the box office.

Determining audience readiness states is critical in developing a communication program that will be cost-effective while inducing the desired response. Make them fall in love before you ask them to open their wallets.

Crafting and delivering messages

Like objectives, messages must gain *attention*, hold *interest*, arouse *desire*, and elicit *action*. Advertising creative teams use this **AIDA model** to develop effective communication appeals. Appeals should be unique to the organization or performance being promoted. The more direct the competition, the more necessary it is to develop a unique selling point (USP).

As with other entertainment activities or destinations, messages directed at audiences must be sent via channels frequently used and easily accessed by that audience. Because many performances are venue-dependent, the Internet is an excellent way to communicate with potential ticket purchasers. Advertising, PR, editorial comment and performance reviews should also be part of the promotional mix for sending messages about live performances.

Internet

Web sites should stimulate visitors to explore a wide variety of information, including photographs of performers, historical information, milestones, upcoming events and highlights with concert schedules and venue information. Seating charts with views of the stage, listing of nearby restaurants and lodging, and online kinks to other attractions should also be included. Special discount ticket offers for web visitors and an order form that can be email or faxed to the box office are also essential components of a performance venue site. The latest in performer news, excerpts of recordings, news and press release pages for media, educational programs, sponsorship and volunteering opportunities should be easily located and accessed. Finally, contact information allows the visitor to send email directly to the directors of ticket service, marketing and PR, information services, education, volunteers and development. The visitor can also arrange to be added to the organization's mailing list.

Editorial and reviews

Source credibility goes a long way in delivering positive, unbiased messages to current and potential audiences. With strategic management of feature stories and critical comments, public relations efforts can enhance marketing's impact.

Press kits, containing performance information, schedules, performer biographies, and suggestions for feature articles, should be delivered to editors of entertainment and calendar sections of local newspapers. Performance trailers placed with television news producers often provide welcome fillers that results in free coverage. Most editorial features are stimulated by paid publicists, and well-placed story ideas are worth their weight in gold.

Reviewers are important to producers of live performances because of their influence on attendance and box office sales. Providing reviewers with advance tickets, interviews with performers and anecdotal material improves your chances for positive commentary, or at least they may curtail negative remarks that can terminate a new show in an untimely fashion.

Finally

Of all entertainment genres discussed in this text, live performance is the least affected by technological advances. Digitization is no substitute for well-scripted productions, talented performers, and the dynamic energy generated by live performances. Yet because of fierce competition from digitized entertainment, effective promotion is key for the success and survival of all types of theatrical, dance and musical productions classified as performing arts.

Never underestimate the role of the Internet for promoting concerts and live performances. Fans always consult Web blogs, calendars and reviews before purchasing tickets, so the design and implementation of an effective, attractive Web site is essential for a complete marketing communications effort.

GOT IT?

Chapter 12 made these important points about marketing performance:

+ Drama, the driving force of entertainment genres, produces conflict and resolution that enables audiences to experience the entire range of human conditions. Promotional efforts must connect audiences with the excitement of a particular genre to be successful.

+ To get audiences to go beyond the reviews and into the theater, advertising, promotions and direct mail are the strategies of choice for marketers.

+ Concert managers budget for three modules: one-sale period, sustaining period, and the panic period when goals have not been met.

+ Corporate donations and government funding are necessary to finance live performances that are part of the non-profit sector.

+ Because public relations forms, maintains or changes public *attitudes* toward the organization or performance genre, events are best used to create an emotional tie with participants and spectators, and to increase brand awareness for an entertainment franchise or corporation.

+ Communication objectives for performing arts audiences are purchase stimulation and performance satisfaction; messages delivered over the Internet, in editorial coverage and positive reviews are most effective for reaching current and potential audiences.

NOW TRY THIS

1. Consult the calendar or entertainment section of your local newspaper and count the number of ads for live performances. How do they compare with ads for mediated events? Sporting events? What do these numbers suggest about audience preferences?

2. Locate three sources on the Internet that provide scheduling information for live performances. How easy or difficult were they to find? What can you suggest for making this process easier?

3. Read three reviews of a single live performance and compare them. Which reviews were most influential? Why? As a result of the reviews, would you attend or simply abide by the consensus of the reviewers?

4. Identify a regional theater in your area and obtain performance information. From the messages and delivery system they use, what can you determine about their marketing effectiveness? What can you suggest for improvement?

QUESTIONS FOR DISCUSSION AND REVIEW

1. What elements are involved in planning a promotional campaign for theatrical productions? What type of research is necessary to determine promotional strategies?

2. Discuss the similarities and differences of marketing the five different types of concerts presented in this chapter.

3. Explain the types of funding appropriate for marketing and promoting a concert or live performance presented by a nonprofit organization.

4. How would you use public relations to enhance the promotion program for a circus that was being picketed for abuse by animal rights groups?

5. Why are editorial and reviewer commentary so important for the success of a live performance? How can use these sources to best serve your organizational client?

MORE STUFF TO READ ABOUT MARKETING LIVE PERFORMANCES

www.thebuzzfactor.com

www.aandronline.com

Beat Wire (PR the for music industry)

Harold Vogel (2001), *Entertainment Industry Economics* 5th edition. Cambridge University Press.

CAMPAIGN CASE STUDY

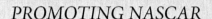

PROMOTING NASCAR

Client: NASCAR

Problem: Reaching and keeping the sport exciting enough for women.

Campaign objectives: Increase female fan participation and create NASCAR products and events relevant for this market segment. Provide sponsors with target audience research.

Situation Analysis: NASCAR, in only a few years, graduated from a regional weekend pastime to a national phenomenon, creating personalities with rock-star popularity and causing an audience least expected to watch gear-head heroes race around a circle—Women.

Of NASCAR's 75 million fans in 2007, 40% were women. Women spent $250 million that year on NASCAR-licensed products, signaling continued growth for this market segment. And all without trying. NASCAR didn't set out to attract women to the sport, but they were caught by the buzz from fans and became fans themselves.

The nation's number one spectator sport, NASCAR was the second-most-watched sport in the United States, after the NFL. More than 21% of fans were minorities, and more than 50% of 7 to 17 segment report they are NASCAR fans. Loyalty prevails, as fans switch brands to support their favorite drivers, and willingly spent more to buy event-sponsored products. Female fans reported they would buy non-racing-related items, such as detergent, if they had NASCAR logos on the packaging.

SWOT Analysis: Strength:

- Sport provides excitement and social connections.

- Weakness: Male domination both in drivers and fans.

- Opportunity: Increase female fan base using technology.

- Threat: Competition from other sports that appeal to women.

Target Audience: Women 18–35.

Promotion Strategies and Tactics:

1. Strategy: Create an attractive lifestyle brand for NASCAR by capitalizing on life stories of drivers, crew chiefs, and pit crew members.

   Tactic: Combine the down-to-earth personalities of drivers with the drama of a life-threatening activity that is clean, female friendly, and patriotic.

2. Strategy: Develop partnerships that appeal to women.

   Tactic: Establish a partnership with Harlequin romance novels to support the publication of three NASCAR-theme books, featuring NASCAR drivers on the covers.

3. Strategy: Use new technologies that allow fans to follow the race from inside the car and via communication between drivers and their crews and provide commentators who can translate that technology into something women viewers can understand.

   Tactic: Use blogs and drive Web sites to elicit fan response and to maximize word-of-mouth advertising on the Internet.

4. Strategy: Service sponsors and provide them with assessments of how well a driver is connecting with fans.

   Tactic: Troll message boards, podcasts, social networking sites, and blogs to locate mentions of drivers.

Results: An increase of female fans indicated by gate statistics and product purchases; increased Internet usage; healthy Harlequin book sales.

Source: Jim Gann for the *Columbia Business Times,* 9/22/07

Question for discussion: *As campaign manager, how would you use sponsors to provide other incentives for women to become NASCAR fans? How would you measure its success?*

---

[i]Erik Piepenburg, "The Fine Art of Selling a Show," *The New York Times,* Sunday, March 21, 2010.
[ii]http://www.broadwayleague.com/editor_files/Touring-Broadway-Facts_08-09.pdf
[iii]Opinion of Bill Wyman for the *New York Times,* June 12, 2005.
[iv]From Robert Hughes' Entertainment column in the *Wall Street Journal,* June 17, 2005.

[v]By Brook Barnes for the *Wall Street Journal*, Oct. 23, 2005.

[vi]C. S. Huntington (2004), "Marketing Professional Ballet," University of Illinois, Institute for Entrepreneurial Studies.

[vii]www.operawarhorses.com/2010/03/05/opera-in-live-performance-thoughts-and-assessments-at-the-end-of-2009-part-two/#more-8500

[viii]From Julie Bosman's Advertising column, *New York Times*, Aug. 29, 2006.

[ix]Robin Pogrebin for the *New York Times*, Oct. 9, 2006, A1.

[x]By Anthony Tommasini for the *New York Times*, Dec. 25, 2005.

[xi]From an article by Daniel Wakin for the *New York Times*, Aug. 21, 2005.

[xii]Sisario, Ben (2010), "A front-row seat, to go? Rock fans pay for perks with stars," *New York Times*, Sunday, May 23, D1.

[xiii]economist.com, May 4, 2006.

[xiv]Scott Donaton, *Advertising Age*, 8/1/2005, 76(31), p. 12.

[xv]From Barry Avrich (2002), *Selling the Sizzle: The Magic and Logic of Entertainment Marketing*. Maxworks Publishing Group, p. 82.

[xvi]Based on similar steps cited in Philip Kotler & Joanne Scheff (1997), *Standing Room Only*. HBS Press, pp. 306–8.

13

PROMOTING DESTINATIONS AND TOURIST SERVICES

> *Not bound to swear allegiance to any master, wherever*
> *the wind takes me I travel as a visitor.*
>
> Horace

Chapter Objectives

After reading this chapter, you will be able to answer these questions:

+ What are the elements of the *travel cycle* and *tourism market?*

+ How does marketing *places* differ from other types of travel and tourism marketing?

+ How are *destination brands* established, built, and maintained over time?

+ What *promotion strategies* are appropriate for branding destinations and places?

+ How do we market *tourism services?*

The tourism and travel industry employs more people worldwide than any other industry. Many local and regional economies are sustained through tourism-related revenues, including transportation, hospitality, food and beverage, recreation, and amusement-based attractions. This chapter begins with an introduction to the principles and dimensions of the travel and tourism market. Next we focus on city and nation destination marketing and present promotional strategies appropriate for bringing attention to place brands. Our final section presents the marketing of tourist services, including resort/hotel/spa, transport, and tour businesses.

INDUSTRY TERMINOLOGY AND DIMENSIONS

Like other leisure-based industries, the travel business has its own jargon. These classifications and measurements were standardized by the World Trade Organization (WTO):

- **Visitor**—any person out of his or her home
- **Tourist**—a person who stays over one night and collections mementos
- **Same-day visitor**—cruise passenger, border shopper, or day tripper
- **Traveler**—commuters, diplomats, migrants, transport workers, and business people
- **Passengers**—non-revenue travelers such as infants or discount fares
- **Tourism**—visitor activities both international and domestic
- **Tourism industry**—provides services of hospitality (hotels and restaurants), transportation, tour operators, travel agents and attractions.

Three basic **tourism units** include: *domestic travel* where residents visit their own country; *inbound tourism* when nonresidents travel in a given country; and *outbound tourism* as residents traveling in another country. Units of tourism are combined in a variety of ways to form **tourism categories**: *internal tourism* (domestic and inbound), *national tourism* (domestic and outbound) and *international tourism* (inbound and outbound).

The travel or tourism market is defined by five criteria:

1. Purpose of the trip—business, leisure, and family emergencies are among the main reasons for travel; only leisure travelers are considered to be tourists
2. Distance of travel—100 miles or more to be considered a tourist distance
3. Duration of trip—travelers who stay away from home for at least one night
4. Residence of traveler—where people live rather than their individual nationalities
5. Mode of transportation—how tourists and travelers get from home to their destination

Reasons for travel (the 'purpose of trip' criteria above) fall into categories according to popularity and potential for revenue generation; they are 1) leisure, recreation and holidays; 2) visiting friends and relatives; 3) business and professional; 4) health treatment; 5) religious or pilgrimages; and 6) homeland or cultural discovery. For each classification, messages must be directed at the appropriate market segment to acknowledge the reasons for their travel and the benefits of particular destinations or hospitality selections.

Tourism promotion is similar to other forms of entertainment promotion in its challenges and problems:

- Intangibility—a trip can't be seen or sampled before purchase

- Perishability—travel is fixed in time and cannot be stored for future use

- Heterogeneity—there is no standardization among destination offerings

- Inseparability—production and consumption are simultaneous

PRINCIPLES OF TRAVEL & TOURISM

Travel is the process of getting from one place to another; **tourism** is the business of hosting guests and selling them things. The entertainment industry, while interested in both travel and tourism, focuses on tourism activities. The **travel cycle** plots a tourist's journey.

For our purposes, a **tourist** is simply someone who travels for pleasure. The cycle begins at home with trip planning, takes tourists out of their homes and onto transportation, and ends with arrival at a destination. Once there, tourists collect mementos and buy souvenirs, then use transport to return home where they relive their trip through photographs. Marketing opportunities occur at each stage of the travel cycle. Marketing destinations to travelers and tourists requires a basic understanding of consumer demands and motivations, the units and categories of tourism, and market segmentation. Tailoring the development of the travel promotional message is also important.

Tourism market segments

Seven of the most important travel segments are: purpose of travel; needs, motivations and benefits sought; the characteristics of travel usage; demographic, economic, and geographic profiles; psychographics; geodemographics; and price. The major travel market segments and corresponding travel motivations can be generalized into six groups, as listed in Exhibit 13.1

Plans trip > leaves home > uses transportation > arrives at destination > collects souvenirs >

Travel Cycle   V

recalls trip with photos, souvenirs   < returns home   <   uses transportation <

EXHIBIT 13.1 Major Travel Market Segments, Motivations and Sales Messages

TRAVELER SEGMENT	CHARACTERISTICS	COMMUNICATION MESSAGE
Adventure	15% of the market; long trips with natural challenges; different perspectives; away from normal routine; experience foreign cultures; enjoy the outdoors; take physical challenges	Experience based
Budget	41% of all tourists; travel the most	Value and deals
FAMILY	55%; take domestic trips; motivated to spend time together	"Something for everyone" message
Gay	most growth potential; 2% of travel packaging; travel to be with friends, learn about culture; appreciate solitude	Unique experiences; quiet locations
Luxury	spend most money; 10% of market; seek romance and feeling alive; enjoy being pampered	Special service emphasis
Baby boomer	spend money but don't stay long; 51% of market; travel to relieve stress; schedule-free or retired; prefer being waited upon	Discovery-oriented messages
Eco-travelers	draw from all groups interested in sustainable tourism and natural phenomena; self-select wilderness tours in remote locations	Nature-oriented messages

Source: The Complete 21ˢᵗ Century Travel & Hospitality Marketing Handbook, Prentice Hall 2004.

German researchers developed a criterion-based scheme that yielded a behavioral-intention measurement for deriving distinct travel market segments. The model can be used to identify customers who were most likely to make positive recommendations to others about a destination they previously visited. The research was conducted in 2000 with a population of 1,500 Virginia residents using a stratified sampling procedure delivered through a mail survey. The results provided a useful approach for identifying distinct actionable tourist market segments. Product satisfaction, pricing, and the need for assistance are the three critical factors that influences the recommendations the respondents made to others.[i]

13.1 Tourists visit Red Squre in Moscow.

The study yielded four unique tourist segments, and two of these were characterized as actionable. Tourists in **actionable segments** are characterized as satisfied with products and services received. They are more likely to be female, older, more apt to spend money than other groups, and they make their trip decisions early. The study found that product or service satisfaction was the most significant variable affecting this group's word-of-mouth communication. The study suggested that tourism marketers should treat the actionable segment as the most valuable target market to pursue. This actionable segment yielded useful information for identifying valuable markets. Consequently, in a challenging marketing environment that often leads to narrow profit margins, the discovery of ideal segments is a cost-effective vehicle.

Role of government, organizations, and agencies

The WTO provides standardization and coordination of global travel industry efforts. On a regional basis, National Tourist Organizations (NTOs) cover a limited range of segments. Most NTOs are outweighed by private sector partnership marketing efforts and are relegated to a minor role in the industry. Still, marketers rely on NTOs for a number of services, including research data, representation in markets of origin, workshops and trade shows, familiarization trips, Internet sites, travel trade manuals, support of literature production and distribution, joint marketing ventures, information and reservation systems, consumer assistance and protection, and general industry advisory services. Often NTOs provide the only research available for campaign development.

A strategy of collaboration among travel professionals is necessary to coordinate all the elements of the travel cycle. Government promotional policies, low budgets, range of tourist products and locations, and joint promotions are all elements that tourism marketers must consider.

Travel motivations and markers

When making travel choices, today's tourists are selecting their activity first, destination second. That means marketers need to understand the key activity-based needs that motivate individuals, families and groups. Travel researchers[ii] have identified three groups of tourist needs:

+ **Hedonism**—gifting oneself with good food, wine, sunshine, beaches, nightclubs, culture, and mounds of self-indulgence.

+ **Self-improvement**—acquiring new skills or improving existing ones in sports, cultural pursuits, and artistic and culinary immersion.

+ **Spiritual needs**—taking pilgrimages, visiting retreats and meditation centers, or simply getting away.

An important component of hedonistic travel is *collecting*—everything from pictures and mementoes to local art and indigenous products. Collected items are considered to be souvenirs or **travel markers**. Travel markers come in all forms, but can be classified into these categories:

+ *Local arts, crafts and products*—pottery, jewelry, wool, wine, and foodstuffs like cheese or jam

+ *Markers*—clothing and artifacts with the place name written on them

+ *Miniatures*—replicas of an attraction or place icon, such as mini Eiffel Towers or cable cars

+ *Pieces of the rock*—natural elements taken from the landscape

+ *Treasures*—artifacts discovered at flea markets, garage sales, or antique shops

+ *Visual representations*—photographs, postcards, home movies, and place-based picture books

Souvenirs generate revenue for local businesses and artisans and give tourists an activity that helps define their overall experience of a particular place. Once you understand the needs and segments of tourists, you can begin developing promotional strategies to reach a particular segment and messages to stimulate trip and tour purchases.

Tourism marketing is about selling trips and tours; **destination marketing** is about selling places.

PROMOTING PLACES

In the first chapters of this text we made distinctions between product, service, and experiential marketing. Marketing places involves aspects of selling products (souvenirs), aspects of selling services (hotels) and aspects of selling experience (gaming and other activities). Because a **destination** or place is a total experience that encompasses all types of goods and services, it takes on a character of its own.

In principle, product and place marketing are the same. It's all about identifying, developing and communicating the parts of place identity that are favorable to some specified target groups. In reality, analyzing target group perceptions and developing brand building activities for places are much more complex tasks than those involved with products. Altering country brands is more difficult than changing even established product brands; obviously a country can't replace its beaches with mountains, or grow bananas if its climate produces snow. Although it may be possible for a nation to attract more foreign-directed investments or shift its economic base, there will always be some constraints over which a country has little or no control. Manufacturers, on the other hand, are free to make product improvements or alter their physical appearance as needed.

The most important challenges currently facing place-marketing efforts are: the lack of unity of purpose, difficulty in establishing actionable and measurable objectives, lack of authority over inputs and control over outputs, restricted flexibility, and relative lack of marketing know-how. Consider these challenges:[iii]

+ Place promotion involves multiple stakeholders, some with competing interests. Trying to market a country to tourists as a mountain hideaway inhabited by indigenous people may not serve the interests of those wishing to promote the country's budding industrial infrastructure to foreign investors.

+ Measuring the effectiveness of place promotion is fraught with difficulties. The decision of a multinational firm to locate a plant on an island nation may have little or nothing to do with promotional activities by members of the host country.

+ Unlike product marketing, place promotion is seldom under the control of a central authority. Government or industry associations are rarely in a position to dictate policy to stakeholders. A typical business will have more experience with marketing issues than most countries. Many government officials who become involved in country branding are drawn to product marketing approaches because their countries are in desperate need of exports, tourism, or direct foreign investment. But few in government have the skill sets required to design major promotional campaigns.

+ Promoters have far less control over place brands than over product brands. Besides country marketing campaigns, people may learn about a country in school; from media sources (including newspapers, books, TV and movies); from purchases; and from trips abroad or from contact with citizens or former residents.

- Natural disasters and wars impact promotion. In 2010, Haiti and Chile promotion suffered when earthquakes devastated parts of both countries, and Middle Eastern country promotional efforts were stifled from constant violence and turmoil. Mexico's border wars kept travelers away from the country's seaside resorts in spite of advertising and special discounts intended to retain tourism.

In spite of the obvious challenges, there are many paths to achieving a unique national identity. Spain has made tremendous strides in branding itself as a modern and developed country, while Denmark has successfully branded all of its government ministries and departments with graphic identities. In the past five years, Croatia has been working to reform its image in sports and tourism, and Poland has begun asserting itself in foreign policy. In other cases, promoting a country has involved identifying spokespeople, product brands, and events that can favorably influence public opinion in other countries about the destination.

One of the chief difficulties for many countries has been deciding who should run its national marketing campaigns, which are inspired at least partially by governments that want quick results. Since they may not remain in power for very long, governments are wise to work closely with the private sector when developing marketing strategies.

In spite of the challenges, global destinations continue to use sophisticated elements of marketing techniques. Competition between destination brands need not be a zero-sum game; there will always be room in the global marketplace for many brands, including niche brands and brands that compete on cultural excellence. The presence of multiple country brands in the market place will almost certainly enhance overall interest in the offerings.

DESTINATION BRANDING

Places are the world's biggest tourism brands, and branding is the most powerful marketing weapon available to destination marketers. Most destinations will claim to have superb resorts, hotels, and attractions or a unique culture and heritage—and the world's friendliest people. Clearly, these amenities are relatively useless as differentiators. Instead, branding is about making lifestyle statements that communicate image and build emotional relationships. Differentiation through loyalty and emotional appeal is more important for destination branding than tangible benefits.

To achieve successful destination branding, marketers must be in the business of delivering meaningful experiences rather than simply crafting clever identities with slogans and logos. Destination marketers must address political impacts, conduct ongoing and comprehensive research to identify brand values, and build partnerships across stakeholder groups. A destination success is achieved through the strength of the brand's emotional relationship with the traveler.

Positioning destination brands

Many leading destination brands position themselves as place brands (Disneyland, Las Vegas), whereby whole countries, states, and regions focus on brand building initiatives that include tourism and economic development. Positioning the brand often involves a relationship with events, such as the Olympics, held at the destination. Destination cities offer favorable economic conditions for businesses, (i.e., no sales tax or affordable real estate). The Internet facilitates the creation of strong, highly branded sites and a much stronger presence for individual tourism suppliers. Positioning themes, branding, and images are keys to successful destination marketing.

The best tag lines for tourist destinations are:

+ Based on product values that can be delivered—"What happens in Las Vegas stays in Las Vegas"; "Make San Antonio Your Business Address"

+ Easily understood at the point of purchase—"Canada … the world next door"

+ Easy to use in promotional efforts—"I love New York"

+ Transferable onto souvenirs and clothing—"Experience Montana"

What's does the destination mean to its tourist market segment? That's the question you need to answer to position a destination. Research tells you how to add value to any experience and find a unique selling opportunity. Good branding of a unique position must be sustainable, believable, and relevant. The "100% New Zealand" campaign conveyed the essence of the destination rather than any physical attributes of the country. Instead, focus was upon "pure romance," "pure spirit" and "pure adventure," tying each emotion with the appropriate market segment.

A CLOSER LOOK AT DESTINATION RESEARCH

Branding Western Australia

Tourism to Australia's east-coast cities is flourishing—Sydney, the Gold Coast, and Great Barrier Reef are popular tourist attractions. The west-coast cities, however, are relatively unknown to tourists in Europe and the U.S. In order to bring tourists to the less-populated region of the country, marketers conducted research to help them develop a relevant promotional campaign. This section is a closer look at problem-solving through tourism research.

Problem: Tourists have an unclear image of Perth and the surrounding west coast area of Australia, which has not differentiated itself from other Australian destinations.

Research objectives:

- Identify a set of possible competitive advantages.

- Define a core personality of the Western Australia brand.

Research components:

1. Interview end users (past and present tourists) of brand Western Australia.

2. Use market research to determine national and international markets and global tourism trends.

3. Select appropriate travel consumer target markets and study their decision-making process.

4. Determine the best message and media to reach each location-based target segment.

Market segments:

Using WTO and other migration data, five segments emerged as valuable targets for campaign development. They included:

- Australian national market—Sydney and Melbourne residents, adults 30–59 years who were high income travelers that take long vacations.

- Singapore—urban-based travelers ages 18–35 who take short holidays.

- Indonesia—residential travelers ages 25–45 who take short breaks from work.

- Malaysia—young Chinese families 18–29 who take annual vacations.

- UK—upper-income tourists ages 30–59 who take long holidays.

For each market segment, research was conducted to determine *access* (what airline, type of visa), *growth* (rate of outbound and visitation), *value* (market share of visitors), and *synergy* of online activity.

What research found out:

- Respondents were asked to describe WA with relevant adjectives. Adjectives used to characterize Western Australia's personality were "fresh, natural, free and spirited." These elements were used by the design team to develop logo and collateral materials.

- By choosing from among their reasons for travel, tourists revealed that Western Australia was perceived to be a holiday destination; this information was used in positioning.

- Respondents chose from a variety of the destination's strengths and weaknesses to reflect their travel experience; these helped marketers identify the message focus that would address both concerns.

Integrated strategy and promotion mix:

The campaign strategy modified the 4Ps for campaign development:

· The *destination* (*as product*). *Branding* centered on nature-based regional experiences.

· *Value* (*as price*). Western Australia was positioned as a value-for money destination.

· *Message delivery* (*as place*). Broadcast media were selected as communication channels.

· *Incentives* (*promotion mix*). Celebrity endorsements were used for advertising; events were promoted with discounts for tourists.

Repositioning campaign objectives developed from research findings:

Research allowed marketers to re-position the destination to better suit the identified segments and their perceptions. These steps were taken:

· Fix top-of-mind awareness of destination to position WA as 'nature-based fun.'

· Create lifestyle broadcasts on travel channels featuring kayakers, surfers and hikers.

· Use tactical incentives to stimulate travel during slow periods using tie-ins with airlines for travel discounts and package deals.

· Establish a visiting journalist program to stimulate travel-based editorial for global newspaper and magazine exposure.

· Design a consumer web site for the segment database in each of the three market languages.

· Build convention business among global corporations through liaisons with convention bureaus and conferences.

Campaign promotion:

The $400,000 campaign integrated a rolling television schedule, featuring a different region television commercial each week. Weekly activity was supported with online paid search activity and a campaign specific webpage containing a mix of informative and rich media and content www.westernaustralia.com/breaks. The Web page varied depending on the region that was being promoted in the television commercials and linked through to the relevant Regional Tourism Organizations' Web site.

Campaign results:

The television media schedule over-achieved on all levels, with the campaign reaching over 1.3 million Western Australians, who saw the promotion an average of 19 times each. The television commercials were also very popular online, with over 6,000 video views from the campaign site.

An "Experience Extraordinary" promotion was executed in 2010 based on the research conducted and responses to video advertising in 2008. The new brand was launched in intrastate, interstate, and international advertising, PR, online communications, travel trade, and events.

Post-campaign research

In order to maintain the brand and to evaluate the success of the campaign, marketers conducted a survey to determine:

- the perceived knowledge of Western Australia as a holiday destination.

- the propensity for travelers to consider Western Australia for their holiday.

- visitor data such as length of stay and spending levels.

What do you think?

1. What kind of research would be necessary to determine American images and perceptions of Western Australia?

2. How would marketers use that information to position the brand to the U.S.?

3. How might this market be segmented?

4. What kind of promotions would be necessary to get Americans to travel across the Pacific to Western Australia?

Achieving destination celebrity

Image is the most important communication vehicle for a destination. Places rich in emotional meaning have great conversation value and hold high anticipation for potential tourists. These are the places that become brand celebrities. Celebrity destinations have high added value and high emotional pull, as shown in Exhibit 13.2.

Similar to a product's life cycle, a brand's **fashion curve** migrates a destination through stages of being fashionable to being famous, then familiar, and finally fatigued. The fatigued or mature phase of the lifecycle necessitates a refreshment or reinvigoration for survival in the competitive global marketplace. Whether it's a newly established destination in fashion, or one that has fallen from grace, the process of building or refreshing a destination brand is important for maintaining brand equity.

Building destination brands

A well-executed branding campaign requires an initial investment of public funds supported by private funds in both marketing and destination partnerships. This in turn enhances the destination experience, thanks to brand loyalty and world-of-mouth recommendations. Brands

EXHIBIT 13.2 Destination Brand Positioning Map

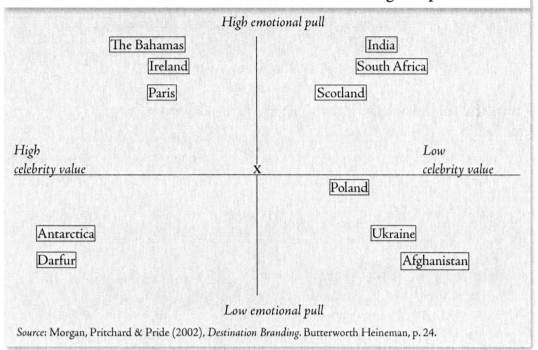

Source: Morgan, Pritchard & Pride (2002), *Destination Branding*. Butterworth Heineman, p. 24.

FOCUS ON CELEBRITY REAL ESTATE AS DESTINATION

For Rent: Stars' Malibu Getaways

Villas of the World Company rents and manages real estate belonging to stars and celebrities Mick Jagger's four-bedroom beachfront property in the West Indies rents for $13,000 a week. The market for celebrities offering their vacation homes and other getaways as private rentals is growing. Bruce Willis offered his three-villa compound in the Caribbean's Turks and Caicos Islands near the Parrot Cay resort for $15,000 to $20,000 per night. Mel Brooks leases out his 1927 Malibu beach cottage for $55,000 per month, and Pierce Brosnan's oceanfront Malibu home goes for $100,000 per month, as does Sting's Malibu getaway. These destinations do good business on the landlord's name; about 10% of the people who rent are attracted specifically to the idea of living among the star's personal effects.[iv]

Promotion tip: If it takes a star to get travelers to a destination, all cities should capitalize on their famous residents and market the place as "Second home to (<u>star's name goes here</u>)."

with emotional roots encourage local food, drinks, and craft brands to partner with the destination brand's values and emotions for their promotions. For instance, the key selling tool of Bushmills and Guinness is its Irishness—the values of authenticity, heartiness, and craftsmanship that imbue Ireland's brand. Guinness puts Ireland's brand mark on much of its international advertising.

Brand building involves two distinct phases: research and identity development, as previously detailed in Chapter 9. Within each phase are several stages of destination brand development.

Market investigation, analysis and strategic recommendations

The first stage in building a brand is establishing the core values (ideals most dear) of the destination that are durable, relevant, communicable, and hold saliency for potential tourists. The key point with destinations is the positioning and values have to be rooted in the fundamental truths about the destination and its culture. Determining those values results from careful and systematic research on the brand's target audience. By surveying visitors, non-visitors, business people, and regional economists, marketers can determine brand value with existing and potential visitors.

Brand identity development

In stage two, the brand identity (visualization) is developed. This graphic identity should communicate the brand values; logos and designs should reinforce these values. To create a successful emotional attachment, a destination brand has to be: credible, deliverable, and differentiating; it must convey powerful ideas, appeal to trade partners, and resonate with tourists. Destination benefits provide a brand with most of its identity. You can use the brand benefit pyramid to distill the essence of the brand's advertising position.

Exhibit 13.3 diagrams how a brand's character (personality, credibility) determines its brand value (economic worth), which in turn consists of psychological benefits and emotional rewards, benefits from destination features, and measurable place characteristics.

Branding nations

Successful global product brands come from countries that have strong brand images of their own—the product is linked with the nation's brand image. Think of Ferrari and you think of Italy—innovative design, speed and style. Champaign gets its chic from its country of origin—who else but France could produce the world's best bubbly?

© Matt Trommer, 2010. Used under license from Shutterstock, Inc.

13.2 Canada's brand logo

EXHIBIT 13.3 Destination Brand Benefit Pyramid

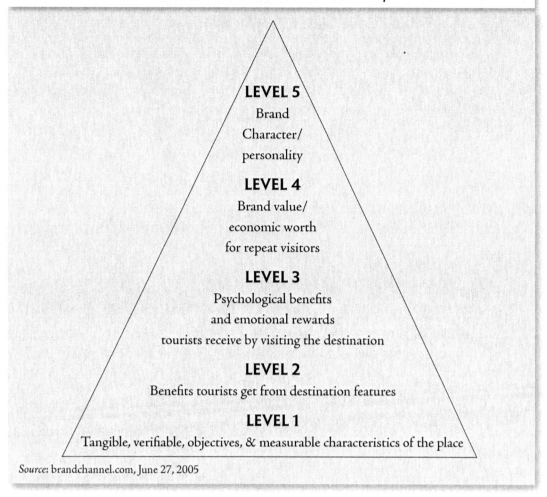

LEVEL 5
Brand
Character/
personality

LEVEL 4
Brand value/
economic worth
for repeat visitors

LEVEL 3
Psychological benefits
and emotional rewards
tourists receive by visiting the destination

LEVEL 2
Benefits tourists get from destination features

LEVEL 1
Tangible, verifiable, objectives, & measurable characteristics of the place

Source: brandchannel.com, June 27, 2005

A nation's brand behaves just like a product's brand when it acts as an umbrella of trust and guarantee of quality. A great deal of equity can be added to brands by leveraging the image of the country of origin. The movement of international capital is influenced by perceptions of countries as brands, and confidence comes along with investments. So brand positioning and brand management have become critical for a country to attract global capital. A country's brand image profoundly shapes its economic, cultural, and political destiny. China is a good example of this fact, as explained in the discussion of re-branding in the following section.

The Philippines re-branded itself many times over the past 30 years, with slogans ranging from "Pride of the Orient" to "Fiesta Islands" to "Philippines: the last bargain in Asia." Its 2006 slogan, "Wow Philippines!" was intended as much to instill national pride as to attract overseas visitors.

Repairing China's Country-of-Origin Image

The increasing competition ongoing from China into global brand markets is the result of a deliberate two-pronged strategy—organically grown brands produced to create new meaning that reflect the changes in China itself, and acquiring credibility and equity of established brands. It reflects a transition from a country viewed as a land of original-equipment manufacturers (one that remains in the background by supplying global brands with unbranded products), to one that creates and manages leading global brands.

China's objective is to acquire leading companies and brands. The People's Republic has executed a 'go global' initiative of US$15 billion set asked for such acquisitions. A 2005 survey on Chinese branding completed by 243 executive-level branding professionals included respondents from North America (41%), Europe (32%), Asia/Pacific (15%), Latin America (9%), and 3% from other countries. A brief synopsis of that survey is presented here to reflect the importance of country of origin on brand image.

Q1. Do you believe the 'Made in China' label helps or hurts Chinese brands?

A1: 79% of respondents said the label hurts brands associated with China

Q2. Provide three words that represent your impression of Chinese brands today.

A2: Chinese brands suffer from negative perceptions, attributing these adjectives in order of importance: cheap, poor value, unreliable, unsophisticated, innovative, lack of track record, dated, unknown, and aggressive.

Q3. Provide comments on Chinese brands and their future for competing internationally.

A3: Answers included:

- The need to overcome the lack of quality perception

- The need to enhance communications to grow awareness

- China is well positioned for brand success

- The need to quickly become brand professionals and practice ethics in patent infringement (knock-offs)

The survey results provided these insights and conclusions:

- Chinese brands have the ability to threaten entrenched brands within specific industries

- China must move away from being low-cost originals to creating and managing dominant global brands.

- Attributes of prestige, trust and safety are not associated with Chinese brands, yet innovation and reliability fare well.

A recommended strategy for China involves traits of all good branding: emotion, uniqueness, adaptation, recognition and consistency. In other words China must:

1. Compete along *emotional* dimensions and symbolize a promise people can believe in.

2. Brand products with a *unique position* to both internal and external audiences and across international markets.

3. *Adapt* to the local marketplace while fulfilling a global mission.

4. Gain strong brand *recognition* by industry leaders.

5. Develop a *consistent identity* across borders.

Current commercial perceptions of China are clearly hurting Chinese enterprise. To combat negative connotations for the phrase "Made in China," the Chinese government launched a TV ad campaign. Counteracting the poor perception of Chinese brands by U.S. consumers who were alarmed by reports of poor quality and deadly oversights, these ads featured products with an international twist. Each "Made in China" example highlighted Chinese manufacturers' collaboration with other countries. For example, MP3 players are shown with the phrase, "Made in China with software from Silicon Valley." Apparel carries the label "Made in China with French designers."

According to *China Daily*, the campaign is intended to show that "Chinese companies work with international firms to produce quality products." Developed by ad agency DDB's Chinese affiliate, the campaign was produced under the direction of China's Ministry of Commerce. But because of the tainted milk scandal that caused the deaths of at least six children and sickened 300,000. the campaign launch was postponed.

Chinese brands can leverage their dominance in their home market and they can benefit from the ingrained positioning as low cost providers. Based on their business model and efforts to gain brand sophistication China's image can only improve.

What do you think?

1. How would you advise China to proceed with its re-branding to the U.S.? To Europe?

2. What media strategies would you recommend?

3. Can you suggest a tag line for a China image campaign?

Source: J. Swystum, F. Burt & A. Ly (2005), "Strategies for Chinese Brands," *Interbrands*.

Coming back from its "Shrimp on the Barbie" campaign in 1984, Australia's newest slogan rocks: "So Where the Bloody Hell Are You?" The Australian Tourism Ministry's $135 million campaign promoted the tagline in commercials aimed at Western tourists. The old slogan, "See Australia in a Different Light," wasn't doing the trick, so Sydney agency M&C Saatchi spent $4.6 conducting focus groups for six months. After testing the line on 47,000 people in seven countries, the agency found the tagline's response positive enough to adopt. Australia's new, creative tagline underscores the challenge that any tourist destination has in trying to distinguish itself among rivals targeting the same audience.[v]

An award-winning destination campaign for Australia in 2006 used the phrase "Where the Bloody Hell Are You?" View the commercial at: http://www.youtube.com/watch?v=TebeNC-_VjA. Or view the print ad at: www.guardian.co.uk/media/2008/may/08/advertising.marketingandpr. Controversy over their campaign slogan gave Australia more publicity and media coverage than promoters could have afforded to buy.

The "rootedness" of many global brands gives them their power—a strength of identity or character—not matched by many corporate constructs which aspire to become a new generation of global brands. The British consulate general foresees a day when the most important part of foreign policy is image, and when counties protect and promote their images through coordinated

FOCUS ON TOURISM SLOGANS

Revamping Old Taglines

Country	Old ad slogan	New ad slogan
Bangladesh	Exotic Bangladesh	Bangladesh-before the tourists
India	None	Incredible India
Singapore	New Asia	Uniquely Singapore
South Korea	Dynamic Korea	Korea: Something More
Thailand	Happiness on Earth	Amazing Thailand
Uganda	Pearl of Africa	Gifted by Nature
Indonesia	My Indonesia	Ultimate in Diversity

Destination decoding: Not every branding effort is a success. Here are some reviews of country campaign slogans:

- Australia's *Where the bloody hell are you?* gained some free P.R., but not always positive, as it was banned in some countries.

- *I Feel Slovenia* is an awkward slogan that makes this beautiful country with lovely people sound something like "Molvania: A Land Untouched by Modern Dentistry."

- A consumer favorite was Alaska's *B4UDIE*—BEFORE YOU DIE!

- *Chile: All Ways Surprising* is so bad it was changed in 2010.

Exercise: Develop two slogans for your home state and poll ten people to see which they choose.

Source: Wall Street Journal research

branding departments. The editor of the journal *Place Branding* predicted that the days when countries essentially open their own in-house marketing shops are right around the corner. To this end, governments try to achieve some kind of control over their images. They realize that image maintenance isn't just about reeling in tourists.

Branding cities

In a study conducted on city branding, the researcher found that successfully branded cities have the same qualities as strong product brands; they focus on reflecting the city's history, quality of place, lifestyle, culture, and diversity. City branding is proactive and forms cooperative partnerships between city municipalities and government.[vi] Cities in need of a re-branding have confusing, non-distinctive images. Their brands are not identifiable and lack awareness. This study identified a crucial group—the Creative Class. These economically influential people—working in science, engineering, architecture, education, arts, music, and entertainment—can offer a city new ideas, new technology, and new creative content. City brands need to appeal to this group of people.

It is possible for a city to have a brand image that evolves into a "quality of place." This in turn establishes brand loyalty, which is essential to a city's survival. It is also possible for a poorly branded city, with the right strategy, to turn itself into a success. This cannot be done by branding alone, of course, as there are so many economic and social factors at play.

The way brands work for a city is how these qualities are projected: by word-of-mouth, public relations, and in some cases, advertising. These attributes must be based on something substantial. The city must be "livable" and attractive to individuals. Much city branding is based on peoples' experience. Although we have the most technologically advanced ways of reaching people with advertising, most information is still communicated the old fashioned way: by word-of-mouth.

How a population is perceived is an important component of city branding. Take New York: when people think of New York, the normal associations are: cosmopolitan and rich. New York offers inhabitants and visitors everything one could demand of a city: finance, commerce, industry, colleges and universities, historical sites, and an enormous array of cultural as well as economic opportunities.

In order for a city to have a brand, it has to stand for something. San Francisco, named the "City by the Bay," has stood for industry, technology, and culture. The rolling hills of California surrounding the city and an attraction considered one of the world's most famous suspension bridges have been key in San Francisco's tourist economy. Images that have defined San Francisco for the better part of the twentieth century have created a powerful city brand.

FOCUS ON COMMUNICATING PLACE

Marketing the City of Dubai

Until the economic recession hit in 2009, Dubai was one of the fastest growing city-brands that has historically earned its reputation as an international commercial center with an innovative, dynamic and entrepreneurial business culture.

Strategically located at the crossroads of trade and commerce between East and West, Dubai, the city-state is the gateway to access markets spanning the Middle East, North and South Africa, the Indian Subcontinent. Dubai transitioned from a limited oil-resource based economy to an investment-driven economy. Leveraging its strategic location, Dubai developed a world-class infrastructure, air connections and port facilities, making it the best-connected city in the region. According to the GDP, Dubai is a twenty-four billion dollar brand. "Excitement " is the underlying brand personality factor, connoting daring, spirited, and competitive.

Influential brands periodically do a brand assessment and make mid-course corrections with a view to achieve their strategic brand intent. Whether products, services, or cities have two facets, one visible and another invisible and larger facet. The visible facets of a brand are its name, logo, advertising, communications, and so on. The invisible aspects considered as critical would encompass quality, production, R&D, service levels, and so on.

The visible aspects of Brand Dubai have been painstakingly built over the years with an enviable brand image as a trading and shopping hub, clusters built around real estate, and trade and tourism. But because visible aspects are easily duplicated by competing destination brands, the true measure of a brand that endures is often the less visible. These invisible aspects are primarily responsible for a brand's enduring competitive advantage, transforming that brand with an image of esteem and reputation.

Recommendations for improving the invisible aspects of the Dubai brand image are:

1. **Creating Systems, Processes, and Institutions:**

   Although Dubai has world-class infrastructure, it does not have world-class systems, processes and institutions. Very few homegrown private businesses in Dubai could replicate their business model on a global scale.

2. Fortifying the Educational Backbone:

Knowledge Village, an education cluster, was set up to develop Dubai into a destination for education for both regional and international learners. This new education and training hub also Complementing a Free Zone's two clusters, Dubai Internet City and Dubai Media City provide facilities to train the clusters' future knowledge workers. These "teaching shops" must deal with inadequate management bodies before they undermine the emerging educational structure.

3. Streamlining the Labor Market:

Reported instances of default on basic labor practice standards include Many a responsible Nike and Gap, both of which have acknowledged the mistakes of producing low-cost goods in sweatshops and re-invented their supply-chain strategy. To build future Dubai, unskilled and underprivileged workers must be treated with due respect and compensated adequately.

Doing a self-critical brand assessment and making sincere efforts to correct misperceptions are the touch-points of Brand Dubai. As an emerging global city-brand it must also focus on building its critical intangible brand assets and make the world applaud Dubai as an "exciting and caring" city brand.

Promoters of brands entering the Dubai market suggest that communication:

- Avoid religious and cultural sensitivities and wrongful language associations.

- Acknowledge the widely diverse languages, backgrounds, beliefs and age groups in Dubai when developing advertising or PR campaigns.

- Align brands with Dubai-based Louvre and Guggenheim museums that have located there in the Abu Dhabi Media Zone, which has invested heavily in talent and organizations such as the New York Film Academy, Sorbonne, and Formula 1 racing.

What do you think?

1. How and when should Dubai market itself to Western nations?

2. What strategy would you recommend to separate the city from the stigma that Americans attach to the Middle East?

Source: Brandchannel.com articles by Suni Varighese, June 27, 2005 and Ali Sabbagh, March 31, 2008.

An important element of city branding is appearance. What a city actually looks like and the physical characteristics it possesses are extremely important. Cities now are largely defined by location, function, or cultural attainments. Rotterdam, Amsterdam, Barcelona, and San Francisco are known primarily for their harbors. Zurich and New York are famed as banking centers. Boston, Chicago, and Atlanta are places filled with American architecture and history. For example, Boston's appearance reinforces its reputation as an "old" city by American standards. Boston will not allow its historical gems to be bulldozed in order to make room for commercial developers soliciting the highest price. This stability is a positive attribute for Boston, and an advantage for its promoters.

Branding on the Web

Despite the plethora of services under one brand umbrella, formation of a brand identity can be achieved using Internet images to give national destinations a common marketing purpose and direction. Electronic commerce offers great flexibility for tourism suppliers operating in volatile markets. Promotional messages can be changed quickly, and perishable capacity (hotels under repair, natural disasters) can be effectively managed.

The fundamental distribution channel on the travel industry is made up of three important players—principals, intermediaries, and consumers.

- *Principals* provide travel services to end users.

- *Intermediaries* pass on information about the services to consumers and try to influence niche markets to use their channel.

- *Consumers* use their own research using global distribution networks that have replaced global distribution system (GDS) that once offered a closed, dedicated connection of terminals to travel agents. Distribution channels facilitate the multidimensional flow of information and transactions. The Internet has facilitated direct access between supplier and travelers with the need to resort to an intermediary.

A destination's marketing position can be defined and reinforced on the Internet more effectively than traditional brochures, and destination databases can be developed and used for traveler targeting and request fulfillment. Destination databases include BOSS system in Canada, CULLIVER in Ireland, SWISSLINE in Switzerland, and ATLAS in Australia. However, having a Web site in itself is not enough to enjoy continuing success of a tourist destination—there must be a coherent strategy in place to develop, position, and promote the Web presence. Repeat business is only likely to develop if tourists' expectations are met.

PLACE BRAND PROMOTION STRATEGIES

Promoting a destination or place requires some creative ingenuity and partnership development. Specific marketing strategies can extend place brands beyond the traditional media delivery systems. Using destinations as film and fashion locations, special advertising sections, and production partners for television series are three strategies profiled in this section.

Film and fashion locations

Film locations are an excellent way for destinations to gain brand recognition. New Zealand is especially adept at attracting blockbusters to its two islands, and Eastern Europe is currently luring studios with low production costs and historical locations. By hosting film making, countries can enhance the destination's image and capitalize on the exposure enjoyed by hit movies.

13.3 Cappadocia, Turkey, where the first *Star Wars* was filmed.

In 2002, a report commissioned by the New Zealand's Kiwi government found a strong film and TV production industry would be a key to economic prosperity. That year, *The Lord of the Rings* and *Whale Rider* were filmed on location, beginning a solid, profitable and fun year of filming. By establishing a New Zealand Screen Council with a $280,000-a-year operating grant, New Zealand achieved sustainable foreign exchange earnings of $280 million a year in 2008.[vii] To date, more successful films produced on location in New Zealand include *River Queen*, *The World's Fastest Indian*, *King Kong*, and the *Chronicles of Narnia*.

In the U.S., network television series CSI: continued to popularize its show locations: Las Vegas, Miami, and New York in 2010. Those three cities, as well as Los Angeles (NCIS:LA), offer incentives to attract production companies to locate shows in those cities.

Another promotion tactic for branding destinations is using a location as a backdrop for fashion photography shoots. Saks Fifth Avenue set its fall fashion catalog in Morocco, integrating the scenery, native costumes, and people with models in designer gowns. The publication was produced in conjunction with Royal Air Maroc, Almeraie Golf Palace, La Mamounia Hotel, Imperial Morocco Tours, and the Moroccan National Office of Tourism. The partnership showcased the country and several attractions, and the association proved to be mutually beneficial to the retailer and the destination.

Media and product liaisons produce branded entertainment

Another place promotion tactic involves place as a virtual main character in film or television travel features. Kahlua coffee liqueur, for example, launched a branded entertainment television campaign: Kahlua and *Conde Nast Traveler* teamed up to present "Bring Home the Exotic," a television show that delved into the realm of exotic travel and home entertaining experiences. The first product to create, produce, and maintain full ownership of a show, Kahlua presented a five-part series on the Oxygen Network in 2005 with original episodes airing on Saturdays. The audience traveled with a *Conde Nast*

Image 13.4

Branding the City by the Bay

The area first began to develop as a city known as Yerba Buena in 1822 and remained a small town until the Mexican American war in 1846, and was then taken over by a naval force and in the name of the United States was renamed "San Francisco" on January 30th, 1847. The California Gold Rush started in 1848 and led to considerable immigration into San Francisco and the surrounding areas. During this time, San Francisco Bay became one of the world's greatest seaports, dominating shipping and transportation in the American West.

The Chinatown district of the city is still one of the largest and has the largest concentration of Chinese in any single city outside of China. Many businesses started to service the city during this time such as Levi Strauss, Ghirardelli Chocolate, and Wells Fargo bank, and still exist there today. Like many cities, the political situation in early San Francisco was chaotic. Military government was present to clean the city of crime and corruption, and soon San Francisco became the largest city west of the Mississippi River. Completed in 1936, The Golden Gate bridge is the most recognized landmark in San Francisco and declared one of the modern Wonders of the World. Progress and expansion were always priorities to San Francisco, and branding began early in its history.

Attractions

Among the many attractions, the city offers visitors these special places: Golden Gate Bridge, Golden Gate Park, The Presidio, Sausalito, Treasure Island, Alcatraz, Chinatown, Fisherman's Wharf, and many museums, art galleries, restaurants, hotels, architecture, in addition to regional attractions such as Muir Woods, Half Moon Bay, Silicon Valley, Napa Valley, Monterey and Carmel. San Francisco is the fourth-largest city in the state of California.

The creative community of San Francisco evolved in a similar way to the underground movements in Paris and New York, but San Francisco's counter-cultural movement came much later. San Francisco experienced her cultural renaissance in the 1960s as countless groups of nonconformist young people made the town their home, The already liberal city turned exotic as "freaks," hippies, and "ethnics" created a hip cultural renaissance, especially in the Haight-Ashbury district. Street art flourished, color flooded the nation, and the city played a big part in the national cultural renaissance that occurred during this time. The Haight still maintains a bohemian atmosphere and has become a major tourist attraction, and it still manages to attract the homeless and teen runaways. To solve the homeless problem, a "Care Not Cash" plan, was set up, in which welfare checks that homeless people previously received were replaced by vouchers for housing. This is a problem that is real for San Francisco, and will continually need to be addressed, no matter who is in charge of running the city. Also in the 1960s and 1970s large numbers of gay people moved to San Francisco. Today the gay population remains hugely important to the diverse community and the city's economy.

NICKNAME: *The City By the Bay*

Branding efforts

Destinations must be in the marketplace to remind busy consumers that they exist. They have to find new ways to maintain their brand awareness in the consumer population, and that's leading them to think more about promotional possibilities. San Francisco has a lot of branding advantages, but since its dot.com bust and the added economic consequences of September 11th, San Francisco has suffered like many other cities. In June of 2004, the San Francisco Convention and Visitors Bureau launched a new branding campaign developed by Eleven, an integrated brand marketing agency that came up with the tagline "Only in San Francisco" to try to reestablish a new and improved brand identity. The main point was to enhance tourism's economic recovery.

Only in San Francisco do you have people from all over the world that are focused on their common humanity. San Francisco has many brand advantages. It's a place unique from the ground up because of its geography, landmarks, originality, traditions, cultures, tolerance, and diverse inhabitants.

Cities, however, are aiming for attracting more than just visitors. There has been a shift in how cities are thinking about themselves; they're more aware that they have certain assets, and if they're deployed in a strategic fashion instead of waiting for companies to come to them, they stand to benefit more. In this way, it appears that the strategy behind branding a city is being handled in the same way agencies are branding commercial products.

Economics and tourism

Tourism is one of San Francisco's largest industries and the largest employer of city residents. The Pacific Stock Exchange, and many major American and international banks and venture capital firms are located here. Companies headquartered in San Francisco include Anchor Brewing, SEGA, Bechtel, Charels Schwab, CNET, The GAP, Ghirardelli, Levi Strauss & Co., Macromedia, Pacific Gas & Electric, The Sharper Image, Viz Communications, Wells Fargo, and many others. 40–50 miles south of San Francisco lies the famous Silicon Valley, which is home to Apple Computer, Symantec and many other electronic and digital companies.

The city is serviced by several public transit systems including Muni which is the city-owned public transit system and the famous Cable Cars. BART, which stands for Bay Area Rapid Transit, connects San Francisco with the East Bay and San Mateo County communities on the San Francisco Peninsula. In addition, a commuter rail service called Caltrain operates between the city and San Jose and Gilroy, making it fairly appealing and convenient to travel locally as well as regionally.

People: residents and visitors

San Francisco, like New York and Paris, is extremely diverse. There are many different ethnic groups that make up the city and for the most part, visitors encounter friendly residents and locals. The climate tends to be reasonable any time of year, strongly influenced by the cool currents of the Pacific. The air is dry and the weather is remarkably mild, with a so-called Mediterranean-climate. The charm that San Francisco possesses is evident in her attractions as well as her parks, coastline, and unique neighborhoods such as Pacific Heights and Chinatown, where restaurants, homes, streets, and architecture are famous. The history of Alcatraz (the once famous prison turned tourist attraction) attracts people from around the world.

What do you think?

1. Given the unusual "small-town" attractions, climate, people, diversity, history and values that offer many opportunities for branding success, how would you position San Francisco as a brand?

Traveler editor and a selected couple to exotic locations around the world where they explored the terrain, were treated to local foods and beverages, stayed in unique accommodations, met compelling real-life characters and experienced new cultures. Upon returning home, the travelers hosted a themed party during which they recreated their exotic travel experiences for family and friends.

The television show created a platform to promote and communicate Kahlua's ongoing brand strategy, and to engage the target adult audience in a meaningful way that was relevant to their lifestyles. The program was fully integrated with on- and off-premise efforts including a stand-alone insert in *Conde Nast Traveler* to reach 30+ year-old women across the country with a natural connection to travel.

Magazine special advertising sections

Cooperative advertising is not new, but sponsored sections in upscale publications are becoming an economical way to market destinations, transportation, and travel accessories in a single effort. For instance, *the New York Times, Sunday* produces quarterly travel magazines that combine locations with transportation companies, resorts and attractions. Such sponsor-based advertising is common in travel magazines as well as special tourism-based sections in general consumer-based publications. Subscribers, many of whom are doctors and executives, are likely to read the narratives and note the brands because the content is specifically directed at the up-market traveler. And by advertising brand constellations—groups of products and brands clustered around a single experience—sponsors benefit from the image transfer produced by associating with other high-end brands.

PROMOTING TOURISM SERVICES

The services industry is comprised of four major segments: hotels, tour operators, transport operators and attractions, each with its own set of target audiences with specific needs, motivations and spending patterns. *Hotels* target corporate clients, groups on package tours, independent vacationers. and visitors taking weekend package breaks. *Tour operators* target singles and couples 18–30, families with children, retired people, seniors, empty nesters, sports or activity participants, and culture seekers. Many alumni association establish education-based tours as well. *Transport* operators target passengers in first, club and standard classes as well as charter groups. *Attractions* focus on local residents, day visitors from outside local areas, domestic and foreign tourists, and school parties.

Tourism services are affected by seasonal demand patterns. Their high fixed costs of operation and a fixed capacity at a point in time must factor in rent, wages, marketing, equipment, salaries, and so forth. The interdependence of tourism products such as hotels, transportation, catering and recreation also impact the tourism services industry. Because other texts cover hospitality marketing in much greater detail, we limit our focus to successful strategies in segments that provide examples relevant for entertainment marketing. This section overviews hospitality, specifically resort accommodations and their rating systems, cruise ships and their ports, and packaged tours. Attractions are covered in the next chapter.

Promoting accommodations

The hospitality industry is dedicated to providing tourists with motels, hotels, resorts and spas to ground their travel around a pleasant accommodation experience. Global resorts and spas engage in a constant quest for upscale visitors. Accommodations are both serviced and non-serviced. Serviced hotels and resorts have a staff on the premises and target luxury travelers. Non-serviced facilities include furnished units and hostels that focus on the budget market as well as flathotels (furnished flats rented by the week or month), time shares, parks, cottages, and apartments. A five-star rating is a marketer's most visible tool.

While prestigious ratings help lure upscale visitors, top-tier hotels don't need much of a boost from rating services. Amid a resurgence in business travel and a growing corps of leisure travelers who are willing to spend freely on luxury options, room rates at luxury hotels average $250.00 per night. In major cities like New York, San Francisco, Washington, DC, and Chicago where rooms are increasingly filled all week and demand outweighs supply, the priciest hotels often ask for and get upwards of $1000.00 per night.

Fine hotels are ideally suited to succeed in an experiential economy.

Luxury hotels in the top 25 U.S. markets are over 150 in number with several hundred properties worldwide. But as traveler demands change, so does the definition of luxury. To determine luxury standards, travel magazines conduct annual reader polls, and travel guides and reviewers have their best lists and recommendations. Guests surveyed agree that comfort, style, service and pampering are among their expectations in luxury hotels. Most crucial is the degree to which a hotel reflects its surroundings and delivers an experience that evokes the community.

Using PR, in the form of editorial content, is a successful method of promoting both destinations and tourism brands, as shown in Exhibit 13.4 below.

Luxury has gone global; Four Seasons, for example, has 58 hotels and resorts in 27 countries. Premium brands targeting affluent global travelers need an effective sales force to inform and support travel channels, and work with distribution partners in the meeting, incentive and wholesale segments of the travel industry. Marketing luxury hotels involves effective PR, image

EXHIBIT 13.4 Advertising Editorial Sections and Sponsors

ARTICLE TITLE/TOPIC	SPONSOR/ADVERTISER
"What to know before you go"	Malarone pharmaceuticals
"Family Matters"	Embassy Suite Hotels
"Going with the Flow"	Tumi luggage
"La Dolce Getaway"	Silversea Cruises
"New Season on the Isles"	Brand Britain
"It's Like a Whole Other Country"	Travel Texas
"The Caribbean's Dutch Treat"	Curaccao Tourism
"Natural Wonders"	Brand Colorado

FOCUS ON CAREERS

Profile of a Travel Planner

For the past ten years, Bridget Marnane has been the Director of Incentive Travel Planning for WORLD CLASS Travel by Invitation, a San Diego-based incentive travel company. The incentive travel business serves corporations that reward their top performing employees or best clients with trips developed specially for them. We also help plan and direct trips for corporate meetings. Working within their budgets, we locate places, plan activities and produce an ultimate experience for travel groups. To become knowledgeable about places to stay, we are guests of resorts, cruise ships and five-star hotels that all vie for our group bookings.

After graduating with a B.A in Business with an emphasis in Marketing from the University of San Diego, Bridget worked as bank loan processor and new accounts supervisor before assuming her current job. She was personally introduced to company president Nikki Nestor at a party, and followed up with a phone call to schedule an interview. "She was looking for a person with marketing skills, and hired me on the spot."

Bridget has a variety of responsibilities, which include: negotiating with hotels and other travel service suppliers, preparing budgets and creating proposals for new and continuing clients. She attends educational seminars several times a year, and conducts site inspections in locations where clients will travel. She also prepares contracts, organizes details of the incentive programs, and ultimately travels with the groups as trip director.

"My favorite part of the job is traveling with the groups. It is most rewarding to see the incentive program come to fruition and to witness the excitement of the guests as they experience all that we have been planning for 12–18 months." The job's only downside, according to Bridget, is preparing the final accounting after programs are completed. "It's often a very long and tedious process."

In her words..............

Just part of the job

"Last year, Prince Ranier of Monaco died while our group was in the air on their way to an incentive program in Monte Carlo, Monaco. The small principality was in a state of mourning, which included a moratorium on all entertainment and other forms of revelry in public areas. Within 24 hours, the on-site staff changed venues for two of the major events and greatly revised a third event. The gala evening, specifically, required many modifications, which included moving the event from the Grand Casino in Monaco to a Palace in Nice, adding transportation for almost 300 guests (as the original venue was within walking distance of the hotel), moving and adding entertainment at the new venue and modifying the décor to fit a different room size. It ended up being a very successful trip and many of the guests didn't even realize that the program had been changed because the revised itinerary ran so smoothly."

Advice for newcomers...

When you first enter a new industry or company, it is helpful to locate someone whose success and work ethic you admire. Ask this person to act as your mentor; over the next few months, watch and learn from this person. Learning "on the job" is the best way to become adept at your chosen profession, but it also helps to learn from others' accomplishments and failures, especially if they hold the position you eventually hope to assume yourself!

Reprinted with permission of Bridget Marname.

advertising and branding. Magazine and newspaper editorials function as effective sources of information for luxury travelers. Image advertising can raise awareness levels and enhance a resort's reputation that result in an ability to generate premium pricing.

The spa market

Even in an economic downturn, physical well being is important to consumers. As of June 2008, there were 18,100 spas in the U.S., an increase of 24% over the previous year. In 2008, $10.9 billion of revenue was generated by the U.S. spa industry staffed by 143,200 full-time and 112,000 part-time, and 48,500 contract employees.[viii]

Four types of spas predominate: club spas, day spas, resort and hotel spas, and other spas. According to PricewaterhouseCoopers, the average profit margin for all types is 17.3%, with the highest profits coming from day spas.[ix] The International Spa Association reported industry revenues increasing at 75% per year since 2000. Hotels and resorts met increased demand by providing dedicated facilities for guests and day visitors. Cruise ships and hotel chains added independently run spas or partnering up with established spa brands to attract guests who want both luxury accommodations and personal pampering. Growth in resort spa will be in square footage allocation and the number of qualified operators employed. In 2008, around 300,000 people were employed by spas across the United States.

Despite the fast growth, the spa industry remains surprisingly fragmented—the approximately 5,700 spas in the U.S. are operated by roughly 5,000 different organizations. Currently, two companies are poised as potential front-runners to become chain spas: Steiner Leisure of Nassau, Bahamas, and Miami-based Elizabeth Arden. Hotels continue to be a major destination for spas because hotels can finance spas and vacationers usually don't bat an eye at the spa's costly treatments. Many hotel spas are also open to the general public to attract a wider clientele. Some hotel chains, such as the Mandarin Oriental, are known equally well for their spas as their rooms.

Fairmont, whose Willow Stream spas are located within its hotels, spent around $20 million on six spas in Scottsdale, Arizona, Bermuda, and Mexico, among other locations, and has plans to add nine more in the future. A top priority was to lure more men to the spas, since 50% of the hotel guests are men, so one part of the budget went to pay a cultural anthropologist who quizzed men and women about their bathing habits and least/most favorite body parts. The anthropologist learned that men feel uncomfortable parading around in bathrobes, so Willow Stream issued men boxer shorts in a program dubbed "Keep your shorts on."

According to the founder of Canyon Ranch, the intention of their spas is to provide inspiration, guidance, education, and support to further the achievement of healthier living.[x] Rather than selling simply vacations, spas promote a direct, emotional connection experience

TRENDS FOR SPA PROMOTIONAL CONSIDERATION

International Spa Association has pinpointed the following spa trends for 2010 that have an impact how they might be promoted:

Use Social Media—spas to offer up-to-the-minute deals by tweeting or posting a Facebook message. Ad-Ology research shows that 57% of 18 to 24 year olds and 48.5% of 25 to 34 year-olds say social media influenced their choice of a hair salon or day spa.

Provide Customer Service—87% of ISPA member spas utilize customer feedback mechanisms to ensure they're exceeding consumers' needs. Also, 48% of ISPA member spas have implemented customer loyalty programs, allowing them to offer discounts or rewards while incentivizing frequent visits to the spa.

Offer a Spa Sampler Menu—Mini services offered at lower price points are popular ways consumers get a taste of treatments. Forty-six percent of spas see an increase in shorter (30 minutes or less) treatment bookings, and 86% offer shorter treatments.

Advocate Preventive Care—Spa treatments like massage, acupuncture and meditation have been proven to aid in stress reduction and recovery time for pre- and post-op patients.

Form Spa Partnerships—Partnerships with established franchises, hotels and local businesses benefit spas. Recent pairings like Murad Inc. and Massage Envy will allow consumers to enjoy the benefits of a total spa experience for an affordable price. Forty-six percent of day spa members partner with local businesses to incorporate spas into their workplaces. Popular partnerships include: developing wellness programs at local hospitals, accommodating guests at local hotels without spa facilities and service discount trades between spas and local business employees.

Develop Cell Phone Applications—"Spa-ing" is easier than ever with the convenience of doing it from a cell phone. The Four Seasons' app allows visitors to browse spa services and check room availability for their next stay. The Hot Springs and Spa Finder—California app guide consumers to road-side soaks, spiritual retreats, and commercial spas. Plan a spa vacation from anywhere with Tripology's app. The Find a Spa app displays search results for spas in your location proximity.

Use Philanthropy—Spas are offering promotions and free services to people who serve the community such as teachers, hospice workers, and military personnel. Community outreach is a great way to generate business and show how easy it is to incorporate spa into your life.

Market to Millennials—This group, now outnumbering baby boomers, is being lured to spas through social media outlets. Born during the exercise craze of the 1980s, they were the first generation to watch their parents indulge and they have now embraced the experience themselves in large numbers.

Offer Simplified Spa Menus—No-frills treatments that offer a return on investment are what consumers are demanding.

Source: experienceispa.com

devoted entirely to self-pampering. In the quest for a sense of control and authentic experiences, Boomer consumers seek the sanctuary and camaraderie provided by the spa vacation community. Fitness facilities, healthy dining establishments, spa services and treatments, and lifestyle boutiques are necessary components for successful experience delivery.

Whether tied to an established hotel brand or positioned as a spa brand, spa promotion strategy is intricately associated with developing feature articles for travel and lifestyle magazines and providing video segments for broadcast on travel and entertainment channels. Listed below are the ten top spas in America according readers of *Travel & Leisure* and *Spa Magazine*.

Kids market segment

Hoping to lure the littlest guests and their families, old-line resorts are adding million-dollar kids' centers and golf clinics for toddlers. Once resorts had super-sized their spas, they began wooing guests in a new way—with million-dollar child entertainment programs that promise adults time off on family vacations. Going way beyond kiddie pools and teen clubs, resorts offer everything from manicures for 2-year-olds to hour-long Spanish classes for kids barely old enough to read.

To attract upscale families, the Kerzner International destination resorts spent over $1 million on its KidsOnly program in Los Cabos, Mexico for golf clinics for 4-year-olds and pool-sized sandboxes. With family travel up 8% a year, travel research firms set out to discover family vacations without theme parks or characters from Sesame Street. Their investigation of 12-resort property's kid programs yielded some interesting marketing tactics.

The Ritz-Carlton in Puerto Rico was popular with kids for their free poolside hair braiding; kids at the Greenbrier in West Virginia liked bowling and air-hockey. Nemacolin Woodlands Resort took kids for Hummer rides; La Quinta Palm Spring Resort's kid visitors loved the strawberries that replaced fries in their dinners; Palm Beach Breakers challenged its kids with an

America's Top Spas in 2010

1. Canyon Ranch, Tucson, AZ

2. Golden Door, Escondido, CA

3. Oaks at Ojai, Ojai CA

4. Mii amo at Enchantment, Sedona AZ

5. The Greenhouse Spa, Arlington, TX

6. Red Mountain Spa, Ivins, Utah

7. Lake Austin Spa Resort, Austin, TX

8. Westglow Resort Spa, Blowing Ridge, NC

9. Cal-a-Vie, Vista, CA

10. Green Valley Spa, St. George, UT

outdoor maze; and the Hyatt Regency Kauai manage their kids' clubs on the point system to the delight of vacationing parents.[xi]

Club Med traditionally is a good bet for their kids programs with age-appropriate activities—kite flying for young kids, horseback riding, and martial arts for older ones. And for the whole family? Meringue lessons, of course. Resort marketing, like any innovative branding program, addresses the needs and wants of its most sought-after consumers.

Promoting timeshares

In the 1990s, Marriott and other resort property companies developed time-shares, an economic boon for most hoteliers. By selling a week's stay at the resort, marketers get up-front cash to build alliances with global properties so their members can stay during their prescribed week. Scheduling vacation time around time-share availability and encountering unsatisfactory lodging diminished sales, however. The business became so complicated that memberships dropped, and the only activity was in re-sales.

Today's time-shares have been re-branded as destination clubs that are sold by private organizations to give members unlimited access to A-list vacation retreats around the world in exchange for club dues. These clubs deliver the kind of luxury home-away-from-home amenities that are similar to what is offered with luxury hotels without the hassles. They are popular because the downsides of time-shares (like scheduling conflicts) and vacation home maintenance and mortgages don't enter the experience.

With a limited member-to-property ratio, the clubs allow year-long access to residences for New York shopping, Outer Banks golf, and Colorado skiing. One-time membership deposits tend to rival the costs of a vacation home, but they offer those with wanderlust the perfect travel option. Depending on membership level, Private Escapes Destination Club charges from $85,000 to $190,000; Abercrombie & Kent Destination Club fees start at $250,000 and Exclusive Resorts charge $375,000 to join. In addition, annual dues range from about $7,000 to $25,000.[xii] Destination clubs advertise and plant feature articles in *Lexus Magazine*, *Robb Report*, and *Executive Golfer*. It seems there is no shortage of luxury travelers willing to cash in their vacation real estate, preferring to live on their money rather than in it.

Equity sharing, where millionaires buy into a private community that offers exclusive accommodation and activity privileges around the world, have decreased in the recent economic downturn. Properties such as the Yellowstone Club in Big Sky, Montana, have succumbed to takeovers, fraud and bankruptcy.

Internet hotel and resort rating systems[xiii]

In spite of their inconsistencies, ratings are significant marketing tools. Entities such as the Forbes Travel Guide's 2010 lists its 53 five-star properties in destinations throughout North America, ten of which are in California. These award-winners are selected annually using rankings that are derived from property inspectors who pose as guests. Inspectors might call housekeeping to ask for extra toothbrushes, request a last-minute dry cleaning, or order room service and see if the bottled water is opened and poured by the staff.

In down times, three-star hotels depend on tactical marketing promotional efforts to secure marginal sales. The most effective are: short-term price discounts, partnership deals, retail incentives, deep price discounts for tour operators, sales force, advertising, Internet deals, and loyalty program bonuses.

Some properties market themselves as five star resorts to attract luxury travelers. Rating systems, which used to be quantitatively ranked only by the *Mobil Travel Guides*, AAA, or Michelin internationally, have been replaced by individual hotel booking Web sites that have their own star (or diamond) rating systems. The same property can be assigned a different number of stars by each rating service, making star-based positioning a tenuous strategy.

There really is no Internet standard for hotel rating systems, but several sites are trying to bring some standardization between the rating systems currently used by each hotel booking vendor. Also, because of the lack of authority and standardization in hotel ratings systems, it really helps to know how liberal or conservative a particular rating service tends to be.

Most tourists either book or shop for destination accommodations on line. Below is a sampling of *four-star hotel ranking criteria* used by the leading Internet travel sites:

- **Expedia**: First-class accommodations with an emphasis on hospitality and premium customer service. Highly reliable hotels offering a fine-dining restaurant, a range of amenities, and facilities for the sophisticated traveler; also appropriate for the business traveler.

- **Travelocity**: These superior properties distinguish themselves with a high level of service and hospitality, as well as a wide variety of amenities and upscale facilities. A well-integrated design, stylized room décor, excellent restaurant facilities, and landscaped grounds are all present. The comfort and convenience of the guest is the staff's prevailing concern.

- **Orbitz**: Deluxe/upscale hotels: Find comfort, class and quality that you can count on. These hotels will usually be in a prime location and other amenities may include: proximity to desirable shopping areas and restaurants, valet parking, concierge service, room service, well-equipped fitness centers and state-of-the-art business centers. These properties may be newly constructed or recently renovated, and offer tasteful decor in each room or suite.

- **AAA**: These establishments are upscale in all areas. Accommodations are progressively more refined and stylish. The physical attributes reflect an obvious enhanced level of quality throughout. The fundamental hallmarks at this level include an extensive array of amenities combined with a high degree of hospitality, service, and attention to detail.

- **Priceline**: Four-star hotels will have the following amenities: Remote Control TV with Premium Channels, Telephone with Voicemail, Radio Alarm Clock, Iron and Ironing Board, Hairdryer, Business Services, 24-Hour Front Desk, Restaurant Room Service, Bellman, Concierge, Fitness Center Access. Four-star hotel examples include Hyatt Regency, Hilton, Sheraton, Marriott, and Swissotel.

- **Hotels.com**: Mostly large, formal hotels with smart reception areas, front desk service, and bellhop service. The hotels are most often located near other hotels of the same caliber and are usually found near shopping, dining, and other major attractions. The level of service is well above average and the rooms are well lit and well furnished. Restaurant dining is usually available and may include more than one choice. Some properties will offer continental breakfast and/or happy hour delicacies. Room service is usually available during most hours. Valet parking and/or garage service is also usually available. Concierge services, fitness centers, and one or more pools are often provided. Typical National Chains include Hyatt and Marriott.

- **Hotwire**: These hotels are known for their attention to detail. Rooms are well-adorned with high-quality linens and furnishings. Upscale hotels are usually newly constructed properties or recently renovated, providing guests with the ultimate in updated facilities. Other amenities may include room service, concierge services, valet parking, and fitness centers. These hotels are usually located near popular shopping, fine restaurants and major attractions. Examples include Wyndham, Hilton, and Westin.

To make matters even more confusing, many hotel Web sites use star ratings from someone else. For example, Travelocity.com uses AAA and Travelweb.com often uses the ratings from one of its owners, Priceline.com. Sidestep.com, actually displays the star rating from the Web site where it will eventually send you to book the hotel. So, what's a resort marketer to do? You need to position the property on other qualities not part of the Web booking system criteria to differentiate the property from the competition.

The transport industry

Getting tourists to their destinations include transport industries of airlines, railroads, buses, and cruise ships. Each industry has special considerations for marketing and focuses on efforts to position themselves among a group of competitors that provide the same basic service—transportation. This section concentrates on the fastest growing mode of transportation of the North American travel industry for the past 30 years—the cruise industry. Consolidation has resulted in just ten brands that control over 90% of the market.

Cruise ships and cruise markets

By combining the amenities of a hotel with the adventure of travel, cruising tries to offer a better vacation choice. As competition for the cruise vacation market intensified, cruise lines took advantage of scale economies to build larger ships with more bells and whistles, and the distinction between mass-market and premium lines began to blur. Brands compete for the family market, ethnic markets, and singles—a far cry from its narrow heritage of luxury older adult travelers.

According to some industry experts,[xiv] the marketing focus for the cruise industry should be on attracting non-cruisers who are currently vacationing on land. This

© James Steidl, 2010. Used under license from Shutterstock, Inc.

13.5 Cruise ships have been plagued with on-board illness and accidents that have weakened bookings.

industry has identified their primary marketing goal: increasing trial among first-time users. Carnival Cruises' development of a first-timer base leads the industry with a 50% new-cruiser ratio to repeat travelers. Converting customers from land competitors such as resorts and spas yields a larger market than other lines in the luxury segment. Ad agencies help to refresh Carnival's "fun" brand image to break through the clutter of other cruise liners seeking first timers.

Also important are the repeat cruisers that make up 60% of the industry-wide passengers. Most premium and luxury cruise brands don't even track first-time cruisers, concentrating instead on first time-to-brand cruisers. Dedicating annual budgets to ongoing personnel training, investments in quality food, and service and entertainment upgrades will allow cruise companies to meet the expectations of their repeat customers. Addressing how guests are treated onboard and once they return home is a natural extension of the brand promise for Celebrity Cruises marketing strategy. Loyalty marketing programs seek to create brand loyal consumers through outreach initiatives and special offers to encourage repeat visits.

Cruise *homeport packaging* is another important strategy for this industry. Travelers prefer spending three hours or less getting to their destination. More choices of ports of embarkation make it easier for prospects and past guests to enjoy cruising, so lines constantly work to add new ports to their destination roster. Pricing, distribution, and promotional strategies are also key to reaching both new and repeat cruisers.

Bottom-line, aggressive pricing coupled with product improvements makes cruising an accessible consumer vacation opportunity that is easily booked through Internet travel agents like Expedia, Travelocity, and Orbitz. The development of outbound telemarketing and other direct initiatives enable lines to pursue qualified leads. The core demographic of adults 25–54 has grown to include Boomers who are reached through broadcast advertising on network and cable TV, spot TV, and radio; brand and tactical print advertising in consumer magazines and newspapers; and direct response mailings. Using infomercials as part of the media mix also facilitates direct response initiatives and helps cruise marketers drill down to prospects who are interested in cruising.

Holland-America focuses exclusively on the 50+ market, which is expected to grow to more than 106 million by 2015 when they will account for 45% of the adult population with a spending power of $1.6 trillion.[xv] According to census data, this market is the most affluent of any age segment; they spend more per capita on travel and leisure than any other age group. They travel more frequently and stay longer, making them ideal targets for cruise liners. Seniors who refuse adult living communities can purchase condo-type staterooms on some cruise ship lines, guaranteeing them a constant source of revenue from these passengers-in-residence.

Co-branding is the strategy of Cunard's Queen Mary 2; they paired with exclusive Canyon Ranch resort and Chanel brands to communicate high quality and a distinct brand image. Other luxury brands featured on their lines are a Veuve Cliquot champagne bar for celebrating, Waterford crystal and Wedgwood china for dining, Microsoft X-Boxes for play, and Simmons private label mattresses covered with Frette linens for rest. Co-branding is always a successful brand positioning strategy for attracting luxury travelers.

New ships and new ports keep the cruise business alive. In 2006, six big new ships hit the waters. Royal Caribbean's Freedom of the Seas 3,634-passenger ship supplanted the Queen Mary 2 as the largest ocean liner in the world. Equipped with the FlowRider surf park that is a cross between a resistance swimming pool and Class V rapids, Freedom also offers fitness amenities including a full-size boxing ring and a studio with eight Pilates machines. Another large launch was Princess Cruise's Crown Princess, which has mini-suites and interconnecting family suites that sleep up to eight people. And although the Mediterranean is the largest cruise draw, the Middle East has become an increasingly popular destination for cruise passengers; Dubai remains hot, and Libya has emerged as a destination. Ports in the Baltic, Northern Africa, and Black Sea are on itineraries as lines roll out shorter cruises. For the first time, Orient Lines' 826 passenger Marco Polo sailed around Iceland with stops in five ports.[xvi]

Packaging niche cruises

Travelers who seek a cruise experience but want to avoid conventional cruise vacations select a niche cruise lines. Ships operated by niche lines are smaller, offer a more intimate cruise experience and concentrate on hands-on ports of call experiences. Marketed by positioning themselves differently than the competition, these lines offer a variety of experience levels and trip durations. Some of the most uniquely positioned are mentioned here.[xvii]

- *American Cruise Lines* offers voyages that travel along the inland waterways through the US, combined with an historical slant. The three-ship fleet offers cruises from Maine to Florida with nine unique itineraries for 7–13 day trips.

- The *American West Steamboat Company* has authentic sternwheeler ships offering a unique cruise experience o the Snake and Willamette Rivers in Oregon and Washington. Open-seating meals and casual ambiance are marketed to budget travelers.

- *Cruise West* provides close-up travel that focuses on the destination with personalized touches on itineraries covering Alaska, Costa Rica, Panama Canal, Baja Mexico, California's wine country, and the Columbia and Snake Rivers.

- *Galapagos Explorer* is a private organization dedicated to promoting Ecuador as a destination for tourism. Offering an ecological theme, the ship is equipped with a special sewage treatment system that minimizes environmental disturbance. During a seven-night cruise, visitors see ten islands as they enjoy exceptional service amenities.

- *Glacier Bay Cruises* has three adventure class small ships called sport utility vessels. The company offers three levels of adventures: low impact for viewing wildlife, high level offering hikes, kayaking and island exploration, and a medium level that combine categories.

- *RiverBarge Excursions* offers a hotel barge experience that travels through America's rivers and inland waterways. They specialize in 4–10 day adventures to places off the beaten path with all-inclusive pricing.

- *Star Clipper* offers yacht-like experiences on tall ships. Clippers take guests to the Far East, Caribbean, and Mediterranean. International cuisine, pampered comfort, and lack of rigid schedule are part of the ambiance marketed to upscale tourists.

Luring cruise ships to a destination brand port

The expanding cruise market often uses a *home-port growth* strategy. As cruising continues to grow in popularity, portage becomes a high yield market for many coastal cities. Canadian coastal cities are embarking on campaigns to lure cruise ships to their ports.[xviii]

The Northern Territory, Australia, refreshed its tourism brand by focusing on marketing and development of cruise shipping. The new brand was launched in March 2005, completing six months of intensive market and consumer research supported by a government committee. The research identified the Northern Territory's target market as "Spirited Travelers" and developed an alignment between the needs of potential domestic and international travelers.

Based on the opportunity for greater alignment for positioning the Northern Territory in key markets, a marketing communications strategy was designed to identify how best to reach and communicate with Spirited Travelers. The process included developing a suite of new visual and verbal tools and a campaign program. The strategy and core positioning of the destination is encapsulated in the Northern Territory's new tagline—*Share Our Story*. The successful development of the brand has resulted in the Northern Territory's use of a common platform for its domestic and international market positioning and associated marketing programs.

Not unlike cities who market to manufacturers and corporations, coastal cities lure prospective cruise lines by promoting benefits for their employees (schools, real estate, public transportation) and economic development.

Promoting packaged tours

The tour operator industry is far more fragmented than the cruise industry, but far less so than the hotel and resort industry. The dynamic packaging capability of online travel agencies presents a serious risk to tour operators without a niche product or differentiation. Consumers are willing to pay more for a known brand associated with expertise in destination or quality. Like cruise lines, the tour industry is focusing on the Boomer generation to grow sales.

All-inclusive and escorted tours have grown in popularity because of their ability to serve niche markets, and their no-hassle approach to travel. Tours are either standardized or all-inclusive. *Standardized packages* are manufactured by contractors who provide separate parts of a total tour, which include these basic elements:

+ Price guarantees

+ Convenience

+ Accessibility to consumers

+ Image and branding in brochures

+ High standards and a sense of security

All-inclusive tours provide two or more service elements in these configurations:

+ Transportation and accommodations packaged well in advance of delivery

+ Accommodations with transport optional; hotels and visitor attractions are marketed together

+ Hybrid or modular packages put together on short notice

Tour programs are retained on a central database and delivered to travelers in printed, glossy brochures or over the Internet. Providers receive bulk-rate airline fares. Tour packages, sold through computerized reservation systems, are developed to match competitor programs and maintain market share. Packagers must respond to the level of traveler sophistication, needs, and motivations.

Tours are subject to uncontrollable factors in the external environment that affect their ability to deliver the promised package. Economic events (exchange rates), political events, natural disasters, technology, and sustainable development requirements all affect the tourism industry and necessitate adaptation. Tactical tour promotions in economic downtimes include: discounting, increased advertising, and consumer promotions including competitions, kids go free, and booking date discounts.

One of the biggest growth trends in the touring industry is experience-based travel where tourists interact with environments. With special interest tours like car racing packages, for instance, participants are often so devoted to the theme that business is guaranteed through stable economic times as well as turbulent ones. From history-based travel packages that include elements of architecture and arts to the merging of ocean cruise vacations with extended on-land hiking adventures, anything goes in today's packaged tour industry.

Big-ticket travels

Some high-cost travel agencies and concierge services pitch one-of-a-kind travel experiences, generally for members who have already paid initiation fees or annual dues. For a real marketing challenge, try developing a travel brochure for these three adventures.

+ *After-hours at the Guggenheim Museum* in Venice offers a private tour and access to the museum after closing, plus sunset champagne and hors d'oeuvres on the roof with the museum director. Cost: Part of a $200,000 two-week trip for a family of four (excluding airfare).

+ *Astronaut training in Moscow* takes travelers to the Yuri Gagarin Cosmonaut Training Center where they don space suits and use flight simulations. The trip also includes dog sledding in Sweden and racecar driving in France. Cost: Part of a $75,000 two-week European excursion.

+ *Four-day cruise on a private yacht* includes a cruise along the French Riviera and dinner for fifty in San Tropez prepared by a celebrity chef. Cost: $1 million for the trip, including air transport and cruise for 50 of your closest friends.

Eco-tourism and sustainable development

Eco-tourism is an industry that hosts visitors for the purposes of education and natural encounters with the environment. Economic benefits of eco-tourism include providing jobs for local residents and securing governmental funds for protecting natural areas. Environmental education and heritage preservation of parks, beaches, and underwater trails are among the industry's benefits for tourists and host regions.

Eco-tours are marketed to appeal to people who want to go beyond collecting souvenirs and markers. Watching whales in Alaska, snorkeling coral reefs in Belize, and photographing seals in the Galapagos Islands are a few of the options from which eco-travelers may choose.

Eco-tourism has helped to reposition the South African tourism brand to reap dividends for local business, residents, and the environment. The process was a cooperative approach between government and private eco-lodges. Kruger game reserve granted concessions to private game lodge owners who wanted to attract serious eco-tourists with deep pockets seeking five-star luxury and personalized service, South African tourism had identified four main brand audiences: luxury, backpacker and party crowd, business entertainment, and a family travel segment. To educate partners and interest local businesses in joining the branding effort, a sales team attended trade shows and workshops to set up one-on-one meetings. South African promotion efforts included print advertising, journalist visits, and consistency in communication materials to help create a strong and stable brand in the marketplace.

One of South Africa's flagship lodges, Singita (voted by *Conde Nast* readers as the best hotel in the world), is a perfect example of a successful eco-brand. Tourists pay top dollar for an all-inclusive experience: professional game drives in luxury vehicles, gourmet meals, and opulent accommodation. Singita was careful to build brand value by providing excellence in all areas of the facility. The lodge promoted its brand by selecting the Born Free Foundation as a strategic alliance partner, and by keeping their name in the paper with aggressive public relations and conservation activities.[xix]

Sustainable development is a philosophy invoked to maintain a healthy balance between visitors and resources. Keeping global environments healthy for future travelers is the aim of sustainable tourism. Responsible entities are host communities, tourism firms and tourists themselves. Every destination's host community is responsible for defining its philosophy and vision for tourism, and for establishing the social, physical, and cultural carrying capacity for the region. In other words they ask crucial questions such as: How many tourists can be accommodated before they out-number hotels and exhaust resources? What is a healthy balance of residents and visitors to insure the comfort and safety of both? Tourism firms must observe regulations set by regions and NTOs, as well as guidelines and practices established by each destination. Tourists need to accept responsibility for self-education about the customs and culture of regions before they visit. Responsible marketers work in conjunction with destination efforts toward promoting sustainability.

Finally

As the world's largest employer, tourism is an industry that deserves attention from experience marketers. Two aspects of the travel business involve marketing destinations and tourist services.

Both functions demand attention to anticipating travelers' needs and motivations, and to maintaining positive consumer perceptions of a place or destination.

In the coming decade, marketing will become the primary driving force to motivate people to change their travel behavior. Just as lifestyles have changed, travel marketers must recognize behavior changes and adjust their product and strategy to accommodate a consumer who has defined leisure time. Research will continue to be an important marketing tool to identify trends for formulating product development and marketing new programs. To embrace the value equation, travel marketers who can save consumers time and energy while customizing an experience will increase repeat business. With insight into tourist attitudes and behavior, effective marketing communication will lay the foundation for future success.

GOT IT?

Chapter 13 made these distinctive points:

- The travel cycle involves leaving home, traveling by transport to a destination, collecting trip markers, returning home and recalling travel through souvenirs.

- Tourist market segments include adventurers, the budget-minded, families, gay travelers, luxury travelers, boomers, and eco-tourists.

- Destination branding is accomplished with unique positioning, building the brand through constant market research, and identity development; marketing challenges include establishing actionable and measurable objectives, unifying marketing efforts and lack of authority and control over marketing input.

- Countries are branded through the strength of their national identity; cities need specific economic, social and climate-based conditions to be attractive destination for both workers and visitors; once identity is established and built, it must be maintained through active research and campaign adaptation.

- Promotion strategies for destinations include using them as film and fashion shoot locations, special advertising sections, and production partners for television series.

- Rating services are inconsistent and vary by Internet booking provider; nonetheless, they are an important function of the place marketing process.

- Packaged, all-inclusive tours and cruise ships provide marketers with guaranteed, reliable products for travelers.

NOW TRY THIS

1. Go online and find out what measures national parks take to insure sustainability. From your investigation, how might parks better control access and use during peak seasons? How should parks promote themselves without impacting the environmental limitations of the park?

2. Select a resort you would like to visit. Check the ratings of that resort from four of the Internet sites listed in this chapter. What did you learn from the ratings? How likely would you be to base your decision on the ratings provided?

3. Take a look at Spain's tourism Web sites. How does this umbrella brand present specific regions to visitors? What collaboration is needed for a unified presentation of the country's various cities? Does the site provide links to specific locations? What recommendations can you make to improve Spain's destination image?

4. Inventory the items you collected from your last trip. How many of the categories discussed in this chapter are included in your collection? How did you use these items to recollect your trip? From this exercise, describe the role souvenirs for providing a memorable experience.

QUESTIONS FOR DISCUSSION AND REVIEW

1. A travel agency's market area has a good potential to sell more eco-tours. How should she proceed to identify prospective buyers for these tours?

2. Describe the various resources available to a destination marketer to brand a place. What is the ideal combination of inputs and financial support to provide a successful marketing effort?

3. What is the image of Brand America? What aspects of the US contribute to the global audiences perception of the country? How can the US brand be redefined to improve its image?

4. For each travel segment outlined in Exhibit 13.1, suggest a destination to match their needs and craft a promotional message that will attract their attention to that destination.

5. Explain the similarities and differences between place marketing and tourist services marketing. What role do the 4Ps play in presenting travel places and services?

MORE STUFF ABOUT MARKETING DESTINATIONS AND ATTRACTIONS

www.centram.org—Center for Travel Marketing, online courses.

www.travelmarketingblog.com—industry newsletter.

www.tia.org/researchpubs—Travel Industry Association, market research.

www.world-tourism.org—provides statistics on tourism arrivals, departures, etc.

www.unwto.org—information on global policies for tourism.

Bob Dichenson & Andy Vladimir (2004), *The Complete Travel & Hospitality Marketing Handbook*. Pearson Prentice Hall.

R. K. Dowling (Ed.) (2006), *Cruise Ship Tourism*. Edith Cowan University, Australia.

CAMPAIGN CASE STUDY

Incredible India

Problem: India was having difficulty bringing in high-net-worth tourists into the country.

Campaign Objective: To develop a positive and memorable brand image for India.

Situation Analysis: India had been a place where many backpackers came. However, there was no interest from rich travelers. Research showed that upper class travelers knew little about India beyond being a place of elephants and the Taj Mahal. With almost thirty different languages, many different cultures and different looking people, India as a destination never had a brand name. Singapore had Uniquely Singapore, Malaysia had Truly Asia. India needed a distinct and unique brand. At a time when alternative medicine, Yoga and Ayurveda were gaining importance across the globe, India needed to consciously promote spirituality in its campaign.

Research told campaign developers that travelers thought the Western world, because of weather and architecture factors, had grey as a predominant color, and that travelers viewed India as full of color. India was always referred to as brighter and more vibrant than other countries; magenta, reds and dark blues defined India.

SWOT Analysis:

- Strength: Diversity in culture and geography

- Weakness: Lack of appeal from high-end North American travelers

- Opportunity: Position India as a desirable destination

- Competition from other Asian tourist locations

Target Audience: Upscale travelers from North America.

Strategy: Use media and technology to project India as a place for physical and mental rejuvenation, cultural enrichment, spiritual evaluation and a modern infrastructure with a positive brand. Use colors as the theme to ground the entire campaign idea.

Tactic 1: Use traditional television and print media to promote India as a destination by packaging India as an experience of the soul.

Tactic 2: Use online blogs and a well-designed web site to convey colors that would enable India to stand out on computer screens and in video-streamed television commercials.

Results: The Incredible India campaign was produced to invoke a colorful street and folk art of India theme revolving around curing twenty-first-century stress. The idea highlighted what was unique to India, put it in an Indian context.

The campaign increased the Indian share in tourism market from three percent to four percent, and it increased the spending to the second highest level in the world, after U.S. So while American tourist's average spending was about thirteen hundred dollars, travelers to India spent about twelve hundred dollars. The website saw sharp increase—200% per year—in terms of traffic. What started out in 2002 with four hundred destinations was eventually scaled to almost a thousand six hundred destinations in 2009. And high-end tourists began out-numbering the backpackers. The Incredible India campaign went on to win twice in one year: the gold for destination campaign of the year at PARTA (the global travel agent association) and the top prize for a Euro Effi.

Sources: Naresh Gupta, Grey Advertising and Sudhir Nair, G2 Interactive, both in South Asia

Question for discussion: As an account manager, how would you target tourists from outside North America? What kind of research would be needed to determine their travel motivations?

[i]Joseph Chen (2003), "Market Segmentation by Tourists' Sentiments," *Annals of Tourism Research* 30 (1), 178–193.

[ii]By Fiona Gilmore (2002), "Branding for Success" in *Destination Branding*, pp. 58–65.

[iii]Randall Frost (2004), "Mapping a Country," brandchannel.com, April 19.

[iv]Ellen Stein for *VLIFE*, Oct. 2005, p. 38.

[v]Bruce Stanley's Advertising column in the Wall Street Journal, March 10, 2006.

[vi]Study conducted by Julia Winfield-Pfefferkorn; downloaded from brandchannel.com, Jan. 2, 2005.

[vii]By Michaela Boland for *Variety*, Nov. 13–29, 2005, p. A4.

[viii]www.experienceispa.com/articles/index.cfm?action=view&articleID=248&menuID=75

[ix]Christina Valhouli, "An Industry Tones Up".

[x]Mel Zuckerman (2004), "Capitalizing on the Canyon Ranch Difference," in B. Dickinson & A. Vladimir, *The Complete 21ˢᵗ Century Travel & Hospitality Marketing Handbook*. Pearson/Prentice Hall, p. 570.

[xi]Reported by Nancy Keates for the *Wall Street Journal*, April 1, 2005.

[xii]By Ali Basye for *Lexis Magazine*, Fall 2005.

[xiii]From David Grossman's Business Travels column in *USA Today*, 8-03-04.

[xiv]Vicki Freed (2004), "Carnival Cruise Lines' Winning Formula," in B. Dickinson & A. Vladimir, *The Complete 21ˢᵗ Century Travel & Hospitality Marketing Handbook*. Pearson/Prentice Hall, Chapter 30.

[xv]A. Kirk Lanterman, (2004), "Adapting the Cruise Product to an Evolving Travel Market," in B. Dickinson & A. Vladimir, *The Complete 21ˢᵗ Century Travel & Hospitality Marketing Handbook*. Pearson/Prentice Hall, Chapter 33.

[xvi]From Amy Gunderson's report on cruises for the *New York Times*, Feb. 26, 2006.

[xvii]Written by Cindy Bertram for the Niche Cruise Marketing Alliance.

[xviii]Northwest Territory Tourist Commission; downloaded from www.nttc.com.au/nt/nttc/industry/strategies/cruise.html Jan. 2, 2005.

[xix]By Ron Irwin writing for brandchannel.com, Oct. 28, 2002.

Chapter 14

PROMOTING ATTRACTIONS AND THEMED SPACES

Mickey is the mouse that roared.

Chapter Objectives

After reading this chapter, you will be able to answer these questions:

+ What are *attractions* and how are they promoted?

+ How are *museums* marketed and how are they changing their focus?

+ What key strategies underlie marketing of *shopping destinations?*

+ What tourist groups do *casinos* attract and how can marketers address their cultural needs?

+ How are *theming* and *branded venues* used to market attractions and servicescapes?

Every tourist destination has attractions to entertain or education visitors. In this chapter, we extend our discussion of tourism entertainment by focusing on attractions and theme-based experiences. First we look at promoting attractions such as museums, shopping malls, and casinos. Then we explore theming concepts and how they apply to promoting restaurants, malls, parks, venues, and even religious programming.

PROMOTING ATTRACTIONS

Attractions are location-based entertainment experiences that have a symbiotic relationship with tourism. Without tourist attractions there would be no tourism, and without tourism there would be no attractions. Attractions draw from local environments, and as such market themselves on their own right. They are diverse and include landscapes to see, activities to do, and experiences to remember. We'll explore promoting three of the most popular attractions, museums, retail locations, and casinos.

What constitutes an attraction?

According to a travel scholar,[i] a phenomenon must have three components to be considered an attraction: a tourist, a site to be viewed, and a marker or image that makes the site significant. Historic sites, amusement parks, and natural spectacles such as Niagara Falls are all attractions.

Three perspectives

Research conducted on tourist attractions has three broad perspectives: definitions and description of attraction types, organization and development of attractions, and cognitive perception and experience of tourist attractions by different groups.[ii] Aspects of each perspective have some relevance for developing marketing strategies.

Descriptive perspective, the most frequent form of attraction typology in tourism research, describes the uniqueness of a site. Attractions are classified using the Standard Industrial Codes (SIC) into similar types, according to industry. This information is published in tourist guidebooks. The World Trade Organization (WTO) uses classifications that include natural beauty and climate, culture and social characteristics, sport, recreation, and educational facilities, shopping and commercial facilities, infrastructure, price levels, attitudes toward tourists, and accessibility. Research surveys incorporate these elements to ascertain their importance to tourists. Results allow an objective comparison between one destination and another.

Organizational perspective focuses on spatial (building and site), capacity (high and low), and temporal nature (visit duration) of attractions. Simple scale continuums are based on the size of the area that the attraction encompasses. Scale considerations provide insight into the organization of tourist attractions, their relationship to other attractions, and the relationship of attraction images to attractions themselves. Tourism marketers promote the images of specific, small-scale attractions to create identifiers for larger attraction complexes. Touring attractions are aimed at travelers who are in transit and characterized by short visits. Destination attractions are major centers of tourism characterized by numerous tourist activities integrated around a central point. For a planner, the primary considerations for smaller sites are mobility and access, while larger site planning focuses on providing a mix of variety and stimulation.

The *cognitive perspective* centers around safety and is based in the natural curiosity that tourists have to see "what's really behind things." The safest attractions occur in a staged, highly structured environment where tourists relate to the promoted or advertised *image* rather than to quote unquote reality, or a direct experience of the site. Research in this perspective has determined that an attraction's staging and level of renown are related to market scale. Globally branded attractions offer less risk to tourists than smaller market attractions. For local venues, safety is the marketing message.

Three less significant measures of attraction research are historical, locational, and valuational variables. *Historical measures* monitor a place over time to determine trends and changes in audience preference. Changes do not necessarily mean negative perceptions. The Coliseum in Rome, for example, has suffered damage from decades of traffic pollution and tourism, yet is still a favorite attraction for visitors to Italy. *Locational measures* compare the same attraction categories across different locations, such as the ancient ruins located at Ephesus near Ismir, Turkey compared to those at Antica Attica outside Rome. *Valuational measures* (numeric ratings) are obtained through visitor preference surveys, tourist attendance and usage rates, guidebook analysis, surveys of experts or professionals, and economic expenditures and income. Marketers then use much of this research to develop campaigns for the attraction.

PROMOTING MUSEUMS

The U.S. has over 15,000 museums that host 865 million visitors each year. Half of these charge only voluntary admission fees. The Smithsonian is the nation's largest museum, with 6,000 employees and 140 million items on display or archived. Traditionally, museums have contained dead things—artifacts from the past, art from old masters, or priceless collections from exotic lands. In the past ten years, however, many museums have undergone serious transformations. Museums don't just compete with other museums, they compete with all other forms of entertainment and attractions. They are complete experiences that integrate art, artifact and replica.

Museum types

Museums are classified by their offerings. Exhibit 14.1 shows museum types by percentage of the total number.

Culture-based museums have to do with satisfying curiosity about other groups and societies; they are places where audiences can experience something authentic. Museum curators mix constructed surroundings with authentic items to produce a realistic scene for viewing and discussion. The Congo Museum in Brussels mixes recreated scenes from tribal life with authentic artifacts to provide a realistic portrayal of African life.

EXHIBIT 14.1 Museum Classifications

TYPE OF MUSEUM	PERCENTAGE OF WHOLE
Historic	29
Historic site	24.5
Art	14.8
General	8.6
Natural history or nature center	6.7
Specialized	5.7
Aboretum/botanical garden	3.9
Science and learning	2.2
Other	3.2

Celebrity museums allow visitors to appreciate a virtual encounter with a star or offer fun "discoveries." At Madame Tussaud's Wax Museum in Las Vegas, visitors might snuggle up to Marilyn Monroe or get married to George Clooney in a wedding-party stage set—wedding gowns provided. The Museum of Jurassic Technology in Los Angeles and the American Sanitary Plumbing museum in Worcester, Massachusetts rely imagination and audience involvement to present pseudo-inventions and whimsical experiences.

Science and learning museums, on the other hand, provide the real thing through hands-on interaction with exhibits and displays. San Francisco's Exploratorium is one example of a museum that offers actual and virtual location activities that entertain through education. Growing in popularity with family audiences, learning museums have substantial online collections with rich content offerings. They offer many different kinds of learning activities suited to different age levels and learning styles. Their Web sites provide virtual visits that increase desire for a "real-time" visit to the museum building.

Specialty museums offer unique environments. The Frick in New York City is housed in one of Fifth Avenue's only remaining mansions. The architecture of San Francisco's Museum of Modern Art takes audiences through a catwalk that simulates being in a giant eye. The Houston's Menil Collection combines modern art with ancient and tribal art in an urban neighborhood of art sites. New York's Museum of Modern art is considered to have the best shopping,[iii] but the Metropolitan Museum is the most intriguing with its vast collections, tomb rooms with Egyptian pyramids, and fascinating array of gifts in its shop. Most museums do have their own retail shops on location as well as extensions in shopping malls to sell collection reproductions and miniatures. Whether displaying Armani collections, Impressionist paintings, or tattoo art, museums truly compete for visitors with all other types of other attractions.

FOCUS ON LEARNING ATTRACTIONS
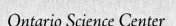

Ontario Science Center

Since opening its doors in 1969, The Ontario Science Center in Ontario Canada has fascinated more than 40 million visitors, boasting over 800 exhibits in eleven exhibition halls. In 2009, the center was forty year old and reached five million visitors through onsite experiences and traveling exhibitions, and generated over seven million online visitors. The Center competes with other national attractions by providing an entertaining and innovative space for family interaction and innovation. The Center includes Family Innovation Experience Areas where visitors help real scientists with real research, use the latest technology to explore the connections between art and science, and work with a variety of new and familiar materials in innovative ways. These experience areas include:

- *Challenge Zone* features a "Challenge of the Day," in which participant teams are encouraged to design and build practical solutions using a variety of common and unusual materials within an allotted time.

- *Citizen Science* is the place to meet scientists and get involved with real research projects. Visitors learn how to hone research questions, collect data, and analyze and visualize results.

- *Media Studios* feature media tools for discovering what happens when the boundaries between music, fashion, art, technology, and science start to blur.

- *Material World* encourages visitors to look at the "stuff of life" in different ways. Visitors work with artisans to explore the creative side of materials science.

- *KidSpark* was designed as a stimulating learn-through-play space for children eight and under It is packed with more than 40 experiences that offer much more than hands-on fun.

Marketers promoted Center sleepovers for school groups, summer day camp for kids of all ages, and group meetings for organizations and businesses to expand upon the normal facility activities. Other promotion strategies include:

- Partnership collaboration with other major attractions to stimulate tourist vacations

- 25 major promotions and increased channels of distribution to drive attendance

- Enhanced community access programs

- Visits by regional school board members

- Corporate sponsorships

Activities used as promotional tools to enhance the museum's audience reach and membership drives include:

- Museum virtual tour for online exploration

- Sleepovers for elementary school students

- Summer day camps

- Meeting center hosts corporate events

- Payload serve allows visitors to participate in research

- Sci Fri: Friday nights for high school students

- Birthday parties

Successful marketing efforts increased two-year memberships by 65% and generated 51% of the Center's expenditures; the Canadian government awarded the balance of financial support.

Source: www.ontariosciencecenter.org, Jan. 4, 2009

Museum research and promotional tactics

The single promotion strategy of museums a few decades ago was "Collect it and they will come." Today, audience needs and wants has become a primary focus for attracting visitors, and the strategy for marketing museums is "Know them and they will come." The process of understanding audience needs and using that knowledge to promote museum brands involves a series of steps, as outlined here.

1. *Involve staff members in research efforts.* You can't equate the *term* audience solely with visitors. Members, donors, staff, and volunteers are audiences too. Looking at them as customers paves the way for marketing to become a museum-wide function. Questions and comments that museum front-line staffers receive from visitors can tell you:

   + What impresses people most about your institution

   + What they wish it had more of

- What services are not being provided that should be

- What the museum may think is working that actually *isn't* working.

Marketing efforts offer staff members a major role in creating the changes that will affect their departments. Don't be afraid to let them participate; chances are they've already given a lot of thought to workable solutions.

2. *Use comment cards to generate feedback.* One of the best ways to generate feedback on museum performance is with this simple listening tool. Comment cards should have two components—an opportunity for visitors to tell their story and a mechanism for responding to them. Not only do the cards provide new ideas, they provide a method for museums to identify and reply to customers who have had a negative service experience and may be at risk of taking their patronage elsewhere. They are a powerful tool for service recovery, which can have effects on the bottom-line by:[iv]

   - Keeping at-risk customers from leaving

   - Minimizing negative word-of-mouth advertising that would undermine marketing efforts

   - Increasing positive word-of-mouth advertising (visitors who have had a problem become vocal advocates of a company).

3. *Promote memberships.* Members are the lifeline of museum organizations and require consistent recruitment and maintenance efforts. Membership development involves two types of solicitations: 1) placing solicitations *on-site* with signs at the admissions desk and gift shop cash registers, offering a premium with on-site membership purchases, using tent cards in the restaurant or cafe promoting membership, proclaiming a Members Month to double promotion efforts, and offering staff and docents incentives and commissions for selling memberships; 2) Conducting *direct mailings* with available in-house lists and by compiling lists of visitors from "free membership" raffle drawings

Membership offerings can be structured by promoting renewals and offering special benefits such as: gift memberships

14.1 Interior of the Natural History Museum in London.

for trustees, boards, staff and members, renewal promotions using special offers in each renewal notice, and a "Renew Online!" message on printed pieces. Enacting membership programming and benefits such as "double-discount days" in the gift shop for members during the holidays are also tactics for membership building.

4. *Establish a speaker's bureau.* Presentations and talks to local clubs, churches, service organizations, and professional groups take a museum's message directly to local audiences and provide an opportunity to begin building relationships with those audiences. The tactic has more of a public relations and marketing research base than an educational one. Set up and promote the bureau as a special event, with press releases, Web site promotions, and community liaisons. Recruit engaging speakers: Toastmasters International is an invaluable speaker resource with 8,500 chapters worldwide.

5. *Maximize hotel concierge services.* Building good relationships with hotel and corporate concierges can result in increased ticket sales, more facility rentals, and additional members, donors, and volunteers. Locate concierges by contacting hotels directly or through their area professional associations. National Concierge Association chapters can be found on their Web site. Appoint a staff member to act as a liaison, and contact concierges on a regular basis to make sure that they're aware of what's happening at the museum. Or assemble a concierge's museum book with staff names and addresses, museum information, and exhibit schedule. Concierge-referred incentives are not always necessary, but ticket discounts are a win-win situation for the museum, the concierge, and the visitor.

6. *Affiliate with business databases.* The GuideStar database (GuideStar.org) contains information about more than 850,000 U.S. nonprofits. Each week, tens of thousands of donors, funders, and members of the media use it to find and compare charities, monitor performance, and give with greater confidence. GuideStar draws its basic listing information from the IRS Business Master File and Forms. Listings can be updated and expanded at no charge. A number of nonprofits have received sizable donations from people who first found them through the GuideStar search engine.

7. *Conduct regular tours.* Tours are excellent mechanism for attracting new visitors and retaining current members. For example, the Silver City Museum, a regional history museum in New Mexico, gives half-hour tours focusing on the city's historic architecture and landmarks. The Delaware History Museum offers 60-minute tours of Wilmington's historic areas that act as a popular add-on to senior tours that include the museum's interactive exhibits. Both of these institutions began their guide service in response to visitor requests. To increase the marketability of a group tour program, announce the service in press releases, add a promotional page to the Web site, and get the word out to tourism promotion organizations. Don't forget group sales departments at nearby restaurants and hotels.

8. *Make the museum a movie star.* To create awareness, feature the museum in motion pictures. Remember the Philadelphia Museum of Art as a backdrop for *Rocky's* triumphant run up the stairs? Did you notice the Metropolitan Museum featuring *Batman* running wild, or the break-in featured in *The Thomas Crown Affair?* If you saw *A League of Their Own,* you may recall the women's team visiting the Baseball Hall of Fame in Cooperstown, New York. In an attempt to bring celebrity to museums, movies are tying themselves to various venues—Imax theaters, for instance, has screens in 55 museums. The Henry Ford Museum and Imax Theater in Dearborn, Michigan have shown Disney and *Star Wars* films to packed houses. Cooperation between private and non-profit organizations allows museums to receive educational materials and speakers. For example, Imax offered study guide to accompany a museum showing of *Apollo 13* for school groups.

9. *Hold special receptions for new exhibits.* Well-publicized events, such as new exhibition celebrations, give members advance previews and generate a sense of excitement. The Laguna Beach Museum of Art, for instance, partners with local restaurants to provide food and beverages for invited members prior to artist receptions and new installations. A 2009 exhibition on surfing art generated great young adult attendance, speaking to an audience not previously associated with art openings and museum visits.

10. *Lease space to corporations and organizations for special events.* The Metropolitan Museum leased space to a large investment firm in conjunction with a Lichtenstein exhibit that brought together the artist Christo, news reporter Diane Sawyer, and financial investors for a special event. Held in the museum's Egyptian tomb room, the evening featured chamber music, a variety of wines, and a six-course meal with a Lichtenstein-based food theme. Financial compensation was not the only benefit: the activity yielded media coverage and a generous gift from the meeting's sponsor. In a similar lease agreement, Armani paid dearly to put his fashion collection in the MOMA. As an alternative for leasing out space, some museums lease their assets to other locations. Boston Museum, for instance, rented 21 Monets to the Bellagio Casino in Las Vegas and continually leases art to shows held in London.

11. *Take the museum brand show on the road.* One a museum has developed a national brand image, it can move beyond its walls. The Guggenheim, for instance, has global locations, including Las Vegas. Madame Taussaude left New York for the Vegas Strip, housing a trendier version in the Venetian Hotel. Exhibitions travel from museum to museum; now, museums can travel to audiences as well.

Twittering museums

Museums use Twitter because its brilliance lies in simplicity. Unlike a Facebook page with photos, videos, and all manner of fluff, it takes truly minimal effort for visitors to post a sentence with what they're doing on Twitter. For both museums and visitors, Twitter has the ability to enhance

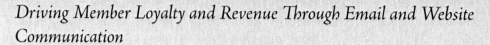

Driving Member Loyalty and Revenue Through Email and Website Communication

The organization

Carnegie Museums of Pittsburgh is a collection of four properties, including Museums of Art, Natural History, Science Center, and Andy Warhol Museum. Reaching more than 1.5 million visitors a year through its four museums, the organization serves 400,000 people through on-site and off-site educational and outreach programs and global traveling exhibitions.

The challenge

With 90% of its membership marketing budget spent on replacing lost members, Carnegie Museums needed a strategic plan for membership retention. The organization understood that the Internet offered a cost-effective opportunity to reach its members more frequently and encourage them to renew, but it faced several obstacles:

- No consistent online relationship with the constituents

- Impersonal text-only messages were sent using a personal email tool without tracking capabilities, and the site lacked member-only content.

- Site had no transaction capability for members to renew online.

Site objectives

1. Develop a strategic plan to develop ongoing relationships through email and Web communication to improve membership retention.

2. Create an online solution to create more effective emails and site content and to provide built-in tracking and reporting capabilities for analyzing online results.

3. Streamline the transaction process and provide an easy way to renew online.

Implementation

- Online member was center created in 2002 with an email marketing system that allow constituents to receive email newsletters and event alerts.

- Online surveys were developed to gather visitor information for targeting online communications.

- Online membership renewal/upgrade campaigns installed to alert donors of upcoming mailings.

Results

Better outreach and member services

- Increased quality and frequency of member communications

- Increased membership renewals

- Increased email list from 12,000 to 50,000

- Survey data revealed that 78% of online members felt more connected with the museum and 89% intended to renew their memberships

Increased membership renewals and revenue

- Email newsletters renewed at a rate of 88% compared to previous 62%

- First-year members renewed at a rate of 58% compared with 40% the previous year

- Multi-year memberships renewed at a rate of 78% versus 73% previously

- Average online transactions on Member Center increased to $131 from $111 offline

- Organization raised $121,000 online after taking membership sales to the Web

Improved efficiency

- Marketing staff communications with members an additional 15–20 times per year

- Online cost effectiveness allows the organization to produce and promote more member-only events

- Easy site management by non-technical staff members

What do you think?

1. Take a look at carnegiemuseums.org and engage in their Web site. Discuss your experience with ease of use, attractiveness, and entertainment value.

2. What additional steps might the organization take to further develop their web site?

Source: www.convio.com/

lectures *during* exhibitions or talks. The speaker speaks and the audience tweets—all in real time. In terms of efficacy for museums, Twitter has the edge over Facebook. Here are some of the ways museums invoke Twitter[v] as part of their promotion tactics.

The Natural History Whale, 10,855 followers. Using a life-sized blue whale painted on its ceiling to twitter, the New York's Natural History Museum provides information about exhibitions and offers amusing comments about its visitors below and the trials of a whale living on the ceiling.

Maryland Zoo—1,074 followers. The zoo's Twitter feed is informative, funny and provides information using bite-sized facts about the it's species of animals, and provides links to additional information updated several times a day.

Brooklyn Museum—21,650 followers. Noted for its effective use of social media, the museum is also one of the first institutions to monetize their Twitter feed with exhibition info and constant dialogue between the museum and its followers. For a $20 a year fee, visitors gain access to an exclusive feed called @1stfans where they can talk directly to artists and get invitations to special events.

SHOPPING ATTRACTIONS

Beyond retail, shopping is now marketed as a global attraction set within a variety of themed and crafted spaces designed to lure both traveling and local customers. Shopping centers have become destinations for Asian, European, and North American tourists seeking brands and bargains. South Coast Plaza in Orange County, California provides a tour for visitors complete with location maps, instant credit, and concierge service. Shopping vacations to Hong Kong are favorites of U.S. consumers who travel to Asia.

Positioning

Positioning differentiates shopping venues. Department store positioning typically involves targeting specific audiences. The two largest department stores in Paris, Le Bon Marche and Les Galeries Lafayette, use three domains of cultural manifestations to differential themselves: the surrounding area, social aspects such as store window dressings, style, and the store itself. Located in a modern building on the Left Bank, Le Bon Marche fashions itself as an upscale shop for local and Parisian shoppers. Les Galeries Lafayette, on the other hand, markets to tourists and mass shoppers by providing an historical setting that is by itself an attraction in the fashionable area adjacent to L'Arc d'Triumph.

Window shopping

Window displays are a favorite marketing strategy for retail locations seeking both local and global shoppers. Club scenes and models in animal costumes have adorned Selfriedge's Flagship store in London. Along with trendy brands and in-store restaurants, such tactics have helped turn the store into a more profitable and profitable one than most of its American rivals. Embracing shopping as a form of entertainment not necessarily linked to buying, Herrods has also turned itself into leisure and tourist destinations with lavish food halls, eateries, bars, and frequent exhibits.[vi]

Loyalty programs

According to retailers and mall managers, customer loyalty drives most and specialty promotion programs. Here are a few examples.[vii]

+ *Mall Credit Card*: In association with VISA and Master Card, special mall cards allow consumers to buy products easily. This helps track purchases and spending patterns.

+ *Drawing*: A drawing program requires shoppers to save their receipts. For every $100 in mall receipts, they received one entry in an annual drawing for a new car. The winner has to be present to win, so drawing day brings lots of shoppers to the mall.

+ *Parking premiums*: Big spenders can receive a free valet service. By taking their receipts to the information desk in the mall to be validated, consumers who maintain a certain spending level get a valet sticker entitling them to free parking services.

+ *Wheels*: Free strollers and wheelchairs to moms and the elderly are an appreciated convenience.

+ *Education rebates*: Partner with local schools and offer a rebate program in which fraction of a percentage of proceeds from parent shoppers goes back to their children's schools.

+ *Points program*: Based on purchases in the shopping mall, customers acquire points for discounts or coupons. The program can be outlet or category specific or apply to all stores in the mall. Prizes also can be status symbols such as club memberships, short holiday resort vacations, or concert tickets.

+ *Frequent spender lounges*: For adult shoppers who use their mall charge cards or accrue spending points, mall lounges provide rest rooms, couches, and soft drinks.

FOCUS ON SHOPPING

India's Malls Lure Foreign Retailers

Shoppertainment has come to India. A sharp rise in malls across the country has changed the way people shop for retail goods. Air-conditioned malls are replacing stuffy mom-and-pop stores in cluttered street locations and crowded outdoor markets. Over 100 malls containing over 30 million square feet of new shopping centre space were projected to open in India by the end of 2010, according to the India Shopping Centre Forum 2009 (ISCF). A recent report, *Mall Realities India 2010*, made a strong case for the continuing robustness in the shopping centre business.

India's fasts-growing middle class has more disposable income than ever and an appetite for world-class shopping. Smaller than European malls, Indian retailers organize around cities where global manufacturers are located. The Saharan Mall in Gurgaon, for instance, receives 150,000 visitors each week thanks to companies like General Electric, Cocoa-cola and IBM that are housed in this location.

Management consultants rank India fifth on a list of the 30 best emerging destinations for foreign investment in the retail sector in spite of the country's heavy regulation. Operating through local franchises, retail giants like Britain's Marks & Spenser sell products in India. International players in India's retail market also include: Landmarc Group (Dubai), Metro (Germany), Shoprite (South Africa), Nanz (Germany), Mango (Spain), and McDonalds, Dominos, and Tricon Restaurants (U.S.).

However, the mall is not only about shopping. It has a movie multiplex and amusement stores for hanging out on weekends. Designer clothes and accessories from Gucci, Arron, Rado, and Opal as well as the Home Store and the Furniture Store are also featured. Shoppers Stop supermarket chain, clothing store Pantaloons, and Waterside clothing are the most prominent local retail chains. Other brands cashing in on available retail space are Adidas and Sony.

Source: www.indiaprwire.com/pressrelease/retail/2009053026418.htm

PROMOTING CASINOS AND GAMING ATTRACTIONS

We covered casinos previously as venues and travel destinations. Here we look at casinos as attraction centers for gaming, live shows, and other engaging activities. Ever since gambling was legalized in some states and renamed gaming, it has been coming closer and closer to favorite pastime status. Casino billboards advertise entertainment shows as the "world's most daring," "most sensual," or "most exciting." A favorite attraction of tourists, casinos are the most popular form of gaming worldwide. More money is spent of gaming and wagering activities than on movies and recorded music combined. People play not only for the thrill of winning, they gamble because it is entertaining.

The U.S. is the leading provider of gambling venues with 1,624 casinos, and France has the second highest number with 448. Other European leaders are Germany (125), Russia (170), and the UK (212). Japan's 37 and Kazakhstan's 25 casinos lead the Asian nations. Macau (China), with 29 casinos. Las Vegas entrepreneur Steve Wynn built an entire waterfront resort in Macau that rivals all other global gambling facilities. In South America, Argentina leads the other countries with 79 casinos. Australia has 370 casinos, and South Africa has the most venues on the African continent with 45 casinos.

A popular casino in the U.S.'s Southeast is in Tunica, Mississippi is now the country's third largest gambling destination. Other locations are racing to catch up. Together, Detroit, and Windsor,

Ontario, which face each other across the Detroit River, are expected to become a significant gambling market as several mega-casinos are being built along river. Casino operator Park Place Entertainment is buying up locally owned riverboat and land-based casinos in the Southeast and Midwest.

Connecticut is home to the most profitable casino in the U.S. and currently the nation's top American Indian tribal gambling market. Foxwood Resort Casino, operated by the Mashantucket Pequot Tribal Nation, averages over 55,000 patrons each day and more than 20 million visitors each year. The nation's largest tribal casino, Foxwood employs over 10,000 people. In the West, Harrah's Entertainment and Trump Hotels have each cut deals to develop and operate tribal casinos in California. Elsewhere, tribes in New York, Florida and Minnesota reap hundreds of millions each year from gaming operations.

The casino business is retailing opportunities for betting and other gaming experiences that are stimulating, exciting, and entertaining. In spite of the fact that they receive nothing tangible in return for the money they spend, gamers tend to come back for repeated visits. The marketing challenge is to use advertising and publicity to get customers into casinos, then to keep them playing for as long as possible with service and frills. Casinos have found it necessary to create marketing images that appeal to the core players they most want to attract. Research determines which incentives are the most profitable to implement for each category of player.

Mandalay Bay (Las Vegas) casino hotel, for example, caters to low and mid-budget players who don't require extensive credit-granting facilities or lavish meal and entertainment services. In contrast, Mirage Resorts and MGM Grand profitably exploit the high-roller niche. Casino management are generally willing to comp (no charge) these guests up to 50% of the amount it expects to win from the players. Players are ranked by a) buy-in amount to the game, b) average bet, c) largest bet, and d) duration of play.

As players' demands shift, casinos must alter the mix of games. New slot machines are so popular they now account for a steadily rising share of overall industry revenues. Tour promoters bring busloads of retired adults to casinos specifically for playing the slots.

Global gaming

One aspect of casino marketing is determining objectives for attracting a variety of players. For example, a goal may be to increase international or domestic ethnic market share. A first order of business is to determine how both existing and potentially new international customers perceive the casino. Research should reveal whether or not the casino is currently seen as capable of satisfying a mixed customer base of both domestic players and international players.[viii]

Perceptions are normally related to visuals. To gain an international image, public signage must in different languages to indicate readiness to serve an international clientele. Brochures and printed materials must be available in different languages and restaurants or menus should offer a variety of foods to satisfy a variety of domestic, ethnic, and international tastes. Another factor for increasing international market share is location. In most instances, location dictates increasing domestic or ethnic business first. Marketing efforts then create a springboard to go after the more costly international or overseas business.

Gaming resorts offer a complex entertainment experience. The entertainment experience is delivered through several elements, both tangible (such as quality of food, type of slot machines) and intangible (such as employee courtesy, ambience of the building). A casino visitor will determine his or her satisfaction and desire to return not based on winning or losing at the gambling tables, but based on the entertainment value created from the whole experience related to his or her expenditures. The value of the gaming experience perceived by each customer will vary because of his or her individual background, variable expectations and valuation criteria, and perception of what happens during the time he or she spends at the casino. Therefore it is extremely important for casino managers to understand how to create and add value each guest's experience.

To succeed overseas in places like Macau, U.S. operators must adapt to a different way of doing business. The vast majority of Macau's gamblers, for instance, wager in private VIP rooms rather than on the wide-open floors in huge Vegas-style casinos; in 2009, Macau hosted more visitors than Las Vegas! Table games such as baccarat generate the biggest profit in Asia; in Vegas, slot machines are the moneymakers.[ix]

A vast casino complex in Singapore, the Marina Bay Sands Resort, that opened in April 2010 cost developers $5.4 billion to build. The 55-story complex has three hotel towers connected by a single rooftop Sky Park, a museum, shops and a Vegas-style casino. Six restaurants featuring six of the world's top chefs and others focusing on regional food, are highlighted by an Asian Pangaea, high-octane mega-club with locations in New York, London, and Spain. Public relations placements of the resort's story were featured in global newspapers and prominently on the Internet (including a Wikipedia entry) to promote the opening.

Customer satisfaction factors, as well as aspects that positively or negatively impact a visitor's experience in a casino, have been the object of many studies. Research suggests that repeated visits to a casino are a function of the casino location, casino physical attributes, games offered, extra amenities of the casino, hospitality attributes, and the skill and attitudes of the casino staff.

Since an attitude by casino staff is so important to business, training programs are developed to increase staff awareness of various groups' cultural values and particularities as well as communication methods so that the interaction between staff and customer can be as smooth as possible. For example, while in the U.S. calling somebody by his or her first name may represent friendliness, the Chinese interpret this practice as a disrespectful way to communicate with an elderly person.

Attracting gamblers from Asia

Las Vegas is a favorite destination for Asians, from groups of budget travelers to high-stake gamblers who can individually affect a casino's bottom line. Gaming is part of the Asian culture. Eighty-five percent of the high rollers that play in Las Vegas come from China, Taiwan, and Japan.[x]

Asians are well known for being among the high-end gaming customers. Sales increases at places such as The Forum Shops at Caesars Palace are directly attributable to the Asian visitors, who are very focused on quality and brand name of products they purchase. The gaming industry is aware of the potential of Asian customers. Understanding their culture, needs, and expectations can lead to an increase in customer service and therefore customer satisfaction, which is a key factor in generating repeat visits to the same casino.

A study published by Bear Stearns market analysts estimates that three-fourths of the Las Vegas Strip's baccarat players come from Asia, indicating that the health of Asian economies has a direct bearing on the bottom line of several Las Vegas casinos.[xi]

To increase these numbers, some gambling companies have strategically placed executives in potential Asian markets such as Hong Kong, Singapore, and Tokyo in order to establish partnerships with local travel agents to send visitors to Las Vegas. But these efforts will only be worthwhile if a prepared team is ready to properly serve these customers when they arrive at the casinos. Getting to the casino is one thing. Having a positive experience while there is another.

Statistics show that in Las Vegas, losses by Chinese visitors have been extraordinary.[xii] Even though the volume of Japanese people visiting Las Vegas is greater than the volume of Chinese visitors, the amount of money the Chinese gamers are willing to gamble is exorbitant. For example, some reports indicate that individual losses at a casino reached US$10 million over an 8-month time frame. Casinos consider the Chinese New Year the best gambling weekend in the year when thousands of Chinese revelers come to Las Vegas to celebrate and gamble.

All these factors have caught the attention of gaming companies for this emerging market. Considering and potential difference that Chinese customers can make to the casino bottom line, casino marketers should be extremely interested in better understanding this customer segment.

PROMOTING THEMED ENVIRONMENTS

Synonymous with entertainment, themed environments pervade global landscapes. A **themed environment** is the ultimate in manufactured experiences that markets authenticity to travelers and visitors within a single space. Theming is prevalent in parks, restaurants, malls, hotels, branded spaces and religious venues. Themes have become a way for all businesses and destinations to differentiate themselves in the hope of attracting and entertaining customers who consume goods and services. The increasing reliance on motifs and themes serves marketers well. In such environments, consumption is fused with fantasy and amusement; Las Vegas is the ultimate themed space.

14.2 The Venetian Hotel brings Venice to Las Vegas by creating a theme around the Italian city.

Staging reality

The process of theming connects the advertising, media, celebrity, fashion and status markers that elevate symbols over substance. What do visitors expect from a themed experience? Theming characteristics include:

1. Being *set apart* with specific boundaries as in theme parks, or as an enclosed structure for a restaurant or hotel.

2. A *predictable* environment; visitors to the Mall of America know they can expect entertainment, shopping, food, and activities.

3. An environment that is *safe and protected from harm*; Disney provides a security staff and accident-free rides to insure visitor safety.

4. Focus on a *single motif* with relevant artifacts, costumes, and architecture; visitors to Ruby's Diners sit on red leather and chrome bar stools or in booths, eat hamburgers and fries, and sip sodas that are served by waiters in 1950s diner attire. The Venetian Hotel uses gondolas, canals, and ceramics to theme their hotel with an Italian motif.

5. Theming enables *licensing*; Hard Rock Café licenses its themed venues, menus and T-shirt designs to establishments worldwide.

The theming strategy works. By incorporating recognizable symbols into everyday environments, marketers provide a way for visitors to experience the feeling of a historical era, faraway place, or exotic culture. The presence of symbols enhances audience enjoyment of almost every activity and attraction.

Theme developers base their marketing on research conducted to determine public preferences and to understand the theme itself. In order to duplicate the historical time period or location settings, information must be gathered. Music, talent, event marketing, and public relations jobs are part of this large and profitable industry.

Themed restaurants

In order to enhance mealtime, roadside diners adorned themselves with symbols of nostalgia, and themed restaurants were conceived. Today, almost all eating establishments use thematic devices or become entirely themed environments. Most themed restaurants are synonymous with the image of their franchise chain in both exterior and interior design. Restaurant themes draw from popular genres such as film, sport, contemporary music, and ethnic cultures. Narrative is communicated non-verbally through the use of props, artifacts, sound, menu, and merchandise. Eating is not the central focus—diners are there to consume the theme as well as the food.

New themed establishments tell new stories, to say the least. At SoHo's chic Casa La Femme, diners sit on the floor in designer tents, are served by waiters on their knees who explain the menu, and can visit a palm reader in her tent between courses. At Red Square in the Mandalay Bay Resort, people dine in the cold train station atmosphere of a Moscow restaurant. Ice cubes in the shape of Lenin's head appear in drinks at the restaurant's tiny vodka bar. Guests huddle in thick coats since they and the vodka bottles are chilled down to Siberian temperatures.

Theming strategies for restaurants vary widely; the most common are reliquary, parodic, ethnic, and reflexive.[xiii]

Reliquary theming involves the use of relics and artifacts connected to a heroic figure or notable era or event that introduce a sense of pilgrimage to the experience. Diners visit to pay homage to the objects as much as to eat. This strategy makes a direct link to the famous. For example, Hard Rock Café's link to music and the film industry gives diners a sense of being in the presence of something special or even sacred in those industries.

Parodic theming (think parody) uses ambiance created through artifacts and decorative devices to create a magical (but knowingly fake) environment based on a strong motif. Jungle-themed Rainforest Café is the best example of this type of parodic theming. No one really believes they are in a rainforest, but they like the experience just the same.

14.3 Hard Rock Cafe boasts a nostalgia theme.

Ethnic themes provide art, décor, music, and in some sense stereotypical signals to reflect a recognizable culture. North of the border, sombreros and mariachi music say "Mexico" to patrons.

Reflexive theming focuses on a brand that becomes a theme. McDonalds, Round Table Pizza. and KFC are examples of branded themes.

Themed restaurants are managed using a business model with these characteristics:

- Rational, standardized, and efficient operations that can be easily replicated

- Chains and franchising that are built upon a successful theming formula

- Merchandising to boost sales and help advertise the restaurant. Hard Rock Café T-shirts make consumers into walking billboards for the brand. Merchandise also serves as markers or souvenirs of tourist visits to exotic locations

Trade journals reporting on themed restaurants identified four problems that contribute to a decline in success: the inability to attract repeat visits; mediocre food and service and high prices; overexpansion; and lack of management focus on the core concept.[xiv] The biggest marketing challenge is getting customers to repeat their dining experiences. Special promotions, occasion parties, and tour packages are a few strategies available to drive repeat visits. Another strategy involves taking themed franchises out of urban areas and into shopping malls. City center locations are highly competitive and an unreliable market frequented by tourists, but suburban enclosed locations get more repeat visitors. Thus, the themed shopping mall moves into center stage.

Themed shopping malls

Overarching motifs and coordinated symbolic schemes in total environments are typical of suburban U.S. malls that marketing themselves as places to be. As destinations, malls require some means of identification and differentiation. Malls are private commercial spaces that are expressly designed to make money and realize capital, yet they may disguise their purpose with motifs built around themes like kitsch or high-tech urban space.

Suburban malls changed the nature of retail competition by adding the dimension of a dedicated entertainment space to the marketing equation. The grand themed environments of malls function as the host to a variety of commercial enterprises and is also attractive as a destination itself.

The newest retail environments structured around theming are "downtown walking areas" adjacent to popular attractions. Downtown Disney in Anaheim is one example of a location built around themed eating experiences. As with malls, the process of reliance on theming as a consequence of increased choice and spatial competition is seen in many types of tourist attractions around the globe.

Theme parks

The Americana themed amusement park industry has evolved into a multibillion-dollar entertainment segment that draws visitors from around the world and spawns many imitations.

The top ten global amusement park and their attendance records in 2008 were:

1. Magic Kingdom, Disney World Resort, Buena Vista, FL / 17,063,000
2. Disneyland at Disneyland Resort, Anaheim CA / 14,721,000
3. Tokyo Disneyland, Tokyo, Japan / 14,293,000
4. Disneyland Paris, Marne-la-Vallee, France / 12,688,000
5. Tokyo DisneySea, Tokyo, Japan / 12,498,000
6. Epcot at Walt Disney World Resort, FL / 10,935,000
7. Disney's Hollywood Studios at Walt Disney World Resort, FL / 9,608,000
8. Disney's Animal Kingdom at Walt Disney World Resort, FL / 9,540,000
9. Universal Studios Japan, Osaka, Japan, / 8,300,000
10. Everland, Yongin, Gyeonggi-Do, South Korea / 6,600,000

In the economic downturn, attendance American Disney theme parks decreased slightly in 2009, especially California Adventure that suffered a 2% decrease; however Hong Kong and other global Disney parks held their own, according to the Themed Entertainment Association Company information, annual reports, and park sources are used to calculate estimates of park attendance. Ticketing and marketing through online channels was reported to be the primary source of revenue for these parks.

In an effort to attract American tourists, a Count Dracula Theme Parks is being built near the Romanian capital rather than Transylvania, the vampire's alleged birthplace. A feasibility study carried out by PriceWaterhouseCoopers claimed the park would attract more than a million tourists a year. Costing about $15.6 million, with an additional $19 million needed for infrastructure improvements, the park will include amusement rides, a golf course, a Gothic castle wired with spooky effects, a zoo, horseback riding, restaurants, and shops.[xv]

Theme parks are brand magnets in any country because they create a brand halo in a wider geographic area than just the theme park alone. Theme parks serve as splashy introductions to new markets and kick the door open to other ventures. Which is why the Chinese government underwrote Disney's Hong Kong project that continues to grow at 7% per year.

Disney began promoting the Magic World of Disneyland in Hong Kong with a television show designed to educate the Chinese about Disney's world and lure them to the $3.2 billion park that opened in September 2005. Hosted by a pop star, the show featured black-and-white clips of Walt Disney explaining his California masterpiece, and modern-day images of the Honk Kong park, which is a replica of the original in Anaheim.

China posed marketing challenges Disney hadn't faced before—translating what are called family values. By bringing America to Hong Kong, park management retained white actors who speak English for their face characters, which is part of a global strategy that aims to best present the characters from the original animated motion pictures. However, bringing the American Dream to China was not the objective of WPP Group's JWT advertising agency that promotes the park for Disney. Because most of what Chinese listen to on MTV is made in China, dreams, they say, must be built around the host country.[xvi]

Making a Magic Kingdom-style park was part of the agreement with the government, which largely financed the venue. To determine what Chinese audiences wanted, Disney conducted research using focus groups—participants said they wanted an authentic Disney Experience. Hoping to avoid accusations of cultural imperialism, Disney bowed in some areas: the park features Chinese and other Southeast Asian foods, and its grounds have correct feng shui design elements. Some rides, such as Jungle Cruise, set amid Cambodian ruins, were tweaked for local tastes.

Because Disney marketing is constrained by strict state media controls, promotional efforts were focused on a new Web site and advertising on Coca Cola cans. To build what Disney calls branded story education, Disney toured south China's malls, wooed travel agents, and teamed up with the Communist Youth League to sell stories in community centers. Theme parks are a cornerstone of Disney's international growth strategy, as they are coveted by local officials around the world who seek revenue-generating attractions. The company reportedly has its eye on Shanghai and South Korea[xvii] for the next park locations.

14.4 Amusement park at the Santa Cruz CA beach.

© Karin Hildebrand Lau, 2010. Used under license from Shutterstock, Inc.

Usually dependent on an unskilled, seasonal workforce with high turnover rates, amusement parks have operating profits that are sensitive to visitor-days (attendance equivalent to the number of separate visitors times the number of days in operation) and average per-capita spending. Park performance depends on region, weather patterns, number of season days, local demographics and income characteristics, and the amount of capital recently invested. New motion simulator rides and other computer-controlled experiences such as those developed in the framework of virtual reality and interactive video games are the new frontiers in the evolution of theme-park concepts. Quality of design, efficiency of service, and public fancy will continue to determine the degree of theme park success.

Branded theme retail venues

Like respectively themed restaurants, branded themes rely on the brand to produce the theme and the theme to reinforce the brand. NikeTown is a retail menagerie of themes, styles, and images revolving around sports. Shoppers become visitors in an atmosphere build around the "just do it" slogan that resembles a spiritual gymnasium or cathedral of consumption. NikeTown is a combination of amusement-centered themed environment and a mega-boutique. Whether consumers are weekend warriors or more committed to participating in sports, Niketown New York will provide every kind of gear needed. The first four of the building's five floors are dedicated to shirts, sneakers, sweats, and sportswear plastered with the trademark swoosh. Specialty items aren't limited to kicks endorsed by NBA stars like LeBron James and Carmelo Anthony or team-specific jerseys for European soccer and the American Dream Team; they extend to running shoes with accompanying iPods that track mileage. The top level offers a change of scenery and stock, going rustic with exposed brick and vents with fashion-oriented offerings.

The Guinness Factory in Dublin is Ireland's most visited attraction. Here, the beer's history, advertising campaigns and brewing process are presented to visitors who pay to experience and sample the legendary beer that is synonymous with Irish culture. Munich's Hofbrauhaus is another beer-branded venue catering to tourists. Promoting branded venues entails transferring the brand image onto a space where visitors can experience the brand in real time.

Religious theming

Theming has come to religion. Trinity Broadcasting Network (TBN), the largest Christian religion-based television network, is headquartered in Costa Mesa, California. The facility entertains visitors with religious souvenirs and reenactments of Christian milestones. TBN features all types of programming—talk shows, quiz shows, kids shows, and reality shows—all based around religious themes. The station's first film, *Six: The Mark Unleashed* starring Steven Baldwin premiered on TBN in 2004.[xviii]

On the cutting edge of technology, Trinity Broadcast Network's virtual reality theaters are operated in Nashville, Dallas, and Costa Mesa. Two more theaters are planned for Hawaii and Jerusalem to present visitors with an experience combining high definition digital video technology and a 48-channel digital audio system. The theaters showcase four original productions from TBN Films. Satellite technology has opened up opportunities for the Gospel to reach global audiences over 33 international satellites. TBN's themed venues and programming are marketed through churches, print advertising and tourism bureaus, making the business a profitable nonprofit.

The Holy Land Experience in Orlando, FL, showcases architectural recreations of Jerusalem, serene landscaping, historical exhibits, and live religious shows including the Passion drama which reenacts the crucifixion and resurrection of Jesus. After operating at a deficit in 2005 and 2006, the park was purchased by Trinity Broadcast Network, which quickly turned around its finances. By the end of 2007, it was operating at a profit.[xix]

Crystal Cathedral, an architectural marvel also located in California, is promoted to tourists of all denominations and hosts regular tours through the facility. Religious theming is used to market celebrity clergy, ideology, and venues of worship that attract visitors who partake in a variety of entertainment-based experiences. The Christianity brand has become so big, in fact, that PR professional Larry Ross claimed he "took a bungee jump for God and helped turn religious public relations into big business."[xx] Representing multiple religious genres—"Passion of the Christ" film, Billy Graham, and the men's ministry Promise Keepers among them—Ross' ministry has been publicity, marketing and branding since 1994. Ross characterizes his job as finding the sweet spot where faith and the culture intersect, because religion on its own often isn't enough to generate mainstream press.

14.5 Crystal Cathedral retains a marketing director.

© Gertjan Hooijer, 2010. Used under license from Shutterstock, Inc.

Theming Las Vegas

A composite of themed attractions, hotels, casinos and restaurants, Las Vegas is the ultimate staged environment. The world capital of show business, every square foot of the city is devoted to entertainment. Neon superlatives like 'best,' 'largest,' and 'biggest' dominate the landscape that dwarfs people and cars and evokes the materialization and megalomania of the town.

Las Vegas is a mega-resort that has repositioned itself from gambling enterprise to comprehensive entertainment capital where slot machines and roulette wheels take their places among top acts in music, comedy, art, and magic. Las Vegas radiates hope, humor and extravagance, endlessly repeating the myth of instant wealth available to anyone who will play. Exploring marquees preach mantras of the Strip: Shop, shop, shop, win, win, win. Composed of vastly incongruous architectural styles and themes that are forced into senseless proximity, Medieval Excalibur is a few blocks from Caesar's Palace of ancient Rome, which is not far from modern New York. Centuries and continents are mixed in together as the ultimate faux-travel experience. By totally immersing visitors in an imaginary world, Las Vegas is completely focused on its one-dimensional essence—razzle-dazzle.

So what can marketers learn from this expertly fabricated entertainment experience? One set of authors writing on Las Vegas offers these tips:[xxi]

- Interactivity is key to consumer enjoyment; always package and market shared experiences.

- Show business thrives on legends and lore—successful marketers create a new mythology for their clients.

- The customer service is king; make certain everyone in the business is informed and inclined to immerse the consumer in service.

- Efficiency and planning yield a successful operation that can be marketed with confidence.

- Try to own some show-business category that showcases the brand. MGM Grand Hotel aspires to 'own' the luxury hospitality segment with its size and grandeur.

- Having a special jargon helps make the brand or experience immersionary; always try to use show-business talk to advertise and promote entertainment.

- If you can't stimulate business where the consumers and audiences are, make the entertainment brand experience a destination Mecca of its own.

- Learn how to implement free show business experiences to bring audiences to your venue or attraction.

If, as the slogan says, *What goes on in Las Vegas stays in Las Vegas*, hospitality and casino promoters can capitalize on the 'forbidden fun' aspect of the destination's entertainment value. After all, what's more exciting than doing what doesn't come naturally!

Finally

As tourism grows, so will attraction development and improvement. Marketing skills are needed to identify trends, reach audience segments and differentiate offerings for audiences of all types. Theming is one strategy that helps set location-based entertainment apart from the competition. However, authenticity has become a scarce commodity in simulated fake environments. Whether or not this trend will continue or yield to realism is yet to be determined. For now, 'fabulous fakes' seem to be the preferred entertainment strategy that marketers must understand and embrace.

GOT IT?

The major points of this chapter are:

+ Attractions provide tourists and residents with place-based experiences that are marketed by the hosting venue.

+ Museums are marketed using research to determine the needs of visitors; staff members are used to implement new programs, and web sites are used to recruit, maintain, and service members.

+ With all forms of service marketing, customer service is a key element for gaining repeat customers and generating positive world-of-mouth promotion.

+ Casinos attract ethic groups and Asians by understanding and addressing their cultural nuances through language-based signage and menu development.

+ Theming is a motif-based marketing strategy to immerse visitors and differentiate eating, shopping, gaming, and playing experiences.

+ Marketing branded tourist attractions, restaurants, malls, parks, and venues involves providing a safe environment, familiar symbols, an enhanced narrative and providing incentives to stimulate repeat visits.

NOW TRY THIS

1. While viewing your city's tourism bureau online, count and categorize the number and type of attractions promoted. What links are provided to connect visitors with each attraction? How do attractions partner with each other to provide tourist packages? What packaging improvements can you suggest?

2. Visit the Web site of a two local museums and compare their membership benefits. Which is more appealing to you? Why? What could you suggest to the other museum to be competitive with your age and lifestyle demographic?

3. Visit an ethnic themed restaurant and make a list of all the icons, artifacts and symbols of the theme. Then ask ten friends what icons, artifacts, and symbols they would choose from that theme. Compare the two. What conclusions can you draw from this comparison that are valuable for marketing ethnic themes?

4. Develop a new themed space idea with the potential for global franchise, Describe the space, retail venue and artifacts you would incorporate into this attraction. What audience would you target? What locations do you recommend? In your answer, consider 1) investment potential, 2) available labor force, and 3) socio-cultural transferability.

QUESTIONS FOR DISCUSSION AND REVIEW

1. What marketing strategies do attractions use to connect with tourism boards? To reach local audiences? Which are most effective? Why?

2. How do museums structure their membership programs to capitalize on exhibit-based experiences? What other business-model methods might they use to generate revenue?

3. Why has theming become so pervasive for marketing location-based entertainment? Which themes are most effective for repeat customers? Why?

4. When marketing casinos, what ethical issues should promoters consider when developing repeat-based incentives? How pervasive is gambling addiction?

5. What marketing measures can you suggest for theme-based restaurants to promote repeat visits? How will franchising expansion impact food-based entertainment revenues?

MORE STUFF ABOUT MARKETING VENUES AND THEMED SPACES

www.designboom.com—marketing theme parks

www.stuff4restaurants—marketing restaurants

www.marketingreligion.net—marketing brands of faith

CAMPAIGN CASE STUDY

Reviving a Park's Popularity to Challenge Disney

Client: China's Ocean Park

The problem: Declining attendance and revenues, loss of visitors to Disney Park

Campaign Objective: Revive local loyalty for Ocean Park; differentiate the park from Disney Hong Kong.

Situation Analysis: Ocean Park had lost around $80 million in 2006 and a cumulative $200 million in the previous five years. Many locals expected the park would close down, particularly as the government had just committed an enormous sum of money to woo Disney to its Lantau Island site at the expense of the older facility of Ocean Park that was an old and tired brand. Marketing research was conducted to determine how the park could differentiate itself from Disneyland, which found that visitors wanted animals as part of their park experience.

SWOT Analysis:

- Strength: A long-standing history of serving Chinese visitors

- Weakness: Dated infrastructure and promotion

- Opportunity: Become a strong Disney competitor

- Threat: Park closing in lieu of competition from Disney

Target Audience: Hong Kong and Chinese families

Strategy 1: Upgrade the park facilities to meet the competition.

Tactic: Revitalize the product by rebuilding the park in a 6-year project intended to double the park's attractions.

Strategy 2: Create a promotional campaign designed to reconfigure sales and marketing plans and revive the brand with media and promotions.

- **Tactic:** "Love Ocean Park, Love Hong Kong" campaign & theme.

Strategy 3: Use external communications to position the park as an interactive experience with giant pandas, and breakfast watching aquarium jellyfish

- **Tactics:**

  1. An online quiz that attracted more than 100,000 responses.

  2. A recognizable icon (like Mickey was for Disney) developed for a sea lion character named Whiskers.

  3. Seasonal events—Halloween, Christmas and Chinese New Year—to spike attendance.

  4. Corporate visits scheduled for evenings when the park was usually dormant.

  5. An annual pass was invoked create loyalty and a real sense of value.

Strategy 4: Use internal communications to develop park employees as park ambassadors.

Tactic: Instigate training sessions, newsletters and incentives for best employee.

Results: Campaign research showed that recognition of Whiskers, combined with the public's association of the mascot with the park, created a successful brand.

Ocean Park became one of the few regional parks in a Disney neighborhood to add 20% more business than its competitor. By 2009, the park ranked 15th in the world and number one in China, outpacing Disneyland. In fiscal year 2007/2008 a record 5.3 million guests went through the gates, and the first quarter in 2009 was its best ever.

Question for discussion: *How should Ocean Park expand its promotion to include online and mobile phone advertising? How can the park further differentiate itself from Disney?*

Source: By: Tony Kelly, Hong Kong; www.themelt.com/TEAERA2008 and www.marketinginteractive.com/news/515

---

[i] James MacCannell (1976), *The Tourist*, p. 109.
[ii] Alan Lew (1987), "A Framework of Tourist Attraction Research," *Annals of Tourism Research* 14 (4).
[iii] L. Delp, C. Ryan & L. Sanders (2000) for *Travel Holiday*, November.
[iv] By Kathleen Khalife on museummarketingtips.com, Jan. 4. 2006.
[v] www.museumstrategyblog.com/museum_strategies/marketing/.
[vi] By Cecilie Rohwedder for the *Wall Street Journal*, May 5, 2003.

[vii]From www.marketingprofs.com/ea/qst_question.asp?qstID=3074 Jan. 7, 2006.

[viii]By Stephen Karoul, "Casino Marketing – Perception Or Reality" March 3, 2002.

[ix]Peter Sanders in "Heard on the Street" for the *Wall Street Journal*, March 9, 2006.

[x]Sandara Galletti, (2002) "Chinese Culture And Casino Customer Service" Unpublished paper, Loyola Marymount University – Los Angeles, CA.

[xi]D. Biers, D. (2001). "Bright lights, High rollers." *Far Eastern Economic Review*, March 22.

[xii]J. Pomfret, J. (2002). "China's high rollers find a seat at table." *The Washington Post*, March 26.

[xiii]A. Bearadsworth & A. Bryman (1999), "Late modernity and the Dynamics of Quasification: The case of Themed Restaurants," *The Sociological Review* 47 (2), 228–257.

[xiv]From *Nation's Restaurant News*, Dec. 7, 1998, p. 29.

[xv]Mala Matina at www.newsfinder.org/site/more/dracula_theme_park/ March 17, 2010.

[xvi]Geoffrey Fowler & Merissa Marr for the *Wall Street Journal*, June 16, 2005.

[xvii]Merissa Marr & Geoffrey Fowler for the *Wall Street Journal*, June 16, 2005.

[xviii]From tbn.org.

[xix]DailyFinance: http://srph.it/bFQDCD.

[xx]Strawberry Saroyan for the Sunday *New York Times Magazine*, April 16, 2006.

[xxi]B. Schmitt, D. Rogers & K. Vrotsos (2004), *There's no Business That's Not Show Business*. Prentice Hall, Chapter 14.

Chapter 15

PROMOTING MEDIATED ENTERTAINMENT

> Television?
> The word is half Latin and Half Greek.
> No good can come of it.
> C.P. Scott

Chapter Objectives

After reading this chapter, you will be able to answer these questions:

+ How are *films* positioned, promoted, and distributed?

+ What are the macro and microeconomic *financial factors* affecting film marketing?

+ What is the primary strategy used to market *television* shows?

+ How is *product placement* used in movie and television marketing?

The cultural industries are not only defined by the nature of their cultural products, but also by the industry system in which they are produced and consumed. What is this national fascination with the cult of celebrity?[i] You need to study popular culture to understand the impact of the industry on society. Marketing to an invisible, mass audience is a huge challenge for media marketers, who depend on advertising revenues, ratings, and seasonal fluctuations to judge the success or failure of their efforts.

Film and television marketing consists of three distinct phases: the *production stage* where a script is developed, capital is raised and the movie or show is produced; the *distribution stage* where movies go to theaters and shows are broadcast on network or cable TV; and finally, the *after-market stage* when films go to DVD and television, and when TV shows are syndicated to other channels and global markets. This chapter looks at how marketing for mediated entertainment—movies and television—is developed and executed with these stages in mind.

THE BUSINESS OF MARKETING MOVIES

Far from the glamorous side of the movie business, behind-the-scene financing and mass marketing control success or failure of a film property. Strategic gain for media properties has two stages: 1) first-time success with revenue and acclaim, and 2) the use of success to generate more sales. Moving a character to another genre, putting the film plot in another form, or using the film as an anchor to launch a movie of the same type are all forms of extending a property. To begin, you'll see who watches and what audiences want, then how to reach them using a variety of promotional tools. Finally, you'll learn the basics of finance budgeting for its relevance to taking movies to film audiences.

Who goes to the movies and what do they want to see?

Today's audiences want to be transported away from the gloom of 24-hour news; they want happy endings, but they won't buy a fake one. Audiences are very fickle, and film appreciation varies by segment and genre. So to lure and hold audiences, marketers direct their attention to niche markets. Among the many options, these segments receive special attention from promoters:

+ **Gender:** *Women* generally go to movies about characters, so character development is crucial for attracting and keeping women in the audience. *Men*, of course, prefer action, and today's studios direct most of their attention at shooting up the screen.

+ **Ethnicity:** *Hispanic and African-American audiences* frequent films 30–40% more often than the general population; universal themes, such as family loyalty, appeal to these markets.

+ **Age:** Box office draws are aimed at *teenage audiences*, especially girls, and address topics of family, youthful rebellion, and teen pregnancy. *Boomers* react most favorably to nostalgia and are targeted for period pieces, biographies, and historical fiction.

- **Special circumstances:** *Military groups* and their families and the military personnel stationed overseas have become audiences for movies that deal with anxieties and dilemmas of war and separation.

- **Genre:** Like audience segments, film genres appeal to specific audiences. *War movie* audiences, for example, want films with distinct good guys and bad guys; black and white distinctions. To market a war movie successfully, the film needs to have something at stake: honor or pride or personal dignity. That's why audiences like films about World War II; there's no gray in them. *Fantasy films*—many digitally animated—have wide appeal, allowing parents and children to view the same film for different reasons: adults enjoy special effects while the kids delight to action and super-heroic activity.

- *Special interest*: *Independent filmgoers* are usually urban, at a median age of 33, with above average household income, and more educated than blockbuster film audiences. They want to be stimulated and challenged by film and are not so focused on being entertained. Unlike the happy ending crowd, these audiences don't respond to in-your-face marketing, preferring instead reliance on word-of-mouth, critical reviews, Internet and film Web sites, and wild postings hung around a city.

The newest genre to captivate movie audiences is the Hollywood-style documentary. Released with fanfare and receiving huge revenues in 2005, *March of the Penguins* supplied the emotional and narrative satisfactions associated with popular commercial cinema. Earning more than $75 million at the American box office, *Penguins* became the second highest grossing nonfiction movie ever. Why? This film gave audiences everything they want—an epic journey, a family in peril, moments of humor, tenderness and suspense, and a sonorous voice-over from Morgan Freeman—without using stars or special effects.[ii]

Positioning and selling a film

Marketers traditionally position films by genre, relying on the audiences' selective perception to focus on what has previously best entertained them. Directors sometimes confuse marketability with playability—a movie can preview like gangbusters with a recruited audience, but that doesn't mean it has marketable elements. Several factors play a role in a film's marketing success, including trailers, tie-ins, Oscar nominations, stars, previews and reviews, film festivals, the Internet, and viewing venues. Each of these elements contributes to positioning a film (or the viewing experience) apart from others in the marketplace. These distinctions are discussed here.

Role of trailers

Since the first Internet trailer (for *Stargate*) was shown in 1994, trailers have become the most important marketing tool for movie promotion. Teaser trailers, shown months in advance of release, peak audience interest about a forthcoming film and begin creating awareness of the title.

Full-length trailers, shown prior to the film's release, are produced for theaters and television commercials. When shown as part of a rolling series of previews or at the beginning of a home video, trailers may run as long as five or six minutes.

Trailers can be tailored to specific audience segments by focusing on certain elements of a film. Often two or three trailers are developed for different segments. Shots are typically edited out of the film for use in a buzz-building trailer. Because stars bring their own brand to a film, movie trailers must blend the star's traits with the movie's strengths.

Budgets for trailers run between $500,000 and $2 million. Trailers are adapted for television commercials and used in electronic press kits and as point-of-sale materials in video stores and on DVDs. In style, they are moving away from straight narration to include more music and fewer voice-overs. The best trailers have a beginning and a middle, but no end—audiences must see the movie to find out how the story ends.

Role of tie-ins and merchandising

Movie industry synergy is often created with what is called a *tent-pole film*, which is a hit whose profits often hold up everything else at the studio. By branding movies as *lumps of content*, marketers can create a winning synergy. Once the brand becomes an icon, it can be further exploited through merchandising and promotional tie-ins. Added exposure for family films comes from a close association with toy makers, apparel companies, and fast-food franchises. Movie tie-ins work most effectively with teens, who wear specialty brands and eat at McDonalds and Taco Bell.

15.1 Robert Downey Jr. poses with *Iron Man 2* merchandise.

As mentioned in an earlier chapter, tie-in partnerships have prompted retailers to go into new product lines with filmmakers. In 2010, Disney invested $1 billion to create partnerships with luxury designers for *Alice in Wonderland*-inspired goods. By targeting the film to adults, Disney tie-ins were pricier products that were part of an Alice Lifestyle Program. Check out these top-of-the-line tie-in products:

1. *Alice* **wonderland platform shoes by Versace, $1195.** Versace is known for her whimsical, often psychedelic styles.

2. *Alice* **evening gowns by Sue Wong, $328–630.** Dresses with White Rabbit inspiration include a colorblock dress ($328), a Flower Wonderland Inspired gown ($588) and a Victorian Long Lace Gown ($630).

3. *Alice* **handbag by Furla, $475.** This Italian brand known for classic leather designs created a handbag containing images from the fairytale that included a metal rabbit handclasp.

4. *Alice* **charm bracelet by Stella McCartney, $395.** This British included a necklace for $425 for the occasion.

5. *Alice* **"Couture" costume jewelry by Tom Binns, $175.** Both a high-end *Alice* collection with pieces costing up to $1000, and a more affordable line of costume jewelry that included a string of plastic hearts Red Queen necklace.

6. *Alice* **crystal-encrusted "Tea Party White Donut" by Swarovski, $115.** Four *Alice*-themed pendants, including a Tea Party Tea Pot for $150 were offered by this famous crystal maker.

FOCUS ON MERCHANDISING

Can Tie-Ins Transcend the Kids Market?

The movie licensing industry accounts for one quarter of all toys sold in a single year. Toys, video games, clothing, accessories, iPhone apps, and action figures are big money makers. For kids, Harry Potter tie-ins were the epitome of cool in the far-reaching empire of merchandise and tie-ins. The movies were a boon to retailers who inventoried countless *Goblet*-related items including watches, calendars, music, toys, clothing, collectibles and jewelry. Another example is *Transformers 2*, a movie that led toy sales in 2010 with $592 million after only six months. And movies like *Star Wars* have collected over $8 billion in merchandise sales revenues since 1977.

Films aimed at a youth audience are most suitable for merchandising, but another market is taking shape. Digital Playground, a high-budget porn provider, took a mainstream approach to merchandising by launching a 22-product line inspired by the "Pirates" porn movie series. The world's most expensive porns, complete with CGI and serious plots, *Pirates 1 and 2* product line focuses on pirate inspired vibrators based on characters from the movie.

But in such a low-budget industry, merchandising is capped at about a thousand units and may not be a viable option for the adult entertainment industry. To test the market, one product developer hired two full-time designers and two marketing professionals, met with large distributors worldwide, interviewed a multitude of retailers, tested four different packaging manufactures, hired over 50 test marketers to provide product feedback, developed sales and marketing strategies, and spent a significant amount of money developing the line.

Partnering with major movies has a high-risk level, even with a successful movie like 1988's *Roger Rabbit* whose merchandising flopped. For the adult market, lifestyle products are preferred over movie fan merchandise. Digital Playground based its offering of pirate themed merchandise on the notion that theme transcends movies and can stand on its own. Their female oriented line of products targets an audience that identifies with the product through function and design rather than the movie itself. Instead of relying on movie branding, these products are based loosely on a film's theme.

But movie merchandising may become a bigger trend in the heavily pirated adult industry; some studios are moving towards higher quality productions aimed at viewers who will pay for professional HD content. This is partly because people who are actually willing to pay for porn want HD, high quality porn. Better produced porns could generate merchandise other than hats or t-shirts and become a viable channel for making money in an industry struggling to create content and products that people will pay for.

Source: Lydia Leavitt for crunchgear.com, Feb. 2010

Mel Gibson chose to partner his film with Christian organizations when marketing *The Passion of Christ*. Enlisting 2,000 Christian retailers to build the buzz for the film's release (on Ash Wednesday, an annual Christian holy day), Gibson and Newmarket Films promoted through churches to 120 million parishioners using printed materials and online sermons for preachers. Retail outlets sold packs of witness cards containing spiritual messages on one side and a promotion on the other for $5.95 a pack. Pendants of large and small pewter nails on leather thongs retailed at $13 and $25; 100 thousand were sold. Three thousand behind-the-scenes coffee table books about making the movie sold for $25 in a single week. Framed paintings and prints based on the movie, selling for between $30 and $100, generated sales of 20,000 units in three weeks. *Passion*'s logo was prominent in NASCAR's Daytona 500. Ten-second television trailers were developed featuring specific churches for a cost of $795 to Newmarket and $1000 to the co-sponsor. So in spite of the film's low box office take, licensed goods provided enough revenue for Gibson and Icon Distribution to cover the costs of production and then some.[iii]

Role of stars

A general assumption is that stars are absolutely essential to mainstream film production, both in Hollywood and at cinemas across the globe. Without a doubt, stars are a key element in the overall film package. A weapon in the film financier's armory, stars are essential for creating a promotable film package. However, the popularity of a star-driven film depends the marketing process connected with it.[iv]

Stars must "work" the picture with publicity junkets and media interviews. Shortly before a film is released, appearance schedules are developed with producers of network and cable programs such as *The Today Show*, *Oprah*, *David Letterman*, and *Larry King*. Most stars rely on their publicist or the studio's publicist to develop junket schedules. Others determine their own availability for appearances. Tom Cruise has final approval over all marketing materials on his films and does a smart job of selling his own movies. For the film *Collateral*, for instance, he insisted on an ensemble junket where they appeared together because he knew Jamie Foxx would attract a different audience than he would.[v]

But marketing doesn't always create stars; the public often makes those determinations. Look at Johnny Depp. He's now a gigantic star but he's been a great actor for many years. In spite of good marketing, it took *Pirates of the Caribbean* to make him a big movie star—the audience spoke.[vi] His role in *Alice in Wonderland*, a film traditionally aimed at children, was used to skew the film to an older audience. You'll find more star-powered strategy celebrity marketing in Chapter 16.

Role of screenings, sneaks, and reviews

Test screenings presented at local movie theaters or mall locations measure target audience reaction to movies. Respondents see an unfinished version of a film, then complete a survey with detailed questions regarding plot, characters, and scenes. Producers use these comments to edit the film accordingly. Screenings are valuable pre-release tools.

15.2 "At the Movies" film critics give them thumbs up or down.

© Arkady, 2010. Used under license from Shutterstock, Inc.

To get favorable word of mouth promotion before a film is released, studios schedule sneak previews and capture audience comments as they emerge from the theater. Sneak comments are featured in news clips and video releases to correspond with the film's opening. Well-edited responses become positive testimonials to audience enjoyment and can used to stimulate interest in a specific audience segment. Sneaks are important for generating enthusiasm for a new film.

Professional reviews matter, but they aren't enough to sell a blockbuster film. Roger Ebert, for instance, gives thumbs up to many of the films he reviews, and his comments usually headline print film ads. So no one really pays attention to the "two thumbs up" designation. For independent or foreign films, however, reviews are significant determinants of box office revenues. These audiences may peruse three or four critics' columns before determining whether or not to see a film.

Role of ratings

Ratings have an effect on audience make up and ultimately box office revenues. Getting the ideal balance that includes both teens and adults is tricky; producers need the teens but don't want to deter adults with a PG rating. However, X ratings severely narrow the viewing field.

Determined by the MPAA board majority vote, rating appeals require a two-thirds vote to overturn a board rating. A PG 13 rating is issued when ONE sexually derived word is used as an expletive; more than one requires an R rating. Trailers also require approval prior to release, they must tell the audience which rating the trailer and the movie advertised are assigned. "All audience" rated trailers have a green designation; "restricted" designations have a red background to avoid mismatching.

Role of the Internet

The Internet has brought a dimension to film promotion that exceeds what has been possible through all the other promotional devices combined. By bringing fans together, soliciting comments, and creating buzz, the Internet now has a primary role in movie marketing. Substantial portions of a film's budget are allocated to developing and maintaining an appropriate Web site.

Film Web sites give audiences an opportunity to experience the brand before and after its release. Most sites use games and gimmicks to entertain and involve potential audiences. Blogs, social networks, Twitter, and fan sites are important for stimulating interest, creating buzz, and generating box office revenues.

Role of the Oscars

The leverage of an Oscar nomination is well known; the ceremony is one of the most-watched broadcasts in the world. In terms of box office and DVD sales, a Best Picture Oscar has lasting value. Best Actor and Best Actress only matter to the actor and actress. What really helps is a lot of nominations. In our volume-related society, 10 nominations for one movie is very impressive.[vii]

Even more significantly, nominations for independent and foreign films create new audiences from the recognition and publicity the Oscars generate. Other awards, such as recognition from

A CLOSER LOOK AT PROMOTING SUPERHEROES

Marketing the Fantastic Four

Remaining in the shadow of other comic superheroes like Spiderman and X-Men, the Fantastic Four have stood by while other characters from the Marvel Comics lineup got the full Hollywood treatment. The first Marvel superheroes of the San Lee era, the Fantastic Four established the Marvel trademark of sympathetic heroes. When 20th Century Fox released its $100 million adaptation of the *Fantastic Four*, they hoped it would be their best chance to turn the last superstars in the Marvel collection into a global franchise of video games, action figures and assorted billions in ancillary revenue that follows—a tent-pole film.

One advantage for promoters was the fans who had been waiting decades for the movie. With conventions and Web sites devoted to their beloved comic books, fans were powerful tools for creating and spreading buzz. After decades of shoddy development, Fox needed an outstanding screenplay to position itself among other releases in a competitive summer release season.

Fox and Marvel built the Fantastic Four release around the refrain: *Take the number 4 and repeat it.* Production Chief Avi Arad spent weeks interviewing comic book-nerds at festivals such as Comic-Con in San Diego and Wizard World in Los Angeles. With an audience strangely obsessed with what Hollywood would make of their childhood heroes, Arad faced the promotion challenge head on.

Using Web sites to generate movie rumors and news, Fox sites generated Internet ads and as many as 3 million hits a month. But fans had high expectations and were hypersensitive to changes in characters. Before its release, *Ain't It Cool News* echoed the concern by publishing a blistering critique of a movie rewrite that had been long-since discarded, resulting in a bad buzz.

Fox offered fan sites enough unique content to build and expand their interest in the film. Fan sites were fed bits of news and concept art at strategic intervals. The cast was sent to comic book conventions where publicists distributed plastic vials of "cosmic dust." And the studio held an event for fan site developers, flying correspondents to the set in Vancouver with complementary rooms. Media, given exclusive images from the film for their sites, were allowed interviews with the director and cast members.

Trailers were shipped to 3,200 theaters with Marvel's *Elektra* to introduce Fantastic Four to its target audience; unfortunately *Elektra* was Marvel's biggest flop ever. After releasing *Revenge of the Sith*, Arad learned that courting comic book fans was only part of the game—the general public needed to be introduced as well.

So the movie was promoted in TV, print, and radio ads; Burger King aired its own *Fantastic Four* commercials for both adults and kids. Kraft hawked *Fantastic Four* Lunchables. Star Michael Chiklis (as Ben Grimm) appeared as The Thing in TV spots for Samsung phones with the tagline, "it's fantastic!" Promotions included courting theater owners at the ShoWest industry convention in Las Vegas with an hour-long, celebrity-heavy presentation and a splashy highlight reel that previewed the upcoming Fox lineup.

Ultimately, it was the franchise rather than the film that generated profits. The first weekend box office was $56 million, and total gross revenue came to $155 million after six months. *Fantastic Four* pleased some fans but dismayed others and most reviewers. Roger Ebert gave the PG-rated, 110-minute film a thumbs down, complaining that the picture was "All set-up and demonstrations without any character development."[viii]

What do you think?

1. How else might Marvel have used its fans to help promote the film?

2. How should they have educated the public about the comic book characters?

3. What could the studio have done to control high expectations for the film before it was released so fans were not disappointed?

4. What kind of research might have added to the film's script revision?

Source: Jonathan Bing, *Wired*, July 2005

Sundance and other film festivals, as well as the Golden Globes (which precede the Oscars), add equity to a film brand and usually results in enhanced box office sales.

Role of niche audiences

Film promotion is all about playing to a targeted audience. Disney took grass roots marketing to a new level by providing activities for juvenile detention centers in Los Angeles as a tie-in to the movie *The Chronicles of Narnia: The Lion, the Witch and the Wardrobe*. A class of teenagers enacted a mock trial of Edmund, a character in the movie, made crumpets in a cooking class, and recreated movie sets in construction classes as part of a buildup to see in the film when it was released.[ix]

Disney and its partner Walden Media have reached out to a panoply of special-interest groups, from the Coast Guard Youth Academy to Ronald McDonald House, wooing them with invitations to glitzy presentations on the studio lot and lavishing them with posters, snow globes, and other promotional gear. The team's marketing strategy included pulling a variety of themes from the storyline to build their campaign around. Themes included: World War II historical backdrop, the religious references of the characters, the fantasy element of the story, and such themes as loyalty, courage, good versus evil, and the importance of family.

Disney and HarperCollins, the publisher of the book written by C. S. Lewis, provided books to schools for in-class reading. Nineteen new editions of the novel coincided with the movie, along with activity books with glitter pens and magnets. *Narnia* materials were sent to every elementary and middle school in America, including posters, educational guides, and more than 90,000 copies of the novel and accompanying teaching lesson plans.

To back up these grassroots campaigns, a slew of promotional partners were recruited. Together they brought in marketing efforts valued at $15 million that targeted kids and families at shopping malls with everything from elaborate exhibits to fake snow. Walden has the rights to adapt six other Lewis books in the series and an 18-year franchise deal, so this was only the tip of the impending promotional iceberg.

Role of venues

Movie venues can be in-theater or out-of-theater. New in-theater experiences are being created to lure audiences to movie houses. Out-of theater locations include airline viewing and outdoor locations.

In-flight movies offer marketing value through licensing fees and features in airline magazines. Summer attendance at outdoor movie locations is soaring. Audiences are watching movies among sculptures at the North Carolina Museum of Art in Raleigh, amid the skyscrapers in New York City's Bryant Park, in a parking lot across from a Seattle pub, and from a marble mausoleum in Hollywood's Forever Cemetery[x]. Because **temporary venues** are so flexible in that they can be almost anywhere, the practice is not likely to disappear soon. What the temporary venue really speaks to is how much the idea of novelty is central to the entire viewing experience. Audiences insist on it. Perhaps that has been true all along, but lately it seems that viewers set the pace, and distributors struggle to keep up. The temporary venue is a response to that shift, one that will work until something else comes along and makes it seem obsolete.

Traditional viewing venues are also upping the novelty ante. Theaters located in malls, in an effort to set up the movie-going experience as a special event, are combining adult-only screenings with dinner before the film or with desert following the feature. Such packaged marketing efforts help studios promote movies to specific market segments. Cineplexes also foster multiple viewing options for families with different preferences.

Some movie viewers complain that pre-film advertisements are ruining the experience. To address the complaint, Screenvision, one of two companies that package on-screen advertising for exhibitors, invested $50 million in a digital projection system to improve the viewing quality of advertising. The other company, National CineMedia, is introducing 20-minute packages, which include, along with the ads, behind-the-scenes segments from impressive movie sets. With many audiences preferring home viewing, venues are taking measures to bring them back to theaters, including pre-viewing experiences and in-theater entertainment (dining, interviews with stars) prior to the movie.

Role of aftermarket sales

Almost half of the revenue made by studios on feature films is generated by DVD sales; 23% from theatrical releases, 12% from video rentals, and 17% from other sources such as merchandising and licensing. A high percentage of movie revenues comes from DVD sales from sites like Netflix and Redbox. Redbox, as opposed to Netflix, has two winning promotion tactics. First, they offer consumers an incredibly easy way to rent the most popular movies—run by a convenience store or grocery store and there are movies for only a dollar. Second, they do something for the movie industry that for the most part only Netflix pays minimum guarantees with no returns. In other words, a movie distributor can take an order from Redbox for 500k units at $10 a DVD, with no returns and no resale of the DVD into the aftermarket. Redbox will actually destroy the DVDs. That's a quick and easy $5,000,000 in hassle free revenue. From the studio perspective, that's $5 million in net margin that doesn't require the overhead and actual costs of distribution and returns, along with the opportunity to spend less on marketing and advertising to promote the title. Redbox takes care of all of that. Doing business with Redbox can be good business for larger movie distributors because Redbox reduces the revenue risk and increase the revenue for every title they take. That's hard for any studio to walk away from.

Netflix is the *only* company with an online offering that produces minimum guarantees for movie titles. Everyone else offering online sales and rentals does so on a consignment basis. They put no cash up front. They don't reduce the risk for movie studios, they actually increase the risk. According to Mark Cuban of wallstreetpit.com, the first pure online company that can demonstrate a reliable ability to monetize content online and can offer guarantees, will turn the industry upside down.

To insure continuing sales of aftermarket products, film studios must make their initial marketing efforts strong enough to carry audience momentum to the next stage—buying or renting the DVD or video. Because DVDs are a larger part of Hollywood's revenue stream than any other source, concern over slowing sales runs high.

Role of film festivals[xi]

Much media hype centers around film festivals. The most popular currently is Utah's Sundance Festival, where major and minor players come looking for hits. Being selected for a premiere at a well-known festival is a great accomplishment, however, entrance into the festival is only an opportunity to compete with dozens of other films for the attention of the festival-goers, media and distribution agents.

The atmosphere of a top film festival involves the crush of television cameras and newspaper reporters who hunt for "the buzz" of what's hot. Internationally known movie studios, festival sponsors, distributors, and dot-coms all try to outdo each other in a desperate fight to capture a share of the eyeballs. Here are some guerilla marketing techniques used by low budget productions that provide hip festival marketing campaigns where consistency is key to success.

- **Promotional materials** should have consistent themes, colors and designs. Clean designs are very important; use white space effectively to draw attention away from the sense-deadening clutter. Glossy color reproductions are a must as black and white photocopied materials are a waste of paper and time, considering the competition.

- **Handbills** or postcards handed out by volunteers are the name of the game. Very few festival-goers will refuse a handbill, which guarantees a cursory glance, which is the only opportunity promoters get.

- **Stickers** are risky promotion tactic that is best avoided. A few malicious prankster-placed film stickers can result in vandalism charges.

- **Postering** is the most obvious and the most common element of any promotional campaign. Target unconventional festival locations to distribute posters because the target audience (film attendees) will not be seeing the competition's vast array of other offerings.

- **T-shirts and Hats** are a bit more expensive, but well worth the price. Although there is more space on a T-shirt, hats are closer to eye-level. The most profound psychological effect of promotion is seeing someone wearing clothing that promotes a film. A T-shirt or hat is part of a living, breathing human being who represents the film. It suggests that this particular film has a fan base and a group of supporters behind it, that the film has been seen and liked.

- **Use Promotion Teams:** Dispatching small groups of people into the street to give away promotional items can be extraordinarily effective, especially if your teams are all wearing promotional clothing that ties into giveaways.

- **Create a Scene:** Nothing attracts a crowd like a crowd. Get as many volunteers as possible in a high traffic area and give them something to talk about. The filmmakers and some of the subjects of one documentary dressed up as characters from the film and gathered in the street shortly before the film's screening. One of the subjects of the documentary, a professional impersonator, carried a portable CD player which was blasting songs from the film's sound track. The group of costumed people began dancing to the music, making noise, having a good time, and inviting people to come to the film.

- **Stand Apart:** The most important thing to remember is that you can make the biggest splash by not following the crowd. As with all promotion, originality and creativity are the keys to success; doing things differently will yield rewarding results.

According to agents, producers and buyers, a new class division has been created in the independent market—the so-called *mini-majors*. Most of these "bigger" **indies** (independent films) are actually owned by giant studios, who pursue independent movies with the potential to earn substantial money at the box office. Smaller "micro-distributers" are left with the many titles that could turn a profit at much lower prices. According to a William Morris Independent representative, studios are moving out of the low-budget art-house business, and are looking for surprise hits. Low-budget movies that gross under $5 million are most interesting to smaller studios, such as Lions Gate, which paid nearly $3 million for worldwide rights to *Right at Your Door*, a low-budget thriller about a terrorist attack that paralyzes Los Angeles. The studio offered the production company a percentage of the box-office gross and region/territory openings as well. Roadside studio is another successful player in the new lower-priced indie landscape; they paid more than $600,000 for domestic rights to *Stay*, an offbeat comedy with a bestiality angle.

Role of the global film market

The expanding foreign box office has helped rejuvenate a number of films that have suffered in the U.S. market, especially epics set in ancient times such as *Kingdom of Heaven, King Arthur*, and *Alexander*. Animated films are also getting a boost from foreign interest, and many studios are now focusing more on international releases for both epics and animations.

Creative campaigns for U.S. films don't always translate across borders. For *War of the Worlds*, for instance, a separate creative campaign was designed for Japan to play up the link between the daughter and her father protecting the family—a response to the importance of females in the overall Japanese audience. According to a Warner marketer, Europeans are more character driven, while Asians and Latin Americans prefer action.[xii] Marketing with customized trailers helps bring a cultural focus to insure a movie's success abroad.

In just five years, China has become what Hollywood considers the world's most important producer of foreign-language blockbusters, catapulting beyond France, Spain, or India in global box-office receipts. Why? Chinese filmmakers have combined a formula of high-quality production, exotic setting, gorgeously choreographed action, and universal themes that sell equally well in Boston and Beijing.[xiii]

By marrying low-cost, high-quality projects with U.S. distribution, Chinese producer Bill Kong has made hits grossing a total of $500 million. Yet he's never produced a picture in Los Angeles or in English. His first film, *Crouching Tiger, Hidden Dragon*, was a result of wooing Hollywood to front half of the $15 million budget. By filming in Shanghai, Kong shoots six days a week and has a film completed in four months for $30 million, half the cost of shooting in the U.S.

Filmmakers from Hollywood, Hong Kong, and China have teamed up to duplicate Hollywood's long-successful formula: earn enough money domestically to cover the costs of making a film and then generate big profits through global distribution. In 2008, over 400 films were in production on the mainland. China now offers Hollywood studios a growing audience, and the buzz on Chinese films has sparked a gold rush among investors. The Hengdian Group, a Chinese pharmaceutical company, built a film studio that is equivalent to Universal Studios— both the movie lot and the theme park. Revenues are generated from the 3 million tourists who pay to watch filming in China each year.

Avatar director James Cameron says an era of 3D films began in China in 2009 with a string of 3D films produced both at home and abroad and released on Chinese silver screens. Chinese cinemas have been installed with advance technology 3D film projectors. Audience members are embracing the new experience of watching spectacular films wearing 3D glasses. As a genre of the big screen, 3D films are expected to see its popularity rise over the next two years as more foreign and domestic filmmakers embrace 3D technology.[xiv]

Creating a promotion budget

Although there is no formula for creating a marketing budget for a film, studios consider these variables:

+ Film's potential gross

+ Audience makeup

+ Gross of similar genres

+ Anticipated revenues from foreign or video sales

+ Number of screens used for release

+ Number of markets included in the release

Pitching Natural Born Killers to a UK audience

Rather the pitching to the huge audience aggregation as it had identified in the U.S., Warner Brothers' marketers pitched the Oliver Stone film to a relatively narrow audience of young adult males in Britain. The film combined elements of both a cult film and a mainstream hit and was positioned in the market as something of an outlaw film. But the promotion was not without problems.

The circulation strategy of *Natural Born Killers* in Britain was based upon the film's industrial setting, the film's classification delay, and the presses' response. The film had become a surrounded by discourses of outrage in the period leading up to its British release. Instituted by press commentators and reviewers, anxieties about the film mobilized concerns about direct audience effects of the film's violence. Then reports of "copycat" killings allegedly inspired by the film caused the British Board of Film Classification (BBFC) to delay *Killers* for two months, giving marketers only eight weeks to run its advertising campaign.

The target audience included two main groups: working-class males enthusiastic about violent films and a more discerning cinemagoer group from the middle class who were already fans of the Tarantino-style cult hit *Reservoir Dogs* and *Pulp Fiction*.

Warner Brothers dedicated a more extensive advertising campaign to hooking the "downmarket" audience group, which consisted of "unthinking males" and "new violence" audiences. Cutting across these two groups was a third faction—rock music fans. Copying from the recording industry advertising technique of fly posting, posters were distributed with independent record stores and big name chains. Promotions were held at selected universities with posters and T-shirts, and competitions and coverage in student populations.

Ultimately, the beneficial commercial advertising effects of media hysteria put audience awareness of the film at 77% two weeks before its opening and 83% by the week of its release; an impressive 94% awareness among males under 25 was realized. Once awareness was achieve, marketing efforts were directed a clearing up lingering confusion about whether or not it was banned and to stress its imminent release. Two advertisements were assembled featuring the film's stars: a Woody Harrelson ad was aimed at men and the other, featuring Juliette Lewis, was aimed at women. The ads were placed in television programs with guaranteed male audiences—a boxing match and as a trailer preceding a James Bond film.

The press advertising campaign was aimed largely "downmarket," featuring Harrelson with a tag line, "The controversy starts when you see the film." Heavy publicity schedules were arranged for director Stone and producer Jan Hamsher. In the end, moral panic in the media and the delay in release differentiated the film from other releases and positioned it as an outrageous and attractive product. *Natural Born Killers* opened in UK screens with a moderately successful release.

Source: Thomas Austin, *Hollywood, Hype & Audiences*, 2002

A traditional budget includes 65–70% for TV ads and the balance on print and outdoor, with about 3% for the poster. Once the target audience is identified, a budget can be determined based on size. Major studios allocate advertising budgets as follows:

Newspapers—15%   Internet—9%

Network TV—24%   Spot TV—18%

Trailers—6%   Non-media (tie-ins, publicity)—16%

Other media (radio, outdoor, magazine)—20%

Movie studios are reassessing TV ads because audiences have caught on to studios' tactics for making an event out of every new movie. In a push to cut TV costs, some studios are aligning themselves with different sorts of advertisers. To market *Wedding Crashers*, New Line joined forces with Anheuser-Busch, brewer of Budweiser beer. Budweiser sponsored the movie's New York City premiere, retail promotions, and local screenings and offered *Wedding Crashers* content on its Web site. *Crashers* figured prominently in two Bud TV spots and in an online movie ad called "Crash this Trailer," which allowed users to substitute images of their faces on the bodies of *Crashers* stars Owen Wilson and Vince Vaughn. In another saving move, Fox spread the same money it would have spent on network prime-time spots over a handful of cable channels, and purchased prime-time ads via local stations rather than through national networks.[xv]

Budgeting for independent and short films

Independent and specialty art films require minimal budgets for newspaper advertising, festival participation, and screenings aimed at opinion leaders. By avoiding summer or holiday releases, indies must consider and work around feature release schedules. Sites like boxofficeguru.com or showbizdata.com publicize release dates around which indies should be scheduled to avoid competition with blockbusters and major studio releases. An allowance for reviewer tickets is recommended as well. Marketers need to have films mentioned on reviewing sites like indieclub.com and indietalk.com to began creating buzz. Send news releases to magazines such as *Independent Filmmaker*, *Millimeter*, and *Markee*, and to cable shows that feature short films for public airing.

The most famous buzz-generating indie is *The Blair Witch Project*. By developing an Internet site one year before it hit the screens in 1999, *Witch* producers generated 75 million hits and gained enough investors to see a profit on the film. Filmed in "mockumentary" style by Central Florida Film School pals, *Witch* developers posted messages about the film before it was released. Six months following the release, thousands of other sites appeared, and the hype continued to gain momentum. Editors who hadn't even seen the film posted rave reviews on the Internet, and after its presentation at the Sundance Film Festival, there was no stopping it. Based on the hype, Artisan Entertainment bought the film for $1 million and redeveloped the Web site into an interactive experience that convinced teens the footage was real.

Witch writers made the cover of *Time* and *Newsweek* and took every interview that came along; if none came, they were not ashamed to beg. Based on their success, filmmakers offered these buzz rules for independent filmmakers:

+ It's not always important the people understand you.

+ It's how things seem, not how they really are, that is important to the suits in Hollywood; pretend you have a film.

+ Don't worry about the script, just start a Web site about your movie idea and talk about it as if it's in production.

+ Get busy writing script and hope it works.

Promoting short films on a small budget begins with the Internet, using sites like undergroundfilm.com, ifilm.com and brownfish.com, or producing a self-developed site. Promoting self-developed sites is accomplished with blogs that get the attention of *Ain't It Cool News* as well as *Film Threat*, shortfilminsider.com, and *Internet Video Magazine*. Formal press releases via fax or email and placing the short on TV and cable shows that feature short films are also prudent strategies. Good publicity doesn't have to be expensive, just creative.

MOVIE ECONOMICS

In no other business is a single example of product fully created at an investment of millions of dollars with no real assurance that the public will buy it. In no other business does the public use the product and then take away with them merely the memory of it.[xvi]

Domestic box office revenue increased by 8% in 2009, with motion pictures generating a record $10.6 billion. While ticket sales increased from 1.36 billion in 2008 to 1.41 billion in 2009, they remained lower than the all-time high of 1.6 billion set in 2002.[xvii]

Hollywood keeps worrying about where the money will come from for new feature films. Many of the factors that affect other industries—economic cycles, foreign exchange rates, technological advances, and interest rates—also affect profits and valuations for the film industry. A macroeconomic view suggests the following film industry givens:

+ Seasonal demand patterns are more easily discerned and interpreted than long-wave admission cycles.

+ Ticket sales for new film releases normally are not very responsive to changes in box office prices per se, but there may be sensitivity to the total cost of movie going, which can include fees sitters, meals, and parking.

- Market share data have limited application and relevance for film because consumers have little brand identification with movie distributors and because market share tends to fluctuate considerably from year to year for every distributor.

- Trade effects or "cultural discounts" are low for U.S. films because the basic global language is English.

- Total fees from the licensing of films for use in ancillary markets have collectively far overshadowed revenues derived from theatrical releases.

Doing the Hollywood math involves more than just calculating box office sales; it reflects revenue generated from home viewing on DVD or video, TV, and merchandise licensing as well. For the first time since 2002, U.S. consumers spent more to see Hollywood movies in theaters in 2009 than on buying them on DVD and Blu-ray discs, industry figures that trend is expected to continue.[xviii] Adams Media Research reported that U.S. box office receipts boomed to $9.87 billion in 2009 and overtook DVD and Blu-ray sales of $8.73 billion. Overall DVD and Blu-ray sales including films, television shows, concert videos and other content declined about 10 percent to $13 billion in 2009.

In 2010, in spite of softening box office revenue, profits were booming, thanks to the home market, sales to television, and rapid growth overseas. Record revenues of over $50 billion are also boosted by mega-blockbusters like *Avatar* (which surpassed the $1 billion mark in March 2010) that bring in between $200 and $500 million at the U.S. box office.

Convention-generated revenue

One of the most established media-based fan clubs, Star Trek, continues to generate revenue and create excitement for fans nationwide. At the Las Vegas Convention Center in 2007, the Star Trek Fan Club held a convention to celebrate Episode III of *Star Wars*. Film and series celebrities, archive exhibits of film props and costumes, contests, and exclusive merchandise were all convention features. Sponsorship packages came in a variety of forms and prices:

- "Brought to you by" for $130,000

- Co-sponsorship for $100,000

- Contributing sponsorship for $70,000

- Product or service sponsorship for $40,000

- Special events sponsor for costume contest, auction, Jedi training, a kids' room, concessions, hotels for a range of investment dollars

- Promotional partner sponsorship for $15,000

Sponsorship included two levels of benefits: media and site-based. *Media benefits* included email blasts, online and print collateral materials, on-site exposure and signage, press kit mention, logo on publications and newspaper, online flyers, and ads in the programs. *Site benefits* included a booth, public address announcement, volunteer shirts, press room use, convention badges and hotel discounts, and collectable merchandising. Fan Web sites offered the sponsors substations, communications centers, recreation rooms, and docking bays to promote their brands at the convention, still a great way to promote pop-culture-based extravaganzas.

Financial foundations; microeconomic factors

The movie business is contract driven. Film studios simultaneously engage in four distinct business functions: financing, producing, distributing, and marketing/advertising. We'll now look briefly at these financing aspects.

Some of the most creative work in the industry is reflected in the financial offering prospectuses that are circulated in attempts to find film projects. Financing sources come from the *industry* (distributors, talent agencies, etc), from *lenders* (banks, insurance companies) and *investors* (public and private pools). The most common financing variations available from investors and lenders are: common stock offerings, combination deals with other securities, limited partnerships and tax shelters, and bank loans.

Labor unions have an important influence on the economics of filmmaking for their below-the-line production costs, which can be easily estimated. The major Hollywood unions include:

+ American Federation of Television and Radio Artists (AFTRA)
+ Directors Guild of America
+ International Alliance of Theatrical and Stage Employees (IATSE)
+ Producers Guild of America
+ Screen Actors Guild (SAG)
+ Writers Guild of America

For membership fees, unions negotiate contract terms with a studio's bargaining organization, the Alliance of Motion Picture and Television Producers (AMPTP).

Distributors

Films are first distributed to the market that generates the highest marginal revenue over the least amount of time. The usual sequence has historically been theatrical release, licensing to pay cable distributors, home video, network TV, and local television syndicators. With larger and larger amounts of capital invested in features, pressures for faster recoupment is moving the market earlier opening of all windows. In fact, some studios are simultaneously releasing to all channels of distribution.

Distributors normally design their marketing campaigns with specific target audiences in mind. Some send bid letters several months in advance of a release to theaters located in regions where they expect to find audiences most responsive to a specific film's theme and genre. Theaters that accept bid letter terms receive a sliding percentage of box-office gross after allowance for house (theater) expenses. For many theater owners, box office receipts are secondary to concession stand revenues, over which they have total control of proceeds. Film exhibitors are subject to capacity and competition as well as rentals percentages for which they bid. Volatile over the short run, theatrical exhibition is remarkably consistent over the long haul.

Revenue recognition factors

Revenues from theatrical exhibition is straightforward, consisting of either percentage or flat-rent contracts. The AICPA guide indicates that television license revenues for feature films should not be recognized until the following conditions are met:

1. Film license fee is disclosed

2. Film costs are determined

3. License fee is collectable

4. Licensee accepts film in accordance with license agreement conditions

5. Film is available (distributor retains discretion on availability date)

For inventoried films, costs allocated to secondary markets and that are not expected to be realized within twelve months are classified as *noncurrent* in the following categories of film production: released, completed but not released, in process, and story rights/scenarios.

Big picture accounting

The legal heart of most film projects is the production-financing-distribution (PFD) agreement, which includes: step deals, packages, presales, and private funding. Each of these financial options provides the producer with different trade-offs in terms of creative control and profits. Most important is the distribution-agreement section for allocation of revenue streams.

What happens to a dollar that flows from the box office helps explain the revenue process. Assuming that house expenses are 10%, the remaining 90 cents is a 90:10 split for the first two weeks in favor of the distributor who realizes an 81-cent gross. A 30% distribution fee of 24 cents is subtracted, leaving 57 cents. Advertising and publicity costs (20–25% of rentals) deduct another 20 cents. From a remaining 37 cents, 6 cents is required for miscellaneous distribution expenses (prints, taxes, transportation). A residual pool of on 31 cents of the original dollar remains before negative costs of the picture are calculated. When gross participation to a major actor is factored in (usually 10%), there is 8 cents less with which to recoup negative costs. If the movie is studio financed, half of any profit after recoupment is owed the studios, the other half split among other participants. Despite this risk, many investors find filmmaking financially attractive and worth the risk.

Studios engage in three distinct television-related activities: licensing features to networks, syndication of features to local stations, and production of made-for-television movies. Feature licensing is the most lucrative; it may generate a profit margin of between 40 and 65% for the studio distributor.

The essential strength of major film studios is in their ability to control distribution from the early financing stages to the timing of theatrical releases. The enormous amount of capital required to operate film production and distribution facilities on a global basis presents a significant barrier to entry and reinforces the trend toward vertical integration of the industry. Production or *sunk costs* include most of the expenditures, so exposure to a variety of exhibition windows is essential for realizing a profit.

Threats to the movie industry

Two significant obstacles confront studios before they can see substantial incomes from making movies available to watch anytime of a big-screen TV or tiny iPod: piracy and pricing. According to the U.S. movie industry's trade body (Motion Picture Association of America), one in four people on the Internet have illegally downloaded a film and the problem is set to get worse.

The rise of broadband Internet access and cheap storage, along with the growth of digital content, has enabled digital piracy to flourish around the world.[xix] According to the information technology & Innovation Foundation, these practices threaten not only the robust production of digital content in the future, but U.S. jobs in the present. Unfortunately, many advocates, believing that information should be free, would have government not only turn a blind eye to digital piracy, but actively tie the hands of companies who seek to limit digital piracy.

And although piracy is a serious problem in the United States, it is even more serious in many other parts of the world, especially emerging markets. The Business Software Alliance found, for example, that although software piracy declined or remained the same in over eighty percent of countries, global piracy still increased by 3% in 2008 because of rapidly expanding growth in PC ownership in high piracy regions such as Asia and Eastern Europe. To change social behavior, some content owners have tried to educate users on the impact of piracy through marketing campaigns. These tactics work in parallel with efforts to provide users legal means to access content, such as developing new forms of distribution like the iTunes store or Hulu.

Major film studio representatives say piracy on the Net has cost them billions of dollars, even though box office takings rose by 1.7% domestically and 5.2% worldwide in 2008. The MPAA has attributed the increase in piracy to rising ticket prices as the number of total tickets sold dropped by 2.6% internationally.

EXHIBIT 15.1 Piracy Matrix to Combat Piracy

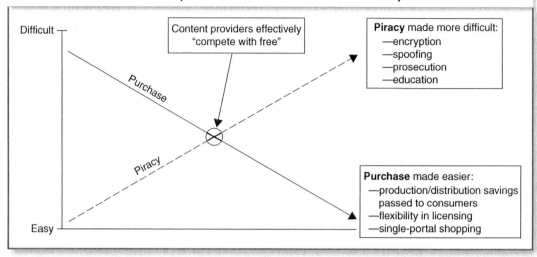

A study conducted by the MPAA questioned 3,600 Internet users who regularly went to the cinema from across the world. It found that a quarter admitted to having downloaded a film from the Internet. In Korea, six out of 10 Internet users download movies.

Motion picture piracy in China costs U.S. studios nearly $300 million a year, according to industry estimates. Though the Chinese allow as many as 20 U.S. theatrical releases into the country each year, the average number of U.S. films admitted is 14.[xx]

More worrying for the film industry, many downloaders said they had cut back on trips to the cinema and were buying fewer DVDs. In a bid to combat piracy, the MPAA launched a global promotion campaign to hammer home the message that piracy is a crime. But it could face an uphill struggle in changing attitudes. The survey found that a fifth of downloaders had no qualms about getting hold of a movie before it was released in the cinema. And a majority said it was okay to download a film once it was available on DVD or video.

PROMOTING TELEVISION PROGRAMS

Unlike movie marketing, promoting television is much more focused on specific audiences and time slots. And it's all about the ratings game—getting a big share of the viewing audience. Rather than being controlled by studios, television production occurs through networks and cable stations (although network and cable station ownership is often held by a major motion picture studio). This section presents an overview of television promotion, including who watches, what they watch, which promotion strategies work, and what are continuing threats to the industry.

Boosting DVD Sales

To invigorate the release of a film on DVD that has been out of the market for a while requires promotional tactics to generate sales. Here are a few suggestions offered by associatedcontent.com:

- Create Media Bundles that include CD soundtracks, downloads, or additional DVD movies.

- Partner with medium-sized retail stores or other product manufacturers to sell films on DVD. Retailers can use them as incentives for customers who spend over a certain amount of money in their store. The same volume of DVD movies can be sold to manufacturers who are launching new products or marketing popular merchandise. By coupling DVDs with products that the film's intended audience would buy is most effective.

- DVD movies can also be used to promote film screenings and other events. Sell copies of the movie to large organization that can use them for the purpose of attracting fundraising event guests.

An integrated online campaign can also help a film become one of the top-selling DVDs.

Brand goals:

- Regenerate awareness of film months after theatrical release

- Create a dominating presence to rise above other home videos and DVDs released around the same time

Campaign elements

- Exclusive home page presence the day of the film's home release with an image of the star built into the background and pointing to a special co-branded site

- Include exclusive "blooper" content taken from the DVD, and a interactive trivia game

- Movie image featured on a puzzle game channel

- Sweepstakes with prizes including a theme-park vacation

- Downloadable film image wallpaper for electronics

Who watches TV

The easy answer is, of course, everyone. But audiences must be understood in terms of specific segments and viewing preferences. Ethnic groups and age or lifestyle segments make a difference in marketing television properties.

Ethnic groups

Television advertisers are recognizing the power of ethnic audiences by adding programming and integrating ethnic actors into popular dramas and situation comedies.

Another growing segment of viewers is the Latino audience, the largest minority group in the U.S. Hispanics retain a strong sense of ethnic identity and use media to help with the process of assimilation and for cultural maintenance. The Hispanic TV audience in the U.S. grew faster in 2009 than for the total TV population with a continued increase of Hispanic TV homes (2.3%) compared with total U.S. TV homes (0.3%) for the 2009–2010 TV season.

Research found that Latinos don't see themselves as one homogenous group, and often travel between two cultures.[xxi] As with African-American viewers, Latino audiences agree that media programming and formats are not meeting their needs. In response to those complains, TV producers have continually added characters and co-stars to network dramatic hits such as the "CSI:" series, "Without a Trace," and "Criminal Minds." According to Nielsen, ad spending data for the first half of 2009 suggests that advertisers are responding to the TV-watching growth in both the Hispanic and African-American markets.

Age and lifestyle cohorts

Kids, teens, gays, and boomers continue to attract viewers and advertisers; they are profiled here.

A booming market, *tot's* TV shows are being produced for the youngest viewers and the smallest eyeballs. Because profits are driven by merchandising, the commercial and creative sides of children's television are fusing in a way that can make them indistinguishable from one another.

TV networks are chasing youngsters because unlike their older siblings, they haven't abandoned TV for the Internet or video games, and they're home a lot. Preschoolers have their own channels, including Viacom's Noggin and PBS Kids' Sprout, and Sesame Workshop. But such kids shows can't rely on advertising revenue because commercials aimed at the very young seldom work. So, networks pay low fees to studios and turn to sales of toys and DVDs to make up the difference.

When Nickelodeon's popular "Kids' Choice Awards" program went to China in 2005, the producers were forced to make some serious modifications. There would be no voting on a favorite burp. Nor would children judge which movie character was the best at breaking wind. Viacom, which dominates youth-oriented programming in the United States and other parts of the world with its MTV and Nickelodeon networks, is aggressively courting Chinese youngsters, hoping to introduce them to its brand of playfully antiauthoritarian programming. After all, China has roughly 300 million people younger than 14, and Viacom executives warm to the idea of capturing even a sliver of a demographic that now exceeds the population of the entire United States. According to MTV, there's no such thing as a global strategy without China. Viacom already has a 24-hour MTV channel in southern Guangdong province. China Central Television and the Shanghai Media Group broadcast Nickelodeon's "Wild Thornberrys," "CatDog" cartoons, and "SpongeBob SquarePants."

Shows for older kids are also booming. *Teens* are not only watching television, they are using all media simultaneously. With more media experience than any generation in history, these media savvy adolescents watch less TV than any other age demographic. Yet teens interact with program text in a variety of ways after the television is turned off. For example, after watching an episode of "Hannah Montana," teenagers are able to visit the Web site and read letters written among particular characters. Teens buy soundtracks of their favorite shows and read about their favorite television actors in magazines. But they don't watch network TV, preferring instead WB, MTV, Comedy Channel, and Nickelodeon.[xxii]

Other audience segments are going through a featured metamorphosis. Shows starring gay males and females, pioneered by "Ellen," "Queer Eye for the Straight Guy," and "The L World" have been phased out in favor integrating gay characters into network and cable programming. Similar to what has occurred with ethnic groups (African-Americans and Latinos), gay character prominence in major shows has quelled the necessity to produce gay-specific programming in favor of character integration into regular programming.

The most desirable segment for advertisers, baby boomer viewers tune into network shows that deliver news or reflect their values. Network shows that are hits with large audiences are:

+ "60 Minutes" and the "CSI:" series (CBS)

+ "Larry King" (CNN)

+ "The News Hour with Jim Lehrer" (PBS)

+ "House" (Fox)

+ "Weeds" (Showtime)

+ "Bill Maher" (HBO)

Advertisers love boomers because of their buying power so they cultivate relationships with producers who determine brand placements, commercial buys, and sponsorships for the boomer audience.

Internet video viewers

The 35–49 year-old viewing segment has gravitated from giant-screen viewing toward Internet video.[xxiii] In April 2009, three of the top five sites, ranked by time spent viewing, were Hulu, ABC.com, and NBC.com. According to Nielsen, this middle-aged demographic helped fuel a significant increase (119%) in time spent watching Hulu between November 2008 and April 2009. Time spent watching on Hulu per viewer increased 20% from 147 minutes to 325 minutes in this same time period. Although this segment represents only 30% of total Hulu viewers, they spent 10% more time on the site than any other age group. This increase surge may be due in part to Hulu's aggressive promotion campaign, which began with a TV ad during the Superbowl.

Hulu, a joint venture among ABC, NBC, and Fox networks, may follow the way of subscription media to increase revenues. As of this writing, unless Hulu increases its number of ads and ad rates on the site, it may seek revenue from the viewers themselves.

FOCUS ON NETWORK PROMOTION

NBC President Speaks Out

During an interview between *Advertising Age* and Adam Stotsky, president of NBC Entertainment Marketing, network television promotion was discussed. Here is a synopsis of that interview.

AA: *In this era of fragmented audiences, how much are you changing the practice of running promos on your own network?*

Stotsky: Broadcast TV is still the most efficient medium to reach a mass, wide, broad audience, and since it is a media asset we have readily available, the value is still significant, and the effect is still quite profound. We don't reach as many people as we once did as often as we once did, but as you've seen from the power of the Olympics' performance or in CBS's performance this year with the Super Bowl, it's still an incredibly powerful driver.

AA: *What other strategies do you use?*

Stotsky: A key driver above and beyond on-air promotion has really been a social-media strategy. The opinions of online thought leaders and the discovery around different shows and different network brands within consumers' own social circles play an increased role in the implementation and design of our marketing strategy.

Networks have to innovate or die. There is a proliferation of consumer media choices, and as a media marketer, we've got to do everything we can to stand out and make consumers take notice. We thought our "Southland" promotion was a really innovative idea that the *L.A. Times* brought to us for a show that was based in Los Angeles and that was about the Los Angeles Police Department. Having a hometown paper collaborate with us was a good way to reach audiences, and it certainly contributed to a strong premiere of the show on NBC.

AA: *How did you market late-night comedians?*

Stotsky: Ultimately, our principal challenge in marketing a TV product is to drive initial sampling of the show. Each late-night comedian has his own specific brand of comedy and, certainly, his own unique audience to whom he'll be appealing. We had to create three different campaigns for the different brands and audiences.

1. Jimmy Fallon was targeted to a young consumer through college-campus initiatives. We did some in-bar activity, some on-premise promotion.

2. Conan was a well-established late-night talk-show host. We had a unique partnership with *Entertainment Weekly*, where for 10 weeks, Conan O'Brien and "The Tonight Show" sort of hosted TV reviews and more importantly, the *Entertainment Weekly* "Must List."

3. With Jay, the challenges were self-evident. The key call was disrupting consumer behavior and actually playing into one unique aspect of the format. What we set out to do strategically with Jay Leno at 10 was remind people that this was fresh comedy, comedy about the day's events, that if you DVR it, you wouldn't be up to speed with what's happening in the world.

AA: *Why use "snipes" (graphic elements at the bottom of the screen?)*

Stotsky: We try not to disrupt the viewing experience, but consumers say there is a benefit to knowing what's coming on next, so we keep a constant monitor in our qualitative consumer focus-group research on how we're doing. Some networks have intensive animated or live-action lower-third graphics. We choose not to do that.

AA: *What are your best promotional tools?*

Stotsky: Build buzz through digital media, give viewers an incentive to spread the word, and tie everything back to a larger campaign.

Source: Brian Steinberg for *AdAge*, March 15, 2010

What do audiences watch?

Measuring television audience viewing has been the exclusive property of Nielsen Inc. for years. In February 2010, however, Rentrak Corporation, a leader in multi-screen media measurement serving the advertising and entertainment industries, merged with DISH Network L.L.C. to commercially integrate DISH Network's TV viewing data with Rentrak's TV Essentials audience measurement service. Contributing the largest national TV viewing data set, DISH Network provides Rentrak the ability to become the only company to offer media measurement in all 210 TV markets, with more than 15 million televisions nationwide when combined with telco TV and cable viewing information. So what? Viewing information statistics will have a second source of reporting, benefiting advertisers and promoters alike.[xxiv]

Networks argue that television advertising is not dead. Viewer data from a range of sources shows that Americans spend on average more hours watching TV per week than they do online, suggesting that TV advertising is most likely to be effective when it forms emotional bonds between the brand and its consumers. Product placements and tie-ins also offer advertising opportunities in a variety of show genres.

Exhibit 15.2 features the most popular shows that advertisers loved and viewers watched during the spring 2010 season:

Based on audience ratings, television programming has evolved or morphed into a plethora of reality shows and sitcoms of all forms. Because of their popularity with global audiences, we'll look at profiles of both formats. Then we'll look at what's brand new.

EXHIBIT 15.2 Advertisers' Best Buys

SHOW	NET	18–49 RATING AVG./ AD REVENUE
NBC SUNDAY NIGHT FOOTBALL	NBC	7.5/1.00
AMERICAN IDOL-TUE	FOX	10.3/.38
GREY'S ANATOMY	ABC	5.4/.32
HOUSE	FOX	5.2/.31
AMERICAN IDOL-WED	FOX	9.5/.31
BIGGEST LOSER 8	NBC	4.2/.30
NCIS	CBS	4.3/.29
CSI: MIAMI	CBS	3.8/.26
DESPERATE HOUSEWIVES	ABC	5.2/.25
CRIMINAL MINDS	CBS	3.9/.24
NCIS: LOS ANGELES	CBS	3.7/.24
THE MENTALIST	CBS	4.0/.22
SAT NIGHT FOOTBALL	ABC	2.0/.22
THE BACHELOR	ABC	4.3/.22

DANCING WITH THE STARS	ABC	3.9/.21
PRIVATE PRACTICE	ABC	3.7/.21
CSI: NY	CBS	3.4/.21
CSI:	CBS	3.9/.21
THE BIG BANG THEORY	CBS	5.4
EXTREME MAKEOVER: HM ED	ABC	2.9
THE GOOD WIFE	CBS	2.8
BIGGEST LOSER 9	NBC	4.0
TWO AND A HALF MEN	CBS	4.9
BONES	FOX	3.3
BROTHERS & SISTERS	ABC	3.5
TV Ratings 2009 from The Nielsen Company.		

Reality TV shows

Why are there so many reality shows on television? Because they are economical, often interactive and create an avenues to fame for viewers. By keeping production costs low, using non-celebrities and tying in with advertisers, reality television producers have less to lose and more to gain than producers of sit-coms or dramas that rely on established star-power and top-notch writers.

Accounting for 69% of television shows worldwide, television audiences are exposed to a plethora of characters, plots and topics. Sub-categories include:

+ docu-soaps ("Big Brother")
+ celeb-reality ("Osborne's," "Celebrity Rehab")
+ game shows ("Dating in the Dark")
+ contest shows ("Biggest Loser," "American Idol," "Next Top Model")
+ sports shows ("Contender," "Ultimate Fighter")
+ makeover shows ("How do I Look?")
+ multiple combinations of the sub-categories ("Apprentice," "Survivor")

Even the former Alaska governor is getting into the act by teaming with uber-producer Mark Burnett to shop a reality series for 2011 about her home state, network sources confirm. Palin and her family would be followed on-camera in the show.

The genre has interchanged the role of audience member and audience subject by looking into the daily lives or ordinary people. According to a recent study, many reality viewers watch because of a personal desire for prestige and status.[xxv] Others are fascinated with status and prestige gained from participating, which fulfills their needs for their 15 seconds of fame. Voyeuristic programs allow participants to gain a type of celebrity status.

Reality shows are economical and travel well across boundaries. One drawback, however, is the loss of revenue from reruns that would defeat the notion of "real-time" action for viewers. But because audience members are able to influence and determine program content, new episodes and programs are destined to be crowd pleasers.

Success for the reality show *Survivor* was a result of a variety of factors, but the most important include:

- Co-branding with exotic travel destinations
- Creating excitement and hype through the contestant auditioning process
- Maintaining secrecy about coming seasons
- Promoting removed participants as celebrities to hype new episodes
- Using spot commercials to preview series events
- Maintaining an active Web presence
- Survivor finales and reunions at seasons' end

Part of the fascination with reality shows are the casting calls and audition phases where thousands of would-be cast members try out to appear on shows. Web site castingbackstage.com provides hopefuls with audition news about future and current reality-based shows.

Sitcoms

A favorite genre since the onset of television in the fifties, the sitcom, or situation comedy, has generated more fans over the years than any other type of programming. Loyal fans track sitcom characters and action over the decades, often viewing with several generations of their families. Para-social relationships—fans bonding with stars and treating them as real friends—are consistently formed between sitcom viewers and actors.

Taking fan loyalty to its heights, Fox asked fans of its beloved sitcom "Arrested Development" to make a formal declaration of their devotion. The brainchild of Fox executives who were increasingly leery about the show's future, the loyalty oath offered fans a chance to speak out and take action against the show's potential hiatus because of sinking ratings. Viewers pledged never-ending loyalty and allegiance to the show and promised to tune in for every episode in the third season. Fox claimed 100,000 signatures, but may have used the tactic as a rationale against its demise because of fan disloyalty![xxvi]

Promoters use gaming experiences to promote and retain sitcom audiences. Games often mimic sensibilities of the show that inspired them; "The OC" entwined players in an intricate social scene from the program. The experiences allow players to move freely through a simulated "OC" environment, said a Gameloft designer who developed the game. Producers like game promotion because it involves people with the show even when they're not watching.[xxvii]

GoTV helped viewers use their phones to catch up on the complex plotlines of ABC's "Desperate Housewives" and "Lost" through short recap clips. Major wireless carriers feature content inspired by many of the season's biggest shows, providing another promotional tactic for entertainment marketers.

Miniseries

Viewing among adults ages 18–49, the group that advertisers pay a premium to reach, was up considerably during Discovery Channel's "Life" series. Promotions for "Life" in 2010 centered around narrator Oprah Winfrey who was selected for her ability to draw viewers.

Similarly, HBO used Tom Hanks' star-power as producer and narrator to promote their miniseries "The Pacific." Promoting to a niche of war veterans and museum goers, the cable channel used Civic Entertainment Group (CEG) to developed a campaign. For the promotion, installed HBO-branded kiosks were installed in 16 World War II-themed museums around the U.S. The kiosks, which operated like an ATM, allowed visitors to record a video tribute thanking veterans and active military for their service. The 30-second messages, recorded free of charge were be sent to HBO, which compiled the tributes for a montage appearing on its website and distributed to the troops. Museum databases and organizations such as the American Legion and Operation Gratitude were used to promote the kiosks and their exhibits.

Using an offbeat tactic to promote the first season of the Sci Fi Channel's "Bermuda Triangle" miniseries, marketers dropped errant black socks into lockers and laundry baskets at gyms and Laundromats that contained the message "nothing stays lost forever" and the address for the show's Web site. In one of the biggest promotional splashes ever undertaken by the channel, Sci Fi also lavished outdoor and print ads along with a radio campaign centered on a fake mayday distress call. On a bet that the mystery would appeal to a wide audience, the channel gave "Triangle" an advertising blitz to keep viewers tuned in.

Soaps

As the economy weakens, daytime viewing increases. And although senior viewers are not being replaced in the same numbers, a few soaps linger to capture a favorite demographic of advertisers. According to Nielsen ratings, the top soaps in the 2009–10 season and number of viewers are shown in Exhibit 15.3.[xxviii]

News

Local television news appears to be losing its audience at an accelerating pace. In 2009, viewership at affiliates of the four major networks, which produce most of the local television news in the U.S., declined across all timeslots, according to Project for Excellence in Journalism's analysis of data from Nielsen Media Research. For early evening and late news, viewership decreases were steeper than in 2008. And in 2009, there were declines in early morning local newscasts as well, which had been stable the previous two years.

The declines were also seen across all four networks, with CBS and Fox the hardest hit as well as NBC's late night news. These numbers reveal a clear pattern across more than 200 markets, roughly 800 stations. These declines appeared to worsening because the rate of decline for early evening and late news was steeper than the year before. On average, local TV newscasts lost twice as many viewers in 2009 (4.1 million viewers) across the three sweeps periods compared to the 2008 loss (2 million viewers).[xxix] Not good news for advertising aimed at baby boomers that make up the largest segment of news viewers.

EXHIBIT 15.3 America's Top Daytime Soaps

SOAP	VIEWERS
1. The Young and the Restless	5,016,000
2. The Bold and the Beautiful	3,209,000
3. Days of our Lives	2,973,000
4. All My Children	2,728,000
5. General Hospital	2,582,000
6. One Life to Live	2,463,000
7. As the World Turns	2,431,000

TV audiences as fans

Before the Internet, fans dedicated to television shows and characters were limited to conventions for connecting with other fans. Today, hundreds of sites and blogs bring fans together electronically. Fans are especially important to marketers for their purchasing power of licensed goods and for viewing, which in turn translates into audience ratings that dictate advertising rates and revenues.

Another channel through which media companies can reach fans is the opportunity to extend interaction beyond television and the computer into real life. Foursquare sends pings created by member network shows to remind viewers to tune in using branded tips and badges. When users check in to Foursquare, they can see notes left by friends that are related to the show/movie's characters or themes. So for example, followers of the movie Valentine's Day will see tips about the most romantic places and experiences in New York City, San Francisco, Chicago, Los Angeles, and Boston.[xxx]

How are TV shows placed and promoted?

Placement is concerned with where and when and how a firm chooses to compete in the national television marketplace. Three positioning strategies predominate: stable, complementary, and competitive. *Stable* strategy places a show by time slot and length of time on the air; *complementary* strategy places the show immediately following a show of same type; *competitive* strategy is selected when there are few attractions or competing shows. Networks determine positions to retain audiences and to take audiences from other networks or cable stations by packaging their most popular series together.

Most television series are promoted using traditional methods: TV, print, radio, outdoor, Internet, and publicity. Commercials feature characters from the sitcom or weekly drama with laugh or music tracks that are familiar to the viewing audience. But what about the viewers who don't watch specific shows? If they've never seen the show, what is the incentive to do so?

One solution is to create promotions that connect nonviewers to the show and get them to sample a show. The plan is not to describe the show, but rather to draw viewers in on an emotional level. By building advertising platforms into the show itself, networks can multiply the pool of potential viewers. Internal promotion may connect a show with an enormous number of people who have not seen it so viewers are motivated to sample, and existing viewers are reminded to tune in again.[xxxi] Strategies can promote the show and advertise the sponsoring product simultaneously. ABC's "Extreme Makeover: Home Edition," for example, used all Sears' Craftsman power tools, and host Ty Pennington mentioned that connection all the time. The convergence of advertiser with program content is slowly invading network and cable programming. Is this the wave of the future? An educated guess from the author suggests that it is.

To generate buzz for one fall season, networks went all out.[xxxii] For the medical sitcom "Out of Practice," CBS plastered ads on drugstore prescription bags and water coolers. NBC pushed reality series "Three Wishes" by slapping yellow stickers on real 100,000 bills. Head-shaving parties were part of Fox's marketing blitz for "Prison Break" dramatic series. Why so outrageous? The growth of cable channels has eroded network share to less than 50%, down from 90%. On-demand cable, videogames, and the Internet are adding to competition for viewers' leisure time. As a result, shows need a wider array of marketing ploys.

Two promote the second season premiere of "Chuck," a critical and fan favorite, NBC ordered 19 more episodes for the 2010 season based on a new plotline, a Subway sponsorship deal and a "save Chuck" Internet campaign that was fueled by fans. Because of low ratings and few advertisers, series producers agreed to slash costs by eliminating some characters, reducing the roles of others and cutting the production schedule from 8 to 7 days per episode.

In a stunt for Disney's "Lost," ABC scattered 10,000 plastic bottles on beaches with a flier inside reading, "I'm Lost. Find me on ABC." By spending 80% of the fall marketing budget on "Lost" and "Desperate Housewives," the network drew 20 million and 30 million viewers respectively. For their re-launch the following season, issues of *TV Guide* came with a preview DVD for "Lost" attached to the front cover, and "Desperate Housewives" logos were slapped on dry cleaner bags with the tagline "New dirty laundry."

Technology has enabled more sophisticated promotional opportunities. Although promotion campaigns linking outdoor advertising with Bluetooth technology (point-to-point wireless connection that allows text, sound, pictures and video to be sent to mobile devices) prevail in Europe, CBS was the first U.S. network to promote its new fall season with Bluetooth.[xxxiii] In a New York City promotion, the network brought to life five of Grand Central station's static billboards that allowed people standing within 36 feet of the board to activate Bluetooth-enabled mobile phones and download a 30-second clip. Bluetooth technology provides advertisers a way to provide video clips directly to consumers, bypassing the Internet and downloading content directly from subway stations, shopping malls, and athletic arenas.

FOCUS ON TELEVISION

Selling an Idea to the Networks

Simon Cowell's "American Idol," created for the benefit of his record label, became an international hit. But only after being rejected by every American television network.

Coming into the U.S. music reality show realm, "American Idol" followed Britain's "Pop Stars" and "Fame Academy." After shooting "Pop Idol" in England with four judges, Cowell believed he could combine fun with candid and finally fan voting to choose a winner in almost a soap opera format. At the time Cowell tried to market the show in the U.S., however, ABC had already experienced a failed music show, "Making the Band," and had declined. WB network tried a similar format with a show called "Pop Stars" that found only a niche audience. They said no to "Idol." NBC's reality executives also passed, and CBS's reality division rejected the idea during an initial phone call.

That left Fox. Pitching the idea with fervent passion, Cowell's colleague impressed Fox with the notion that the format would essentially be all audition, complete with a lot of really woeful early performances. In this show, the audience would rule. Needing fresh summer programming, Fox accepted the show. The network, however, agreed to air the program only if it could be a fully sponsored broadcast.

As talks with Fox dragged on, execs at News Corporation (Fox's owner) were witnessing the success of England's "Pop Idol." The daughter of the corporation's founder, Rupert Murdoch, loved the show. With a call to the top decision-maker at the Fox network, Murdoch ordered a buy. In spite of faltering advertising sponsorship, Fox closed the deal as a 15 episode series like it had been in Britain. As part of the deal, Fox wanted Cowell's charismatic figure on the judging panel.

Cowell worried both about his lack of knowledge about American music and whether American television would insist that he water down his critiques of the contestants. Although the name was changed to "American Idol," the British format was retained to the letter. Fox believed that American audiences were ready to rebel against what Cowell called "the terrible political correctness that invaded America and England."

The other judges were smoothly selected. Randy Jackson, former Journey band member, and Paula Abdul, who had her own solid musical and dance career, came on board. The judges were limited to three to avoid ties.

As the show progressed, Cowell unleashed his lash on every offending wannabe. He told one girl to get a lawyer and sue her vocal coach. Others he labeled with terms as wretched, horrid, and pathetic. As it turned out, "Idol" was an instant hit, with opening ratings of 10 million viewers, the most-watched show on American television on its first night. The second night it added a million viewers. Among coveted audience members in the 18–35 group, "Idol" finished first and second for the week.

Cowell embarked on a round of publicity, doing 50 interviews with American radio stations in one day alone. Within a matter of weeks, Fox was making arrangements to bring "Idol" back in the regular season. The show became more than fresh programming, it became a business-changer for all of network television.

Source: Bill Carter for *The New York Times*, Sunday Business Section, April 30, 2006

Threats to the television industry

Technology keeps change constant, and with change comes a period of readjustment. Podcasting and Internet television are changing the way money is made in media.

Podcasting

After Steve Jobs announced Apple's release of the video iPod in 2005, podcasting became an Internet alternative to broadcasting through subscription Web sites that post audio and video programs. Video podcasts—made and published on the Web by both producers with large budgets and no budgets—enabled homegrown media makers to distribute their programming directly to global audiences. With thousands of blogs providing online audiences with content, broadcasters worry whether or not podcasting might replace television broadcasts.[xxxiv]

One iPod user anchors a daily three-minute mock TV news report she shot with a camcorder. Edited on a laptop and posted on a blog called Rocketboom, the show reaches more than 100,000 fans a day. Providing consistently entertaining daily episodes, the 14-month-old **vlog** (video log) type of podcast costs about $20 a day to produce. The rapid expansion in the number of vlogs offering podcasts strongly suggests how bored viewers are getting with standard commercial TV. Out with networks, in with podcasts. Two of the best vlogs, Scratch Video and Minnesota Stories, can turn personal narrative about the tedious or mundane into micro documentaries of wit, beauty, or intelligence. After signing a deal with TiVo, Rocketboom provides podcasters with all types of shows sent directly to computer, portable players, or the TiVo box for viewing at your leisure.[xxxv]

FOCUS ON LISTENING

RIP: Is Radio Dead?

One of the first forms of broadcasting, radio has been challenged by new technology for the last decade. **Traditional or terrestrial radio**, providing analog signals for AM/FM stations, is fighting for survival. Technological change has taken away the AM/FM monopoly on mass-appeal audio entertainment and information. The talk-radio universe is affected by the economy, and the recession has been brutal to all advertising-based media. Talk radio has a huge following from baby boomers that grew up with personalities who meant something in their lives. However, today's kids don't even have radios. The younger generation doesn't think of radio as an institutional component of day-to-day life, which diminishes the value of owning a license to broadcast. That's why traditional radio is in trouble.

Clear Channel, CBS, and Disney are all trying to get out of the radio business by selling stations, and radio advertising growth is slow. In times of recession, however, many folks will shift towards traditional free services such as broadcast TV and radio. So, even though the audience is shrinking, radio is still an important and reliable medium for advertising.

HD radio, which transmits digital radio and data alongside existing AM/FM, provides CD quality sound. HD Radio even gives consumers access to other media platforms, such as iTunes tagging, where you can download an on-air song to your iPod. These units are also picking up steam as automobile makers are including them in new models, and standalone versions. Digital radio coordinates with GPS, satellite, and Internet technologies to deliver extremely targeted advertising as well as consumer services like traffic, lodging, restaurant, and other information.

Satellite radio, or digital radio over satellite, provides talk, music, and news by subscription. The merger of Sirius and XM provides hundreds of commercial-free choices and listening options. Satellite radio technologies give listeners the opportunity to engage with radio content and build their own formats, which can increase the demand for radio and offer a competitive alternative to multi-media players. Sirius XM ended the second quarter of 2009 with 18,413,435 total subscribers, a decrease of 1% from 2008. Total revenue for Sirius XM Radio Inc., however, grew by 1% in 2009 to $608 million, up from $601 million.

Internet radio, with global streams, requires software or a website to enable audio streaming. Companies like last.fm and imeem have done deals with the leading rights holders to give them permission to stream music over the Internet. Streaming can be done "on-demand," meaning if you want to listen to the new song, you inform your favorite Web music service of your choice and it plays. Music can also be streamed in various forms of smart playlists that track your favorites. Popular playlist sources include hypemachine, Pandora, and Jango.

The next generation of listeners will have their favorite web music services, all supported by advertising, just like traditional radio stations, and all of them licensed by rights holders (eventually), and all of them paying the rights holders every time their song is played. And because these services will be free to anyone who wants to listen, they will be very popular. Never before have listeners been able to decide they want to listen to something they don't currently own and then just play it. No searching on Limewire or bittorrent, no waiting for the download, just type in the name of the song and hit play. These services will soon be coming to mobile phones, making obsolete our limited iPod library. The WiFi revolution has quietly spread across the globe, providing wireless Internet, mobile, and broadcasting to a whole new level. WiFi units offer thousands of online radio stations including internet-only channels and hybrid technology that includes fully integrated iPod/MP3 functionality. Internet advertising expenditures have increased over the last five years, as seen in Exhibit 15.4:

EXHIBIT 15.4 Online Ad Spending

US ONLINE ADVERTISING SPENDING, BY FORMAT, 2006–2011(MILLIONS)

	2006	2007	2008	2009	2010	2011
Paid Search	$4,871	$6,484	$7,910	$8,622	$9,209	$10,590
Display	$2,273	$3,556	$4,089	$4,016	$4,289	$4,718
Classifieds	$1,998	$2,719	$3,127	$3,183	$3,413	$3,686
Internet Video/ rich media	$1,224	$1,319	$1,854	$2,221	$2,774	$3,328
Internet radio	–	–	$200	$260	$292	$351
Podcast	–	$22	$25	$28	$32	$43
Others	$1,674	$2,011	$2,313	$2,267	$3,043	$4,564
Total	**$12,490**	**$16,111**	**$19,519**	**$20,957**	**$23,050**	**$27,279**

Note: excludes alliance deals and partnership program; at current prices; numbers may not add up to total due to rounding
Source: ZenithOptimedia, "Advertising Expenditure Forecast - March 2009," provided to eMarketer, April 14, 2009

Sources: www.seekingalpha.com/article/140094-the-uncertain-future-of-radio
www.hear2.com/2008/04/the-future-of-m.html
www.digitalsyndicate.net/radiodead.html

Content

Virtually limitless content could revolutionize television viewing and eliminate cable companies completely. Internet access to television means instant access to hard-to-find content and on-demand episodes of prime-time fare. Electronics hardware that brings Internet video to television screens includes: Intel's Vivi, which facilitates hooking computers into TVs; Cisco's DP600 DVD player, which has a broadband connection for pulling content off the Web; Microsoft's Xbox 360, which routes video and other content from media center computers to TVs; AT&T/EchoStar's Homezone satellite TV service, which provides video on demand via the Internet; Panasonic's PX500 line of TVs, which have computer inputs that can display any content off the Internet or a computer.

PRODUCT PLACEMENT: ON-SCREEN AND IN-PROGRAM ADVERTISING

Branded entertainment, which embeds brands and products in the content of movies, TV shows, online, and on cell phones and in video games, has become increasingly important to marketers as they seek alternatives to commercials and other traditional forms of advertising.

Both film and television productions rely heavily on revenues from products placed in film and on TV. The practice has become so widespread that it has fostered an industry and trade association of its own. The Entertainment Marketing Association is made up of three constituent groups, each with a vested interest in the practice: corporations and manufacturers looking to place their brands, studios and production companies looking to defray costs with brand placements, and placement agencies. The impact and value of product placement is evident from quantifiable research data.

What has been euphemistically called "brand integration" by network television and Madison Avenue may be better characterized as steroid-enhanced product placement deals. Advertising companies—from Omnicom to MediaVest to Carat Americas—have started their own branded entertainment divisions to solidify their relationships with their corporate clients and the cash that comes with them.[xxxvi] This section shows how branded products are integrated into film and television.

Placing products in film

Product placement is now big business. Film studios have departments dedicated to sending out bids for products and negotiating contracts with corporations interested in placement opportunities. Likewise, brand managers assign the placement function to a negotiator. Media buyers allocate budgets for placement, and research companies monitor the brand awareness generated by film placements.

For films that are not tent-pole blockbusters, product placements serve to provide revenue for movie studios. Used for revenue generation, brand placements in 2009 films were presented on brandchannel.com. Comments from reviewers provide an audience member's perspective of the branding effort.[xxxvii]

Product placements are an art, and not all art is good—much of it, in fact, is terrible. Moviegoers know what they are paying for: to watch movies, not commercials. When product

The Perfect Fit Award

Which brand/film association had the best chemistry?

The product placement business offers no guarantees, but there are instances when the matching game between movies and starring brands are simpatico and fit not only the film's brand identity, but the product's placement as well. Here are the nominees for matches made in movie heaven.

Aston Martin in *Quantum of Solace*	54%
Gran Torino in *Gran Torino*	8%
Jagermeister in *The Hangover*	26%
Purina Dog Chow in *Marley & Me*	5.5%
Louis Vuitton in *The Proposal*	4.5%

The Bomb Award: *Which brand cameo ruined your enjoyment of a film/scene?*

placements are overtly obvious, blatant, and simply inept, moviegoers cringe as the suspension of disbelief is broken and a scene is ruined, or in some cases the entire film undermined, by bad product placement.

Nokia in *Star Trek*	34%
McDonalds in *The Day the Earth Stood Still*	9.5%
American Spirit in *He's Just Not That Into You*	07%
Apple in *The Proposal*	08%
Cisco WebEx in *Transformers*	41%

Placing products on television

With over 1,000 product placement instances since it launched in 2009, "The Jay Leno Show" had by far the most product placements of any primetime show in the same year. From its inception, "The Jay Leno Show" was a business strategy first, an entertainment program second. And although it lasted only a short time, Nielsen released an interesting year-end list that found the show had succeeded at one of its aims: becoming an attractive venue for in-show ads.[xxxviii] According to tunedin.com, TV's top 10 product-placers are shown in Exhibit 15.5:

For television producers, these sophisticated plugs are a way to offset rising production costs. Advertisers end up buying more ordinary 30-second ads and paying a separate integration fee to

EXHIBIT 15.5 Top Television Product Placements

SHOW	PLACEMENTS
1. The Jay Leno Show	(1015)
2. WWE Monday Night Raw	(787)
3. The Biggest Loser	(704)
4. American Idol	(553)
5. Extreme Makeover: Home Edition	(483)
6. The Celebrity Apprentice	(428)
7. Top Chef: Las Vegas	(412)
8. America's Next Top Model	(380)
9. Project Runway	(350)
10. Dancing With the Stars	(331)

the network, which splits the money with the studio. Or, instead of an integration fee, advertisers may include the show in their marketing efforts, such as mall promotions, magazine ads, and newspaper stuffers.

Some genres work better for placement than others. Reality shows, for instance, lend themselves to brand integration—thirsty, starving islanders will gobble and guzzle Doritos and Mountain Dew after vanquishing their opponents in a "Survivor" episode, and viewers usually accept the products' presence. But scripted shows are trickier—some feel like commercials and offend audiences. Successful placements grow out of characterizations, such as a Campbell Soup tie-in with NBC's "American Dreams" instituted to portray a character's wholesomeness. After a junior high student bribed schoolmates to send entries to an annual

© Shaun Heasley/Reuters/Corbis

15.3 "Seinfeld" was one of the first television shows to use product placements in volume.

Campbell's Soup essay-writing contest, three times the number of entries were received from viewers of "American Dream" than had been previously received from a typical number of people.

Gannett sells product placement on local talk shows for about $2,500 a pop. The midmorning shows, which replace local news, talk programs, or syndicated fare, are a way for stations to underwrite local programming while milking a little more money from their daytime schedule. According to one station executive, these shows could increase the time period's revenue take between 50% and 100%. These broadcast *slotting fees* are the on-air equivalents of the slotting allowances that package goods pay retailers to get shelf space. Each station makes its own decision whether to launch the shows, but the introduction of the pay-to-appear shows is often corporate driven.

Local advertisers using placements have included cosmetic dentists, homebuilders, and auto dealer groups. More regional and national advertisers are beginning to take advantage of the shows through local *unwired buys*—buys made at the corporate ownership level. In an unwired buy with Gannett, The Richard Group, Dallas, coordinated holiday appearances on two shows, "Colorado & Co." and "Atlanta & Co.," for its client Honey Baked Ham. This format helps advertisers integrate products into more of an editorial-style environment on a local level. The shows are the property of the sales and marketing department rather than the newsroom and, at the end of each segment and again at the end of the show, a host mentions that the segment was paid for by the advertiser. Denver's KUSA, the first Gannett-owned station to introduce the current format, has been moderately successful with slightly increased ratings.[xxxix]

Some products help develop show set. Assuming an "also starring" role in NBCs "The Apprentice" was Poggenpohl, a German kitchen cabinet maker. The company sent out news releases to alert media that viewers could learn all about its pricey cabinets by visiting the TV show's Web site. Makers of furniture and appliances are getting in on the placement act—brands from Bosch appliances to Big John Toilet Seat—by wooing set designers and cozying up to TV and movie stars.

Popular tool company Barbara K. Enterprises works with a product placement company to gets its female-friendly kits in movie and television scenes. Appeals to set designers and production companies landed the firm a big part alongside Brad Pitt and Angelina Jolie in the film *Mr. & Mrs. Smith*. After placing pieces of furniture on "The Real World," Blue Dot Design's sales of featured chairs and shelving units rose along with brand awareness.[xl]

Plot placement

Integrating a brand or product into a significant and engaging role in a storyline is **plot placement**. This technique is most prevalent in television programming. According to media buyers, becoming a central plot element is worth ten times the cost of running a commercial in the same television program for product brands. Plot placements in television and film include Revlon's corporate espionage plot line on soap opera "All My Children," and Mini Cooper's central role in a heist featured in the movie *The Italian Job*.

Using products to promote television

The coming together of product brands and television shows can be seen in the two examples of such unions featured here:

Bertolli, a Unilever brand of Italian pastas, used both conventional advertising and webisodes to launch a mini-series created to showcase the secrets of Italian cuisine. According to *Brandweek*, a 15-second equity spot and a 30-second trailer (aired during the 2010 Oscars) were part of a new ad campaign launch and Web series promotion. The campaign used digital and social media, as well as celebrities, to drive traffic to "Into the Heart of Italy," a mini Web series. It also included homepage takeovers and bi-weekly, behind-the-scenes segments on media properties like Yahoo.com and Extra, respectively.

Two advertising heavyweights teamed up for a two-hour "Secrets of the Mountain," to be broadcast on NBC in April, 2010. The movie, which focuses on a single mother, highlights values—such as generosity, honesty, and togetherness—that Wal-Mart and P&G executives said were in short supply on television. According to the *Wall Street Journal*, ads for both companies ran during commercial breaks, and the film included product placements for both. P&G spent $4.5 million to produce the film and paid for airtime for the broadcast. Wal-Mart paid some of the costs, including a fee to P&G for the right to be "presenting sponsor."

Placement evaluation methods and the Q-Ratio

Measuring a product placement's effectiveness is the domain of companies such as iTVX and IAG Research. It's still an inexact science but some results cannot be ignored, such as pre-selling 1,000 Pontiac Solstice cars in the 41 minutes following an episode of "The Apprentice," which plugged the car. Most networks believe that the benefits of branded integration outweigh any hypothetical downsides. After all, television is self-selecting; if audiences don't like product placements, they turn off the show.

To examine the complexities of branded entertainment, the industry needs to decipher who, what, why, and how much branding was involved. One source of examining branded entertainment's effectiveness is *ratings*, which do not consider the quality of the placement. A second, stand-alone *quality component*, in addition to the ratings, helps measure the value of product integration.

iTVX developed a Q-Ratio™ that measures the quality of the product placement. The ratio represents a relative value, which is either expressed as a fraction of a 30-second commercial, or as the number of commercials it is equivalent to. For example, a placement with a .756 Q-Ratio signifies that the quality of that particular placement is valued at approximately 75% of a 30-second commercial.

The importance of having such a valuation is exemplified by the fact that the Q-Ratio™ does not change with the commercial cost. This Q-Ratio measures over 50 variable factors pertinent to the quality of the product placement. Once tabulated, this Q-Ratio remains constant, allowing the marketer to multiply privy costs per 30 seconds by the Q-Ratio to get an estimated valuation of that integration. According to the company that provides this service, the methodology creates a logical standard of accountability.[xli]

Because advertisers expect a high degree of specificity in knowing the effectiveness of their ads, there is pressure on traditional forms of old media to improve their ability to measure how consumers respond to product placement. Among companies vying to become the place where advertisers look for product placement measures, Nielsen spent $225 million to acquire IAG Research, one of the biggest companies to measure the effectiveness of advertising and product placement. IAG comes up with its product placement ratings by asking 2.5 million people to fill out surveys online after watching their favorite shows. The surveys ask whether viewers remember the brand, think more positively about it or want to purchase it, and whether the placement disrupted their viewing experience.

Evaluating the effects of using branded content

Raising the branded content bar, new methods to evaluate TV offerings are in place to determine how effective branded TV content offerings are at meeting advertisers' ROI goals. Ground rules, consisting of questions posed by advertisers to suppliers, may help evaluate whether or not to invest in a scripted series. Let's look at five criteria advertisers use for evaluating television placements.

1. *How will the show generate and maintain high ratings?* If the goal is to increase ROI, the sitcom or drama must generate high levels of sampling and maintain viewer loyalty so the brand will connect with a maximum number of people in a target audience.

2. *How likely is the show to be purchased by another network?* Once the season is over, cable channels may bid for the rights to broadcast. The better received the original series, the more likely it will be an attractive purchase for other distribution outlets.

3. *How will the show increase sales?* Placements that offer two-second product shots, banners, and name mentions only increase name recall. For a placement to be worth the money, the brand's benefits must be organically integrated into the show for sales to increase.

4. *How will the integration be a natural and logical element of each episode?* The brand must grow out of the story line so it is not an obvious commercial that suppresses results.

5. *How will the network's marketing extensions increase brand sales and show ratings?* Expect more than increased name awareness from promotional programs and Web sites.

Product films

As commercials become TiVoed out, companies are looking to digital and other types of entertainment media to promote their brands more effectively than could be accomplished with a 30-second spot. So instead of placing their brands into other people's films, some companies are financing or producing their own branded movies. Automobile companies BMW, Ford, and Cadillac produced their own films for the Internet starring their products and brands that were hits among brand fans.

FOCUS ON ETHICS

Reality TV Lets Marketers Write the Scripts

According to critics, the advertising industry is fighting back against TiVo and other ad-skip technology by altering preexisting content in ways that could threaten the visual and editorial integrity of television programming.[xliii] They claim that brand integration is largely responsible for the reality TV genre as we know it and not vice versa.

The trend was pioneered with "Survivor," which CBS greenlighted only after its executive producer explained that instead of the network paying actors, advertisers would pay the network for a starring role. Envisioned as a commercial vehicle as much as a TV drama, "Survivor" is a pretext for contestants to interact with brands. According to *Advertising Age*, CBS thought it was one of the best bargains in TV history. Behind the program's long-term impact was the relentless promotion of the series by CBS's parent company, Viacom. To generate buzz, more than 100 affiliate radio stations ran segments, including dozens of drive-time interviews with Burnett, while 16 of CBS's TV stations and Viacom's MTV and VH1 covered "Survivor" as if its ins and outs were news.

By the time "American Idol" appeared, placing branded products gave way to placing branded wannabe pop stars themselves. Fox has reaped millions by making "Idol" contestants literally do backflips over corporate logos in mini-commercials disguised as music videos. The contestants who succeed are as much commodities as the product they hawk.

The argument against advertising-integrated program content is that the stronger the foothold, whether through ad buys or product placement, the more power advertisers have to define our collective values. Mike Darnell, Fox's reality guru, told *Entertainment Weekly* that his dream project would be a beauty pageant featuring female prisoners: "You give them a chance to get a make-over and it's a 40-share special." So will Miss San Quentin sashay her way into prime time? Only viewers have the power to say.

What do you think?

1. Is the reality-show platform a natural context for branded products, or are corporations designing reality content around their brands?

2. Who should ultimately determine the amount and type of product placement appropriate for television audiences?

The first brand to finance a film was a sneaker company who wanted to showcase its brand. A documentary about skateboarding won several prestigious awards at major independent film festivals such as Sundance. Growing from a three-city release into a major phenomenon, *Dogtown and the Z-Boys* received extraordinary coverage from mainstream press, MTV, and National Public Radio. What made this film unique was its financing—Vans sneaker company gave the director $65,000 to keep its shoes on the feet of everyone onscreen. By connecting teen fascination with skateboarding events with their movie-going habits, Vans' investment yielded revenues of $1.4 million before overseas distribution, DVD sales, and television licensing. And the company raised its profits up 66% from increased U.S. sales.[xliii]

It's the engagement, stupid!

Inserting itself between traditional marketing activities and an increasing demand for ROI assessments, the metric of consumer engagement will soon become the Holy Grail for marketers and advertisers alike. **Engagement** can be defined as the outcome of advertising and marketing activities that substantively increases a brand's strength in the eyes of the consumers (and actually predicts sales and profitability). Engagements are being used more and more to allocate marketing budgets.[xliv]

Engagement comes in many forms. On-demand video content, for instance, is available for singles who are bored with the bar scene. Comcast, the country's largest cable provider, offers "Dating on Demand," so singles can use their remotes to view hundreds of potential dates' video profiles. They make contact with their choices through online dating sites that work with Comcast, primarily the hurrydate.com site. On-demand technology stores video content in central offices that can be accessed over cable lines anytime. Previously used to order movies, the on-demand service allows viewers to make their own mini-casts at home and upload them to the cable company over the Internet.[xlv]

Experiential marketing is another avenue to generate engagement. Research suggests that audiences believe that participating in experiential marketing increases their purchase consideration.[xlvi] Marketers are responding to this notion by shifting experiential marketing into the heart of the marketing mix. PR and advertising campaigns have become extensions of brand experiences—not the other way around. For instance, the Pontiac Solstice was launched with a live concert by Jet in New York's Times Square, an event that was rebroadcast on the *Jimmy Kimmel Show*. Street teams went out in full force the following morning to keep the buzz alive and facilitate live national and local news spots featuring VH1 VJ Rachel Perry. Programs like these root their creative efforts in the live experience and its aftermath, recognizing its power to galvanize PR and inspire viral word-of-mouth advocacy. A trade group, the Live Brand Experience Association (LBEA) was created to help marketers understand and embrace experiential marketing's potential.

Coming next? Experiential movie trailers may be the next thing. By borrowing techniques from playgrounds, game play, and theme park design, a new innovation in developing trailers drives emotional branding in entertainment marketing via Web streaming. Using a mixed reality technique, boundaries between real and virtual content merge into a full spectrum of simulation in trailer development and presentation.

One movie promoter created both micro and macro experiences to bring to life its film *Where the Wild Things Are*. In a promotion that stretched boundaries, the tourism arm of New York executed Wild Things Week NYC, an event that included a month-long exhibit at the Morgan Library and Museum that featured the original drawings and manuscripts

15.4 American actor Max Records poses during a photocall for Spike Jonze's film. *Where the Wild Things Are* in Madrid on December 10, 2009.

© *Emilio Naranjo/epa/Corbis*

for the children's book, written by Maurice Sendak, on which the movie is based. The promotion featured giveaways of crowns like those worn by the protagonist, at hotels, restaurants and retailers; and a curriculum put together by the New York City Department of Education based on the book and film and posted on the department's Web site for teachers across the country to use as a reference.

Immersive advertising

An evolutionary step forward in the traditional marketing practice of product placement, Neopets virtual animal kingdom has become a placement paradise. Neopia's Web site collapses the boundaries between content and commercials with corporate sponsored zones (Firefly Mobile Phone Zone) and branded games (Nestle Ice Cream Frozen Flights, Pepperidge Farms Goldfish Sandwich Snackers, and McDonald's Meal Hunt). Wins are rewarded with NeoPoints for purchasing Neopet toys.

This marketing strategy provides a link from Neopia Central, the site's shopping district, which takes members to a splash page for the Cereal Adventure zone. This home of breakfast mascots, including Trix rabbit and Cocoa Puffs cuckoo, leads to a game called Lucky Charms: Shooting Stars!, in which kids navigate a series of marshmallow treats to earn more NeoPoints. Visitors can also surf into the Disney Theater where they can buy their pets some popcorn and settle into to watch previews for *Lilo & Stitch 2*. And they can also earn Neopoints by answering a market research survey linked from the homepage with questions like: "When was your last visit to Wal-Mart?" and "Are you aware of the new Power Rangers DVD?"

The roster of clients who have set up shop inside the land of Neopia runs from Atari and DreamWorks to Frito-Lay and Lego. While passive product placement has become standard in TV and film, the Neopets approach emphasizes interaction and integration. The seamless interweaving of marketing and entertainment is an advertiser's dream come true according to a Jupiter Research analyst. The only drawback is an ethical dilemma: should kids earn points for watching commercials for sugary cereals? For the time being at least, Neopia and its virtual economy (regulated by the Neodaq) thrive by pairing generations with a game they can play together—matching new users with old Neopets—while keeping the future of Neopia promising. This is marketing at a very sophisticated level.

Cell phone entertainment and promotion

In 2006, News Corporation created a mobile entertainment store called Mobizzo and a production studio to focus exclusively on developing cell phone entertainment. Capitalizing on the growing appetite for video, graphics, and music on cell phones, the store was the first virtual mobile shopping mall by a major media company. What makes it different from other offerings is its direct sales to consumers, bypassing the exclusive arrangements common with wireless phone companies. Its competitors—MTV and CBS—are all vying for the same market.

Mobizzo acquired 2,000 pieces of content from a Hollywood tattoo designer, a Chinese art collective, and a Los Angeles street artist. Aspiring to make Mobizzo a global brand, Rupert Murdock's company is even pursuing products created by teenagers based on comic books for the 13–24 crowd. News Corp. committed tens of millions of dollars to a marketing campaign of TV, print, and online advertising, and hired a team to promote the service during spring break in Florida.[xlvii] Media giants have devoted sizeable efforts to grow their own mobile businesses to capitalize on the exploding thirst for mobile phone entertainment such as games, film clips, and news flashes.

Finally

This chapter has presented an overview of television and film audiences, budgets, and marketing strategies. Promoting movies involves millions of dollars dedicated to creating an opening weekend blitz; television promotion, on the other hand, focuses on keeping audiences interested enough to tune in for another season of network or cable programming. Ever-improving technology and venue consolidation allow us to view media in the palms of our hands wherever and whenever we choose. How to keep audiences visiting advertising-based broadcasts and box office venues is a challenge marketers of this generation must face and overcome.

GOT IT?

- Positioning films is best accomplished with trailers that can be used in TV commercials, press kits, post-of-sale materials, and on DVDs. Internet sites give audiences an opportunity to explore the movie brand before and after release; Oscar nominations enhance a films brand image and stimulate attention.

- Global distribution complements national film distribution and revenue generation by reaching international audiences through theaters and DVD sales.

- Promotional budgets for marketing films are determined by these factors: potential gross, audience makeup, gross of similar genres, anticipated revenues from foreign or video sales, number of screens used for release, and number of markets included in the release.

- The macroeconomic financial factors affecting film marketing are seasonal demand, movie-going costs, market fluctuations and licensing fees: microeconimic factors include financing sources, labor unions, and distribution recoupment.

- Reality shows and sitcoms have the strongest appeal for global television audiences; their fans use the Internet to purchase licensed merchandise, support programming, and influence content. Marketers cultivate audiences from fans.

- Product placement in film and video is big business, involving brands, content, negotiation and advertisers; ratings and quality measures are available to evaluate placement effectiveness.

NOW TRY THIS

1. Visit the Web site of your favorite sitcom or reality show. What interactive tools are used to engage viewers? How are fans connected? How important is the Web site for viewers like you?

2. Google your favorite film star and visit several of the sites listed. What kinds of information is generated for the star? What sources provide this information? How reliable are they? What role does this star play in marketing his/her own films?

3. Assuming that you are an aspiring reality show contestant, what avenues are available for you to get an audition? Where are auditions held? What steps are required for getting an interview? Are there any costs involved? Do you need an agent? What does this information tell you about the contestants who are finally selected for the show?

4. Locate four separate reviews for a mainstream Hollywood film of your choice. After reading them, how likely are you to go or not go based on their comments? Why? What does your attitude suggest about the importance of reviewers comments for audience generation?

QUESTIONS FOR DISCUSSION AND REVIEW

1. When marketing a film that has no top star billing, what strategies would you use to position and promote the movie to a national audience? A global audience?

2. What are the various ways marketers use the Internet to promote a television show or a movie? Which medium is most reliant on the Internet? Why?

3. Suggest a marketing plan for a small independent film about a jazz musician in post-hurricane New Orleans that combines documentary segments with fictional characters and plot. Which festivals would you target? Would you develop a trailer as part of your strategy? Why?

4. What brands or products would you consider placing to help finance the film described in question 3? What criteria are necessary for making the most appropriate selections?

5. Make some predictions about movie attendance in the next five years and provide a rationale for your prediction. Do the same for television viewership.

MORE STUFF ABOUT MARKETING MEDIATED ENTERTAINMENT

www.multichannel.com—How video and interactive programming get marketed to customers of multimedia services.

www.mymarketingtv.com—Free Internet marketing television show for entrepreneurs who want to start their own home-based business.

www.theepochtimes.com—Current articles on online TV advertising.

CAMPAIGN CASE STUDY

Promoting a Television Series Using an Integrated Communications Approach

Client: ABC's *Lost*.

Problem: The series loses fans during the summer hiatus, making it difficult to get them back for a new season.

Campaign Objective: Retain current fans and stimulate new viewers of the series during the summer prior to its third season; stimulate viewing audience for series final season.

Situation Analysis: The fifth season of the series began airing on ABC in January 2009 and concluded with a two-hour season finale in May and continues the stories of the survivors of the fictional crash of Oceanic Airlines. Some of them were rescued and those still stranded seemingly disappear to an unknown location and time with the island that they inhabit. The storyline follows two different time periods and the cast is largely broken into two groups: Those who have left the island and those who remain on the island as they erratically jump through time. Season 5 continued *Lost*'s decline in ratings, with the season premiere and its next episode being watched by the lowest season premiere in the series' history. Michael Emerson won an Emmy for Outstanding Supporting Actor in a Drama Series.

SWOT Analysis:

- Strength: Strong characters and fan base following.
- Weakness: Ratings decline and loss of viewers for season premiere
- Opportunities: Reinvigorate fan base and raise ratings
- Threats: Competition, viewer loss of interest

Campaign Objective: Retain current viewers during the summer and stimulate interest for the 6th season premiere.

Target Audience: Current *Lost* fans and fans who had stopped watching.

Strategy 1: Fuse media channels.

Tactic: use websites, fan message boards, websites with character details, podcasts, text-message updates, print magazines and newsletters, and video-on-demand.

Strategy 2: Use publicity stunts, video games to give a real feel to the show without compromising plan's integrated nature to blur the lines between reality and fiction by using fictitious ads in different media. Engage the fan base with a game designed to reveal secrets about the show.

Tactics:

- ABC provided free *ad-supported episode*s on the Internet including downloads of Lost on iPods via iTunes.

- *Video games*—both console and mobile phone-based—were also developed as show promotion incentives. "Losties" online community was a viable force for spreading interest in the series. "The Lost Experience" took viewers through the everyday lives of plane crash survivors stranded on a mysterious tropical island.

Strategy 3: Incorporate a tie-in between the show and another medium.

Tactic: Launch *Bad Twin*, a tie-in book authored by a fictitious character from the show.

Strategy 4: Promote the show's final season by using a contest for American *Lost* fans 18 or older.

Tactic: Using either ABC's Flash-based online "mash-up" editing tool or their own video editing tools, fans were encouraged to produce and submit their own 35-second promo for the *Lost* finale episode aired May 23, 2010. The contest deadline was March 21. ABC.com users voted from among 5 finalists selected by contest judges. The winning promo aired on television and earned its creator a trip to Los Angeles to attend the series' special finale party on May 13.

Results: A successful new season premiere for series ratings and advertisers alike. Tom Lowry of *BusinessWeek* wrote, "Using podcasts, interactive games, websites, and good, old-fashioned hype, ABC has turned a cult-style show into a cross-media sensation." Here are the campaign results:

- Web site Lostpedia.wikia.com boasted 6319 articles dedicated to the show in the spring of 2010.

- The 2nd most pirated TV show in 2009.

- Most recorded series on TV.

- Ratings for the premiere of the sixth and final season was up from the 2009 premiere, giving big late-evening numbers to ABC.

- *Bad Twin* became a best seller.

- "The Lost Experience" became the largest global game ever based on a TV series.

Source: www.icmrindia.org/CaseStudies/catalogue/Marketing/MKTG156.htm

Question for Discussion: *As account manager, would you advocate merchandising for the series once it has ended? How else could you extend the brand to generate revenue from a past success?*

[i]J. Wemple, J. Shamsie & T. Lent (2005), *The Business of Culture: Strategic Perspectives of Entertainment and Media*.

[ii]By A.O. Scott for the *New York Times Magazine*, Dec. 11, 2005.

[iii]By Theresa Howard for *USA Today*, Feb. 24, 2004.

[iv]Justin Wyatt (1994), *High Concept: Movies and Marketing in Hollywood*. University of Texas Press.

[v]Terry Press quote

[vi]Terry Press quote

[vii]From an interview of Terry Press by Lynn Hirschberg for the *New York Times*, Nov. 14, 2005.

[viii]From rogerebert.suntimes.com/reviews, Dec. 21, 2005.

[ix]From an article on advertising from the *Wall Street Journal*, Nov. 25, 2005.

[x]From an article by Charlotte Kaiser for the *Wall Street Journal*, July 8, 2005.

[xi]FilmFestivals.com reporter Glen Berry

[xii]By Gabriel Snyder and Ian Mohr, "H'wood's New World Order," *Variety* Sept. 26–Oct. 2, 2005.

[xiii]From an article by Geoffrey Fowler and Karen Mazurkewich for the *Wall Street Journal*, Sept. 14, 2005.

[xiv]China.org.cn, Feb. 20, 2010.

[xv]By Kate Kelly and Brian Steinberg for the *Wall Street Journal*, Aug. 19, 2005.

[xvi]Quoted in Harold Vogel (2001), *Entertainment Industry Economics*. Cambridge University Press, p. 99.

[xvii]www.thefreelibrary.com/Motion+picture+distributors:+ranked+by+2009+domestic+box+office...-a0217604836

[xviii]www.reuters.com/article/idUSTRE5BU0HS20100105

[xix]http://www.itif.org/files/2009-12-15.DigitalPiracy.pdf

[xx]Reported by the BBC on newslbbc.co.uk/1/hi/technology Dec. 16, 2005.

[xxi]A study conducted by Maruth Figueroa, graduate student at California State University, Fullerton, Dec. 2005.

[xxii]Aaron Patrick for the *Wall Street Journal*, Jan. 27, 2006.

[xxiii]www.marketingcharts.com/television/middle-agers-help-hulu-grow-490-9125/nielsen-growth-spent-time-viewing-per-viewer-demographic-group-april-2009jpg/

[xxiv]vbythenumbers.com/2010/02/08/dish-network-®-and-rentrak-announced-landmark-television-audience-measurement-agreement/41420

[xxv]S. Reiss & J. Wiltz (2001), "Why America Loves Reality TV. *Psychology Today* 34 (5), 52.

xxviBryan Curtis for the *New York Times Magazine*, Dec. 11, 2005.

xxviiBy Karen Idelson for "Hollywood Calling" in *Variety*, Sept. 26–Oct 2, 2005.

xxviiien.wikipedia.org/wiki/List_of_US_daytime_soap_opera_ratings#2010s

xxixwww.stateofthemedia.org/2010/local_tv_audience.php

xxxAlison Mooney for *AdAge* for digitalNEXT, Feb. 8, 2010.

xxxiDeveloped by Ken Convoy of New Paradigm TV, Santa Barbara, CA, April 5, 2005.

xxxiiBy Brooks Barnes for the *Wall Street Journal*, Sept. 2, 2005.

xxxiiiEmily Steel's Advertising column for the *Wall Street Journal*, Aug. 24, 2006.

xxxivRobert Mackey for the *New York Times Magazine*, Dec. 11, 2005.

xxxvIbid Mackey, "TV Stardom on $20 a Day."

xxxviFrom "On Television, Brands go from Props to Stars," by Lorne Manly for the *New York Times*, Oct. 2, 2005.

xxxviihttp://www.brandchannel.com/features_effect.asp?pf_id=489

xxxviiitunedin.blogs.time.com/2009/12/11/jay-leno-is-1/

xxxixFrom *AdAge*, Dec. 7, 2005.

xlBy Cheryl Lu-Lien Tan for the *Wall Street Journal*, Sept. 22, 2005.

xliFrank Zazza, CEO of iTVX, in a Web site address featured on itvx.com, Dec. 2005.

xliiJennifer Pozner (2004), "Triumph of the Shill: Part II," *Bitch Magazine* 24, Spring, p. 56.

xliiiBernard Schmitt, David Rogers & Karen Vrotsos (2004), *There's no Business that's not Show Business*. Financial Times/Prentice Hall, chapter 3.

xlivFrom the *Wise Marketer*, Dec. 9, 2005.

xlvBy Peter Grant for the *Wall Street Journal*, Dec. 15, 2005.

xlviBy Josh McCall for the Jack Morton Worldwide newsletter, Dec. 17, 2005.

xlviiReported by Laura Holson for the *New York Times*, Feb. 27, 2006.

Chapter 16

PROMOTING STARS AND CELEBRITIES

> *I am my own industry.*
> *I am my own commodity.*
> Elizabeth Taylor

Chapter Objectives

After reading this chapter, you will be able to answer these questions:

- What is *stardom* and what are the components of a *star system*?

- What are the components of *celebrity* and *fame*?

- Who are the people making up star and celebrity *audiences*?

- How are celebrities and stars marketed as *brands*?

Hollywood stars, fame, fans, and media celebrities are the topics of this chapter. Stardom is an outgrowth of film and television image production, and it recently has been established as an area of academic study. James Monaco's taxonomy of fame includes three categories: 1) a *hero*, or someone who has actually done something spectacular (fireman in 9/11), 2) a *star*, or someone who achieves prominence through development of a public persona that is more important than his or her professional profile (Donald Trump), and 3) a *quasar* or accidental celebrity, or someone who becomes a media darling inadvertently (Monica Lewinsky).

Our focus is on people who became **stars** through their roles in popular film, or became **celebrities** recognized for their television appearances or media hype. Both stars and celebrities become properties of their own right that can be sold to audiences and fans. The selling part is what we address in this chapter, focusing on the roles of movie stars and television celebrities for audience development and revenue generation. After exploring the nature of stars and celebrities and their audiences, we review branding for its relevance to marketing famous people.

WHAT IS STARDOM?

Stars are the key elements in the overall film package. Stars are defined as a "group of people whose institutional power is very limited or non-existent, but whose doings and way of life arouse a considerable degree of interest."[i] The basic conditions for stardom are a 1) thriving economy in a 2) large-scale society that 3) enables social mobility. As an elite and privileged group, stars cannot know everyone, but everyone can know them; and anyone may become a star. While the development of the star turned the individual into a commodity to be marketed and traded by the industry, it also gave the star access to a new kind of power—a relationship with the audience that was independent of the vehicles in which they appeared. This section presents stars as production and consumption, the studio and star systems, stars as capital, and star images.

Stars as a phenomenon of production and consumption

The audience-star relationship is market controlled. Stars are typically *produced*, that is, they arise out of what filmmakers promote. They are also consumption-based, because they arise from what the audiences demand. Stars' physical makeup fixes a type of beauty that defines and reflects norms of attractiveness. Many stars develop to become nationally advertised trademarks.

Stars can be viewed in terms of their function in the economy of Hollywood, including their role in the manipulation of film audiences. Charisma has proved a marketable commodity, and as such adds an intrinsic property to stardom. Stars are a studio's capital. They represent a large financial investment and are used to sell films. The film industry spends an enormous amount of money, time, and energy building up star images through publicity, promotion, fan clubs, and merchandising. Stars are challenged, however, for top billing by special effects and the star director.

Studio system

In order to understand the role of stars in Hollywood, you have to know about the star's controlling body, the studio. The situation in Hollywood in the 1920s through the 1950s was an *oligopoly*, an economic condition where a market is completely dominated by a small number of companies limiting competition. In 1930, eight studios dominated Hollywood;[ii]

- The Big 5 (majors): MGM, Paramount, RKO, Fox, Warner Brothers
- The Little 3 (minors): Columbia, United Artists, Universal

The majors were *vertically integrated*, meaning they exercised control over production, distribution, and exhibition. The minors did not control exhibition but had access to the major's distribution circuit.

The major studios made, released, and marketed their films; they even owned the cinemas in which they were shown. Exhibition was the most profitable sector of the film industry. Before TV and video, box-office receipts were the source of income for recouping the money spent on making films. It made sense for the film studios to want all of those profits for themselves. They did not own all the cinemas in the U.S., but the ones that they did own were the "first-run" cinemas that got the most popular films exclusively before their competitors (as a result they delivered 75% of all theatrical revenues). The advantages of this system were that the majors controlled the money and power within the film industry. They also controlled the stars, who were obligated to act for one studio until their contracts ran out. During the twenty years between 1930 and 1950, the studios made the stars. They selected their parts, prepared their promotion, and dictated when and where they appeared in public.

Production system

In order to meet audience demand during this period in history, each of the studios was producing on average one film per week. Studios modeled themselves on factories to achieve such vast production. Other than the producer, everybody involved with making the film (actors, cameramen, scriptwriters, prop makers, and so on) was simply *salaried staff*, there to perform their function in the overall process of making a film.

The only person who saw the film through the complete process was the associate producer, who monitored the shooting schedule and budget for each film. The associate producers were answerable to the head of production, who was ultimately responsible for making sure the studio made money.

Stars are categorized as performance specialists: they are required to execute certain tasks. During pre-production, stars read scripts and learned lines; when in production, stars rehearsed and shot scenes; in post-production, stars dubbed or post-synchronized voice during sound re-recording. In addition, star labor involved participating in promotional tasks such as press interviews, premiere appearances, and television show interviews.

The contract system

As part of this approach to filmmaking, all staff involved with producing a film were signed to long-term, permanent contracts with the studios. Stars were typically contracted to a studio for seven years. The contracts were such that the star had no choice in the films that they had to make or how many. Despite being crucial to the marketing of films, stars had very little power. If they refused to do a film they would be suspended without pay and their contracts would then be extended. Frequently stars would be lent out to other studios.

The star system

Today, star contracts are based on conditions of exclusivity. The work of stars is based on selling a distinctive identity, and contracts must determine the rights to the exploitation of a star's image. The rights to use a star's name, voice and likeness are used to carry the star's image into other media, designed for commercial and promotional use. Stars' exposure is governed by the star system.

The **star system** refers to the institutional hierarchy established to regulate and control the employment and use of all actors. Stardom is a system of usage by three entities: 1) the film industry that tries to manage audience demands for films; 2) distributors that use stars to sell films to exhibitors in domestic and overseas markets; and 3) exhibitors who own and run theaters showing films that use stars to draw audiences. In this circuit of exchange, stars are a form of capital, a form of asset deployed with the intention of gaining advantage in the entertainment market and making profits.[iii]

Stars as capital

As a form of capital, stars are valuable assets for a production company; stars are a form of investment. Increasingly marketed through star differentiation, films have relied on star power for decades. During the studio era, stars stabilized demand, creating a consistent box office performance for a star's films. From an economic perspective, stars are thought of as a monopoly on personality.[iv] Star monopolies are based on the belief in unique individuality—there is only one Johnny Depp.

As negative costs rise, stars become even more central to the packaging of a project and

16.1 Legendary movie star Clint Eastwood appears on a Guinea stamp.

securing production financing. Since moving to a package-unit system of production, the powers of agents to act as key mediators in the industry has achieved new importance. The most powerful agencies are Creative Artists (Gwyneth Paltrow, Vince Vaughn, Demi Moore), International Creative Management (Jodie Foster, Eddie Murphy, Julia Roberts), and the William Morris Agency (Clint Eastwood, Bruce Willis, Kate Winslet). Artists Management Group (Cameron Diaz, Leonard DiCaprio, Robin Williams) and Endeavor (Robert DeNiro, Ben Stiller) are smaller agencies managing powerful stars. Since 2008, intra-agency trades have escalated because of growing anxiety over the future of the film business.

Agencies, their clients, and the studios remain in a situation of mutual dependence. Because stars are no longer bound by contract to agencies, agency power is limited somewhat. It is the studios that hold the money, and agents are only rich and powerful to the extent that they can place clients in packages that receive financial backing.

Stars may choose to be paid based on a film's performance (back-end deal), with payment based on a star participating in a percentage of the profits. Participation deals vary depending whether payments are made on the basis of gross receipts (based on the sale of the film in all markets) or net profits (what remains after gross receipts meet a break-even level). Compared to net points, gross points are of greater value, and the agents of top stars negotiate for these.

Box office performance has allowed stars economic and symbolic power in the film industry, yet even high-profile stars cannot always stabilize demand with their differentiation. Popularity does not always translate into profitability. Some stars become involved in film projects as joint producers through their own companies. Extra control acts as insurance against disaster—or so they hope.

Star images

Stars need to appear in the right type of vehicle for their existing image or persona. The popularity of a star-driven film depends upon its marketing.

Images are complex configurations of visual, verbal, and aural signs.[v] Stars' images come not only from their movies but also from forms of publicity and promotion, as well as from critical review and commentary. Images are also developed from the characters stars play and the style of performance they use to portray that role. Stars are categorized by social variables of age, gender, race, and nationality. Stars are mediated identities—audiences get images rather than a real person. As moviegoers form impressions of the star, the star becomes a collection of meanings.

Through their images, stars appear to be ordinary people, but they are also shown to be exceptional and apart from society. Their images are interpreted in many different ways and can be historically transformed (Madonna, for instance, shows different images of herself as over time). Star images are circulated in various forms of media and in many different contexts.

Cinema audiences make choices based on star vehicles as well as personalities. Some stars manage their image through associations with forms of performance other than film. Kenneth Branagh's association with classical Shakespearean theater draws on the cultural status of theater to distinguish himself from other popular film performers. Mick Jagger, on the other hand, has used his music-based celebrity to his advantage in a starring role with Angelica Huston that modified his rock image.

Star vehicles

Films are promotional vehicles for a star. A star combines two methods of product differentiation: the personal monopoly of a star's image and the familiar conventions that establish generic expectations.[vi] According to Richard Dyer,[vii] a vehicle provides:

16.2 Rocker Ice-T and Coco attend the 8th Annual Tribeca Film Festival "Burning down the house: the story of CBGB" premiere in 2009 in New York City. He transitioned from music to TV and film.

© Dziekan/Retna Ltd./Corbis

+ A character of the type associated with the star (Reese Witherspoon's ditzy blonde roles; Clint Eastwood's tough guy roles)

+ A situation, setting or generic context associated with a star (Hugh Grant in romantic comedies)

+ An opportunity for a star to do his/her thing (Jim Carey as a funny guy)

Film genres play an important role in defining star identities, setting limits on the contexts in which a star performs. However, with the mixing of genres and stars' traversing genres to expand their range of acting, these limits are not necessarily confining.

Special effects as stars

A recent rise in the emphasis of special effects as cinematic elements has given special effects a starring role. According to some motion picture analysts, special effects action/adventure movies with huge budgets seem to be the only reliable moneymakers. Startling special effects that are highlighted in commercials and trailers generate unstoppable momentum that even bad reviews cannot deter. One analyst pointed out that smart marketing showed that special effects could replace the traditional cornerstones of Hollywood films: *Avatar* proved that a special effects

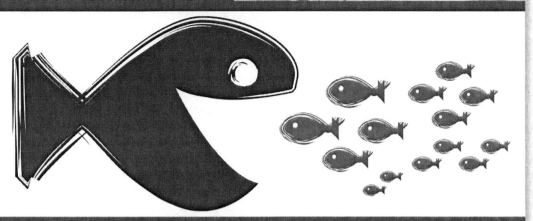

Image 16.3 Big fish/small fish.

PR Firms Shift Tactics in Post-Merger Hollywood

Hollywood studios and talent agencies are not the only groups that get restructured by mergers. Public relations companies, whose billings are under pressure and whose star clients' lives are under ever-increasing scrutiny, are undergoing their own shake-out. As a result, two decidedly different strategies are emerging—stick with stars or profit with corporations. Star clients generate far less revenue for agencies than corporate clients. For instance, talent flacks typically receive $5,000 a month to represent star clients, but corporate clients pay six-figure sums for brand management, product integration, communication strategy, targeted marketing, promotions, and event management. Just one large corporate account could equal the revenue lost from 20 existing star clients.

The latest merger is a melding of two of Interpublic's stand-alone public-relations powerhouses, PMK and BNC, which two months ago saw PR gurus get bigger roles and several other high-profile players pick up and leave. The rationale for combining the firms depends on whom you ask.

The "aggressive" evolution of BNC's model to position it "on the attack" prompted Interpublic to reward the group. Stan Rosenfield, whose firm represents George Clooney, Robert DeNiro, and Helen Mirren, speculated that Interpublic's purchases of PR firms PMK, HBH, BNC, and Rogers & Cowan were designed to give its ad agencies better access to talent. And although the same people who were representing the same talent three months prior were still repping the same people, what changed was the name of the companies doing the business.

Celebrity- and entertainment-based media continue to be a popular segment. Being part of a bigger agency where branding is the buzz word doesn't sit well with everyone, however. Five talent publicists left their agencies to form Slate. Two other veterans left to create a company called Viewpoint. Unlike Slate's focused approach that centers around looking after their talents' careers, Viewpoint aims to consolidate efforts around a current list and grow to become a complete destination for talent.

Big Fish Philosophy: The merger of HBH and PMK with BNC offers clients 100 staff in Los Angeles and a New York office of about 50, not to mention PMK's longtime cachet in entertainment PR, the combo is a force with which to be reckoned. In fact, PMK-BNC could be the prototype for a new, more vertically integrated PR firm, analogous to a major talent agency with its various related activities and economies of scale. The combined billings of PMK/HBH and BNC (about $70 million) likely make it the largest entertainment PR firm in the U.S. They service both corporate and celebrity clients.

Stand-Alone Philosophy: Independent PR outfits feel they have an advantage in the shifting landscape because of their focus on clients and ability to devote time to the task of public relations without justifying actions to a parent company. Success, though, often is limited to the ongoing ability of a specific publicist to serve a specific client. Unlike bigger firms, indie shops are more vulnerable to the everyday limitations and idiosyncrasies of the people at the core of these relationships with talent. Here, the entire focus is on stars and their management.

In 2010, the stars and their PR agencies include the following:

Who reps whom

PMK-BNC

Mariah Carey, Eric Clapton, Cameron Diaz, Colin Farrell, Kate Hudson, Jimmy Kimmel, John Legend, Eva Mendes, Jessica Simpson, and Barbara Walters

Slate

Jennifer Aniston, Daniel Craig, Benicio Del Toro, Johnny Depp, Kirsten Dunst, Tom Ford, Ryan Gosling, Anne Hathaway, Jude Law, Sam Mendes, Demi Moore, Gwyneth Paltrow, Sarah Jessica Parker, Zachary Quinto, and Ridley Scott

Viewpoint

Christian Bale, Pierce Brosnan, Matt Damon, Jesse Eisenberg, Calista Flockhart, Katherine Heigl, Lisa Kudrow, Shia LaBeouf, Chris Pine, and Keri Russell

Source: Elliot Kotek for Reuters, Feb. 19, 2010

3-D film with few stars could still win big at the box office, and *Hurt Locker* (hand-held camera effect) proved that neither stars nor a story were essential for winning an Oscar. Special effects films are also popular in foreign markets where U.S. films now derive half of their revenues.

Directors as stars

During the 1990s, marketers and publicists began to promote films based on the name of their directors. Steven Spielberg's popular movies mark him as a superstar; all questions of wealth, politics, and aesthetics became irrelevant to his star persona—he could do no wrong. In *vanity deals*, studios have helped some stars created their own production companies to pursue their own projects. Clint Eastwood has been one of the most successful star-directors. Recently, however, a

16.4 Director/star woody Allen.

series of financial disasters and shareholder objections have caused studios to all but cease offering such deals to stars. Still, studio advertising incorporates expressions such as "From the Director of ……", director's cuts are now added to DVD movies along with director's commentary, and specials on directors appear in a plethora of film magazines.

Virtual stars

From the big screen to the computer, all forms of animated and actual stars can be viewed and perused on the Internet. One of the most popular new forms of stars is a descendent of the Japanese printed cartoon (*manga*) and animated film (*anime*). Unlike American comic superheroes, anime characters grow and develop over time, and contain an underlying spiritual optimism. These virtual stars continue to gain popularity in games and feature-length films, and appeal to both children and adults.

Hundreds of Hollywood stars enjoy Internet stardom generated by Web-browsing fans. Hundreds of sites dedicated to stargazing enable even the homebound to connect with their favorite screen star. Marketers use the Internet as a tactic to generate buzz and to maintain a positive image for client stars. Exhibit 16.1 shows ranking for top actors.

The limits of stardom

The notion of stardom has also been described as a discrete and recognizable episode in the life of a star. It is the period of inevitability where personality intersects with history. Every episode of stardom carries within it the seeds of its own demise. This "iron law" dictates that, because personalities can grip the general attention for only so long, stardom only lasts three years.[viii] Is this notion a useful one for marketing professional?

EXHIBIT 16.1 Top Ten Actors for 2009

STARMETER REPORTS

Selections are based on the search behavior of 57 million users of the IMDb.com movie database.

1. Robert Pattinson
2. Kristin Stewart
3. Johnny Depp
4. Megan Fox
5. Taylor Lautner
6. Brad Pitt
7. Christian Bale
8. Dakota Fanning
9. Zooey Deschanel
10. Ryan Reynolds

WHAT IS CELEBRITY?

Public figures become celebrities at the point at which media interest in their activities is transferred from reporting on their public role to investigating their private lives. We may describe **celebrity**, then, as a commodity traded by the promotions, publicity, and media industries that produces interest beyond a person's public role.[ix] Celebrities are generated from sports, politics, the arts, religion, business, science, the professions, academia, and, of course, entertainment.

Celebrities differ from stars in several ways: where film creates stars, television creates personalities; where stars play roles, personalities perform themselves. Stars are able to continually accrue meaning through successive appearances, while television personalities, by contrast, are in danger of exhausting the meanings they generate by continually drawing upon them in order to perform at all. The film star is structured through the discourses of individualism, while the television personality constructs his or her celebrity through conceptions of familiarity.

This section looks at the celebrity industry, fame and reality television, celebrity economy, the manufacture of celebrities and how celebrities are consumed.

Celebrity industry

A celebrity's name has attention-getting, interest-catching, and profit-generating value. A mishmash of cultural and economic processes culminates in the wildly lucrative celebrity industry. The quest for celebrity, many critics say, indicates a shift towards a culture that privileges the momentary or sensational over the enduring.

Celebrities can be heroic, accidental, or public. We can type celebrity status according to how it's earned: *ascribed* (Prince Harry), *achieved* in competition (Tiger Woods), or *attributed* by the media (Michael Jackson). But it's important to remember that what constitutes celebrity in one cultural domain may be quite different in another. Our focus here is on American culture and its media-generated iconic symbols.

In a world where everyone has access to a camera, a screen, or both, it is easier than ever to find fleeting fame. Whether, like Tiger Woods, a celebrity earns status through accomplishment, or through generating millions of dollars in ticket and merchandise sales for films as George Lucas has, or being the nation's leading talk-show host for 27 years as is the one and only Oprah Winfrey, the famous stand out. According to the *Celebrity Register*, a celebrity is a name that, once made by news, now makes news by itself. The best paid celebrities (in descending order) are actors, athletes, authors, chefs, directors/producers, kid stars, magicians, models, musicians, and personalities from other areas, such as religion and politics.

A variety of services track the movements of celebrities in various sectors and sell access to celebrities. One such service, Celebrity Service International, charges subscribers $3,000 a year for bulletins. The modeling agency Celebrity Look-a-Likes by Elyse provides talent to advertising agencies for commercials. Home office and road staffers also serve the industry, as well as limousine drivers and bodyguards. Forbes' top ten celebrities are listed in Exhibit 16.2.

Fame

As the saying goes, some are born famous, some work hard to achieve fame, and others have fame thrust upon them.[x] People from politics and business were once successful and then famous, but now people in the entertainment industry are made famous by the media. Fame is now disconnected from achievement completely. The dream of fame has become inseparable from the idea of personal freedom.

EXHIBIT 16.2 World's Most Popular Celebrities, 2009

According to a *Forbes* magazine poll, the top stars were:

1. Angelina Jolie
2. Oprah Winfrey
3. Madonna
4. Beyonce Knowles
5. Tiger Woods
6. Bruce Springsteen
7. Steven Spielberg
8. Jennifer Aniston
9. Brad Pitt
10. Kobe Bryant

Compare these celebrities to the top ten stars above. What do the combined lists say about our preoccupation with stars?

Source: Forbes.com, 2009

Some of the factors of fame are exhibitionism, charisma, drive, and names. Demi Moore's nude appearance on the cover of *Vanity Fair* magazine during her pregnancy was an act of exhibitionism that certainly made her more famous. Charismatic figures reflect a self-assurance that is attractive to audiences. From the beginning, Hollywood stars changed their names because of their sound, country of origin, or prior exposure. As for drive, even Marilyn Monroe had to fight very hard for recognition.[xi]

FOCUS ON NAMING

The Celebrity Effect

Dramatic surges in the use of names belonging to stars and celebrities occur as their popularity increases according to research by the Social Security Administration, which has tracked the top 1000 most popular names for boys and girls since 1879. In 1956, for example, "Elvis" rose almost 60% after *Heartbreak Hotel* was released. And once Washington starred in Mo' Better Blues, the name "Denzel" increased 55% from the previous year.

Although parents may not name their babies after stars, the repetition of any name causes familiarity, liking and eventually adoption for personal use. To be popular, names must be compatible with the larger cultural moment to wield any influence. Perhaps that's why there weren't thousands of little Madonnas running around playgrounds in the eighties!

Here are the most popular names for 2009. * = a celebrity-based name.

RANK	MALE NAME	FEMALE NAME
1	Aiden*	Amelia
2	Noah	Isabella*
3	Liam*	Ava
4	Cayden	Sophia*
5	Ethan*	Olivia*
6	Jackson*	Madeline
7	Landon*	Lilly
8	Jacob	Abigail
9	Caleb*	Chloe*
10	Lucas*	Emma

Go to ssa.gov and search for your own name to see what other names were popular the year you were born. Any matches with famous folks?

Source: babynames.com

Andy Warhol claimed that everyone gets his or her 15 minutes of fame. Like stars, people who possess political, economic, or religious power can also become famous. The establishment of personal Web sites offers the possibility of fame and public visibility to anyone with a computer and a camera. Certainly the number of contestants auditioning for reality television can attest to the truth of this statement. Which is why we turn our attention to the *ordinary celebrity*, as created and nurtured by reality television.

Reality show fame

According to the Nielsen Media Research, reality shows account for about 66% of all of American TV shows (both in cable and broadcast). They amount to about 79% of all of the world TV shows (in cable and in broadcast).

The media's interest in manufacturing celebrities, especially on commercial reality television, has transformed media from being the end-user of celebrity to being the producers themselves. By using ordinary people with no special abilities and achievements as the talent in their programming, reality producers turn out a series of celebrities each season who are dependent upon the program that made them visible—because they have no other platform from which to address their audience.

The publicity and promotion potential of the reality show format is varied: the program can be promoted as news, cultural phenomenon, a launching pad for new celebrities, a contest, or just entertaining television. As each member of the "Survivor" team is ejected, he or she can be cycled through channel, network, or sponsors' promotions or act as a presenter in new programming ventures. When the season is over, the entire cast is processed through various program formats all over again, with retrospectives, reunions, and so on. Cross-promotions between networks, cable, newspapers, magazines, and radio is fundamental. "Survivor" participants are the epitome of the fabricated celebrity. Contestants want to be on television long enough to be famous, and fame becomes a personal justification.

The growing importance of the camera as a means of validating everyday reality is implicit; reality TV offers to display our everyday identities as spectacle, as an experiment and as entertainment. Even the genre term *reality* sets out to eliminate the distance between television and everyday existence. The reality genre has cashed in on the promotional possibilities that fuel the production and consumption of celebrity with the promise of media validation for just being who you are, every day.

Reality show casting calls have become events in their own right. Web sites post calls, and books offer hints for getting auditions and pointers for being chosen for a part. So who makes money on reality show fame? Almost everyone. Agents are paid to get their clients' work, brand managers pay winners to endorse products, show advertisers are exposed to millions of viewers, and producers sell their low-budget hits to global outlets.

The economies of reality shows help them proliferate. Both the lower cost of production and payout to stars keep studios profitable; yet these shows have little value in the aftermarket product for television. DVD sales of seasonal episodes account for some sales revenue, but the profit in reality shows comes mainly from product placement and sponsorships.

The economy of celebrity endorsements

Promoters seem to think celebrity endorsements actually persuade consumers to buy things. One example of the soaring rate of television advertisements screened during the 2010 Grammy Awards. An annual study of Grammy ads by media licensing consultancy GreenLight found that Black Eyed Peas, Eric Clapton, Drew Barrymore and Luke Wilson were just a few of the celebrities pitching Target, T-Mobile, Olay, AT&T and other brands during the year's biggest TV music show.

FOCUS ON PERSONAL BRANDS

Nicknaming

Nicknames have been around for centuries, long before the digital age, but the process of acquiring a nickname changed with email in the 1980s when users had to create their email handles. Unlike the name given by parents, nicknames can be awarded by people themselves. Nicknames can convey something about a person's demeanor that a birth name cannot.

According to Minya Oh, writer and radio personality in New York, regular people can be stars in their own minds and in their own circle of friends. "It's all about the Everyman becoming the Superman," she said. Names have meaning and are imbued with varying degrees of potency. Movie stars often change their names to suit create a screen image, and singers often adopt short or single word names (Ice-T, Cher). Internet users create nicknames for themselves to display their alter-ego, or to convey attitude. Internet sites like MySpace.com and YouTube.com have enabled everyone to feel like a celebrity.

The Internet has several nickname generators, where one can acquire all manner of monikers, from Western-theme to porn-star-worthy. But the most popular are organic—they spring up from an event, physical trait, or hobby. As millions of people continue to express themselves with instant messaging, email, blogs, forums, and Web sites, they will create new digital genres.

What do you think?

1. What does your email nickname say about your?
2. How might nicknames become personal brands?

Source: Stephanie Rosenbloom for *The New York Times*, April 13, 2006

In 2009, brands cut costs by focusing mostly on the licensing of pop music to maintain some celebrity presence in their ads. A year later, brands are once again partnering with celebrities and using pop music to maximize brand awareness and forge emotional connections with consumers. In total about 15% of the 2010 Grammy ads featured celebrity endorsements, a 150% spike from the previous year, and were dominated by U.S. car makers.

And there is also big money for U.S. celebrities who endorse brands abroad. Stars can net between $1 and $5 million for a single overseas ad campaign on the condition that no one will see them outside the country in which they were made. Britain is seen as a place where a celebrity's good name can be protected; for their eyes only! Michael Madsen, Ed Harris, and Samuel L. Jackson are among stars willing to make a buck abroad without compromising their image at home by endorsing uncharacteristic brands.[xii]

When a celebrity is the center of controversy, many advertisers choose to distance themselves before their own reputations are tarnished. Kobe Bryant's family-friendly endorsement deals with Nutella and McDonald's came to a quick end after he was accused of rape. Pepsi shied away from Madonna after her Like a Prayer video aired. Dell quietly let spokesman Benjamin Curtis's contract expire after he was arrested for allegedly trying to buy marijuana. Sears and FedEx yanked their sponsorships of *Politically Incorrect* after host Bill Maher called Americans "cowards" for "lobbing cruise missiles from 2,000 miles away," post 9-11. All of Tiger Wood's sponsors except Nike bailed on him after news of his infidelity surfaced.

Promoters must keep in mind that when a company signs a celebrity endorses, they are signing an image to pair with their own logo. Meaning the star must be compatible with the brand, be squeaky clean, and not be featured on dozens of other ads simultaneously. For instance, Dennis Rodman would not be a good choice for endorsing a line of children's toys, nor SpongeBob SquarePants for endorsing a brand of beer. Companies have to evaluate the individual's image and reputation to make sure it matches their own needs. Because people never forget. Businesses must take every means necessary to protect their own reputation by aligning themselves with appropriate celebrity spokespersons.

Manufacturing celebrity

Celebrities are developed to make money. As property, they are financial assets to those who stand to gain from their commercialization. Celebrity is produced, traded, and marketed by the media and publicity industries. Its cultural function is purchased identity—a branding mechanism for media products.

Celebrity industries include:

+ Entertainment—theaters, music and dance halls, sports arenas, and movies studios

+ Communications—media

- Publicity—PR, advertising

- Representation—agents, managers

- Appearance—costumes, makeup, hair styling

- Coaching—music, dance speech

- Endorsement—souvenirs, toys

- Legal and business services

Each of these entities contributes to the development, production, distribution, or maintenance of celebrities. After tourism, the industry is one of the world's largest, and it continues to thrive in step with the world population's need for stars, celebrities, and famous people to admire, emulate, and desire.

Consuming celebrity

Audiences place individual celebrities somewhere along a continuum that ranges from seeing them as objects of desire or emulation to regarding them as spectacular freaks. As objects of desire, they create a process of audience bonding.

Celebrity magazines exploded in 2008, but the economic recession has hurt traditional celebrity media so hard that it forced consolidation of the nine magazines covering the territory. As advertising and circulation erode, and even the market's dominant Web sites should be "looking over their shoulders."

According to a report from DeSilva + Phillips, a New York-based media banking firm, the rise of online alternatives and the recession have sped up the decline of some celebrity media franchises. *People*, the report notes, is perhaps the only magazine to prove itself as a multi-platform leader—accounting for 24% of the category's print circulation, 28% of its ad pages and 43% of its revenues.[xiii]

Entertainment and celebrity media span a diverse and wildly competitive landscape. Glossy magazines, TV tabloids, and countless websites all vie for audience and advertising. Everyone hopes that a sinking GDP means America needs entertainment more than ever. Some of the star media trends are:

- Sinking readership and defecting advertisers for entertainment and gossip magazines are causing online alternatives that may be more profitable.

- Celebrity programming has held its audience as TV provides a secondary platform for some stars. A challenger is web video with its increased reach and sophistication.

- Evolving mobile web popularity that serves up bite-sized celebrity content—news briefs, photos, professional and UCG videos are replacing traditional programming.

Oscar Drives Husbands Away

2010 Oscar winner, Sandra Bullock left her husband over allegations that he cheated. Jesse James reportedly had been going behind Bullock's back with a tattoo model who refers to him as the Vanilla Gorilla and wears patent leather pumps to bed.

If history is any indication, an Oscar win for a woman may result in castration her man. In 1938, after Jane Wyman won an Oscar, she and Ronald Reagan divorced. Other instances of fool-around fellas include Reese Witherspoon whose husband Ryan Phillipe was caught cheating after she won a Best Actress Oscar for *Walk the Line*. And two years after Halle Berry took home gold for *Monster's Ball*, she and R&B singer Eric Benét filed for divorce following allegations that Benét was unfaithful.

Hilary Swank split with Chad Lowe after her second Oscar win (for *Million Dollar Baby*). Ditto for Helen Hunt and Hank Azaria; and sweethearts Julia Roberts and Benjamin Bratt. Another Oscar curse casualties were Kate Winslet and director Sam Mendes, who separated a year after she received her first Academy Award for *The Reader*, and he went home empty-handed for *Revolutionary Road*.

Women earning big awards have strained marriages in other industries, but such occurrences by stars receive media hype, making their transgressions very public. Many celebrities have fragile egos, and media become their realities. According to one psychologist, the typical reaction for a man who feels professionally threatened, and thus insecure in a relationship, is to cheat. Infidelity is a way of taking control away from the woman.

What do you think?

1. How would you handle a promotion for a star with a cheating husband? Would blame or avoidance be the best strategy? Why?

Source: Nicole LaPorte for thedailybeast.com

STAR AND CELEBRITY AUDIENCES

Audiences accept stars and celebrities as a form of public personality with whom they identify, in whom they invest and maintain a personal interest, and to whom they ascribe a value that is cultural or social rather than merely economic. This section explores the psychological, playful, and fan relationships that occur between audiences and people who have gained fame in the movies and on television.

Star-celebrity relationship

Psychologists have determined that people's favorite stars and celebrities are usually those of the same sex, a fact which indicates a relationship built predominantly on self-identification.[xiv] One model of star classification identifies four categories of star-celebrity/audience relationships.[xv] They are:

+ *Emotional affinity*—a loose attachment of audience member to star; based on a star's charismatic attraction and the audience's motivation to care for and feel attached to figures on the screen

+ *Self-identification*—a state in which the audience member puts himself or herself in the person or situation of the star

+ *Imitation*—most common among young viewers, the condition in which a star serves as a role model for an audience member

+ *Projection*—a state where the audience member bonds psychologically with star; a parasocial (one-way) relationship is developed

Modeling theory[xvi] suggests that an audience member sees a star, imitates his or her actions, and receives a consequence from the new behavior. Among audience members of all types, imitation is a form of acquiring new ideas and behaviors from mediated people. As very visible role models, stars and celebrities often contribute to the formation of a viewer's identity. Self-identity has become increasingly interwoven with mediated symbolic forms, and in some cases leads beyond modeling to a parasocial relationship. Here, stars can be regular and dependable companions to provide advice and support—they allow audience members to imagine alternatives of how they may create their own identities. Stars and celebrities enable viewers to experiments with their self-images. Experimentation yields opportunities for marketing—from star fashions and branded cosmetics to celebrity endorsed products bought by star-struck audiences, the fans.

Watchers and gazers

Fans, readers, and viewers have their own menu of personalities for which they maintain interest, and some appear to be gullible about the truth of what they see, hear, or read about celebrities and stars. Celebrity and star watchers have been categorized into a typology of audience types.[xvii]

1. *Traditional audiences* regard text about the celebrity from media sources as realistic. They believe that celebrity stories as arise naturally through the news media rather than through promotions and publicity. Their interaction with celebrity involves modeling, fantasy. and identification.

2. *Second order traditional audiences* see a more complex narrative where publicity plays a part but did not pose an obstacle to esteeming celebrities. They believe in the deserving celebrity, and their interaction is more negotiated than traditional audience members.

3. *Postmodern audiences* see media coverage as fictional and know about celebrity manufacture. They often seek out evidence and detail, rejecting or ignoring the story of the naturally rising celebrity as naïve and false. They have an active interest in the techniques of manufacturing celebrity.

4. *Game players* regard the content of media as semi-fictional and aren't bothered about where the stories come from of whether or not they are true. They make use of celebrity material for play and their own cultural activities. This audience type consists of two sub-groups: gossipers and detectives. *Detectives* consider celebrity production a giant playground, and *gossipers* think of celebrity media as a rich social resource. The game-playing group is a dominant form of audience type inscribed into mainstream media formats.

In all groups, those audience members who believe most in media truth about celebrity are those who know least about the production process. *Play* is an accurate description of audiences' mode of engagement with celebrity. They see pleasure in the social exchange of gossip and stories the media develop about famous people. Fans are characterized by their enthusiastic mode of play-type engagement.

According to an audience involvement scale, levels of involvement with stars and celebrities determine their marketing priority. Audience scale levels include:

+ Invisible—seek out local celebrities but don't travel to Hollywood

+ Watchers—passive viewers

+ Seekers—the largest group and the biggest spenders have a stronger attraction to celebrities; they go to performances and spend the most money on entertainment

+ Collectors—buy souvenirs

+ Fans—need personal interaction with stars

+ Insiders—groupies who are celebrities by associating with them

+ Entourage—the star's inner circle or network of close associates

+ Ensnared—an obsessed fan

A celebrity marketer's objective is to move an audience member up the scale from being invisible to becoming a fan.

Fan behavior

Fans are prime marketing targets for manufacturing celebrities and stars through mediated vehicles, and for cultivating audiences that insure box office and advertising revenues. Because of their important role when developing marketing strategies, fans merit attention in any discussion of entertainment marketing.

Again, fans construct parasocial, imagined connections to stars or celebrities who fulfill their needs for friendship; such interactions are substitutes for real relationships. "Fandom" is a surrogate relationship where audience members live vicariously through the lives of famous people.[xviii] This "intimacy" is mediated by television, movies, and the Internet; contact is constantly available one mass media conduit or another. Some associations even take on religious connotations, such as fan adoration for dead celebrities Elvis, Princess Diana, and James Dean; shrines, memorials, and gatherings signify religious dedication.[xix]

PROMOTING STARS AND CELEBRITIES

A visibility industry exists: its function is to design, create, and market celebrities as brands. Professionally managed and directed, celebrities receive power from media who give equal amounts of attention to a variety of famous types. A definable, publicizable personality can become a nationally advertised trademark. Sylvester Stallone was the first star to become a registered trademark. Arnold Schwarzenegger talked about his career as a brand name product and exploited it with the same dedication as a fast food chain. To create a star or celebrity brand, marketers use the same strategy as that used to brand products. A huge group of sub-industries— from venue managers to the beauty industry to the legal world—provide services to produce and promote personal brands.[xx]

Celebrity branding

Celebrity brands are both homemade and licensed; when an individual produces a powerhouse company, a homemade Martha Stewart brand is created. When celebrities are hired to make a brand, such as Michael Jordan for Nike or Tiger Woods for Buick, they have become licensed brands themselves. The importance of the celebrity as a branding mechanism for media products has assisted their fluent translation across media formats and systems of delivery.

Three branding strategies are recommended for promoting celebrities:[xxi]

1. **Pure selling** where the agent presents a client's qualifications to an intermediary, such as when a singer's tapes are sent to a talent scout who solicits a record company. Here the celebrity is sold to distributors, akin to getting shelf space for a cola.

2. **Product improvement** where an agent works with a client to modify certain characteristics to increase his or her market value. Madonna's transformation from East Village punk to a lacy virgin, to a cowgirl and again to a kids' author, is an example of transforming a product in response to current trends.

3. **Market fulfillment** where an agent scans the market to identify unmet needs, finds a person that meets those needs, and develops a saleable product. Spice Girls and 'N Sync were created by assembling photos of young singers and developing a hybrid that would sell records.

A CLOSER LOOK AT MARKETING CELEBRITIES

© Simone Cecchetti/Corbis

Image 16.5 Singer Madonna performs onstage in her 'Sticky & Sweet Tour' in 2009, displaying one of her many brand images.

Madonna's Marketing Magic

In recent years, Madonna has become THE idiosyncratic female icon. Along with a discussion of her promotion strategy, we recount Madonna's images of herself during the course of her career.

Physical transformation strategies

Material virgin with a boy toy

Madonna represents a fantasy of what fans and critics own gendered or sexual identities might mean. The term 'postmodernism' came into vogue in the 1980s when Madonna was born on MTV with the release of her video 'Lucky Star', 'Into the Groove' is a song associated with the height of her 'boy toy' phase, coming soon after her first number one single 'Like a Virgin',

Body builder

Madonna's next major image overhaul came after she resculpted her body through aerobics and weight training, dyed her hair Marilyn Monroe blonde, and began wearing self-designed body-armor style lingerie. Styling herself after American female retro-icons in her 1984 'Material Girl' video, Madonna's 'Express Yourself' gave viewers a whole new series of image references to gendered and sexual icons with an entirely new level of irony.

Dominatrix

During the early 1990s, Madonna again altered her image and identity with the releases of *Truth or Dare*, the book *Sex*, and the videos 'Erotica', 'Vogue', and even the recent 'Deeper and Deeper'. A postmodern icon of gender and sexuality, Madonna understood her identity as a series of images which could be distinguished from each other through specific references. If an audience didn't already know her real identity, her varying personas might have seemed less like entertainment and more like schizophrenia.

Media maven

The powerful seductiveness of her multiple identity-images, reside in Madonna's ability to remain uncontaminated by multiple images. Madonna is permanently a part of history, strategically positioned as a famous marginalized person when such identities have become powerful and recognizable. As a way of coping with an inevitable disappearance from the mass media limelight, she has used images of sexual minorities and postmodernism in her work for shock value.

Image maintenance

What is important to think about here is Madonna's relationship to the well-managed maintenance of her identity. When a product is profitable, those who promote the product want to repeat the formula that fostered such success. Madonna is quite aware that she is in the profit business. But instead of simply *repeating* the product/image formula that gave her success, Madonna chose to make fun of her 'boy toy' self, which many young adults had come to copy with their own style of dress. By offering her audience a slightly differentiated Madonna image, she kept them coming back for more products, which was good business sense.

So after 20 years, Madonna consistently reaps profits. Reinventing herself in almost clockwork fashion, Madonna morphed herself into a virgin, material girl, boy toy, dominatrix, media maven to working mom. The genius of reinvention and understanding of the inevitable end of the business cycle have kept Madonna on top of revenue generation. Marketers should take advice from this branding expert. By using the Madonna strategy, marketers have several avenues to magnify and reinvent their client's star-celebrity brand. The most important tactics are:

1. **Communication:** Trailers, Web sites, advertising with graphic uniformity, audience-focused messages, and continuity of message delivery.

2. **Audience Loyalty:** To maintain loyalty, reinvent and re-analyze the brand's image to address audience perceptions.

3. **Failure Analysis:** Analyzing and anticipate failure to optimize it and double the brand marketing success rate.

4. **Reinvention:** The keys to reinvention are simple:

   a. Die a thousand deaths and come out on the other side.

   b. A star's brand image is money in the bank. Migrate it, don't ever change it.

What do you think?

1. What lessons can entertainment marketers learn from Madonna's transformative branding strategy?

2. What suggestions do you have for her brand maintenance for the next five years?

Sources: unpublished article by Analee Nemitz, English Graduate Student, University of California, Berkeley; Sean De Souza for www.psychotactics.com/artmadona

Managing the star-celebrity brand

If not managed properly, star brands can become a huge liability. *Brand asset management* is one strategy for driving profitable growth from star brands. As developed by Scott Davis,[xxii] the management process has four phases and eleven steps. Here is a short adaptation of his asset management platform for managing star brands.

Phase one: develop a brand vision

The ultimate vision for most stars and celebrities is to become a household name and to earn as much money as possible. But that's not always the case. Some personalities prefer to remain private (Kevin Spacey) or have as their goal to be recognized for their talent or ability as a performer (Sean Penn). Whatever the vision, agents, marketers, and stars must agree on a single vision that defines the best brand-based strategies to pursue. A brand's vision may determine whether to recreate the brand by re-positioning, or to increase its value perception through brand extensions (merchandising, new endeavors).

Phase two: determine the brand's image

This step is research-driven, and it involves understanding audience perceptions of the star relative to the competition and opportunities for growth. To determine the star's brand image, audience members are asked about: the brands consistency across audience segments, the star's perceived strengths and weaknesses, and what audiences want from the star-brand in the future. By uncovering audience beliefs about a brand, marketers can work toward improving, changing, or maintaining the beliefs.

Phase three: develop an asset management strategy

This phase includes determining the right brand-based strategies for achieving the goals set in Phase One and from the audience perceptions discovered in Phase Two. There are four steps to the process.

1. *Establish a unique position.* Should the star be positioned by genre, as is an adventure star like Sylvester Stallone? Or should the star be positioned as a comedian, such as Jim Carrey? The trick is not to limit the position, but to focus attention on that aspect of the star's abilities so audiences associate that quality with the star within the genre of film or television roles. Stars are sometimes positioned with tag lines, such as "Oscar winner" or "Emmy nominee" to enhance the position.

2. *Extend the brand.* Most stars prefer to accept new challenges, such as changing genres, supporting philanthropic causes, or endorsing consumer products. Moving stars beyond their usual role extends both exposure and revenue generation potential for the brand. Brand extenders are discussed in more length in the next section.

3. *Communicate the brand's position.* Communication is about determining the right mix of media and place-based vehicles that will maximize the potential for achieving the image goals. Communication vehicles include advertising, Internet, public relations, and event marketing. All communication should achieve specific and measurable goals.

4. *Determine the brand's worth.* Not quite a pricing strategy, determining worth involves setting fees for performing, guest appearances, and product endorsements. A factor of the star's popularity, the fees are predicated upon the star's talent, the audience size, and the star's compatibility with branded products.

Phase four: measure the return on brand investment

Since you can't manage what you can't measure, evaluation must be constant and appropriate. Common measures of branding success and star power include but are not limited to:

+ Paid attendance as box office receipts

+ Media coverage

+ Google hits

+ Fan base and club activity

+ Award nominations

+ Special appearances

+ Endorsed product sales

+ Polling research of audience perceptions of celebrities

+ Arbitron, Nielson, and other rating services

+ *Q factor*, which measures the degree of like or dislike by audiences based on familiarity and appeal (see Chapter 6).

+ *The Great Dinner Party* question where fans disclose which star's party they would prefer to attend (see Chapter 6).

FOCUS ON SUPERSTAR ECONOMICS

Do Stars Always Equate to Profits?

A growing number of academics are studying how movies are made, financed and distributed; most are finding that the studio's assumption that big stars will increase a movie's bottom line is simply wrong. According to a Rutgers economics professor, there is no statistical correlation between stars and success.

Superstar economics was first used to explain the astonishing fees of top lawyers and star chief executives. When applied to movies, the dynamic means that improvements in technology that would make it easier for top performers in a field to serve a larger market would not only increase the revenue generated by stars, but would also reduce the revenue available to everybody else.

The Hollywood star system is built upon the premise that stars bring many different kinds of benefits: they are easier to market, they help sell more tickets and they help drive home-video sales. But studio chiefs acknowledge that a star does not guarantee success.

Extending the star or celebrity brand

Keeping the star-celebrity brand alive in a mediated world means constant exposure through as many means as marketing provides. In this section, we discuss media star stories, product endorsements, and political affiliations for their value as brand extensions.

Star stories as brand extensions

Media vehicles are useful for bring stars and celebrities to audiences; biographies made for television broadcast and published as best sellers give stars depth as "real people." Placement on talk shows, appearances on "Inside the Actors' Studio" (PBS), and stints hosting game shows are other vehicles that give a client face time in front of audiences.

Featuring stars as models in magazine fashion layouts presents an opportunity for co-branding between star and fashion brand.

Politics and brand extension

Celebrities incorporate themselves into party politics, especially in the U.S. Stars and celebrities are involved with electioneering, fund-raising, lobbying, and so on. Such involvement contributes to the overall professional strategy of marketing celebrities and it gives stars political influence within their party. Some

© C3396 *Hubert Boesi/dpa/Corbis*

16.6 Sean Penn uses his stardom to bring awareness to social causes.

even run for political office themselves—such as former President Ronald Reagan and California's Governor Arnold Schwarzenegger.

Celebrities and stars take up political and philanthropic causes and are known to contribute time and money to emergency situations such as natural disaster, aid for small farmers, global overpopulation, health issues such as AIDS and cancer, and moral considerations such as a woman's Right to Choose. Their media presence in association with a cause brings attention to all forms of global strife and inequities. Good for the cause, better for the star's image. Angelina Jolie's adoption of children from Darfur brought both the plight of children and the little-known country to global media and fan attention. This marketing strategy is one that should not be ignored when promoting a star or celebrity.

Celebrity endorsement

Brands clamor for the perfect celebrity to endorse their products. Celebrities project their image onto the advertised brand, transforming it from a simple product into an enhanced extension of a famous personality. Celebrities themselves are anxious to receive the exposure advertising provides, to say nothing of the millions of dollars in revenue. This section will discuss the dynamics of celebrity endorsement for products, pharmaceuticals and nonprofit causes as well as political affiliations.

Studies show that celebrity endorsers make advertisements more believable, enhance the recognition of a brand, create a positive attitude toward the brand, and create a distinct personality for the brand.[xxiii] Evidence suggests that endorsement is most effective in sustaining ad recollection and brand name regardless of the product category.[xxiv] According to advertising research, the economic worth of celebrity endorsers justifies the large costs they incur and are worthwhile investments. Research on the impact of celebrity endorsements proves that these contracts are positively associated with financial returns.[xxv] Consumer familiarity with the celebrity engages consumers at a deeper level; they aspire to be and live as the celebrities do with the products they use.

Baby boomers, after all, have Sally Fields advocating a monthly pill to stop bone loss, and Jamie Lee Curtis telling people to keep regular with a special yogurt. Boomers themselves, these stars resonate with their television audience in a way no other aged celebrity could.

Matching celebrities with brands is usually a function of the advertiser, but agents often solicit specific brands for their celebrity clients. The most important factor of successful endorsement is the celebrity-audience match-up. Boomers respond to stars such as Candice Bergen and Alan Alda who had similar backgrounds, while younger adults are likely to emulate Tiger Woods or Mary Louise Parker, who represent attractive lifestyles. Kermit the Frog is perfect to endorse milk when kids are targeted. Match-ups between celebrity and brand are also important; products must be something the star would use for an obvious benefit—Woods and Tag Heuer, for instance.

Celebrities Hawking Drugs

Celebrity endorsement is the stable of advertising campaigns seeking differentiation for their brand. One aspect of the celebrity endorsement phenomenon involves companies that hire celebrities to attract attention to the latest drugs and the diseases that go with them. Wyeth hired supermodel Lauren Hutton to promote hormone replacement therapy for menopause. GSK contracted football star Ricky Williams to publicize social anxiety disorder, helping make Paxil the world's top-selling antidepressant. Celebrities have become integral to drug marketing strategies that include paid advertising and aggressive public relations campaigns to produce media appearances on *Oprah* and *The Today Show*. According to celebrity brokers, the star's remuneration package, though always confidential, can range from $20,000 to $2 million.

According to a senior marketing executive at Amgen, the partnership between celebrity and brand has an intangible sort of magic. Amgen is the Californian biotech firm that hired star Rob Lowe to help market an anti-infection drug for a reported fee of more than $1 million. To be effective, pharmaceutical marketing must 1) use an A-list celebrity, 2) find a "news-hook" that links the celebrity and the product, 3) develop simple messages, and 4) make sure the celebrity delivers those messages during every appearance.

On-air talk-show appearances on media venues like *Oprah* can be better forums for celebrities than straight advertisements, which are governed by regulations. The great advantage to celebrity endorsement over advertising is that the airtime is practically free, and there is no equal time for candidates to worry about. The downside with a media interview is that the situation is less controllable than a scripted ad. It can be tricky for the celebrity to ensure that all product messages are delivered. Advertisers, urged to rate their prospective celebrity with a Q score, used Rob Lowe because his Q score was high with women over fifty, a key target of the Amgen campaign.

The 2010 spring season saw famous sneezers like reality star Alison Sweeney endorse McNeil Consumer's Zyrtec Liquid Gels, and American Idol judge Kara DioGuardi spoke for Merck's Claritin. Sweeney, a longtime "Days of Our Lives" star and host of "The Biggest Loser", took part in a Zyrtec event dubbed "Race Against Your Allergies," in New York City's Madison Square Park. DioGuardi served as the face of Claritin's Living Clear campaign, a user-generated content effort that invited users to submit videos to LivingClear.com to show what Claritin's non-drowsy formula did for them. Votes from site visitors decided the ultimate winner, who pocketed a $10,000 prize and won a chance to star in a Claritin online ad, while five finalists took home $1,000 and a one-year supply of Claritin products.

Campaigns touting new drugs—and mature products seeking a sales boost late in their lifecycle—helped spending on consumer drug ads rise by 4% to $4.8 billion in 2009, according Kantar Media.

Pharmaceuticals outperformed the general advertising market, due primarily to the timing of new drug launches and marketing activity among brands with significant sales potential.

Internet advertising also showed growth in 2009. Former "Extra" host and broadcast journalist Dayna Devon offered personal tips on Allergan to Facebook fans invited to share her experience with Juvederm through the social networking site. Website visitors could upload a photo to see how they might look after using Juvederm. The site also let them find a doctor, and sign up for "customized e-mails, exclusive offers and special event invitations. GlaxoSmithKline recruited tennis great John McEnroe for an awareness campaign about prostate cancer. A public service campaign in print featured an image of McEnroe having blood drawn with a tagline, "Get serious" that urged men over 40 to get tested for the disease. Ads ran in magazines like *Fortune, People* and *Sports Illustrated* where McEnroe was placed to get the attention of men in the target age cohort. Stand Up To Cancer partnered with Amgen on another recent celebrity-driven educational campaign that featured Edie Falco and Cynthia Nixon, advising patients on the risk of infection during treatment in 30- and 60-second broadcast spots, print ads, and a Web site.

Novo Nordisk enlisted action film star and ex-wrestler Dwayne "The Rock" Johnson for its Diabetes Aware campaign with the Entertainment Industry Foundation. Past celebrity associations with the campaign included Halle Berry, Cuba Gooding, Jr., Dustin Hoffman, Kevin Kline, and Jon Lovitz. An unbranded effort, the campaign aimed to reach the 24 million Americans living with diabetes as well as the estimated 6.2 million Americans unaware that they had the disease.

What do you think?

1. What ethical issues are present with celebrity endorsements of pharmaceuticals?
2. If you were a star's agent, how would you advise him or her regarding an appearance for a specific drug? Why?

Sources: Marc Iskowitz **and** Mathew Arnold for www.mmmonline.com

Proper match-ups establish celebrity credibility with target audiences and maximize cross-promotional opportunities.

Celebrity matches differ by level of product involvement. Routinely selected products that are usually lower in cost—toothpaste, cosmetics—require little consumer involvement in the purchase process. Products that carry more risk (an incorrect choice means considerable loss of money or esteem)—car or travel—require a high level of involvement before making a purchase selection. As we saw in Chapter 10, some entertainment contents are sold using a rational approach by providing information; others rely on emotion to drive the purchase, and use a transformational approach to advertise. The trick is matching the star to the correct approach.

	INFORMATIONAL ADS	TRANSFORMATIONAL ADS
Low involvement	expertise	likeability
High involvemen	objectivity	similarity

Low involvement products that require information are best suited to celebrities with product expertise; motor oil should maybe be endorsed by a NASCAR driver. Low involvement products sold with emotional need likable celebrities to be effective; Bill Cosby sold a lot of Jell-O. High involvement products needing information seek objective celebrities; a travel show host is a good choice to recommend a hotel brand. Emotionally sold high involvement products are best promoted with celebrities similar to the audience segment; an actor playing an attorney on "The Good Wife" may be right for a life insurance brand.

The only real problem with product endorsement for celebrities and stars is overkill; redundancy can turn off the viewing public when a single personality is associated with too many products. Credibility levels drop for both the product and the endorser when a personality has multiple brand associations.

Four celebrities signed in 2010 to be brand boosters were:

+ Rapper/Singer Drake for Sprite. His first commercial, titled "Unleashed," aired during the NBA All Star Games and depicted Drake struggling to find inspiration in the studio while recording his hit song "Forever."

+ Charles Barkley rapped about a $5 box deal for Taco Bell in a commercial that premiered during the 2010 Super Bowl.

+ Shaquille O'Neal pops out of a bottle of Muscle Milk high energy drink when consumers show the number 33 to a computer webcam.

+ "Avatar" star Zoe Saldana has become the face of Avon's latest fragrance, "Eternal Magic."

Valuing celebrities

The arcane field of measuring celebrity appeal yields Q Scores that tell advertisers and media outlets how much the public likes actors, news anchors and sports figures.[xxvi] Q Scores are prepared by Marketing Evaluations of Manhasset, New York using mail surveys to ask about celebrities' likeability and familiarity to groups of people selected from a 100,000-strong database.

A push from marketers for more-detailed research on the effectiveness of advertising resulted in a services offered through Omnicom's Davie-Brown entertainment marketing operation. Known as the Davie-Brown Index, the measure is based on regular surveys of people drawn from a 1.5 million-member research panel provided by a Dallas online market-research firm called *i.think*. A list of more than 1,500 celebrities is presented four times a year, asking to respondents whether they view the famous person as a trendsetter, trustworthy and is influential, and whether the celebrity's endorsement of a product would be believable. The Davie-Brown Index uses eight criteria for its evaluation: appeal, notice, trend setting, influence, trust, endorsement, aspiration, and awareness.

Resulting scores enable advertisers and ad agency personnel to determine if a particular public figure will motivate consumers who see them in an ad to purchase the product advertised. One of the risks of celebrity endorsement is overexposure, so number of previous endorsements is a prime consideration for valuing celebrity brands. Other measuring devices include e-Polls and focus groups where people react to actual commercials featuring celebrities.

Celebrities and cause marketing

Celebrities can bring visibility, credibility, and attract media attention to **cause marketing campaigns**. Successfully contacting, negotiating, and working with celebrities requires critical research and specialized rules of protocol, according to the president of the Celebrity Source, Inc. The firm has partnered Kareem Abdul Jabar with Energizer Batteries and the International Fire Chiefs Association and Robert Guillaume with Quaker Oatmeal and the American Heart Association, among many others.

Being global

Although Hollywood is the most influential industry within the global film economy, the operation of stardom exists in other large markets, most notably in East and South Asia. Thanks to careful marketing, Jackie Chan became a global phenomenon in the late 1990s. Indian screen legend Amitabh Bachchan has starred in popular Hindi cinema since the 1970s. The large number of cinemagoers in India and distribution of his vehicles in markets as diverse as Africa and Russia make him a very recognizable global star.

Stardom has also played an important part of the popular cinemas of Europe, although some European film still suffers from its equation with art-house productions.

In Asia, a Korean movie boom, or "Hallyu," for popularized Lee Byeong-Heon who launched his latest movie *G.I. Joe: The Rise of Cobra* with director Stephen Sommers (who made *The Mummy 3* in 2008) in 2010. Shahrukh Khan, a superstar of Indian cinema, turns out fans by the thousands. Boosted by a proliferation of international film festivals, stars previously unknown are receiving attention from American directors.

Nowhere is the age of celebrity more apparent than in London, where celebrity faces and magazine titles take up most of the space in newspaper stalls. Celebrity sells everywhere, as reflected in London's rise as one of the main hubs of the international celebrity and marketeering circus.[xxvii]

Celebrities and Luxury Fashion Brands

The use of celebrity endorsement is especially valuable to brands in the luxury fashion sector, which have doubled in the past ten years. Versace (Italy) has used Madonna, Demi Moore, and Halle Berry in its print ads; Julia Roberts appeared in Fianfranco Ferre's ads, and Louis Vuitton ads have featured Jennifer Lopez, Scarlett Johansson, and Uma Thurman.

Celebrity endorsements are important to luxury brands for the following reasons:

· Brand awareness for new luxury brands

· Positioning and reposition existing brands

· Sustaining a brand's aura

· Revive and revitalize staid brands

· Generate PR leverage and opportunities for brands

· Create global brand awareness

· Promote a brand's products and appeal

Image 16.7 Venezuelan Actress Alicia Machado came out with her own line of perfume "Malice by Machado" to capitalize on her stardom.

© Zayra Morales/EFE/Corbis

Although the most widely used method is paid-for media advertisements in fashion magazines and TV, additional ways that celebrities are used to endorse brands include:

· Product use in movies and TV programs

· Fashion spreads at different events and locations

· Promotion photographs using products from a brand

· Mention of brands in music lyrics

· Inviting celebrities to be co-creators and partners in designing specific products

· Naming products after celebrities

Celebrity endorsement transfers the personality and status of the celebrity directly to the brand. To achieve maximum impact, matching a celebrity with the right brand should adhere to these five rules:

1. **Credibility**—high level of talent or expertise in a field (George Clooney).

2. **Global appeal**—known worldwide and appreciated by majority of people in the consumer and fashion society (Charlize Theron).

3. **Personality**—celebrity and brand personalities must match in a positive way (Nicole Kidman for Chanel).

4. **Uniform power**—celebrity must not overshadow the brand.

5. **Constancy**—celebrity must have lasting power, maintaining high appeal after the campaign is over.

Public controversies and professional or personal circumstances that compromise the celebrity's image may also compromise the brand. Promoters must to use caution and do their research before signing a celebrity to endorse an entertainment brand.

Source: Uche Okonkwo for brandchannel.com, April 7, 2006

Because English is a common language in the UK and U.S., major studios choose London for their international premiers and press junkets. However, the city's notorious tabloid press poses some dangers for visiting stars, making it just as hard to stay out of the tabloids as getting into them.

The tabloid business has become a sort of entertainment industry in its own right. Its business model has two distinguishing features. First, celebrity has become the product—rather than just a device for marketing films. The talent owes its standing chiefly to the celebrity machine and not to any particular gift. It therefore depends on the attentions of the press to make money. Second, celebrities, agents, photographers, and picture desks have found that the most efficient way to create an endless supply of celebrity news is to work together. A business that used to be based on intrusion has discovered a preference for collaboration.

The tabloid business is also expanding abroad. Northern & Shell launched an American edition of *OK!*, a celebrity magazine that already has Australian, Chinese and Middle Eastern editions. The *National Enquirer*, a hard-nosed American scandal sheet famed for pushing back the boundaries of taste—and of free speech—was re-launched and stuffed with alumni of British tabloids and magazines.[xxviii]

Media management is a global phenomenon. Developed in symbiosis with newly aggressive modes of reporting and newsgathering, *spin* is now so widespread across so many national media

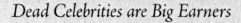

Dead Celebrities are Big Earners

The 13 iconic figures on Forbes' list grossed a collective $886 million in 2009! Jok termed the "summer of death," 2009 became a parade of news and media attention. Commemorative magazine issues, television specials and social media soapboxes provided an outlet for the public's curiosity.

The most significant death in terms of coverage was Michael Jackson's on June 25. According to the Pew Research Center's Project for Excellence in Journalism, the pop star's passing occupied 18% of the news the week of his death, and 17% for the two weeks thereafter. The Magazine Information Network estimated that Michael Jackson's death resulted in $55 million in additional revenue for the magazine industry in the two months following the event, thanks to special issues and book-a-zines dedicated to memorializing his life.

Jackson's three-hour memorial was shown live on 18 cable and broadcast networks, pulling in 31.1 million viewers, according to Nielsen Media Research, representing millions of dollars in airtime. ABC and CNN attracted the largest audiences with 5.3 million viewers, while NBC pulled in 5.1 million, CBS earned 3.9 million, Fox News drew 2.2 million and MSNBC had 1.4 million.

On the day of Jackson's death, Google traffic was so high that they thought hackers had taken control of their servers. According to Mashable.com, a third of all messages on Twitter referenced the pop star. In the week following Jackson's death, the top 10 most visited sites, including Time Warner's TMZ, Yahoo!'s omg and Wenner Media's US Magazine.com, collectively registered nearly 30 million unique users—nearly double the previous week's traffic according to comScore.

News of Farrah Fawcett's cancer battle raised *Entertainment Tonight's* ratings 17% the week of May 12. A week later, Fawcett's documentary attracted 8.9 million viewers on NBC. *Vanity Fair's* August Heath Ledger cover sold 485,000 copies on the newsstand, the top for the year and more than the Jackson/Fawcett split cover, which posted newsstand sales of 437,000, according to the Audit Bureau of Circulation's Rapid Report.

The media's coverage of famous deaths is nothing new. *Time* magazine memorialized John Lennon with the headline "The Day the Music Died," and nearly 33 million tuned in to Princess Diana's 1997 funeral. Tabloid and newsweekly magazine covers were also dedicated to Patrick Swayze, Ted Kennedy, and Natasha Richardson.

Source: Lauren Streib, Forbes.com, Oct. 27, 2009

systems that its power has become universal. Management of public personae has become a core activity not only for entertainment, but for contemporary politics as well. Strategies for both are derived from public relations models of crisis management or from the celebrity industry's methods for building the public identity of the celebrity commodity.

Finally

Marketing celebrity and star brands involves the same skills and strategies needed to successfully market products. Audiences are fickle and must be constantly reminded of a personality's presence. Spin, gossip, and hype are the tools of the publicity trade for movie and television marketers. And with large amounts of capital invested in star-power, marketers' tactics must justify the bottom line costs spent on manufacturing celebrity.

With a celebrity society in place, there is plenty of opportunity for alliance with all forms of celebrity marketing. Advertising, public relations, agents, event promotion, and media relations are among the business most involved with celebrity management.

GOT IT?

- Stardom is a condition based on a thriving economy and social mobility; the star system includes audience demands on the industry, movie distributors and exhibitors, all of whom rely on the selling power of stars for their success.

- Celebrities are commodities traded by media industries; mostly, they are television personalities who play themselves; factors of fame include exhibitionism, charisma, drive, and names.

- Most celebrity audience members are game players who get pleasure from social exchange of gossip and media-generated stories about famous people; fans construct para-social relationships with stars and celebrities.

- Celebrity branding strategies include: pure selling, product improvement, and market fulfillment; brand asset management is a strategy that drives profitable growth for star and celebrity brands.

- Marketers coordinate celebrity endorsers with qualities of expertise, objectivity, likeability and similarity with the audience's level of involvement with a product or brand.

NOW TRY THIS

1. Visit a Borders or Barnes & Noble bookstore magazine section and inventory the periodicals focused on celebrities and stars. Peruse them to see what products are advertised in them. What do the products tell you about the readership of these magazines? What do the story titles tell you about what fans want to know?

2. Using your favorite movie star as a subject, use Google and star-based Web sites to trace his or her career. How much of what you read is generated by the star's publicist? How much is reported by news media? What other sources provide star information? What can you conclude about marketing strategies for your star from this investigation?

3. Using your favorite television celebrity, suggest several products that s/he might be likely to endorse. Poll ten of your friends and see which product they would be most likely to purchase if endorsed by your celebrity choice. Which of the match-up criteria are most appropriate to their selections: expertise, likeability, objectivity, or similarity?

4. Invoke your creativity to develop a reality show that is designed to bring members of a Boomer audience segment into the public eye. What would the prizes be? Who would host the show? How might the winning contestants be manufactured into celebrities?

QUESTIONS FOR DISCUSSION AND REVIEW

1. Make the best match-up between stars/celebrities/personalities and products from the list below and provide a rationale for your choice. Answers follow Question 5.

   1. Musician P. Diddy
   2. Athlete Lance Armstrong
   3. TV show host Oprah Winfrey
   4. CNN reporter Anderson Cooper
   5. Ex-president Bill Clinton
   6. Author J. K. Rowling
   7. Actor Johnny Depp
   8. Radio show host Howard Stern
   9. Comedian Dave Chappelle
   10. Actor Kate Hudson

   a. Mont Blanc watch
   b. American Express
   c. L'Oreal hair color
   d. Nature Power Bar
   e. Sony electronics
   f. Motorola Razr mobile phone
   g. Oliver Peeples eyeglass frames
   h. Red Cross
   i. Bose speakers
   j. Xerox copy machines

2. How can the Internet be maximized to brand a star or celebrity? Which branding principles apply to this strategy?

3. How would you differentiate branding a film star or television celebrity from branding a sports or music personality? How are they different from mediated personalities?

4. Are stars better off without the studio system? What did they lose and gain from the demise of studio-based contracts?

5. Using criteria such as salary, endorsements, appearances, etc., calculate the approximate worth of a star or celebrity brand. How would you manage this asset over the next five years? What brand extensions would you consider?

Answers to Question 1: 1-f, 2-d, 3-b, 4-g, 5-h, 6-j, 7-a, 8-e, 9-i, 10-c

MORE STUFF ABOUT MARKETING STARS AND CELEBRITIES

www.celebrities.suite101.com—articles on the latest ways celebrities are promoted.

www.zoomerang.com—daily marketing trends polls.

www.sourcewatch.org—how marketers use celebrities for products and causes.

CAMPAIGN CASE STUDY

Developing a Heart Throb

Client: Leonardo DiCaprio

Problem: Making the top ten popularity list in Hollywood isn't easy, but becoming a movie heart-throb is even harder. Promoters want De Caprio to rise above Johnny Depp and Brad Pitt as a must-see for the next generation of film-goers.

Campaign Objective: Build an iconic celebrity brand build an iconic celebrity brand like Johnny Depp, Clint Eastwood, and George Clooney that will outlast typical Hollywood pretty boys.

Situation Analysis: Sex appeal makes ladies love leading men like DiCaprio and Johnny Depp, and talent makes men want to be like them. Becoming one of the Hollywood greats was the ambition of Leonardo. His rise to fame culminated in 2010 with Martin Scorcese's new film, *Shutter Island*, that earned $40.2 million in its opening weekend, a record for the director. *Shutter Island* is the latest in a string of extraordinary performances by the Hollywood actor. With incredible cinematic performances in *Gangs of New York*, *The Departed*, and *Blood Diamond*, DiCaprio is clearly building an iconic celebrity brand that could outlast typical Hollywood pretty boys. However, media focus on Depp and Brad Pitt challenge his ability to shine above those actors and gain true acting acclaim.

SWOT Analysis:

- Strength: Solid acting role, high visibility.

- Weakness: Vulnerable to being pigeon-holed as 'pretty boy' and not being taken seriously by critics.

- Opportunities: Break free from traditional film roles to expand and enhance his image.

- Threats: Scandals, competition, and pigeon-holing.

Target Audience: Movie goers 18–55 and media critics.

Promotion Strategy: Invoke three distinct stages to transition a pretty-boy image into building a leading-man celebrity brand and achieve Depp-like iconology.

Stage 1: Break through as a heartthrob using looks and sex appeal in a starring role. In the 1990s, DiCaprio built his celebrity brand in dramatic leading roles with his pretty-boy charm and good looks: *Man in the Iron Mask* (1998), *Titanic* (1997), *Romeo + Juliet* (1996), and *Marvin's Room* (1996) focused on DiCaprio's good looks, much like *21 Jump Street* (1987–1990), *Cry Baby* (1990) and *A Nightmare on Elm Street* (1984) did for Johnny Depp and *Johnny Suede* (1991).

Stage 2: Transition into more serious roles to get respect and reinforce celebrity status. Let DiCaprio shine through the clutter. Looks can only take one so far in Hollywood; heartthrobs have expiration dates. While an actor might reach celebrity status with his good looks, talent is key to developing a sustainable celebrity brand. That means taking on more diverse acting roles that don't just leverage those good looks, but capitalizes on talent. DiCaprio transitioned from pretty boy to serious actor with *The Beach* (2000) and *Catch Me If You Can* (2002), followed by more complex roles in *Gangs of New York* (2002), *The Departed* (2006), *Blood Diamond* (2006), and *Shutter Island* (2010). Johnny Depp did a 180 from his pretty-boy role in *21 Jump Street* by starring as a disfigured man in *Edward Scissorhands* (1990) and a creepy B-movie director in *Ed Wood* (1994).

Stage 3: Expand DiCaprio by pushing boundaries and moving outside of his comfort zone and partner with other stars. Music diva, Madonna, who constantly pushed her boundaries by re-inventing her image—from music sex goddess to enlightened diva to cowboy lover—is a perfect model to follow. Johnny Depp's career parallels Madonna in many ways. He re-invented himself in Edward *Scissorhands*, again in *Ed Wood* and again in *Pirates of the Caribbean* and *Alice in Wonderland*. Beyond that, Depp partnered with Tim Burton on the majority of projects. *Charlie & the Chocolate Factory* (2005), *Corpse Bride* (2005), *Sweeney Todd* (2007), and *Alice and Wonderland* (2010) are Tim Burton films that starred Depp. DiCaprio could partner with George Clooney or Clint Eastwood in a series of serious drama or intelligent comedies.

Results: Considering DiCaprio's relationship with Martin Scorcese (starring in Scorcese's *Shutter Island, The Departed, Gangs of New York, The Aviator*), he could easily follow Johnny Depp's path. As of April 2010, his *Shutter Island* was top of the box office with $75.5 million, maintaining an edge of past Scorsese-DiCaprio collaborations.

Question for Discussion: *As DiCaprio's agent, how would you construct his future film associations and roles? What re-inventions can you suggest to launch the star from Stage Two to Stage Three?*

[i] Francesco Alberoni, "The Powerless Elite," p. 75.

[ii] www.studymedia.co.uk/hollywood_studio_system.htm, downloaded Dec. 27, 2005.

[iii] Paul McDonald (2000), *The Star System*. Wallflower, p. 5.

[iv] From J. Stacey (1994), *Star Gazing: Hollywood cinema and Female Spectatorship*. Routledge, pp. 85–153.

[v] Richard Dyer (1998), *Stars*. British Film Institute, p. 34.

[vi] OpCit McDonald p. 93.

[vii] OpCit Dyer, p. 62.

[viii] Louis Menand (1997), "The Iron Law of Stardom," *New Yorker Magazine*, March 24.

[ix] Graeme Turner (2004), *Understanding Celebrity*. Sage, p. 9.

[x] Andrew Evans & Glenn Wilson (1999), Fame: *The Psychology of Stardom*. Satin Pubication, p. 45.

[xi] Ibid Evans & Wilson, p. 51.

[xii] Samuel Blake (2004), "From Hollywood, For Our Eyes Only". *New Statesman* 133, issue 4709, p. 16.

[xiii] foliomag.com/2009/outlook-celebrity-magazines-may-never-recover-recession.

[xiv] Leo Handel (1976), *Hollywood Looks at its Audience: A report of film audience research*.

[xv] By Andrew Tudor as presented in Richard Dyer's (1998) *Stars*, p.18.

[xvi] A. Bandura (1977), *Social Learning Theory*. Prentice-Hall.

[xvii] Developed by J. Gamson (1994), Claims to Fame: Celebrity in Contemporary America. University of California Press, p. 147.

[xviii] From C. Rojek (2001), *Celebrity*. Reaktion.

[xix] From J. Frow (1998), "Is Elvis a God? Cult, culture and Questions of Method," *International Journal of Cultural Studies* 1 (2), pp. 197–210.

[xx] Irving Rein, Philip Kotler, Michael Manlin & Martin Stoller (2006), *High Visibility: Transforming your Personal and Professional Brand*, 3rd edition. McGraw-Hill, p. 46.

[xxi] Ibid, Rein, Kotler, Manlin & Stoller.

[xxii] Scott Davis (2000), *Brand Asset Management: Driving Profitable Growth Through Your Brands*. Jossey-Bass.

[xxiii] J. Agrawal & W. Kumakura (1995), "The Economic Worth of Celebrity Endorsers," *Journal of Marketing* 59, 56–68.

[xxiv] H. Friedman and L. Friedman (1979), "Endorser Effectiveness of Product Type," *Journal of Advertising Research* 19, 63–71.

[xxv] OpCit Agrawal & Kumakura.

[xxvi] From Brian Steinberg's Advertising column in the *Wall Street Journal*, Feb. 13, 2006.

[xxvii] By Hatja Hoffman reporting in Inside London for *Variety*, Sept. 26–Oct. 2, 2005.

[xxviii] From the *Economist*, Sept. 1, 2005.

IS THE INTERNET DESTROYING MEDIA CULTURE AS WE KNOW IT? OR IS IT SIMPLY RE-SHAPING CULTURE?

DISCUSSION FOR DEBATE

The following is excerpted from an article by Michiko Kakutani, writing for the *Sunday New York Times*, March 21, 2010 that presents two sides of the argument 'is traditional media dead or does it act to reincarnate content on the Internet?' This question can be used as a platform for classroom debate or discussion.

In a summary of media propelling the twenty-first century, the author reviews books and promotional tactics that drive a culture of what he calls "Text Without Context." Including passages from newly released books, Kakutani looks into the past for a view of the future. His overview should generate thought and contemplation for promoters of entertainment caught in the digital age conundrum of originality versus recap. (Links to video examples can be found on nytimes.com/arts.)

In *Reality Hunger*, David Shields's book in defense of 'recombinant' or appropriation art underscores the issues of copyright, intellectual property and plagiarism in a world where the Internet makes copying and recycling a slam dunk. In Jaron Lanier's book, *You are Not a Gadget*, focuses on how online collectivism, social networking and popular software designs are changing the way people think and process information. He suggests that it's difficult to tell an original creation from a 'mash-up- of ideas from others and suggests that Web 2.0 has created a 'digital forest of mediocrity,' that substitutes speculation for expertise.

Other results of digital media are: the blurring of news and entertainment, a growing polarization in national politics, a deconstructionist view (readers decide on how to interpret the content), postmodernism (mashing-up), and cultural relativism advanced on the left by radical feminists and on the right by creationists. Lanier purports that Kindle and iBook reading devices will foster online chatter that travels into a multitude of Google pages, all vying for attention.

Many viewing audiences only tune in to TV special events like the Super Bowl and the Oscar Awards specially choreographed for the digital chatter on Twitter and Google Wave that precedes or follows each event. Rather than verifying sources of news stories, to obtain news, listeners prefer a video clip and sound bite. The author calls today's world a "global water-cooler culture" where people send each other emails, text messages, tweets and YouTube links. He thinks that gossip, rumors, weird anecdotes and visuals have gone from staying in the office to blanketing the entire world.

A squeaky-wheel theory, where the loudest gets the grease, characterizes contemporary mediascape. The constant bombardment of trivia causes loud, blatant personalities get more attention than subtle ones. For instance, Sarah Palin's every move and pronouncement was followed by TV news, talk-show hosts, and pundits from both parties. Today, pundits squeeze out reporters using tell-all memoirs, talk-show confessionals, self-dramatizing blogs and carefully tended Facebook and MySpace pages.

Another sign of the future is the amount of time professionals and scientists spend, "not on seeking cancer cures or safe drinking water, but schemes to send digital pictures of teddy bears and dragons between adult members of social networks," said author Lanier. The Web's interactivity prompts user feedback where fan bulletin boards serve as audience focus groups. In an effort to appear on 'most-e-mailed lists,' TV writers listen to fans for making programming decisions and developing series plot lines.

Author Neal Gabler (*Life the Movie: How Entertainment Conquered Reality*) asserted that celebrity is "the great new art form of the 21st century." He claims that celebrity competes with movies, plays, books and television, steakubg frin old media their role in reflecting culture. Online culture,

Shay Sayre, Ph.D., is professor emeritus at California State University, Fullerton. Recipient of a Fullbright-Hays grant to study in Hungary, Sayre has taught graduate degree programs in Brussels, Hong Kong, and Brisbane, Australia. Previously with Young & Rubicam Advertising, Sayre directed promotional programs for Paramount Pictures and served as marketing director for the San Diego Symphony. She is the author of *Qualitative Methods for Marketplace Research* (Sage), *Campaign Planner for Promotion, IMC* (Southwestern), *Entertainment and Society* (Routledge), and numerous book chapters and journal articles in publications such as the *Journal of Advertising; Consumption, Markets & Culture; Journal of Professional and Business Ethics; Advances in Consumer Research; and Research in Consumer Behavior*. She divides her time between Ennis, Montana and Laguna Beach, California.

he said, dominated by trivial mash-ups and fandom, is one of reaction without action. Lanier claims that the Web is killing old media, causing a situation where culture is effectively "eating its own seed and stock."

What do you think?

In a group or with another person, form a **debate**. One person takes the side of defending the Web and digital media's role in creating culture; the other speaks against the Internet for destroying traditional media and creating a world of dumbbells.